The New Testament

A STUDENT'S INTRODUCTION

Eighth Edition

STEPHEN L. HARRIS

Professor Emeritus

California State University, Sacramento

McGraw Hill Education

THE NEW TESTAMENT: A STUDENT'S INTRODUCTION, EIGHTH EDITION

Published by McGraw-Hill Education, 2 Penn Plaza, New York, NY 10121. Copyright © 2015 by McGraw-Hill Education. All rights reserved. Printed in the United States of America. Previous editions © 2012, 2009, and 2006. No part of this publication may be reproduced or distributed in any form or by any means, or stored in a database or retrieval system, without the prior written consent of McGraw-Hill Education, including, but not limited to, in any network or other electronic storage or transmission, or broadcast for distance learning.

Some ancillaries, including electronic and print components, may not be available to customers outside the United States.

This book is printed on acid-free paper.

1 2 3 4 5 6 7 8 9 0 DOC/DOC 1 0 9 8 7 6 5 4

ISBN   978-0-07-811913-2
MHID   0-07-811913-8

Senior Vice President, Products & Markets: *Kurt L. Strand*
Vice President, Content Production & Technology Services: *Kimberly Meriwether David*
Managing Director: *William R. Glass*
Brand Manager & Managing Editor: *Sara Jaeger*
Executive Director of Development: *Lisa Pinto*
Associate Marketing Manager: *Alexandra Schultz*
Brand Coordinator: *Adina Lonn*
Director, Content Production: *Terri Schiesl*
Content Project Manager: *Lisa Bruflodt*
Buyer: *Susan K. Culbertson*
Media Project Manager: *Jenny Bartell*
Cover Designer: *Studio Montage, St. Louis, MO*
Cover Image: *Courtesy National Gallery of Art, Washington*
Compositor: *Aptara®, Inc.*
Typeface: *10/12 ITC New Baskerville Std*
Printer: *R.R. Donnelley*

Excerpts from the *New English Bible* C. 1961, 1970 Oxford University Press and Cambridge University Press. Used with permission of Cambridge University Press.

All credits appearing on page or at the end of the book are considered to be an extension of the copyright page.

Library of Congress Cataloging-in-Publication Data

Harris, Stephen L., 1937–
    The New Testament : a student's introduction / Stephen L. Harris, Professor Emeritus, California State University, Sacramento. — Eighth Edition.
        pages cm
    ISBN 978-0-07-811913-2 (alk. paper)
    1. Bible. New Testament—Introductions. 2. Bible. New Testament—Textbooks. I. Title.
    BS2330.3.H37 2014
    225.6'1—dc23
                                                                                      2013049770

The Internet addresses listed in the text were accurate at the time of publication. The inclusion of a website does not indicate an endorsement by the authors or McGraw-Hill Education, and McGraw-Hill Education does not guarantee the accuracy of the information presented at these sites.

www.mhhe.com

For Geoffrey Edwin, Jason Marc, and Kevin L.

Preface to the Eighth Edition

Like its predecessors, the eighth edition of *The New Testament: A Student's Introduction* is designed for undergraduates beginning their first systematic study of the Christian Greek Scriptures. The purpose of this introductory text is twofold: to familiarize readers with the contents and major themes of the New Testament and to acquaint them with the goals and methods of important biblical scholarship.

Rearrangement and New Features

To facilitate students' learning experience, material in the new edition has been rearranged into six parts. The first chapter of Part One provides an overview of the New Testament and its relationship to the Jewish Scriptures, known to Christians as the Old Testament. After surveying the literary genres that early Christian authors adopted to express their beliefs, this chapter describes the usefulness of scholarly—historical and analytical—approaches to studying the sacred writings. Greatly expanded, the second chapter traces the gradual development of the New Testament canon, illustrating the importance of historical events, such as the Jewish Revolt against Rome and the patronage of the emperor Constantine, respectively, to the contents and the final tally of New Testament books.

In Part Two, "The Three Worlds in Which Christianity Originated," the text reviews the three major forces that largely shaped and defined the new faith: Judaism, Greek culture, and Roman political power. As twenty-first-century scholars increasingly emphasize the historical context of Christian origins, this textbook integrates vital new research on the Jesus movement's interaction with imperial power. Closer focus on the tension between Christ and Caesar appears not only in the fuller coverage of emperor worship (Chapter 5), but also in the discussion of the Book of Acts, where Paul's "gospel" of Jesus' kingship sparks riots and seems to undermine Roman social stability (Chapter 12). To many in the Greco-Roman world, the message that the kingdom of God is superior to the Roman Empire seems to subvert the government's legitimate authority.

Part Three, "Diverse Portraits of Jesus," discusses the four Gospel accounts of Jesus' life and teaching. While emphasizing the theological orientation of the Gospel writers, Chapter 6 now also underscores scholarly contributions to our understanding of the Gospels' composition, including the Synoptic Problem and the two-document hypothesis. The presentation of John's unique Gospel—strikingly different from the three Synoptic accounts—offers a more nuanced analysis of the author's realized eschatology, particularly his creative handling of the early apocalyptic expectations that Jesus would soon return to earth (Chapter 10).

Coverage of scholarly attempts to recover the "historical Jesus" has been expanded to include recent modifications of the quest. At the same time, the discussion has been streamlined for greater clarity (Chapter 11).

Part Four features the Book of Acts, in which the author of Luke's Gospel presents an idealized account of the early church. The writer's candor about the destabilizing social effects of the Christian message is brought into sharper focus, a theme that carries over into Part Five, "Paul and the Pauline Tradition." In addition to outlining the influence of the Roman patron-client model

v

on Paul's thought, this section also offers greater coverage of his theology, especially the paradigm-changing nature of new critical interpretations. The controversial issue of pseudonymity—composing documents in the name of a deceased writer, such as Paul or Peter—is given further attention, as is the church's inclusion of pseudonymous letters and other works in the New Testament canon.

Part Six, "General Letters and Some Visions of End Time," highlights characteristic anxieties of the church in the decades shortly before and after the turn of the first Christian century. Many of these later New Testament documents were apparently composed in response to doctrinal disputes or reflect disappointment in believers' apocalyptic expectations. Whereas John of Patmos, the author of Revelation, paints a lurid scenario of End Time that will "soon" culminate in Jesus' Second Coming, some later writers, such as the pseudonymous author of 2 Peter, deal specifically with failed hopes of an early Parousia. Like the other catholic epistles confronting a church in crisis, the three letters from the Johannine community—the same group that had produced the Gospel of John—reveal quarrels over doctrine and conduct that bitterly divided their members.

A new chapter—"Outside the Canon: Other Early Christian Literature"—reviews important documents that the church ultimately did not accept into the New Testament. These rejected works include pseudonymous Gospels, such as those ascribed to Thomas, James, Peter, and Judas. Discovered in 1945, the Gospel of Thomas contains versions of Jesus' sayings that may be as old or older than those incorporated into the canonical Gospels. Other writings, such as the Didache (Teaching of the Twelve Apostles), represent the worship practices of early Jewish-Christian communities, some of which rituals are remarkably similar to contemporary church services. In its present form, the Didache probably dates from about 100 CE, and is thus older than several of the catholic epistles (see Chapter 20).

Other new features include the addition of several boxes highlighting important themes or subjects, such as "The Role of Women in John's Gospel" (Box 10.6); "The Christian Message's Disruptive Effect on Greco-Roman Society" (Box 12.4); "Through a Glass Darkly: Justification and Unconditional Love" (Box 15.1); and "Gnosticism" (Box 18.3). In addition, many sections of the text have been rewritten to incorporate trends in current scholarship, including an extensive updating of the "Recommended Readings."

Pedagogical Aids

This text offers numerous devices to help students learn the material quickly and easily. As in previous editions, each chapter begins with a concise summary of key topics/themes, and important terms are printed in **boldface**, listed at the end of every chapter, and then defined in the expansive Glossary at the back of the book. To help readers remember essential information, each chapter includes pertinent Questions for Review, as well as aids to facilitate class dialogue, Questions for Discussion and Reflection. The extensively updated Recommended Readings refer students to publications available at most college and university libraries. Representing the work of leading scholars, the books listed provide crucial insights and analytical tools for enhancing our understanding of the New Testament and the sociohistorical environment in which it developed.

Online Resource

Additional resources for *The New Testament* can be found on the Online Learning Center at www.mhhe.com/harris8e. Students will be able to access multiple choice, true/false, and essay quizzes to test comprehension as well as chapter summaries. Instructors can take advantage of an Instructor's Manual with testbank questions and PowerPoint lecture slides.

Acknowledgments

I am deeply grateful to the colleagues who have provided generous commentary and advice for improving the book's quality and usefulness in the classroom: Terry Burden, University of Louisville; Bryan Burkhead, Guilford Community College; Pamela Hedrick, High Point University; Bradley Nystrom, California State University-Sacramento; Ronnie Prevost, Logsdon Seminary, Hardin-Simmons University; Cherie Hughes, Tulsa Community College.

I would also like to express appreciation to my managing editor, Sara Jaeger; Richard Wright, the copyeditor; and the project manager, Lisa A. Bruflodt.

In addition, I'd like to thank two friends and colleagues: Professor Brad Nystrom, for his readable translation of Cleanthes' "Hymn to Zeus," and the late Rev. Dr. James Straukamp, for his permission to use his excellent photographs of biblical sites. Finally, I am grateful to Geoffrey E. Harris for his expertise in correcting the printed text.

Contents

CHAPTER 9   Luke's Portrait of Jesus

CHAPTER 10   John's Reinterpretation of Jesus

Illustrations

PART ONE

An Invitation to the New Testament

CHAPTER 1

An Overview of the New Testament

Here begins the Gospel of Jesus Christ. Mark 1:1*

Key Topics/Themes A collection of twenty-seven Greek documents that early Christians appended to a Greek edition of the Hebrew Bible (the Old Testament), the New Testament includes four Gospels, a church history, letters, and an apocalypse (revelation). The early Christian community produced a host of other writings as well, which scholars also study to understand the diverse nature of the Jesus movement as it spread throughout the Greco-Roman world.

People read the New Testament for an almost infinite variety of reasons. Some read to satisfy their curiosity about the origins of one of the great world religions. They seek to learn more about the social and historical roots of Christianity, a faith that began in the early days of the Roman Empire and that today commands the allegiance of more than 2 billion people, approximately a third of the global population. Because Christianity bases its most characteristic beliefs on the New Testament writings, it is to this source that the historian and social scientist must turn for information about the religion's birth and early development.

Most people, however, probably read the New Testament for more personal reasons. Many readers search its pages for answers to life's important ethical and religious questions. For hundreds of millions of Christians, the New Testament sets the only acceptable standards of personal belief and behavior (see Box 1.1). Readers attempt to discover authoritative counsel on issues that modern science or speculative philosophy cannot resolve, such as the nature of God, the fate of the soul after death, and the ultimate destiny of humankind.

Jesus of Nazareth, the central character of the New Testament, provides many people with the most compelling reason to read the book. As presented by the Gospel writers, he is like no other figure in history. His teachings and pronouncements have an unequaled power and authority. As an itinerant Jewish prophet, healer, and teacher in early-first-century Palestine, the historical Jesus—in terms of the larger Greco-Roman world around him—lived a relatively obscure life and died a criminal's death at the hands of Roman executioners. His followers' conviction that he subsequently rose from the grave and appeared to them launched a vital new faith that eventually swept the Roman Empire. In little more than three centuries after Jesus' death, Christianity became Rome's official state religion.

*Unless otherwise noted, all New Testament quotations are from the New English Bible (New York: Oxford University Press, 1976); (see Chapter 2, p. 36).

BOX 1.1 The New Testament: A Relatively Modern Artifact

A printed, bound copy of the New Testament that readers can hold in their hands is a relatively modern development. Until the fourth century CE, the New Testament did not even exist as a coherent entity—a single volume containing the twenty-seven books in its now-familiar table of contents. Before then, believers, and even church leaders, had access to individual Gospels or subcollections, such as compilations of Paul's letters, but not to a comprehensive edition of the entire text.

Even after Rome made Christianity the state religion and imperial patronage encouraged the production of an official Christian Scripture, New Testaments were extremely rare. Not only were manuscript copies prohibitively expensive, but the vast majority of people in the Roman Empire could neither read nor write. It was not until the printing press was invented in the fifteenth century CE, permitting the eventual mass production of Bibles, that the New Testament as we know it came into being.

Clearly, the New Testament authors present Jesus as much more than an ordinary man. The Gospel of John portrays him as the human expression of divine Wisdom, the Word of God made flesh. Jesus' teaching about the eternal world of spirit is thus definitive, for he is depicted as having descended from heaven to earth to reveal ultimate truth. About 300 years after Jesus' crucifixion, Christian leaders assembled at the town of Nicaea in Asia Minor to decree that Jesus is not only the Son of God but God himself.

Given the uniquely high status that orthodox Christianity accords the person of Jesus, the New Testament accounts of his life have extraordinary value. Jesus' words recorded in the Gospels are seen not merely as the utterances of a preeminently wise teacher but also as the declarations of the Being who created and sustains the universe. The hope of encountering "God's thoughts," of discovering otherwise unattainable knowledge of unseen realities, gives many believers a powerful incentive for studying the New Testament.

What Is the New Testament?

When asked to define the New Testament, many students respond with such traditional phrases as "the Word of God" or "Holy Scripture." These responses are really confessions of faith that the Christian writings are qualitatively different from ordinary books. Some students express surprise that non-Christian religions also have **scriptures**—documents that these groups consider sacred and authoritative (having the power to command belief and prescribe behavior). In fact, many other world religions possess holy books that their adherents believe to represent a divine revelation to humankind. Hindus cherish the Vedas, the Upanishads, and the Bhagavadgita; Buddhists venerate the recorded teachings of Buddha, the "enlightened one"; and followers of Islam (meaning "submission" [to the will of Allah]) revere the Quran (Koran) as transmitting the one true faith. Ideally, we approach all sacred writings with a willingness to appreciate the religious insights they offer and to recognize their connection with the cultural and historical context out of which they grew.

Given the historical fact that the New Testament was written by and for believers in Jesus' divinity, many readers tend to approach it as they do no other work of ancient literature. Whether or not they are practicing Christians, students commonly bring to the New Testament attitudes and assumptions very different from those they employ when reading other works of antiquity. The student usually has little trouble bringing an open or neutral mind to exploring stories about the Greek and Roman gods. One can read Homer's *Iliad*, an epic poem celebrating the Greek heroes of the Trojan War, without any particular emotional involvement with the Homeric gods. However, this objective attitude toward supernatural beings is rare among persons studying the New Testament.

To be fair to the New Testament, we will want to study it with the same open-mindedness we grant to the writings of any world religion. This call for objectivity is a challenge to all of us, for we live in a culture that defines its highest values largely in terms of the Judeo-Christian tradition. We can most fully appreciate the New Testament if we begin by recognizing that it developed in, and partly in reaction to, a society profoundly different from our own. To a great extent, the New Testament is the literary product of a dynamic encounter between two strikingly different cultures of antiquity—the Jewish and the Greek. A creative synthesis of these two traditions, early Christianity originated in a thoroughly Jewish environment. But in the decades following Jesus' death, Christianity spread to the larger Greek-speaking world, where it eventually assumed the dominant form that has been transmitted to us.

The Jewish world of Jesus and his first disciples was centered in **Palestine,** an area at the eastern end of the Mediterranean Sea now partly occupied by the modern state of Israel (see Figure 1.1). According to the biblical Book of Genesis, God had awarded this territory—the **Promised Land**—to his chosen people, the Jews.* In Jesus' day (the first third of the first century CE[†]), however, the land was ruled by Rome, the capital of a vast empire that surrounded the entire Mediterranean basin, from France and Spain in western Europe to Egypt in northeast Africa and Syria-Palestine in western Asia (see Figure 1.2). As a Palestinian Jew, Jesus experienced the tension that then existed between his fellow Jews and their often-resented Roman overlords

*Jew, a term originally designating the inhabitants of Judea, the area surrounding Jerusalem, also includes all members of the covenant community living outside Palestine.

[†]CE (the Common Era), a religiously neutral term used by Jews, Christians, Muslims, and others, is synonymous with the traditional AD, initials representing *anno domini*, Latin for "in the year of the Lord." BCE (before the Common Era) corresponds to BC (before Christ).

(see Chapters 5–10 for discussions of Gospel references to Jewish-Roman relations).

Although many students automatically ascribe their own (twenty-first-century North American) values and attitudes to Jesus' world, it is important to recognize that, even today, inhabitants of the eastern Mediterranean region do not view life as Americans typically do. In the Mediterranean's agrarian, conservative peasant society, old ideas, values, and practices contrast sharply with those in the West's technologically sophisticated democracies. Two thousand years ago, the degree of difference—social, religious, and political—was even greater, a fact that must be considered when studying the Gospel accounts of Jesus' interaction with Palestinian villagers and Roman officials. The more we learn about first-century Palestinian-Jewish and Greco-Roman customs, social institutions, and religious beliefs, the better we will understand both Jesus and the writers who interpreted him to Greek-speaking audiences (see Chapters 3–5).

The New Testament and the Hebrew Bible

Before considering the second great historical influence on the creation of the New Testament—Greek thought and culture—it is helpful to describe what the New Testament is and how it relates to the older Jewish Scriptures, the **Hebrew Bible** (so called because it was originally composed in the Hebrew language, with a few later books in a related tongue, **Aramaic;** see Boxes 1.2 and 1.3). Basically, the New Testament is a collection of twenty-seven Christian documents, written in Greek and added as a supplement to a Greek edition of the Hebrew Bible known as the **Septuagint** (see below). The Christian Bible, therefore, consists of two unequal parts: the longer, more literarily diverse Hebrew Bible (which Christians call the Old Testament), and a shorter anthology of Christian writings (the New Testament). Bound together,

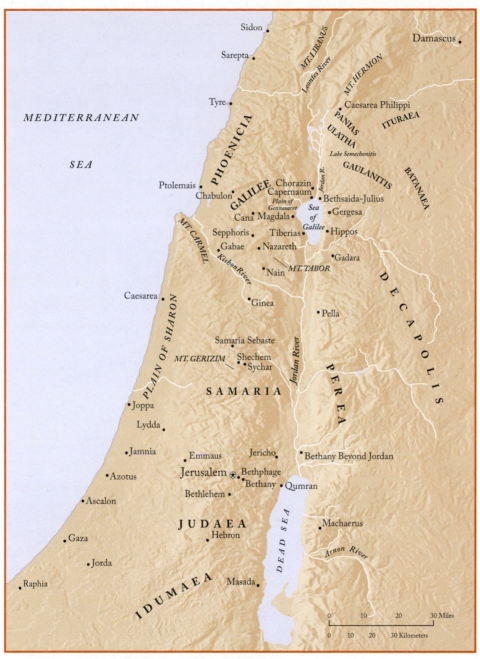

FIGURE 1.1 Palestine at the time of Jesus (early first century CE). Located at the eastern margin of the Mediterranean Sea, this region promised to Abraham's descendants was then controlled by Rome (see Figure 1.2).

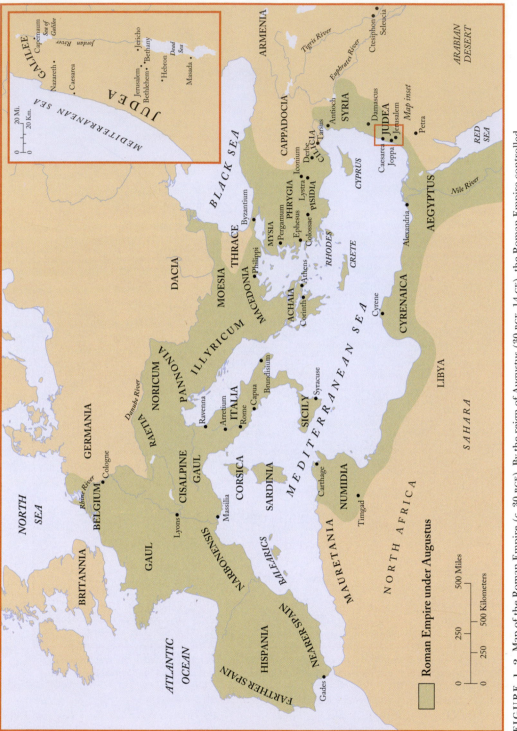

BOX 1.2 **Hebrew Bible and Apocrypha**

TORAH

Genesis
Exodus
Leviticus
Numbers
Deuteronomy

PROPHETS

Former Prophets
    Joshua
    Judges
    Samuel (1 and 2)
    Kings (1 and 2)
Latter Prophets
    Isaiah
    Jeremiah
    Ezekiel
The Twelve (Minor Prophets)
    Hosea
    Joel
    Amos
    Obadiah
    Jonah
    Micah
    Nahum
    Habakkuk
    Zephaniah
    Haggai
    Zechariah
    Malachi

WRITINGS

Psalms
Job
Proverbs
Ruth
Song of Solomon
Ecclesiastes
Lamentations
Esther
Daniel
Ezra-Nehemiah
Chronicles (1 and 2)

DEUTEROCANONICAL BOOKS (APOCRYPHA)

1 Esdras
2 Esdras
Tobit
Judith
The rest of the chapters of the Book of Esther
The Wisdom of Solomon
Ecclesiasticus, or the Wisdom of Jesus Son of
    Sirah
Baruch
A Letter of Jeremiah
The Song of the Three
Daniel and Susanna
Daniel, Bel, and the Snake
The Prayer of Manasseh
1 Maccabees
2 Maccabees

the two testaments form the Christian Bible. **Bible,** a term derived from the word *biblia* (meaning "little books"), is an appropriate title because this two-part volume is really a compilation of many different books composed over a time span exceeding 1,100 years.

In considering early Christians' use of the Hebrew Bible, however, we must remember that the Jewish Scriptures did not then exist as an easily accessible bound volume. At the time of Jesus and the early church, the Hebrew Bible existed only as a collection of separate scrolls

(see Chapter 2). Few Jews or early Christians owned copies of biblical books or read them privately. Instead, most Jews and Jewish Christians only heard passages from the Mosaic Torah or prophetic books read aloud at religious services in the local synagogue or at a Christian house church. If at the latter, they likely heard the Scriptures read not in the original Hebrew but in Greek translation.

That the early Christian movement appropriated the Hebrew Bible, which had been created by and for the Jewish community, is

BOX 1.3 Organization of the Hebrew and Christian Greek Scriptures

The contents of the New Testament are arranged in a way that approximates the order of the Hebrew Bible, which is also called the Tanakh, a term whose consonants represent the three principal divisions of the Hebrew Scriptures: the *Torah* (Mosaic Law or instruction), the *Nevi'im* (Prophets), and the *Kethuvim* (Writings).

OLD COVENANT (TESTAMENT)

T *Torah* (five books of Moses)
A
N *Nevi'im* (Prophets)
   Histories of Joshua-Kings
   Books of the Prophets
A
K *Kethuvim* (Writings)
H Books of poetry, wisdom, and an apocalypse (Daniel)

NEW COVENANT (TESTAMENT)

Four Gospels (story of Jesus)

Book of Acts (church history)
Letters of Paul and other church leaders

Book of Hebrews, catholic epistles, and an apocalypse (Revelation)

---

extremely significant. Believers who accepted Jesus as the Jewish **Messiah** (Anointed One, a term applied to all of Israel's kings; see Chapter 3) looked to the Jewish Scriptures—the only written religious authority for both Jews and early Christians—to find evidence supporting their convictions. When New Testament authors refer to "Scripture" or "the Law and the Prophets" (cf. Luke 24:27, 32), they mean the Hebrew Bible, albeit in a Greek (Septuagint) edition. In composing their diverse portraits of Jesus, the Gospel writers consistently clothed the historical figure in images and ideas taken from the Hebrew Bible. In Matthew's Gospel, for example, virtually every word or action of Jesus is interpreted in terms of ancient biblical prophecy (see Chapter 8).

Testament and Covenant

The very term *New Testament* is intimately connected with the Hebrew Bible. In biblical usage, **testament** is a near synonym for **covenant,** which refers to an agreement, contract, vow, or bond. To appreciate the New Testament concept of the bond between God and humanity, we must examine the Hebrew Bible's story of God's relationship with **Israel,** the ancient Near Eastern people with whom the Deity forged a binding covenant, making them his exclusive partner. Exodus, the second book of the Hebrew Bible (Tanakh), recounts the solemn ceremony in which the Israelites conclude their central covenant with **Yahweh** (the sacred name of Israel's God) (Exod. 19–20; 24). Under the terms of the **Mosaic Covenant** (so called because the Israelite leader **Moses** acts as mediator between Yahweh and his chosen people), the Israelites swear to uphold all the laws and commandments that Yahweh enjoins upon them. These legal injunctions are contained in the books of Exodus, Leviticus, Numbers, and Deuteronomy. Together with the Book of Genesis, which serves as an introduction to the framing of the Mosaic Covenant, this section of the Hebrew Bible is known as the **Torah** (see Figures 1.3 and 1.4). Meaning "law," "teaching," or "instruction," the Torah is also referred to as the **Pentateuch** (a Greek term for the first five books of the Bible, Genesis through Deuteronomy). According to Mark's Gospel,

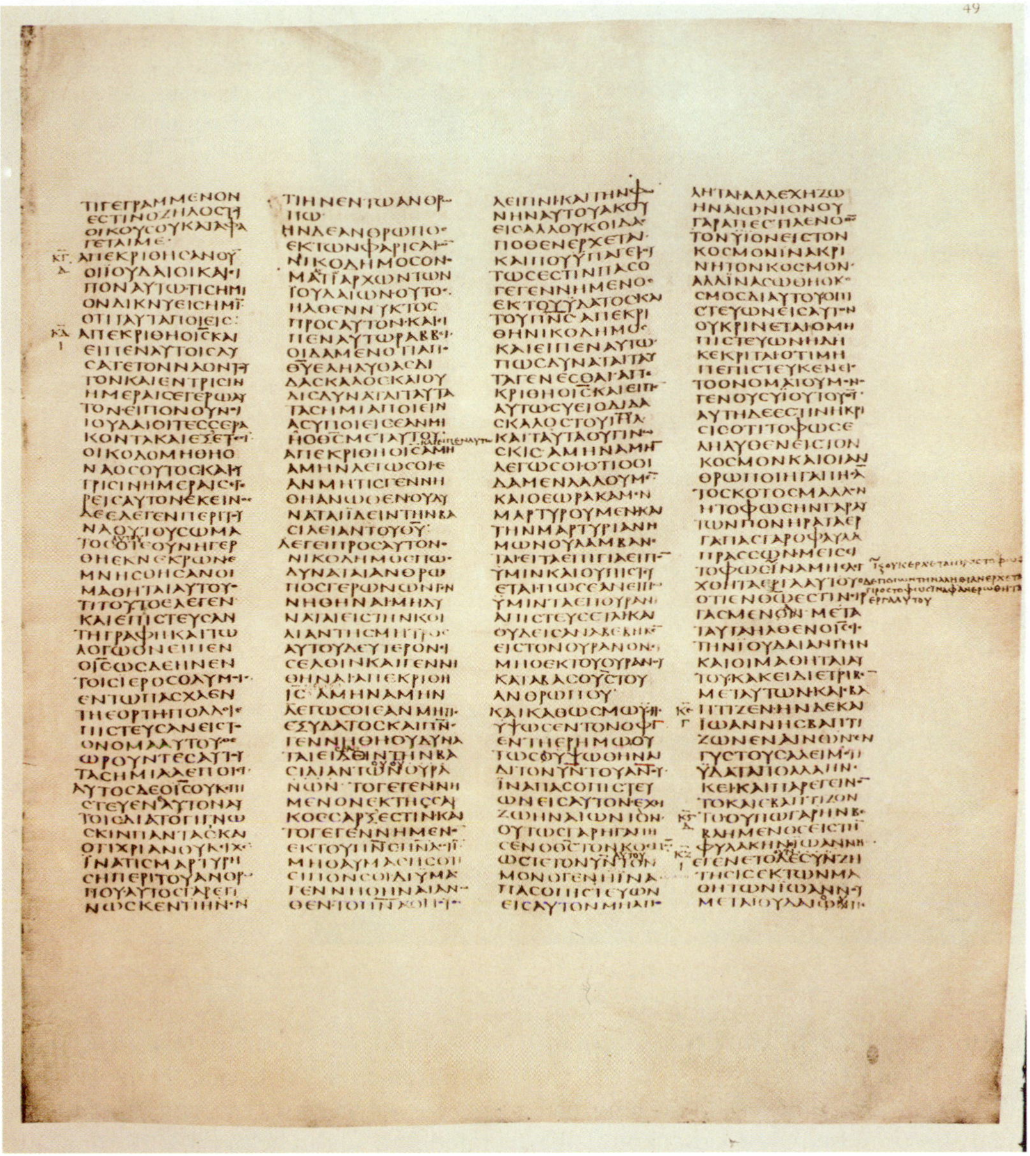

FIGURE 1.3 A page from John's Gospel in the Codex Sinaiticus. The oldest complete copy of the New Testament, the Codex Sinaiticus was produced about 330–350 CE.

when Jesus is asked to state Israel's most essential teaching, he cites Torah commands to love God and neighbor (see Mark 12; cf. Deut. 6:4–5 and Lev. 19:18).

According to stipulations of the Mosaic Covenant, Yahweh's vow to protect Israel is contingent upon the people's faithfulness in keeping Yahweh's instructions; failure to obey the more than 600 covenant laws will result in Israel's destruction (Deut. 28–29; see Box 3.1). Some of Israel's later prophets concluded that the people had been so disobedient that Yahweh eventually rescinded his covenant vow, abandoning Israel to its enemies. Writing about 600 years before the time of Jesus, the prophet Jeremiah promised that Yahweh would replace

FIGURE 1.4 A Torah scroll.
Copies of the Mosaic Torah are kept
in every Jewish temple or synagogue.
This elegant manuscript is approximately one-third the size of the
standard Torah scroll.

the old Mosaic agreement with a "new covenant
[testament]" (Jer. 31:31).

The Gospel writers believed that Jesus had
instituted the promised New Covenant at the
Last Supper he held with his disciples. "And he
took the cup, and gave thanks, and gave it to
them, saying Drink ye all of it: For this is my
blood of the new testament . . ." (Matt. 26:27–28,
King James Version). The adjective *new*, not
present in the earliest manuscripts, was added
to emphasize the change in God's relationship
with humankind. (Most modern English translations, including the New Revised Standard
Version, the New Jerusalem Bible, and the
Revised English Bible, omit the interpolated

"new" and use "covenant" instead of "testament"
in this passage.) Believing themselves to be the
people of the New Covenant that Jesus inaugurated the night before his death, Christians
eventually called their collection of Gospels,
letters, and other sacred writings the New
Testament. Although the Hebrew Bible, which
dealt with the older Mosaic Covenant, became
known as the Old Testament, many scholars
suggest that it would be more appropriate to call
it the First Testament. Because Christians believed that the covenants and promises made to
Israel were fulfilled in Jesus, they retained their
Greek version of the Hebrew Bible as authoritative and suitable for religious instruction.

The Septuagint

Although New Testament writers regarded the Hebrew Bible as their principal source for documenting their claim that Jesus was Israel's prophesied Messiah, they did not quote from the original Hebrew text. Instead, they used a popular Greek translation of the Hebrew Bible that had been produced for Greek-speaking Jews who lived in **Alexandria,** Egypt, then one of the world's largest centers of literary and scientific research. Beginning about 250 BCE with a rendition of the Pentateuch into Greek, the Septuagint grew in discrete stages as historical, prophetic, and other books were added over time. According to a tradition preserved in the Letter of Aristeas, however, the Septuagint was almost miraculously produced. In the Aristeas account, which most scholars believe to be legend, the Septuagint was the work of seventy-two Hebrew scholars (divided into twelve groups of six) who labored seventy-two days to create a set of identical translations, their remarkable agreement signifying divine guidance in the project. Abbreviated in informal usage to "the work of the seventy," the Septuagint (represented by the roman numeral LXX) became the standard biblical text for Jews throughout the Greco-Roman world and is the version quoted most frequently in the New Testament.

Language and Literature of the New Testament

Koinē Greek

The New Testament was written in the same kind of *koinē* (common) Greek as the Septuagint. The most widely spoken language of the early Christian era, *koinē* became the dominant tongue of the eastern Mediterranean region after the conquests of Alexander the Great (356–323 BCE; see Chapter 4). Although less polished and elegant than the classical Greek of the great Athenian poets and philosophers, *koinē* was then spoken by so large a percentage of the population that it communicated far more effectively than Hebrew or Latin.

Major Contributors to the New Testament

Most of the New Testament's twenty-seven books were composed during the half-century between about 50 and 100 CE, although a few did not appear until the early decades of the second century CE (see Box 1.4). The oldest surviving Christian documents are the letters of **Paul,** a Greek-educated Jew who wrote the first—and by far the most influential—interpretations of Jesus' death on the cross. For Paul, Jesus' humiliating execution by Roman soldiers was not a historical accident, but an essential event in God's plan for reconciling humanity to its Creator. Written between about 50 and 62 CE, Paul's letters to newly-founded congregations in Greece, Italy, and Asia Minor (modern Turkey) were highly controversial at the time of their composition. Paul, who claimed that he received his unique "gospel" directly from the risen Jesus (Gal. 1:11–12), argued that God had graciously extended his covenant to people of all nationalities. In Paul's view, moreover, Gentiles (non-Jews) did not have to obey Torah requirements, such as circumcision and dietary laws—a claim that seemed too radical for many believers. As Gentiles flocked in ever-increasing numbers to the church, however, Paul's innovative doctrines not only prevailed but eventually became central to mainstream Christianity.

Paul's legacy greatly influenced Christian editors who assembled the New Testament books. His genuine letters, as well as several that were ascribed to him by later Pauline disciples (see Chapter 17), constitute about a third of the New Testament. In addition, an idealized portrayal of Paul dominates the second half of the Book of Acts, a selective account of the early church. Composed by the same author, the Gospel of Luke and Acts together make up another third of the New Testament collection.

BOX 1.4 New Testament Books: Approximate Order of Composition

APPROX. DATE (CE)	TITLE OF BOOK	AUTHOR
c. 50	1 Thessalonians	Paul
	2 Thess. (if by Paul)	
c. 54–55	1 and 2 Corinthians	Paul
c. 56	Galatians	Paul
c. 56–57	Romans	Paul
c. 61	Colossians (if by Paul)	Paul
c. 61	Philippians	Paul
c. 62	Philemon	Paul
c. 66–70	Gospel of Mark	Anonymous
66–73	**Jewish War Against Rome: Destruction of Jerusalem and Temple**	
c. 80–85	Gospel of Matthew	Anonymous
c. 85–90	Gospel of Luke, Book of Acts	Anonymous
c. 85–95	Hebrews, 1 Peter, Ephesians, James	Anonymous/Pseudonymous*
c. 95	Revelation (the Apocalypse)	John of Patmos
c. 95–100	Gospel of John	Anonymous
c. 100–110	1, 2, and 3 John	Anonymous
c. 110–130	1 and 2 Timothy, Titus	Pseudonymous
c. 130–150	Jude, 2 Peter	Pseudonymous

*Pseudonymity—the literary practice, common among ancient Greco-Roman, Jewish, and early Christian writers, of composing books in the name of a famous religious figure of the past.

If we also add the Gospel of John and the three letters (1, 2, and 3 John) that originated in the same distinctive community, it's apparent that a relatively small group of writers collectively produced about three-fourths of the New Testament's total length. Although these few authors—Paul, Paul's disciples, the compiler of Luke-Acts, and the author of the literature ascribed to John—effectively define the Christian revelation, other writers also made important contributions. Certainly the author of the Gospel ascribed to Matthew, which contains the fullest collection of Jesus' teachings, had a major impact on Christian thought. Revelation, brimming with mystical imagery of angels and dragons, has never ceased to capture the Christian imagination.

The Supreme Importance of Jesus

To an incalculable extent, every book in the collection is a celebration of Jesus' significance: He is not only the chief agent of human salvation but also a figure of cosmic dimensions. Regarding Jesus' life and teachings as the culmination of God's revelation to humankind, the author of Hebrews asserts that Jesus is absolutely unique:

> When in former times God spoke to our forefathers [in the Hebrew Bible], he spoke in fragmentary and varied fashion through the prophets. But in this the final age, he has spoken to us in the Son whom he has made heir to the whole universe, and through whom he created all orders of existence.

(Heb. 1:1–2)

From the Christian perspective, Jesus is the heir to all God's promises to Israel, intrinsically superior to any previous biblical figure or angelic member of the heavenly court. Only he is essential to God's creative process and only he perfectly expresses the divine nature: "The Son," Hebrews declares, "is the effulgence of God's splendor and the stamp of God's very being, and sustains the universe by his word of power" (1:3). Despite his present exalted status, however, the human Jesus validated his position as divine son through painful testing. Submitting fully to God's will, "son though he was, he learned obedience in the school of suffering, and, once perfected, became the source of eternal salvation for all who obey him" (Heb. 5:7–10). Obedient unto death, Jesus posthumously ascended to heaven, where he is now seated "at the right hand of Majesty on high, raised as far above the angels, as the title he has inherited is superior to theirs [other members of the celestial assembly]" (Heb. 1:3–4). According to Hebrews' author, to Jesus alone has God declared: "Thou art my Son; today I have begotten thee" (Heb. 1:5), a statement that was traditionally spoken at the coronation of Israel's kings when they were ceremonially adopted as God's sons (Ps. 2:7; see the discussion of Israel's Messiah in Chapter 3).

Jesus' central position in the New Testament is affirmed from the first book in the collection, the Gospel of Matthew, to the last, John's visions of the cosmic Christ in Revelation. Matthew opens his Gospel with a genealogy showing Jesus' descent from great figures of the Hebrew Bible, including **Abraham,** traditional progenitor of the Jewish people, and David, the ruler of Israel to whom God promised an eternal line of kings. In recounting the story of Jesus' birth, Matthew introduces an astronomical image that reappears—with major changes—in Revelation and that imparts a cosmic frame to the entire New Testament collection. In Matthew, a mysterious star leads foreign astrologers to visit Jesus' birthplace, inadvertently inciting King Herod's attempt to kill the child (Matt. 2:1–12). In Revelation's description of the risen Jesus, the once vulnerable infant has become a gigantic figure dominating the sky and holding a vast constellation of stars in one hand (Rev. 1:8–2:1). Editors thus gave the New Testament a linear narrative structure that begins with Matthew's endangered child and closes with visions of a future new creation ruled by that same Jesus, now transformed into ruler of the universe.

New Testament Literary Forms

The New Testament contains several different genres (categories) of literature, although it has considerably less variety than the Hebrew Bible. Early Christian editors arranged the contents not in chronological order according to dates of composition, but according to the documents' literary classification, beginning with the Gospels and ending with the Book of Revelation.

The Gospels The only literary category that early Christians invented, the English word **"Gospel"** translates the Greek *evangelion,* meaning "good news." Designed to proclaim the "good news" about Jesus, the Gospels tell the story of Jesus' ministry, death, and resurrection. The term **Evangelist** refers to the writer of an *evangelion* (Gospel).

In the Greek-speaking world of New Testament times, *evangelion* commonly was used to denote public proclamations about the Roman emperor. The emperor's military victories, welfare policies, and elevation to the status of a god were typical examples of Roman "good news" to be "evangelized" (see the discussion of the imperial ruler cult in Chapter 5). Paul uses *evangelion* to describe his message about salvation through faith in Jesus. Matthew also employs it to denote Jesus' oral teachings (Matt. 4:23; 9:35; 24:14; 26:13). To distinguish *gospel,* an oral message, from *Gospel,* a literary work about Jesus, we will capitalize the term when it refers to the written Gospel form.

By definition, a Gospel must involve the deeds and/or words of Jesus. Although all four New Testament Gospels are narratives—they tell a story—about Jesus' actions and teachings, early Christians also produced Gospels, such as the Gospel of Thomas, that include only Jesus' sayings. Recovered in 1945 from the desert sands of Egypt, the Gospel of Thomas, among many other early Christian writings, is not accepted among the New Testament's officially recognized books (see the discussion of canon in Chapter 2).

Although they present Jesus' activities in ostensibly chronological order, the Gospels are not real biographies in the modern sense. They do not attempt to present a complete life of Jesus or to explain what forces—social, psychological, cultural, historical, or political—caused him to become the kind of man he was. Only two of the Gospels—Matthew and Luke—include traditions about Jesus' birth and infancy. None gives even a scrap of information about his formative years, education, friendships, or other experiences that modern historians would regard as essential. Luke recounts a single incident of Jesus' youth, a pilgrimage from his hometown of Nazareth to Jerusalem, Judaism's holy city (Luke 2:22–40). But the Gospels tell us nothing about what happened to Jesus between the ages of twelve and "about thirty" (Luke 3:23), when he suddenly appears at the River Jordan for baptism. All four concentrate exclusively on the last phase of Jesus' life, the period of his public ministry when his teachings both attracted devoted followers and created bitter enemies.

In all four Gospel accounts, only the final week of Jesus' human existence is related in detail—the events leading up to and including his arrest, trial, and execution by the Romans. The significance of Jesus' suffering and death (known as the **Passion**) is the central concern of each Evangelist. Even the **Fourth Gospel** (John), which includes a longer version of Jesus' public career than any other, devotes nearly half of its narrative to retelling the story of Jesus' last few days on earth. Observing this emphasis of the Evangelists, New Testament scholars have described the Gospel form as a Passion narrative with a long introduction. All incidents in Jesus' life leading up to his crucifixion are rigorously

subordinated to the climactic circumstances of his death. The Gospels' form and content are shaped not by purely historical or biographical considerations, but by their respective authors' theological viewpoints. Combining the Greek *theos* (God) with *logos* (word or logical analysis), **theology** means "a study of God." It is a religious discipline involving the study of God's nature, will, and activity among humankind. The theologian typically defines and interprets systems of belief that express a religion's essential worldview. The Gospel writers are theologians, and like all New Testament authors, the Evangelists write primarily to voice their individual understanding of Jesus' religious or theological significance.

By placing four different versions of Jesus' story at the head of the New Testament collection, Christian editors not only highlighted the diverse ways in which Jesus could be interpreted acceptably by four different Christian writers but also affirmed the supreme importance of Jesus' achievement. The order of contents thus emphasizes the primacy of Jesus' story, the four Gospels together forming a composite foundation document for the Christian religion. No matter how influential the writings that appear later, such as Paul's letters with their innovative declaration that salvations comes to Jew and Gentile alike through faith in Christ, they must always be weighed against the initial presentations of what Jesus said and did.

An Account of the Early Church To a large extent, the books that follow the Gospels either explore the consequences of Jesus' life and death or offer interpretative meditations on their meaning. A continuation of Luke's Gospel, the Book of Acts portrays Jesus' followers carrying on his work, directed by the same divine Spirit that had animated Jesus. Opening with a brief description of the resurrected Jesus' ascension to heaven and ending with Paul's preaching activity in Rome, Acts narrates a series of crucial episodes in Christianity's early development, covering the years from about 30 to 60 CE.

Letters Whereas Acts gives a theological overview of Christianity's rapid expansion in the Roman Empire, the New Testament's twenty-one letters (some of which are actually sermons or tracts) offer close-up views of individual Christian communities and their difficulties in trying to follow Jesus in a sometimes hostile world. Letters by (or attributed to) Paul form a major unit of the collection. Written before the Gospels appeared, the authentic Pauline letters vividly reflect the struggle for unity of thought and purpose taking place in the Greek-speaking congregations that Paul served.

The miscellaneous documents comprising the final part of the New Testament echo the hopes and troubles of widely scattered churches in the late first and early second centuries CE, a period well after that of Paul's missionary tours. Whereas the Book of Hebrews is anonymous, the seven short works known as the catholic epistles are ascribed to early leaders in the original Jerusalem church, the apostles **Peter** and **John** and two of Jesus' kinsmen, **James** and **Jude.** Although several of the epistles were not accorded undisputed scriptural status until the late fourth century, they express the postapostolic church's ongoing anxieties, particularly the problems raised by false teachers and the inexplicable delay in Jesus' promised return (see Chapter 18).

An Apocalypse The Book of Revelation represents the fourth and final literary category in the Christian Scriptures. The title *Revelation* translates the Greek noun *apokalypsis,* which means an "uncovering" or "unveiling." Like other **apocalyptic literature,** Revelation features visions of an unseen world inhabited by spirit creatures both good and evil. It highlights the cosmic struggle between God and Satan, a conflict involving both heaven and earth that ultimately sees evil defeated, God's kingdom triumphant, and the creation of a new earth and heaven (Rev. 12; 16; 20–21). Revelation's message is urgent, demanding that believers hold firm in the faith because, like Paul, the author of Mark's Gospel, and

other apocalyptic writers, the author believes that the universal war he envisions is about to begin. This climactic event "must shortly happen" because Jesus is "coming soon" (Rev. 1:1, 3; 12:12; 22:7, 11, 12).

Apocalyptic ideas played an extremely important role in early Christian thought and dominate many passages in the New Testament. As we study the Gospel accounts of Jesus' preaching, we will find numerous apocalyptic concepts, commonly involving **eschatology.** Derived from two Greek phrases—*to eschaton* (referring to the world's end) and *ho logos* (meaning "study of")—eschatology refers to beliefs about events occurring at the End of time. On a personal level, eschatology involves momentous events at the end of an individual's life: death, posthumous judgment, heaven, hell, and resurrection. On a more general level, it relates to developments that culminate in the End of human society and history as we know them.

Although the twenty-seven documents composing the New Testament generally fit into one of four broad literary genres, most also contain a number of subgenres. The Gospels, for example, include not only biographical narratives about Jesus but also such disparate forms as genealogies, parables, aphorisms, confrontation stories, miracle stories, prayers, reconstructions of conversations, and, in the case of John's Gospel, long metaphysical discourses. The Book of Acts similarly incorporates public speeches, private dialogues, anecdotes about individual figures, and perhaps even excerpts from a diary or travel journal.

Some documents grouped in the third section—the Pauline letters and catholic epistles—are technically not forms of correspondence. Except for its opening phrases, the Book of James is more like a collection of traditional wisdom sayings than a letter. The Book of Hebrews is actually an elaborate sermon, whereas 1 John and Jude resemble tracts directed against opponents who were (or had been) part of their respective authors' religious communities.

Diversity and Unity in the New Testament Documents

The New Testament's variety of literary genres is paralleled by the diversity of its authors' thoughts. Whereas all canonical writers are unified in their conviction of Jesus' supreme value, they respond to his life and teachings in significantly different ways. Modern scholarship has increasingly come to realize that early Christians not only were an ethnically and theologically diverse group but also produced a literature—including the New Testament books—reflecting that diversity. Scholars such as Raymond E. Brown and James D. G. Dunn (see "Recommended Reading") have explored the intellectual, social, and theological forces operating in—and in some cases dividing—different early Christian communities.

Paul's genuine letters, written to largely Gentile (non-Jewish) congregations between about 50 and 62 CE, advocate a Christian's total freedom from the "bondage" of Mosaic Law. In contrast, the Gospel of Matthew, probably composed in Antioch for Jews converted to Christianity, promotes continuing obedience to the Mosaic heritage. A third group, which emphasized the unique divinity of Jesus, issued the Gospel of John as its foundation document. That community, based on the teachings of "the disciple whom Jesus loved," later split into factions debating the question of Jesus' physical humanity, a division reflected in the letters of 1 and 2 John.

After Paul's death, a variety of writers claimed his authority for their particular group. While one Pauline school created the Book of Ephesians, updating Paul's thought to deal with new issues and situations, another composed the Letters to Timothy and Titus, promulgating church structure, administrative authority, and the power of received tradition (see Chapter 17). Whereas these pseudo-Pauline works were eventually accepted into the New Testament, others also attributed to the apostle, such as the apocryphal Acts of Paul and Thecla, were not.

After Roman armies destroyed Jerusalem in 70 CE—and along with it Christianity's parent church (see Chapters 2 and 5)—New Testament

writers differed in their attitude toward the secular government. Although he generally adopts a policy of cooperation with Roman authorities, the author of Luke-Acts also reveals that missionaries' preaching often provoked riots and other disturbances in many Greco-Roman cities, causing serious problems for public officials (see chapter 12). The fiery visionary who wrote Revelation rejects the imperial system altogether and predicts its imminent destruction (see Chapter 19).

Other Early Christian Literature

In addition to the twenty-seven documents comprised in the New Testament, the early Christian community produced a large number of other writings, most of which are in the same literary genres as the New Testament books—Gospels, letters, and acts of the apostles (see Box 1.5). Some of these works, once included in church lists of "recognized books" along with familiar New Testament titles, are as old as or older than many documents that Christians eventually included in their bibles. No one knows why some documents were accepted by the early churches and others were not. Paul wrote letters other than those now in the New Testament (1 Cor. 5:9–11); we cannot be sure that their exclusion was the result of their being destroyed or otherwise lost. Specific works may have been accepted or rejected primarily because of their relative usefulness in supporting what was later regarded as **orthodoxy**—"correct teaching" promoted by church leaders.

Although many early Christian writings have disappeared and are known only by title, enough remain to indicate that the early Christian community was extremely diverse and created a literature that expressed that diversity. Rather than a monolithic organization in which all members embraced a single "true faith," Christianity, for the first three centuries of its existence, interpreted Jesus in a variety of ways. Whereas some

BOX 1.5 Selected List of Early Christian Gospels, Apocalypses, and Other Writings Not Included in the New Testament

WORKS FORMERLY APPEARING IN SOME NEW TESTAMENT LISTS

The Epistle of Barnabas (attributed to Paul's Jewish-Christian mentor)

The Didache (supposedly a summary of the Twelve Apostles' teachings on the opposing ways leading to life or death)

1 Clement (a letter by the third bishop of Rome to the Corinthians)

The Apocalypse of Peter (visions of heaven and hell ascribed to Peter)

The Shepherd of Hermas (a mystical apocalyptic work)

GOSPELS POSSIBLY PRESERVING SOME OF JESUS' TEACHINGS OR OTHER HISTORICAL INFORMATION ABOUT HIM

The Gospel of Thomas (a compilation of 114 sayings of Jesus found in the Nag Hammadi Library)

The Gospel of Peter (a primitive account of Jesus' crucifixion, burial, and resurrection ascribed to Peter)

The Egerton Papyrus 2 (a fragment of an unknown Gospel that may have provided a source for some of the Johannine discourses)

The Apocryphon of James (a private dialogue between Jesus and two disciples, Peter and James)

OTHER GOSPELS, MOST SURVIVING ONLY IN FRAGMENTARY FORM

The Protoevangelium of James (complete)
The Dialogue of the Savior

The Gospel of Judas
The Gospel of the Egyptians
The Gospel of the Hebrews
The Gospel of the Nazoreans
The Gospel of the Ebionites
The Infancy Gospel of Thomas (complete)
Papyrus Oxyrhynchus 840

MISCELLANEOUS OTHER WORKS

The Acts of Pilate
The Acts of John
The Epistula Apostolorum
2 Clement
The Epistle to Diognetus

OTHER IMPORTANT EARLY CHRISTIAN WRITINGS

The Epistles of Ignatius:
  To the Ephesians
  To the Magnesians
  To the Trallians
  To the Romans
  To the Philadelphians
  To the Smyrnaeans
  To Polycarp
The Epistle of Polycarp to the Philippians
The Martyrdom of Polycarp

Jewish-Christian groups in Palestine and Syria regarded Jesus as fully human, a man whom God adopted as his "son" to represent him on earth, some Christians in Rome claimed that Jesus was entirely divine, a spirit being who only appeared to be human. If we were to travel back in time to the second century CE, visiting individual congregations of believers in different geographical regions—from Galilee (where the Jesus movement began), to Antioch in Syria (where Peter had taught), to Ephesus (from which Paul conducted missionary journeys to non-Jewish peoples), to Rome (where different interpreters of Jesus' nature passionately clashed)—we would find a diversity not unlike that which prevails in different denominations today. All of these groups, ancient and modern, emphasized the importance of Jesus in God's plan for humanity, but as their literary remains testify, they understood his role in very different ways.

Because it is the only early Gospel not in the New Testament to survive complete, the Gospel of Thomas has great significance in illustrating some of the variations in early Christian beliefs. This "Fifth Gospel," discovered in 1945 near the Egyptian village of Nag Hammadi, consists almost exclusively of sayings of the risen Jesus. Unlike the New Testament accounts of Jesus' life, the Gospel of Thomas contains neither reports of his miraculous deeds nor narratives about his death and resurrection. Instead of presenting Jesus as a sacrifice for human sin or an eschatological king who will someday return to judge all humanity, Thomas has little to say about Jesus' eschatological role. Although scholars disagree on its interpretation, Thomas seems to show Jesus as guiding his disciples toward an awareness that God's kingdom already rules, although the unenlightened majority of people fail to perceive it. Many scholars believe that Thomas, which contains numerous statements paralleling those in Matthew, Mark, and Luke, nonetheless represents a tradition independent of the New Testament Gospels and may preserve some of the earliest forms of Jesus' sayings. Interestingly, Thomas also includes themes and concepts that are otherwise found only in the Gospel of John. (For a discussion of Thomas and other early works excluded from the New Testament, see Chapter 20.)

Scholarly Approaches to the New Testament

The presence of numerous similarities, as well as some striking differences, in both the New Testament books and other early Christian writings suggests the need for a careful comparison of these documents if we are to understand the complex forces that helped shape Christianity. To help untangle the complexities, and even contradictions, apparent in formative Christian literature, modern scholarship has devised several methodologies for analyzing the texts. In approaching the New Testament analytically, it is important to remember that studying the Bible in a college or university classroom necessarily differs from reading it in church as part of an act of worship. At a religious service, whether Catholic, Orthodox, or Protestant, short excerpts to be read aloud usually are chosen to encourage listeners to behave ethically: Stories of biblical heroes or villains offer models for worshipers to emulate or avoid. In a devotional setting, the Bible speaks with largely undisputed authority.

In a university environment, however, the Bible is studied in the same way as any other literary document from the ancient world. Using techniques similar to those applied in the disciplines of history, anthropology, sociology, linguistics, and literary studies, students investigate such topics as the question of a document's date and authorship, the implied audience and social setting, the historical context, and the writer's apparent assumptions and goals. It is essential to read carefully to perceive what a text actually says (as opposed to what one may have been told about it elsewhere) and to compare it to similar works written at approximately the same time and under the same cultural influences. Comparative study of the Gospels, which were composed between about 70 and 100 CE, reveals much about their individual authors' distinctive theological concerns, helping to explain reasons for both similarities and differences in their accounts.

Since the eighteenth-century Age of Enlightenment, when scientists and other scholars developed analytical tools to clear away long-held misconceptions about both the natural and the social worlds, virtually all forms of traditional authority have been challenged. In physics, the work of Newton—Einstein in the twentieth century—and other scientists revolutionized our understanding of the universe. In the political arena, rebels challenged the claim that kings ruled by divine right, triggering the

BOX 1.6 Helpful Tools for Studying the New Testament

Several one-volume Bible dictionaries offer concise alphabetized mini-essays on important topics:

> Brown, R. E.; Fitzmeyer, J. A.; and Murphy, R. E., eds. *The New Jerome Biblical Commentary*. Englewood Cliffs, N.J.: Prentice-Hall, 1990. Although slightly dated, provides excellent discussions of all canonical books by leading Catholic scholars.

> Evans, Craig A., and Porter, Stanley E., eds. *Dictionary of New Testament Background*. Downers Grove, Ill.: InterVarsity Press, 2000. Contains essays by generally conservative scholars.

> Freedman, David Noel; Myers, Allen C.; and Beck, Astrid B., eds. *Eerdmans Dictionary of the Bible*. Grand Rapids, Mich.: Eerdmans, 2000. Current and scholarly, an excellent resource.

> Powell, Mark A., ed. *The HarperCollins Bible Dictionary* (Revised and Updated), New York: HarperOne, 2011. Concise, comprehensive, and generally reliable.

Multivolume bible aids include the following:

> Coogan, Michael D., ed. *The Oxford Encyclopedia of the Books of the Bible*, 2 vols. New York: Oxford University Press, 2011. Up-to-date scholarly essays on each book of both the Old and the New Testament.

> Keck, Leander, ed. *The New Interpreter's Bible*, 12 vols. Nashville, Tenn.: Abingdon Press, 1994–. A series featuring the complete text of the Bible, in both the NRSV and NIV translations, with detailed scholarly commentary.

> Sakenfeld, Katherine D., ed. *The New Interpreter's Dictionary of the Bible*, 5 vols. Nashville, Tenn.: Abingdon Press, 2006–2010. Up-to-date scholarly discussions of each biblical book as well as many crucial topics, from the afterlife to Yahweh.

American and French revolutions. In the social world, long-accepted institutions, such as slavery, exploitative child labor, and the subjugation of women, were questioned or replaced by more just practices. Religious claims, including authoritarian uses of the Bible, were similarly scrutinized. During the past two centuries, an international community of scholars—Jewish, Catholic, Protestant, and others—has developed innovative methods to illuminate the nature and growth of biblical documents. This cosmopolitan body of scholars, historians, textual experts, literary critics, linguists, anthropologists, sociologists, and theologians includes thousands of university faculty, clergy, seminary instructors, and academic researchers. Collectively, their efforts have provided us with an increasingly precise and well-documented study of the New Testament literature and the environment out of which it grew. Virtually every textbook used in college and seminary

courses today, including this one, draws heavily on these scholarly resources. (At the end of each chapter in this text, readers will find a list of publications by major New Testament scholars, offering valuable references for further study; see also Box 1.6.)

Some of the principal methods that scholars use to study the New Testament are summarized in Chapter 6; here, we will briefly clarify the term *biblical criticism*. For some people, the term *criticism* may awaken negative feelings, perhaps implying faultfinding or a derogatory judgment. But in biblical studies, it is a positive means of understanding scriptural texts more accurately and objectively. *Criticism* derives from the Greek word *krino*, which means "to judge" or "to discern," to exercise rational analysis in evaluating something. In the fields of art and literature, it involves the ability to recognize artistic worth and to distinguish the relative merits or defects of a given work. In New

Testament studies, various critical methods are used, ranging from techniques for investigating the oral traditions that preceded the written Gospels to literary analysis of their final form, structure, and content.

Because, for hundreds of millions of believers, the New Testament embodies their deeply held convictions and spiritual aspirations, approaching it objectively is difficult. For some readers, the rigorous application of dispassionate logic to documents thought to reveal the divine will seems inappropriate. For many people, however, spirituality, reverence for concepts of divinity, love of the biblical tradition, and critical study are not incompatible; from this perspective, thinking analytically about religious texts and the cultural environment that helped shape them is both a tribute to the texts' intrinsic value and a means of better understanding them. Many scholars believe that the scriptures of most world religions, including the Vedas, Hebrew Bible, New Testament, and Quran, were composed to express authentic human experiences of divine power—represented by such classic moments as Moses encountering God at a burning bush on the slopes of Mount Sinai, Jesus hearing a heavenly voice after his baptism at the Jordan River, and Paul beholding the glorified Christ on the road to Damascus. These unique religious experiences, which seem to transcend the ordinary limits of human life, if they are to be preserved for others, must be articulated in human language that is ill equipped to express unearthly realities. Writing of Jesus' apparently supernatural abilities and personal vision of God's kingdom, the New Testament authors inevitably depicted them in terms of the prevailing culture, using then-current images and metaphors to approximate the inexpressible. Although scholarship cannot investigate the world of the spirit or the elusive dimension of religious transcendence the biblical authors explore, it offers enormous help in examining the means—cultural, social, historical, and literary—by which ancient writers conveyed these phenomena to us.

The New Testament Read from Different Social Perspectives

In recent years, scholars have become increasingly aware that the meaning of any book—including biblical texts—is to a large extent dependent on the reader's individual experience and viewpoint. In the United States, this is particularly true when readers belong to social groups such as ethnic or other minorities that the dominant culture may commonly undervalue or otherwise marginalize. Viewing New Testament passages from a specific social location—such as the African American, Hispanic American, Asian American, Native American, or feminist community—is likely to give these stories a meaning that is distinctly different from interpretations traditionally promoted by society's male Caucasian leadership. When an African American whose forebears were plantation slaves reads the New Testament admonition for servants to submit cheerfully to their masters, no matter how abusive (1 Pet. 2:18–20; Col. 3:22; Eph. 6:5), the command is likely to resonate differently for her than it will for the descendants of white slave owners.

As feminist scholars have pointed out, women of all nationalities may read the Christian Scriptures from a perspective fundamentally different from that of most men. Paul's flat refusal to permit a woman to teach in his churches (1 Cor. 14:34–35) or the pastor's insistence that the first woman must be blamed for humanity's downward spiral into sin and death (1 Tim. 2:13–14) may spark feelings of incredulity or resentment unknown to men reading the same texts. But, as feminist commentators have also observed, the same apostle who allegedly forbade women to address the congregation also recognized the role of women prophets (1 Cor. 11:5) and women as church officeholders, as well as "fellow workers" in the Christian fold (Rom. 16:1–5). Some scholars believe that the restrictions imposed on women in 1 Corinthians 14 are a later copyist's interpolation, to make Paul's instructions conform to the anti-feminist passages in a later (non-Pauline) letter (1 Tim. 3:11; see Chapter 14). (For discussions of the importance of women in Jesus' ministry and in the Pauline congregations, see Chapters 9, 13, and Box 10.6; a discussion of the noncanonical Acts of Paul and Thecla, a legendary female disciple, appears in Chapter 20.)

At his most insightful, Paul endorses a vision of radical equality—legal, ethnic, social, and sexual: "There is no such thing as Jew and Greek, slave and freeman, male and female; for you are all one person in Christ Jesus" (Gal. 3:28). For most societies, Paul's goal of an equal and united Christian fellowship is yet to be realized; most religious groups seem content to accept his more conventional statements regulating the social/sexual hierarchy. Both male and female scholars have come increasingly to see, however, that not only Paul but much of our biblical heritage contains disparate elements that are almost inextricably blended: material that is at once marked as severely limited by its origin in intensely traditional ancient Near Eastern and Mediterranean societies and at the same time material that seems to transcend its culture-bound limitations to express universal principles of divine love and the humane treatment of all peoples. Consistent in all the traditions about Jesus' teaching is his emphasis on the supremacy of love, the transforming practice of selfless devotion that redeems interpersonal relationships and makes possible divine rule on earth (cf. Mark 12:28–31; Matt. 5:44–48; John 14:34–35; 15:9–10; 1 Cor. 13, etc.). The challenge to discern such abiding values in the biblical message will shape the contours of our journey through the diverse literature of the New Testament.

Summary

One among many of the world's sacred books, the New Testament is a collection of Greek documents that early Christian writers composed between about 50 and 140 CE. It forms the second part of the Christian Bible, the larger first section of which is the Hebrew Bible (Tanakh), an older anthology of writings than the Jewish community produced. Besides the twenty-seven books included in the New Testament, early Christian authors also created many other religious works, only a few of which, such as the Gospel of Thomas, have survived. Because it combines aspects of both Jewish and Greek thought, scholars study the New Testament in the context of the culturally diverse environment in which it originated. Analyzing such elements as authorship, date of composition, literary form, thematic concerns, and theological content of New Testament texts, modern scholars endeavor to increase our understanding of these enormously influential documents.

Questions for Review

1. Define the term *testament,* and explain the relationship of the Old Testament (the Hebrew Bible) to the New Testament.
2. What version of the Hebrew Bible did early Christians use? In what common language were the Septuagint and New Testament written?
3. Define and describe the major literary forms (genres) contained in the New Testament.
4. Which part of the New Testament was written first? Who was the author, and when did he write?
5. Describe the overall structure of the New Testament. In what specific ways does the figure of Jesus dominate the entire collection of books?
6. What is an apocalypse? Define the terms *apocalyptic* (adjective) and *eschatology* (noun), and explain their application to the early Christian worldview.
7. What evidence do we have of diversity in the early Christian community? What portrait of Jesus was painted in the "Fifth Gospel" of Thomas?

Questions for Discussion and Reflection

1. Try to define and describe the New Testament to someone who has never before heard of it. In what ways does this collection of early Christian documents resemble the scriptures of other world religions? In what ways does the New Testament differ from other sacred books?
2. The literary form or category in which writers choose to convey their ideas always influences the way in which those ideas are expressed. Why do you suppose early Christian writers invented the Gospel form to express their views about Jesus? Why do you think all four Gospel authors focused on the last week of Jesus' life?

3. Only one Gospel writer also wrote a history of the early church, continuing his story of the Jesus movement with additional stories about a few of Jesus' followers. Given that the New Testament contains *four* different accounts of Jesus' ministry, why do you think there is only *one* narrative about the church?

4. Of the twenty-seven New Testament books, twenty-one are nominally letters. Why do you suppose the letter form was so popular among early Christians? In a church scattered throughout the Roman Empire, what advantage did letter writing have over other literary forms?

5. How can modern scholarship help us better understand the origin and growth of the New Testament? Discuss ways to distinguish essential religious experiences and spiritual insights from "culture-bound" interpretations of them.

Terms and Concepts to Remember*

Abraham	*koinē*
Alexandria	Last Supper
apocalyptic literature	Messiah
Aramaic	Mosaic Covenant
Bible	Moses
covenant (testament)	orthodoxy
eschatology	Palestine
Evangelist	Passion
Fourth Gospel	Paul
Gospel	Pentateuch
Hebrew Bible (Old Testament)	Peter
	Promised Land
Israel	scriptures
James	Septuagint
Jesus	theology
John	Torah
Jude	Yahweh

Recommended Reading

Bailey, James L., and Vander Broek, Lyle. *Literary Forms in the New Testament: A Handbook.* Louisville, Ky.: Westminster/John Knox Press, 1992. An excellent discussion of literary categories found in the New Testament.

Brown, Raymond E. *The Churches the Apostles Left Behind.* New York: Paulist Press, 1984. A brief but authoritative survey of seven different Christian communities—and their distinctive

theologies—that produced major parts of the New Testament literature.

Dunn, James D. G. *Unity and Diversity in the New Testament: An Inquiry into the Character of Earliest Christianity,* 2nd ed. London/Philadelphia: SCM Press/Trinity Press International, 1990. Contains a detailed examination of theological differences manifested in different New Testament books, as well as a summary of nine themes contributing to theological unity of canonical authors.

Ehrman, Bart D. *The New Testament and Other Early Christian Writings: A Reader.* New York: Oxford University Press, 1998. Includes Gospels, letters, and apocalypses not in the New Testament.

Evans, Craig A., and Porter, Stanley E., eds. *Dictionary of the New Testament Background.* Downers Grove, Ill.: InterVarsity Press, 2000. Contains extended entries on both Greco-Roman and Jewish topics relating to early Christianity, from a generally traditional perspective.

Gamble, Harry Y. *Books and Readers in the Early Church: A History of Early Christian Texts.* New Haven, Conn.: Yale University Press, 1995. Explores such topics as the extent of literacy in the Greco-Roman world, the interaction of oral and written materials in the early Christian community, and the community's production and circulation of books.

Gneuse, Robert. *The Authority of the Bible: Theories of Inspiration, Revelation and the Canon of Scripture.* New York: Paulist Press, 1985. A brief but thoughtful review of biblical authority and the nature of divine inspiration.

Massey, James E. "Reading the Bible as African Americans." In *The New Interpreter's Bible,* Vol. 1, pp. 154–160. Nashville, Tenn.: Abingdon Press, 1994. Briefly surveys issues involving slavery and African American churches' use of Scripture.

Newsom, Carol A., Ringe, Sharon H., and Lapsley, Jacqueline E., eds. *Women's Bible Commentary,* 3rd ed. Louisville, Ky.: Westminster/John Knox Press, 2012. Scholarly essays interpreting each book of both the Old and the New Testament from a feminist perspective.

Osiek, Carolyn. "Reading the Bible as Women." In *The New Interpreter's Bible,* Vol. 1, pp. 181–187. Raises pertinent feminist issues.

Reid, Barbara. *Taking Up the Cross: New Testament Interpretation Through Latina and Feminist Eyes.* Minneapolis: Fortress Press, 2007. Explores the Passion story, relating Jesus' suffering to situations of women in Latin America.

Wicker, Kathleen; Dube, Musa; and Spencer, Althea, eds. *Feminist New Testament Studies: Global and Future Perspectives.* New York: Palgrave Macmillan, 2005. Feminist readings of the Christian Scriptures emphasizing a multiethnic and international context.

*Key terms appear at the end of each chapter and are defined in the Glossary at the back of the book.

CHAPTER 2

How the New Testament Was Formed and Handed Down to Us

The use of books is endless. Ecclesiastes 12:12

Key Topics/Themes Although the early Christian community produced many writings during the period when the New Testament books were composed (c. 50–140 CE), most were not accepted into the canon, the official list of church-approved documents. The process of canonization continued for several centuries; it was not until 367 CE that a canonical list corresponding exactly to the present New Testament first appeared, and even afterward church lists of approved books differed. Because no original copies of any canonical work survive and there are hundreds of variations in extant manuscripts, scholars must compare many different versions in creating a plausible Greek text from which modern translations are made. Although the first translators of the Bible into English, Wycliffe and Tyndale, were condemned by the church of their day, the Christian Scriptures are now available in many excellent English editions.

Formation of the New Testament Canon

For Jesus and his earliest followers, the only authoritative Scripture was the three-part Hebrew Bible. According to the Gospel of Luke, written perhaps fifty-five or sixty years after Jesus' death, the risen Jesus instructed his disciples in the proper application of the Jewish Bible, which was to interpret it as a series of prophecies about his role as Messiah. "'Everything written about me,'" Jesus states, "'in the Law of Moses and in the prophets and psalms was bound to be fulfilled.' Then he opened their minds to understand the scriptures" (Luke 24:44–45).

When New Testament writers, who were active between about 50 and 140 CE, quote Scripture, they quote exclusively from the Hebrew Bible, albeit in an expanded Greek edition.

The earliest contributor to the New Testament, Paul repeatedly emphasized that the Jewish holy writings not only anticipated Jesus' ministry and death but were directly relevant to the Christian movement. The Genesis story of Abraham, for example, was written "for our sake," for the benefit of Paul's contemporaries (Rom. 4:22–24). In fact, "all the ancient scriptures were written for our own instruction" and for Christian "encouragement" (Rom. 15:4). In urging the church at Corinth to refrain from complaints, Paul explains that stories of Israelite

23

"grumblings" were composed to preclude similar Christian errors: "All these things that happened to them [the Israelites] were symbolic and were recorded for our benefit as a warning. For upon us the fulfillment of the ages has come" (1 Cor. 10:11). For Paul, believers in Jesus are living at the brief overlap of two contrasting eras, the "present age of wickedness" (Gal. 1:4; cf. 1 Cor. 2:6), and the new age to come when God and Christ will reign completely (see Chapter 14).

Paul's genuine letters (others are attributed to his later disciples) were sent individually to disparate small congregations scattered throughout Asia Minor, Greece, and Italy. Perhaps the first step in creating the New Testament occurred toward the end of the first century CE when one or more of Paul's admirers searched the archives of the various Pauline churches for surviving copies of his correspondence, gathering them together in a single unit. This anonymous Pauline disciple began an anthology of early Christian literature to which the Gospels, Acts, and other documents gradually were added, forming a New Testament canon.

A word derived from the Greek *kanon*, canon refers to a standard or measurement, the norm by which something is evaluated or judged acceptable. In religious usage, a canon is the official inventory of books, like those various churchmen assembled from the late second century on. Individual lists varied significantly and it took many centuries before the church as a whole recognized the twenty-seven books in the now familiar New Testament table of contents. The earliest canonical reference to any Christian writing as "scripture" appears in 2 Peter, which so designates Paul's letters (2 Peter 3:16). Most scholars date 2 Peter to about 130–140 CE and regard it as the last-written document in the New Testament canon (see Chapter 18).

At no time did a single church authority or council of church leaders formally decide on the contents of the Christian Scriptures. The long process by which the present New Testament gradually assumed its final form involved a variety of complex developments, including controversies over doctrine, particularly the nature and degree of Jesus' divinity (see the discussion of Marcion below). A document's usefulness in regulating belief—an "apostolic" understanding of essential principles—undoubtedly influenced a specific book's status. Shortly after the close of the second century CE, four Gospels, Acts, Paul's letters, and several other books were generally acknowledged, although at this point individual lists of acceptable documents showed marked contrasts. Different canons abounded, some including titles that would be totally unfamiliar to most of today's churchgoers, such as the Epistle of Barnabas or the Shepherd of Hermas. During the first several centuries of its development, Christianity was enormously diverse and produced an equally diverse body of literature, including numerous Gospels and other documents that claimed to be written by apostles. In the end, it was not so much a matter of what to include in the canon, but what to leave out. In the meantime, political events, as well as debates over doctrinal issues, directly or indirectly influenced the canonical process.

The Jewish Revolt Against Rome and Its Consequences

About thirty-five years after Jesus' death, the Jews of Palestine rose in open revolt against their Roman overlords (see Chapter 5). When Roman armies breached Jerusalem's walls, they slaughtered tens of thousands of Jews, burned the holy city, and demolished the Jerusalem Temple, the center of Jewish worship (70 CE). The "great tribulation" that marked Rome's destruction of the Jewish state—along with the parent church of apostolic Christianity—offers a chaotic background to the gradual formation of the New Testament, as well as to the closing stages of the Hebrew Bible canon.

At the time of the Jewish Revolt against Rome (66–73 CE), only a few books of what became the New Testament collection then existed: Paul's authentic letters; a compilation of Jesus' sayings known as the source (Q) document; and the Gospel of Mark (see Box 1.4). Most of the Christian Greek Scriptures were yet to be written, and it would be centuries before the church agreed on their exact contents. Echoes of the Jewish Revolt figure prominently in the first three Gospels—Matthew, Mark, and Luke—which devote considerable space to Jesus' prediction of the Temple's fall and to the sufferings of Jews and Christians that Jerusalem's destruction entailed. Significantly, the first three Evangelists also associate events of the Jewish Revolt, particularly the Temple's demolition, with Jesus' promised return as the glorious Son of Man (Matt. 24–25; Mark 13; Luke 21; see Chapters 7–9).

Although all parts of the Hebrew Bible were completed well before the Jewish wars against Rome, the precise number of books to be included had not yet been determined. Following their suppression of the Jewish rebellion, the Romans apparently encouraged Jewish scholars who had not participated in the uprising to assemble at Jamnia (Yavneh) on the Mediterranean coast to help reorganize postwar Judaism. Led by Rabbi Yohanan ben Zakkai, a small group of rabbis ("masters" or "teachers") discussed ways to cope with the crisis—loss of Temple, priesthood, and homeland—and to provide religious leadership for the Jewish community. As noted in Chapter 3, the rabbis did not formally close the biblical canon, but they seem to have applied several criteria that excluded numerous books that many Greek-speaking Jews used outside Palestine. Accepting the thesis that inspired prophecy had ceased shortly after the time of Ezra (c. 400 BCE), the Jamnia scholars evidently rejected documents clearly composed after that period, such as the Wisdom of Jesus Son of Sirach (Ecclesiasticus) and the books of Maccabees. Of all the extant apocalypses, only Daniel was accepted, perhaps because the author plausibly claimed to write during the sixth century BCE. Books that

contradicted the Torah or that were not originally written in Hebrew, such as the Wisdom of Solomon, were also excluded. The Christian community, however, which adopted the Greek Septuagint as its preferred edition of the Bible, generally recognized the deuterocanonical status of these books the rabbis rejected. Known as the Apocrypha, these later books were eventually included in an official Latin Bible, the Vulgate (see the discussion of Jerome and the Vulgate below).

As a result of the rabbis rejecting later documents not composed in Hebrew or Aramaic, the Hebrew Bible or Tanakh has fewer books than Catholic or Orthodox Old Testaments, which include the later documents, such as Tobit, Judith, and the Wisdom of Solomon, contained in the Septuagint. By contrast, Protestant editions of the Old Testament typically follow the rabbinical model and exclude the apocryphal material (see Chapter 1).

In appropriating a Greek version of the Jewish Scriptures—and rechristening this collection as the Old Testament—the Christian movement also transformed the older Jewish writings into a Christological statement. In Christian eyes, the Old Testament served primarily to reveal Christ, not only through prophecy but also by analogy to specific biblical characters. Christian reinterpretations thus give startlingly innovative meanings to familiar Old Testament passages. Jesus of Nazareth becomes Eve's "seed" (Gen. 3:15), his death and resurrection are foreshadowed in Abraham's near-sacrifice of Isaac (Gen. 22), and his universal rulership is anticipated by the reigns of Davidic Kings (2 Sam. 7; Pss. 2, 110; Isa. 7, 11, etc.).

The order in which Christian editors finally arranged the New Testament books emphasizes both Jesus' connection to characters in the Old Testament and his fulfillment of God's promises to Israel. First in the New Testament canon is Matthew's Gospel, which proclaims "Jesus Christ, son of David, son of Abraham," the culmination of the covenant people's prophetic hopes. The other Gospels, Acts, Pauline letters, and catholic epistles similarly explicate biblical foreshadowings of Jesus' role and work. Although it took several centuries to assume this format, the Christian canon ultimately closed with the Book of Revelation and its image of Christ triumphant, subduing all nations and peoples in his universal kingdom. Because Christianity emerged historically as a messianic and apocalyptic moment within first-century CE Judaism, it is appropriate that the canonical climax occurs with Revelation's assurance that Christ is "coming soon," asserting that Jesus' return to earth—the Parousia or Second Coming— is imminent (Rev. 22:17–21) (see Chapter 19).

Before the end of the first century CE, some Christians were keenly aware that expectations of the Second Coming had failed to materialize. Neither Jesus nor the kingdom had rescued believers from life's sorrows or from Rome's intermittent persecutions. The author of 1 Clement (c. 96 CE) addresses Christians' disappointment in the delayed Parousia:

> Let that Scripture be far from us which says: "Wretched are the double-minded, Those who doubt in their soul and say, 'We have heard these things [predictions of Jesus' return] even in our fathers' times, and see, we have grown old and none of this has happened.'"
>
> (1 Clem. 23:3–5)

A generation or two after 1 Clement was composed, in a work attributed to the apostle Peter, the problem of frustrated apocalyptic hopes was again raised. Skeptics complained that Jesus' promised coming had proved to be a non-event; everything "continues exactly as it has always been since the world began" (2 Pet. 3:1–10). The writer responds to this criticism by asserting that a delayed world judgment allows time and opportunity for sinners to repent and thus is an act of divine mercy.

Nevertheless, Jesus' failure to return visibly may have provoked a crisis of belief among second-century Christians, as the author of 2 Peter testifies. As Christians struggled to understand God's intentions in human history and his plan for the church, they simultaneously began to assemble an anthology of writings that most effectively expressed their core beliefs and

hopes. Foremost was the meaning of Jesus' life and death, as interpreted by the preeminent Christian theologian and missionary, the apostle Paul. By the first half of the second century CE, at least some Christian groups already regarded Paul's letters as "scripture" (2 Pet. 3:16). Although all four of the accepted Gospels had been composed by the close of the first century CE, historians doubt that most believers were familiar with all four. It appears that each Gospel was probably created for a distinct Christian group in a particular city or region. Matthew, for example, seems to have been directed to a congregation at Antioch in Syria, where it probably served as a foundation document for Jewish Christians living there (see Chapter 8). Many scholars believe that the last Gospel written, the account ascribed to John, served to define the distinctive ideas of a religious community based on the teachings of a "disciple whom Jesus loved." Neither the name of the Beloved Disciple nor the original location of his group is known (see Chapter 10). Justin Martyr, a church leader executed in Rome about 165 CE, cites the "memoirs of the Apostles" or "Gospels" as though they had by then attained an authority equal to that of the Hebrew Bible/Old Testament.

The titles by which we now know the canonical accounts of Jesus' life—"The Gospel According to Matthew," or "According to" Mark, or Luke or John—did not become part of the New Testament tradition until more than a century after they were composed. Until the late second century CE, Christian writers generally cite the Gospels anonymously. A notable exception is Papias (c. 140 CE), who refers specifically to the Gospels of Mark and Matthew (see Chapters 7 and 8).

Only gradually did the Gospels come to be regarded as the work of Jesus' initial **apostles**— persons whom Jesus himself had called to be his close followers—or of later companions of the apostles, such as Mark and Luke, who were not eyewitnesses to Jesus' ministry. When Justin Martyr insists that the church should acknowledge only four Gospels—presenting suspiciously labored arguments—he indicates that other Gospels were then in circulation and competed with the four that eventually became canonical. Indeed, the author of Luke's Gospel states that "many [early Christian] writers have undertaken to draw up an account" of Jesus' life (Luke 1:1). Although scholars agree that Luke used Mark's older Gospel as one of his chief sources, we do not know what other very early Jesus biographies the author had in mind (see Chapter 9). We do know that a host of other Gospels were circulating by the second century CE—accounts ascribed to prominent New Testament figures such as Peter, Thomas, James, or Mary Magdalene. Most of the noncanonical Gospels survive only as titles in later church writings denouncing them and/or in badly preserved manuscript fragments. Only one survives complete, the Gospel ascribed to Thomas. Discovered in 1945 near the village of Nag Hammadi in Egypt, the Gospel of Thomas contains 114 sayings of the risen Jesus. Even more recently discovered is an extremely tattered manuscript of the Gospel ascribed to Judas, the first English version of which was published in 2006 (see Chapter 20).

The notion that a single, consistent Gospel—rather than the four sometimes contradictory accounts—should be the church norm was expressed in the *Diatessaron* by a scholar named Tatian, compiled in about 170 CE and now lost. This composite version, which for centuries prevailed in the East, particularly in Syria, ingeniously wove together the contents of Matthew, Mark, Luke, and John, as well as elements from oral tradition, into a unified narrative.

Different Church Canons

Not until late in the fourth century CE did a church leader produce a list of books that corresponds precisely to the twenty-seven books in our New Testament, although in a different order. In 367 CE, Athanasius, then bishop of Alexandria, made an inventory of accepted Christian documents part of his Easter Letter. Even after Athanasius issued his seemingly definitive tally, however, for centuries various churches continued to use New Testament collections that differed significantly from one another.

The Muratorian Canon Scholars formerly dated the list known as the **Muratorian Canon** to the late second or early third century CE but now think that it was probably assembled in the fourth century (c. 350–375 CE). The Muratorian inventory is probably typical of the mixed bag of both (ultimately) canonical and spurious books found in different church catalogues. Listing twenty-four documents, the Muratorian Canon includes the four Gospels, Acts, thirteen letters ascribed to Paul (but not Hebrews), Jude, 1 and 2 (but not 3) John, the Wisdom of Solomon, Revelation, and the Apocalypse of Peter. The Muratorian list excludes five books that eventually achieved canonical status, but it includes a Greek Wisdom book that was later assigned to the Old Testament Apocrypha and an "apostolic" vision of hell that was ultimately not included in any canon.

The Codex Claromontanus is a sixth-century Greek-Latin manuscript that contains a list also thought to derive from the fourth century CE. Besides enumerating most of the present canonical works, this codex includes the Epistle of Barnabas, the Shepherd of Hermas, the Acts of Paul, and the Apocalypse of Peter—all four of which eventually were omitted from the canon. Even the Codex Sinaiticus, one of the oldest (fourth century) and most important manuscripts containing all twenty-seven New Testament books, also includes the Epistle of Barnabas and the Shepherd of Hermas. As late as the fifth century, a Greek manuscript known as the Codex Alexandrinus included both 1 and 2 Clement as part of the Christian Scriptures.

1 Clement, attributed to an early bishop of Rome, is a letter sent to the church at Corinth, perhaps in the mid-90s CE. Concerned that the Corinthians have rejected their duly appointed leaders, the author primarily cites texts from the Hebrew Bible/Old Testament to correct their perceived misbehavior, a practice typical of Christian writers of the period. The writer, however, also quotes passages from Hebrews and from the sayings of Jesus, though it is not certain whether he quotes from written Gospels or from oral tradition.

Like the Apocalypse of Peter, 2 Clement is pseudonymous—composed by an unknown writer in the name of a famous person. The practice of **pseudonymity** was common among both Jewish and Christian authors in the Greco-Roman era. Whereas the church repudiated many pseudonymous documents that claimed authorship by Peter, Paul, James, or other well-known figures in early Christianity, apparently some pseudonymous writings were included in the New Testament canon (see Chapters 17 and 18).

Writing in the early fourth century CE, the church historian **Eusebius** (c. 260–340 CE) observed that, even after Christianity had been legally validated by the Roman government, the New Testament canon was not yet fixed. In describing the church's current opinion of a given book's authenticity, Eusebius divided contenders for official canonization into three categories. The universally "acknowledged" works number twenty-one, including the Gospels, Acts, Paul's letters, and some of the catholic epistles. The "disputed" books, accepted by some churches but not others, include six that eventually entered the canon: Revelation, James, Jude, 2 Peter, and 2 and 3 John. Five other candidates for official inclusion ultimately failed to make the cut: the Acts of Paul, the Shepherd of Hermas, the Apocalypse of Peter, the Epistle of Barnabas, and the Didache, a fascinating compendium of late first-century Christian rituals and moral teachings (see Chapter 20). Eusebius's "rejected" books are the Gospels ascribed to Peter, Thomas, and Matthias and the Acts attributed to Andrew, John, and other apostles, all pseudonymous works.

Whereas some Christian groups endorsed books later barred from the canon, others repudiated works that were finally canonized. Such celebrated writings as Revelation and the Gospel of John fail to appear in many New Testament lists. Several important churches, including those at Alexandria and Antioch, resisted accepting Revelation, partly because it was not believed to be the work of John the Apostle. Although eventually canonized, among Eastern churches Revelation did not attain the same authority as most other New Testament books. The Syrian churches consistently denied it canonical honors.

(Box 1.4 lists the canonical books and their approximate order of composition.)

Marcion's Disputed Role Many scholars formerly thought that the notion of fashioning a Christian Scripture distinct from the Old Testament received its initial stimulus from the proposals of **Marcion.** A wealthy Greek shipbuilder who settled in Rome, Marcion (c. 140 CE) enthusiastically supported Paul's doctrine of salvation by faith. He also found the Old Testament ethically objectionable, especially its portrayal of Israel's God, which he denounced as violent and savage. Insisting that Christianity begin afresh, Marcion advocated wholesale rejection of the Jewish Scriptures and their replacement with an exclusively Christian text. Only Paul's letters and an edited version of Luke's Gospel, purged of its Old Testament references, should be the Christian Bible. According to an older scholarly view, church leaders began to see the importance of defining a New Testament canon only after Marcion had proposed his severely abbreviated list of acceptable documents.

Although Marcion's challenge to define a uniquely Christian Scripture undoubtedly had its effect, most scholars now believe that the evolution of the New Testament canon resulted from a broader set of social and historical circumstances. Noting that Paul's letters had already been collected before Marcion, recent scholars also point out that by 140 CE individual Gospels were already being employed in different churches, although few, if any, churches had accepted all four accounts. Locally approved Gospels and selected documents supposedly of apostolic origin were already regularly and extensively used in worship services and in teaching converts. Read aloud in churches from Syria to Gaul (France), some Gospels, Pauline letters, and other works were in the process of demonstrating their long-term value in maintaining a literary connection with Jesus and his early disciples.

In general, it seems that the New Testament canon evolved to serve two related purposes. First, canonization of certain texts clarified within the Christian community what beliefs church leaders considered true and acceptable.

Questioners like Marcion and his numerous followers could thus be confronted with an officially sanctioned list of books that largely defined the faith. Second, the canon provided a unifying force for churches dispersed throughout the Roman Empire, imparting a firm written authority for universal belief and practice. Citing approved books (but not others), church leaders could distinguish **orthodoxy** (correct teaching) from **heresy** (ideas that church authorities judged deviations from the truth).

The Role of Constantine

The emperor **Constantine** (reigned 306–337 CE) introduced a momentous change in the Roman government's attitude toward Christianity, a change that also may have influenced the finalization of the New Testament canon. Following his victory at the Milvian Bridge over Maxentius, his rival for the imperial throne (312 CE), Constantine effected one of the most unexpected reversals in human history. According to tradition, the emperor experienced a vision in which Jesus was revealed as the divine power that enabled him to defeat his enemies. Undergoing a slow process of conversion to the Christian faith, Constantine ultimately championed Christ as his chief god. This imperial conversion had immense repercussions throughout the empire, altering forever the relationship of church and state (see Figure 2.1).

Shortly before Constantine began his long reign, his predecessor, Diocletian (284–305 CE), had initiated the most thorough and devastating persecution that Christians had yet endured, an ordeal that ended only with Diocletian's abdication and death. When Constantine issued his celebrated decree of religious toleration, the **Edict of Milan** (313 CE), and subsequently began restoring confiscated church property, consulting Christian leaders about official affairs, and appointing bishops to high public office, it was as if a miraculous deliverance of God's people had occurred. To many who benefited from Constantine's policy, it seemed that Revelation's seventh angel had sounded his

FIGURE 2.1 Head of Constantine. Only the head and other fragments of this colossal statue remain, but they reflect the enormous power wielded by this remarkable general and administrator. Seeking the support of a unified church, Constantine summoned and presided over the Council of Nicaea (325 CE), which, amid intense theological controversy, formulated the Trinitarian creed affirming that the Son is co-equal, consubstantial, and co-eternal with the Father.

trumpet: "the sovereignty of the world has passed to our Lord and his Christ" (Rev. 11:15).

In a more modest metaphor, the church historian Eusebius, who later became Constantine's biographer, compared the emperor's increasingly enthusiastic support of the church to the dawn of a brilliant new day, opening up glorious possibilities for the Christian religion. With the exception of Julian (361–363 CE), who was known as the Apostate for trying to revive Greco-Roman cults, all of Constantine's successors to the imperial throne were nominally Christians.

Constantine's influence on the future course of Christianity probably went far beyond his personal acceptance of the faith and his administration's consequent patronage of the church. Not only did the (as yet unbaptized) emperor directly preside over the Council of Nicaea (325 CE)—at which the divinity of Jesus and his co-equality with God were affirmed—he seems to have helped determine the final contents of the New Testament. As Eusebius reports, even three centuries after Jesus' death, Christians in different parts of the Roman Empire had not yet agreed on a fixed canon. Whereas some parts of the church accepted controversial books such as Revelation, James, and 2 Peter, many others did not. In some churches, works like the Dicache, the Epistle of Barnabas, and 1 Clement evidently continued to enjoy quasi-canonical status. When Constantine ordered church leaders to produce fifty parchment copies of the Christian Greek Scriptures for official use, however, ecclesiastical editors may have felt obliged to present the emperor with a consistent list of accepted books. We do not know the exact contents of Constantine's New Testament, but it may have included Revelation and other works that, according to Eusebius, were still "disputed" in his time.

The Latin Vulgate Canons at individual churches continued to differ even after Constantine had ordered official transcripts of the Christian Scriptures and after Athanasius issued his Easter list of approved books later in the fourth century. The event that was perhaps decisive in permanently establishing the New Testament canon was Jerome's translation of the Bible, both the Old and the New Testament, into Latin. Beginning in 382 and continuing until 404 CE, Jerome translated directly from the original Hebrew and Greek, producing the **Vulgate** (from *vulgatus*, the "common" language of the western Roman Empire). This Latin edition remains the official Bible of the Roman Catholic Church. One of his era's great scholars and theologians, Jerome followed Athanasius's canon and included all seven catholic (general) epistles, as well as the controversial Hebrews and Revelation. Jerome's translation excluded other "disputed" writings, however, including the Epistle of Barnabas and the Apocalypse of Peter; once regarded as virtually equal to what we think of as "genuine" New Testament works, these texts were henceforth relegated to obscurity.

Transmitting the New Testament Texts

No original author's copies of any New Testament books have yet come to light. Our oldest transcriptions are fragmentary copies dating from about 200 CE, about a century to a century and a half after the original texts were composed. The earliest surviving **manuscript** is a tiny scrap of the Gospel of John containing four verses from chapter 18. On the basis of its calligraphy (form of handwriting), historians date it to about 125–150 CE, a mere twenty-five to fifty years after the Gospel was written (see Figure 2.2).

Most of these early manuscripts survive only in small fragments, and all were found in

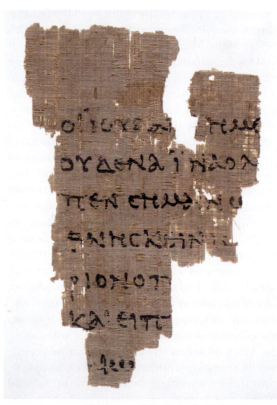

FIGURE 2.2 Fragment of the Gospel of John, the oldest surviving manuscript of a New Testament book. Dating from about 125–150 CE and preserved for 1,800 years in the dry sands of an Egyptian grave, the tiny scrap of papyrus contains four verses from John 18.

BOX 2.1 Copyists' Modifications of New Testament Manuscripts

No two ancient Greek manuscripts of New Testament books are precisely alike. Although most differences in the texts were probably caused by unintentional errors in copying, some textual variations seem to have resulted from deliberate changes, many of which may have been motivated by theological considerations. A few of the oldest manuscripts, including the Codex Sinaiticus, do not contain the phrase "son of God" in Mark 1:1, leading some scholars to think that the phrase was inserted at the beginning of the Gospel to refute a belief that Jesus became God's adopted son at his baptism (see Chapter 7). Another possibly intentional change, made for the same purpose, may appear in Luke's account of Jesus' baptism; some early manuscripts have God declare, "You are my son; *this day* I have begotten you," a quotation from Psalm 2 (Luke 3:22; emphasis added). Most modern translations use an alternative phrasing that avoids the adoption issue, having God say, "in you I am well pleased" or "in you I delight" (New English Bible).

Similar concerns about an orthodox understanding of Jesus' origins apparently influenced manuscript changes in Luke's story of the youthful Jesus' being left behind in the Temple. Mary's reprimand to the child, "your father and I have been anxiously searching for you," was, in some manuscripts, changed to "*we* have been searching for you" (Luke 2:48; emphasis added), ostensibly to avoid any implication that Joseph was Jesus' real father. A theological belief in Jesus' omniscience may have prompted deletion of references to "the Son" from some copies of Matthew's statement that "about that day and hour [of the End] no one knows, . . . not even the Son; no one but the Father alone" (Matt. 24:36).

Perhaps the most striking New Testament interpolation appears in very late manuscripts of 1 John 5:7–8, where a scribe inserted the Bible's only explicit reference to the Christian doctrine of the Trinity, asserting that God exists in three persons and that "these three are one." This trinitarian statement occurs in no manuscript dating prior to the fourteenth century.

Some scholars argue that theological controversies over such issues as Christ's eternally divine nature and equality with God prompted some scribes to emend manuscripts so that they conformed to the orthodox position (see Ehrman in "Recommended Reading" at the end of this chapter).

Egypt, where the dry climate aided preservation of the papyrus on which they were written. The oldest extant copies of the New Testament as a whole, the Codex Sinaiticus and Codex Vaticanus, were compiled in the fourth century CE (see the discussion of "codex" in the next section). These famous texts are written on parchment, an expensive writing material made from sheepskin or goatskin, and much more durable than papyrus.

The fourth-century parchment editions reflect the newfound prosperity of the Christian church. They appeared shortly after Christianity became the favored religion of the Roman emperors. The literary productivity that Constantine strongly encouraged contrasts sharply with conditions a few years earlier under the emperor Diocletian. During the **"Great Persecution"** (303–305 CE), Diocletian ordered the imprisonment or execution of Christian leaders and the burning of Christian books. Diocletian's systematic attacks on the church help explain why we have no complete New Testament texts dating prior to Constantine's time.

Problems in Transmission

The large gap between the time that most of the New Testament was composed (c. 50–100 CE) and the age of the oldest complete manuscript copies (fourth century CE) creates a problem for textual scholars. Questions about whether surviving copies accurately represent the authors' original work are compounded by the fact that no two extant manuscripts or manuscript fragments are precisely alike (see Box 2.1).

BOX 2.2 From Scroll to Codex

Although our word *Bible* derives from the Greek *biblia* (little books) and appropriately describes its nature as a literary anthology, some scholars warn that this designation is somewhat misleading. Modern English books are printed on paper pages that are bound together between covers and read consecutively from front to back, enabling readers to find specific passages with relative ease. By contrast, for most of their early history, the biblical documents existed only as a series of individual scrolls that bore little resemblance to a modern book. Consisting of sheets of papyrus 9 or 10 inches long and 5 or 6 inches wide that were stitched or glued together to form documents up to 25 to 30 feet long, scrolls were extremely difficult to use. To find a particular passage, readers were commonly obligated to unroll brittle papyrus documents for many feet, a process that was awkward and time-consuming.

Because scrolls were expensive to produce and because most people in the ancient world could neither read nor write, the majority of first-century Jews and Christians merely listened to biblical texts read aloud at their local synagogue or house church. In Luke's Gospel, the author shows Jesus, at a synagogue service in Nazareth, searching to find the correct place in a scroll of Isaiah, reading it aloud to the congregation, and then interpreting the passage as being fulfilled in him. "Today," he announces, "in your very hearing this text has come true" (Luke 4:16–22). Luke also refers to the three-part Hebrew Bible—"the Law of Moses" and "the prophets and psalms" (representing the Writings)—that then existed only as an open collection of disparate scrolls. In the days of Jesus and his first disciples, the exact contents of the Jewish Scriptures (Old Testament) had yet to be determined, and the New Testament had yet to be written (see the discussion of the Dead Sea Scrolls in Chapter 3).

It was not until the fourth century CE that the early Christian community generally adopted the **codex,** a manuscript forerunner of the modern book. The most important surviving editions of the New Testament were produced in codex form, which consisted of parchment sheets folded over and sewn together to create a series of easily turned pages featuring a continuous text. Of particular value is the Codex Sinaiticus, a fourth-century manuscript discovered during the 1800s in the monastery of Saint Catherine at the foot of Mount Sinai. Besides the entire New Testament (including books not now in the canon), the Sinaiticus also contains much of the Greek Old Testament.

Although scholars have reconstructed what most believe to be a reliable version of the New Testament Greek text, it is impossible to confirm that we possess exact copies of the letters that Paul dictated or the Gospels as they first circulated in their respective authors' communities. Some scholars suggest that, besides making relatively minor errors of transmission, generations of Christian scribes who copied New Testament books may have edited various passages to make them conform more closely to evolving doctrines of the church. Scribes also commonly modified the wording of one Gospel to make it conform to that in another, a practice known as *harmonization*. A number of scribal additions have long been recognized and omitted in modern translations—such as interpolated trinitarian passages in 1 John—but, in the absence of first- or second-century manuscripts, scholars can only speculate about the nature and degree of many scribal modifications.

In preserving their sacred writings, Christians pioneered the use of the codex. Rather than continuing to record texts on scrolls—long sheets of papyrus or parchment rolled around a stick—Christian scribes assembled page-sized manuscript sheets bound together in the manner of a modern book (see Box 2.2 and Figure 2.3).

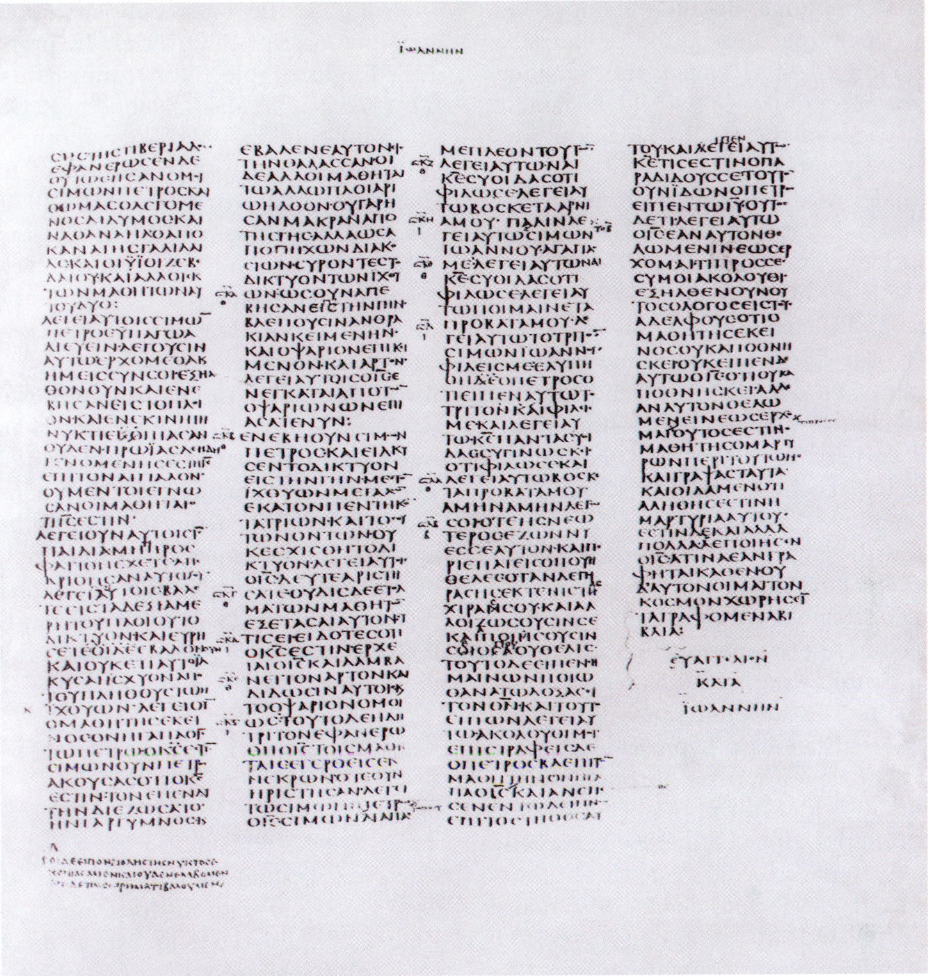

FIGURE 2.3 Ancient codex. Christians pioneered the use of the codex, manuscript pages bound together like a modern book. This Greek text from the Gospel of John contrasts with older copies of New Testament books, which typically survive only in fragmentary form. After Constantine recognized Christianity as a legal religion in the early fourth century, New Testament manuscripts increased in number and quality.

The great fourth-century codex editions of the New Testament were written in uncial characters. Also called "majuscules," uncials are large or capital letters written in continuous script without spaces between words and usually without punctuation. Later manuscripts, called "minuscules," were written in small cursive letters, with individual letters connected to form groups and syllables.

Assembling a Composite New Testament Text

The uncial codices are the most important basis of the text from which modern translations into English or other languages are made. The most valuable is the **Codex Sinaiticus,** a mid-fourth-century manuscript discovered during the mid-1800s in the monastery of Saint Catherine at foot of Mount Sinai. Besides the entire New Testament (including the Epistle of Barnabas and the Shepherd of Hermas), the Sinaiticus also contains most of the Greek Old Testament. Additional pages of the Codex Sinaiticus were discovered as late as 1975.

Even older is the **Codex Vaticanus** (early fourth century), but it lacks part of Hebrews, several Pauline letters, and Revelation. Together with the slightly later uncial editions—the Codex Alexandrinus, which incorporates 1 and 2 Clement and a book of Jewish poetry called the Psalms of Solomon, and the Codex Bezae, which includes a Latin translation of the Greek text—these landmark editions provide scholars with the foundation on which to reconstruct the Greek texts of the New Testament.

The fourth-century codices represent only the beginning of the laborious process of textual reconstruction. Scholars must consult many hundreds of manuscript fragments; abundant quotations from church writers of the second, third, and fourth centuries; various minuscule editions; and scores of translations in Latin, Syriac, Coptic, and other languages spoken throughout the Greco-Roman world. With no fewer than 5,700 ancient manuscript copies of the New Testament, most in fragmentary form, we have an abundance of texts from which to deduce a "standard text." The problem is that no two of these 5,700 texts are identical. Some contain passages that other equally authoritative texts do not; some manifest remarkable differences in the wording or the arrangement of material.

Creating a Standard Greek Text Beginning in the early sixteenth century, European scholars like Desiderius Erasmus, one of the most brilliant leaders of the northern Renaissance, attempted to establish a reliable Greek text from which translations could be made. Although scholars in almost every Western nation have labored for centuries to produce a definitive Greek text, at present there is no standard edition that commands universal scholarly acceptance. Contemporary translations are typically based on a variety of carefully edited Greek texts that incorporate the latest scholarship, including new manuscript discoveries. In preparing the New English Bible (NEB), translators followed *The Greek New Testament*, edited by R. G. V. Tasker and published in 1964. After another major resource, the twenty-sixth edition of the *Novum Testamentum Graece*, was issued in 1979, scholars also consulted this text for the Revised English Bible (1989). Translators of the New Revised Standard Version of the Bible employed the third edition of *The Greek New Testament* (1983).

Thanks to recent manuscript discoveries and the work of modern linguists and textual critics, it is possible today to produce a much more accurate translation than ever before, although absolute certainty remains elusive. Where modern translations differ from the long-familiar readings in the King James, or "Authorized," Version of the Bible, it is commonly because contemporary translators work from a far better Greek text than was available to the King James editors when their version was first published in 1611.

English Translations

The New Testament circulated in its original *koinē* Greek throughout the eastern half of the Roman Empire (later known as the Byzantine Empire). In the west, however, where Latin was the dominant tongue, Latin translations of the Septuagint and New Testament began to appear during the early centuries CE. This movement culminated in Jerome's masterful translation of the Vulgate, a monumental work of biblical scholarship. After barbarian invasions triggered the collapse of the western empire in the late fifth century CE, both education and literacy declined precipitously. During the Dark Ages of the early medieval period, new European languages gradually developed among the politically fractured regions and states of Europe. Latin remained the official language of the Roman Catholic Church, however, and for nearly 1,000 years no major new translations of the Bible appeared (see Figure 2.4).

FIGURE 2.4 Ninth-century book cover showing Saint Gregory and the three scribes. Scholarly priests copied and transmitted the New Testament texts.

Isolated scholars occasionally undertook to translate selected books of Scripture into one of the new European languages. The first person credited with doing so was the Venerable Bede, a Benedictine monk and historian of Anglo-Saxon England, who translated the Bible into his native English. In the 730s, Bede rendered part of Jerome's Latin Vulgate into Old English. During the tenth and eleventh centuries, a few other Bible books, including the Psalms and Gospels, also appeared in English. Not until the fourteenth century, however, did the entire Bible become available in English. This pioneering translation was the work of an English priest named John Wycliffe, who wished to make Scripture accessible to Christian laypeople who did not know Latin. Wycliffe finished his task of translating both the Old and New Testaments by about 1384. The national church, however, fearing the consequences of the Bible's being read and interpreted by laypersons, condemned Wycliffe's version in 1408 and forbade any future translations.

The Invention of Printing

Two historical events ensured that the Bible would find a large reading public in English. The first was Johannes Gutenberg's invention of movable type in 1455, a revolutionary advance that made it possible to print books relatively quickly rather than copying them laboriously by hand. The second was a strong religious movement known as the **Protestant Reformation,** begun in Germany in 1517. In that year, a German monk named Martin Luther vigorously protested administrative corruption and other practices within the Roman Catholic Church. Luther's German translation of the Bible (1522–1534) was the first version in a modern European language based not on the Latin Vulgate, but on the original Hebrew and Greek.

The first English translator to work directly from Hebrew and Greek manuscripts was William Tyndale; under the threat of church persecution, he fled to Germany, where his translation of the New Testament was published in 1525 (revised 1534). Official hostility to his work prevented him from completing his translation of the Old Testament, and in 1535–1536, he was betrayed, tried for heresy, and burned at the stake. Tyndale's superb English phrasing of the New Testament has influenced almost every English translation since.

Although the church forbade the reading of Wycliffe's or Tyndale's translations, it nevertheless permitted free distribution of the first printed English Bible—the Coverdale Bible (1535), which relied heavily on Tyndale's work. Matthew's Bible (1537), containing additional sections of Tyndale's Old Testament, was revised by Coverdale, and the result was called the Great Bible (1539). The Bishop's Bible (1568) was a revision of the Great Bible, and the King James Version was commissioned as a scholarly revision of the Bishop's Bible. The Geneva Bible (1560), which the English Puritans had produced in Switzerland, also significantly influenced the King James Bible.

The King James Bible (Authorized Version)

By far the most popular English Bible of all time, the King James translation was authorized by James I, son of Mary, Queen of Scots, who appointed fifty-four scholars to compose a new version of the Bishop's Bible for official use in the Anglican (English) Church. After seven years' labor, during which the oldest manuscripts then available were diligently consulted, the king's scholars produced in 1611 the Authorized, or King James, Version. One of the masterpieces of English literature, it was created at a time when the language was at its richest and most vivid. In the beauty of its rhythmic prose and colorful imagery, the King James Version remains unsurpassed in literary excellence. It has had a pervasive influence on subsequent English culture, with its phrasing of the Scriptures remarkably memorable and quotable.

Despite its wonderful poetic qualities, however, the King James Version has grave disadvantages as a text for studying the Bible. The very attributes that contribute to its linguistic elegance—the archaic diction, poetic rhythms, and Renaissance vocabulary—tend to obscure the explicit meaning of the text for many readers. Translated by scholars who grew up on the then-contemporary poetry of Edmund Spenser and William Shakespeare, the King James text presents real problems of comprehensibility to the average contemporary student. Students who have difficulty undertaking *Hamlet* cannot expect to follow Paul's sometimes complex arguments when they are couched in terms that have been largely obsolete for centuries. Even more important for serious Bible students,

its translators lacked access to ancient manuscripts that have since been discovered and to recent linguistic studies that have greatly increased our understanding of Greek language and thought.

Modern English and American Translations

Realizing that language changes over the years and that words lose their original meanings and take on new connotations, Bible scholars have repeatedly updated and reedited the King James text. The first Revised Version of the King James was published in England between 1881 and 1885; a slightly modified text of this edition, the American Standard Revised Version, was issued in 1901. Using the (then) latest studies in archaeology and linguistics, the Revised Standard Version (RSV) appeared between 1946 and 1952. Because modern scholarship continues to advance its understanding of biblical languages and textual history, an updated edition, the New Revised Standard Version (NRSV), with the Apocrypha, was published in 1991.

Readers can now choose from a wide selection of modern translations, most of which incorporate the benefits of expert scholarship that draws on interdisciplinary fields of linguistic, historical, and literary studies (see Box 2.3). These include the Jerusalem Bible (JB) (1966), which transliterates several Hebrew terms for God—notably, the personal name Yahweh and the title El Shaddai—into the English text. An updated edition, the New Jerusalem Bible, appeared in 1989. The New English Bible (NEB) (1970, 1976), the product of an international body of Catholic, Jewish, and Protestant scholars, was further refined and reissued as the Revised English Bible (1989). Unless otherwise indicated, all biblical citations in this textbook are from the NEB.

The widely used New International Version (NIV), completed in the 1970s, reflects a generally conservative Protestant viewpoint. A popular Catholic translation, the New American Bible (NAB) (1970), is also highly readable. Like the Jerusalem Bible and the New (and Revised)

BOX 2.3 Comparative Translations of Selected New Testament Passages

JOHN 1:1

KING JAMES VERSION

In the beginning was the Word, and the Word was with God, and the Word was God.

NEW REVISED STANDARD VERSION

In the beginning was the Word, and the Word was with God, and the Word was God.

REVISED ENGLISH BIBLE

In the beginning the Word already was. The Word was in God's presence, and what God was, the Word was.

THE FIVE GOSPELS (SCHOLARS VERSION)

In the beginning there was the divine word and wisdom. The divine word and wisdom was there with God, and it was what God was.

FOUR TRANSLATIONS OF THE LORD'S PRAYER

KING JAMES VERSION

Our Father who art in heaven,
Hallowed be thy name,
Thy kingdom come,
Thy will be done,
    On earth as it is in heaven.
Give us this day our daily bread,
And forgive us our debts,
    As we have forgiven our debtors;
And lead us not into temptation,
    But deliver us from evil.

NEW REVISED STANDARD VERSION

Our Father in heaven,
    hallowed be your name.
Your kingdom come.
Your will be done,
    on earth as in heaven.
Give us this day our
    daily bread.
And forgive us our debts,
    as we have also forgiven our debtors.
And do not bring us to the time of trial,
    but rescue us from the evil one.

REVISED ENGLISH BIBLE

Our Father in heaven,
May your name be hallowed;
Your kingdom come,
Your will be done,
    on earth as in heaven.
Give us today our daily bread.
Forgive us the wrong we have done,
    as we have forgiven those who have
    wronged us.
And do not put us to the test,
    but save us from the evil one.

THE FIVE GOSPELS (SCHOLARS VERSION)

Our Father in the heavens,
    your name be revered.
Impose your imperial rule,
enact your will on earth as you have in heaven.
Provide us with the bread we need for the day.
Forgive our debts
    to the extent that we have forgiven those in
    debt to us.
And please don't subject us to test after test,
    but rescue us from the evil one.

(For different translations of a controversial passage in Paul's Letter to the Philippians, see Box 16.1.)

BOX 2.4   Useful Abbreviations

ABBREVIATIONS OF NEW TESTAMENT BOOKS

Acts	Acts of the Apostles
Col.	Colossians
1 Cor.	1 Corinthians
2 Cor.	2 Corinthians
Eph.	Ephesians
Gal.	Galatians
Heb.	Hebrews
James	James
John	John (Gospel)
1 John	1 John (Epistle)
2 John	2 John (Epistle)
3 John	3 John (Epistle)
Jude	Jude
Luke	Luke (Gospel)
Mark	Mark (Gospel)
Matt.	Matthew (Gospel)
1 Pet.	1 Peter
2 Pet.	2 Peter
Phil.	Philippians
Philem.	Philemon
Rev.	Revelation (the Apocalypse)
Rom.	Romans
1 Thess.	1 Thessalonians
2 Thess.	2 Thessalonians
1 Tim.	1 Timothy
2 Tim.	2 Timothy
Titus	Titus

OTHER ABBREVIATIONS

BCE	Before the common era; dates correspond to dates BC
CE	Common era; dates correspond to dates AD
KJV	The King James Version of the Bible, also called the Authorized Version (AV)
NAB	New American Bible
NEB	The New English Bible
NIV	The New International Version of the Bible
NJB	The New Jerusalem Bible
NKJV	The New King James Version of the Bible
NRSV	The New Revised Standard Version of the Bible
NT	The New Testament
OT	The Old Testament
SV	The Scholars Version of the Bible

English Bible, it includes fresh renderings of the deuterocanonical books (the Apocrypha). Most of these new translations are available in paperback editions, which contain extensive annotations, maps, and scholarly commentary. (Box 2.4 lists some useful abbreviations for New Testament books and other related terms and concepts.)

Some translations that many students favor need to be used with caution. Whereas the Good News Bible offers a fluent paraphrase of the original languages in informal English, many scholars think that the Living Bible strays so far from the original texts as to be unreliable and misleading. Some doctrinally oriented versions, such as the New World Translation published by the Watchtower Society (Jehovah's Witnesses), consistently tend to render controversial passages in a way that supports their distinctive beliefs.

The multivolume Doubleday Anchor Bible, a cooperative effort by Protestant, Catholic, and Jewish scholars, is an excellent study aid. Each volume in the series is the work of an individual translator, who provides extensive interpretive commentary. The Scholars Version (SV) is another in-progress multivolume translation with extensive annotation. Intended as an aid in discovering the historical Jesus, the Scholars Version of *The Five Gospels* (1993) (including the Gospel of Thomas) uses a color code to indicate the relative authenticity of sayings ascribed to Jesus. Sayings considered most likely to be accurate versions of Jesus' actual words are printed in red or pink, doubtful sayings in gray, and those deemed not to represent his authentic voice in black (see Chapter 11). Adopting an idiomatic, conversational style, the SV translators have also issued *The Complete Gospels,* which compiles all known canonical and noncanonical Gospel material from the first three centuries of Christianity, including the fragmentary Secret Mark and Gospel of Peter (see Chapter 20).

An important recent contribution to understanding both the original Jewish and Greek milieu in which the Christian Scriptures developed is Willis Barnstone's *Restored New Testament,* which consistently uses the Aramaic forms by which Jesus and his disciples were probably known in their lifetimes. Thus the name "Jesus," an anglicized form of the Greek *Iesous,* is rendered *Yeshua,* a later Aramaic form of the Hebrew *Yehoshua,* from which the English "Joshua" derives. Similarly, *Yeshua's* first-called disciples are given their proper Jewish names: the two sets of Galilean brothers *Shimon* and *Andreas* (Simon [Peter] and Andrew) and *Yaakov* and *Yohanan,* sons of *Zavdai* (James and John, sons of Zebedee). *Yeshua's* mother and the other Marys also receive their authentic name, *Miryam,* as do the Greek-named Gospel writers, *Markos* (Mark) and *Loukas* (Luke). Further illustrating the diverse nature of early Christianity, Barnstone's edition includes three noncanonical Gospels, those ascribed to Thomas, Judas, and Mary of Magdala.

Summary

A process that spanned more than three centuries, the formation of the New Testament canon was long and complex. With the possible exception of Luke-Acts, each of the twenty-seven (eventually) canonical books originated separately and at first circulated independently of the others. Although the four Gospels, Acts, and Paul's letters were generally accepted by about 200 CE, other books, such as James, Revelation, and 2 Peter, were disputed well into the fourth century. Only gradually were these writings gathered together into a single volume with contents identical to those of today.

Although approximately 5,700 manuscripts containing all or part of the New Testament survive, only a few small fragments date back as early as the first half of the second century CE. The oldest extant manuscripts of a few individual books were transcribed about 200 CE, but the earliest copies of the complete New Testament were not produced until the time of Constantine (c. 325 CE). Because none of the authors' original documents exist (we have only several generations of copies) and no two of the surviving manuscript copies are precisely alike, it is extremely difficult for scholars to compile a reasonably reliable text of the Christian Greek Scriptures from which English translations can be made.

Based on the pioneering labors of Wycliffe and Tyndale, the King James Bible (Authorized Version, 1611 CE) became the most popular translation in the English-speaking world. More recent translations, however, such as the New Revised Standard Version and the New English Bible, are based on older manuscripts than were available to the King James scholars and offer more exact approximations of the original Greek.

Questions for Review

1. Briefly summarize the formation of the New Testament canon. Why did the early church decide that it needed a Scripture comparable to the Hebrew Bible? Discuss the role events such as the Jewish Revolt and the proposals of Marcion in this process.

2. How do some of the early New Testament canons (lists of accepted New Testament books) differ from the present New Testament? Which books were included in most lists, and which books were commonly omitted? Why do you think that certain books were widely recognized as authoritative (possessing the authority to express correct teaching) while others were not?

3. In determining the books accepted as part of the New Testament canon, what forces or needs of early Christianity were at work? When did the first list of New Testament contents identical to today's canon appear?

4. In what manuscript forms was the New Testament preserved during the first three centuries CE? What is the oldest surviving fragment of a New Testament book, and where was

it found? Why do we have more complete textual copies after the time of the emperor Constantine?

5. Given that no two copies of the New Testament texts are identical, how did Bible scholars compile a relatively reliable version of the Greek text? List some recent editions of the Greek text.

6. Discuss Jerome's role in providing a standard Latin edition of the Old and the New Testament. What is Jerome's translation called, and when was it produced?

7. Summarize the historical events that stimulated the translation of the New Testament into modern languages like English. Discuss the roles of Wycliffe, Luther, and Tyndale.

8. Describe the strengths and weaknesses of the King James Bible (Authorized Version) for the modern reader.

Questions for Discussion and Reflection

1. Point out some of the problems scholars face in trying to compile a reliable Greek text of the New Testament. Can you cite specific passages that some Christian scribes may have intentionally changed? What do many scholars think motivated copyists to make these changes?

2. Discuss the advantages for classroom study of modern English translations like the New American Bible, the New Revised Standard Version, the Scholars Version, and the New English Bible (the version used in this textbook).

Terms and Concepts to Remember

apostles	heresy
canon	manuscript
codex	Marcion
Codex Sinaiticus	Muratorian Canon
Codex Vaticanus	orthodoxy
Constantine	Protestant Reformation
Edict of Milan	pseudonymity
Eusebius	Vulgate
the Great Persecution	

Recommended Reading

Barnstone, Willis. *The Restored New Testament: A New Translation with Commentary, Including the Gnostic Gospels Thomas, Mary, and Judas.* New York: W. W. Norton, 2009. A classicist's poetic rendering of the Greek text, with Jewish and Greek names restored.

Bruce, F. F. *The New Testament Documents: Are They Reliable?* Grand Rapids, Mich.: Eerdmans, 2003. Argues for the historicity of the New Testament writing.

Dungan, David. *Constantine's Bible: Politics and the Making of the New Testament.* Minneapolis: Fortress Press, 2007. Examines the religious and political forces at work in determining the final content of the Christian Scriptures.

Ehrman, Bart D. *Misquoting Jesus: The Story Behind Who Changed the Bible and Why.* San Francisco: HarperOne, 2007. Argues that scribes changed New Testament manuscripts for theological reasons.

———. *The Orthodox Corruption of Scripture: The Effect of Early Christological Controversies on the Text of the New Testament.* New York: Oxford University Press, 1993. Provides detailed analysis of variations in ancient manuscripts, demonstrating that copyists' intentional changes are typically motivated by theological concerns.

Eusebius. *The History of the Church from Christ to Constantine,* rev. ed., Translated by G. A. Williamson with an introduction by Andrew Louth. Baltimore: Penguin Classic Books, 1990. Our principal source for the study of the growth and development of early Christianity.

Farmer, William R., and Farkasfalvy, D. M. *The Formation of the New Testament Canon: An Ecumenical Approach.* New York: Paulist Press, 1983.

Gamble, Harry Y. *The New Testament Canon: Its Making and Meaning* (reprint of 1985 edition). Eugene, Ore.: Wipf and Stock, 2002. Argues that the contents of the New Testament were determined by church tradition.

Lewis, Jack P. *The English Bible from KJV to NIV: A History and Evaluation.* Grand Rapids, Mich.: Baker Book House, 1982. A scholarly review of major English translations from the King James to the New International Version.

McDonald, Lee Martin. *The Biblical Canon: Its Origin, Transmission, and Authority,* 3rd ed. Peabody, Mass.: Hendrickson, 2007. Analyzes the historical process of canon formation.

———. "Canon of the New Testament." In *The New Interpreter's Dictionary of the Bible,* Vol. 1, pp. 536–547. Nashville, Tenn.: Abingdon Press, 2006.

Metzger, Bruce M., and Ehrman, Bart D. *The Text of the New Testament, Its Transmission, Corruption, and Restoration,* 4th ed. New York: Oxford University Press, 2005. A scholarly investigation of the process of textual transmission.

Wegner, Paul D. *The Journey from Texts to Translations: The Origin and Development of the Bible.* Grand Rapids, Mich.: Baker Book House, 2000. A readable investigation of the Bible's literary evolution.

PART TWO

The Three Worlds in Which Christianity Originated

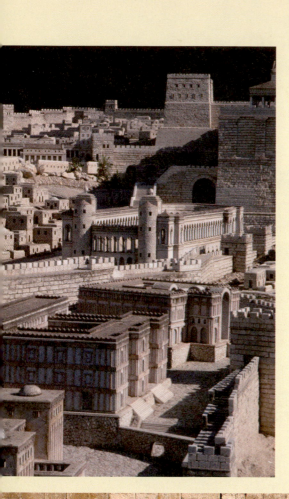

King Herod I (ruled 40–4 BCE) reconstructed Jerusalem (*left*, a scale model) as a lavishly decorated Greco-Roman city, one of the finest in the Roman Empire. Even in Judea, heart of the Jewish faith, Hellenistic culture profoundly influenced language, thought, art, architecture, and social customs. Using vast quantities of marble, gold leaf, and other expensive building materials, Herod completely renovated the Jerusalem Temple (*above*, a scale model), expanding its colonnades and courtyards to cover 172,000 square yards. Begun about 20 BCE, the renovations were completed only a few years before Roman armies destroyed the Temple in 70 CE. Today Jews gather to pray at the Wailing Wall (*below left*), the only portion of Herod's Temple expansion that survives.

Looming behind the ruins of Qumran, which most scholars think was an Essene monastic community that the Romans demolished in 68 CE, are steep cliffs honeycombed with caves in which the Dead Sea Scrolls were found (*above*). Beginning in 1947, archaeologists discovered hundreds of manuscripts, many in small fragments, of virtually every book in the Hebrew Bible, as well as documents containing sectarian Essene writings. In this marble statue (*right*) from the late third century CE, Christ appears as the Good Shepherd, carrying a lamb on his shoulders in the manner of the Greek god Apollo. Anticipating the later lamb-bearing figures of Apollo and Christ, a Minoan sculptor on the island of Crete—more than a millennium before Jesus' birth—fashioned a bronze youth in a similar pose (*far right*). Comparable motifs from ancient Mediterranean culture permeate early Christian art and ritual. ■

CHAPTER 3

The Diverse World of First-Century Judaism

*You [Israel] are a people consecrated to Yahweh your God; it is you
that Yahweh our God has chosen to be his very own people out of all
the peoples of the earth.* Deuteronomy 7:6 (Jerusalem Bible)

Key Topics/Themes Reverence for the Mosaic Torah, for the land God had promised to Israel, for the Jerusalem Temple, and for the God whose invisible presence sanctified it was a unifying force in first-century Judaism. The Jewish religion of Jesus' day, however, was extremely diverse, with adherents split into numerous parties and factions, the most prominent of which included the Sadducees, Pharisees, Essenes, Samaritans, and Zealots. Although the majority of Jews did not then belong to any particular party, many held eschatological convictions (beliefs about the imminent End of the world) similar to those of the Essenes, the group that, as most scholars believe, produced the Dead Sea Scrolls.

The Three Worlds of the New Testament Era

Three major forces largely shaped the world in which Christianity was born and developed: the Scriptures and traditions of Judaism, the culture of Greece, and the political power of Rome. These three forces represent the context in which the New Testament was written. After composing the Gospel of Luke, the same author followed his story of Jesus' life with an account of early Christianity's geographical expansion from its Jewish homeland in Palestine to the great cities of Greece and, ultimately, to Rome, the imperial capital. In the first volume of his two-part work, Luke places Jesus' ministry firmly within the Jewish biblical tradition. However, in his second volume

on Christian origins, the Book of Acts, the author shows Jesus' followers moving away from Palestine to urban centers of Greek culture, a transition that had profound consequences for the subsequent development of the new faith. Although first planted in Jewish soil, the Jesus movement experienced its most significant growth in the larger Greco-Roman world, the environment in which it eventually defined itself as distinct from its parent religion, Judaism.

The One God, Yahweh

Historically, Christianity acquired its characteristic form and self-understanding as it expanded to Greek-speaking populations throughout the

Roman Empire, but it also continued to see itself as firmly grounded in the Jewish biblical tradition. Because both Jesus and his original disciples were children of Israel, born and raised in the Jewish faith, Jesus' message is primarily explainable in terms of Jewish customs and beliefs. Although Judaism of the first century CE was extremely diverse, encompassing many conflicting groups and sects, virtually all practicing Jews held certain tenets in common that set them apart as a distinctive religious community. Many of these shared beliefs were based on the Hebrew Bible, primarily the Torah and the words of Israel's prophets. Foremost was the **Shema,** which proclaimed the oneness of Israel's God:

> Listen, Israel: Yahweh your God is the one Yahweh. You shall love Yahweh your God with all your heart, and all your soul, and all your strength.
>
> (Deut. 6:4–5, Jerusalem Bible)

This directive, which Jesus reportedly cited as his people's "greatest" commandment (Mark 12:28–30), represents Israel's primary obligation—to worship Yahweh exclusively. Alone among the religions of antiquity, first-century Judaism, in all its manifestations, was rigorously monotheistic, accepting the existence of a single God, who was Creator, Ruler, and Judge of all heaven and earth (Isa. 40–43).

According to Exodus 3:13–16, Israel's Deity revealed himself to Moses as **Yahweh,** a personal name that apparently is based on the Hebrew verb "to be" and that occurs almost 7,000 times in the text of the Hebrew Bible. Speaking in the first person, Yahweh declared that he is the eternal "I Am," the One who brings all things into existence, including his chosen nation, Israel. Because of the Torah's prohibition against taking Yahweh's name "in vain" (Exod. 20:7), by the final centuries BCE, most Jews had begun to substitute the title *Adonai* (commonly translated as "Lord") when referring to Yahweh, whose sacred name was considered too holy to be pronounced by ordinary persons. Although some modern English translations, such as the Anchor Bible and the Jerusalem Bible, retain the name

Yahweh, most recent translations follow Jewish custom and indicate the presence of the sacred name by printing LORD or GOD in small capitals when it appears in Hebrew manuscripts.

In the New Testament, the Deity's personal name survives in such expressions as "hallelujah," which means "praise Jah," a shortened form of Yahweh. The divine name is also preserved in the name **Jesus,** an English form of the Hebrew *Yeshua* or *Yehoshua* (Joshua), which means "Yahweh saves" (cf. Matt. 1:21).

Yahweh's character differed radically from that of other gods known in the ancient world. The many gods of Greece, Rome, Egypt, and other polytheistic societies did not object to sharing with fellow deities the sacrifices and rituals of human worship. In contrast, Yahweh describes himself as "the Jealous One" (Exod. 34:14; cf. Exod. 20:5), his jealousy a "consuming fire" that tolerates no divine rivals (Deut. 4:24). Because their God demanded total allegiance and forbade any recognition of other divinities, the Jews did not permit images of other gods in their homeland, a position that Rome officially acknowledged as their legal right and, with some exceptions, respected. This exclusivity, as well as the profound conviction that there is only one correct way to please the One God, Judaism passed on to Christianity (1 Cor. 8:5) and later to Islam, which is also strictly monotheistic.

As the only true God, Creator and absolute Ruler of the universe, Yahweh was all-powerful (omnipotent) and all-knowing (omniscient). In praising his irresistible might and infinite wisdom, many writers of the Hebrew Bible likened Yahweh to a warrior, a divinity who fought for his people, crushing their enemies. A Hebrew poet extols Yahweh for his military defeat of the Egyptian army, drowning Pharaoh's soldiers in a turbulent sea:

> Yahweh I sing; he has covered himself in glory, horse and rider he has thrown into the sea . . .
> *Yahweh is a warrior;*
> Yahweh is his name.
>
> (Exod. 15:1, 3, Jerusalem Bible; emphasis added)

According to the Book of Joshua, Yahweh's prowess also enabled the Israelites who fled Egypt to conquer the land of Canaan (Palestine), which God had promised to their ancestors (Josh. 5:13–15). Similarly, it was Yahweh's martial strength that inspired the young David to kill the giant Goliath, for "Yahweh is the lord of the battle" (1 Sam. 17:47, Jerusalem Bible).

As Israel's thinkers over many generations increasingly emphasized their God's uniqueness and strength, however, Yahweh's omnipotence seemed strangely at odds with his people's historical situation. Although Yahweh announced that he had "chosen [Israel] to be his very own people out of all the peoples of the earth" (Deut. 7:6), this nation—selected for a special relationship with God—repeatedly suffered humiliating defeats by nations that did not recognize or worship Israel's God. By Jesus' day, when imperial Rome controlled the Jewish homeland, Israel had not enjoyed full national independence or freedom from foreign domination for 600 years (the sole exception was the short-lived Maccabean kingdom; see Chapter 5). A bitter tension existed between belief in Yahweh's might and his failure to intervene on his people's behalf. Why did God allow Rome, viewed as an empire of idolaters, to exploit those who at least tried to worship him? Why did he remain silent? (See below for a discussion of Jewish hopes for a Messiah who would deliver them from their oppressors.)

The Torah

In addition to its allegiance to a single God, a second cohesive force in Judaism was the **Torah,** divinely revealed instruction contained in the first five books of the Hebrew Bible (Genesis through Deuteronomy). While Genesis presents colorful tales of Israel's ancestors—Abraham, Isaac, and Jacob—and their descendants' migration to Egypt, the other four books relate Israel's escape from Egypt and the covenant it concluded with Yahweh at Mount Sinai. Called the Mosaic Covenant because Moses acts as

mediator in the formal agreement between God and Israel, it stipulates hundreds of laws, statutes, and ordinances that the Israelites must obey to ensure Yahweh's favor.

Although the Ten Commandments (listed in Exod. 20 and Deut. 5) are the most famous part of the covenant requirements, the many other legal edicts regulating almost every aspect of Jewish daily life were considered equally important and binding (see Box 3.1). Mosaic legislation included far more than the covenant pledge to worship Yahweh alone, to abstain from fashioning images of him, to observe a code of ethical conduct toward one's fellow human beings, and to keep an official day of rest—the **Sabbath**—on which it was a capital offense to do any kind of work. All Israel was also required to adhere to a host of complex dietary restrictions, avoiding not only pork and shellfish but all kinds of other foods as well; regularly to perform elaborate rites involving animal, fruit, and grain sacrifices; and scrupulously to observe **purity laws** that define the concept of holiness, rigorously separating ritually "clean" objects and activities from those deemed "unclean." The priestly Book of Leviticus enumerates long lists of actions or conditions that disqualify one from participating in the covenant community's religious functions, including contact with corpses, menstruating women, mothers of newborn children, or objects contaminated by them. Because Mosaic Law prohibited the eating of so many foods, it was virtually impossible for Jews to share meals—or even socialize—with **Gentiles,** a category encompassing all people who were not Jews, including Greeks, Syrians, and Italians. Given that Gentile males did not practice **circumcision** (the surgical removal of the foreskin from the penis), the physical mark identifying members of the covenant people (cf. Gen. 17), Gentiles were permanently disqualified from full participation in Yahweh's worship. The great barriers between Jew and Gentile, erected by faithful Torah observance, became one of the first major issues to divide the early Jewish Christian community (Acts 15; Gal. 1–5).

According to the Book of Deuteronomy, adherence to Mosaic teaching was required not

BOX 3.1 **The Covenant: A Divine–Human Bond**

In the Hebrew Bible, God's preferred means of establishing a relationship with humans is through a **covenant** (Hebrew, *berith*). A common sociopolitical concept in the ancient Near East, *covenant* means "agreement," "pact," "vow," or "treaty," and commonly takes the form of a divine promise to confer specific benefits on a human partner. According to Genesis, after drowning almost all life forms in a global deluge, Yahweh makes the first of four biblical covenants, promising not to bring another world flood and (somewhat paradoxically) affirming the sacredness of human and animal life (Gen. 9:1–17). God later promises a single individual, Abraham, that his descendants will possess a permanent homeland, Canaan (Palestine), and that through Abraham he will "bless all the families on earth" (Gen. 12:1–3; 17:1–27). He also promises King David to keep David's progeny on Israel's throne "forever" (2 Sam. 7:11–17; Ps. 89).

Whereas these three covenants are unilateral—with God unconditionally conferring benefits on favored individuals or groups—the pact he makes with Israel as a whole is highly conditional upon the people's continuing obedience to his instructions. Four books of Torah (Exodus, Leviticus, Numbers, and Deuteronomy) outline Yahweh's specific requirements—ethical, ritual, and religious—that Israelites must keep to remain in divine favor (Exod. 20–23; 32–34; Deut. 28). For most biblical authors, Israel's endless sufferings and loss of political freedom are the direct result of its collective failure to maintain covenant vows.

---

only of the Israelites who personally swore to uphold the Sinai pact but of all future Israelite generations as well (Deut. 29:13–15; 30:11–14). In his farewell speech, Moses states that Israel's future success as a nation—including the blessings of abundant crops, economic prosperity, and victory in war—is entirely dependent on unwavering obedience to its covenant obligations. Conversely, disobedience will bring national disaster, including plagues, crop failures, famines, military defeats, and, eventually, exile and domination by Gentiles (Deut. 28–29; cf. Lev. 26).

Numerous biblical writers, including the prophet Jeremiah and the authors of the books of Kings, blamed all of Israel's political reversals on the people's collective failure to honor their covenant vows (see Box 3.2). Jeremiah viewed Babylon's destruction of Jerusalem in 587 BCE and the subsequent Babylonian captivity (587–538 BCE) as the direct result of covenant breaking. Although successive waves of Jewish leaders returned from Babylon to Jerusalem during the late sixth and fifth centuries BCE, the Jewish people did not regain political independence, remaining under the successive domination of Persia, Greece, and

Rome (see Chapter 5). With its ancient monarchy and national autonomy gone, the covenant community was increasingly led by priests and scribes who were also the official editors, caretakers, and interpreters of the Hebrew Bible.

Constantly pressured by the dominant Gentile powers that controlled their political and economic environment, the priests and Torah instructors struggled to maintain Jewish identity, creatively reinterpreting the Mosaic heritage to fit the people's changing circumstances. Because keeping Torah commands was seen as a covenant member's primary duty, the Mosaic Law and its correct implementation assumed an overwhelming importance in Jewish daily life, a trend reflected in Hellenistic-Jewish literature. The noncanonical Book of Jubilees, for example, which is a Pharisee writer's retelling of Genesis and part of Exodus, presents the Torah as not only supreme but also eternal: It existed before God created the universe. Because it was delivered through Moses as a perfect and infallible expression of the divine will, the Torah could never be abrogated. Significantly, Jubilees also makes the oral law—orally transmitted commentaries about how the

BOX 3.2 Biblical Divisions of Israel's History

Editors of the Hebrew Bible divide Israel's national history into approximately five distinct epochs.

1. Era of the Ancestral Fathers and Mothers Genesis tells the stories of Israel's distant forbears, beginning with Abraham and Sarah and ending with tales of Abraham's twelve grandsons, such as Judah and Joseph, the putative founders of the traditional twelve tribes of Israel (Gen. 12–50).

2. Era of the Exodus and Desert Wanderings Exodus continues the story of Yahweh's bond with Israel, narrating the story of Moses' confrontation with Egypt's pharaoh; Yahweh's miraculous deliverance of his people at a chaotic sea; the covenant made at Mount Sinai (also called Horeb); the giving of 600 legal ordinances and regulations, which Israel pledges to obey; and the Israelites' preparation to invade Canaan, the territory promised Abraham's descendants (Exodus through Deuteronomy).

3. Era of the Conquest of Canaan and the Judges In the Book of Joshua, Joshua leads the Israelites on a lightning-fast military conquest of Canaan; in the Book of Judges (which may preserve a more realistic depiction of Israel's early history), the Israelites, constantly battling neighboring tribes and small princedoms, struggle to maintain a toehold in the Promised Land.

4. Era of the Monarchy Threatened by the militarily superior Philistines (a sea people who settled in Canaan about the same time as the Israelites),

Israel's tribes temporarily unite to form a central government, with Saul as its first king. After Saul's death, his rival David establishes a stable dynasty with its capital at Jerusalem (c. 1000 BCE).

After the death of David's son Solomon, who had built Yahweh's Temple in Jerusalem, the ten northern tribes secede from the Davidic kingdom, creating the larger northern state of Israel and the weaker southern state of Judah, which retains its Davidic rulers. In 721 BCE, Assyrian armies destroy Israel; in 587 BCE, Babylonian armies destroy Jerusalem, burn Solomon's Temple, and deport Judah's ruling class to Babylon. This mega-narrative—often called Israel's national epic—runs from Genesis 12 through 2 Kings 25.

5. Era of Exile and Partial Restoration After almost fifty years of exile in Babylon, some leading Judeans return to Judah, supported by a decree of Cyrus the Great of Persia, who captured Babylon in 539 BCE. Successive waves of returning exiles eventually rebuild the Temple, restoring Yahweh's formal worship. Fragments of the postexilic history appear in the books of Ezra and Nehemiah, but no comprehensive account of Judah's experience under the ensuing political dominations of Persia, Greece, and Rome was added to the canon. The deuterocanonical books of 1 and 2 Maccabees describe a brief later episode, a successful Jewish revolt against Syrian-Greek occupation forces in the mid-second century BCE, the last narrated events of the Old Testament period. (For summaries of historical milestones in postbiblical history, see Box 5.1 and Figure 5.11.)

Torah is to be applied in specific situations—equally binding.

Readers will find that individual New Testament authors express differing attitudes toward Torah keeping. Whereas the writer of Matthew's Gospel insists that the entire Torah will remain in force until "heaven and earth disappear" (Matt. 5:17–19, Jerusalem Bible), Paul's letters argue that the Law's power ended with

Jesus' sacrificial death (Gal. 3–5). The Gospels typically show Jesus disputing with Pharisees and other opponents over legal issues, including Sabbath observance (Mark 2:23–28), fasting (Mark 2:18–22), dietary prohibitions (Mark 7:14–23), and divorce (Mark 10:1–12). As Gentiles joined the originally Jewish-Christian community in increasing numbers, however, questions about such Torah-mandated rules as circumcision and keeping a kosher diet (abstaining from foods prohibited by the Law) generated heated controversy in the ethnically mixed group. Christian Jews faithful to the Mosaic Torah were appalled by converted Gentiles who adopted Paul's radical "gospel"—that Gentiles were not required to keep any of the Law (Gal. 3–6; Rom. 2–8; Acts 15). In time, the vast influx of Gentile converts that overwhelmed the early churches made the Torah issue largely irrelevant within the Christian fold. Although the Pauline idea of "freedom" from Torah obligations eventually prevailed in the church, the issue of obedience to the Mosaic Law continues to divide Christians from Jews to this day.

The Divine Promises

Besides the covenant bond to Yahweh, manifest in the daily observance of Torah regulations, another major factor helping to unite the Jewish community was the series of promises that God made to Israel's ancestors. Grouped together in Genesis 12–50, the promises begin when Yahweh first appears to **Abraham,** regarded as the chief progenitor of the Jewish people, vowing to multiply Abraham's descendants into a mighty nation, give them the land of **Canaan** (Palestine), create from them a line of kings, and make them a source of blessing to all peoples of the earth (Gen. 12:1–3; 17:1–9; 22:15–18; cf. Rom. 9:4; John 8:33, 39). According to the Genesis promises, collectively known as the Abrahamic Covenant, Yahweh guaranteed Israel a high destiny among the international family of nations: It was to be a populous country, blessed by God's presence in its midst and governed by a divinely appointed royal dynasty.

After Israel's twelve tribes had been politically united under a single king, **David** (c. 1000–961 BCE), Yahweh further promised David that his royal heirs would possess Israel's throne "forever." In the **Davidic Covenant,** Yahweh declared that he might punish individual Davidic kings for wrongdoing but that the dynasty itself would be "everlasting" (2 Sam. 7). It was for only

a brief period, however, that Davidic rulers exercised control over the entire territory described in the Abrahamic pact. After the death of David's son **Solomon** (c. 961–922 BCE), the united kingdom split into the two smaller states of Israel and **Judah,** which, in turn, were swept away by the greater Near Eastern powers of Assyria and Babylon. By Jesus' lifetime, the area promised to Abraham's progeny had been successively occupied by Persians, Greeks, Syrians, and Romans. Free control of their own land was only a distant memory for most Jews, many of whom by then lived outside Palestine in the **Diaspora** ("scattering" of Jews among foreign regions). To some patriotic Jews, however, driving foreigners from their native soil was a sacred duty. To such "Zealots," as they were later called, loyal Judaism and political nationalism were inseparable.

The Jerusalem Temple

A more tangible unifying symbol for many in the Jewish faith was the great **Temple** of Yahweh in Jerusalem. According to Deuteronomy 12, Yahweh recognized only one site on earth as the place where the animal sacrifices required by the Torah were acceptable to him. King Solomon, famous for his wisdom, wealth, and building projects, was the first to errect a monumental sanctuary on Zion's hill in Jerusalem. Solomon's Temple housed the **ark of the covenant,** the sacred chest containing the implements of the Mosaic faith. It was believed that Yahweh's *kavod,* or "glory," dwelt in the innermost room, called the **Holy of Holies.** After the Babylonians destroyed Solomon's magnificent sanctuary in 587 BCE, a smaller building was constructed on the site and rededicated in about 515 BCE. Extensively restored and enlarged by Herod the Great, this second Temple was commonly known in New Testament times as Herod's Temple (see Figures 3.1 and 3.2).

Devout Jews, whenever possible, made annual pilgrimages to the Jerusalem sanctuary, for only there would Yahweh accept their obligatory

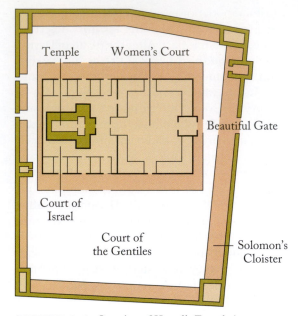

FIGURE 3.1 Overview of Herod's Temple in Jerusalem. With its great courtyards and porticoes, the Temple covered many acres. The main sanctuary, however, was a simple rectangular building with an outer porch, a long inner room, and an innermost chamber known as the Holy of Holies. A heavily bejeweled curtain separated the two inner chambers.

offerings of grain, firstfruits, and unblemished sacrificial animals. According to Luke's Gospel, Jesus' family is especially scrupulous about Temple observances. Mary journeys there from Bethlehem to undergo the purification rites necessary after childbirth, and her infant son is presented there as required by Law (Luke 2:22–39; Exod. 13:2; Lev. 5:7). The Temple is where the twelve-year-old Jesus first manifests an awareness of his special calling (Luke 2:41–50) and where Jesus' family goes to observe the holy days of the Jewish religious calendar (John 7:2–10).

Jesus' family repeatedly traveled to Jerusalem from Galilee, but many pious Jews made arduous pilgrimages to the Temple from distant parts of the Roman Empire. Members of the large Jewish colonies established in Alexandria, Damascus, Antioch, and Rome itself journeyed to the Temple to offer sacrifices and participate in the ceremonies of such solemn occasions as the **Day of Atonement (Yom Kippur).** Held in the fall of

the year, the atonement ritual required Israel's High Priest to present sin offerings for the people so that their God could absolve them both individually and collectively for their wrongdoing. On this special day alone, the High Priest entered into the Temple's Holy of Holies to present a sacrifice on the people's behalf and to utter the sacred name of Yahweh.

In studying the various manifestations of Judaism during the New Testament period, it is important to remember that Jewish identity was more than a matter of belief and religious practice, such as participating in worship and sacrifice at the Jerusalem Temple. Whether they observed Torah regulations or not, as physical descendants of Abraham, all Jews inherited an ethnic and cultural as well as religious identity.

First-Century Jewish Diversity

The Gospel writers mention several distinct Jewish groups—the Sadducees, Pharisees, Herodians, and Samaritans—but these are only a fraction of first-century Judaism's bewildering variety. The more scholars learn about the period before 70 CE, when Roman armies destroyed Jerusalem and the Jewish state, the more diverse Judaism appears to have been. Besides the four groups that New Testament authors commonly depict as Jesus' opponents, the Jewish historian **Flavius Josephus,** an important source of background on first-century Judaism, also describes the Essenes, an apocalyptic sect that anticipates several Christian beliefs and practices, and the Zealots, a nationalistic sect that played a crucial role in the Jewish Revolt against Rome. Keeping in mind that the religious parties discussed here constitute a mere sample of Jewish pluralism, we will survey the six best-known groups alluded to in Josephus or the New Testament. As recent archaeological studies of Galilee (Jesus' home district) have shown, Judaism in the first century CE was divided not only by party and faction, but also by geographical location. (For a description of the social, religious, and

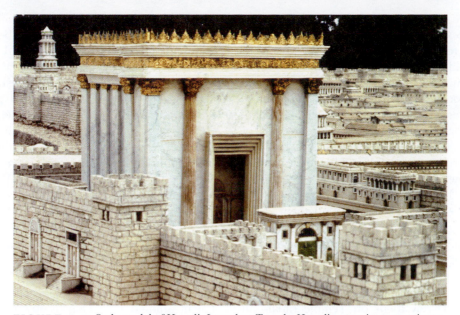

FIGURE 3.2 Scale model of Herod's Jerusalem Temple. Herod's extensive renovations of the Temple, begun about 20 BCE, had been completed only a few years before the Romans destroyed it in 70 CE. According to Josephus, the bejeweled curtain veiling the sanctuary's innermost room, the Holy of Holies, depicted a panorama of heaven. Visible through the main entrance, the curtain is said to have been "torn in two from top to bottom" at the moment of Jesus' death (Mark 15:38). In Mark's Gospel, this event corresponds to the heavens being "torn open" at the time of Jesus' baptism (Mark 1:10).

cultural forces that characterized Jesus' Galilee, see Freyne in "Recommended Reading.")

The Sadducees

Because none of their writings survive, we know the **Sadducees** only through brief references in the New Testament and in other secondary sources, such as Josephus. Represented as among Jesus' chief opponents, the Sadducees were typically members of the Jewish upper class, wealthy landowning aristocrats who largely controlled the priesthood and the Temple. Their name (Greek *Saddoukaioi,* from the Hebrew *Zaddukim* or *tsaddiqim*) means "righteous ones" and may be descriptive, or it may reflect their claim to be the spiritual heirs of Zadok, the High Priest under David and Solomon (1 Kings 1:26). Because the prophet Ezekiel had stated that only the "sons of Zadok" could "approach Yahweh" in the Temple service (Ezek. 40:46), the Sadducees, the officiating priests at the Jerusalem sanctuary,

emphasized their inherited right to this role. High Priests like **Caiaphas** (who condemned Jesus) were apparently always of their number. Along with their opponents the Pharisees, the Sadducees dominated the Great Council (Sanhedrin), Judaism's highest court of religious law.

The Sadducees and the Romans Although the New Testament and Josephus give us an incomplete picture of the group, the Sadducees seem to have acted as chief mediators between the Jewish people and the occupying Roman forces. As beneficiaries of the Roman-maintained political order, the Sadducees had the most to lose from civil disorder and typically opposed a Jewish nationalism that might attempt to overthrow the status quo. Their adoption of Hellenistic customs and their friendship with the Romans made it possible for them to manipulate some Palestinian political affairs. The Sadducees' determination to preserve the uneasy accommodation with Rome is revealed in their eagerness to condemn Jesus, whom they apparently regarded as a potential revolutionary and a threat to Judea's political security. Their view that rebellion against Rome would lead to total annihilation of the Jewish nation was vindicated during the Jewish Revolt (66–73 CE), when Roman troops decimated Jerusalem and Judea.

As conservative religiously as they were politically, the Sadducees practiced a literal reading of the Torah, rejecting the Pharisees' "oral law" and other interpretations of the biblical text. It is uncertain how much of the Prophets or Writings they accepted, but they apparently did not share Pharisaic beliefs about a coming judgment, resurrection, angels, or demons (Mark 12:18; Acts 23:8). As a group, the Sadducees did not survive the first century CE. Their close association with Rome; their refusal to accept developing ideas based on the Prophets, the Writings, and the Apocrypha; and their narrow focus on Temple ritual—all spelled their doom. After the Temple's destruction in 70 CE, the Sadducees disappear from history. The Pharisees, emphasizing education and progressive reinterpretation of Scripture, became the leaders in formulating post-70s Judaism.

The Pharisees

The Gospels' bitter attacks on the **Pharisees,** who are shown as Jesus' leading opponents, have made Pharisee synonymous with hypocrisy and heartless legalism (Matt. 23). To the Gospel writers, the Pharisees and their associates the **scribes** are "blind guides" who perversely reject Jesus' message and thereby doom their people to divine punishment (Matt. 21:33–46; 22:1–14; 23:37–39; Luke 19:41–44). Modern historians recognize, however, that the Gospels' picture of the Pharisees is overly severe. According to most scholars, the Evangelists' antagonism toward the group stems not so much from the historical Jesus' debates with the Pharisees as from the historical situation at the time the Gospels were composed. Written several decades after Jesus' death, the Gospels reflect a period of intense ill feeling between the early Christian community and the Jewish leadership.

Hostility between the church and synagogue climaxed following the Roman destruction of

Jerusalem in 70 CE. In the years immediately after Jerusalem's fall, the Pharisees became the dominant force within Judaism and the chief spokesmen for the position that Jesus of Nazareth was not the expected Jewish Messiah. Although Jews and Christians had previously worshiped side by side in the Temple, following the failure of the Jewish Revolt against Rome, Jewish-Christian relations deteriorated rapidly. After about 90 CE, some Jewish Christians were expelled from the synagogues and condemned as perverters of the Jewish heritage (see John 9). The Gospels preserve the Christian response in their rancorous denunciations of the Pharisees.

Whatever their quarrel with the historical Jesus may have been, as a group, the Pharisees were completely devoted to the Mosaic Torah and its application to all the concerns of daily life. The meaning of their name is obscure, although it seems to have been derived from the Hebrew verb for "to separate." As spiritual descendants of the Hasidim, who separated themselves from what they saw as the corrupting influence of Hellenistic culture, the Pharisees rigorously observed a code of ritual purity. They scrupulously segregated themselves from contaminating contact with anything the Law forbade.

Strict Torah Observance Many Pharisees were deeply learned in the Torah and skilled at its interpretation. Josephus states that the common people regarded them as the most authoritative interpreters of the Mosaic Law. Unlike their rivals the Sadducees, the Pharisees accepted not only the written Law contained in the Mosaic Torah but also a parallel oral law. Pharisaic oral teachings, which the Gospel of Mark calls the "tradition of the elders" (Mark 7:3), were intended to extend the laws of Temple purity to virtually every aspect of daily life, including Sabbath observance, dietary regulations, almsgiving, and prayer.

After many generations of oral transmission— the effect of which was to "build a fence around the Torah"—this vast body of commentary and case law was codified in the Mishnah. The **Mishnah,** compiled about 200 CE by Rabbi Judah ha-Nasi, is the first document of a more unified

Judaism that emerged following the failure of the two great wars against Rome. An informal term meaning "master" or "teacher" in Jesus' day, after about 70–90 CE, **rabbi** became a title designating scholars ordained or officially recognized as authoritative in their practice and exposition of Jewish tradition. In time, the Mishnah (literally, "that which is learned by repetition") became the basis of further commentary, resulting in the **Gemara** (completion), which was added to the Mishnah to form the **Talmud** (teaching), an immense compendium of rabbinic scholarship containing about 2.5 million words. Two Talmuds developed, one in Palestine (also known as the Jerusalem Talmud) about 400 CE and one in Babylon about 550 CE. The Babylonian Talmud, in thirty-six tractates or books, became the supreme guidebook of mainstream **Judaism,** and its case laws the regulators of Jewish life.

Although many scholars believe that Pharisaism evolved into the rabbi-led Judaism that eventually produced the Talmud—and hence modern Judaism—the rabbis who compiled it never refer to themselves as Pharisees and seem to avoid the term. After the Temple's destruction, however, it was the Pharisaic emphasis on reapplication of the Torah to the Jewish people's radically changed circumstances that helped make possible the survival of their religion and distinctive way of life.

Despite his remembered disagreements with Pharisees on how the Law should be practiced, Jesus is known to have been on good terms with some of their number, dining at their homes and even benefiting from a friendly warning about a plot on his life (Luke 7:36–50; 13:31–32). Matthew's Gospel depicts Jesus as sharing the Pharisees' view that the Law is eternally binding (Matt. 5:17–19) and that they interpret it correctly (Matt. 23:2–3). On numerous matters of belief, Jesus and the Pharisees saw eye-to-eye (Mark 11:18–26). Unlike the Sadducees, they believed in a coming judgment day, resurrection of the dead, a future life of rewards and penalties based on deeds in this life, and the existence of angels, demons, and other inhabitants of the invisible world. By devotedly studying the Hebrew Bible and flexibly adapting its principles to the constantly changing situation in which Jews found themselves, the Pharisees depended on the possession of neither the Temple nor the Promised Land to perpetuate the Jewish faith. Some may have been rigid or overly ingenious in their application of the Torah's requirements, perhaps making the Law impossible for the poor or ignorant to keep (Matt. 23:6–23). As a group, however, they pursued a standard of religious commitment and personal righteousness that was virtually unique in the ancient world.

Gamaliel According to the Book of Acts, it was Rabbi **Gamaliel,** a leading first-century Pharisee, who protected the early Jesus movement from excessive repression by the Jerusalem authorities (Acts 5:34–42). Depicted in Acts as the apostle Paul's teacher and an advocate of religious tolerance, Gamaliel is rarely mentioned in the Mishnah, although it observes that "when he died the glory of the Torah ended." Acts portrays Paul, even after his conversion to Christianity, as remaining proud of his Pharisaic background and appealing for support from his fellow Pharisees when he stood trial before the Jerusalem religious council (Acts 23:6–9; Phil. 3:4–7).

The Academy of Jamnia (Yavneh)

After Rome's destruction of the Jewish state in 70 CE, Roman authorities apparently wished to show their goodwill toward prominent Jews who had not advocated violent revolt against the empire. The leading force behind this Roman-endorsed movement to reorganize the postwar Jewish faith was Yohanan ben Zakkai (c. 1–80 CE), an eminent Pharisee. According to one tradition, during the Roman siege of Jerusalem, ben Zakkai—who favored a peaceful settlement with Rome—escaped from the city by feigning death and being carried in a coffin outside Jerusalem's walls for burial. Like the historian Josephus, who also went over to the Romans, ben Zakkai won the favor of Vespasian, the general (and later emperor) whom Nero had dispatched to quell the insurrection. Ben

Zakkai received Vespasian's permission to travel to Jamnia (also called Yavneh or Jabneh), a city west of Jerusalem on the Mediterranean coast that had not participated in the Jewish Revolt.

At Jamnia, ben Zakkai gathered other Pharisaic teachers together and presided over an already-existing Jewish council there, the Bet Din (House of Judgment). During the years following 70 CE, the pronouncements of ben Zakkai and other sages of the **Academy of Jamnia** (although it had no offical authority) significantly influenced Judaism, which thus entered into a new stage of development known as formative Judaism. The Jamnia rabbis successfully confronted the challenge of enabling Judaism to survive without the Temple, an officiating priesthood, or even a homeland. It is said that when ben Zakkai visited the ruins of Jerusalem with another rabbi, his companion lamented the fact that with the Temple gone their religion had no means of making the atonement sacrifices necessary to cleanse the people from sin. Ben Zakkai reportedly answered that henceforth "deeds of love"—humanitarian service—would replace the old system of animal sacrifice. He then quoted the Scripture in which God declares, "I require mercy, not sacrifice" (Hos. 6:6), a passage that Jesus is also said to have emphasized (Matt. 9:13).

After his retirement or death, ben Zakkai was succeeded by Gamaliel's grandson, Gamaliel the Younger (c. 30–100 CE). In addition to debating the canonical status of a few biblical texts, such as Ecclesiastes and the Song of Songs, the Jamnia scholars sought to define the essential requirements—and limits—of Judaism. According to a Talmudic tradition, the benediction against the Minim (heretics) was formulated during this period (about 90 CE). Many scholars believe that this interdiction was aimed at the Christians, whose beliefs about Jesus' superiority to Moses, transmitter of God's Torah, increasingly separated them from Jamnia's views of acceptable Judaism. It seems probable that after 85 or 90 CE Jewish Christians were sporadically expelled from the synagogues, causing a bitter division between the Christian and Jewish communities. The Gospel of John appears to reflect this exclusion of Jesus' followers (John 9:22, 34), as does the Gospel of Matthew, which vehemently denounces Pharisaic policies while simultaneously commending their general teachings (Matt. 23).

The Samaritans

Named for the capital city, Samaria, of the ancient northern kingdom of Israel, the Samaritans were a distinctive Jewish group who occupied the territory lying between Judea and Galilee. Although 2 Kings 17 depicts Samaritans as the descendants of Mesopotamians whom Assyrian conquerors settled in the area during the late eighth century BCE—and therefore not "authentic" Jews—this picture is historically inaccurate. By the time of the Roman occupation of Palestine, Jews in Judea regarded the Samaritans as an alien people who practiced a false version of the Jewish religion.

Whereas Jews worshiped at the Jerusalem Temple on Mount Zion, Samaritans viewed Mount Gerizim, near the ancient Israelite sanctuary of Shechem, as God's approved holy place (John 4:20). When the Hasmonean king John Hyrcanus invaded Samaria in 108 BCE, however, he destroyed the Samaritan temple erected on Mount Gerizim. For most observant Jews, the Samaritan branch of Hellenistic Judaism—which recognized only the Mosaic Torah, and not the Prophets or other biblical writings, as binding Scripture—was little better than a Gentile cult.

In contrast, New Testament writers generally portray the Samaritans favorably, offering none of the blistering denunciations they heap upon the Sadducees and Pharisees. The author of Luke-Acts not only shows Jesus conducting a brief ministry in Samaria (Luke 17:11–19) and making a Samaritan the hero of a famous parable (Luke 10:33–36) but also presents Samaria as the first step beyond Judea on the church's worldwide mission (Acts 1:8; 8:1–40). In John's Gospel, after Jesus holds a long discussion with a Samaritan woman about the differences between her people and the Jews of Jerusalem, she perceives that he is the Messiah and, acting as one of his first missionaries, persuades her fellow villagers to become Jesus' disciples (John 4). Some of Jesus' adversaries even label him a Samaritan (John 8:48)!

Although these Gospel anecdotes suggest that early Christianity found a friendlier reception among some Samaritans than among many adherents of Palestinian Judaism, most Samaritans did not become Christians. Among the various Jewish parties cited in Josephus and the New Testament, the Samaritans are unique in being the only group—apart from what became rabbinical Judaism—that survives to the present day. A Samaritan community continues to practice its ancient rites at Mount Gerizim, near the modern city of Nablus.

The Essenes and the Dead Sea Scrolls

A series of sensational discoveries beginning in 1947 have revolutionized scholars' understanding of Judaism's complexities during the early New Testament period. According to one version of the story, in that year a Bedouin shepherd boy, who had been idly throwing stones into the mouth of a cave near the Dead Sea, heard a sound like shattering pottery. When he climbed into the cave to investigate, he found pottery jars full of ancient manuscripts, now world famous as the **Dead Sea Scrolls** (see Figure 3.3).

Before the young shepherd made his astonishing find, scholars had almost no Jewish literature dating from the centuries immediately before or during the formative period of Christianity. Books of the Hebrew Bible date back considerably farther than the time of Jesus, and the Mishnah was compiled almost two centuries after his death. With the unexpected discovery of the Dead Sea Scrolls, however, scholars now have an entire religious library that was composed or transcribed between the mid-second century BCE and late first century CE. The scrolls not only encompass the period when Christianity first developed but also originated in a place near the Judean wilderness where John the Baptist held his revival campaign—the locale in which Jesus began his ministry.

A large majority of scholars are convinced that the scrolls were produced by the **Essenes,** an ascetic Jewish sect that flourished in Palestine from about 140 BCE until 68 CE, when it was destroyed or dispersed by Roman armies. First-century Jewish authors, such as Josephus and **Philo Judaeus** of Alexandria, had described some of the Essene beliefs and practices. But only after 1947 did their own extensive writings—found in eleven different caves—gradually become available. When some of the Dead Sea Scrolls were first published in English, a few scholars theorized that the Essene group represented an early form of Christianity. More recently, some commentators have speculated that the "Teacher of Righteousness"—the sect's founder and early leader—was none other than Jesus of Nazareth or perhaps his brother (kinsman) **James,** who was known as "James the Righteous." Other critics have claimed that Paul, who rejects Torah keeping in favor of divine grace, is the "wicked priest" whom the scrolls condemn. One commentator has even assigned the "wicked priest" role to Jesus!

Despite a few extreme—and almost universally repudiated—claims, the scholarly consensus holds that the primary value of the scrolls in relation to Christian origins is the evidence they provide for the Palestinian roots of earliest Christianity. Many ideas, terms, and phrases previously thought to have arisen in a non-Palestinian Hellenistic environment were actually present in Jesus' homeland during his lifetime. Documents outlining the Essenes' mode of worship, communal meals, purification rites involving immersion in water, and conviction that they alone formed a "New Covenant" community representing true Israel reveal abundant parallels to Christian teachings. Rather than prove that the Jesus movement developed out of Essene beliefs, however, the scrolls generally show that a marginal Jewish religious group anticipated a number of Christian practices. Certain rituals, such as a shared meal of bread and wine or water baptism of initiates, are not unique to Christianity but are paralleled in earlier Essene practices, just as Greco-Roman myths about a dying and rising savior

FIGURE 3.3 Passage from one of the Dead Sea Scrolls (1Q Isa. 49:12). Placed in clay jars and hidden in caves near the Dead Sea, the Essene library from the Qumran monastery includes the oldest surviving copies of the Hebrew Bible (Old Testament).

deity foreshadowed theological interpretations of Jesus' life, death, and rebirth.

Qumran Some investigators dispute this claim, but the large majority of scholars believe that the ruins of **Qumran,** a settlement located about 8.5 miles south of Jericho and overlooking the northwest shores of the Dead Sea, mark the site of an Essene community that produced the Dead Sea Scrolls (see Figure 3.4). According to most scholars, a particularly rigorous group of Essenes

inhabited Qumran, where they pursued a monastic way of life, apparently renouncing marriage, holding all possessions in common, and unquestioningly obeying their priestly superiors. The Qumran community may have been founded shortly after the Maccabean Revolt when Hasmonean rulers assumed the office of High Priest, a practice the Essenes abhorred as an illegal usurpation that polluted the Temple. Withdrawn from the world in their isolated desert community, the Essenes patiently awaited the

FIGURE 3.4 Ruins at Qumran, near the northwest shore of the Dead Sea. Although some scholars dispute this, the majority believe that the Essenes, an apocalyptic sect that awaited Yahweh's call to battle the Romans, maintained a monastic colony here. After the Essenes had hidden their library—the Dead Sea Scrolls—in nearby caves, the Roman army destroyed Qumran (68 CE), the ruins of which have since been excavated.

arrival of two Messiahs—a priestly Messiah descended from **Aaron,** Moses' brother and Israel's first High Priest, and a second "Messiah of Israel," a leader descended from King David. The only Jewish sect known to expect two such leaders, the Essenes may have influenced the author of the New Testament Book of Hebrews, which is unique in presenting the risen Christ as both a Davidic and a high priestly Messiah. Essene interest in **Melchizedek,** a mysterious king-priest mentioned briefly in the books of Genesis and Psalms, is similarly reflected in Hebrews' comparison of Christ to Melchizedek, the only canonical writing to make this connection (see Chapter 18).

Contents of the Qumran Library Archaeologists have recovered more than 900 manuscripts from eleven different caves in or near Qumran, most of which were written on leather. Although a few scrolls are well preserved, most suffered severe damage from climate, insects, and animals. In Cave 4, for example, approximately 600 manuscripts had disintegrated into more than 15,000 fragments. Many fragments contained only a few words or letters.

The Dead Sea documents, which the Essenes may have hidden in caves shortly before the Roman armies razed Qumran, are enormously important for biblical research. First, the manuscripts contain the oldest surviving copies of the Hebrew Bible, some fragments of which date back to the third century BCE. The youngest manuscripts were made during mid-first century CE, when New Testament figures such as Peter and Paul were already preaching that the crucified Jesus of Nazareth was Israel's Messiah. With the exception of Esther, the Dead Sea Scrolls contain every book eventually included in the Hebrew canon. A spectacular find, the complete scroll of Isaiah, perhaps a thousand years older than any previously known Isaiah manuscript, shows few variations from the Hebrew **Masoretic Text (MT),** the medieval edition of the Hebrew Bible from which most modern translations are made. Other Qumran copies of Scripture, however, differ significantly from the "standard" Masoretic edition.

Extensive variations between some of the Qumran biblical texts and later copies of the Hebrew Bible suggest that by the first century CE, Jewish scholars had not yet adopted a universally recognized version of their sacred writings. The remarkable variation in different textual traditions among the Dead Sea Scrolls indicates that the biblical text remained fluid and subject to scribal changes well into the early Christian era.

Whereas the medieval Masoretic scholars were renowned for their care and accuracy in copying the Hebrew Bible, some Dead Sea copyists were less meticulous. A comparatively short fragment of Jeremiah (4Q Jer3) manifests an unusual number of scribal corrections. After the first scribe copying Jeremiah 7:28–9:2 had omitted a lengthy passage (Jer. 7:30–8:3), a second copyist showed great ingenuity in trying to restore the missing text. Although he managed to insert part of the omitted section (Jer. 7:30–31) into the space between Jeremiah 7:29 and 8:4, he was forced to copy another part (7:32–8:3a) perpendicular to the left margin of the main text, and to write verse 8:3b upside down at the bottom of the page. (See VanderKam and Flint in "Recommended Reading.")

Some recent English editions of the Bible, such as the New Revised Standard Version (NRSV), have utilized the scrolls in restoring texts present in the Dead Sea Scrolls but missing in the MT. Among the innumerable corrections made possible by ongoing study of the scrolls, along with early parallel translations such as that in the Septuagint, is the NRSV's rendering of a controversial passage in Deuteronomy that describes how various gods were assigned the patronage of different nations:

> When the Most High apportioned the nations,
>   when he divided humankind, he fixed the
>   boundaries
> of the people according to the number of the
> gods; the LORD's [Yahweh's] own portion was
> his people, Jacob [Israel] his allotted share.
>
> (Deut. 32:8–9)

Masoretic copyists, apparently troubled by the passage's reference to multiple "gods," amended the text to read "according to the number of the sons of Israel." Although some contemporary translations, such as the New International Version, retain the MT rendering, many scholars believe that the NRSV's translation is correct.

Noncanonical Scrolls   Besides the 200 manuscripts representing books that ultimately became part of the biblical canon, the Dead Sea scribes also produced copies of documents that Jewish scholars eventually excluded from the Hebrew Bible. These include the Book of Tobit (considered deuterocanonical in Catholic and Orthodox Bibles), as well as works of the **Pseudepigrapha,** such as 1 Enoch, an apocalyptic work (see Chapter 19), and the Book of Jubilees, a priestly revision of canonical Genesis and Exodus 1–15. The presence of literature ascribed to Enoch (mentioned in Genesis 5:21–24)—fragments of which were also found at the nearby fortress of Masada (see Figure 3.5)—interspersed among works later included in the Tanakh suggests that at least some Jews of the first century CE regarded these books as sacred and worthy of preservation. Like the Essenes who studied the Enoch documents, the author of the New Testament Book of Jude also saw them as authoritative, quoting a passage from 1 Enoch verbatim (see Chapter 18). A recent English edition of the Hebrew Bible based entirely on the Dead Sea texts was published in 1999 (see Abegg et al. in "Recommended Reading").

Commentaries on Biblical Texts   The Dead Sea writers also composed extensive commentaries on individual books that were later recognized as canonical, such as those on the prophets Habakkuk, Isaiah, Hosea, and Micah. The Habakkuk commentary is particularly illuminating because it shows that the Essenes used the same methods of interpreting biblical texts that many New Testament writers employed. Gospel authors such as Matthew regarded the Hebrew Bible as a repository of prophetic texts foretelling events fulfilled in his own day and in his own community, an approach that the Essene interpreter of Habakkuk also followed. For the Essene writer, the ancient prophet had predicted events related to the creation of the Essene movement and the

FIGURE 3.5 Masada. Built as a fortress retreat by King Herod, during the Jewish Revolt Masada served as the rebels' last holdout against Roman troops. According to Josephus, in 73 CE Masada's occupying force of 1,000, including some women and children, committed mass suicide rather than become Roman slaves.

experiences of its leaders. Other manuscripts cover such topics as the Blessing of Jacob, the Admonition of Moses, an anthology of messianic predictions, and a compendium of eschatological signs marking the last days. Both Essene and New Testament writers characteristically view their own group as enjoying a special covenant relationship with God and as the only worshipers who acceptably carry out the divine will. As such, they alone will be vindicated at God's impending judgment on all humanity.

Sectarian Literature Besides preserving the earliest extant copies of canonical and noncanonical texts related to the Hebrew Bible and composing commentaries on biblical passages that anticipate the interpretive methods of early Christian writers, the Dead Sea Scrolls also include numerous works produced exclusively by and for the Essene community. Although a minority of scholars

argues that the Qumran literature represents a cross-section of Hellenistic Jewish beliefs, most still believe that the nonbiblical manuscripts envisioning imminent eschatological judgment and outlining elaborate rules for living in a monastic society represent genuine Essene thought. Containing many previously unknown documents, this category of scrolls reveals the hopes and worldview of a people who believed themselves God's only true servants, a people who rigorously practiced ritual and ethical purity.

A defining document, the "Manual of Discipline" specifies requirements and regulations for life in the Essene community. Also called the "Community Rule," this manuscript features a dualistic view of the world, dividing the human race into two mutually exclusive classes: (1) The "children of light" are guided by a "spirit of truth" and are ruled by the "Prince of Light"; (2) by contrast, the "children of falsehood" walk in darkness under an "Angel of Darkness." This truth–error and light–dark dichotomy also typifies the language of John's Gospel.

On a less mystical level, the manual also offers practical guidance for screening and admitting members of the monastic community. This compendium of rules sets standards of age, physical condition, strict Torah observance, ritual purity, and doctrinal orthodoxy for initiates who adopt the Essene way of life. Besides the practice of holding material goods in common, which also characterized the first-generation Christians in Jerusalem (Acts 2), the Essenes further anticipated the early church by participating in a solemn meal of bread and wine that strikingly resembles Gospel accounts of Jesus' Last Supper. Additional organizational instructions and rituals appear in the "Zadokite Document," which describes a "New Covenant" made in "the land of Damascus," presumably a code expression for Qumran, where the Essenes had their desert monastery. Unlike the other sectarian scrolls, the Zadokite Document was previously known to scholars; a version had been found at a Cairo synagogue in the 1890s.

The Essene library encompassed many different literary genres, including liturgical hymns modeled on the canonical Psalms, which were probably sung during worship services. Because the Essenes judged the Jerusalem Temple as thoroughly contaminated by the Sadducees who controlled the official priesthood, they apparently tried to duplicate some Temple rituals and ceremonies in their own settlement. Consistent with their division of all humanity into children of "light" or "darkness," the liturgies included lists of blessings upon the obedient and curses on the "wicked."

Eagerly anticipating God's intervention into history, the Essene sectarians also composed a lengthy narrative outlining the "War of the Sons of Light Against the Sons of Darkness," which seems to envision a military conflict with the Romans, who then occupied Palestine. Involving both earthly armies and heavenly forces of good and evil, this climactic battle—an Essene Armageddon—would result in victory for true Israel (the faithful Essene community) and the triumphant reign of God.

The Gospels and the Essenes   The New Testament is silent on the Essenes, their desert monastery, and their austere lives of pious scholarship. The absence of references to the Essenes may reflect the fact that, by the time the Gospels were written, the sect had ceased to exist as an identifiable group. Some historians, however, suspect that the Gospels' silence may reflect their authors' consciousness that Jesus and his first disciples may have been influenced by Essene teachings.

Although a few scholars argue that Jesus spent the "lost years" between ages twelve and thirty as a member of the Essene community, the suggestion has not been widely accepted. In contrast, **John the Baptist**—whom the Gospels paint as a desert ascetic condemning Jewish religious and political leadership and preaching a doctrine of repentance before an impending cataclysm—seems to echo some of the Essenes' characteristic views. What relationship John might have had to the Essene movement, however, remains conjectural.

The Zealots

Known for their passionate commitment to Jewish religious and political freedom, the **Zealots** formed a party dedicated to evicting the Romans from Palestine. Opposition to the Roman occupation, which began in 63 BCE, flared repeatedly during the first century CE, climaxing in the Jewish War against Rome (66–73 CE). In 6 CE, a Jewish patriot known as **Judas the Galilean** led an armed rebellion that fueled nationalistic hopes but that the Romans crushed easily. **Simon,** one of Jesus' disciples, is called a "zealot" (Luke 6:15; Acts 1:13), and in Acts, a parallel is drawn between Jesus' activity and that of Judas (Acts 5:37–39), leading some historians to suspect that Jesus may also have been involved in some form of rebellion against Rome. Most scholars, however, believe that Simon's designation as a "zealot" probably refers to his zeal or enthusiasm for the Law and that Jesus firmly refused to become involved in any political schemes (Mark 8:33; 10:38–39; Luke 24:21; Acts 1:6).

Although many Jews had fought against foreign oppression since the time of the Maccabees, the Zealots did not constitute an identifiable political party until shortly after the revolt against Rome began in 66 CE. According to Josephus, the Zealots' blind nationalism launched the Palestinian Jews on a suicidal course. In his history of the Jewish War, Josephus argues that it was the Zealots' refusal to surrender, even after Jerusalem had been captured, and their occupation of the Temple precincts that compelled the Romans to destroy the sanctuary. According to Josephus, General Titus, the Roman commander in chief, had not originally intended to commit this desecration. This catastrophe and the later bar Kochba rebellion of 132–135 CE discredited both the Zealot party and its apocalyptic hope of divine intervention in achieving national liberation. Thanks to the Zealot failures, both armed rebellion and end-of-the-world predictions were henceforth repudiated by mainstream Judaism.

The Messiah: First-Century Expectations

Jewish-Christian Debates on Jesus' Messiahship

According to Mark's Gospel, Jesus is already halfway through his public ministry before a single close disciple identifies him as "the Messiah" (Mark 8:27–29; cf. Matt. 16:13–17). In this episode, Mark assumes that *the* "Messiah" is a universally recognized concept that his audience will instantly grasp. It is not, however, a clearly defined technical term in the Hebrew Bible, early Christianity's primary authority for its messianic beliefs. Derived from the Hebrew word *mashiah*, **Messiah** means "Anointed One" and refers to the ceremony in which priests anointed (poured oil on) the heads of various persons whom God selected and consecrated for some special undertaking. In the Hebrew

Scriptures, *mashiah* is most frequently applied to the kings of ancient Israel, particularly those descended from King David (Pss. 18:50; 89:20, 38, 51; 132:10, 17). The word thus denotes a political figure, particularly a royal military leader who defends Israel against its enemies.

For many biblical authors, the prototype of God's anointed king was David, the first ruler to establish a powerful Israelite state (c. 1000 BCE), a kingdom that many Jews believed foreshadowed God's reign on earth. In 2 Samuel 7, Yahweh concludes an "everlasting covenant" or treaty with David's "house [dynasty]," promising unconditionally to maintain an uninterrupted line of David's heirs on Israel's throne. "When your life ends," Yahweh tells David,

> and you rest with your forefathers, I will set up
> one of your own children to succeed you and
> I will establish his kingdom. It is he [Solomon,
> David's successor] shall build a house [the
> Jerusalem Temple] in honor of my name, and
> I will establish his royal throne for ever. I will
> be his father and he shall be my son. . . . My
> love will never be withdrawn from him. . . .
> Your family shall be established and your king-
> dom shall stand for all time in my sight, and
> your throne shall be established for ever.
>
> (2 Sam. 7:13–16)

In Psalm 89, Yahweh further vows never to abandon David's royal descendants; he would punish disobedient rulers, but will

> not deprive him [David's heir] of my true love
>   nor let my faithfulness prove false;
> I will not renounce my covenant nor change
>   my promised purpose.
> I have sworn by my holiness once and for all,
> I will not break my word to David:
> his posterity shall continue for ever,
> his throne before me like the sun;
> it shall be sure for ever as the moon's return,
> faithful as long as the skies remain.
>
> (Ps. 89:30–37; cf. 2 Sam. 7:14–16)

Perhaps as a result of this "royal covenant theology," David's heirs ruled in Jerusalem for nearly 400 years (961–587 BCE). (After Solomon's death, Israel split into two nations, the larger kingdom of Israel in the north, and the smaller and poorer kingdom of Judah, with its capital at Jerusalem, in the south.)

Disastrous End of the Davidic Dynasty David's line of reigning kings came to an abrupt end in 587 BCE, when Nebuchadnezzar of Babylon destroyed Jerusalem, burned Solomon's Temple, and removed the last Davidic monarch, Zedekiah, from the throne. Probably referring to this national disaster, the psalmist accuses Yahweh of breaking his sworn oath to David:

> Yet thou [Yahweh] hast rejected thy
>   anointed king,
> thou has spurned him and raged against
>   him,
> thou hast denounced the ["everlasting"]
>   covenant with thy servant [David],
> defiled his crown and flung it to the
>   ground. . . .
> Thou hast put an end to his glorious rule . . .
> and covered him with shame.
>
> (Ps. 89:38–45)

Besides bringing Davidic rule to a permanent end, Nebuchadnezzar also deported much of Judah's upper class to his imperial capital. When a devoted remnant of Judah's leadership returned to Jerusalem from Babylon in 538 BCE, the Davidic monarchy was not restored. After the Persian Cyrus I conquered Babylon in 539 BCE, ending the Babylonian Empire and making Persia the Near East's dominant power, Cyrus installed local governors over Judah. The first of these Persian-appointed governors was Zerubbabel (his name means "born in Babylon"), a descendant of the Davidic family. For a brief period, Jewish hopes for national revival apparently focused on Zerubbabel. Although the prophets Haggai and Zechariah seemed to regard him as a potential restorer of David's kingdom (Hag. 2:20–23; Zech. 2:10; 6:12), Zerubbabel, perhaps on Persian orders, quietly disappeared from history. Despite Yahweh's explicit vow, Israel was never again to have a Davidic king, the "anointed of God."

During the long years of Persian rule, the Jewish people looked mainly to the spiritual leadership of their High Priest, who was also anointed with holy oil when installed in office (Lev. 4:3, 5). The High Priest and his many priestly assistants administered the rebuilt Temple and provided a focus of communal religious identity. Without a king or political autonomy, Judah became increasingly a theocratic (God-ruled) community, guided by a hereditary priestly class that supervised the Temple sacrifices and interpreted the Mosaic Torah.

Israel's Hope for a New Davidic King

Even after centuries of foreign domination, as tiny Judah was successively ruled by Babylonians, Persians, Greeks, Syrians, and Romans, Israel's collective memory of the Davidic Covenant did not fade. Yahweh's sworn oath that his people would have a Davidic heir to rule them forever (2 Sam. 7; 23:1–5; Ps. 89:19–31) was reinforced by Israel's prophets, who envisioned a future golden age when God would at last remember his promise to David.

Isaiah of Jerusalem, who staunchly supported the Davidic monarchy during the eighth century BCE, had delivered unforgettable oracles (prophetic words) from Yahweh:

> For a boy has been born for us, a son given to
>   us to bear the symbol of dominion on his
>   shoulder;
>   and he shall be called
>   in purpose wonderful, in battle
>   God-like,
>   Father for all time, Prince of peace.
> Great shall the dominion be and boundless
>   the peace
>   bestowed on David's throne and on his
>   kingdom,
>   to establish it and sustain it with justice and
>   righteousness from now and for evermore.
> The zeal of the LORD [Yahweh] of Hosts
>   shall do this.
>
> (Isa. 9:6–7)

Isaiah's further allusions to a righteous king "from the stock of Jesse [David's father]" (Isa. 11:1–9) and visions of a prosperous Jerusalem to which the Gentile nations would flock

(Isa. 2:1–4) not only enhanced the prestige of the Davidic royal family but also associated it with the coming earthwide reign of Yahweh.

All of Israel's Davidic kings were literally "messiahs [*mashiah*]," "anointed of God." They reigned as Yahweh's "sons," adopted at the time of their consecration or coronation: "'You [the Davidic ruler] are my son,' [God] said; 'this day I become your father'" (Ps. 2:7). Because the prophets had envisioned these divinely adopted rulers as warrior-kings like David—God's agent in establishing an earthly kingdom—the messianic leader was typically seen as fulfilling a military-political role. His function was to demonstrate the omnipotence of Israel's God by setting up a theocratic state whose righteous government would compel the Gentiles' respect for both Yahweh and his chosen people (Isa. 11; Dan. 2:44).

Psalm of Solomon 17

The most striking description of Israel's expected deliverer was written only five or six decades before Jesus' birth. Ascribed to Solomon, the progenitor of Israel's wisdom tradition, a collection of prophetic poems known as the Psalms of Solomon describes a righteous king who would drive the hated foreigners (Roman occupational forces) from Jerusalem and establish a just sovereignty over both Gentiles and Jews. Psalm of Solomon 17 is the first known work of Jewish literature to use the terms *son of David* and *Lord Messiah* (Christ), distinctive titles that New Testament writers apply to Jesus.

Although Psalm of Solomon 17 sees the Messiah as sinless and powerful, he is clearly a human rather than a supernatural figure, God's agent but not a divine being. His promised activities include gathering together "a holy people" who will be "children of their God," cleansing Jerusalem (presumably including its Temple), and ruling compassionately over the Gentiles. Although a Davidic heir, this "Lord Messiah" achieves his dominion without military conquest because he is "powerful in the holy spirit" and strengthened by "wisdom and understanding."

This vision of a peaceful Messiah subduing opponents through "the word of his mouth [his teaching]" is much closer to that adopted by the Gospel authors than the traditional expectation of a warrior-king like the historical David (see Box 3.3).

A Revisionist View of the Messiah

As presented in the Gospels, Jesus of Nazareth takes a view of the messianic role and the kingdom of God that was disappointing or perplexing to many. Despite some modern commentators' attempts to associate him with the Zealot or revolutionary party, Jesus (as portrayed by the Evangelists) does not present himself as a military or political savior of Israel. As John's Gospel concludes, his "kingdom does not belong to this world" (John 18:36).

Many scholars believe that during his lifetime Jesus did not claim to be Israel's Messiah, but that after the experience of his resurrection—regarded as proof of divine vindication—his followers claimed the title for him. In recognizing Jesus as the Messiah, however, Jewish Christians were faced with a dilemma: They were convinced that he was David's predestined heir, the royal figure whom Isaiah and other prophets had foretold, but, as their detractors pointedly observed, he had "failed" in the essential messianic task of reestablishing David's kingdom. In Luke-Acts, the writer expresses this tension between Christians' belief in Jesus' authentic messiahship and the seeming incompleteness of his earthly work. Repeatedly, the disciples voice their expectation that Jesus will finally make God's kingdom a reality (Luke 19:11) and that he will "establish once again the sovereignty of Israel" (Acts 1:6). Ordered not to speculate about when or how God's imperial domain will actually arrive, the disciples are instead assigned the task of carrying Jesus' message "to the ends of the earth" (Acts. 1:7–8).

Convinced that Jesus *was* God's anointed and that he *would*—eventually—fulfill all the biblical promises to Abraham and David, Christians soon made an enormous leap of faith.

BOX 3.3 **Psalm of Solomon 17**

See, Lord, and raise up for them [Israel] their king,
   the *son of David* [emphasis added] to rule over your servant Israel
   in the time known to you, O God.
Undergird him with the strength to destroy the unrighteous rulers,
   to purge Jerusalem from gentiles
   who trample her to destruction;
   in wisdom and righteousness to drive out
   the sinners from the inheritance; . . .
To destroy the unlawful nations with the word of his mouth;
At his warning the nations will flee from his presence,
   and he will condemn sinners by the thoughts of their hearts.
He will gather a holy people
   whom he will lead in righteousness. . . .
For he shall know them
   that they are all children of their God. . . .
He will judge peoples and nations in the wisdom of his righteousness.
And he will have gentile nations serving him under his yoke
   and he will glorify the Lord in (a place) prominent (above)
   the whole earth.
And he will purge Jerusalem
   (and make it) holy as it was even from the beginning,
   (for) nations to come from the ends of the earth to see his glory,
   to bring as gifts the children who had been driven out, . . .
And he will be a righteous king over them, taught by God.
There will be no unrighteousness among them in his days,
   for all shall be holy,
   and their king shall be the *Lord Messiah* [emphasis added].
(For) he will not rely on horse and rider and bow,
   nor will he collect gold and silver for war.
Nor will he build up hope in a multitude for a day of war.
The Lord himself is his king,
   the hope of the one who has a strong hope in God.
He shall be compassionate to all the nations
   (who) reverently stand before him. . . .
And he himself (will be) free from sin, (in order) to rule
   a great people.
He will expose officials and drive out sinners
   by the strength of his word.
And he will not weaken in his days, (relying) on his God,
   for God made him powerful in the holy spirit
   and wise in the counsel of understanding,
   with strength and righteousness. . . .
Faithfully and righteously shepherding the Lord's flock,
   he will not let any of them stumble in their pasture.
He will lead them all in holiness
   and there will be no arrogance among them,
   that any should be oppressed.
This is the beauty of the king of Israel
   which God knew,
   to raise him over the house of Israel
   to discipline it. . . .
Blessed are those born in those days
   to see the good fortune of Israel
   which God will bring to pass in the assembly of the tribes.

Jesus, God's *mashiah,* will make a second visit to earth to accomplish what was left unfinished at his first coming. Although the Hebrew Bible, the source of both Jewish and Christian messianic ideas, says nothing about the Messiah dividing his work into two separate installments—an initial earthly career that culminates ingloriously in a criminal's death and a second (long-delayed) reappearance as an all-powerful supernatural king—early Christianity readily embraced this belief in a two-part messianic sequence. In the oldest surviving Christian documents, Paul urges his Gentile converts to be prepared for Jesus' imminent return as world judge (1 Thess. 4–5; 1 Cor. 1:7–8; 7:29–31). Paul fully expects to witness Jesus descending in glory from heaven to gather up his loyal followers, who will be "caught up in clouds to meet the Lord in the air" (1 Thess. 4:16–17; cf. 1 Cor. 15:51–55).

For those living in the protracted interval between Jesus' ascension to heaven and his return to earth, New Testament writers emphasize the spiritual significance of Jesus' innovative messiahship. Instead of coming to earth to conquer political enemies and forcibly establish a theocratic monarchy, Jesus is seen as having appeared primarily to conquer less tangible but more formidable foes—human sin, evil, and death. After his sacrificial death, paying the ultimate penalty to redeem humankind, Jesus then ascends to the celestial throne room, standing at God's "right hand" (a position symbolic of his unity with God) (Acts 8:55–56; cf. Rev. 1:11–20, etc.). In thus being portrayed as God's co-regent, an immortal being of cosmic stature, the ascended Jesus, ruling invisibly but eternally over human minds and hearts (Phil. 2:6–11), becomes infinitely more powerful than a Davidic Messiah. In Christian reinterpretation, traditional expectations of a renewed Davidic kingdom are transformed into the concept of a heavenly messianic reign, one in which believers—joined by sacrament and spirit—can participate.

The strongly apocalyptic nature of much (not all) New Testament Christianity serves to direct believers toward a culminating future, when the Deity's intentions will be accomplished "on earth, as in heaven," an omega point (ultimate goal) toward which all creation is now moving. The Christian concept of its Messiah is thus a paradox, a God-anointed king who is rejected and killed, but whose voluntary death is a triumph over forces of darkness and an unfailing sign of hope for humankind.

Mainstream Jews rejected Christian claims about Jesus of Nazareth for a variety of reasons, which will become clearer as we study the Gospels (see Chapters 6–10). Among other things, Jews could point to the fact that Jesus did not accomplish what Israel's prophets said David's anointed heir was commissioned to do: He did not deliver the covenant people from their Gentile enemies, reassemble those scattered in the Diaspora, restore the Davidic kingdom, or establish universal peace (cf. Isa. 9:6–7; 11:7–12:16, etc.). Instead of freeing Jews from their oppressors and thereby fulfilling God's ancient promises—for land, nationhood, kingship, and blessing—Jesus died a "shameful" death, defeated by the very political powers the Messiah was prophesied to overcome.

Indeed, the Hebrew prophets did not foresee that Israel's savior would be executed as a common criminal by Gentiles (John 7:12, 27, 31, 40–44), making Jesus' crucifixion a "stumbling block" to scripturally literate Jews (1 Cor. 1:23). To many Jews, the manner of Jesus' death at Roman hands explicitly disqualified him from messianic status. According to Deuteronomy 21:

> When someone is convicted of a crime punishable by death and is executed, and you *hang him on a tree,* his corpse must not remain all night upon the tree; you shall bury him that same day, for *anyone hung on a tree is under God's curse.*
>
> (Deut. 21:23, New Revised Standard Version; emphasis added)

A literal reading of Deuteronomy indicates that when Jesus was officially condemned and hung on the cross—made from a tree—he was necessarily accursed (Acts 5:30). Confronted with such texts, Christians reinterpreted them creatively, as offering clues to the *meaning* of Jesus' execution. In Paul's letter to the Galatians, he skillfully turns a potential weakness into a strength, citing Deuteronomy and arguing that, through his crucifixion, Jesus voluntarily accepted the Law's curse. In his "accursed" suffering, Jesus bore the punishment deserved by others, sinners whom the Law had condemned (Gal. 3:13; see Chapter 15).

Although no canonical prophet specifically predicted that the Messiah would die as a criminal (or be resurrected thereafter), several biblical passages speak of an unidentified righteous man who suffers unjustly. The most famous of these occurs in Isaiah 53, which describes an anonymous "servant" whose pain and humiliation are borne for the sake of others. This concept of vicarious suffering—in which an innocent person willingly endures unmerited punishment as a substitute for those who are actually guilty—became an important factor in the Christian interpretation of Jesus' death. In the Hebrew Bible, however, none of these suffering servant texts is directly linked to prophecies about the Messiah.

In Mark's Gospel, which scholars believe was the earliest written, the author reveals his awareness of Jewish objections to Jesus as Messiah by emphasizing the unexpected or "hidden" quality of Jesus' messiahship. Mark also utilizes the notion of vicarious suffering, stating that Jesus generously gave his life "as a ransom for many" (Mark 10:45). Of all the Gospel authors, Matthew makes the most sustained effort to defend Christians' messianic claims, literally ransacking the Septuagint edition for passages, or even single words, that could provide scriptural support for the unusual kind of Messiah that Jesus proved to be (see Chapter 8).

Confronted with challenges that Jesus had not fulfilled many scriptural promises, the early Christian movement sometimes found ingenious ways of refuting criticism. According to a tradition contained in both Matthew and Luke, when Jesus resisted the devil's temptations by quoting from the Hebrew Bible, the devil retaliated in kind, citing verses from Psalm 91. This psalm, which states that the truly righteous

person will enjoy God's certain favor, includes categorical assurances that Yahweh will protect his favored one from all physical harm:

> A thousand may fall at your side,
> ten thousand close at hand,
> but you it [misfortune] shall not touch; . . .
> For you the LORD [Yahweh] is a safe retreat;
> you have made the Most High your refuge.
> No disaster shall befall you,
> no calamity shall come upon your house. . . .
>
> (Ps. 91:7, 9–10)

God unequivocally promises to deliver the one whose "love is set on me":

> I will lift him beyond danger, for he knows
> me by my name . . .
> I will rescue him and bring him to honor.
> I will satisfy him with long life
> to enjoy the fullness of my salvation.
>
> (Ps. 91:14–16)

Dying without "honor" or achievement of "long life," traditional signs of divine approval, Jesus appeared to many not to be the godly person whom the psalmist described. Convinced, however, that Jesus had suffered only temporary defeat and, through his resurrection, attained "the fullness of [God's] salvation," the Gospel authors indicated that it was inappropriate to apply the optimistic guarantees of Psalm 91 to Jesus' experience. If opponents cited such passages as evidence that Jesus (who was not rescued by divine intervention) could not have been God's chosen one, Christians had an effective defense: Quoting Scriptures that do not support their claims is the devil's work!

Messianic Claimants Before and After Jesus

Jewish Uprisings Against Rome

Judea's troubled relationship with Rome inspired a series of prophets, revolutionaries, and other leaders who typically promised the Jewish people relief from Roman economic and social oppression. Some rebel leaders reputedly claimed the title of Jewish king, the crime for which Pontius Pilate executed Jesus. Most of those aspiring to royal status claimed not to be a "*son* [descendant] of David" but merely to be "*like* David," a previously obscure youth who was raised from among the common people to become Israel's champion against a foreign military threat. It could be said of these popular national leaders what the psalmist's God said of David: "I have conferred the crown on a hero, and promoted one chosen from my people" (Ps. 89:19).

In his accounts of peasant uprisings against the Romans or their Herodian puppets, the Jewish historian Flavius Josephus reports that several prominent rebels were also messianic pretenders (i.e., they assumed the function of Israel's *anointed* kings). Most of these popular kings appeared either during the turmoil following the death of Herod the Great (4 BCE) or during the greater upheaval of the Jewish War against Rome (66–73 CE; see Chapter 5). After Herod's death, a rebel named Judas, son of a brigand or terrorist named Hezekiah, led Galilee in a revolt against Roman occupational forces. According to Josephus, this Judas was motivated by an ambition to achieve "royal rank" (*Antiquities,* 17:271–272). Simon of Perea, the territory east of Galilee, similarly donned "the diadem," symbol of kingly status, and plundered Herod's palace in Jericho. After leading a band of unruly followers, Simon was captured by the Romans and beheaded, a fate anticipating that of John the Baptist. A third would-be king, Athronges, resembled David in beginning his career as a shepherd, after which he also wore a royal diadem and, supported by his brothers and their armed followers, attacked both Roman and Herodian armies. Roman retaliation against such popular uprisings was swift and severe: In 4 BCE, the Galilean town of Sepphoris, which had aided the rebels, was burned and its inhabitants sold into slavery. Located only a few miles from Nazareth, Sepphoris was lavishly rebuilt during Jesus' early years, a project on which it is remotely possible that he and his "carpenter [artisan]" father worked.

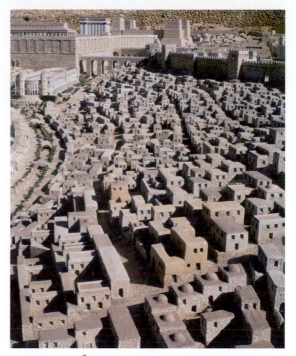

FIGURE 3.6 Scale model of Jerusalem, first century CE. The simple flat-roofed tenements housing the general population contrast with the monumental public buildings that Herod I (40–4 BCE) erected. The heavily fortified Temple area appears at the top.

Early in the first Jewish Revolt against Rome (c. 67–68 CE), several large groups of bandits or guerrilla fighters who had been plundering the countryside infiltrated Jerusalem and occupied the Temple area, which they made their headquarters (see Figure 3.6). This impromptu coalition formed a party of radical nationalists—the Zealots. Composed largely of peasants, the Zealots appear to have been as dedicated to overthrowing the Jerusalem ruling class—which they accused of exploiting the poor and collaborating with Rome—as they were to freeing their land from foreign domination.

Whereas the Zealots derived from the rural poor, the Sicarii (from the Latin *sicarius,* meaning "dagger") were a group of urban terrorists and assassins. Well organized, the Sicarii carried out a carefully plotted series of murders, eliminating priests and other Jerusalem authorities who favored compromise with Rome. According to Josephus, one of the Sicarii leaders, Menachem—the son or grandson of the rebel Judas—assumed the trappings of kingship. Menachem ostentatiously entered Jerusalem as the people's king, a warrior-monarch in the tradition of David.

Another Sicarii pretender, Simon **bar** (son of) Giora, who also had messianic pretensions, led the largest and most powerful force resisting the Roman reconquest of Jerusalem. Josephus states that, after Titus's soldiers had captured and demolished the Temple, Simon, arrayed in royal robes, suddenly appeared among the ruins. If he hoped for a last-minute divine intervention to vindicate his kingly aspirations, he was disappointed: The Romans took him as a prisoner to Rome, where he was executed.

The most famous messianic claimant was **Simon bar Kochba,** who led the second Jewish Revolt against Rome in 132–135 CE. Akiba, a prominent rabbi, proclaimed that bar Kochba fulfilled the promise in Numbers 24:17 that "a star shall go forth from Jacob." While Rabbi Akiba and other supporters called Simon "bar Kochba," which means "son of the star," his detractors derisively labeled the revolutionary "bar Koziba"—"son of the lie." His attempt to liberate Judea and restore a theocratic state was doomed by Roman might, which again annihilated Jewish armies and brought a terrible end to Jewish political messianic hopes.

Summary

As New Testament documents reveal, their authors present Jesus as far more than a Davidic king. Taken together, the canonical writings present Jesus as a composite figure, one who represents the sum of all Israel's heritage. He is not only the anointed monarch whom David foreshadowed; he is also a lawgiver and prophet like Moses, a blameless and humble servant who suffers for others, a heavenly sacrifice and eternal priest, a teacher of supreme wisdom, and the icon or "image of the invisible God" by, through, and for whom the universe was created.

Translating the Hebrew *mashiah* as the Greek *Christos,* the New Testament writers commonly speak as if Christ were not a title but part of Jesus' proper name. Composed in a Hellenistic context and for a Greek-thinking audience, the New Testament books present Jesus almost exclusively in his function as Christ, a universal savior whose role goes far beyond that of the Davidic ruler. In interpreting Jesus' religious meaning, the New Testament authors apply to their hero many different concepts borrowed from the rich vein of Hellenistic Jewish ideas about a messianic figure.

Questions for Review

1. Describe the concepts or beliefs common to most groups of first-century Judaisms. How was the ideal of Jewish monotheism related to Torah practice and the Temple cult?
2. Define some essential differences between the Sadducees and Pharisees. Which party controlled the Jerusalem Temple and was apparently on better terms with the Romans?
3. Discuss some of the beliefs that Pharisees, Essenes, and Christians held in common. What connection did the Essenes have to the Dead Sea Scrolls and possibly to John the Baptist?
4. Discuss the role that the Zealots played in the Jewish Revolt against Rome. What happened to the Jewish state and religion as a result of the revolt? How does Josephus contribute to our understanding of the Jewish war for independence?
5. Summarize the concept of the messianic king found in the Hebrew Bible. To what degree is the biblical Messiah a political figure related to the restoration of King David's royal dynasty? How do New Testament writers modify the concept of the Davidic Messiah?

Questions for Discussion and Reflection

1. How do you account for the extreme diversity of first-century Jewish religious groups, all of whom believed they were following the Mosaic Torah? Why do you think the Essenes regarded themselves as the only "true" Israel, the sole group loyal to its covenant obligations? Discuss the similarities between the Essenes' conviction that they alone served God's plan and the

later Christian belief that their community uniquely represented the "true Israel."

2. Most passages in the Hebrew Bible present a messianic leader as an heir of King David who, as a God-empowered conqueror, would restore Israel to its former political independence and prosperity. Because Jesus did not deliver the covenant people from their oppressors, the Romans, or restore David's throne, how can he be accepted as the Messiah whom Israel's prophets envisioned?

Terms and Concepts to Remember

Aaron	Judaism
Abraham	Judas the Galilean
Academy of Jamnia	*kavod*
ark of the covenant	Masoretic Text (MT)
bar	Melchizedek
Caiaphas	Messiah
Canaan	Mishnah
circumcision	Pharisees
covenant	Philo Judaeus
David	Pseudepigrapha
Davidic Covenant	purity laws
Day of Atonement	Qumran
(Yom Kippur)	rabbi
Dead Sea Scrolls	Sabbath
Diaspora	Sadducees
Essenes	scribes
Gamaliel	Shema
Gemara	Simon
Gentiles	Simon bar Kochba
Holy of Holies	Solomon
James	Talmud
Jesus	Temple
John the Baptist	Torah
Josephus, Flavius	Yahweh
Judah	Zealots

Recommended Reading

Abegg, Martin, Jr.; Flint, Peter; and Ulrich, Eugene. *The Dead Sea Scrolls Bible.* San Francisco: Harper-SanFrancisco, 1999. An English translation of the Hebrew Bible based on the Dead Sea manuscripts (many of which are fragmentary).

Bauckham, Richard. *The Jewish World Around the New Testament.* Grand Rapids, Mich.: Baker Academic, 2010. A series of essays placing early Christianity clearly in its first-century Jewish matrix.

Cohen, Shaye J. D. *From the Maccabees to the Mishnah,* 2nd ed. Philadelphia: Westminster John Knox Press, 2006. A readable survey of evolving Jewish religious ideas that gave birth to both rabbinic Judaism and Christianity.

Cross, Frank M. *The Ancient Library of Qumran,* 2nd ed. Grand Rapids, Mich.: Baker Book House, 1980.

———. *Qumran and the History of the Biblical Text.* Cambridge, Mass.: Harvard University Press, 1975.

Elledge, C. D. *The Bible and the Dead Sea Scrolls.* Atlanta: Society of Biblical Literature, 2005. A clear and concise overview of the scrolls and their significance.

Finkelstein, Louis. *The Pharisees,* Vols. 1 and 2. Philadelphia: Jewish Publication Society of America, 1962. Provides reliable information.

Freyne, Sean. *Jesus, a Jewish Galilean: A New Reading of the Jesus Story.* London: T&T Clark International, 2004. Places Jesus' life in the historical, social, and religious life of first-century Galilee.

Hengel, Martin. *Jews, Greeks, and Barbarians: Aspects of the Hellenism of Judaism in the Pre-Christian Period.* Philadelphia: Fortress Press, 1980.

Horsley, Richard A. "Messianic Movements in Judaism." In D. N. Freedman, ed., *Anchor Bible Dictionary,* Vol. 4, pp. 791–797. New York: Doubleday, 1992. An excellent introduction to political messianic claimants at the time of Jesus.

Horsley, Richard A., and Hanson, John S. *Bandits, Prophets, and Messiahs: Popular Movements at the Time of Jesus.* Minneapolis/Chicago/New York: Winston Press, 1985.

Josephus, Flavius. *Josephus: Complete Works.* Translated by W. Whiston. Grand Rapids, Mich.: Kregel Publications, 1960. A dated translation but contains the complete texts of *The Antiquities of the Jews* and *The Jewish War,* as well as the "Discourse on Hades."

———. *The Jewish War,* rev. ed. Translated by G. A. Williamson; edited by E. M. Smallwood. New York: Penguin Books, 1981. The most important contemporary source for conditions in Palestine during the first century CE.

Mason, Steve. *Josephus and the New Testament,* 2nd ed. Peabody, Mass.: Hendrickson, 2003. Examines Josephus's works for illumination of early Christian background.

Mendenhall, George E., and Herion, Gary A. *Ancient Israel's Faith and History: An Introduction to the Bible in Context.* Louisville, Ky.: Westminster John Knox Press, 2001. An authoritative analysis of archaeological and biblical evidence that places Israel's story in its Near Eastern context.

Murphy, Frederick J. *The Religious World of Jesus: An Introduction to Second Temple Palestinian Judaism.* Nashville, Tenn.: Abingdon Press, 1991. A survey of pertinent cultural and religious groups at the time of Jesus.

Newsome, James D. *Greeks, Romans, Jews: Currents of Culture and Belief in the New Testament World.* Philadelphia: Trinity Press International, 1992. A superbly researched compendium of historical documents relevant to Jewish religious thought and practice during the era of Christianity's inception.

Rainey, Anson F., and Notley, R. S. *The Sacred Bridge: Carta's Atlas of the Biblical World.* Jerusalem: Carta, 2006. A well-illustrated survey of biblical historical geography, including the New Testament period.

Shanks, Hershel, ed. *Christianity and Rabbinic Judaism,* 2nd ed. Upper Saddle River, New Jersey: Pearson, 2012. A collection of scholarly essays profiling the parallel development of Christianity and formative Judaism.

Talmon, Shemaryahu, ed. *Jewish Civilization in the Hellenistic Period.* Philadelphia: Trinity Press International, 1991. A collection of scholarly essays about the fusion of Hebraic and Hellenistic culture that gave birth to rabbi-led Judaism and Christianity.

VanderKam, James, and Flint, Peter. *The Meaning of the Dead Sea Scrolls: Their Significance for Understanding the Bible, Judaism, Jesus, and Christianity.* San Francisco: HarperSanFrancisco, 2002. An authoritative and up-to-date analysis of the scrolls and the light they have thrown on the origins of rabbinical Judaism and early Christianity.

Vermes, Geza. *The Complete Dead Sea Scrolls in English.* New York: Penguin Books, 1998. An authoritative translation of the Essene writings, omitting the biblical texts.

———. *An Introduction to the Complete Dead Sea Scrolls.* Minneapolis: Fortress Press, 2000. A standard work in the field.

CHAPTER 4

The World of Greek Thought and Culture

Jews demand signs [divine revelation], Greeks look for wisdom
[rational argument]. 1 Corinthians 1:23

Key Topics/Themes Although Jesus' life and teachings took place entirely within the context of Palestinian Judaism, his followers quickly spread his message abroad in the Greco-Roman world, where Greek-speaking converts interpreted him in ways that paralleled some previously existing Greek ideas and traditions. The rich diversity of Hellenistic religion and philosophy, which combined Greek culture with older cultures of the Near East, provided the dynamic environment in which early Christianity evolved.

Alexander and the Diffusion of Greek Culture

The fact that the New Testament is written entirely in Greek—as opposed to the Hebrew and Aramaic languages of the Old Testament—can be largely explained in a single word: Alexander. The most spectacular, and in many ways the most influential, of all ancient leaders, **Alexander the Great** conquered the entire eastern Mediterranean region, as well as the older civilizations of the ancient Near East (including Palestine) in the late fourth century BCE. The son of Philip II, king of Macedonia (a region in northern Greece), Alexander (reigned 336–323 BCE) came to the throne at age twenty. A brilliant military strategist and magnetic commander who won and held the devotion of his troops, Alexander embodied some of the most admired virtues of his age. Tutored by the philosopher-scientist Aristotle, he was both a practical man of action and a passionate disciple of Greek culture. Viewing himself as a new Achilles, the warrior-hero of Homer's *Iliad*, he was said to have kept a copy of the epic poem under his pillow, as if determined even in sleep to absorb its message of valor and personal honor. By the time he was thirty, Alexander had led his Macedonian armies to an unprecedented series of military victories that created the largest empire the world had yet known. Extending from Greece eastward through the ancient realms of Egypt, Babylonia, Persia, and Afghanistan into western India, Alexander's empire included most of the (then-recognized) civilized world (see Figure 4.1). At the age of thirty-two, stricken by a sudden fever, Alexander died in Babylon (323 BCE). He did not live long enough to consolidate his far-flung conquests and achieve his presumed goal of a single world government united under the flag of Greek civilization.

71

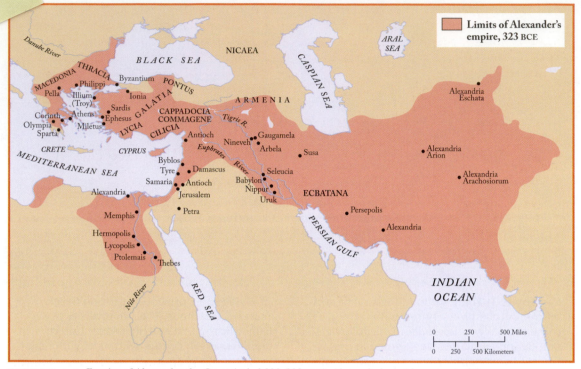

FIGURE 4.1 Empire of Alexander the Great (ruled 336–323 BCE). Alexander's rapid conquest of the older Persian Empire created a new Greek-speaking empire that included all of the ancient centers of civilization from Greece eastward to India. Influenced by Greek language, ideas, and customs, the resultant new international culture is known as Hellenistic.

Both Alexander and his successors (see Chapter 5) actively promoted **Hellenism,** the adoption of Greek language, literature, social customs, and ethical values. (The term derives from *Hellas,* the classical Greeks' name for their country.) Alexander's policy of founding hundreds of new cities—some located thousands of miles from the Greek homeland—that perpetuated the Hellenic way of life created an international Greek-speaking culture and began a new historical era known as **Hellenistic.** Arbitrarily dated as beginning with Alexander's death in 323 BCE, the Hellenistic era chronologically overlapped the period of Roman military expansion and continued as a cultural force into the early centuries CE. During this epoch, which spanned 500 years, the last books of the Hebrew Bible, the entire New Testament, and an additional large body of noncanonical Jewish and Christian literature were composed. Most of these works were significantly influenced by some aspect of Greek thought.

Along with a new form of the Greek language, the *koinē* spoken by Alexander's soldiers, Hellenistic culture introduced a creative flowering of art, architecture, philosophy, science, literature, and religion. It also produced, among educated classes at least, new ways of thought and expression, including a larger worldview in which Hellenistic peoples saw themselves as citizens not merely of a particular city-state (the *polis*) but of the world (*cosmos*) as a whole. This *cosmopolitan* outlook helped break down barriers between different traditions, allowing an integration of Greek with other ethnic customs, a widespread process by which even the Palestinian Jewish community became partly Hellenized.

Many prominent Jews gave their children Greek names and embraced Greek styles of education, dress, behavior, and other social practices. *Koinē* became so widely spoken that the Jews of Alexandria, Egypt's largest city, found it necessary to translate the Hebrew Bible into *koinē*

Greek, beginning about 250 BCE with the Torah and gradually adding other books. This Greek edition, the Septuagint (see Chapter 1), was used not only by Jews of the Diaspora but also by the early Christian churches, which produced their own Scripture, the New Testament, in *koinē* Greek.

Among leading thinkers throughout the Greco-Roman world, the Greek influence was all-pervasive. The Greek love of learning, intense intellectual curiosity, and confidence in the power of reason to discover truth became near-universal standards in the Hellenistic educational experience. Archaeologists have recently discovered that even Galilee, previously thought to be a rural backwater, had a cosmopolitan Hellenistic city, Sepphoris, which was located only four miles from Jesus' home village of Nazareth. Although the Gospel authors depict Jesus' ministry as largely confined to Galilean villages and small towns, some scholars think that Jesus may have had direct experience of Hellenistic culture there. Sepphoris, which the Romans had burned to the ground following a revolt in 4 BCE, was later lavishly rebuilt by Herod Antipas, the area's Roman-appointed ruler. It is theoretically possible, some historians believe, that the youthful Jesus, the "carpenter's son," may have worked on the rebuilding project, perhaps acquiring some knowledge of Greek ideas.

As a Greek book, the New Testament profoundly reflects its Hellenistic background. In many important ways, the New Testament writers combine their Jewish biblical heritage with Greek philosophical concepts. To understand the dual legacy that the Christian Greek Scriptures transmit to us, we must review briefly some major aspects of Hellenistic philosophy and religion.

Greek Philosophy

A term meaning "love of wisdom," *philosophy* is an attempt to understand human life and its place in the universe by applying rational analysis to a body of observable facts. At first indistinguishable from primitive science, Greek **philosophy** began in the late seventh century BCE in Miletus and other Greek cities along the coast of western Asia Minor. By the fifth century BCE, Athens had emerged as the intellectual center of the Greek world, home to numerous schools of thought that used the tools of logic to discredit old superstitions and to construct new theories about the universe.

Socrates, Plato, and the Immortal Soul

Greek philosophers such as Socrates and Plato gave birth to a new interpretation of the universe, some aspects of which lead in a direct line to important Christian doctrines. Almost five centuries before the inception of Christianity, these Athenian thinkers postulated a worldview that later Christian theologians routinely adopted, including a dualistic understanding of the universe, the soul's immortal nature, and a belief that behavior on earth determines the soul's ultimate destiny in the afterlife. Regarding the cosmos as possessing two separate dimensions—an invisible and eternal spirit realm and the visible material world of this life—Socrates and Plato emphasized the necessity of preparing the soul for eternity.

Socrates (c. 469–399 BCE) typically pursued ethical questions, particularly the mental disciplines required to lead the "good life," a life worthy of responsible and intelligent humans (see Figure 4.2). Combining brilliant originality with an impish sense of humor, Socrates regarded human life as an ongoing quest for truth, a pilgrimage toward the highest ideals of the spirit. Questioning every belief that his fellow Athenians cherished as "obviously" true, Socrates good-naturedly cross-examined artisans, teachers, and politicians alike—demanding to learn how people could be so sure that their beliefs were valid.

While attracting a small circle of devoted followers, Socrates also irritated many of Athens' most influential citizens, some of whom viewed this "gadfly" and his stinging questions as a threat to conventional morality. His critics eventually placed Socrates on trial, where he was convicted and executed for introducing "new gods" and corrupting Athenian youth, charges that masked his adversaries' real complaint. Socrates

repudiating materialistic goals, and paid the supreme penalty for voicing ideas that leaders of their respective societies deemed subversive. Despite their cultural differences, both men were sages who taught that the ultimate realities were divine powers before whom all people's conduct would be judged posthumously.

Plato's Profound Influence The historical situations for Jesus and Socrates are also alike in that neither one left anything in writing. In both cases, their teachings were reconstructed by later writers whose accounts of their subjects' lives may owe as much to editorial interpretation as they do to biographical fact. Socrates' youthful disciple **Plato** (c. 427–347 BCE) made his teacher the hero of a series of philosophical dialogues in which a saintly and humorous Socrates always outargues and outwits his opponents. Because virtually all of Plato's compositions, which he continued to produce until his death at eighty years of age, feature Socrates as the chief speaker, separating Plato's ideas from those of his mentor is difficult. New Testament scholars face a similar problem in trying to distinguish Jesus' authentic sayings from the added commentary of the Gospel writers, who wrote between forty and seventy years after Jesus' death (see Chapter 11).

Although he was a philosopher and logician, Plato profoundly influenced the history of Western religion, particularly later beliefs about the immortality of the soul and the effects that decisions made in this life can have on posthumous rewards and punishments. Plato's dualistic view of reality also deeply affected subsequent religious thought. He posited the coexistence of two distinct worlds: one the familiar physical environment of matter and sense impressions, and the other an invisible realm of perfect ideal forms. In this dualistic vision our bodies belong to the material sphere, where we are chained to the physical process of change, decay, and death. Our souls, however, originate in the unseen spirit world and after death return to it for postmortem judgment. Education involves recognizing the superiority of the soul to the body and cultivating those virtues that prepare the soul for its

FIGURE 4.2 Statue of Socrates (c. 469–399 BCE). Condemned to death for challenging the religious assumptions of his fellow Athenians, Socrates lives on in the dialogues of his great disciple, the philosopher Plato.

was the only person in Athens' long history to be put to death for expressing unpopular ideas.

Many readers find suggestive parallels between the respective careers of Socrates and Jesus, both of whom followed a divine calling, advocated cultivating spiritual values and immortal destiny. Hence, the person who truly loves wisdom, the genuine philosopher, will seek the knowledge of eternal truths that make real goodness possible, helping others along the way to realize that ambitions for worldly power or riches are false idols. The wise seek the perfect justice of the unseen world and, with the pure spirits of divinity, find everlasting life.

Over the centuries, Plato's ideas were modified and widely disseminated until, in one form or another, they became common knowledge during the Hellenistic era. Some New Testament writers, such as the author of Hebrews, used Platonic concepts to illustrate parallels and correspondences between the spiritual and physical worlds (Heb. 1:1–4; 9:1–14). The book's famous definition of Christian faith is primarily a confession of Platonic belief in the reality of the invisible realm (Heb. 11:1–2).

Stoicism and Stoic Endurance

Another Greek philosophy that became extremely popular among the educated classes during Roman times was **Stoicism.** Founded in Athens by Zeno (c. 336–263 BCE), the Stoic school emphasized the order and moral purpose of the universe. In the Stoic view, Reason is the divine principle that gives coherence and meaning to our universe. Identified as **Logos** (a Greek term for "word" or "cosmic wisdom"), this universal mind unifies the world and makes it intelligible to the human intellect. Human souls are sparks from the divine Logos, which is symbolized by cosmic fire and sometimes associated with a supreme god.

Stoic teaching urged the individual to listen to the divine element within, to discipline both body and mind to attain a state of harmony with nature and the universe. Stoics rigorously practiced self-control, learning self-sufficiency and noble indifference to both pleasure and pain. The Stoic ideal was to endure either personal gain or loss with equal serenity, without any show of emotion.

Many celebrated Romans pursued the Stoic way, including the philosopher Seneca (Nero's tutor), the Greek slave Epictetus, and the emperor Marcus Aurelius (161–180 CE). The hero of Virgil's epic poem *The Aeneid,* with his rigid concept of duty toward the gods and unselfish service to the state, is intended to embody the Stoic virtues. When Paul discusses self-discipline or the ability to endure want or plenty, he echoes Stoic values that were commonplace in Greco-Roman society (Phil. 4:11–14).

Epicureanism

A strikingly different philosophical outlook appears in the teachings of **Epicurus** (c. 342–270 BCE). Whereas the Stoics believed in the soul's immortality and a future world of rewards or penalties, Epicurus asserted that everything is completely physical or material, including the soul, which after death dissolves into nothingness along with the body. The gods may exist, but they have no contact with or interest in humankind. Without a cosmic intelligence to guide them, people must create their own individual purposes in life. A major goal is the avoidance of pain, which means that shrewd individuals will avoid public service or politics, where rivals may destroy them. Cultivating a private garden, the wise forgo sensual indulgences that weaken physically and mentally. Using reason not to discover ultimate Truth, but to live well, the enlightened person seeks intellectual pleasures because mental enjoyments outlast those of the body.

Epicurus's stress on the material, perishable nature of both body and soul found support in the philosopher Democritus's atomic theory. Democritus (born about 460 BCE) taught that all things are made up of tiny, invisible particles called atoms. It is the nature of atoms to move and collide, temporarily forming objects, including sentient ones like animals and humans, and then to disintegrate and re-form as other objects elsewhere. Wise or foolish, all persons are merely chance collections of atoms destined to dissolve without a trace.

Cynicism

A school of philosophy deriving from Antisthenes, one of Socrates' disciples, **Cynicism** included several famous teachers, particularly Diogenes of Sinope (c. 404–323 BCE) and his student Crates of Thebes (died c. 270 BCE). Teaching that virtue is the greatest goal in life, Cynics emphasized strict self-discipline and opposition to prevailing social custom and values, such as respect for money or political power. Demonstrating their antimaterialistic beliefs by their actions, Cynics were famous for scorning all creature comforts and traveling about thinly clad and barefoot, earning a meager subsistence by teaching and/ or begging. Some scholars find elements of Cynic principles in Jesus' injunctions to his disciples, who were to wander barefoot throughout Israel, preaching the kingdom and relying on handouts to survive (Mark 10; Luke 10:1–10).

According to the Book of Acts, early Christian missionaries and Greek philosophers had their first significant encounter in the university city of Athens about 50 CE. Acts reports that the apostle Paul debated Stoic and Epicurean philosophers, to whom he presented the novel idea of Jesus' resurrection. Living up to their reputation as champions of intellectual freedom, the Athenians invited Paul to speak at the Areopagus (a public forum). Acts states that Paul's audience listened politely until he preached about Jesus rising from the dead, a notion foreign to Greek thought, which conceived of posthumous survival in the form of an immaterial soul. Paul apparently did not succeed in establishing a new congregation of believers in Athens as he did in some other Greek cities; tension between the conflicting claims of Greek reason and Judeo-Christian revelation would characterize the church for many centuries.

Greco-Roman Religion

The Twelve Olympians

In contrast to Jewish **monotheism** (belief in a single, all-powerful God), Greco-Roman religion was characterized by **polytheism** (belief in many gods). Although the Greeks and Romans accepted the existence of innumerable deities, the highest gods were only twelve in number.

Because they dwelt on Mount Olympus, the loftiest peak in northern Greece, they were known as the Olympians. **Zeus,** whom the Romans called **Jupiter** or Jove, ruled as king of the Olympian gods, all of whom were part of a divine family consisting of Zeus's brothers, sisters, and children. The champion of justice, lawful order, and cosmic harmony, Zeus was a sky-god associated with both daylight and storm, a patriarchal deity who enforced his rule by obliterating opponents with his thunderbolt (see Figure 4.3).

Wiser than the older generations of gods whom he had overthrown to assume universal sovereignty, Zeus willingly shared power with

FIGURE 4.3 Statue of Zeus (or Poseidon) holding a (vanished) thunderbolt. In this larger-than-life bronze (c. 460 BCE), Zeus is both a personification of storm and lightning and the heavenly enforcer of justice, lawful order, and cosmic harmony. Unlike the Judeo-Christian God, who is eternal, Zeus is the descendant of older generations of gods who ruled the universe before him.

the other Olympians, each of whom had a distinctive function or sphere of influence. Zeus's hot-tempered brother Poseidon (the Roman Neptune) was lord of the sea and earthquakes, while his other brother, **Hades** (Pluto), known as the "Zeus of the Underworld," presided over a subterranean realm that housed the dead. Representing a sinister aspect of divinity, Hades lent his name to the gloomy kingdom he ruled, a name that New Testament writers also used to designate the soul's posthumous abode (Rev. 20) (see Box 4.1).

Zeus's sister-wife Hera (Juno) was queen of heaven and guardian of marriage and domesticity; his sister Demeter (Ceres) promoted the fertility of earth's soil that yielded life-sustaining grain; and his sister Hestia (Vesta) embodied the fixity and stability of the hearth and home. An important temple to Vesta stood near the Roman Forum, where a sacred flame was kept burning, symbol of the eternal city's vital force.

Zeus's eldest child was Athene (Minerva), goddess of wisdom, who—like a divine thought—had emerged fully formed from her father's head. Zeus also fathered Apollo, god of self-discipline, health, manly beauty, prophecy, and the creative arts; and Apollo's twin sister, Artemis (Diana), virgin patron of wildlife and the hunt. Zeus's other Olympian children were Hermes (Mercury), messenger of the gods and guide of souls to the Underworld; Ares (Mars), god of war and aggression; Aphrodite (Venus), personification of feminine beauty and sexual allure; and Dionysus, god of wine and ecstasy. (When Zeus's son Dionysus ascended to Mount Olympus, Hestia was customarily demoted to keep the total number of Olympians at twelve.)

The Hymn to Zeus

Although the **Olympian religion** has long since been supplanted by Christianity, nonetheless it was once capable of inspiring some worshipers with a deep sense of spiritual feeling. In his "Hymn to Zeus," the Stoic poet Cleanthes shows a profound reverence for the king of heaven, praising him in terms not unlike those found in the biblical psalms:

> O Zeus, most glorious of immortals,
> many-named, almighty and eternal,
> lord of nature who guides all things
> in accordance with law,
> it is fitting that all mortals
> should call upon you,
> *for we are your children. . . .*
> Obedient to your direction
> as it rolls around the earth,
> all the universe submits willingly to your rule.
> Your invincible hands hold nothing less
> than the eternal thunderbolt—two-edged,
>   flaming—
> whose stroke causes all nature to shudder. . . .
> Apart from you, lord, nothing is done on
>   earth,
> in the sacred heights of heaven, or in the sea,
> except those things the wicked do in their
>   folly.
> Indeed, you are able to make wrong things
>   right
> and to create order out of chaos.
> In your sight even worthless things are worthy,
> for you have so fitted together
> all things good and evil
> that supreme Reason reigns forever over all.
>
> (Translated by Brad Nystrom; emphasis added)

Cleanthes' reference to the fatherhood of God—"we are all your children"—expressed the Stoic belief in the universal brotherhood of all humanity. Another Stoic writer, Aratus, who voiced the same idea, is quoted in Acts 17, thus becoming part of Christian Scripture (Acts 17:28).

Gods Offering Worshipers a Personal Relationship

When Augustus assumed imperial leadership of Rome in the first century BCE, the Olympian gods were still honored in the public sacrifices and rituals of the state-supported religion, but to many people, they seemed increasingly remote from ordinary human concerns. Only a few deities associated with the Olympian cult apparently offered a satisfying personal relationship with their worshipers. Two of the most

BOX 4.1 **The Three-Story Universe**

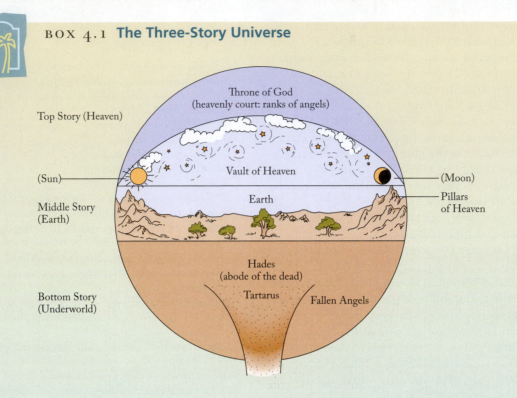

Most ancient writers, including the authors of the Hebrew Bible and the New Testament, postulated the existence of a vertically structured universe. A concept that both Israel and Greco-Roman society inherited from Mesopotamia (modern Iraq), site of the oldest Near Eastern civilizations, this three-tier universe encompassed both spiritual and material dimensions. The top story, located somewhere above the vault or dome of heaven, was the invisible home of the immortal gods; the middle level, earth's surface, supported human society; and the bottom level, a dank subterranean cavern, housed the dead. In Greek myth, this Underworld was named for the deity who ruled it, Hades (the Roman Pluto), a term the New Testament also applies to the soul's posthumous abode (Luke 16:23; Rev. 1:18; 6:8; 20:14). According to Greek mythology, an even more dismal pit existed beneath Hades' gloomy kingdom, a kind of cosmic sub-basement called Tartarus, which served as a prison for defeated gods and notorious sinners.

The biblical tradition makes this infernally dark abyss the place to which God consigned rebellious angels who had mated with mortal women to produce a race of famous heroes (Gen. 6:1–4). The noncanonical Book of 1 Enoch, which is quoted as Scripture in the New Testament Book of Jude, contains vivid elaborations on the Genesis "fallen angel" motif. Alluding to these divinely condemned angels, 2 Peter 2:4 explicitly places them in the mythical Tartarus, which the New English Bible renders as "the dark pits of hell." A Christian variation of the Greek hero myth infers that Jesus, like the celebrated figures of Dionysus, Orpheus, Heracles (Hercules), and Aeneas, descended (presumably after the Crucifixion) into these "dark pits," where he "made his proclamation to the imprisoned spirits" (1 Pet. 3:19; cf. 1 Pet. 4:6). After having experienced both earthly life and a postmortem descent to the Underworld, Jesus then ascends to the uppermost realm of the three-tier cosmos. (A sketch of the Hellenistic multilevels of heaven appears in Figure 14.4.)

FIGURE 4.4 Asclepius and suppliant. The son of Apollo and a mortal woman, Asclepius, the first physician, is patron of the healing arts. A wise, compassionate god who was concerned about the welfare of individual human beings, Asclepius was worshiped throughout the Greco-Roman world. Ministering to both mind and body, the god invited patients to sleep overnight at his shrine, where he appeared in their dreams to prescribe remedies and, sometimes, to perform miraculous cures.

accessible figures were Asclepius and Dionysus, both of whom were born mortal and underwent suffering and death before achieving immortality, experiences that allowed them to bridge the gulf between humanity and divinity.

Asclepius, the most humane and compassionate of Greek heroes, was the mortal son of Apollo and Coronis, daughter of a king in Thessaly (see Figure 4.4). Inheriting from his divine father the gift of miraculous healing, Asclepius became the archetypal physician, devoting himself to curing the sick and maimed. When his skill became so great that he was able to raise the dead, however, Zeus killed him with a thunderbolt for disrupting the natural order. After attaining posthumous divinity, Asclepius, as the supreme patron of medicine, extended his benevolence throughout the Greco-Roman world. Professional healers, known as the Sons of Asclepius, officiated at hundreds of sanctuaries, such as Epidaurus in Greece, where patients flocked to be relieved of their afflictions.

Reports of miraculous cures abounded, causing Asclepius to be hailed as the "savior" and friend of humankind.

People seeking divine help at Asclepius's many shrines commonly underwent treatment that combined faith healing with the practice of scientific medicine. To create a direct relationship with the god, patients usually began their cure by spending several nights sleeping at his temple, during which time Asclepius was said to appear in their dreams, asking questions about their health and giving advice. Attending physicians then prescribed a variety of therapies, ranging from changes in diet and exercise to surgical procedures. Grateful patients commemorated their restoration to health by dedicating inscriptions and plaster replicas of the body parts that the kindly god had healed. Although Asclepius demanded strict ethical behavior of those he helped, he was also acclaimed for welcoming the poor and disadvantaged to his sanctuaries.

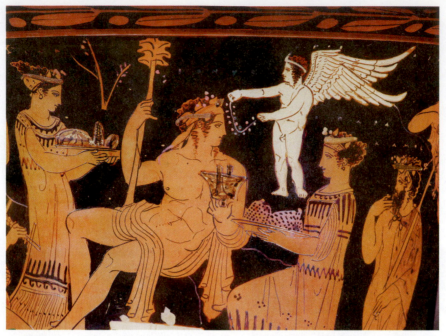

FIGURE 4.5 Dionysus pictured as a young man. A god who inspires both joy and terror, Dionysus, also called Bacchus, embodies the principles of mutability and transformation in both external nature and the human psyche. The inventor of wine, his chief gift to humanity, he offers an escape from life's burdens, bringing intoxication, spiritual ecstasy, and, in his mystery cult, the promise of immortal life. As the son of Zeus and the mortal Semele, Dionysus experienced death, a descent to the Underworld, and ascension to heaven.

Dionysus of Thebes and Jesus of Nazareth

Whereas Asclepius's compassionate nature and benevolent works anticipate aspects of Jesus' ministry, the myth of **Dionysus** foreshadows some later Christian theological interpretations of Jesus' cosmic role (see Figure 4.5). Although Jesus is a historical figure and Dionysus purely mythical, Dionysus's story contains events and themes, such as his divine parentage, violent death, descent into the Underworld, and subsequent resurrection to immortal life in heaven, where he sits near his father's throne, that Christians ultimately made part of Jesus' story (see Box 4.2).

Like Asclepius, Heracles, Perseus, and other heroes of the Greco-Roman era, Dionysus has a divine father and human mother. The only Olympian born to a mortal woman, he is also the only major deity to endure rejection, suffering, and death before ascending to heaven to join his immortal parent. The son of Zeus and Semele, a princess of Thebes, Dionysus was known as the "twice-born." The future god's two births took place in this way: Motivated by jealousy of her husband's human mistress, Hera deceived Semele, then pregnant with Dionysus, into compelling Zeus to reveal himself in his true form. The resulting blaze of lightning incinerated Semele, but Zeus snatched the unborn child from her womb and placed it in his own body, from which the infant Dionysus had a second birth. In one version of the myth, Hera released the Titans, ancient gods whom Zeus had chained in Tartarus (the dark abyss below Hades), who attacked the young Dionysus, dismembered his body, and ate it (see the section "Dionysus and Orphism"). In another tradition, the risen Dionysus descended to the netherworld

BOX 4.2 Parallels Between Dionysus of Thebes and Jesus of Nazareth

Scholars of world religion and mythology detect numerous parallels between the stories of heroes and gods from widely different cultures and periods. Tales of mortal heroes who ultimately become gods characterize the ancient traditions of Egypt, Mesopotamia, India, Greece, and Rome, as well as the native cultures of Mesoamerica and North America. In comparing the common elements found in the world's heroic myths, scholars discern a number of repeated motifs that form a distinctive pattern. Although Jesus is a historical figure and Dionysus a mythic being, their received life stories reveal components of an archetypal pattern, including the hero's birth to a divine parent; his narrow escape from attempts to kill him as an infant; his "missing" formative years; his sudden appearance as a young adult manifesting miraculous gifts; his struggle with evil forces; his return to his place of origin, commonly resulting in rejection; his betrayal, suffering, and death; and his resurrection to divine status, followed by the establishment of a new cult honoring his name.

DIONYSUS

Is son of Zeus, king of the Greek gods

Is son of Semele, a virgin princess of Thebes

Survives an attempt by Hera to kill him as an infant

Performs miracles to inspire faith in his divinity

Battles supernatural evil in the form of Titans

Returns to his birthplace, where he is denied and rejected by family and former neighbors

Invents wine; promotes his gift to humanity throughout the world

Suffers wounding and death at the hands of the Titans

Descends into the Underworld

Rises to divine immortality, joining his father, Zeus, on Olympus

Evangelizes the world, establishing his universal cult

Punishes opponents who denied his divinity

JESUS

Is Son of God (Mark 15:39)

Is son of Mary, a virgin of Nazareth (Luke 2)

Survives an attempt by King Herod to kill him as an infant (Matt. 2)

Performs healings and other miracles (Mark 1–2)

Resists Satan; exorcizes demons (Mark 1–3; Matt. 4; Luke 4)

Returns to his hometown, where he is rejected and threatened with death (Mark 6; Luke 4)

Transforms water into wine (John 2); makes wine the sacred beverage in communion (Mark 14)

Suffers wounding and crucifixion at the hands of the Romans (Mark 15; John 19)

Descends into the Underworld (1 Pet. 3:19; 4:6)

Resurrected to glory; reigns in heaven at God's right hand (Phil. 2; Acts 7:55–57)

Directs followers to evangelize the world (Matt. 28:19–20)

Will return to pass judgment on nonbelievers (Matt. 24–25; Rev. 19–20)

(See "Dionysus" in S. Hornblower and A. Spawforth, eds., *The Oxford Classical Dictionary*, 3rd ed. [New York: Oxford University Press, 1996], pp. 479–482.)

to retrieve his mother, Semele, and install her on the celestial Olympus. Having experienced an agonizing death and journey to Hades' realm, Dionysus, alone among Olympians, personally knew what it is to suffer and die.

Wine, the Beverage of Communion Between Gods and Humans As the inventor of wine making, Dionysus bestowed upon humanity a beverage that is a two-edged sword: It can liberate people from their cares, temporarily giving them

FIGURE 4.6 Dionysus riding a panther. This mosaic from Delos pictures Dionysus mounted on a wild beast, symbol of the wine god's potential violence and affinity with unpredictable, savage nature. As the patron of Greek drama, he presided over both tragedy and comedy, two seemingly contradictory aspects of human existence.

the freedom of a god, but its potentially negative aftereffects can also deliver a painful reminder of human limitations, the inability to assimilate a divine gift with impunity (see Figure 4.6). Most authors of the Hebrew Bible similarly regard wine as a mixed blessing, overindulgence in which can bring misery but which, in general, represents God's benefaction, one that produces a "merry heart" (Ps. 104:15) and "gives joy to life" (Eccles. 10:19). Sacrificed to Yahweh in Israelite worship (Lev. 23:13; Num. 28:14), wine was also the drink to be served at the future messianic banquet celebrating God's ultimate dominion over the earth (Isa. 25:6).

Long before Jesus linked wine and bread as part of the Christian liturgy (Mark 14:22–25; Luke 22:17–20), the two tokens of divine favor were associated in the Dionysian tradition. In the *Bacchae* (Bacchae were worshipers of Bacchus, another name for Dionysus), the Athenian playwright Euripides (c. 485–406 BCE) has the prophet Tiresias observe that Demeter and Dionysus, respectively, gave humanity two indispensable gifts: grain or bread to sustain life and wine to make life bearable. Tiresias urges his hearers to see in Dionysus's gift of wine a beverage that brings humans into communion with the divine:

This new God [Dionysus] whom you dismiss,
no words of mine can attain
the greatness of his coming power in Greece.
    Young man,
two are the forces most precious to mankind.
The first is Demeter, the Goddess.
She is the Earth—or any name you wish to
    call her—
and she sustains humanity with solid food.
Next comes the son of the virgin, Dionysus,
bringing the counterpart to bread, wine
and the blessings of life's flowing juices.
His blood, the blood of the grape,
lightens the burden of our mortal misery.

When, after their daily toils, men drink
their fill,
sleep comes to them, bringing release from
all their troubles.
There is no other cure for sorrow. Though
himself a God,
it is his blood we pour out
to offer thanks to the Gods. And through him,
we are blessed.

(Translated by Michael Cacoyannis)

Consumed in thanksgiving, and symbolic of the god's shed blood, wine bestows a blessing upon humanity.

Emblematic of divine generosity, bread and wine were tangible evidence of the gods' care for humankind. In this context, the Gospel tradition frames Jesus' public ministry with momentous feasts involving bread and/or wine. In John's Gospel, Jesus' first miraculous act is to change water into vintage wine at a Jewish wedding, a "sign" of his divinity that seems to mimic the wine-making magic of some Dionysian priests. In the Gospels of Mark, Matthew, and Luke (but, strangely, not John), Jesus hosts a final Passover dinner with his friends at which he announces that the bread he is disbursing is his "body" and the wine he is sharing is his "blood" (Mark 14). The next day, Roman soldiers execute him; his wounding and crucifixion represent a form of *sparagmos,* the ritual tearing asunder of a male sacrificial victim, a fate reminiscent of Dionysus's at the hands of the Titans.

In interpreting the theological meaning of Jesus' life to a Greco-Roman audience, New Testament authors did not present their hero as a new version of Dionysus, but nonetheless they told his story in ways that strikingly parallel the Dionysian tradition. The Gospel accounts of Jesus' return to Nazareth, the Galilean town where he grew up, strongly resemble the myth of Dionysus's return to Thebes, his birthplace. In both cases, family and former neighbors fail to recognize the hero's divinity—that he is God's son—and reject him, even threatening him with death (Mark 6:1–6; Luke 4:16–30). In Euripides' *Bacchae,* the unvalued god exacts a fearful revenge on those who are blind to his divine

nature, whereas in the Gospel tradition, Jesus emphasizes forgiveness of those who reject and kill him (Luke 23:34). The author of Revelation, however, portrays the glorified Christ as behaving with Dionysian violence when he returns to punish nonbelievers (Rev. 19–20).

The Mystery Religions

In addition to the public state rituals honoring the principal Olympians, Greco-Roman society fostered a number of "underground religions" that exerted a wide influence. Known as the **mysteries** (Greek, *mysteria*) because their adherents took oaths never to reveal their secrets, these cults initiated members into the sacred rites of gods who were thought to welcome human devotees, becoming their spiritual guardians and protectors. Because Greco-Roman deities did not demand exclusive devotion, people commonly were initiated into more than one mystery religion, simultaneously cultivating a mystic bond with such diverse gods as Dionysus, Demeter, Persephone, Isis, Osiris, or Mithras. Although scholars question the extent to which these esoteric cults anticipated Christian rites, in some cases participants shared a communal meal in which their god was invisibly present, perhaps allowing them to absorb the divine body into themselves and thus partake of the deity's immortality.

Dionysus and Orphism

Although Dionysus was the most widely celebrated Greco-Roman example of the dying and rising god, other cults centered around such figures as **Orpheus,** a mortal poet and musician whose music delighted both gods and humans, exerting a power to calm even savage beasts. When Orpheus bravely descended into Hades' realm to rescue his deceased wife, Eurydice, he reputedly learned the mysteries of the next world. The poetry later written in Orpheus's name supposedly contained instructions for purifying the soul to attain a happy afterlife and magic formulae that deceased souls could recite to guarantee their safe journey through netherworld darkness. Orphism, based on a body of occult literature ascribed to Orpheus, may not have been a unified cult, but its arcane teachings significantly influenced many Greco-Roman ideas about the soul and its fate after death.

Orphic teachers promoted a distinctive version of Dionysus's story that emphasized both the wine god's triumph over death and his intimate connection with human nature. According to Orphic tradition, Dionysus was originally the son of Zeus and Persephone, a daughter of Demeter (goddess of the soil's fertility) and queen of the Underworld. Because his son combined heavenly power with earth's secret wisdom, Zeus planned to enthrone Dionysus as king of the universe. When the Titans attacked and killed Dionysus, Athene managed to save the young god's heart, carrying it to her father, Zeus. After Zeus swallowed the heart, integrating it into himself, he fathered his son anew by Semele, who gave the child a second birth as Dionysus Zagreus.

Zeus punished the Titans by obliterating them with his thunderbolts. Orphic religion taught that the human race sprang from the Titans' remains, which accounts for humanity's dual nature: Humans are rebels against the gods, but they also contain elements of the divine, the flesh of Zeus's son, which the Titans had consumed. Although flawed by destructive impulses (the Titan heritage), humanity is partly redeemed by an inherent spark of divinity (Zeus's son Dionysus).

Because they house a "god within," humans can be awakened to their divine potential. Through ritual purification and ethical behavior, initiates could, in the next world, eventually share their god's eternal life. The material body (Greek, *soma*), meanwhile, was the soul's prison (*sema*); death was merely the freeing of the soul to attain its ultimate home, the celestial realm above.

In Orphic doctrine, the Underworld became a place of regeneration and eventual rebirth, commonly through the soul's reincarnation in new bodies until a state of spiritual purity and salvation was reached.

Because Orphism foreshadowed some of the themes and symbols of Christianity, it is not surprising that early Christian artists commonly used the figure of Orpheus—or even Dionysus—to depict Christ.

Mithras and Mithraism

Perhaps the most rigorously organized and politically effective mystery cult in the Roman Empire was that of **Mithras,** which became Rome's official state religion in the third century CE. Although Mithras, whose name means "covenant," was originally a Persian god embodying the divine power of light, his mysteries did not appear in the Greco-Roman world until the first century CE. Scholars believe that, although Mithraism used names taken from ancient Persian mythology, it developed as a new cult in the West under the influence of Hellenistic astrology. Pictorial carvings decorating the walls of the caves in which Mithraic rituals were performed show that Mithras was a solar deity who presided over the stars, planets, and other astronomical features of the celestial zodiac. He was born from a rock on December 25, then calculated as the winter solstice, the crucial turning point of the solar year when the days begin to lengthen. After his birthplace was visited by shepherds, Mithras went forth to slay a bull (the zodiacal sign of Taurus), from whose blood and semen new life emerges (see Figure 4.7).

His sacred myth identifies Mithras with the invisible forces ruling the universe, his sacrifice of the cosmic bull a manifestation of his omnipotence. Although we do not know how Mithras's story relates to the rites practiced in the underground chambers where men were initiated into his mysteries, the initiation ceremony represented a spiritual rebirth, making the worshiper a soldier of his god, committed to the principles of light and life that Mithras personified. Enormously popular among ordinary soldiers and merchants, Mithraism established sanctuaries in virtually

FIGURE 4.7 Mithras slaying sacred bull. The principal rival to Christianity during the first three centuries CE, the cult of Mithras was extremely popular with soldiers, merchants, and traders throughout the Roman Empire. Men (women were excluded) initiated into the god's mysteries received a cleansing baptism with the blood of a sacrificial animal and participated in a ritual meal. As with the religions of Isis and Dionysus, Mithraism offered adherents glimpses of the spirit realm and assurances of the soul's future life.

every part of the Roman world, from Britain and Germany to Mesopotamia and Egypt.

Christianity's leading competitor during the first three centuries CE, Mithraism featured some rituals paralleling those of the church, including baptism, communal meals, and oaths of celibacy. As Christians were figuratively washed in the "blood of the Lamb" (Rev. 7:14), Mithraic initiates were sprinkled and purified with the blood flowing from a sacrificed bull. Despite the fact that it apparently fulfilled its members' emotional and spiritual needs, Mithraism had a fatal flaw: Women could not be admitted to the god's service. When the Christian church, which baptized women as well as men, overcame its chief rival, however, it retained one of Mithraism's most potent symbols, the natal day of its lord. Because the winter solstice appropriately signifies the birth of God's Son, "the light of the world" (as well as the rebirth of the Mithraic sun), the church eventually chose Mithras's birthday—December 25—to celebrate as that of Jesus.

The Mother Goddesses

Other mystery religions emphasize the importance of a female figure, a mother goddess who can offer help in this life and intervene for one in the next world. Demeter, who gave the world grain—the bread of life—and her daughter Persephone were worshiped at Eleusis and elsewhere in the eastern Mediterranean. Originally concerned with agricultural fertility and the cycle of the seasons, the Eleusinian Mysteries developed into a mystical celebration of death and rebirth.

Isis Even more popular in Roman times was **Isis,** an Egyptian mother goddess whom artists typically depicted as a madonna holding her infant son Horus (see Figure 4.8). Representing motherly compassion allied with divine power, Isis was the center of a mystery cult that promised initiates personal help in resolving life's problems, as well as the assurance of a happy existence after death. As an embodiment of

FIGURE 4.8 Statuette of Isis holding the infant Horus (c. 600 BCE). Originally an Egyptian goddess, in New Testament times Isis was worshiped throughout the Roman Empire as the embodiment of wisdom who offered worldly success and divine protection to persons initiated into her cult. Commonly pictured as a tender mother nursing her son, Isis became a prototype of the Christian Madonna and child.

creative intelligence and cosmic wisdom, Isis was known as the goddess of "a thousand names," a deity whom the whole world honored in one form or another. Offering the individual worshiper far more comfort than the official state religions of Greece or Rome, the Isis cult found dedicated adherents throughout the Roman Empire (see Box 10.4).

In his novel *The Golden Ass,* the Roman author Apuleius (second century CE) reveals more about the mystical effects of initiation into a mystery cult than any other ancient writer, describing his visionary experience in which the goddess Isis became his personal savior. Like countless others before and after him, Apuleius seems to have undergone a religious awakening that transcended normal reality and bound him to a beneficent and caring deity who redeemed him from his animal nature, unveiled heavenly secrets, and imparted new meaning to his life.

The myth of Isis involved her male consort **Osiris,** originally a mortal ruler of ancient Egypt. Like Dionysus, Osiris suffered death by being torn to pieces but was restored to life as god of the Underworld. Osiris owed his postmortem existence to his sister-wife, Isis, who had searched throughout the world to find and reassemble the pieces of his dismembered corpse. By Greco-Roman times, the cults of Isis and Osiris, king and judge of the dead, had developed mystical rituals that promised worshipers a posthumous union with the divine.

Summary

Although remaining firmly anchored in the Jewish biblical tradition, during its crucial formative years Christianity grew and developed in a society dominated by Hellenistic ideas and values. The multiplicity of Hellenistic philosophies and religions, both public and secret, with which early Christianity competed suggests that many people in the Greco-Roman world not only felt a need to find spiritual direction and purpose in their lives but also took action to fulfill their spiritual aspirations by being initiated into various mystery religions. Offering practical help in this world and immortality in the next, many Hellenistic mystery cults focused on the promise inherent in myths dramatizing the death of a young male figure, such as Dionysus or Osiris, who is subsequently reborn to eternal life in the spirit realm. Others emphasized the wisdom and compassion of a mother goddess, such as Isis. Many of these cults involved a ritual or sacred meal in which worshipers communed with a patron deity who guided them through the mysteries of spiritual regeneration.

During the first century after Jesus' death, his followers interpreted his cosmic role—his posthumous descent into the Underworld, his ascent to heaven, and his invisible reign as universal king—in terms that echoed some ancient traditions about Greco-Roman gods and heroes. In addition to well-known myths about mortal heroes whose redemptive labors earned them postmortem divinity, the Hellenistic and Roman practice of awarding divine honors to great rulers, such as Alexander, Julius Caesar, and Augustus, provided contemporary precedents for the transformation of favored humans into gods (see Chapter 5 for a discussion of the emperor cult). Although most scholars do not think that New Testament writers directly borrowed theological concepts from older cults, their portrayal of Jesus' supernatural status nonetheless paralleled previously existing narratives and rituals. Operating in a thought world shaped by Greek philosophy and religion, early Christian authors, perhaps inevitably, forged their theology of Jesus in images and symbols that Greek readers would readily comprehend.

Questions for Review

1. Define the term *philosophy,* and summarize Plato's teaching about the immortality of the soul and eternal spirit world.
2. How did the Stoics and Epicureans differ in their views of reality? How did ideas expressed in Cleanthes' *Hymn to Zeus* become part of the New Testament?
3. Identify the major Olympian gods and their principal attributes. In what ways does the Greek myth of Dionysus anticipate elements in Jesus' story? Name some parallels between the two "sons of God" who suffered, died, and attained posthumous immortality.
4. What were the "mystery religions"? What benefits did initiation into the cults of Dionysus, Demeter, Mithras, Isis, and Osiris confer on the worshiper? Enumerate some of the resemblances between some mystery cults, such as that of Mithras, and early Christianity.

Questions for Discussion and Reflection

1. Religion was an important part of life in the Greco-Roman world. How can we explain the parallels between some pre-Christian cults, such as those of Asclepius, Dionysus, and Mithras, and early Christianity? Why do you suppose the idea of a hero with a divine father and mortal mother, one who suffered pain, died, and descended into the Underworld, had such appeal to the Hellenistic imagination? Why did humans tend to regard their heroes and saviors as possessing the qualities of both god and man?

2. As the inheritor of two distinct and contrasting traditions—Jewish and Greek—early Christianity struggled to assimilate two ostensibly incompatible approaches to knowledge—divine revelation and human reason—creating a tension that persists to this day. According to the Jewish biblical view, true wisdom is available only through supernatural revelation of God's will, as expressed in Scripture. In contrast, the Greek emphasis on rational inquiry—the basis of contemporary science—assumes that human intellect, properly disciplined, can achieve a valid understanding of the cosmos. Are these two worldviews really incompatible? How would you reconcile the authority of biblical tradition with the values and insights of philosophy and science?

Terms and Concepts to Remember

Alexander the Great	mysteries
Asclepius	Olympian religion
Cynicism	Orpheus
Dionysus	Osiris
Epicurus	philosophy
Hades	Plato
Hellenism	polytheism
Hellenistic	Socrates
Isis	Stoicism and
Logos	Epicureanism
Mithras	Zeus/Jupiter
monotheism	

Recommended Reading

Boring, M. Eugene; Berger, Klaus; and Colpe, Carsten. *Hellenistic Commentary to the New Testament.* Nashville, Tenn.: Abingdon Press, 1995. An invaluable resource that provides extensive parallels between ideas in the New Testament and concepts appearing in Hellenistic literature.

Ferguson, Everett. *Backgrounds of Early Christianity*, 3rd ed. Grand Rapids, Mich.: Eerdmans, 2003. Provides a comprehensive survey of the Greco-Roman and Jewish environments in which early Christianity developed.

Fox, R. L. *Pagans and Christians*. New York: Knopf, 1987. A comprehensive and insightful investigation of Greco-Roman religious life from the second to the fourth century CE.

Hornblower, Simon, and Spawforth, Antony, eds. *The Oxford Companion to Classical Civilization*. New York: Oxford University Press, 1998. Includes brief essays on leading authors, historical leaders, and periods of Greco-Roman history.

Hubbard, Moyer V. *Christianity in the Greco-Roman World: A Narrative Introduction*. Peabody, Mass.: Hendrickson, 2010. Enumerates many specific parallels between Greco-Roman ideas and practices and New Testament literature.

Jeffers, James S. *The Greco-Roman World of the New Testament Era: Exploring the Background of Early Christianity*. Downers Grove, Ill.: InterVarsity Press, 1999. Attempts to re-create in detail the environment in which the new faith spread through Hellenistic society and the Roman state.

Johnson, Luke T. *Among the Gentiles: Greco-Roman Religion and Christianity*. (The Anchor Yale Bible Reference Library). New Haven: Yale University Press, 2010. Illustrates how Greco-Roman religious traditions and practices helped shape early Christianity.

Koester, Helmut. *Introduction to the New Testament*, Vol. 1, *History, Culture, and Religion of the Hellenistic Age*, 2nd ed. Philadelphia: Fortress Press, 1995. An informative and scholarly study.

Lieu, Judith M. *Neither Jew nor Greek? Constructing Early Christianity*. London: T and T Clark, 2003. Scholarly essays exploring the complexity of Christian origins.

Martin, Luther H. *Hellenistic Religions: An Introduction*. New York: Oxford University Press, 1987. A solid introduction to the principal Greco-Roman religious movements and cults.

Turcan, Robert. *The Cults of the Roman Empire*. Translated by A. Nevill. Cambridge, Mass.: Blackwell, 1996. Provides a lucid survey of the major cults and mystery religions that rivaled early Christianity.

CHAPTER 5

The World of Roman Political Power

The woman [riding the symbolic beast] you saw is the great city that
holds sway over the kings of the earth. Revelation 17:18

Key Topics/Themes After the death of Alexander of Macedonia (323 BCE), his empire, which encompassed most of the known world from Greece eastward to western India, was eventually divided among his successors, including the Ptolemaic dynasty of Egypt and the Seleucid rulers of Syria. Following the Seleucid occupation of Palestine, Antiochus IV introduced a policy of enforced Hellenization, compelling his Jewish subjects to abandon their traditions and adopt Greek customs. Although many Jews readily complied, the Hasidim (Torah loyalists) resisted. Led by the Maccabees, a family of guerrilla fighters, the Jews drove out Antiochus's forces and established an independent Jewish state ruled by the Hasmonean dynasty (142–63 BCE). Under control of the Roman Empire after 63 BCE, the covenant people were successively ruled by Roman-appointed Herodian kings and a series of Roman governors, such as Pontius Pilate. Widespread political discontent flared into a massive rebellion against Rome (66–73 CE), which resulted in the destruction of Jerusalem and the Jewish state.

According to the Gospels of Matthew and Luke, before Jesus began his public ministry, he was first tempted to imitate Greek and Roman leaders who had succeeded in conquering the world. The Gospel authors present the temptation to become another Alexander the Great or **Caesar** Augustus as if it originated with Evil incarnate—the **devil** (Greek, *diabolos*). Offered "all the kingdoms of the world and their splendor," Jesus is pictured as vigorously rejecting a "devilish" goal that would inevitably involve military violence (Matt. 4:1–9; Luke 4:3–13).

To appreciate the Gospel writers' view that a single individual could achieve global rulership, one must realize that recent Greco-Roman history had provided people in Jesus' era with outstanding examples of men who had gained control of enormous empires (see Figure 4.1; also see Figures 5.2, 5.4, and 5.5). The first-century-CE social and political environment was largely shaped by the exploits of several extraordinary conquerors, beginning with Alexander the Great (see Figure 5.1) and ending with Augustus, the emperor ruling when Jesus was born (Matt. 1:5; Luke 2:1). Shortly before Jesus' birth, a devastating series of power struggles in the Mediterranean world had been resolved in favor of Augustus's one-man rule of the vast **Roman Empire,** which included the Judean homeland.

FIGURE 5.1 Bust of Alexander the Great. Although he managed to conquer most of the known world before his death at age thirty-two, Alexander's dream of unifying East and West under a single government was never achieved.

The possibility that a new charismatic leader, such as Jesus, could reverse the status quo and seize power for himself was, in some minds at least, still conceivable (Luke 24:21; John 6:15; Acts 1:6–8). Many of Jesus' compatriots, in fact, eagerly anticipated a God-sent ruler who would forcibly evict occupying Roman forces from Palestine and restore the Israelite kingdom of David (see Chapter 3).

Alexander and His Successors

In a single decade, as his armies swept eastward from Macedonia to India, Alexander succeeded in subduing virtually all the known world, setting an example of "global" domination that inspired later military leaders—particularly those of Rome—to emulate his achievement (see below).

After Alexander's death, his empire slowly disintegrated, but large sections remained under the control of his successors, known collectively as the Diadochi. By about 300 BCE, three distinct powers had emerged to dominate the eastern Mediterranean basin. One of Alexander's ablest generals, **Ptolemy I,** founded a dynasty that ruled Egypt for nearly three centuries. Another of Alexander's successors was **Seleucus,** who established the **Seleucid dynasty,** which controlled Syria, then a large territory that stretched from western Asia Minor (now Turkey) to Mesopotamia (modern Iraq). Eventually, the son of a third successor, Antigonus, governed Macedonia and parts of Greece. Sporadic efforts to reunite Alexander's empire failed, but the descendants of his commanders continued to rule Greece and the Near East until their various kingdoms were gradually incorporated into the Roman Empire.

Antiochus's Persecution and the Maccabean Revolt

Palestine and the Hellenistic Kingdoms

From the biblical perspective, the two most important nations derived from Alexander's empire are Ptolemaic Egypt and Seleucid Syria (see Figure 5.2). When Ptolemy took control of Egypt, he also acquired Palestine, the Jewish homeland. We know little about events during this period (c. 300–200 BCE), but it appears that under the **Ptolemaic dynasty** the Jews inhabiting **Judea**—the territory surrounding Jerusalem—enjoyed relative peace and prosperity. Shortly after 200 BCE, however, the Ptolemaic forces were driven out of Palestine, and the Seleucid kings of Syria assumed control. Conflict between the Syrian monarchs and the Jews reached a climax during the reign of Antiochus IV (175–163 BCE).

Antiochus, who called himself Epiphanes (God Manifest), attempted to unify the many diverse religious and ethnic groups in his empire by

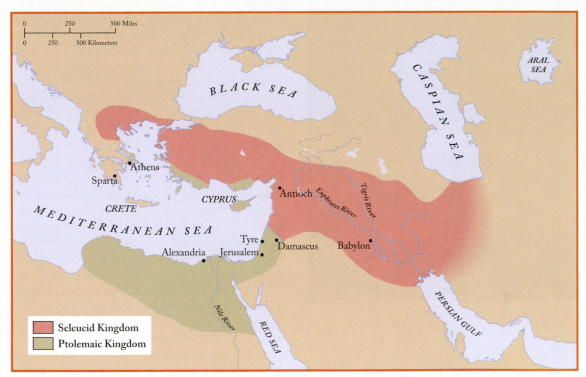

FIGURE 5.2 The Seleucid and Ptolemaic kingdoms. After Alexander's death in 323 BCE, his vast empire was divided among his military successors. General Ptolemy assumed control of Egypt, while another general, Seleucus, ruled Syria and Mesopotamia. The Ptolemaic and Seleucid dynasties repeatedly fought each other for control of Palestine.

actively promoting Hellenization, forcing on his subjects the adoption of Greek culture, customs, and religion (see Figure 5.3). Attracted by Greek ideas and social institutions, many Jews voluntarily abandoned their ancestral traditions to embrace the Greek way of life. Eager to become members of the gymnasium, the equivalent of a municipal athletic club, many Jewish youths underwent surgery to disguise the marks of circumcision (the ritual removal of the male's foreskin prescribed by Mosaic Law) so that they could not be identified as Jews when exercising nude. Mass adoption of Hellenistic practices, particularly among the Jewish upper classes, threatened to destroy Jewish ethnic distinctiveness.

Whereas many Jews willingly joined Hellenistic society, others firmly resisted the process. Aware that some Jews publicly opposed his policy of cultural and political assimilation, Antiochus determined to outlaw the ancient

rituals and practices that made the Jews so different from other peoples in his empire. Departing from the usual Greek attitude of tolerance toward non-Greek religions, Antiochus attempted to eradicate the ancient Jewish faith. He forbade reading or teaching the Mosaic Law, ordered copies of the Hebrew Bible burned, executed women who had their sons circumcised, and ordered the infants' bodies tied around their mothers' necks. Keeping the Sabbath was also declared a crime punishable by death.

Besides making traditional Jewish religious observances a capital offense, Antiochus also ordered an attack on the Jerusalem Temple, where Yahweh's "glory" dwelt invisibly. After stripping the Temple of its treasures to pay for his wars against Egypt, Antiochus erected an altar to the Olympian Zeus in the sanctuary courtyard and polluted Yahweh's altar by sacrificing pigs there. (This desecration is the "abomination" described

FIGURE 5.3 Greek coin showing the profile of Antiochus IV, Epiphanes (ruled 175–163 BCE). Antiochus was the Seleucid ruler of Hellenistic Syria who profaned the Jerusalem Temple by erecting an altar to Olympian Zeus there, an "abomination" that resounds through the books of Daniel and 1 Maccabees and resurfaces as a sign of End time in the Gospels of Mark and Matthew (Mark 13:14; Matt. 24:15–16).

in the Book of Daniel and echoed in the Gospel predictions of the Roman destruction of the Temple [Dan. 9:27; 12:11; Mark 13:14; Matt. 24:15–16].) Devout Jews who refused to eat swine's flesh, an act prohibited by Mosaic Law, or who otherwise refused to compromise their ancestral religion were slaughtered by royal command. These "pious ones" who preferred death to giving up cherished traditions became known as the **Hasidim,** religious loyalists from whom the Pharisees and members of other Jewish denominations of Jesus' day were descended.

Torah Loyalism, Martyrdom, and the Reward of Future Life

The persecutions of Antiochus mark the first time in biblical history that Jews died not for defending their country militarily against foreign invaders but merely for practicing their faith. The Book of 2 Maccabees paints horrific pictures of faithful Jews paying for their integrity by

being tortured, mutilated, and executed. When Eleazar, a ninety-year-old Torah instructor, spits out the pig's flesh that Antiochus's soldiers have forced on him, he is bludgeoned to death. Even worse are the agonies endured by seven young brothers who similarly refuse to pass the king's test of religious conformity by eating what the Torah forbids. One by one, before their mother's eyes, they are scalped, their heads flayed, their tongues cut out, their hands and feet lopped off, and then, still conscious, thrust into huge pans and slowly fried alive (2 Macc. 7).

As martyrs who willingly died in a religious cause, the anonymous seven brothers not only served as models for other Jews forced to choose between life and Torah loyalty but also voiced a belief that their unspeakable sufferings would be compensated for in a future life. Expressing a conviction that God will resurrect the faithful dead—a view that enters the biblical record only with the Hellenistic Book of Daniel (Dan. 12:1–3)—the second brother places his martyrdom in the light of eternity: "The King of the world will raise us up, since it is for his laws that we die, to live again for ever" (2 Macc. 7:9). Appearing initially in the crisis ignited by enforced Hellenization, the concept that enduring a painful but holy death would lead to immortality ultimately exerted a pervasive influence on the early Christian community.

The Maccabean Revolt

To some Jewish thinkers, Antiochus's savage attacks on the Hasidim seemed to represent the "great tribulation" heralding the end of the world. The apocalyptic parts of Daniel (chs. 7–12), with their eschatological visions of God's overthrow of Antiochus's tyranny, are believed to have been written at this time.

For the Hasidim, the situation was desperate, but help came from an unexpected quarter. When Syrian commissioners tried to compel an aged village priest named **Mattathias** to sacrifice to the state-imposed cult, the old man killed first a fellow Jew who had sacrificed and then the king's representative. The author of 1 Maccabees places this defiant speech on Mattathias's lips:

Although all the nations within the king's dominions obey him and forsake their ancestral worship, . . . yet I and my sons and brothers will follow the covenant of our fathers, . . . nor will we deviate one step from our forms of worship.

(1 Macc. 2:19–22)

Fleeing with his five sons to the hills, Mattathias organized a band of guerrilla fighters that proved surprisingly effective against the Syrian army. After Mattathias's death, his most capable son, **Judas Maccabeus** ([God's] Hammer), carried on the revolt. In December 164 BCE, Judas's followers recaptured and purified the Jerusalem Temple, an event later commemorated annually as the **Feast of Dedication** (1 Macc. 4) and known today as **Hanukkah.**

Following Judas's death, leadership of the Jewish war for religious freedom passed to various Maccabean brothers, who eventually succeeded in forcing the Syrians to grant Israel national independence (142 BCE). Despite protests from other Jewish groups, including many of the Hasidim, the **Maccabees** made themselves kings, establishing the **Hasmonean** dynasty (named after a Maccabean ancestor, Hasmoneas).

The Domination of Rome

The Maccabean political and social legacy was less impressive than their military accomplishments. The Hasmonean period (142–40 BCE) was largely one of intrigue, ambition, and treachery—a series of tragically missed opportunities for achieving Jewish unity and peace. Eventually, rivalry among the Hasmonean rulers led to a decision fatal to Jewish national autonomy: an invitation to involve Rome militarily in Jewish affairs. In 63 BCE, a claimant to the Hasmonean throne, John Hyrcanus II, asked Rome for help in ousting his younger brother, Aristobulus II, who had made himself both High Priest and king. In response, Rome dispatched Pompey, whose troops overthrew Aristobulus and installed John Hyrcanus as High Priest and "ethnarch" (63–40 BCE) over a Jewish state much reduced in size and prestige. The change in title from "king" to "ethnarch" (provincial governor) is significant, for after 63 BCE, Jewish rulers were mere puppets of Rome, and the Holy Land merely another province in the empire.

The Herod Family

No family was more instrumental in the stormy transition from Hasmonean to Roman domination of Judea than the Herods. **Antipater** (c. 100–43 BCE), the father of **Herod the Great,** the monarch ruling Palestine for the Romans when Jesus was born (Matt. 2:1; Luke 1:5), was a nobleman of **Idumea,** the Greco-Roman name of ancient Edom, a traditional enemy of the Jews. While supporting the claims of John Hyrcanus II as Jewish ethnarch, Antipater also managed to forge strong links with Rome, a talent for winning—and keeping—Roman favor that characterized most members of the royal dynasty founded by his son Herod (73–4 BCE).

Although both Antipater and Herod were apparently Torah-observant (the people of Idumea were forcibly converted to Judaism when John Hyrcanus I conquered the region in 129 BCE), many Jewish leaders did not trust them. Antipater had made Herod governor of Galilee in 47 BCE, but when the Roman Senate appointed Herod king of Judea seven years later, the new king had to overcome armed resistance to gain his throne. By 37 BCE, Herod had captured Jerusalem and begun a long reign marked by a strange combination of administrative skill, cruelty, and bloodshed. Politically, Herod was remarkably successful. Enjoying Roman support, he extended the boundaries of his kingdom almost to the limits of David's biblical empire. Under Herod, the Jewish state expanded to include the districts of Samaria and Galilee (where Jesus grew up) and territories east of the Jordan River (see Figure 5.4).

Herod's building program matched his political ambitions. He constructed monumental fortresses, the best known of which is **Masada** on the western shore of the Dead Sea (see Figure 3.5). He also founded the port city **Caesarea Maritima,** which later became the Roman administrative capital. Herod's most famous project, however, was rebuilding the Temple in Jerusalem, transforming it into one of the most magnificent sanctuaries in the ancient world (see Figure 3.2). This was the

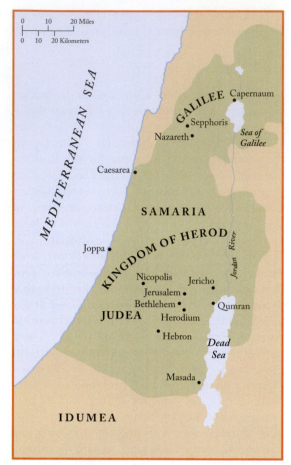

FIGURE 5.4 Herod's kingdom. Appointed ruler by the Romans, Herod the Great (ruled 40–4 BCE) expanded the boundaries of the Jewish state to include most of the land once held by King David (1000 BCE). At his death, Herod's kingdom was divided among his three sons.

means of attracting tourists to his magnificently rebuilt capital. (See Figure 7.7 for a surviving inscription warning Gentiles not to trespass into precincts reserved for Jews only, an offense punishable by death.) Begun in 20 BCE, the Temple embellishments were not completed until about 62 CE, only eight years before the Romans destroyed them.

Despite his grandiose achievements, Herod's treachery and violence made him hated by most of his Jewish subjects. He murdered his Hasmonean wife Mariamne and their two sons, Alexander and Aristobulus, as well as other family members. His fear that some conspiracy would rob him of his throne and his ruthless elimination of any potential rival provide the background for the Gospel story that Herod massacred Bethlehem's children (Matt. 2:16–17).

Herod's Successors

When Herod died in 4 BCE (according to modern calendars, Jesus was probably born a few years BCE), his kingdom was divided among his three surviving sons. **Philip** (4 BCE–34 CE) became tetrarch of the areas north and east of the Sea of Galilee. He seems to have been a competent ruler, and we hear little of him. His brother **Herod Antipas** (4 BCE–39 CE) was given the territories of Galilee and Perea, a region east of the Jordan River. This is the Herod who beheaded John the Baptist (Mark 6:14–29; Matt. 14:1–12) and whom Jesus characterized as "that fox" (Luke 13:31–32). As ruler of Galilee, Jesus' home district, Herod reportedly examined Jesus at Pilate's request (Luke 23:6–12). A third brother, **Herod Archelaus,** inherited the southwestern portion of Herod the Great's realm (Judea, Samaria, and Idumea), but he proved a vicious and incompetent ruler. The Romans removed him in 6 CE and in his place appointed a series of prefects (later **procurators**) to govern the region directly for Rome. The most celebrated of these local governors was the prefect **Pontius Pilate** (26–36 CE), the man who sentenced Jesus to death.

Two other members of the Herodian dynasty, both named Herod Agrippa, play prominent roles in the New Testament Book of Acts. A grandson of Herod the Great, **Herod Agrippa I** was raised in

Temple where Jesus and the disciples worshiped (Mark 11:27–13:2; Luke 2:22–38, 41–50; 19:47–48; 20:1–21:7; Acts 2:46; 3:1–10; 21:18–30).

Most of Herod's renovations involved a major expansion of the platform on which the Temple stood, including a series of courtyards and columned and roofed walkways that surrounded the building. Close to the Sanctuary was "Court of Israel," for Jewish males who had been ritually purified in order to approach the holy place, and a large courtyard for Jewish women directly in front of the shrine (see Figure 3.1). Herod's main innovation in reconstructing the Temple area was introducing a special court for Gentile visitors, a

Rome, where he won the friendship and financial support of two future emperors, Caligula and Claudius. When Claudius came to power, he appointed Herod Agrippa I (ruled 41–44 CE) king of Judea and Samaria, restoring the Palestinian territories over which his grandfather had reigned. Apparently a devoted adherent of the Mosaic Law and a strong supporter of the Pharisees, Herod persecuted some apostolic leaders of the Jerusalem church, imprisoning Peter and beheading James, the son of Zebedee and brother of John. According to Acts 12, Herod Agrippa died suddenly—"eaten up with worms"—after a visiting delegation had honored him as a god.

His son, **Herod Agrippa II,** the last of the Herodian line to hold a kingdom, later was made ruler of Philip's old territory, as well as parts of Galilee and Perea. Notorious for a lifelong incestuous affair with his sister Bernice, who joined him in interrogating Paul (then a prisoner at Caesarea Maritima), Herod Agrippa II reportedly exclaimed that Paul almost persuaded him to become a Christian (Acts 25:13–26:32). Loyal to Rome during the Jewish Revolt, which began in 66 CE, after the rebellion was suppressed, he regained his throne with Roman help. Later moving to Rome, he died there in 93 CE.

The Roman Emperors

Although Pilate and representatives of the Herod family are the most prominent political figures in the Gospel accounts, the real center of political power in Jesus' world lay in the person of the Roman emperor. At Jesus' birth, the emperor **Augustus** (originally named Gaius Octavius, ruled 27 BCE–14 CE) reigned over an empire even larger and more diverse than Alexander's (see Figure 5.5). Rome controlled

FIGURE 5.5 The Roman Empire at the death of Augustus in 14 CE. With the city of Rome as its administrative capital, the empire governed most of the known world. Its subjects included people of virtually every race, language group, and ethnic background.

not only Asia Minor and Egypt, but also most of Europe and North Africa. Military conquests had reduced the Mediterranean Sea to the status of a large Roman lake. Located at the eastern margin of the empire, the Jewish homeland was only an insignificant, although politically troublesome, part of an international colossus. As a further insult to Jewish sensibilities, the Romans adopted the Greek name for this area, calling it **Palestine** after the Philistines, a seafaring people who had once been Israel's chief enemy (Judg.; 1 Sam.).

The Beginning of Imperial Rule

Rule of the empire by a single man who could wield almost unlimited power had been instituted only a short time before Jesus' birth. The grandnephew of Julius Caesar, Gaius Octavius (the future Augustus), joined with Mark Antony to defeat Brutus and Cassius, Caesar's assassins, at the Battle of Philippi (42 BCE). With Lepidus, another of Caesar's supporters, Octavius and Mark Antony formed the Second Triumvirate (the first had been an unofficial alliance between Julius Caesar, Pompey, and Crassus) and shared the governing of Rome. The real power was divided between Mark Antony, who took control of the eastern empire, and Octavius, who administered Italy and the western dominions. Competition between the two men culminated in the battle of Actium (31 BCE), a naval engagement in which Octavius's forces defeated those of Antony and his paramour, Cleopatra VII, a descendant of Alexander's general Ptolemy, who then ruled Egypt. Antony's death and Cleopatra's suicide (30 BCE) allowed Egypt to be incorporated into the empire and left Octavius the sole ruler of the Roman state.

After decades of civil war, Rome was finally at peace. A grateful Senate voted Octavius the title of "princeps" (27 BCE), recognizing him as the undisputed head of state. The ascension of Octavius (henceforth called Augustus) marked the end of the ancient Roman republic and

cost the citizens of Rome many of their traditional political rights. The Romans, however, seemed willing to exchange civil freedom for the restoration of public order, political stability, and economic prosperity that Augustus's reign brought (see Figure 5.6).

Augustus was succeeded by his stepson **Tiberius** (ruled 14–37 CE), the emperor reigning during Jesus' ministry (Luke 3:1). It was Tiberius's governmental appointee Pontius Pilate who found Jesus guilty of treason against Rome (Matt. 27:11–44; Mark 15:2–32; Luke 22:66–23:38; John 18:28–19:22). (Box 5.1 chronicles some key events that helped shape Jesus' world.)

FIGURE 5.6 Head of Augustus (Gaius Octavius), first emperor of Rome (ruled 27 BCE–14 CE). Defeating all rivals for control of the Roman Empire, Augustus ended centuries of civil war and introduced a new era of peace and political stability.

BOX 5.1 Some Representative Events That Shaped the World of Jesus and the Early Church

ALEXANDER AND HIS SUCCESSORS

c. 334–323 BCE — Alexander's conquests create a new international culture, the Hellenistic, bringing Greek language, literature, ideas, and customs to the entire Near Eastern world, including Palestine. This broad diffusion of Greek philosophic and religious thought plays a major role in the development of both Judaism and Christianity.

323–197 BCE — The Ptolemaic dynasty, established by Ptolemy I, general and one of Alexander's successors, controls Palestine. Many Jews are attracted to Greek learning and the Hellenistic way of life.

200–197 BCE — The Seleucid dynasty of Syria, descendants of Alexander's general Seleucus, ends Ptolemic rule over Palestine and begins a new reign over the Jews (197–142 BCE).

168–164 BCE — The Seleucid ruler Antiochus IV, "Epiphanes," attempts to eradicate the Jewish religion, forbidding Torah observance, and erecting an altar to the Olympian Zeus in the Temple precincts ("the abomination" of Daniel 9:27). Mattathias, a Torah loyalist, and his five sons initiate the Maccabean Revolt.

164 BCE — Led by Judas Maccabeus, a Jewish guerrilla army recaptures, purifies, and rededicates the Temple, an event later commemorated in the festival of Hanukkah.

142–63 BCE — By 142 BCE, the Jews have expelled the Syrian armies and established an independent state governed by Hasmonean (Maccabean) rulers.

THE ROMAN EMPIRE

63 BCE — Pompey's legions occupy Palestine, annexing it as part of the Roman Empire.

40 BCE — The Roman Senate appoints Herod (Herod the Great), a nobleman of Idumea (the ancient Edom), king of Judea.

37–4 BCE — After laying siege to Jerusalem, Herod takes the city by force; he then lavishly rebuilds the Jerusalem Temple.

27 BCE–14 CE — Gaius Octavius becomes undisputed ruler of the entire Roman Empire. Renamed Augustus by the Roman Senate, Octavius ends the civil wars that had divided Rome for generations and establishes a long period of civil order called the Pax Romana (Roman Peace).

The Life of Jesus

c. 6–4 BCE — Jesus is born to Mary and Joseph, citizens of Nazareth.

4 BCE — After Herod the Great's death, his kingdom is divided among his three sons. Herod Antipas (4 BCE–39 CE) rules Galilee and Perea; Herod Philip (4 BCE–34 CE) rules territories north and east of Galilee; Herod Archelaus (4 BCE–6 CE) rules Judea, Samaria, and Idumea but is deposed. His territories henceforth are administered directly by Roman officials.

14–37 CE — Tiberius, stepson of Augustus, rules Rome.

(continued)

BOX 5.1 continued

26–36 CE	Pontius Pilate, appointed by Rome, governs as prefect of Judea (26–36 CE).
c.27–30 or 29–33 CE	Jesus' public ministry: Jesus and a small band of disciples tour villages and cities in and around Galilee. A final journey to Jerusalem results in Jesus' rejection by religious authorities and his execution by Pilate on charges of treason.

The Evolution of the Christian Community and Its Scriptures

c. 30 or 33 CE	A number of Jesus' followers are convinced that they have seen him risen from the dead. Gathered in Jerusalem, a commune of believers is inspired to begin carrying the oral gospel of Jesus' resurrection to Jews and (somewhat later) Gentiles. The Christian church is born.
c. 33–35 CE	Saul of Tarsus, a zealous Pharisee then persecuting Christian "heretics," experiences a vision of the risen Jesus on the road to Damascus.
c. 50–62 CE	Paul, now the preeminent Christian missionary to the Gentiles, composes a series of letters to various Christian communities in the eastern Mediterranean region. These letters are the earliest parts of the New Testament to be written.
c. 62 CE	James, Jesus' kinsman, is killed in Jerusalem.
c. 64–65 CE	Following a major fire in Rome, the emperor Nero persecutes Christians there. According to tradition, Peter and Paul are martyred then.
c. 66–70 CE	The first account of Jesus' public ministry is written (the Gospel according to Mark).

66–73 CE	Led by the Jewish nationalists and other revolutionaries, the Palestinian Jews revolt against Roman tyranny. Titus, son of the new emperor Vespasian, captures and destroys Jerusalem and its Temple (70 CE).

THE POSTAPOSTOLIC ERA

c. 80–85 CE	The Gospel of Matthew is written (in Antioch?).
c. 85–90 CE	Luke-Acts is published.
c. 80–100 CE	The books of James, Hebrews, and (possibly) 1 Peter are written.
c. 90 CE	Leading rabbis and Jewish scholars hold a council at Jamnia, to restructure postwar Judaism. Christians are expelled from Jewish synagogues.
c. 90 CE	The Letter to the Ephesians is included among Paul's correspondence.
c. 95–100 CE	The Gospel of John is produced by the Johannine community. The letter of 1 Clement is written in Rome.
c. 95 CE	John of Patmos writes the Book of Revelation.
c. 100–110 CE	Letters of John are written.
c. 100–130 CE	The Didache, Shepherd of Hermas, and Epistles of Ignatius are composed. The canonical New Testament books of 1 and 2 Timothy, Titus, and Jude appear.
132–135 CE	The bar Kochba rebellion against Rome is crushed by the emperor Hadrian (117–138 CE).
c. 130–150 CE	2 Peter is written.
367 CE	Bishop Athanasius of Alexandria publishes a list of twenty-seven New Testament books corresponding to the present New Testament canon.

The Pyramidal Structure of Roman Society

Like most ancient sociopolitical systems, the society of imperial Rome had the shape of a pyramid, with a single enormously powerful ruler at the apex and a vast powerless majority at the base (see Figure 5.7). In contrast to modern democracies, in which the people elect their representative officials, the Roman Empire was governed by rulers who either inherited their position or achieved it through military conquest. Concentrated almost exclusively in the person of the emperor and a small hereditary aristocracy, power flowed in only one direction, from the top down. A large and rigorously trained army, responsible to the emperor, maintained public order and ruthlessly crushed any attempted rebellion, as it did in the case of the two Jewish revolts (66–73 CE and 132–135 CE).

Landownership and wealth were also mostly confined to the top of the social pyramid, where perhaps 5 percent of the total population effectively controlled the economy, which was based primarily on agriculture and trade. Whereas a few elite groups enjoyed relatively secure lives of leisure, luxury, and literacy, most people, illiterate and impoverished, were compelled to work extremely hard to maintain even a subsistence level of existence. Many lived in such extreme penury that having enough to eat each day seemed to require divine intervention (Matt. 6:11). However, as Jesus pointed out, Roman imperial society had a few well-placed *patrons*, wealthy and/or politically influential aristocrats, who could dispense favors (money, grants of land, administrative or military appointments) to their social inferiors, chosen beneficiaries known as *clients* (Luke 22:24–27). The patron–client relationship, in which the

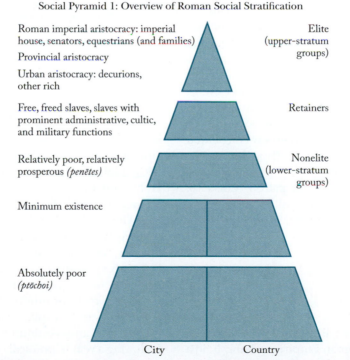

Social Pyramid 1: Overview of Roman Social Stratification

Roman imperial aristocracy: imperial house, senators, equestrians (and families)

Provincial aristocracy

Urban aristocracy: decurions, other rich

Elite (upper-stratum groups)

Free, freed slaves, slaves with prominent administrative, cultic, and military functions

Retainers

Relatively poor, relatively prosperous *(penētes)*

Nonelite (lower-stratum groups)

Minimum existence

Absolutely poor *(ptōchoi)*

City   Country

FIGURE 5.7 Pyramid figure is reprinted from *The Jesus Movement* by Ekkehard W. Stegemann and Wolfgang Stegemann, English translation by O. C. Dean, Jr., copyright © 1999 Fortress Press. Used by Permission of Augsburg Fortress. For a detailed discussion of the New Testament social world, including the patronage system and Jesus' theological role as divine broker, see the entries by Malina and Stegemann and Stegemann in "Recommended Reading."

powerful shared some of their advantages with the less privileged, fostering a social network of implied gratitude and obligation, characterized the society in which Christianity emerged.

The worldview assumed by most New Testament writers reflects to a remarkable degree the structure and practices of imperial Rome, paralleling its pyramidal shape and patron–client arrangement. As the ultimate governing authority, God occupies a position in the Christian cosmos analogous to that of the emperor in Roman society. As the emperor is surrounded by courtiers of aristocratic birth, so the Deity's throne is encompassed by privileged spirit beings (called the *bene ha elohim* [sons of the gods] in the Hebrew Bible), typically regarded as "angels" (Greek for "messengers"), who carry out divine orders (Job 1:6; 2:1; cf. 1 Kings 22:19–22; Zech. 3:1–10; Rev. 7:11; 8:2, etc.). As imperial patronage is commonly administered through intermediaries, designated agents or appointees of the emperor, so, in the New Testament, Jesus becomes God's appointed channel for divinely conferred benefits—mercy, forgiveness of sins, spiritual guidance, and salvation. In the last-written Gospel, that ascribed to John, the author explicitly claims that Jesus is the sole access to God. In John 14:16, he is represented as declaring that he alone is "the [true] way . . . no one comes to the Father except by me." Mediating between heaven and earth, the risen Jesus heads a Roman-like hierarchy over his earthly subjects, functioning as exclusive broker of the divine patron (Col. 1:16; 2:10, 15). (See the discussion of Paul's service to his divine patron in Chapters 13 and 15.)

The Jewish Revolt Against Rome

Although most Jews living in cities scattered throughout the Roman Empire probably held a wide variety of views about their Gentile rulers, most seem to have accepted the political realities of imperial domination. The case was fatally different in the Jewish homeland.

FIGURE 5.8   Portrait of the emperor Vespasian (ruled 69–79 CE). Appointed by Nero to crush the Jewish Revolt (66–73 CE), Vespasian conquered Galilee but withdrew from the war after Nero's suicide. A year later, he became emperor. He then appointed his son Titus to carry on the siege of Jerusalem.

About thirty-five years after Jesus' crucifixion, the Palestinian Jews rose in armed revolt against Rome. Led by passionate Jewish nationalists, many of whom believed it sinful even to allow idol-worshiping Gentiles to occupy the Holy Land, the Jewish Revolt (66–73 CE) proved an overwhelming disaster for the Jewish people.

When the Jewish Revolt broke out in 66 CE, the emperor **Nero** sent a veteran military commander, **Vespasian,** to crush the rebellion (see Figure 5.8). Galilee fell easily to the Roman army, but before Vespasian could occupy Judea, the territory in southern Palestine of which Jerusalem was the capital, Nero was driven from the throne and committed suicide (68 CE). Following a year of political chaos, Vespasian was acclaimed emperor by the Roman legions and confirmed by the Senate. Leaving his son **Titus** in charge of the Jewish War, Vespasian returned to Rome (see Figure 5.9). After a siege of six

FIGURE 5.9 Portrait of the emperor Titus (ruled 79–81 CE). When his father, Vespasian, left him in charge of putting down the Jewish Revolt, Titus laid siege to Jerusalem, capturing the city and burning its Temple in August 70 CE. He succeeded his father as emperor in 79 CE but died after a brief reign.

months, Titus captured and destroyed Jerusalem, burning Herod's splendidly rebuilt Temple in 70 CE (see Figure 5.10). (Box 5.2 lists the Roman emperors of the New Testament period.)

Our main source of information about the war is **Flavius Josephus,** a first-century Jewish historian who first participated in the rebellion but later became an ally of the Romans. An eyewitness to many of the events he describes, Josephus wrote to explain and defend his countrymen's action in revolting against Roman oppression. In *The Jewish War,* he vividly recounts the Roman capture of Jerusalem and the slaughter of many thousands of men, women, and children. While attempting to evoke sympathy for his people and to make their religion comprehensible to his Greek and Roman readers, Josephus also blames what he portrays as a small minority of political fanatics for their refusal to negotiate a compromise settlement with the Roman forces. According to Josephus, the extreme revolutionary party, the **Zealots,** virtually forced General Titus to destroy the holy city and its Temple by their obstinate refusal to accept the Roman terms of peace. Many historians doubt Josephus's sometimes self-serving interpretation

FIGURE 5.10 Detail from the Arch of Titus, which the Roman Senate erected in the Forum of Rome about 100 CE. Created in honor of Titus's victories in the Jewish War, this frieze depicts Roman soldiers carrying off loot from the Jerusalem Temple, including the Menorah—the seven-branched candelabrum formerly housed in the sanctuary.

BOX 5.2   Roman Emperors of the New Testament Period

The imperial form of government, in which a single man ruled the entire Roman Empire, was established by Augustus a generation before the birth of Jesus and continued until the collapse of the western empire in 476 CE. Emperors reigning during the rise of early Christianity, and some of the principal events that affected the Christian community, are given here.*

THE JULIO-CLAUDIAN DYNASTY

Augustus (30 BCE–14 CE): Establishment of Pax Romana; Jesus' birth, c. 6–4 BCE; Jesus' youth in Nazareth, Galilee

Tiberius (14–37 CE): John the Baptist's revival campaign; Jesus' ministry in Galilee and Judea; the Crucifixion c. 30 or 33 CE; the conversion of Paul

Gaius (Caligula) (37–41): Threatened installation of the emperor's statue in the Jerusalem Temple

Claudius (41–54): Expulsion of some Jews from Rome (c. 49); earliest letters of Paul

Nero (54–68): Persecution of Christians in Rome; outbreak of the Jewish War; Vespasian's and Titus's suppression of the Jewish Revolt; executions of James (Jesus' kinsman), Peter, and Paul

THE YEAR OF THE FOUR EMPERORS AND THE FLAVIAN DYNASTY

Galba (68–69); Otho (69); Vitellius (69)

Vespasian (69–79): Destruction of Jerusalem (70) and Masada (73); Mark written

Titus (79–81)

Domitian (81–96): Luke-Acts' positive view of Rome; sporadic persecutions; Revelation's visions of Rome's fall; community of the Beloved Disciple's production of the Fourth Gospel

THE ADOPTIVE AND ANTONINE EMPERORS

Nerva (96–98)

Trajan (98–117): Letter of Pliny the Younger describing the persecution of Christians in Asia Minor

Hadrian (117–138): Second Jewish Revolt, led by bar Kochba (132–135); Jews barred from Jerusalem

Antoninus Pius (138–161): Marcion's excommunication in Rome; composition of 2 Peter, the last canonical document written

Marcus Aurelius (161–180)

Commodus (180–192)

---

*How important the Roman emperors were to early Christianity is indicated by Eusebius (c. 260–340 CE), who organizes his *History of the Church* according to the reigns of specific emperors.

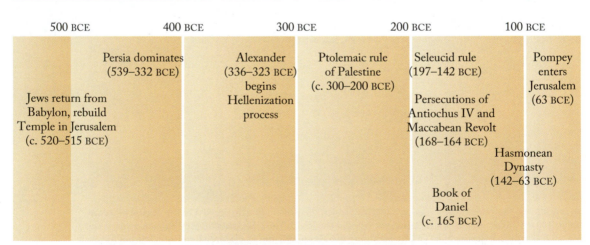

500 BCE	400 BCE	300 BCE	200 BCE	100 BCE
	Persia dominates (539–332 BCE)	Alexander (336–323 BCE) begins Hellenization process	Ptolemaic rule of Palestine (c. 300–200 BCE)	Seleucid rule (197–142 BCE)	Pompey enters Jerusalem (63 BCE)
Jews return from Babylon, rebuild Temple in Jerusalem (c. 520–515 BCE)				Persecutions of Antiochus IV and Maccabean Revolt (168–164 BCE)	
					Hasmonean Dynasty (142–63 BCE)
				Book of Daniel (c. 165 BCE)	

FIGURE 5.11   Time line: From Alexander's conquests to the Second Jewish Revolt.

of events, but his surviving works, including a history of Israel called *Antiquities of the Jews,* are an invaluable record of this turbulent period.

A second Jewish rebellion against Rome (132–135 CE) was led by a young man popularly known as **bar Kochba** (Son of the Star), whom many Palestinian Jews believed to be the Messiah who would restore David's kingdom. Brutally suppressed by the emperor Hadrian, the bar Kochba rebellion resulted in a second Roman destruction of Jerusalem (135 CE). A Roman shrine was then constructed on the site of Yahweh's Temple, and Jews were forbidden to enter their city on pain of death (see Figures 5.11 and 5.12).

Questions About God's Justice

Because Yahweh was believed to be the Lord of history—his will enacted through historical events—the Roman destructions of Jerusalem raised painful questions. Why did God inflict such suffering on his covenant partner? Why did he permit a Gentile power, which did not acknowledge him as God, to triumph over a people who at least tried to worship him?

For many faithful Jews, Rome had become the new Babylon, reenacting Nebuchadnezzar's violation of Yahweh's sanctuary and reducing tens of thousands of Abraham's descendants to slavery and public humiliation. For loyal, Torah-observant Jews of the late first century CE, the lament of Psalm 44 rang with special resonance:

> All this has befallen us, but we do not
>   forget thee
> and have not betrayed thy covenant:
> we have not gone back on our purpose,
> nor have our feet strayed from thy path.
> Yet thou hast crushed us as the sea-
>   serpent was crushed
> and covered us with the darkness of death.
>
> (Ps. 44:17–19)

It was in their role as Yahweh's devout worshipers that the covenant people suffered:

> Because of thee we are done to death all
>   day long,
> and are treated as sheep for slaughter.
>
> (Ps. 44:22)

About thirty years after Titus demolished the Temple in 70 CE, the author of the Book of 2 Esdras expressed similar bewilderment at God's failure to protect his people, while at the same time allowing an "ungodly" nation (Rome) to rule the earth:

> My heart sank, because I saw how you [God] tolerate sinners and spare the godless; how you have destroyed your own people, but protected your enemies. You have given no hint whatever to anyone how to understand your ways. Is Babylon [Rome] more virtuous than Zion? Has any nation except Israel ever known you? What

1 CE		50 CE		100 CE
Herod appointed king (40 BCE) Temple rebuilt	Pontius Pilate procurator (26–36 CE) Ministry of Jesus (c. 27–30 CE)	Jewish Revolt against Rome (66–73 CE)	Academy of Jamnia (c. 90 CE)	Second Jewish Revolt (132–135 CE)
		Letters of Paul (50–c. 62 CE) Destruction of Jerusalem (70 CE)		Gospel of John
Birth of Jesus (c. 6–4 BCE)		Oral traditions about Jesus		
Death of Herod (4 BCE)		Gospel of Mark (c. 66–70 CE)		

FIGURE 5.12   Arch of Titus. Commemorating Rome's triumph in crushing the Jewish Revolt (66–73 CE), this monumental arch honors Titus, son of Vespasian, who led the siege of Jerusalem in 70 CE. After capturing and burning the city, Titus razed Herod's Temple, the center of Jewish worship.

tribes have put trust in your covenants as the tribes of Jacob have? . . . Has any nation ever kept your commandments like Israel?

(2 Esd. 3:30–32, 36)

(For a discussion of 2 Esdras's **theodicy,** an attempt to explain an all-powerful God's tolerance of evil and undeserved suffering, see Chapter 19.)

New Testament Attitudes Toward Rome: Tensions Between Caesar and Christ

We do not know what role, if any, the small Christian communities in Galilee or Judea played in the Jewish Revolt against Rome, though it seems probable that they suffered from both Roman devastation of the region and Zealot intolerance of Gentile-friendly groups. New Testament attitudes toward Rome are complex, even ambiguous. Mark's Gospel, perhaps written at the height of the revolt, indirectly reflects contemporary views of Rome during Jesus' ministry. Many first-century Judeans regarded Rome as "the evil empire" and bitterly resented its presence in their homeland. This negative

view seems to echo in Mark's story of Jesus exorcizing the Gerasene demoniac, a man possessed by "unclean spirits" who announce that their name is "legion," the term designating a Roman military unit of about 5,400 soldiers, "because there are so many of us" (Mark 5:1–13). The sensitive issue of paying taxes to support an idolatrous Gentile government, which troubled many Jews, is addressed in Jesus' famous directive to "pay Caesar [the Roman emperor] what belongs to Caesar, and God what belongs to God," a pronouncement that reaffirms the covenant people's primary allegiance to Yahweh (Mark 12:17). As Jesus presents it, the "kingdom of God," a concept central to his teaching, is both an implicit criticism of and an exciting alternative to Roman imperialism.

Jesus' choice of the phrase "the kingdom of God"—rather than "the people of God" or "the community of God"—may have had political connotations for some of his contemporaries. If one is to come wholeheartedly under the rule of Israel's God, what is one's relationship to Roman rule? Certainly, Pontius Pilate, Rome's representative in Judea, demands to know Jesus' connection to the "kingdom": "Are you the king of the Jews?" When Jesus does not deny this charge, Pilate has him executed for treason (Mark 15:1–20). According to John's Gospel, Pilate also posted a notice on Jesus' cross stating the crime for which he was crucified—"Jesus of Nazareth King of the Jews" (John 19:19–22)—a public reminder that Rome tolerated no competition to Caesar.

Luke's trial scene makes clear that Jesus' accusers could easily misinterpret his message as politically seditious: "We found this man subverting our nation, opposing the payment of taxes to Caesar, and claiming to be Messiah, a king" (Luke 23:1–4). In his sequel to the Gospel, the Book of Acts, Luke is equally candid about critical responses to Christian preaching. According to their opponents, Paul and other missionaries "flout the Emperor's laws, and assert that there is a rival king, Jesus" (Acts 17:7). In fact, the Jesus movement is seen as "unpatriotic" and "un-Roman" because, as some residents of Philippi claim, it advocates "customs which it is illegal for us Romans to adopt and follow" (Acts 16:21–22). When he describes Nero's savage treatment of Roman Christians, whom the emperor falsely blamed for the fire that ravaged the capital (64 CE), the historian Tacitus (c. 55–117 CE) shows that anti-Christian propaganda had shaped his opinion of the movement. Although he notes that the martyrs "were sacrificed to [Nero's] brutality rather than to the national interest," Tacitus nonetheless condemns Christians for their alleged "anti-social tendencies" and judges them "guilty" and deserving of "ruthless punishment," presumably for subverting hallowed Roman traditions (*Annals* 15.44; see Box 12.4). How could people who pledged their allegiance to Jesus, crucified for treason, possibly be loyal to the state?

In the two-volume Luke-Acts, the author insists that, false accusations to the contrary, both Jesus and his early followers were innocent of political sedition (see Chapters 9 and 12). Although the Gospel writers portray Jesus as a political victim of Rome's determination to eliminate any potential leader who might oppose its absolutism, they also tend to absolve Rome of guilt for killing Jesus. In all four Gospels, Roman soldiers typically play positive roles. When Luke describes a group of Jewish leaders identifying a Roman centurion as a "friend of our nation . . . who built us our synagogue" (meeting place), he adds that the man deserves to have Jesus heal a favorite servant. Impressed by the Roman officer's trust in his curative powers, Jesus exclaims that "not even in Israel have I found such faith" (Luke 7:1–10; Matt. 8:5–13). Another centurion in effect returns the compliment at Jesus' execution, recognizing him as "a son of God" (Mark 15:39), or in Luke's version, pronouncing him "innocent" of sedition against Rome (Luke 23:47). By placing favorable judgments of Jesus on the lips of Roman soldiers, the Evangelists anticipate the historical fact that Jesus' disciples achieved far greater success among Greeks and Romans than among their fellow Jews.

In his letter to the church at Rome, Paul urges believers to submit to Roman laws and institutions (Rom. 13:1–7). Paul likely thought of this submission to governmental authority as only temporary, however, for Jesus' return to establish the kingdom was imminent. Immediately following his admonition to pay taxes and to respect Roman magistrates, Paul adds that "deliverance is nearer to us now that it was when first we believed," for "the day [of the Lord] is near" (Rom 13:11–13). Writing perhaps forty years after Paul dispatched his letter to the Romans, the mystic who composed Revelation took a much bolder stance against Rome. Symbolizing the Roman Empire as both a wild beast and a seductive "harlot," John of Patmos urged Christians to "come out" of the imperial system altogether (Rev. 18:4). God has adversely judged "the great city that holds sway over the kings of the earth" (Rev. 17:18) and Jesus, who is "coming soon," will destroy it (Rev. 17–18; 22:12, 20).

Scholars increasingly emphasize that the sociohistorical context in which Christianity emerged and defined itself is that of Roman power. As Greek influence permeated almost every aspect of social culture, so did Roman political might shape and control the lives of people living throughout the empire. If Jesus and his early followers proposed a "new way" to live (Acts 9:2), they inevitably encountered suspicion from their neighbors and, eventually, resistance from local authorities. Instead of imitating the social norms by seeking power and riches, Jesus' followers were to be distinguished by sharing their material goods (Luke 18:18–30; Acts 2:43–45; 4:32–35) and by avoiding the economically exploitative nature of Roman society. In a memorable directive, Jesus instructs his disciples not to mimic the Roman patron–client arrangement:

> In the [Greco-Roman] world, kings lord it over their subjects; and those in authority are called their country's "Benefactors." Not so with you: on the contrary, the highest among you must bear himself like the youngest, the chief of you like a servant. . . . I am among you like a servant.
>
> (Luke 22:25–27)

When they brought the "good news" of Jesus' gracious kingship to the Greco-Roman world, Paul and his fellow missionaries could easily be seen as also attacking Greco-Roman religions, including those that the state endorsed. As he wrote to the congregation in Corinth, the empire's population worshiped "many 'gods' and many 'lords,'" whereas he and his converts honor only "one God, the Father" and "one Lord Jesus Christ" (1 Cor. 8:5–6). In attempting to bring a new version of Israel's monotheism to Greek and Roman cities, Paul showed little respect for the established cults. The sacrificial rites that "the heathen offer are offered" "to demons," and not to God (1 Cor. 10:20). The Olympian deities and such savior figures as Isis and Mithras, Paul implies, are demonic, malign spirits opposed to Israel's God. In fact, Paul asserts that people who reject his message are "so blinded by the god of this passing age [Satan]" that they remain in darkness (2 Cor. 4:4). As the Gospels of Matthew and Luke suggest, the source of imperial power is the devil, who can offer Jesus "all the kingdoms of the world" because they have "been put into my hands and I can give [them] to anyone I choose" (Luke 4:6–7). Although Jesus rejected this political temptation, the devil had more success (as many early Christians believed) in giving his "dominion" to Rome and its empire.

The Cult of the Roman Emperor

In the ancient world, it was commonly assumed that military leaders who conquered enormous territories probably did so because the gods favored them. It was appropriate, then, for people to acknowledge that a major conqueror had won divine approval or was perhaps even divine himself, a view that goes back to the pharaohs of Egypt. Egyptian religion identified a living pharaoh with the god Horus while a deceased pharaoh was identified with Osiris, lord of the dead. In the Greco-Roman tradition, the practice of worshiping a successful leader as if he were a god began with Alexander the Great. Shortly after Alexander conquered Egypt in 331 BCE, a priest of the god Ammon at Siwa in the Libyan desert is said to have hailed him as the son of Ammon-Ra, the chief Egyptian deity, whom the Greeks identified with Zeus. As the newly crowned king of Egypt, Alexander was by custom entitled to this form of address, which was accorded to all pharaohs. Because the oracle of Ammon enjoyed great prestige, however, many Greeks seem to have taken the priest's words literally. Ruler of most of the known world, Alexander apparently promoted the concept of his own divinity and encouraged the establishment of a cult in his honor.

Alexander's successors, particularly the Ptolemaic and Seleucid dynasties, also found it politically useful to elicit divine honors from their subjects. Many Hellenistic cities competed with one another in revering the king as their divinely empowered benefactor, offering sacrifices and performing other rites modeled on those granted the Olympian gods. Although many Greeks opposed treating human beings as if they were divine, the ruler cult was so widely practiced that the Romans eventually adopted it.

By the fourth century BCE, Romulus, the legendary founder of Rome, was given posthumous deification and identified with a minor Italian deity named Quirinus. After his assassination, the Roman Senate formally declared Julius Caesar (c. 100–44 BCE) henceforth a god. In his *Metamorphoses,* the Latin poet Ovid vividly described the soul of Julius Caesar ascending—like a radiant comet—to celestial glory. Jupiter (the Roman Zeus), Ovid states, guaranteed Caesar's entry into heaven "as a god," who would also "have his temples on earth" (see Figure 5.13).

As Caesar's adopted son and designated heir, Octavius, the future emperor Augustus, was known as *divi filius,* "son of God." Upon his death in 14 CE, the Senate acclaimed Augustus a god in his own right. Roman coins, imprinted with the emperor's image, typically also carried inscriptions proclaiming his divinity. Thus every monetary transaction throughout the empire involved handling objects that advertised imperial worship, a fact that resonates in the story of Jesus holding a coin bearing Caesar's portrait and suggesting it be returned to the ruler (Mark 12:13–17).

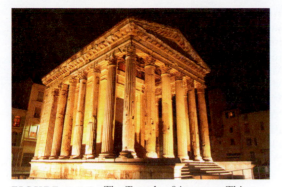

FIGURE 5.13 The Temple of Augustus. This remarkably well preserved Roman temple in Nimes, France, dedicated to the deified Augustus, illustrates the widespread cult of emperor worship. Brilliantly illuminated in this night photograph, the temple seems to glow, as if radiating the light of a divine presence that the Romans officially associated with their deified ruler.

In a recently recovered inscription from the late first century BCE, a Roman governor, Paulus Fabius Maximus, suggests that the cities of Asia Minor (modern Turkey) should revise their calendars so that Augustus's birthday, September 23, marked the beginning of the New Year. "Born as a common blessing to all," the governor states, Augustus, who had decisively defeated his enemies and established peace throughout the Roman world, should be universally acknowledged as "the beginning of life and living" for every inhabitant of the empire.

Twenty years after this proclamation, the governor received a golden diadem and an official commendation for discovering a "way to honor Augustus that was hitherto unknown . . . , namely to reckon time from the date of his nativity." Equally extravagant praise was heaped on Augustus's successors, even unworthy emperors such as Caligula, whose reign all people "had hoped and prayed for" because it showed that "the happiest age for mankind had now arrived" (see Reed in "Recommended Reading"). These superlatives typically present the emperor as fulfilling humanity's deepest aspirations for a utopia, an administration of perfect justice and peace.

Most important for New Testament study is the term Paulus Fabius used to describe his promotion of the imperial cult: *evaggelia,* the plural of "good news," the same term that Paul and the Gospel writers would later use to proclaim the "glad tidings" about Jesus (see Chapter 1). When a Lukan angel, on the night of Jesus' birth, tells shepherds that he has "good news for you" and "great joy coming to the whole people" because "a deliverer [savior, the same term applied to Roman emperors] has been born to you," he is effectively appropriating laudatory terms commonly reserved for Rome's rulers and reapplying them to Jesus (Luke 2:8–14).

Although many cities and provinces throughout the Roman Empire intermittently sponsored emperor worship, scholars caution that there was never a single government-sanctioned cult. Not only did Rome not impose a centralized rite, but emperor worship took many different forms and was commonly integrated into previously existing cults of other state-recognized gods. As the Book of Revelation makes clear, some Christians saw the tension between Jesus, a king now enthroned in heaven, and a human ruler who controlled much of the earth, as a clash between invisible spiritual forces of good and evil. According to Revelation's author, that conflict would inevitably culminate in Rome's fall and the triumph of God's reign. In the meantime, Christians' refusal to participate in the emperor cult—on the grounds that only "one God" and "one Lord" is entitled to worship—could bring official persecution, resulting in confiscation of property, imprisonment, or even death.

 ## Summary

The period of Jesus' life is chronologically framed by two Jewish wars for religious and political independence. The first, led by the Maccabees, created an autonomous Jewish state. The second, a generation after Jesus' death, resulted in national annihilation. Bar Kochba's later attempt to restore Jewish fortunes met a similar defeat. From this time until 1948, when the modern nation of Israel was established, the Jews were to be a people without a country.

Questions for Review

1. Summarize the achievements of Alexander the Great. After his death, how was Alexander's empire divided among his successors?
2. What did the Greek-Syrian king Antiochus IV attempt to accomplish in his policy toward his Jewish subjects? How did the Hasidim oppose Antiochus's enforced Hellenization, and what part did the Maccabees play in Jewish resistance to assimilation?
3. After the Romans conquered Palestine, what role did Herod and his successors play in Jewish history? Describe the functions of Roman governors such as Pontius Pilate.

Questions for Discussion and Reflection

1. How did belief in a single holy God who requires exclusive devotion affect Jewish behavior during the persecutions of Antiochus IV? Why were Jews willing to suffer torture and death rather than disobey Torah commands? How is the concept of martyrdom related to notions about compensation in the afterlife?
2. Discuss Jewish relations with Rome. What led to the Jewish Revolt of 66–73 CE, and what were its consequences for the Jewish people? In what different ways did New Testament authors regard Rome?
3. Describe the practice of posthumously awarding divine honors to Greek and Roman rulers. With whom did the custom begin, and how might it have prepared the way for people in the Roman Empire to accept the idea of a crucified Jewish prophet as the resurrected Son of God? Why was it perhaps easier in the Hellenistic world to accept the idea of supernatural intervention and postmortem deification than it is today?

Terms and Concepts to Remember

Antiochus IV	Flavius Josephus
Antipater	Hanukkah
Augustus	Hasidim
bar Kochba	Hasmoneans
Caesar	Herod Agrippa I
Caesara Maritima	Herod Agrippa II
Dedication, Feast of	Herod Antipas
devil	Herod Archelaus
Herod the Great	procurators
Idumea	Ptolemaic dynasty
Judas Maccabeus	Ptolemy I
Judea	Roman Empire
Maccabees	Seleucid dynasty
Masada	Seleucus
Mattathias	theodicy
Nero	Tiberius
Palestine	Titus
Philip	Vespasian
Pontius Pilate	Zealots

Recommended Reading

Brodd, Jeffrey, and Reed, Jonathan L., eds. *Rome and Religion: A Cross-Disciplinary Dialogue on the Imperial Cult.* Atlanta: The Society of Biblical Literature, 2011. A collection of scholarly debates on the interaction of early Christianity and the diverse manifestations of emperor worship.

Carter, Warren. *The Roman Empire and the New Testament: An Essential Guide.* Nashville: Abingdon Press, 2006. Shows how Roman social structures and customs impinged upon Christian lives in the New Testament world.

Edwards, M. J.; Goodman, M.; Price, Simon; and Rowland, C., eds. *Apologetics in the Roman Empire: Pagans, Jews, and Christians.* New York: Oxford University Press, 1999. Places Jewish and Christian literature in the broad context of historical forces operating in the Greco-Roman world.

Goodman, Martin. *The Ruling Class of Judea: The Origins of the Jewish Revolt Against Rome, AD 66-70.* New York: Cambridge University Press, 1993. An authoritative analysis of events crucial to both Jewish and Roman history.

Hanson, K. C., and Oakman, Douglas E. *Palestine in the Time of Jesus: Social Structures and Social Conflicts.* Minneapolis: Fortress Press, 1998. Examines the biblical social world, emphasizing its differences from later Western cultures.

Holmberg, Bengt. *Sociology and the New Testament: An Appraisal.* Minneapolis: Fortress Press, 1990. Surveys sociology's contribution to our understanding of the sociopolitical environment assumed by the New Testament.

Josephus, Flavius. *The Jewish War,* rev. ed. Translated by G. A. Williamson; edited by E. M. Smallwood. New York: Penguin Books, 1981. The most important contemporary source for conditions in Palestine during the first century CE.

Malina, Bruce. *The Social World of Jesus and the Gospels.* New York: Routledge, 1996. Discusses the analogy between the Roman patron–client relationship and Jesus' theological role as broker of divine benefits.

Reed, Jonathan L. "Archaeological Contributions to the Study of Jesus and the Gospels." In Amy-Jill Levine, Dale C. Allison, Jr., and John Dominic Crossan, eds. *The Historical Jesus in Context.* Princeton, N.J.: Princeton University Press, 2006. Surveys archaeological discoveries that shed light on Jesus' Galilean environment and the Evangelists' attitudes toward Rome.

———. *The HarperCollins Visual Guide to the New Testament: What Archaeology Reveals About the First Christians.* San Fransisco: HarperOne, 2007. A lavishly illustrated survey of Greco-Roman archaeological sites and monuments related to early Christianity.

Rubenstein, Richard E. *When Jesus Became God: The Epic Fight over Christ's Divinity in the Last Days of Rome.* New York: Harcourt Brace, 1999. Traces the theological and political debates in which a Jewish prophet was ultimately transformed into a Gentile god.

Stegemann, Ekkehard W., and Stegemann, Wolfgang. *The Jesus Movement: A Social History of Its First Century.* Translated by O. C. Dean, Jr. Minneapolis: Fortress Press, 1999. A comprehensive study of Greco-Roman sociopolitical structures in general and the first-century-CE Palestinian social environment in particular.

PART THREE

Diverse Portraits of Jesus

Most scholars agree that the stone ossuary (*right*) inscribed "Joseph, son of Caiaphas," found in Jerusalem, likely contained the bones of Caiaphas, the High Priest who presided over Jesus' trial at the Sanhedrin (Mark 14:53–15:1). Water still flows through a stone channel that archaeologists believe marks the remains of the Siloam Pool in east Jerusalem (*below*), the site where Jesus healed a man born blind. Unearthed in 2004, steps leading down to the pool suggest that it may have been used for ritual immersion. According to John 9, Jesus made a paste of mud mixed with his spittle, which he applied to the blind man's eyes. Following Jesus' instructions, when the man washed off the mud in the Siloam Pool, he was able to see for the first time. Found in the 1950s at the port of Caesarea, an inscribed stone (*top of facing page*) dedicated to the emperor Tiberius mentions the name of Pontius Pilate, prefect of Judea (26–36 CE), the Roman official who condemned Jesus to crucifixion. It is one of the few archaeological confirmations of a New Testament character's historical existence.

The ruins of Capernaum (*below left*), a fishing village on the northwest shore of the Sea of Galilee, reveal a setting in which Jesus was said to be "at home" (Mark 2:1, 15). Sheltering about 1,500 inhabitants during the first century CE, Capernaum's houses were generally small, crudely built of rough stone blocks and roofed with thatch. Excavations of a first-century house church there, its walls bearing graffiti by Christian pilgrims, suggest that it incorporates the remnants of Peter's simple dwelling. A first-century-CE Galilean boat (*below right*), buried for almost two millennia under sediment in the Sea of Galilee, was discovered in 1986. Such fishing boats were a common sight in Jesus' day. ▶

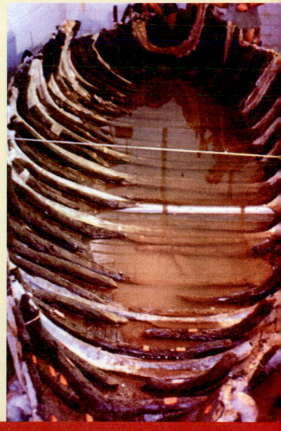

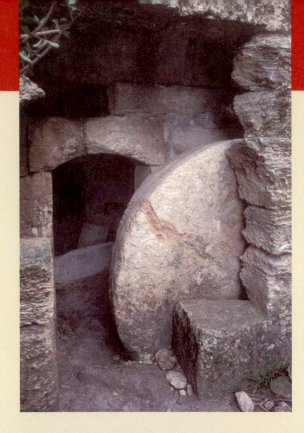

Located south of Jerusalem, the first-century burial cave of Midras (*left*), with its circular stone that rolls laterally to seal the tomb entrance, resembles the Gospel descriptions of Jesus' sepulcher. Several sites near Jerusalem claim to be Jesus' burial place. Still bearing the iron spike that pierced his heel bone and fastened him to a wooden panel, a bone fragment (*below*) of a crucified man was discovered in an ossuary in a Jerusalem tomb. ■

CHAPTER 6

The Gospels
Form and Purpose

Many writers have undertaken to draw up an account of the events that have happened among us [the early Christian community] following the traditions handed down to us by the original eyewitnesses and servants of the Gospel. Luke 1:1–2

Key Topics/Themes Each a product of a different group within the early Christian community, the four canonical Gospels are our major source of information about the life and teachings of Jesus. More interested in presenting a theological interpretation of Jesus' words and actions than a purely factual account of his life, the Gospel writers portray Jesus as unlike any other figure of history, able to perform miracles, rise from the dead, and ascend to heaven. The first three Gospels—Matthew, Mark, and Luke—are so similar that scholars call them the Synoptics, their parallel accounts capable of being seen together "with one eye." By contrast, the Fourth Gospel, that ascribed to John, gives Jesus' life a different chronology and presents his teachings, in both style and content, in an entirely different way. Challenged by both their similarities and their differences, scholars attempt to explain how the Gospels were created and how accurately they portray the historical Jesus.

Unlike virtually all other extant literature from the Greco-Roman world, the New Testament writings were not composed by members of the ruling class. Viewing Rome's hierarchal society from outside the power elite, most early Christian authors, particularly those active after Rome's destruction of Jerusalem in 70 CE, do not support the imperial system, much less its cult of the divine emperor. Instead, most canonical writers generally appeal to an audience that suffers socioeconomic oppression, the poor and politically powerless, the same disadvantaged multitudes to whom Jesus largely directed his ministry (Luke 6:20–26; Matt. 11:28–30, etc.).

In fact, some New Testament writers, such as James, argue that too cozy a relationship with Roman society's exploitative values makes one God's enemy (James 5:5).

In presenting their stories of Jesus, the Gospel writers offer a powerful alternative to the Roman system, with its succession of "divine" emperors flatteringly hailed as world rulers and "saviors." For the Evangelists, Jesus is the rightful king that Roman monarchs could only pretend to be, imperial propaganda notwithstanding. Pontius Pilate, representing Rome, had executed Jesus as "King of the Jews" (Matt. 27:11, 37), but God had raised him to immortal life and made him ruler over the entire cosmos. As the risen Jesus announces to his disciples, "Full authority in heaven and on earth has been committed to me," transforming Rome's victim into universal sovereign (Matt. 28:18). Moreover, this same Jesus would soon return in glory to judge all "nations," including the imperial power that had crucified him (Matt. 25:31–46). As we study the Evangelists' accounts of Jesus' life and death, we discover that their main goal is to persuade readers of Jesus' supreme importance to all humankind and to win their allegiance to a king infinitely superior to any earthly ruler.

The Gospel Writers' Emphasis on Jesus' Religious Meaning

If we carefully analyze the four Gospel narratives, it becomes clear that the Evangelists are less concerned about purely historical facts than in expressing a particular theological viewpoint. Like all New Testament authors, the Evangelists write primarily to voice their individual understanding of Jesus' religious or theological significance.

John's Gospel contains the most explicit statement about the author's theological purpose and selective use of the Jesus tradition. Appended by a later editor, a note at the Gospel's conclusion states (with some rhetorical exaggeration) that the author chose to utilize only a relatively small portion of the information available to him:

> There is much else that Jesus did [that is not included in the Gospel]. If it were all to be recorded in detail, I suppose that the whole world could not hold the books that would be written.
>
> (John 21:25; cf. 20:30)

As John's author explains, his standard for deciding what material to include does not primarily involve goals of historical accuracy or biographical completeness. Acknowledging that he had many relevant facts about Jesus that were "not recorded in this book [his Gospel]," John adds that

> Those [deeds of Jesus] here written have been recorded in order that you may hold the faith that Jesus is the Christ, the Son of God, and that through this faith you may possess life by his name.
>
> (John 20:31)

The writer's objective, then, is clear: to inspire life-giving faith in his readers. All of John's fellow Evangelists probably shared his theological orientation, chiefly because they were uniformly convinced that Jesus was not an ordinary figure of history, but a person of supernatural abilities whose teachings and sacrificial death had the power to confer salvation and immortality on those who believed in him. For the Evangelists, it might have seemed irrelevant to depict Jesus the way a modern, science-inspired biographer would today, using strict criteria of historical accuracy and rational skepticism. In the early Christian view, it was far more important to portray Jesus as their faith revealed him to be, God's ultimate revelation to humanity.

Because the Evangelists were committed believers in Jesus' divine Sonship and saw their writing tasks as more theological than historical, scholars find it difficult to separate what may be authentic memories of Jesus' words and actions from later theological interpretation (or embellishment) of them. For the last several decades, many contemporary scholars have focused on a quest to understand the historical Jesus more accurately (see Chapter 11). The difficulty of distinguishing the Jesus of history from the Christ of faith is compounded by the Evangelists' tendency to portray the living man in the light of his post resurrection splendor, a trend most pronounced in John, the Gospel that makes the most extensive claims for Jesus' divinity.

In a speech appearing only in John, the author highlights the role of the Paraclete (a term variously translated as "Advocate," "Helper," or "Comforter"), the divinely sent Spirit that guides John's religious community after Jesus' departure. According to John, Jesus promised the disciples that after his death "the Holy Spirit will teach you everything, and will call to mind all that I have told you" (John 14:26). In other words, only after the Crucifixion and Jesus' ascension to heaven would his followers, in retrospect, be able to comprehend the meaning of his life and deeds. The author of John's Gospel therefore portrayed the earthly Jesus in radiant colors that reflected his community's perception of Jesus' celestial "glory" (John 1:14), clothing him in the attributes of the cosmic Christ. Although the extent to which John depicts the mortal Jesus as already manifesting divinity is unique to his Gospel—and accounts for many of his differences from the other three Evangelists—all Gospel authors interpret Jesus in the light of their respective communities' post resurrection faith.

The Synoptic Gospels

In contrast to John, with its distinctive emphasis on Jesus' divinity, stand the first three Gospels—Matthew, Mark, and Luke. Despite some important differences, these three accounts are strikingly similar: They have so much material in common that one can arrange their contents in parallel columns and compare—at a single glance—their three versions of the same saying or incident in Jesus' life (see Box 6.1). In general, Matthew, Mark, and Luke—unlike John—follow the same order of events in narrating Jesus' public ministry: All three begin with his baptism in the Jordan River, followed by descriptions of his tours through the villages of rural Galilee, where he heals the sick, expels demons, teaches the crowds, and debates issues of Torah observance with opponents. In all three, Jesus makes only one trip to Jerusalem (John reports many visits there), where he is arrested, condemned, and crucified. Because they present Jesus' story from essentially the same viewpoint, they are called the **Synoptic Gospels:** They can be read together, "with one eye."

Only one of the Synoptic authors, Luke, gives us a specific statement about his authorial intentions and methodology. In a formal preface

to his narrative, Luke makes clear that he did not personally know Jesus and that his work depends entirely on secondary sources, including oral traditions and previously existing Gospels:

> The author to Theophilus: Many writers have undertaken to draw up an account of the events that have happened among us, following the traditions handed down to us by the original eyewitnesses and servants of the Gospel. And so I in my turn, your Excellency, as one who has gone over the whole course of these events in detail, have decided to write a connected narrative for you, so as to give you authentic knowledge about the matters of which you have been informed.
>
> (Luke 4:1–4)

Although brief, Luke's introduction outlines the general procedures he followed in compiling a Gospel that built on the work of his predecessors. Acknowledging that "many writers" had already preceded him in documenting Christian origins—the "events" that had occurred "among us" (the Christian community)—Luke also makes clear that he stands some chronological distance from the developments he describes. Living perhaps two or three generations after the "original eyewitnesses" and other (later?) "servants of the Gospel," he must use the techniques of a researcher, investigating "in detail" the "whole course" of the Jesus movement. His goal is to create a "connected narrative" (according to accepted Hellenistic literary standards) so that his readers can receive "authentic knowledge" to take the place of the oral teachings on which they had formerly depended.

To understand Luke's intent in adding yet another Gospel to those already in existence, it is important to recognize that he was also the only Evangelist to compose an account of the early church, to follow a life of Jesus with a narrative about what Jesus' disciples accomplished after their Master's death. Aware that Christianity had undergone enormous changes during its first few decades—growing from an exclusively Palestinian Jewish movement to a largely Gentile faith in the Greco-Roman world—Luke felt the necessity of retelling Jesus' story in the light of its

BOX 6.1 Parallels and Differences in the Four Gospels

In comparing the contents of the four canonical accounts of Jesus' life, it is striking that, while events in Mark generally have close parallels in Matthew and Luke, much of the material in John has no parallel in the three Synoptic Gospels. As we will discover in Chapter 10, the differences between John and the other three Gospels are even greater than appears in this chart: Even when John deals with the same events, such as Jesus' assault on the Temple and his arrest, trials, and crucifixion, he uses a different chronology and gives different descriptions of what happened.

TOPIC/EPISODE	MARK	MATTHEW	LUKE	JOHN
Jesus as eternal Word	—	—	—	1:1–14
Word made "flesh"	—	—	—	1:14
Birth story	—	1:18–2:23	1:5–2:40	—
John's baptizing work	1:9–11	3:1–17	3:1–21	1:6, 15, 19–28
Temptation by Satan	1:12–13	4:1–11	4:1–14	—
Teaching primarily or "only in parables"	4:1–24	13:3–35	8:4–18; 13:18–21	—
Teaching primarily in long, metaphysical discourses				
Conversation with Nicodemus	—	—	—	3:1–21
Conversation with Samaritan woman	—	—	—	4:1–42
"I am" speeches				
Bread of life	—	—	—	6:26–66
Good Shepherd	—	—	—	10:1–21
True vine	—	—	—	15:1–17
Farewell discourses (divine nature and return to the Father)	—	—	—	13:12–17:26
Exorcisms (casting out demons)	1:23–28; 5:1–20; etc.	8:28–34	8:26–39	—
Feeding multitudes	6:32–44; 8:1–10	14:13–21	9:10–17	6:1–13
Resuscitation of dead				
Daughter of Jairus	5:35–43	9:18–27	8:49–56	—
Lazarus	—	—	—	11:1–46
Return to Nazareth	6:1–6	13:54–58	4:16–30	—
Assault on Temple	11:15–19	21:12–17	19:45–48	2:13–27
Prediction of Jerusalem's fall	13	24–25	21	—
Crucifixion	15:21–47	27:32–66	23:26–54	19:17–42
Empty tomb	16:1–8	28:1–8	24:1–9	20:1–3
Post resurrection appearances				
In Galilee	—	28:16–20	—	21:1–19
In Jerusalem	—	28:9–10	24:13–53	20:10–29

subsequent impact among non-Jews. Composing Luke-Acts as a literary unit, the author then portrays Jesus' ministry as anticipating the missionary activities of the later church, a literary agenda that helps to explain the way in which he revises the traditions of Jesus' return to Nazareth to make it a foreshadowing of the church's Gentile mission. In Mark's Gospel, which scholars believe was one of Luke's principal sources, Jesus revisits his hometown, where his former neighbors show so little respect that their lack of trust renders him *unable* to perform the kind of miraculous works he had achieved elsewhere among strangers (Mark 6:1–6). Luke shifts this incident from the middle of Jesus' ministry, where both Mark and Matthew place it, to the beginning, omitting any suggestion that his protagonist's powers were limited and then expanding the story to include an Old Testament reference to Israelite prophets who performed miracles for non-Jews. When the Lukan Jesus states that both Elijah and Elisha healed Gentiles rather than native Israelites, it rouses the Nazareans to murderous fury. Their attempt to kill Jesus—an element found only in Luke's version of the Nazareth episode—serves to foreshadow Jesus' later rejection and death in Jerusalem (Luke 4:16–20; compare Matt. 13:52–58). Luke's account also functions to anticipate a major theme in Acts, that Gentiles, even more than Jews, will benefit from the Christian "good news."

Despite their intermittent differences—most resulting from an individual Evangelist's characteristic themes and particular theology about Jesus—the three Synoptic Gospels agree fully on the form and method of Jesus' teaching. According to both Mark and Matthew, Jesus consistently taught in figurative language: "He never spoke to them [the public] except in parables" (Mark 4:34; Matt. 13:34–35). The signature style of Jesus' teaching, a **parable** (Greek, *parabole,* meaning a "placing beside" or "a comparison") usually takes the form of a brief fictional narrative, typically comparing some familiar object or practice to the dawning kingdom of God. In the Synoptic accounts, Jesus commonly likens God's kingdom to a germinating mustard seed, the unexpected discovery of a valuable pearl, or a woman kneading bread. Otherwise, Jesus typically debates points of the Mosaic Torah or delivers **aphorisms,** terse, quotable statements that his audience will remember, such as "The Sabbath was made for the sake of man and not man for the Sabbath" (Mark 2:27) or "It is easier for a camel to pass through the eye of a needle than for a rich man to enter the kingdom of God" (Mark 10:35). In the Synoptic Gospels, Jesus keeps his speeches short, dispensing memorable one-liners or creating unexpected reversals of social/ethical conventions in vivid parables, such as those evoking a father's love for his disobedient son, a religious outsider (a Samaritan) caring for a helpless Jew, and a "sinful" tax collector who prays better than a righteous Pharisee.

By contrast, John's Gospel contains not a single parable of the Synoptic kind, using homely metaphors drawn from rural peasant life. Instead, the Johannine Jesus delivers long, philosophical discourses, typically about his divine nature, his origin from and imminent return to heaven, and his special relationship to the Father (see Boxes 10.3 and 10.4). Rather than debate Pharisees or other opponents about Mosaic principles or announce the arrival of God's kingdom, John's Jesus dwells largely on his personal divinity and his significance to believers as the "way," "truth," and "life." Only in John does Jesus descend from heaven to "become flesh" (the divine Word incarnate), and only in John do the crowds threaten to stone him for claiming "equality" with God (John 8:56–59). Approximately 90 percent of John's material has no parallel in the Synoptic accounts. John's insistence on Jesus as a divinity walking the earth in human form—and the almost total absence of topics that characterize Jesus' Synoptic message—cause scholars to doubt the Fourth Gospel's historical value. In terms of the Synoptic Gospels and their sources—the early Markan tradition, a hypothetical collection of Jesus' sayings, and special material peculiar respectively to Matthew or Luke—John is outvoted four to one (see the discussions of

BOX 6.2 From Oral *Kerygma* to Written Gospel: Hypothetical Stages in the Gospels' Historical Development

New Testament scholars employ a variety of critical methods to discover the processes by which originally oral traditions about Jesus gradually evolved into written form. Historical and literary analysis of the Gospels suggests that they developed over a relatively long period (c. 30–100 CE), undergoing several discrete stages of growth. The following list provides a hypothetical reconstruction of events and movements leading to the Gospels' creation.

DATE	EVENT OR DEVELOPMENT

I. Period of Exclusively Oral Traditions

30 CE	Oral preaching by Jesus in Galilee, Samaria, and Judea
30–33 CE	Crucifixion
30–50 CE	Oral preaching about Jesus by Aramaic-speaking disciples in Galilee, Samaria, Judea, and neighboring regions; formation of the first Christian community at Jerusalem, led by Peter, John, and James; formation of additional Aramaic-speaking communities throughout Palestine; development of a second major Christian center at Antioch in Syria
40–60 CE	Missionary tours of Paul and associates; establishment of new, larger, Gentile, Greek-speaking churches in Asia Minor, Greece, and Italy

II. Period of Earliest Written Documents

50–70 CE	Oldest surviving Christian documents (Paul's letters to Gentile congregations) composed; collection of Jesus' sayings, in Greek (the Q document), compiled; possible collection of Jesus' miraculous works, the Signs Gospel (later incorporated into the Gospel of John); possible first edition of the Gospel of Thomas (like Q, a sayings Gospel)

III. The Jewish Revolt Against Rome and the Appearance of the First Canonical Gospel

66 CE	Outbreak of the Jewish War
66–70 CE	Mark's "wartime" Gospel composed, relating Jesus' suffering to that of his persecuted followers
70 CE	Roman destruction of Jerusalem, the Temple, and the original Christian center

IV. Production of New, Enlarged Editions of Mark

80–90 CE	Composition of Matthew and Luke, who use Mark and Q as their primary sources (plus their individual special sources, respectively M and L)

V. Production of New Gospels Promoting an Independent (Non-Synoptic) Tradition

90–100 CE	Composition of the Gospel of John, perhaps incorporating the older Signs Gospel; second edition of the Gospel of Thomas, incorporating the older Thomas sayings collection

Gospel sources in Chapters 8, 9, and 10). Because both the Synoptic Gospels and John cannot be right about the form and content of Jesus' teaching, scholars generally focus on the Synoptic accounts in their search for the historical Jesus, regarding John as essentially a theological meditation on Jesus' life (see Chapter 11).

From Oral Preaching to Written Gospel

The Oral Period Luke's reference to the fact that he used both oral and written sources (Luke 4:1–4) encourages scholars to trace several distinct stages of the Gospels' development over time (see Box 6.2). The first stage was entirely oral, represented initially by Jesus' spoken teachings and then by his earliest followers' preaching about him. For approximately forty years—between the time of the Crucifixion (c. 30 or 33 CE)—and the appearance of Mark's Gospel (c. 66–70 CE)—the Christian *kerygma*—the proclamation about Jesus—was entirely by word of mouth. Paul's letters were composed during this period (c. 50–62 CE), but Paul rarely mentions events in Jesus' life or quotes his teachings. (For exceptions, see Jesus' words at the Last Supper [1 Cor. 11:23–26] and the received tradition about Jesus' post resurrection appearances [1 Cor. 15:3–7].)

The oral proclamation began in Judea, Galilee, and adjoining regions where Aramaic was spoken. When Christian missionaries carried their message into Greek-speaking territories, however, important changes had to be made. Not only were Jesus' Aramaic sayings necessarily translated into *koinē* (common Greek), but they had to be explained, reinterpreted, and applied to urban conditions very different from those in rural Palestine where they originated. Busy merchants in crowded Hellenistic marketplaces might require an explanation of Jesus' parables, initially designed for poor villagers and peasants in an agricultural economy, that perhaps challenged missionaries' ingenuity. Similarly, Christian preachers themselves eventually needed reinterpretations of some teachings. Jesus' homely parable of the laborer sowing seeds ultimately was transformed into an allegory illustrating Christians' diverse experiences as preachers in the Hellenistic world, where they were sometimes welcomed, often rejected, and occasionally persecuted. (See Mark 4, with its elaborate application of the sower parable to conditions in the early church.)

As scholars have learned from studying the growth of oral traditions in different cultures around the globe, transmitting stories orally to new audiences inevitably produces variations in phrasing and emphasis as the speaker adapts the tale to different hearers and situations. Until a tradition is finally fixed in writing, it is characterized by extreme fluidity, changing with each fresh recitation. In the case of Jesus' sayings, which presumably were venerated even at the earliest stages of transmission, Christians probably made every effort to repeat them accurately. Even so, the Gospels show a wide range of variation in what appear to have been the same sayings. To cite only one example among many, in Mark, Jesus states that "he who is not against us is for us," whereas in Matthew he says the opposite: "He who is not with me is against me, and he who does not gather with me scatters" (Mark 9:40 and Matt. 12:30). To complicate the matter further, Luke preserves both forms of the sayings (Luke 7:50; 11:23). The degree of variation in some traditions is so great that the meanings become mutually exclusive, as in the strikingly different versions of the wedding feast parable, which appears in two canonical Gospels, Matthew (22:2–13) and Luke (14:16–23), as well as in the apocryphal Gospel of Thomas (saying 64). (See Box 9.5 for a detailed examination of the parable.)

Divergent oral renditions of Jesus' sayings and parables multiplied in widely separated geographical areas, including important Christian centers at Jerusalem, Antioch in Syria, Ephesus in Asia Minor, and Corinth in Greece. Each center undoubtedly cultivated distinct traditions closely associated with the earliest missionaries, teachers, and prophets in their respective communities. Given the multiplicity of variations that developed, it is difficult, if not impossible, to recover the original form of a given saying. Inheritors of a complex process of oral transmission, the Gospel writers compiled not necessarily what Jesus exactly said or did, but what the believing community collectively understood to be the tenor of his actions and sayings.

Different Approaches to Reading the Gospels

How we approach studying the Gospels depends largely on our preconceptions about their nature and the kind of religious authority they embody. Attitudes toward the Gospels range from uncritical acceptance of every statement at face value to intense skepticism that denies the works any historical credibility. Between these two extremes lie a great variety of viewpoints, each with its characteristic assumptions—ideas or beliefs that one takes for granted, assuming them to be true without first carefully examining their validity. These sometimes unconscious assumptions can profoundly influence the reader's understanding of the Gospel text, predetermining its meaning.

In studying the Gospels systematically, it is helpful to clear away some common misconceptions that tend to inhibit thinking logically about them. One typical assumption is that, because the New Testament writings are sacred literature, revered by millions as containing divine revelation, they must be factually accurate in every respect. This view equates historical accuracy with religious truth and is commonly expressed in an either-or formula: Either the Gospels derive from God, and are therefore literally true, or they are of human origin and so are false. Insisting that Scripture must be inerrant—entirely free from all error—if it is to have any real value, this approach creates a false dilemma, forcing people to choose unnecessarily between two extremes. This black-and-white fallacy, characteristic of some fundamentalist beliefs, is not supported by the Gospels, none of which claim to be error-free.

A religious movement that began early in the twentieth century among conservative Protestants, chiefly in North America, **fundamentalism** arose partly in response to post-Enlightenment scientific rationalism, which was regarded as undermining the certainties of Christianity. Asserting that every biblical passage, whether involving science, history, or theology, is inerrant, fundamentalists assume that, in the act of writing Scripture, biblical authors transcended the ordinary limitations of time, place, and culture to produce absolutely infallible documents.

Most scholars, whether Catholic or Protestant, do not accept fundamentalism's "all or nothing" approach, which tends to make enemies of faith and intellect. Rather than fearing or ignoring the discoveries of science and other academic disciplines, they think it more productive to use a variety of critical methodologies in studying biblical texts. This author believes that the Gospels are best served when examined in the context of the Greek-speaking Jewish community that produced them. This historical-critical approach assumes that, the more we know about the first-century Jewish and Hellenistic language, literary forms, social customs, philosophical ideas, and religious beliefs, the better equipped we are to understand the New Testament message.

In this regard, Jesus' preferred mode of teaching—the parable—offers a helpful way to understand how religious discourse functions. The meaning or spiritual force of a parable does not depend upon its literal truth. When Jesus tells of a Samaritan traveler befriending a man who had been beaten and left for dead or of a father who cherishes his sinful son as much as he loves his righteous child, it does not matter that the characters in the parable are entirely fictional. Expressing his ideas in short stories, metaphors, and other figures of speech, Jesus conveys insights about human relationships—including a message that illustrates the practice of unconditional love—that do not need to be historically factual to be religiously and ethically "true." The Gospel narratives in which Jesus' parables are embedded at times may function in a similar manner, reporting stories intended to illuminate Jesus' unique value instead of slavishly reproducing the events of a limited historical moment.

The Gospels and Modern Scholarship

As students of the New Testament, we benefit enormously from more than two centuries of Western *biblical criticism,* which has illuminated much about the Jewish environment in which Jesus lived, the Greco-Roman society in which his followers brought their message to non-Jews, and the process by which oral preaching about Jesus eventually took written form in the Gospels. As many readers have discovered, using the tools of biblical criticism to understand more clearly the nature and purpose of the early Christian writings is an empowering experience. In analyzing the Gospels rationally, we also heed Jesus' version of the Hebrew Bible's "greatest commandment": to "love the Lord your God with . . . all your *mind*" (Mark 12:30, emphasis added). To Deuteronomy's demand that the Israelites must loyally adhere to Yahweh with all their "heart and soul and strength" (Deut. 6:4-5), Jesus adds the concept of the human intellect, the mental capacity to discern probabilities and to evaluate evidence (see Chapter 1). Because logical reasoning is indispensable in comprehending the Gospels' historical and religious significance, we will apply scholarly techniques of rational inquiry as we investigate the individual accounts of Jesus' life, allowing each Gospel writer to express his particular vision of Jesus' message and meaning.

Historical Criticism

Like much recent New Testament commentary, this book approaches the Gospels employing a combination of critical methods to explain both the historical process by which they were created and the end product of that evolution, the literary texts themselves. **Historical criticism** involves the analysis of documents that purport to record historical events, investigating the historical setting in which the texts originated. Using standards of evidence analogous to those in the social sciences, historical critics test a given account against several criteria, including such standards as factual accuracy, historical plausibility, and authorial presuppositions. Historians ask such questions as: Is this event likely to have occurred in the way the author presents it? Does it accord with what we already know about this particular historical situation? What is the writer's bias or personal agenda, and how does it affect what he reports? Historical critics investigate such issues as a document's authorship, its date and place of composition, the intended audience, and the social and cultural circumstances that produced it.

The Gospels present almost insurmountable challenges for historical critics. Because the Gospel authors believed in Jesus' divinity—that he was qualitatively different from every other character in history—their presentation is colored by their faith. In the Gospels, Jesus wins every argument, triumphs over his opponents in every debate, possesses unimpeachable authority, and even defies the laws of nature by calming a storm and feeding thousands with a few fish (see Figure 6.1). Like

FIGURE 6.1 Typical example of early Christian art in the catacombs of Rome. This wall painting shows communicants celebrating the Eucharist, or communal meal. The fish and the baskets recall Jesus' twin miracles of feeding 4,000 and 5,000 in Mark's Gospel.

many of their Hellenistic contemporaries, the Evangelists present a world populated by supernatural beings, assigning speaking roles to both angels and devils. Jesus is shown on various occasions holding conversations with Satan or his "legion" of demons, malignant spirits who are identified as the unseen cause of disease and madness. Although many people in antiquity uncritically accepted the existence of such entities, they are not part of the universe as modern science defines it and as most people now experience the world in their daily lives.

Scholarly recognition that the Evangelists embraced a worldview significantly different from our own and that their concerns were more theological than biographical means that historians must approach the Gospels carefully, judiciously distinguishing between recoverable historical fact and religious claims that lie beyond the reach of historical investigation. Because the historian's sphere is necessarily restricted to the material realm, which operates according to widely agreed-upon laws of probability, he or she cannot evaluate nonmaterial phenomena, reported events that are not repeatable in the laboratory or otherwise open to scientific scrutiny. Using archaeological evidence, such as an inscription identifying Pontius Pilate as governor of Judea for the years equivalent to 26–36 CE, historians can confirm that Pilate represented Rome during Jesus' lifetime. They cannot confirm, however, that the man whom Pilate crucified overcame death and rose from the grave.

For many, however, it is precisely these unrepeatable manifestations of supernatural power that give the Gospels their incomparable value as guarantors of purpose and meaning in human life. The Evangelists' assertions that Jesus is the Son of God and that he presently reigns in heaven are, for countless believers, incontrovertible facts. However, such claims of faith, which posit a spiritual dimension of existence outside the physical world, are inaccessible to historical verification.

Although they can neither confirm nor deny the historicity of Jesus' resurrection, historians can investigate the religious movement led by disciples who believed so completely in it that they were ready to die for their beliefs. Historical criticism also helps us understand the Evangelists' presentation of supernatural themes by studying what people in Hellenistic society commonly accepted as true, including magic, sorcery, and witchcraft. Discovering what many Palestinian Jews thought about miracles, divine interventions in history, and the prevalence of demonic possession during the first century CE enables us to see why such supernaturalism pervades the Gospel accounts (see Chapter 7).

In the following discussion, we will examine the problems facing modern scholars as they attempt to discover the Gospels' complex interrelationship and the evolutionary development the Gospels underwent before reaching their present form. Awareness of the historical, social, theological, and literary forces at work in producing the Gospel texts will help us to understand the reasons for both their similarities and their differences.

Form Criticism

Recognizing that originally Palestinian oral traditions about Jesus had been modified to accommodate a new, ethnically and religiously diverse Gentile audience, early twentieth-century German scholars began to emphasize the implications of such adaptations. The critical method that attempts to identify the oldest oral form underlying the Gospels' written texts is called **form criticism.** Form critics operated on the theory that the Gospels are made up of many individual units—brief narrative episodes, discrete conflict stories, pronouncements, parables, and sayings—that presumably circulated orally and independently of one another before the Gospel authors gathered them together and placed these units in a narrative context.

Mark's Gospel, for instance, seems to consist of a string of relatively brief incidents, anecdotes, and sayings that are very loosely connected to one another. The individual units, such as the accounts of Jesus exorcizing demons or performing miraculous cures, are generally brief, self-contained narrative episodes that have clear-cut beginnings and endings and that can stand alone. During the oral period, these units were thought to be autonomous, existing free of a narrative framework. Jesus' pithy statements comparing God's kingdom to a mustard seed or a priceless pearl, for example, do not depend on the larger Gospel context to convey their message. Such detachable units are called **pericopes.** Derived from the Greek *peri* (about) and *koptein* (to cut), the term denotes the individual, orally transmitted building blocks from which the longer Gospel account was presumably constructed.

The form critic searches for the *Sitz im Leben,* the probable "life-setting" or social circumstances from which stories about Jesus originated and that early followers orally transmitted. The first Christians spoke about Jesus in many different situations and for many different purposes—preaching to fellow Jews, defending their beliefs to Greek or Roman officials, instructing new converts, settling disputes among themselves, and conducting worship services. By establishing the probable prewritten form of a particular saying or incident, an individual pericope, the form critic hoped to demonstrate how the different Gospel writers edited these previously free-floating units to express their respective views about Jesus.

In recent decades, some scholars have questioned the form-critical assumption that Mark, regarded as the earliest Gospel, was stitched together of previously isolated oral units, individual episodes illustrating Jesus' words and deeds. These scholars point to relevant studies in folklore, oral history, and oral literature showing that oral traditions about a hero figure commonly coalesce into an extended oral narrative. Like other storytellers in the Greco-Roman world, early Christians probably gave public performances narrating tales about the healer-prophet from Galilee, stories that rapidly grew and developed by absorbing additional oral traditions at each recitation.

According to this view, Mark inherited not merely a series of fragmented anecdotes and sayings but a well-developed oral story about Jesus' public ministry that he, in turn, orally transformed into his distinctive Gospel. As many scholars have observed, Mark's Gospel shows many signs of oral composition and probably continued to be recited orally at Christian gatherings both before and after it was committed to writing about 66–70 CE.

Literary Analysis of the Gospels

Possessing the complete written texts of five Gospels (including the apocryphal Thomas), scholars can compare these documents using the tools of **literary criticism.** Rather than analyzing a text to determine its historical background and oral or written sources, literary critics study the finished product, a skill that many careful students have already acquired. Every experienced reader practices literary criticism to some extent, studying a text not only to gain information but also to detect its principal concerns and themes. Like all literary narratives, the Gospel stories have the basic elements of setting, character, dialogue, plot, style, and rhetorical techniques, such as the use of irony. Readers automatically assimilate clues—characteristic words, images, and repeated phrases—that indicate how the author intends them to react toward a character's particular statements or behavior.

Redaction Criticism

In recent decades, scholars have increasingly focused on the role of the individual Gospel writer in editing, revising, and reshaping the oral and written traditions he inherited. A form of literary analysis, **redaction criticism** (from the German *Redaktions-geschichte*) emphasizes the redactor's (author-editor's) importance in assembling, rearranging, and reinterpreting his sources. Matthew and Luke do not slavishly follow their primary sources—Mark and a hypothetical collection of Jesus' sayings—but freely adapt them to express their individual theological viewpoints. The recognition that the Gospel writers were not mere compilers of older material but active interpreters of it, creatively modifying traditions to make a theological point, deepens our understanding of differences in the three Synoptic accounts. By scrutinizing the way Matthew and Luke edit their sources and the changes they make in rendering the same saying or parable, scholars can discover their particular theological orientation. When Matthew or Luke revise Mark or give a different version of a shared saying, they invariably do it for theological reasons.

As readers become familiar with an Evangelist's distinctive views, they will eventually be able to explain why Matthew's rendition of the wedding feast parable, for example, differs from that of Luke or Thomas. In each case, the author edits the parable to fit his religious perspective (see Box 9.5). At crucial moments in his narrative, such as Jesus' crucifixion, each Evangelist emphasizes his particular understanding of the event by ascribing different last words to Jesus. Whereas Mark and Matthew agree that the dying Jesus utters a single despairing cry, the other two Gospel authors present final statements that reflect a totally different mood and meaning, with Luke and John highlighting their hero's serene confidence and control of the situation (see Box 10.7). In their distinctive death scenes, the four authors ascribe to Jesus a climactic utterance consistent with the distinctive theological picture of Jesus depicted throughout their respective Gospels.

Narrative Criticism

A method of literary interpretation that is increasingly applied to studying the Gospels, **narrative criticism** emphasizes such factors as the manner in which a story is constructed, the point of view from which it is told, the author's

implied attitude toward his subject or characters, and even the use of geographical settings to convey authorial intent. The Gospel authors do not tell their stories in the first person, nor do they present themselves as eyewitnesses to the incidents they describe. Instead of introducing themselves to readers and citing their personal credentials as historians of Christian origins, the Gospel writers all assume the role of an anonymous but omniscient narrator— fully but inexplicably aware of everything that occurs. They presume to know Jesus' private thoughts, his opponents' secret motives, and even words spoken when there are no witnesses present to overhear, as when Jesus prays alone in Gethsemane while all his disciples sleep (Mark 14). The Gospel authors almost never intrude directly into their stories—the chief exception being the narrator of John's Gospel in his description of the Crucifixion and his statement of authorial purpose (John 20–21). The effect of the omniscient storyteller, who reports the speeches of heavenly voices, exorcized demons, and angelic visitors in exactly the same way that he records ordinary human conversations, is to impress on readers the narrator's comprehensive authority.

Gospel authors also use geographical locations to express value judgments. In Mark's Gospel, the author presents Jesus' career in terms of two opposing territories. In the first half of Mark's story, Jesus recruits disciples and enjoys considerable success in his native Galilee, the largely rural area of peasant farmers north of Samaria and Judea. Mark sets the final part of his Gospel in Jerusalem, where his hero performs no miracles and is betrayed, tried for treason, and crucified. When a tiny group of women find Jesus' tomb empty on the first Easter morning, Mark has an angel tell them *not* to look for their risen Lord there—in Jerusalem—but to look back "in Galilee."

Mark's negative attitude toward Jerusalem (and its original church?) contrasts with Luke's positive view of the Jewish capital. In Luke's account, all of Jesus' post resurrection appearances take place in or around Jerusalem. Luke reports that Jesus explicitly commands his followers to *remain* in Jerusalem and wait for an outpouring of the Spirit. He also devotes the first part of Acts, the sequel to his Gospel, to describing the flowering of the Jerusalem community, which he presents as the Spirit-guided nucleus of Christianity's expansion into the larger world (Acts 1:8). Readers influenced by Mark are likely to differ significantly from Luke's readers in their opinions of Jerusalem's desirability or its importance in the Christian scheme of things.

In his presentation of Jesus' opponents—scribes (scholars) and Pharisees—Luke guides readers to a relatively sympathetic attitude toward Jews rejecting the Christian message. The Lukan author describes those who played a part in instigating Jesus' execution as more to be pitied than condemned, picturing them as acting in ignorance. In contrast, Matthew portrays Jesus' religious opponents as vicious hypocrites, threatening them with the fires of **Gehenna,** a symbol of posthumous torment (Matt. 23). Unfortunately for the history of relations between Judaism and Christianity, Matthew has thus far proven the more persuasive narrator, his negative picture of Jewish leaders helping to fuel two millennia of Christian persecution of Jews.

Synoptic Problem

If readers, in quick succession, scan through the contents of all three Synoptic Gospels, they may wonder why Matthew, Mark, and Luke cover so much of the same material, and generally in the same sequence of events (see Box 6.3 for the Gospels' major characters). Why are these three accounts so similar when John's example shows that Jesus' life could be portrayed in such different fashion? Scholars' efforts to unravel the complex interconnections among the three Synoptics, to account for their duplications and repetitions—as well as for material

that appears in both Matthew and Luke entirely absent from Mark—is called the Problem. **Source criticism,** the investigation of a writer's use of various sources, is remarkably useful in solving the puzzle.

In carefully analyzing the three Synoptic accounts, scholars recognize a number of shared characteristics that suggest a solution. First, in sharp contrast to John, Mark, Matthew, and Luke tell basically the same story, narrating Jesus' ministry in such similar ways that their broad agreement implies a literary interconnection. One of the Synoptic writers must have used at least one of the other Gospels as a source. The shared material, which includes both the same general sequence of events and some teaching, is called the *triple tradition*. In addition, Matthew and Luke include a large quantity of Jesus' teaching that does not appear in Mark. Known as the *double tradition*, this material—absent in Mark but appearing in both Matthew and Luke—represents some of Jesus' best-known sayings, such as the Lord's Prayer, the golden rule, and the Beatitudes, blessings that he pronounces on the poor, the meek, and the peaceable. In many cases there is almost a word-for-word agreement on the passages incorporated into both Matthew and Luke but which occur nowhere in Mark.

In examining the narrative order in the Synoptic triple tradition, scholars also noticed that either Matthew or Luke may sometimes deviate from Mark's arrangement of events, but almost never do they differ from Mark in the same place and in the same way. In general, when Matthew departs from the Markan sequence, Luke does not; when Luke disagrees with Mark, Matthew does not. This pattern indicates that Mark is the determining factor in shaping the other two Synoptic writers' version of Jesus' story, that his account is the basis for the other two.

Another factor suggesting that Mark is a primary source for Matthew and Luke, rather than an abbreviation of them, is the relative amount of space each Evangelist devotes to recounting episodes that the three Gospels have in common. If Mark wished to produce a more concise account of Jesus' life by abridging Matthew and Luke, as a small minority of scholars propose, his version of events that all three include should be the shortest, a brief summary of the other two. However, the opposite is true. In almost every case, Mark's description of a specific incident is longer than the parallel version in Matthew or Luke. Whereas Mark takes ten verses to narrate Jesus' cure of the woman afflicted with a chronic hemorrhage (Mark 5:25–34), Matthew tells the same story in only three verses (Matt. 9:20–23). Similarly, Matthew reports the raising of Jairus's daughter in six verses (Matt. 9:18–19, 23–26), while Mark's account is almost twice as long (Mark 5:22–24, 35–43). In this and numerous other instances, Matthew appears to have abridged Mark rather than the other way around.

How, then, can we account for passages in Matthew and Luke that give an expanded narration of events merely alluded to in Mark, such as Jesus' confrontation with Satan in the wilderness? Mark mentions briefly that the devil tempted Jesus but provides no details (Mark 1:12–13). By contrast, Matthew and Luke offer elaborate dramatizations of Jesus' resisting the tempter, using almost identical language (Matt. 4:1–11; Luke 4:1–13). Most scholars agree that, although Matthew and Luke draw on Mark for a shared narrative sequence, they also incorporate other sources into their larger Gospels.

After realizing that Mark was the source for the chronological framework in Matthew and Luke, scholars also identified a second major source to account for the extensive teaching material that does not appear in Mark but that Matthew and Luke share. According to this theory, Matthew and Luke not only used Mark but also partly incorporated a written collection of Jesus' sayings, including many of his parables. This hypothetical collection is called the **Q** document (from *Quelle,* the German word for "source") (see Figure 6.2).

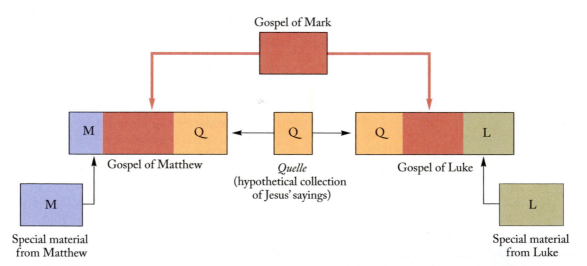

FIGURE 6.2 The two-document theory of the literary relationship of the three Synoptic Gospels. Note that this theory takes Mark's Gospel as a major source for Matthew and Luke. In addition, both Matthew and Luke incorporate teaching material from Q (*Quelle,* a hypothetical collection of Jesus' sayings). Matthew also uses special material unique to his Gospel, here designated M; Luke similarly includes material found only in his account, here labeled L.

The Q (Source) Document

Most scholars now agree that Matthew and Luke employed two principal sources in composing their Gospels, Mark and Q. Although Q does not survive as a separate document—a potential weakness in the **two-document theory**—its contents can be reconstructed from passages that both Matthew and Luke include but that are absent in Mark. According to this view, at a relatively early date Christians began collecting Jesus' remembered sayings, eventually compiling them in written form between about 50 and 70 CE to produce the Q document.

The Q passages—non-Markan material Matthew and Luke have in common—total more than 200 verses and contain some of Jesus' most memorable teachings, including much of Matthew's Sermon on the Mount (Matt. 5–7) and Luke's parallel Sermon on the Plain (Luke 6). (See Box 6.3 for a sampling of the collection's inferred contents.) An increasing number of scholars ascribe enormous importance to Q, for this Sayings Gospel, at least in its first edition, may preserve one of the earliest forms of Christianity. It seems to have been written in Greek and assembled by a community of itinerant preachers living in Galilee or western Syria who regarded Jesus as both prophet and wisdom teacher. Containing virtually no narrative, Q presents Jesus as one "greater than Solomon" (the traditional founder of Israel's wisdom school) who is the last in a long line of God's prophets and sages. Q apparently included no theology interpreting Jesus' death as a saving act, focusing almost exclusively on the living man's ethical teachings, parables, and spiritual insights. Before being assimilated into Matthew and Luke, Q was apparently a Gospel in its own right, providing the first written witness to Jesus' primary message. (See Robert Miller and John Verbin et al. in "Recommended Reading.")

Besides integrating sayings from Q into Mark's narrative framework, Matthew and Luke also incorporated sources (perhaps from oral tradition) unique to their respective Gospels. Scholars designate Matthew's special material with the abbreviation **M,** which includes his genealogy of Joseph, Jesus' legal father; his distinctive birth story; the dream of Pilate's wife; a mysterious resuscitation of Jerusalem "saints"; and an Easter morning earthquake (see Boxes 8.3 and 8.4). Luke's individual material, known as **L,** includes some of Jesus' most famous parables, such as the prodigal son, the good Samaritan, and Lazarus and the rich man (see Boxes 9.2 and 9.3).

The Griesbach Theory Although most scholars agree that the two-source theory most satisfactorily explains the literary relationship of the Synoptic Gospels, a small minority deny Markan priority. According to this view, Mark is a conflation (blending together) of the other two Synoptics. Known as the **Griesbach theory,** after J. J. Griesbach (1745–1812), who first published this solution to the Synoptic Problem, this hypothesis has been revived by several contemporary scholars, notably William Farmer. These dissenting scholars emphasize the fact that a few short passages in the triple tradition (material present in all three Synoptics) show Matthew and Luke agreeing *against* Mark. Proponents of the two-source theory, however, argue that such "minor agreements" merely suggest that both Mark and Q had some limited material in common, that in a few instances they overlapped. Other defenders of the majority theory suggest that the minor agreements are the result of early scribal attempts to make the Synoptic texts more consistent, "harmonizing" the verbal differences (see Box 2.1). (For a discussion of deliberate scribal changes to the ancient Greek manuscripts, including scribal attempts to harmonize the Evangelists, see Ehrman in "Recommended Reading.")

More recently, several scholars have emphasized the difficulties inherent in the Q theory, questioning that Q ever existed. While accepting that Mark was the first Gospel written, Mark Goodacre, E. P. Sandars, and other

BOX 6.3 The Probable Contents of Q

Although we lack absolute proof that Q, a hypothetical collection of Jesus' sayings, ever existed, many scholars believe that it is possible to reconstruct its contents. By carefully isolating teaching material contained in both Luke and Matthew but absent from Mark, scholars have compiled a list of more than 200 verses they believe were originally part of Q. These passages include some of Jesus' most characteristic teachings, including the Beatitudes, his command to love one's enemies, his commissioning of the disciples, and his renunciation of material possessions.

Because Luke seems to have preserved Q's original order better than Matthew, Q sayings are customarily cited by Lukan chapter and verse. Although in many cases the two Gospel writers show an almost verbatim agreement on Q's wording, in places where they disagree, scholars can typically reconstruct the original phrasing by taking the two Evangelists' editorializing tendencies into account. The saying about having a rafter lodged in one's eye (Luke 6:41–42/Matt. 7:3–5), for example, reveals Luke and Matthew in total agreement. In the Beatitudes, however, Matthew appears to modify Jesus' original commendations of the literally poor and hungry, making them "poor in spirit" and hungry for "justice" or "righteousness," a characteristic Matthean term.

Because it contains little narrative and few references to Jesus' martyrdom, Q appears to have originated in a community that remembered Jesus primarily as a wisdom teacher and prophet whose death resembled those of Israel's earlier prophets. Mark, however, made Jesus' death of paramount importance, God's means of redeeming humanity. By combining Q's wisdom teachings with Mark's theology of the cross, Matthew and Luke demonstrated that the two ways of regarding Jesus' significance were not necessarily mutually exclusive.

The following summary of some representative Q material lists parallel verses in Luke and Matthew.

Q MATERIAL	LUKE	MATTHEW
The ministry of John the Baptist	3:7–9, 16–17	3:1–17
The testing of Jesus by Satan	4:1–13	4:1–11
The Beatitudes	6:20–26	5:3–12
The admonition to love one's enemies and abide by the golden rule	6:27–36	5:44–48; 7:12
The healing of a Roman officer's slave	7:1–10	8:5–10, 13
The differences between Jesus and John	7:31–35	11:16–19
The Lord's Prayer	11:2–4	6:9–13
The sign of Jonah	11:16, 29–32	12:38–42
The avoidance of anxieties and reliance on God	12:22–31	6:25–33
The great feast	14:16–24	22:1–10
The rejection of family ties	14:26–27	10:37–39
The parable of invested money	19:12–26	25:14–30

For a complete reconstruction of Q's probable contents, see "The Sayings Gospel Q," in Robert J. Miller, ed., *The Complete Gospels,* 4th ed. (Salem, OR: Polebridge Press, 2010).

critics have raised serious issues about the hypothetical Q. Despite these objections, the scholarly majority still regards the two-source hypothesis as the most adequate explanation of both the general similarities and the individual differences in the Synoptic Gospels. (For arguments opposing the majority agreement, see works by Farmer, Goodacre, and Sandars and Davies in "Recommended Reading.")

Differences Between the Three Synoptic Gospels and the Gospel of John

Contemporary scholarship has produced a vast body of work on the Gospels, analyzing their contents, probable mode of composition, and the degree to which they represent the historical Jesus accurately. If all four Gospels fully agreed on the sequence of events in Jesus' life and on the precise nature and manner of his teaching, scholars might find their work much easier. Comparative study of the Gospels, however, reveals inconsistencies and problems of historical plausibility that require careful attention. In reading the Gospels vertically (perusing each individually from top to bottom, beginning to end), most people will probably not notice many of the differences they contain (review Box 6.1). Almost everyone recognizes a few major discrepancies—that John places Jesus' assault on the Temple's moneychangers at the beginning of his ministry, whereas the Synoptic Gospels place it at the end—but few readers initially detect the significant differences in the way that Matthew and Luke present some of the stories they share, such as Jesus' return to his hometown, Nazareth. When the Gospels are read horizontally, with the reader consecutively studying all three versions of the Nazareth episode, however, it becomes clear that each Synoptic writer approaches the incident not as an objective reporter of factual events but as an interpreter of its religious or thematic significance. In the Gospel of Mark, which scholars believe is the earliest version, the author emphasizes that Jesus' former neighbors fail to value Jesus, a lack of trust that renders him unable to perform the kind of miraculous works he had accomplished elsewhere (Mark 6:1–6). Matthew tells the Nazareth story somewhat differently, avoiding any implication that Jesus may have had limited powers and stating merely that Jesus "did not work many miracles there" (Matt. 13:54–58; see Box 8.2 for examples of specific differences between Mark's and Matthew's respective accounts of the same tradition).

Four Distinctive Portraits of Jesus

The fact that the early Christian community generally did not promote a single, uniform edition of Jesus' life or adopt one "official" version free of seeming contradictions is significant. Instead of an "authorized biography," the church accepted the four canonical Gospels, perhaps recognizing that different Christian groups scattered throughout the Roman Empire had already adopted one or more different Gospels as foundation documents of their particular communities. Although individual churches, such as Antioch where Matthew may have been written, would not relinquish their Evangelist's work in favor of another, by the late second century CE many seem to have accepted two or three of the Synoptic accounts. John, which some early church leaders condemned as a Gnostic fabrication, took longer to be accepted by the church at large. Its position as the Fourth Gospel may reflect its relatively late inclusion in the canon. (Box 6.4 summarizes the extensive cast of characters appearing in the Gospels—many shared but some unique.)

As Jesus elicited widely different responses during his lifetime, so he inspired the Evangelists to represent him in significantly different guises, ranging from the Galilean carpenter-prophet in Mark to the incarnate heavenly Word of God in John. This composite portrait, with all its attendant problems and unanswered questions, is the one deemed appropriate to reflect early Christianity's diverse communities of faith.

BOX 6.4 **The Gospels' Cast of Characters**

Because the four Gospel writers present four distinctive ways of telling Jesus' story, they do not all include the same cast of characters. Although a few personages, such as John the Baptist, Peter, and Pontius Pilate, appear in all four accounts, the three New Testament lists of Jesus' twelve chief disciples differ significantly. John introduces a number of figures, such as Nicodemus and Lazarus, who are not mentioned in the Synoptics. The major players in each of the four narratives, along with representative passages in which they appear, are given here.

CHARACTERS	MARK	MATTHEW	LUKE	JOHN
Jesus' family				
Jesus' mother, Mary	3:20–21, 31–35; 6:3	1:18–25; 2:11, 21	1:26–56; 2:5–7, 16–19, 33–34, 48–51	2:2–5; 19:25–27
Jesus' putative father, Joseph	—	1:16, 18–25; 2:13–14	1:27; 2:4–5, 16, 48; 3:23	1:45; 6:42
Jesus' "brothers" (close kinsmen)	3:31–35; 6:3	13:55–56	—	7:1–9
John the Baptist				
Baptism of Jesus	1:4–11, 14	3:1–17	3:1–22	1:15–36
Comparison between John and Jesus	—	11:7–19	7:24–35	—
Execution by Herod Antipas	6:14–29	14:1–12	3:19–20; 9:7–9	—
Jesus' inner circle of disciples				
Simon Peter and Andrew (brothers)	1:16–18; 9:2–6	4:18; 17:1	9:28	—
Peter's confession	8:27–33	16:13–25	9:18–22	—
Peter's denial of Jesus	14:26–31, 66–72	26:33–35, 69–75	22:31–34, 54–61	18:15–18, 25–27
James and John, sons of Zebedee	1:19–20	4:21–22; 17:1	—	—
Wish to be first in the kingdom	10:35–45	20:20–28	22:24–27	—
Other disciples (in speaking roles)				
Andrew, Peter's brother	—	—	—	1:40–42, 44; 6:8–9
Philip, one of the Twelve	—	—	—	12:20–22
Thomas, one of the Twelve	—	—	—	20:24–28
The unidentified Beloved Disciple	—	—	—	13:23–26; 18:15–16; 19:26–27; 20:2–10; 21:7, 20–24
List of the Twelve	3:13–19	10:1–4	6:12–16	—

CHARACTERS	MARK	MATTHEW	LUKE	JOHN
Persons whom Jesus heals				
The Gerasene demoniac	5:1–20	8:28–34	8:26–39	—
Jairus and his daughter	5:22–24, 35–43	9:18–19, 23–26	8:40–42, 49–56	—
Woman with hemorrhages	5:25–34	9:20–22	8:43–48	—
Syrophoenician (Canaanite) woman	7:14–30	15:21–28	—	—
A man born blind	—	—	—	9:1–38
Lazarus, brother of Mary and Martha	—	—	—	11:1–44; 12:1–11
Women disciples or women whom Jesus befriends				
Galilean women who support Jesus	—	—	8:1–3	—
Woman who anoints Jesus	14:3–9	26:6–13	7:36–50	12:1–8
Samaritan woman	—	—	—	4:7–42
Women at the cross and/or tomb				
Mary of Magdala	15:40–41, 47; 16:1–8	27:55–56; 28:1–11	8:2; 23:49; 24:10–11	19:25; 20:1–10
Mary, mother of James and Joseph	15:40–41, 47; 16:1–8	27:55–56	24:10–11	—
Salome	15:40–41, 47; 16:1–8	27:56; 28:1	24:10–11	—
The sisters Mary and Martha	—	—	10:38–39	11:19–36, 39, 45; 12:1–8
Nicodemus	—	—	—	3:1–12; 7:50–52; 19:39
Figures in the Passion narrative				
Judas Iscariot	14:10–11, 43–46	26:14–16, 21–25, 47–50; 27:1–5	22:3–6, 47–48	13:21–30; 18:2–3
Caiaphas, the High Priest	14:53–64	26:57–66	22:54, 66–71	11:47–53; 18:13–14
Pontius Pilate, Roman prefect	15:1–15, 43–44	27:1, 11–26, 58	23:1–7, 11–25, 52	18:26–19:16, 19–22
Herod Antipas	—	—	23:6–12	—
Barabbas, the terrorist	15:6–15	27:15–26	23:18–25	18:38–40
The Roman centurion who praises Jesus	15:39	27:54	23:47	
Joseph of Arimathaea, who buries Jesus	15:42–46	27:57–60	23:50–54	19:38–42

Summary

This book allows each Gospel to speak for itself, respecting the integrity of the individual Evangelist. We will approach each Gospel as an independent work that embodies the distinctive thought of its particular author. Without trying to make the Gospels conform to ideas expressed in any other New Testament book, we will examine each Evangelist's account of Jesus' life on its own terms and in the context of its author's theological assumptions. By recognizing the distinctiveness of each Gospel account, we can also appreciate the rich diversity of New Testament Christianity, as well as its thematic unity—the unparalleled importance of God's actions through Jesus of Nazareth. In studying the Gospels, Paul's letters, and the other canonical writings, we benefit greatly from all the scholarly research and methodologies that help illuminate the historical origins, the literary development, and the theological insights contained in the twenty-seven documents that collectively became the standard-bearers of the Christian faith.

Questions for Review

1. Why do scholars think that the Gospel writers emphasized their understanding of Jesus' religious or theological meaning more than the basic historical facts of his life? For what purpose does the author of John's Gospel say that he composed his account?

2. How does the author of Luke's Gospel explain his purpose in writing? If he was not an eyewitness to events in Jesus life, on what oral and written sources does he depend? Why does he think it necessary to produce another Gospel when other accounts are already in existence?

3. Why are Matthew, Mark, and Luke called the Synoptic Gospels? Define *Synoptic* and explain its application to the first three Gospels.

4. According to the Synoptic accounts, what were Jesus' characteristic modes of teaching? Define the terms *parable* and *aphorism,* and give examples of each form.

5. Explain the relationship between the oral preaching (*kerygma*) of the first Christians and the later composition of written Gospels. What

does the gap of forty to sixty five years between the time of Jesus' death and the time of the canonical Gospels' composition suggest? Review some of the circumstances that may have caused early Christian communities to produce several different versions of Jesus' life and teachings.

6. Describe some of the scholarly methods used to study the Gospels. Define these scholarly terms, and explain how each functions in analyzing a document: historical criticism, source criticism, form criticism, literary criticism, and narrative criticism.

7. Define and explain the Synoptic Problem. What qualities of the first three Gospels cause scholars to raise this issue? In what ways do scholars believe that Matthew and Luke are related to Mark? Describe the two-document theory.

8. Explain scholars' reasons for postulating the existence of the hypothetical Q document. What kind of material did this presumed collection contain. What do the abbreviations M and L stand for?

9. Summarize the Griesbach theory. How does it differ from the two-document theory?

Question for Discussion and Reflection

1. Scholars recognize that the Gospel authors are not historians or biographers in the modern sense. As you read the Gospel accounts carefully, consider whether the writers are interested primarily in preserving historical facts about Jesus or in interpreting his life in religious terms. Relate the Evangelists' theological concerns to redaction criticism.

Terms and Concepts to Remember

aphorism	narrative criticism
form criticism	parable
fundamentalism	pericope
Gehenna	Q (*Quelle*)
Griesbach theory	document
historical criticism	redaction criticism
kerygma	source criticism
L	Synoptic Gospels
literary criticism	Synoptic Problem
M (Matthew's special sources)	two-document theory

Recommended Reading

Bauckham, Richard. *Jesus and the Eyewitnesses: The Gospels as Eyewitness Testimony*. Grand Rapids, Mich.: Eerdmans, 2006. Argues that the Gospel accounts are based on reliable eyewitness reports.

Boring, M. Eugene. "Gospel, Message." In K. D. Sakenfeld, ed., *The New Interpreter's Dictionary of the Bible,* Vol. 2, pp. 629–636. Nashville: Abingdon Press, 2007. A concise discussion of the Evangelists' principal themes.

Ehrman, Bart. *Misquoting Jesus: The Story Behind Who Changed the Bible and Why*. San Francisco: Harper San Francisco, 2005. Illustrates presumably deliberate scribal changes to the Gospels.

Funk, Robert W., ed. *New Gospel Parallels*, Vol. 1, *The Synoptic Gospels*, Vol. 2, *John and the Other Gospels*. Philadelphia: Fortress Press, 1985. The most valuable scholarly tool for comparing the Gospel texts.

Green, Joel B.; Brown, J. K.; and Perrin, Nicholas, eds. *Dictionary of Jesus and the Gospels*, 2nd ed. Downers Grove, Ill.: IVP Academic, 2013. Scholarly discussions of the historical Jesus quest and the formation of the Gospels, from a generally conservative perspective.

Hengel, Martin. *The Four Gospels and the One Gospel of Jesus Christ: An Investigation of the Collection and Origin of the Canonical Gospels*. Harrisburg, Penn.: Trinity Press International, 2000.

Koester, Helmut. *Introduction to the New Testament*, Vol. 2, *History and Literature of Early Christianity*, 2nd ed. New York: de Gruyter, 2000. Translated from the original German; a major and incisive study of New Testament origins.

Levine, Amy-Jill, and Brettler, Marc Z., eds. *The Jewish Annotated New Testament*. New York: Oxford University Press, 2011. Scholarly essays placing each book of the New Testament in its Jewish context.

Miller, Robert J. *The Complete Gospels*, 4th edition. Salem, OR: Polebridge Press, 2010. Includes all known Gospels in contemporary translations, including a new text of Q.

The Synoptic Problem

Farmer, W. R. *Jesus and the Gospel: Tradition, Scripture, and Canon*. Philadelphia: Fortress Press, 1982. An argument for the primacy of Matthew's Gospel.

Goodacre, Mark. *The Case Against Q: Studies in Markan Priority and the Synoptic Problem*. Harrisburg, Penn. Trinity Press International, 2002. Questions the reality of the Q source.

———. *The Synoptic Problem: A Way Through the Maze*. Edinburgh: T and T Clark, 2004. A lucid analysis of the relationship of the Synoptic Gospels.

Kloppenborg, John S. *The Formation of Q: Trajectories in Ancient Wisdom Collections*. Studies in Antiquity and Christianity. Harrisburg, Penn. Trinity Press International, 2000. A scholarly study of the presumed Q text that finds two layers of traditions, the first presenting Jesus as a wisdom teacher and the second, later edition picturing Jesus as an apocalyptic judge.

Powery, Emerson B. "Synoptic Problem." In K. D. Sakenfeld, ed., *The New Interpreter's Dictionary of the Bible,* Vol. 5, pp. 429–434. Nashville: Abingdon Press, 2009. A clear and concise exposition of the issues.

Robinson, J. M.; Hoffman, P.; and Kloppenborg, J. S., eds. *The Critical Edition of Q: A Synopsis Including the Gospels of Matthew and Luke, Mark and Thomas, with English, German and French Translations of Q and Thomas*. Minneapolis: Fortress Press, 2000. A detailed and comprehensive study of Q.

Sanders, E. P., and Davies, Margaret. *Studying the Synoptic Gospels*. Philadelphia: Trinity Press International, 1989. A thorough scholarly investigation of the Synoptic Problem, skeptical of Q's existence.

Stein, Robert H. *Studying the Synoptics: Origin and Interpretation*, 2nd ed. Grand Rapids, Mich.: Baker Academic, 2001. A readable argument supporting the two-document theory.

Streeter, B. H. *The Four Gospels*. London: Macmillan, 1924. A landmark scholarly study arguing that Mark is the earliest Gospel.

Verbin, John S.; Kloppenborg, John; and Kloppenborg, S. *Excavating Q: The History and Setting of the Sayings Gospel*. Minneapolis: Fortress Press, 2000. An authoritative study of the Q source.

CHAPTER 7

Mark's Portrait of Jesus
The Hidden Messiah and Eschatological Judge

*For even the Son of Man did not come to be served but to serve
and to give up his life as a ransom for many.* Mark 10:45

Key Topics/Themes Between about 64 CE, when Nero began Rome's first official persecution of Christians, and 70 CE, when the Romans destroyed Jerusalem (along with its Temple and the original apostolic church), the Christian community faced a series of crises that threatened its survival. Responding to the wars, revolts, and persecutions that afflicted his group, Mark composed what appears to be the earliest narrative account of Jesus' public career, presenting Jesus' story in a way that was strikingly relevant to the precarious circumstances of Mark's intended readers. Mark's Gospel thus portrays a Jesus who faces attack on three crucial fronts: from Jewish religious leaders, local (Herodian) rulers, and Roman officials. Painting Jesus as a "hidden Messiah" who was misunderstood and devalued by his contemporaries, Mark emphasizes that Jesus came to serve, to suffer, and to die—but also ultimately to triumph by submitting fully to the divine will.

The shortest and probably the earliest of the four canonical Gospels, the narrative "According to Mark" contains relatively few of Jesus' teachings. Instead, the author—who was the first to call his written account an *evangelion* (gospel)—presents Jesus as a miracle-working man of action who is almost constantly on the move, dashing from village to village in Galilee and adjacent regions and, finally, journeying to Jerusalem for a fatal confrontation with its religious and political authorities. Mark's Jesus announces God's kingdom, exorcizes demons, heals the sick, and voluntarily sacrifices himself for others.

Mark's Historical Setting

Several critical methods are helpful in studying **Mark,** beginning with historical investigation of the Gospel's authorship, date, place of composition, possible sources, and social and religious environment (see Figure 7.1). The earliest reference to Mark's Gospel comes from Papias, a Christian writer who was bishop of Hierapolis in Asia Minor about 130–140 CE (see Box 7.1). As quoted by Eusebius, Papias states that Mark had been a disciple of the apostle **Peter** in Rome and based his account on Peter's reminiscences

The Gospel According to Mark

Author: Traditionally John Mark, traveling companion of Paul and "interpreter" for Peter in Rome. The writer does not identify himself in the Gospel text, and scholars, unable to verify the mid-second century tradition of Markan authorship, regard the work as anonymous.

Date: About 66–70 CE, during the Jewish Revolt against Rome.

Place of composition: Rome or Syria-Palestine.

Sources: Primarily oral tradition. Many scholars believe that Mark used a few written sources, such as a collection of Jesus' parables (ch. 4), a compilation of apocalyptic prophecies (ch. 13), and, perhaps, an older account of Jesus' arrest, trial, and execution (chs. 14–15).

Audience: Gentile Christians suffering persecution.

FIGURE 7.1 Social Pyramid 2: Social Stratification of Jewish Society in the Land of Israel (Without Religious Groups). In Jesus' day, Jewish society was sharply divided between two unequal groups: a powerful elite, representing a tiny percentage of the total population, and the nonelite masses. Whereas the elite upper stratum, such as the Roman-appointed Herodian kings, aristocratic chief priests, and large landowners, enjoyed the privileges of political influence, wealth, and prestige, the lower stratum, encompassing the vast majority of the population, lacked access to power or social privilege. Nonelite groups ranged from some relatively prosperous artisans, small farmers, and merchants to large numbers of landless day laborers whose families existed in utter penury. Many of Jesus' parables deal with the social and economic inequities that pervaded his society. See also Figure 5.7 for the pyramidal structure of Roman society. (Pyramid figure is reprinted from *The Jesus Movement* by Ekkehard W. Stegemann and Wolfgang Stegemann, English translation by O. C. Dean, Jr., copyright © 1999 Fortress Press. Used by permission of Augsburg Fortress.)

of Jesus. Papias notes that Mark "had not heard the Lord or been one of his followers" so that his Gospel lacked "a systematic arrangement of the Lord's sayings" (Eusebius, *History* 3.39).

Besides his intention to link Mark's Gospel to apostolic testimony, a consistent trend among church leaders during the second century CE, Papias makes two important historical observations: The author of Mark was *not* an eyewitness but depended on secondhand oral preaching, and Mark's version of Jesus' activities is "not in [proper chronological] order." Careful scrutiny of Mark's Gospel has convinced most New Testament scholars that it does not derive from a single apostolic source, such as Peter, but is based on a general body of oral teachings about Jesus preserved in the author's community.

Mark's author offers few hints about where or for whom he wrote, except for his insistence that following Jesus requires a willingness to suffer for one's faith. Mark's near equation of discipleship with suffering suggests that he directed his work to a group that was then undergoing severe testing and needed encouragement to remain steadfast (see Mark 8:34–38; 10:38–40). This theme of "carrying one's cross" may derive from the effects of Nero's persecution (c. 64–65 CE), when numerous Roman Christians were crucified

BOX 7.1   Papias on the Origin of Mark's Gospel

The oldest surviving reference to Mark's authorship of the Gospel bearing his name comes from Papias, who was a bishop of Hierapolis about 130 or 140 CE. An early church historian, Eusebius of Caesarea, quotes Papias as writing that an unnamed presbyter (church elder) was his source:

> This, too, the presbyter used to say. "Mark, who had been Peter's interpreter, wrote down carefully, but not in order, all that he remembered of the Lord's sayings and doings. For he had not heard the Lord or been one of his followers, but later, as I said, one of Peter's. Peter used to adapt his teachings to the occasion, without making a systematic arrangement of the Lord's sayings, so that Mark was quite justified in writing down some things just as he remembered them. For he had one purpose only—to leave out nothing that he had heard, and to make no misstatement about it."
>
> (Eusebius, *The History of the Church* 3.39)

Eusebius also quotes Papias's declaration that he preferred to learn Christian traditions from the testimony of persons who had known Jesus' companions rather than from written documents, such as the Gospels:

> And whenever anyone came who had been a follower of the presbyters, I inquired into the words of the presbyters, what Andrew or Peter had said, or Philip or Thomas or James or John or Matthew, or any other disciple of the Lord, and what Aristion and the presbyter John, disciples of the Lord, were still saying. For I did not imagine that things out of books would help me as much as the utterances of a living and abiding voice.
>
> (Eusebius, *The History of the Church* 3.39)

Although Papias is a relatively early witness to the Christian tradition, scholars caution that we have no means of verifying the historicity of his claims.

or burned alive. Papias and Irenaeus, another early church leader, agree that Mark wrote shortly after Peter's martyrdom, which, according to tradition, occurred during Nero's attack on Rome's Christian community.

Although Rome is the traditional place of composition, a growing number of scholars think it more likely that Mark wrote for an audience in Syria or Palestine. Critics favoring a Palestinian origin point to Mark's emphasis on the Jewish Revolt (66–73 CE) and concurrent warnings to believers who were affected by the uprising (Mark 13; see Box 7.6). In Mark's view, the "tribulation" climaxing in Jerusalem's destruction is the sign heralding Jesus' **Parousia,** or return in heavenly glory. The association of wars and national revolts with persecution of believers and Jesus' **Second Coming** gives an eschatological urgency to Mark's account.

Even though Papias and other second-century writers ascribe the Gospel to John Mark, a companion of Peter and Paul (Philem. 24; Col. 4:10; Acts 12:12–25; 14:36–40), the author does not identify himself in the text. The superscription—"The Gospel According to Mark"—is a later church

embellishment, for second-century churchmen tried to connect extant writings about Jesus with apostles or their immediate disciples. The Gospel is anonymous; for convenience, we refer to the author as Mark.

Mark's Puzzling Attitude Toward Jesus' Close Associates

Jesus' Family

If scholars are right about assigning the Gospel to a time when the Jewish War against Rome had already begun and the Temple was expected to fall, most of the adult generation that had known Jesus was no longer alive. Even forty years after Jesus' death, however, there must have been some persons who had heard the disciples preach or who had known members of Jesus' family. James, whom Paul calls "the Lord's brother" (Gal. 1:19), was head of the Jerusalem church until his martyrdom in about 62 CE (Josephus, *Antiquities* 20.9; Acts 12:17; 15:13–21;

BOX 7.2 **Mark's Leading Characters***

John the Baptist (1:4–9); executed (6:17–29)

Jesus introduced (1:9); final words (15:34)

Simon Peter and his brother Andrew (1:16–18); Peter's imperfect discipleship (8:27–33; 9:2–6; 14:26–31, 66–72)

James and John, the fishermen sons of Zebedee (1:19–20); wish to be first in the kingdom (10:35–45)

Levi (Matthew), a tax collector (2:13–17)

The Twelve (3:13–19)

Judas Iscariot, Jesus' betrayer (3:19; 14:17–21, 43–46)

Mary, Jesus' mother, and other family members (3:20–21, 31–35; 6:3)

The Gerasene demoniac (5:1–20)

Herod Antipas, ruler of Galilee (ruled 4 BCE– 39 CE) (6:17–29; 8:15)

The Syrophoenician (Canaanite) woman (7:14–30)

A rich young man (10:17–22)

The woman who anoints Jesus at Bethany (14:3–9)

The High Priest Caiaphas (14:53–64)

Pontius Pilate, prefect of Judea (governed 26–36 CE) (15:1–15, 43–44)

Barabbas, the terrorist released in place of Jesus (15:6–15)

Simon of Cyrene, the man impressed to carry Jesus' cross (15:21)

Joseph of Arimathaea, the Sanhedrin member who buries Jesus (15:42–46)

Mary of Magdala (in Galilee) (15:40–41, 47; 16:1)

Mary, mother of James and Joseph (15:40, 47; 16:1)

*Characters are listed in general order of appearance, along with the chief quality or event that distinguishes them in Mark's narrative.

21:16), making him a contemporary of Mark. Through his surviving associates, James presumably would have been an invaluable source of information when Mark began compiling data for a biography of Jesus.

Strangely, Mark does not seem to have regarded Jesus' relatives—or any other ordinary source a modern biographer would consult—as worthy informants. One of the author's prevailing themes is his negative presentation of virtually everyone associated with the historical Jesus. (Box 7.2 lists Mark's leading characters.) From "his mother and brothers" (3:31) to his most intimate followers, Mark portrays all of Jesus' companions as oblivious to his real nature and/or as obstacles to his work. Mark's Gospel consistently renders all Jesus' Palestinian associates as incredibly obtuse, unable to grasp his teachings, and blind to his value.

The Markan picture of Jesus' family implies that they, too, failed to appreciate or support him: "When his relatives heard of this [his drawing large crowds around him], they set out to take charge of him, convinced he was out of his mind" (3:21, Jerusalem Bible). When "his mother and his brothers" send a message asking for him, apparently demanding that he cease making a public spectacle of himself, Mark has Jesus declare "whoever does the will of God is my brother, my sister, my mother." This is a startling repudiation of his blood ties and an implication that in the Markan Jesus' view, his relatives were not doing the divine will (3:31–35). The force of this antifamily episode is intensified because Mark uses it to frame a controversy in which Jesus' opponents accuse him of expelling demons by the power of Beelzebub, another name for the devil. Jesus countercharges that those who oppose his work are defying the **Holy Spirit** (God's presence active in human life), an "unforgivable sin" (3:22–30). At this point in the narrative, Mark shows Jesus' family attempting to interrupt his ministry, thus subtly associating them with his adversaries (see also John 7:1–9).

Mark also depicts Jesus' acquaintances in **Nazareth** as hostile to a local carpenter's unexpected emergence as prophet and healer, questioning his credentials as sage and teacher. "Where does he get it from?" his neighbors ask. "'What wisdom is this that has been given him?' and 'How does he work such miracles? Is not this the carpenter, the son of Mary, the brother of James and Joseph and Judas and Simon? And are not his sisters here with us?' So they [turned against] him" (6:2–3). In this incident in which Jesus revisits his home turf, Mark argues that those who thought they knew Jesus best doubted not only his right to be a religious leader but also his legitimacy—note Mark's reference to "the son of Mary," a contrast to the biblical custom of identifying a son through his male parentage even if his father was dead. The Nazarenes' refusal to see any merit in him results in a troubling diminution of Jesus' power: "He *could work no miracle there*" except for some routine healings (6:6; emphasis added). Mark thus seems to dismiss both family and hometown citizens as acceptable channels of biographical tradition: They all fail to trust, comprehend, or cooperate with his hero.

Mark's allusion to Jesus' "brothers" and "sisters" (see also Matt. 13:54–56) may disturb some readers. Because his Gospel does not include a tradition of Jesus' virginal conception or birth, the existence of siblings may not have been an issue with the Markan community (as it apparently was not for the Pauline churches; none of Paul's letters allude to a virgin birth). Matthew, however, explicitly affirms that Jesus was virginally conceived (Matt. 1:18–25), and Luke strongly implies it (Luke 1:26–38). Some Protestant Christians believe that, following Jesus' delivery, his mother may have borne other children in the ordinary way. According to Roman Catholic doctrine, however, Mary remains perpetually virgin. Jesus' "brothers" (translating the Greek *adelphoi*) are to be understood as close male relatives, perhaps cousins or stepbrothers (sons of Mary's husband, Joseph, by a previous marriage). (An apocryphal infancy Gospel, the Protevangelium of James, which probably dates from the second century CE, depicts James as Jesus' older stepbrother and Mary as eternally virgin; see Chapter 20.)

The Disciples

Mark's opinion of the Galilean **disciples** whom Jesus calls to follow him (3:13–19) is distinctly unsympathetic, although these are the Twelve Apostles on whose testimony the Christian faith is traditionally founded. Almost without exception, Mark paints the Twelve as dull-witted, inept, unreliable, cowardly, and, in at least one case, treacherous. When Jesus stills a storm, the disciples are impressed but unaware of the act's significance (4:35–41). After his feeding of the multitudes, the disciples "had not understood the intent of the loaves" because "their minds were closed" (6:52). The harshness of Mark's judgment is better rendered in the phrase "their hearts were hardened" (as given in the New Revised Standard Version). This is the same phrase used to describe the Egyptian pharaoh when he arrogantly "hardened his heart" and refused to obey Yahweh's commands (Exod. 7:14–10:27). After listening for months to Jesus' teaching, the disciples are such slow learners that they are still ignorant of "what [Jesus' reference to] 'rising from the dead' could mean" (9:9–10). Not only do they fail to grasp the concept of sharing in Jesus' glory (10:35–41), but even the simplest, most obvious parables escape their comprehension (4:10–13). As Jesus asks, "You do not understand this parable? How then will you understand any parable?" (4:13).

Although he has "explained everything" (4:33–34; see also 8:31–32), and the disciples have presumably recognized him as the Messiah (8:27–32), they desert him after his arrest (14:30). Peter, who had earlier acknowledged Jesus as the Messiah, three times denies knowing him (14:66–72). Almost the only character in Mark shown as recognizing the significance of Jesus' death is an unnamed Roman soldier who perceives that "truly this man was a son of God!" (15:39).

Mark's recurring motif that all of Jesus' original associates, including family, former neighbors, and followers, were almost preternaturally blind to his true identity and purpose carries through to the end of his Gospel. At the empty tomb, an unnamed youth in white directs a handful of women disciples not to linger in Jerusalem but to seek their Lord in Galilee, but they are too frightened to obey (16:1–8). The Gospel thus ends with the only disciples who had followed Jesus to the cross—a few Galilean women—inarticulate with terror, unable to cope with the news of his resurrection!

Mark's view that the resurrected Jesus will not be found near his burial site—Jerusalem—contrasts with the Lukan tradition that Jesus instructed his followers to remain in Jerusalem awaiting the Holy Spirit (Luke 24:47–53; Acts 1–2). Whereas Luke makes Jerusalem the center of Christian growth and expansion, the Spirit-empowered mother church led by Peter and James, Jesus' "brother" (Acts 1:4–3:34; 15:13–21; 21:16), Mark paints it as a hotbed of conniving hypocrites who scheme to murder the Son of God.

Mark's antipathy toward the historical Jesus' closest associates and the original Jerusalem church is puzzling. Does this apparent hostility mean that the group for which Mark wrote wished to distance itself from the Jerusalem community, whose founders included Jesus' closest family members, Mary and James (Acts 1:14; 12:17, etc.)? Does Mark's negative attitude indicate a power struggle between his branch of Gentile Christianity and the Jewish Christians who (until 70 CE) headed the original church? Some scholars caution that one should not necessarily postulate a historical tension between the Markan community and Palestinian Jewish Christians. Ancient historians and biographers commonly portray their heroes as enormously superior to their peers, depicting a subject's followers or disciples as constitutionally incapable of rising to his level of thought or achievement. Writing in this literary tradition, Mark may have emphasized the deficiencies of Jesus' contemporaries to underscore his hero's unique status: By magnifying Jesus' image, Mark demonstrates that Jesus alone does God's work and declares God's will.

Mark as a Literary Narrative

Organization and Bipolar Structure

Whatever the historicity of Mark's version of Jesus' career, it eventually exerted a tremendous influence on the Christian community at large, primarily through the expanded and revised editions of Mark that Matthew and Luke produced (see Chapter 6). Because the two other Synoptic Gospels generally follow Mark's order of events in Jesus' life, it is important to understand the significance of Mark's bipolar organization. Mark arranges his narrative around a geographical north–south polarity. The first half of his narrative takes place in **Galilee** and adjacent areas of northern Palestine, a largely rural area of peasant farmers where Jesus recruits his followers, performs numerous miracles, and—despite some opposition—enjoys considerable success. The second half (after ch. 8) relates Jesus' fatal journey southward to Judea and Jerusalem, where he is rejected and killed (see Figure 7.2). Besides dividing Jesus' career according to two distinct geographical areas, Mark's Gospel presents two contrasting aspects of Jesus' story. In Galilee, Jesus is a figure of power, using his supernatural gifts to expel demons, heal the sick, control natural forces, and raise the dead. The Galilean Jesus speaks and acts with tremendous authority, effortlessly refutes his detractors, and affirms or invalidates the Mosaic Torah at will. Before leaving **Caesarea Philippi,** however, Jesus makes the first of three Passion predictions, warning his uncomprehending disciples that he will go to Jerusalem only to suffer humiliation and death (8:30–38; 9:31–32; 10:33–34).

By using the Passion predictions as a device to link the indomitable miracle worker in Galilee with the helpless figure on the cross in Judea, Mark reconciles the two seemingly irreconcilable components in his portrait of Jesus. The powerful Son of God who astonishes vast crowds with his mighty works is also the vulnerable Son of Man who, in weakness and apparent

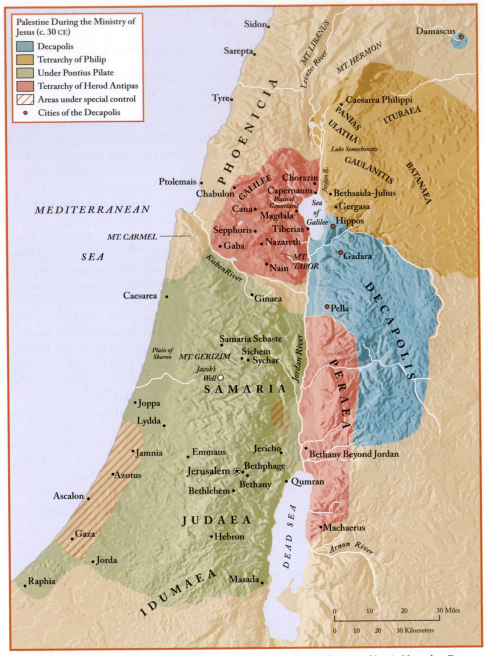

Palestine During the Ministry of Jesus (c. 30 CE)
- Decapolis
- Tetrarchy of Philip
- Under Pontius Pilate
- Tetrarchy of Herod Antipas
- Areas under special control
- Cities of the Decapolis

FIGURE 7.2 Political divisions of Palestine during the ministry of Jesus (c. 30 CE). Note that Rome directly administered Judea and Samaria through its governor Pontius Pilate; Herod Antipas ruled Galilee (Jesus' home district) and Peraea; another son of Herod the Great, Philip, ruled an area to the northeast. The Decapolis was a league of ten Greek-speaking cities on the east side of the Jordan River.

BOX 7.3 Mark's Order of Events in Jesus' Life

BEGINNING OF JESUS' MINISTRY (C. 27 OR 29 CE)

Jesus is baptized by John at the Jordan River (1:9–11).

Jesus begins preaching in Galilee (1:14–15).

Jesus recruits Peter, Andrew, James, and John to be his first disciples (1:16–20).

Jesus performs miraculous cures and exorcisms in Capernaum and throughout Galilee (1:21–3:12).

Jesus appoints twelve chief disciples from among his many followers; he explains the meaning of parables to this inner circle (3:13–4:34).

Jesus returns to Nazareth, where his neighbors reject him (6:1–6).

Herod Antipas beheads John the Baptist (6:14–29).

Jesus miraculously feeds a Jewish crowd of 5,000 (6:30–44).

END OF JESUS' MINISTRY (C. 30 OR 33 CE)

Jesus leaves Galilee and travels through non-Jewish territories in Phoenicia and the Decapolis (7:24–37).

Jesus miraculously feeds a second crowd, this time of Gentiles (8:1–10, 14–21).

Jesus cures a blind man, and near the town of Caesarea Philippi, Peter's eyes are opened to Jesus' true identity as the Messiah; Jesus rebukes Peter for failing to understand that the Messiah must suffer and die (8:22–9:1).

Jesus is gloriously transfigured before Peter, James, and John (9:1–13).

Jesus travels south to Judea, teaching the crowds and debating with Pharisees (10:1–33).

On the road to Jerusalem, Jesus for the third time predicts his imminent suffering and death (the Passion predictions) (8:31–33; 9:30–32; 10:32–34).

EVENTS OF THE LAST WEEK OF JESUS' LIFE

On Palm Sunday, Jesus arranges his public entry into Jerusalem; his followers hail him in terms of the Davidic kingdom (11:1–11).

Jesus drives the moneychangers out of the Temple (11:15–19).

Seated on the Mount of Olives opposite Jerusalem, Jesus predicts the imminent destruction of the Temple (13:1–37).

Jesus' enemies conspire to kill him; Judas betrays Jesus (14:1–11).

Jesus holds a final Passover meal with the Twelve (14:12–31).

After the Last Supper, Jesus is arrested at Gethsemane on the Mount of Olives outside Jerusalem (14:32–52).

Jesus is tried on charges of blasphemy before the High Priest Caiaphas and the Sanhedrin (14:53–65).

On Good Friday, Jewish leaders accuse Jesus before Pontius Pilate; Jesus is declared guilty of treason, flogged, and condemned to crucifixion (15:1–20).

A group of Galilean women witness the Crucifixion; Joseph of Arimathaea provides a tomb for Jesus (15:40–47).

On Easter Sunday, Mary of Magdala and other women discover that Jesus' tomb is empty; a young man instructs them to look for Jesus in Galilee, but the women are too frightened to tell anyone of their experience (16:1–8).

---

defeat, sacrifices his life "as a ransom for many" (10:45). Thus, the author balances older Christian traditions of his hero's phenomenal deeds with a bleak picture of Jesus' sufferings, devoting the last six chapters to a detailed account of the Passion. Although Matthew and Luke follow Mark in his north–south, power–weakness dichotomy, John's Gospel shows that there were other ways to arrange events in Jesus' story. In John, Jesus repeatedly travels back and forth between Galilee and Judea, performing miracles in both regions. As Papias's remark about the Gospel's lack of historical order warned, the Markan sequence of events, with its emphasis on a single, final visit to Jerusalem, appears to express the writer's theological vision of Jesus' life rather than a literal reconstruction of his subject's actual movements (see Box 7.3).

Mark's Gospel can be divided into six parts:

1. Prelude to Jesus' public ministry (1:1–13)
2. The Galilean ministry (1:14–8:26)
3. The journey to Jerusalem (8:27–10:52)
4. The Jerusalem ministry (11:1–15:47)
5. Mark's Passion narrative: Jesus' trial and cruifixion
6. Postlude: the empty tomb (16:1–8)

Prelude to Jesus' Public Ministry

Like the writer of a classical epic, Mark plunges into the middle of the action, providing no background about his hero but introducing him with apocalyptic suddenness. The opening line, "Here begins the gospel [good news] of Jesus Christ" (1:1), simultaneously announces his epic theme and echoes Genesis 1, alerting readers to see that, in Jesus, God has begun a new creative activity. Jesus is the **Christ** (Greek translation of the Hebrew *mashiah*) and "the Son of God," titles that Mark seldom uses in his narrative, for one of his purposes is to demonstrate that in his lifetime the majority of people did not recognize Jesus' divine Sonship. No person calls Jesus "a son of God" until almost the very end of Mark's Gospel (see Box 7.4). Significantly, at that point Jesus is already dead, and the speaker is neither a Jew nor a disciple but a Roman centurion (15:39).

By citing, as if from memory, a blend of passages from Isaiah (40:3) and Malachi (3:1)—that a divinely appointed "herald" and a "voice crying aloud in the wilderness" are preparing a path for the Lord—Mark immediately places Jesus' story in the context of the Hebrew Bible. Mark identifies the "herald" with **John the Baptist,** a desert ascetic then conducting a religious campaign at the Jordan River, where John baptizes converts "in token of repentance, for the forgiveness of sins" (1:4). Jesus, implicitly included among the repentant, appears for **baptism,** perhaps as John's disciple. Mark has

John predict a "mightier" successor, although he does not show the Baptist as explicitly identifying Jesus as such.

The biographer's decision to introduce Jesus at the Jordan River is significant, for the Jordan was the gateway by which the Israelite tribes originally entered Palestine, their Promised Land. Mark may also have expected his readers to remember that "Jesus" is the Greek version of "Joshua," the name of Moses' successor who led Israel across Jordan into its homeland. Mark's brief reference to Jesus' being tested for forty days in the Judean wilderness also has biblical connotations. As the Israelites wandered for forty years through the Sinai wilderness, undergoing trials and temptations, so Jesus is tempted by **Satan** in the desert, the untamed haunt of hostile entities. Jesus vanquishes Satan, just as Joshua conquered the Canaanite nations that opposed Israel (Josh. 1–6).

Mark's allusion to Jesus' overcoming the Evil One introduces another of the author's principal themes: God's Son will break the devil's hold on humanity. Jesus' **exorcisms**—the casting out of demons who have possessed human beings—are an important part of Jesus' ministry and are given proportionately greater space in Mark than in any other Gospel. (In contrast, John's Gospel does not contain a single reference to Jesus' performing exorcisms.)

The Galilean Ministry: Inaugurating the Kingdom

Mark's Eschatological Urgency

Mark launches Jesus' career with a startlingly eschatological message: "The time has come, the kingdom of God is upon you; repent and believe the Gospel" (1:15). Mark's sense of eschatological urgency permeates his entire Gospel, profoundly affecting his portrayal of Jesus' life and teaching. With the tradition that Jesus had prophesied the Temple's fall about to be realized, Mark, writing about 70 CE, sees the

BOX 7.4 Mark's Identification of Jesus as "Son of God"

Although Mark's preferred designation of Jesus is "Son of Man," he also identifies Jesus as **"Son of God"** at strategic places in his narrative. In most editions of Mark, the first reference to Jesus' divine parentage occurs in the opening verse and is addressed directly to readers, who must be aware of Jesus' supernatural identity if Mark's way of telling his hero's story—an ironic contrast between who Jesus really is and who people mistake him for—is to succeed. Because some early manuscripts omit the phrase "Son of God" in Mark 1:1, however, it is possible that the author originally intended for readers to learn of Jesus' special relationship to the Father in the same manner that Jesus did, at his baptism, when a heavenly voice privately confides, "You are my beloved Son; in you I take delight" (Mark 1:11).

The "voice from heaven" paraphrases Psalm 2, a poem sung at the coronation of Israel's monarchs, a royal ceremony at which Yahweh is represented as adopting the newly consecrated king: "You are my son, . . . this day I become your father" (Ps. 2:7). Because Mark contains no reference to Jesus' virginal conception, many scholars think that the author regards Jesus as becoming God's son by adoption, his baptism and visitation by the Holy Spirit the equivalent of Davidic kings' being anointed with holy oil.

In an ironic counterpoint to God's voice, Mark next uses the speech of a demon to reveal Jesus' hidden identity. When driven from a man he has possessed, the demon angrily declares: "I know who you are—the Holy One of God" (1:25). Whereas Mark's human characters fail to recognize Jesus' true nature until after his death, supernatural entities, including "unclean spirits," know and fear him. In a typically Markan paradox, human opponents accuse Jesus of being an agent of Beelzebub, "the prince of demons"—allegedly the source of his supernatural power—while the demons themselves testify that Jesus is "the Son of God" (3:11, 22–28). Mark draws further on the questionable testimony of evil spirits when describing the Gerasene demoniac: The satanic "Legion" boldly announces that Jesus is "son of the Most High God" (5:1–13).

In contrast, when Peter finally perceives that Jesus is "the Christ," he apparently does not also intuit Jesus' divinity, confining his witness to his leader's messianic (political) role. In Mark's narrative, Jesus' closest disciples lack the perceptiveness of Beelzebub's imps! (Compare Mark's account of Peter's "confession" with Matthew's version, where the author has Peter employ a major Christological title, "Son of the living God," absent in Mark [Matt. 16:13–16].) Even after Jesus is miraculously transfigured before their eyes and the celestial voice again affirms that he is God's son (9:8), the Galilean disciples remain oblivious.

At Jesus' trial before the Sanhedrin, Mark presents a darkly paradoxical glimpse of his hero's real identity. When the High Priest asks if his prisoner is indeed the "Son of the Blessed One" (a pious circumlocution for God), Jesus, for the first time in Mark's account, admits that he is—a confession of divinity that condemns him to death. Only when Jesus hangs lifeless on the cross does a human figure—a Roman centurion—belatedly speak of Jesus as "a son of God," a Hellenistic Gentile's recognition that Jesus had died a heroic death worthy of divine honor (see also Box 11.2).

---

eschaton—the end of history as we know it—about to take place (13:1–4, 7–8, 14–20, 24–27, 30, 35–37). He therefore paints Jesus as an eschatological figure whose words are reinterpreted as specific warnings to Mark's generation. In the thought world Mark creates, the apocalyptic Son of Man who is about to appear in glory (13:24–31) is the same as the Son of Man who came forty years earlier to die on the cross (8:31, 38; 9:9–13, 31). The splendor of the one to come casts its radiance over Mark's portrait of the human Jesus (9:1–9).

Mark's style conveys his urgency: He uses the present tense throughout his Gospel and repeatedly connects the brief episodes (pericopes) of his narrative with the transition word *immediately*. Jesus scarcely finishes conducting a healing or exorcism in one Galilean village before he "immediately" rushes off to the next town to perform another miracle. In Mark's breathless presentation, the world faces an unprecedented crisis. Jesus' activity proclaims that history has reached its climactic moment. Hence, Mark measures time in mere days (during the Galilean ministry) and hours (during the Jerusalem episodes). Reduced to tiny increments, time is literally running out.

Mark represents Jesus as promising his original hearers that they will experience the *eschaton*—"the present generation will live to see it all" (13:30). The kingdom, God's active rule, is so close that some of Jesus' contemporaries "will not taste death before they have seen the kingdom of God already come in power" (9:1). The long-awaited figure of Elijah, the ancient prophet whose reappearance is to be an infallible sign of the last days (Mal. 4:5), has already materialized in the person of John the Baptist (9:12–13). Such passages indicate that Mark's community anticipated the imminent consummation of all things.

Mark as Apocalypse

So pervasive is Mark's eschatology that some scholars regard the entire Gospel as a modified **apocalypse** (*apokalypsis*), a literary work that reveals unseen realities and discloses events destined soon to climax in God's final intervention in human affairs. Mark's use of apocalyptic devices is particularly evident at the beginning and ending of his Gospel. God speaks directly as a disembodied voice (a phenomenon Hellenistic Jews called the *bath qol*) at Jesus' baptism and again at the **Transfiguration,** an **epiphany** (manifestation of divine presence) in which the disciples see Jesus transformed into a luminous being seated beside the ancient figures of Moses and Elijah (1:11; 9:2–9). In this apocalyptic

scene, Jesus converses with Moses and Elijah (who represent, respectively, the Torah and the prophets) to demonstrate his continuity with Israel's biblical tradition. Jesus thus embodies God's ultimate revelation to humanity. Mark's declaration that at Jesus' baptism the heavens are "torn apart," suddenly giving access to the spirit realm, anticipates a later apocalyptic vision in the Book of Revelation. Revelation's author similarly describes "a door opened in heaven" and hears a voice inviting him to "come up here" and receive a preview of future history (Rev. 4:1–2).

At the most important event in his Gospel, Jesus' crucifixion, Mark repeats his image of the heavens being "torn" asunder. He states that at the instant of Jesus' death "the curtain of the temple was torn in two from top to bottom," a phenomenon that inspires a Gentile soldier to recognize Jesus' divinity (15:37–39). In describing this incident, Mark apparently assumes that his readers will understand the symbolism of the Temple curtain. According to Josephus, the outer room of the Temple was separated from the innermost sanctuary—the Holy of Holies where God's "glory" was believed to dwell invisibly—by a huge curtain that was embroidered with astronomical designs, images of the visible heavens that hid God's celestial throne from mortal eyes. In Mark's view, Jesus' redemptive death "tore apart" the curtain, opening the way to a heavenly reality that the earthly Temple had symbolized. For Mark, this rending of the sacred veil functions as an apocalypse or revelation of Jesus' supreme significance.

Jesus as Son of Man The author presents virtually all the events during Jesus' final hours as revelatory of God's unfolding purpose. At the Last Supper, Jesus emphasizes that the eschatological "Son of Man is going the way appointed for him" and that he will "never again" drink wine with his disciples until he will "drink it new in the kingdom of God" (14:21, 25). At his trial before the **Sanhedrin,** the Jewish leaders' highest judicial council, Jesus reveals his true identity for the first time: He confesses that he

BOX 7.5 The Synoptic Gospels' Use of the Term "Son of Man"

The authors of the Synoptic Gospels use the expression "Son of Man" in three distinct ways, all of which they place on the lips of Jesus to denote three important aspects of his ministry. The three categories identify Jesus as the Son of Man who serves on earth, the Son of Man who must suffer and die, and the Son of Man who will be revealed in eschatological judgment. Representative examples of these three categories appear below.

THE EARTHLY SON OF MAN

Mark 2:10 (Matt. 9:6; Luke 5:24): Has authority to forgive sins.

Mark 2:27 (Matt. 12:8; Luke 6:5): Is Lord of the Sabbath.

Matthew 11:19 (Luke 7:34): Comes eating and drinking.

Matthew 8:20 (Luke 9:58): Has nowhere to lie his head.

Luke 19:20: Came to seek and save the lost.

THE SUFFERING SON OF MAN

Mark 8:31 (Luke 9:22): Must suffer.

Mark 9:12 (Matt. 17:12): Will suffer.

Mark 10:45 (Matt. 20:28): Came to serve and give his life.

Matthew 12:40 (Luke 11:30): Will be three days in the earth.

THE ESCHATOLOGICAL SON OF MAN

Mark 8:38 (Matt. 16:27; Luke 9:26): Comes in glory of the Father and holy angels.

Mark 14:26 (Matt. 24:30; Luke 21:27): Will be seen coming with clouds and glory.

Mark 14:62 (Matt. 26:64; Luke 22:69): Will be seen sitting at the right hand of power.

Luke 17:26 (Matt. 24:27): As it was in days of Noah, so in days of Son of Man.

For a fuller discussion of the Son of Man concept and its use by the Synoptic authors, see George Eldon Ladd, *A Theology of the New Testament* (Grand Rapids, Mich.: Eerdmans, 1974), pp. 145–158.

---

is the Messiah and that the officiating High Priest "will see the Son of Man seated at the right hand of God and coming with the clouds of heaven" (14:62–63).

This disclosure—found only in Mark—associates Jesus' suffering and death with his ultimate revelation as the eschatological Son of Man. A designation that appears almost exclusively in the Gospels and then always on the lips of Jesus, **Son of Man** is Mark's favored expression to denote Jesus' three essential roles: an earthly figure who teaches with authority, a servant who embraces suffering, and a future eschatological judge (see Box 7.5). Although many scholars question whether the historical Jesus ever used this title, many others regard it as Jesus' preferred means of self-identification. Still other scholars postulate that Jesus may have used the title Son of Man to designate another,

future-coming figure who would vindicate Jesus' own ministry and that the later church, because of its faith in Jesus' resurrection, retrojected that title back into the account of Jesus' life at points where it originally did not appear. In Mark's view, however, Jesus himself is clearly the eschatological Son of Man.

Son of Man in Hellenistic-Jewish Literature The Hebrew Bible offers few clues to what Jesus may have meant if he employed this title. The phrase appears frequently in the Book of Ezekiel, where "son of man" is typically synonymous with "mortal" or "human being," commonly the prophet himself. In the Book of Daniel, however, "one like a [son of] man" appears as a celestial figure who receives divine authority (Dan. 7:14). Most scholars think that this human figure (contrasting with the mystic "beasts" in Daniel's vision) originally symbolized a collective entity, Israel's faithful. By Jesus' time, Daniel's Son of Man apparently had assumed another identity, that of a supernatural individual who will come to judge the world.

The composite Book of 1 Enoch, which belongs to noncanonical Hellenistic-Jewish writings known as the Pseudepigrapha, contains a long section (called the Similitudes or Parables) that prominently features the Son of Man as the one who, at the consummation of history, passes judgment on humanity (1 Enoch 37–71). Although some scholars dispute this claim, many believe that this section of 1 Enoch was written by the first century CE. Fragments of Enoch (but not yet the Similitudes) have been found among the Dead Sea Scrolls, and the canonical Epistle of Jude cites Enoch as if it were Scripture (Jude 14–15). It seems likely that ideas about Enoch's Son of Man were current in Jesus' day and that he—or his immediate followers—applied them to his role in history.

The major element that Mark's Jesus adds to the Son of Man concept is that he is a servant who must suffer and die before attaining the kind of heavenly glory that Daniel 7 and 1 Enoch ascribe to him (cf. Mark 8:30–31; 10:45; 13:26–27; 14:62).

"The Son of Man Has the Right on Earth . . ." It is as the earthly Son of Man that Mark's Jesus claims the right to wield immense religious power (see Box 7.5). As Son of Man, the Markan Jesus assumes the authority to prescribe revolutionary changes in Jewish Law and custom (2:10). Behaving as if he already reigns as cosmic judge, Jesus forgives a paralytic's sins (2:1–12) and permits certain kinds of work on the Sabbath (3:1–5). In both instances, Jesus' pronouncements outrage Jewish leaders. Who but God can forgive sins? And who has the audacity to change Moses' inspired command to forbid all labor on God's day of rest (cf. Exod. 20:8–10; Deut. 5:12–15)?

In the eyes of Jews scrupulously observing Torah regulations, Jesus dishonors the **Sabbath** by healing a man's withered arm on that holy day. The Pharisees interpreted the Torah to permit saving a life or dealing with other comparable emergencies on the Sabbath, but in this case (2:23–28), Jesus seems to have violated the Torah for no compelling reason.

As Mark describes the situation, it is Jesus' flexible attitude toward Sabbath keeping that incites some Pharisees and supporters of Herod Antipas to hatch a murder plot against him (3:5–6). To most readers, Jesus' opponents overreact inexplicably. To many law-abiding Jews, however, Jesus' Sabbath-breaking miracles and declaration that the Sabbath was created for humanity's benefit (2:27–28) seem to strike at the heart of Jewish faith. Many devout Jews believed that the Torah was infallible and eternal. According to the Book of Jubilees, the Torah existed before God created the universe, and people *were* made to keep the Sabbath. Jesus' assertion that the Sabbath law is not absolute but relative to human needs appears to deny the Torah's unchanging validity and to question its status as God's final and complete revelation.

Teaching the Mysteries of the Kingdom

Jesus' Parables Many of Israel's prophets, and virtually all its apocalyptic writers, use highly symbolic language to convey their visions of the divine will. In depicting Jesus as the eschatological Son of Man, it is not surprising that Mark states categorically that Jesus never taught publicly without using parables (or other figures of speech) (4:34). The root meaning of the word **parable** is "a comparison," the discernment of similarities between one thing and another. Jesus' simplest parables are typically **similes,** comparisons using *as* or *like* to express unexpected resemblances between ostensibly unrelated objects, actions, or ideas. Thus, Jesus compares God's kingdom—which he never explicitly defines—to a number of items, including a mustard seed. Like the tiny seed, God's rule begins in an extremely small way, but eventually, like the mustard plant, it grows to an unexpectedly large size (4:30–32).

(Jesus' intent in this parable may have been ironic, for farmers do not want wild mustard plants taking over their fields any more than most people wanted the kind of divine rule that Jesus promoted.) Like the parable of the growing seed (4:26–29), which appears in Mark alone, the mustard plant analogy stresses the unnoticed evolution of divine sovereignty rather than explaining its nature or form. Most parables are open-ended: They do not provide a fixed conclusion but invite the hearer to speculate about many possibilities inherent in the comparison. According to Mark, understanding parables involving germination and growth suggests the "secret" of God's kingdom, a glimpse into the mysterious principles by which God rules.

Other parables take the form of brief stories that exploit familiar situations or customs to illustrate a previously unrecognized truth. In the parable of the sower, a farmer plants seeds on different kinds of ground with distinctly different results (4:2–9). The lengthy interpretation that Mark attaches to the image of sowing seeds (4:13–20) transforms what was originally a simple parable into an allegory. An **allegory** is a complex literary form in which each element of the narrative—persons, places, actions, even objects—has a symbolic value. Because every item in the allegory functions as a symbol of something else, the allegory's meaning can be puzzled out only by identifying what each individual component in the story represents.

Almost all scholars believe that Mark's elaborate allegorical interpretations, equating different kinds of soil with the different responses people make when they receive the "seed" (gospel message), do not represent Jesus' original meaning. By the time Mark incorporated the sower pericope into his Gospel, the Christian community had already used it to explain people's contrasting reactions to their preaching. Jesus' pithy tale based on everyday agricultural practices was reinterpreted to fit the later experience of Christian missionaries. The reference to "persecution" (4:17) places the allegorical factor in Mark's time rather than in the context of Jesus' personal experience in Galilee.

In one of his most controversial passages, Mark states that Jesus uses parables to *prevent* the public from understanding his message (4:11–12). To many readers, it seems incredible that Jesus deliberately teaches in a way intended to confuse or alienate his audience. Mark justifies his hero's alleged practice by quoting from Isaiah (6:9–10), which pictures Yahweh telling the prophet that his preaching will be useless because Yahweh has already made it impossible for the Israelites to comprehend Isaiah's meaning. Mark's attempt to explain why most people did not follow Jesus seems contrary to the gracious goodwill that the Gospel writers normally associate with him and probably does not express the policy of the historical Jesus. In the historical experience of Mark's community, however, it appears that the kingdom's secrets were reserved for a few chosen disciples, such as those whom Mark says privately received Jesus' esoteric teaching (4:11). (In Luke's edition of Mark, he removes Isaiah's pessimistic declaration from Jesus' lips and transfers the saying to his sequel, the Book of Acts, where he places it in Paul's mouth to explain why the apostle gave up trying to convert fellow Jews and concentrated instead on the more receptive Gentiles; cf. Mark 4:11–12; Luke 8:10; Acts 28:25–28.)

Jesus and the Demons Eschatological beliefs are concerned not only with the end of the world but also with visions of invisible spirit beings, both good and evil (see Chapter 19). Apocalyptic literature, such as Daniel and 1 Enoch, typically presents God's defeat of spiritual evil as the ultimate victory that completes God's sovereignty over the entire universe. Given Mark's strongly eschatological point of view, it is not surprising that he makes a battle between supernatural forces—God's Son versus Satan's demons—an integral part of his apocalyptic Gospel. After noting Jesus' resistance to Satan (1:12–13), Mark reinforces the theme of cosmic struggle by making Jesus' first miracle an exorcism. Remarkably, the demon that Jesus expels from a human victim is the first character in the

Markan narrative to recognize Jesus as "the Holy One of God"—who has come "to destroy" the agents of evil (1:23–26).

Following his exorcisms at **Capernaum,** Jesus performs similar feats in Gentile territory, "the country of the Gerasenes." Driving a whole army of devils from a Gerasene madman, Jesus casts them into a herd of pigs. The religiously unclean animals become a fit home for spirits who drive people to commit unclean acts (5:1–20). The demons' name—"legion"—is an unflattering reference to the Roman legions (large military units) then occupying Palestine (and in Mark's day assaulting Jerusalem). When in Capernaum, a Galilean Jewish city, Jesus commands the demons to remain silent, whereas in the Gerasene region, he orders the dispossessed Gentile to tell others about his cure.

Mark arranges his material to show that Jesus does not choose to battle evil in isolation. At the outset of his campaign through Galilee, Jesus gathers followers who will form the nucleus of a new society, one presumably free from demonic influence. Recruiting a band of Galilean fishermen and peasants, Jesus selects two sets of brothers, **Simon Peter** (also called **Cephas**) and **Andrew,** and James and John—sons of **Zebedee** also known as **"sons of thunder (Boanerges)"**—to form his inner circle (1:16–20). Later, he adds another eight disciples to complete the Twelve, a number probably representing the twelve tribes of Israel: **Philip; Bartholomew; Matthew; Thomas; James,** son of Alphaeus; **Thaddeus;** Simon the Canaanite; and **Judas Iscariot** (3:16–19; cf. the different list in Acts 1). Mark states that, when Jesus commissions the Twelve to perform exorcisms (6:7–13), they fail miserably (9:14–18, 28–29), a sad contrast to the success enjoyed by some exorcists who are *not* Jesus' followers (9:38–41).

Jesus Accused of Sorcery In another incident involving demonic possession (3:22–30), Mark dramatizes a head-on collision between Jesus as God's agent for overthrowing evil and persons who see Jesus as a tool of the devil. The clash occurs when "doctors of the law" (teachers and interpreters of the Torah) from Jerusalem accuse Jesus of using black magic to perform exorcisms. Denying that evil can produce good, Jesus countercharges that persons who attribute good works to Satan "slander the Holy Spirit," the divine force manifested in Jesus' actions.

Matthew's version of the incident explicitly links Jesus' defeat of evil spirits with the arrival of the **kingdom of God.** The Matthean Jesus declares, "If it is by the Spirit of God that I drive out the devils, then be sure the kingdom of God has already come upon you" (Matt. 12:28). To both Evangelists, Jesus' successful attack on demonic control is a revelation that through his presence God now rules. Willful refusal to accept Jesus' healings as evidence of divine power is to resist the Spirit, an obstinacy that prevents spiritual insight.

The Existence of Demons Mark, like other New Testament authors, reflects a common Hellenistic belief in the existence of unseen entities that influence human lives. Numerous Hellenistic documents record charms to ward off demons or free one from their control. In Judaism, works like the deuterocanonical Book of Tobit reveal a belief that demons could be driven out by the correct use of magical formulas (Tob. 6:1–8; 8:1–3). Josephus, who was Mark's contemporary, relates a story about Eleazar, who allegedly exorcised a demon in the presence of the emperor Vespasian (69–79 CE), drawing the malign spirit out through its victim's nose (*Antiquities* 8.46–49).

Zoroastrianism A belief in devils and demonic possession appears in Jewish literature primarily after the period of Persian domination (539–330 BCE), when Persian religious ideas seem to have influenced Jewish thought. According to the Persian religion **Zoroastrianism,** the whole universe, visible and invisible, is divided into two contending powers of light and darkness, good and evil. Only after historical contact with Zoroastrian dualism does the figure of Satan emerge as humanity's adversary in biblical literature (Job 1–2; Zech. 3). Angels and demons thereafter populate Hellenistic-Jewish writings, such as the books of Daniel and 1 Enoch.

Belief in Supernatural Evil Although Hellenistic Greek and Judeo-Christian writers may express their beliefs about supernatural evil in terms considered naive or irrational to today's scientifically disciplined mind, they reflect a viewpoint with important implications for contemporary society. Surrounded by threats of terrorism, lethal diseases such as cancer and AIDS, and frightening disregard for human life, people may wonder if the forces of cruelty and violence are not greater than the sum of their human agents. Does evil exist as a power independent of human volition? Such diverse works as the Synoptic Gospels, Ephesians (6:10–17),

and Revelation show a keen awareness of evil so pervasive and so profound that it cannot be explained solely in terms of human acts, individual or collective. Whatever philosophical view we choose to interpret the human predicament, the Gospel portrayal of Jesus' struggle to impart wholeness and health to others expresses the Evangelists' conviction that humanity cannot save itself without divine aid.

Jesus the Healer Physical cures, as well as exorcisms, characterize Jesus' assault on evil. In Mark's portrayal, one of Jesus' most important functions is to bring relief to the afflicted (see Figure 7.3). He drives a fever from Simon Peter's mother-in-law (1:29–31), cleanses a leper (1:40–42), enables a paralyzed man to walk (2:1–12), restores a man's withered hand (3:1–6), stops a woman's chronic hemorrhaging (5:25–34), and

FIGURE 7.3 *Christ with the Sick Around Him, Receiving Little Children*. In this etching by Rembrandt (1606–1669), healing light radiates from the central figure of Jesus and creates a protective circle of illumination around those whom he cures.

resuscitates the comatose daughter of **Jairus,** a synagogue official (5:21–24, 35–43). To Mark, Jesus' restoration of physical health to suffering humanity is an indispensable component of divine rule, tangible confirmation that God's kingdom is about to dawn.

Mark's Narrative Techniques

In assembling from various oral sources a series of brief anecdotes about Jesus' ability to cure the sick, Mark stitches the miracle stories together like pearls on a string. Weaving these originally independent pericopes into the fabric of his narrative, Mark re-creates them with vividness and immediacy. Besides using a wealth of concrete detail to help readers visualize the scene or feel its emotional impact, Mark commonly employs the technique of *intercalation,* inserting one story inside another. This sandwiching device typically serves to make the story placed inside another narrative function as interpretative commentary on the framing story. In telling of Jesus' family's attempt to impede his ministry (3:21, 31–35), for example, Mark inserts a seemingly unrelated anecdote about Jesus' opponents accusing him of sorcery (3:22–30), implicitly associating his "mother and brothers" with his adversaries.

Mark uses the same device of wrapping one story around another when describing the resuscitation of Jairus's daughter, interrupting the Jairus episode to incorporate the anecdote about a hemorrhaging woman into the middle of the narrative. Pushing through the crowds surrounding him, Jesus is on his way to help Jairus's seriously ill daughter (5:22–24) when a woman—who Mark says had suffered for twelve years from unstoppable bleeding (and was therefore ritually unclean)—suddenly grabs his cloak and, as if by force of desperate need, draws into her ailing body Jesus' curative energy. This incident is doubly unique: It is the only Gospel healing to occur without Jesus' conscious will and the Evangelists' only hint about the physical nature of Jesus' ability to heal. Mark states that Jesus can *feel* his power

flow out when the woman touches him, as if he were a dynamo being drained of electrical energy (5:25–34). The Markan Jesus, moreover, does not know at first who is tapping his power.

Mark then resumes the Jairus narrative: Although a messenger reports that the girl has already died, Jesus insists that she is only "asleep." Taking his three closest disciples into the girl's room, he commands her to "get up"— "*Talitha cum,*" an Aramaic phrase that Mark's community probably revered for its association with Jesus' power over death (5:35–43). The author links the two stories by a simple numerical device—the mature woman had been afflicted for a dozen years and the young girl is twelve years old—and by the assertion that it is the participants' *faith* that cures them. The woman demonstrates unconditional trust in Jesus' power, and Jairus presumably accepts Jesus' advice to replace fear for his daughter's safety with "faith."

Mark's Ironic Vision In the Nazareth episode, where Jesus appears as a prophet without honor (6:4–6), Mark invites his readers to share Jesus' astonishment that people who should have known better reject a golden opportunity to benefit from Jesus' help. As Mark presents Jesus' story—which is largely a tale of humanity's self-defeating rejection of God's attempt to redeem it—such disparities abound. Demons steeped in evil instantly recognize who Jesus is, but most *people*—including his peasant neighbors and the educated religious elite—do not. The wind and waves obey him during a storm on the **Sea of Galilee** (4:35–41) (see Figures 7.4 and 7.5), but his disciples ultimately prove disloyal. He miraculously feeds hungry multitudes (an incident Mark records in two different versions [6:30–44; 8:1–10]) and can suspend the laws of physics by striding across Galilee's waters (6:30–52; 8:1–10), but Jesus' closest followers are unable to grasp the meaning of his control over nature. Among the very few who respond positively to him, the majority are social outcasts or nobodies such as lepers, blind

FIGURE 7.4 Fishing boat returning to Capernaum on the Sea of Galilee. The village of Capernaum, home to Peter and his brother Andrew, served as a center for Jesus' early Galilean ministry.

FIGURE 7.5 Excavations at Capernaum. Dated to the first century CE, the ruins of these small private houses are located near the shore of the Sea of Galilee, an appropriate location for the dwellings of fishermen. Archaeologists have found considerable evidence indicating that one of these humble structures belonged to Peter. According to Mark, Jesus cured Peter's mother-in-law of a fever there (Mark 1:29–31; cf. 2:1–12).

mendicants, ritually unclean women, and the diseased. This *irony,* or logical incongruity between normal expectation and what actually happens in the narrative, determines both Mark's structuring of his Gospel and his characterization of Jesus' messiahship.

The Journey to Jerusalem: Jesus' Predestined Suffering

Mark's Central Irony: Jesus' Hidden Messiahship

In chapter 8, which forms the central pivot on which the entire Gospel turns, Mark ties together several motifs that convey his essential vision of Jesus' ministry. Besides repeating the theme of the disciples' obtuseness, chapter 8 also sounds Mark's concurrent themes of the hidden or unexpected quality of Jesus' messiahship—especially the necessity of his suffering—and the requirement that all believers be prepared to embrace a comparably painful fate. In contrast to John's Gospel, in which Jesus' identity is publicly affirmed at the outset of his career, Mark has no one even hint that Jesus is Israel's Messiah until almost the close of the Galilean campaign, when Peter—in a flash of insight—recognizes him as such (8:29). The Markan Jesus then swears the disciples to secrecy, as he had earlier ordered other witnesses of his deeds to keep silent (1:23–24, 34; 3:11–12; 5:7; 7:36; 8:30; see also 9:9). Jesus' reluctance to have news of his miracles spread abroad is known as the **messianic secret,** a term coined by the German scholar William Wrede (1901).

Some commentators have suggested that Mark's picture of Jesus' forbidding others to discuss him merely reflects historical fact: that during Jesus' lifetime most of his contemporaries did not regard him as God's special agent and that he himself made no public claims to be Israel's Messiah. Most scholars, however, believe that Mark's theme of the messianic secret represents the author's theological purpose. For Mark, people could not know Jesus' identity until *after* he had completed his mission. Jesus had to be unappreciated in order to be rejected and killed—to fulfill God's will that he "give up his life as a ransom for many" (10:45).

A conviction that Jesus must suffer an unjust death—an atonement offering for others—to confirm and complete his messiahship is the heart of Mark's **Christology** (concepts about the nature and function of Christ). Hence, Peter's confession at Caesarea Philippi that Jesus is the Christ (Messiah) is immediately followed by Jesus' first prediction that he will go to Jerusalem only to die (8:29–32). When Peter objects to this notion of a rejected and defeated Messiah, Jesus calls his chief disciple a "Satan." Derived from a Hebrew term meaning "obstacle," the epithet *Satan* labels Peter's attitude an obstacle or roadblock on Jesus' predestined path to the cross. Peter understands Jesus no better than outsiders, regarding the Messiah as a God-empowered hero who conquers his enemies, not as a submissive victim of their brutality. For Mark, however, Jesus' true identity must remain shrouded in darkness until it is revealed in the painful glare of the cross (see Figure 7.6).

At the end of chapter 8, Mark introduces a third idea: True disciples must expect to suffer as Jesus does. In two of the three Passion predictions, Jesus emphasizes that "anyone who wishes to be a follower of mine must leave self behind; he must take up his cross, and come with me" (8:27–34; 10:32–45). Irony permeates the third instance when James and John, sons of Zebedee, presumptuously ask to rule with

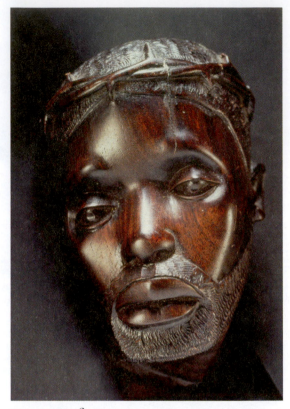

FIGURE 7.6 *Christ with the Crown of Thorns.* In this wooden carving of Jesus crowned with thorns, an anonymous twentieth-century African sculptor beautifully captures both the sorrow and the mystery of Mark's suffering Son of Man.

Jesus, occupying places of honor on his right and left. As Jesus explains that reigning with him means imitating his sacrifice, Mark's readers are intended to remember that when Jesus reaches Jerusalem the positions on his right and left will be taken by the two brigands crucified next to him (15:27).

In reiterating the necessity of suffering, Mark addresses a problem that undoubtedly troubled members of his own community: how to explain the contrast between the high expectations of reigning with Christ in glory (10:35–37) and the believers' actual circumstances. Instead of being vindicated publicly as God's chosen faithful, Christians of the late 60s CE were being treated like outcasts or traitors by Jewish Zealots and like criminals by the Roman emperor. Mark offers fellow believers the consolation that their hardships are foreshadowed by Jesus' experience; Christians must expect to be treated no more justly than their Master.

Mark's device of having a delegation of Jewish leaders conspire against Jesus in Galilee (3:6) and having Jesus repeatedly prophesy his death serves to cast the shadow of the cross backward in time over the Galilean ministry. These foreshadowing techniques help unify the polar opposites of Mark's narrative: They not only connect the powerful healer of Galilee with the sacrificial victim in Jerusalem but also link Jesus' experience with that of Mark's implied readers.

The Jerusalem Ministry: A Week of Sacred Time

In the third section of his Gospel, Mark focuses exclusively on the last week of Jesus' life, from the Sunday on which Jesus enters Jerusalem to the following Sunday's dawn, when some Galilean women find his tomb empty (11:1–16:8). To Mark, this is a sacred period during which Jesus accomplishes his life's purpose, sacrificing himself for humanity's redemption. Mark's Christian Holy Week also corresponds to Passover week, when thousands of Jews from throughout the Greco-Roman world gather in Jerusalem to celebrate Israel's deliverance from slavery in Egypt. As he narrates Jesus' rejection by Jewish leaders and execution by Roman officials, Mark celebrates the irony of events: Blind to Jesus' value, no one recognizes Jesus as a deliverer greater than Moses and a sacrifice that epitomizes the essential meaning of Passover.

The Triumphal Entry

If Mark was aware of Jesus' other visits to Jerusalem (narrated in John's Gospel), he dismisses them as unimportant compared with his last. In bold strokes, the author contrasts Jesus'

joyous reception in the holy city with the tragedy of his crucifixion five days later. A crowd, probably of Galilean supporters, enthusiastically welcomes Jesus to Jerusalem, hailing him as restorer of "the coming kingdom of our father David" (11:9–10). As Mark reports it, Jesus had carefully arranged his entry to fulfill Zechariah's prophecy that the Messiah would appear in humble guise, riding on a beast of burden (Zech. 9:9). Mark thus portrays Jesus suddenly making a radical change in policy: Instead of hiding his messianic identity, Jesus now seems to "go public"—challenging Jerusalem to accept him as God's Anointed. Jesus' appearance as a messianic claimant also challenges Roman authority. Because the Messiah was commonly expected to reestablish David's monarchy, the Roman prefect Pontius Pilate was likely to interpret Jesus' actions as a political claim to Judean kingship and, hence, to Rome, an act of treason (15:2–3).

Focus on the Temple

Once Jesus is in Jerusalem, his activities center around the Temple: His entrance into the city is not complete until he enters the Temple courts (11:1–10). On the Monday following his arrival, he creates a riot in the sanctuary, overturning moneychangers' tables and disrupting the sale of sacrificial animals (11:15–19). This assault on the Sadducean administration brands him as a threat to public order and probably seals his fate with the chief priests and Temple police.

As Mark describes his actions, Jesus visits the Temple, not to worship, but to pronounce eschatological judgment: Jesus' last teaching is a prophecy of the sanctuary's imminent destruction (ch. 13)—a prediction that may lie behind later charges that Jesus conspired to destroy the center of Jewish religion (14:56). Jesus' negative verdict on the Temple begins to take effect at his death, when the jeweled curtain veiling its inner sanctum is split apart (15:38), exposing its interior to public gaze and foreshadowing its imminent desecration by Gentiles (see Figure 7.7).

FIGURE 7.7 Warning inscription from Herod's Temple. Illustrating the barrier erected between Jews and Gentiles, this inscription warned Temple visitors that no Gentile could enter the inner courtyards except on pain of death.

Besides condemning the Temple's sacrificial system and the Sadducean priests who control it, Mark uses other devices to indicate that Jesus' Jerusalem ministry is fundamentally an adverse judgment on the city. Jesus' cursing an unproductive fig tree—the curse (11:12–14) and its fulfillment (11:20–24) bracketing the story of his attack on Temple practices—represents Mark's intent to condemn the Jerusalem leaders who, in his opinion, do not bear "good fruit" and are destined to wither and die.

The parable of the wicked tenants who kill their landlord's son (12:1–11) has the same function: to discredit Jesus' enemies. In Mark's view, the landlord (God) has now given his vineyard, traditionally a symbol for Israel, to "others"—the author's Christian community.

Confrontations at the Temple

In Jerusalem, clashes between Jesus and Jewish leaders intensify, becoming a matter of life or death. Mark pictures Jesus scoring success after success in a series of hostile encounters with representatives of leading religious parties as he moves through the Temple precincts, thronged with Passover pilgrims. The Pharisees and Herod Antipas's supporters attempt to trap Jesus on the controversial issue of paying taxes

to Rome, a snare he eludes by suggesting that people return government coins to their source while reserving for God the rest of one's life.

The Sadducees also suffer defeat when they try to force Jesus into an untenable position they hope will illustrate the illogic of a belief in resurrection to future life. When asked to which husband a woman who has been widowed six times will be married when all the former spouses are raised, Jesus states that there will be no ethical problem because resurrected persons escape the limits of human sexuality and become "like the angels in heaven" (12:18–25). Citing the Torah, apparently the only part of the Hebrew Bible that the Sadducees accept, he quotes Yahweh's words to Moses at the burning bush—that Yahweh is the God of Abraham, Isaac, and Jacob (Exod. 3:6)—arguing that, because Yahweh is "not God of the dead but of the living," the ancient patriarchs must still be alive from the Deity's perspective (12:26–27).

Interestingly, Mark closes Jesus' Temple debates with a friendly encounter in which the Galilean and a Torah expert agree on the essence of true religion. Answering a "lawyer's" question about the Bible's most important requirement, Jesus cites the Shema, or Jewish declaration of monotheism: There is only one God, and Israel must love him with all its force and being (Deut. 6:4–5). To this he adds a second Torah command: to love one's neighbor as oneself (Lev. 19:18). In agreement, the "lawyer" and Jesus exchange compliments. Although not a follower, the Jerusalem leader sees that active love is the essence of divine rule, a perception that Jesus says makes him "not far from the kingdom of God"—a more favorable verdict than Jesus ever passes on the Twelve (12:28–34).

Jesus' Prophecy of the Temple's Fall

In chapter 13, Mark underscores his eschatological concerns. In response to the disciples' question about when his prediction of Jerusalem's destruction will take place, Jesus delivers his longest speech, associating the Temple's fall with an era of catastrophes that culminate in the Son of Man appearing as eschatological judge. The author seems to have composed this discourse from a variety of sources, combining Jesus' words with older Jewish apocalyptic literature and perhaps with prophetic **oracles** from his own community as well. A considerably expanded version of the speech is preserved in Matthew 24, and a significantly modified version of Mark's eschatological expectations appears in Luke 21. John's Gospel contains no parallel to the Synoptic prophecies about the *eschaton.*

Readers will notice that Mark incorporates two somewhat contradictory views of the End. He states that a swarm of disasters and frightening astronomical phenomena will provide unmistakable "signs" that the Parousia is near, just as the budding fig tree heralds the arrival of spring (13:8, 14–20, 24–31). Conversely, neither the Son nor his followers can surmise the time of Final Judgment, so one must keep constant watch, because the End will occur without previous warning (13:32–37).

Oracles of Disaster Mark's strong emphasis on political and social upheavals as portents of the End reflects the turbulent era in which he composed his "wartime" Gospel. If, as historians believe, Mark wrote during the Jewish Revolt, when battles and insurrections were daily occurrences, he seems to have viewed these events as a turning point in history, an unprecedented crisis leading to the final apocalypse. In addition to witnessing the intense suffering of Palestinian Jews, the Markan community was undoubtedly aware of recent persecutions in Rome that resulted in numerous deaths, including the executions of Christianity's two chief apostles, Peter and Paul (mid-60s CE). Between about 67 and 70 CE, Zealots may also have attacked Palestinian Christians who accepted Gentiles into their communities, for those extreme revolutionaries regarded virtually all Gentiles as enemies of the Jewish nation. These ordeals may well account for Mark's references to "persecutions" and assertions that

unless this period of testing was "cut short," no believers could survive (13:9–13).

The "Abomination" Mark incorporates a cryptic passage from the Book of Daniel into his eschatological discourse. When believers see "'the abomination of desolation' usurping a place which is not his," they are to abandon their homes in Judea and take refuge in nearby hills (13:14–20; cf. Daniel 9:27; 11:31; 12:11). Directly addressing his readers, the author alerts them to the importance of understanding this reference (13:14). Some scholars believe that Mark here refers to the Zealots' violent occupation of the Temple in 67–68 CE and their pollution of its sacred precincts with the blood of their victims, which may have included some Christians (see Box 7.6).

This tribulation, which threatens the people of God, will be concluded by the Son of Man's appearing with his angels to gather the faithful. Mark shows Jesus warning disciples that all these horrors and wonders will occur in the lifetime of his hearers, although no one knows the precise day or hour (13:24–32). Mark's eschatological fervor, which Matthew and Luke subsequently mute in their respective versions of the Markan apocalypse (cf. Matt. 24–25 and Luke 21), vividly conveys both the fears and hopes of the author's Christian generation. Mark's eschatology, in fact, closely resembles that of Paul, who—a few years earlier—wrote the church in Corinth that "the time we live in will not last long" (1 Cor. 7:29). As his first letter to the Thessalonians makes clear, Paul fully expected to be alive at the Parousia (1 Thess. 4:13–18; see Chapters 14 and 15).

The Last Supper and Jesus' Betrayal

Following the eschatological discourse, Jesus withdraws with his disciples to a private "upper room" in Jerusalem. On Thursday evening, he presides over a **Passover** feast of unleavened bread, an observance that solemnly recalls Israel's last night in Egypt, when the Angel of Death "passed over" Israelites' houses to slay the Egyptian firstborn (Exod. 11:1–13:16). In a

BOX 7.6 The Desecrating "Abomination" and Mark's Eschatological Community

The longest speech that Mark assigns to Jesus is his prediction of Jerusalem's imminent destruction (Mark 13), suggesting that for Mark's intended audience this event was of great importance, a warning that the Parousia (Jesus' return in glory) was near. Mark's cryptic reference to the "abomination of desolation," an apocalyptic image borrowed from Daniel (Dan. 9:27; 11:31; 12:11), signifies a Gentile pollution of the Jerusalem Temple. Mark pointedly advises his readers to take careful note of this profanation of the sanctuary and, when they see it occurring, abandon their homes in Judea and take refuge in the surrounding hills.

In Daniel, the "abomination" was Antiochus IV's defilement of the Temple by sacrificing swine on its altar and erecting an altar to Zeus, king of the Hellenic gods, in its courtyard. Some scholars suggest that the "abomination" to which Mark refers was the occupation of the Temple area by brigands shortly before the Roman siege began.

According to Josephus, in the winter of 67–68 CE, a mixed band of Jewish guerrilla fighters moved into Jerusalem from the countryside and seized control of the Temple. Led by Eleazar, son of Simon (see Chapter 3), this revolutionary group formed the Zealot party, which resolved not only to expel the Romans but also to purge the city of any Jewish leaders who cooperated with them. Adopting a policy of radical egalitarianism, the Zealots fiercely attacked Jerusalem's wealthy aristocracy and the Temple's priestly administration, which they condemned as traitors to the Jewish nation for having collaborated with the Romans. The Zealots assassinated many of the Jewish landowners and priests, staining the Temple pavements with the blood of Jerusalem's leadership, acts that outraged Josephus and may have been regarded as a polluting "abomination" by other Jews.

The Zealots also held illegal trials for and executions of those they suspected of not sharing their total commitment to the war against Rome. It is possible that Jerusalem's Christian community, which by then included Gentiles (an anathema to the Zealots), suffered Zealot persecution and that the shedding of Christian blood, both Jewish and Gentile, also contaminated the holy place, an "abominable" guarantee of its impending fall.

The church historian Eusebius records that shortly before Jerusalem was obliterated Christians there received an "oracle" inciting them to escape from the city and settle in **Pella,** a mostly Gentile town in the Decapolis, a territory east of the Jordan dominated by a league of ten Hellenistic cities (*Eccl. Hist.* 3.5.3). Scholars still debate the historicity of this episode, but Josephus reveals that such "inspired" predictions about Jerusalem's dire fate were circulating among Jews during the war with Rome. He states that some Jews prophesied that the Temple would be destroyed "when sedition and native hands [the Zealots] should be the first to defile God's sacred precincts" (*The Jewish War* 4.6.3; see also 4.3.10 and 4.3.12). In Christian circles, oral traditions about Jesus' pronouncement on Jerusalem may have been the source of Mark's declaration to flee the city when the "abomination" (Zealot defilement of the sanctuary?) occurred.

For a detailed analysis of the Jewish Revolt's influence on Mark 13, see Joel Marcus, "The Jewish War and the *Sitz im Leben* of Mark," *Journal of Biblical Literature* 3(3) (1992): 441–462.

---

ritual at the close of their meal, Jesus gives the Passover a new significance, stating that the bread he distributes is his "body" and the wine his "blood of the [New] Covenant, shed for many" (14:22–25)—liturgical symbols of his crucifixion. Mark's account of this **Last Supper,** the origin of the Christian celebration of the **Eucharist,** or Holy Communion, closely resembles Paul's earlier description of the ceremony (1 Cor. 11:23–26).

Mark's Passion Narrative: Jesus' Trial and Crucifixion

Mark's Suffering Messiah

In describing Jesus' **Passion**—his final suffering and death—Mark's narrative irony reaches its height. Although the author emphasizes many grim details of Jesus' excruciatingly painful execution, he means his readers to see the enormous disparity between the *appearance* of Jesus' vulnerability to the world's evil and the actual reality of his spiritual triumph. Jesus' enemies, who believe they are ridding Judea of a dangerous radical, are in fact making possible his saving death—all according to God's design.

Jesus' Arrest in Gethsemane Even so, Mark's hero is tested fully—treated with vicious cruelty (14:65; 15:15–20), deserted by all his friends (14:50), and even (in human eyes) abandoned by God (15:34). The agony begins in **Gethsemane,** a grove or vineyard on the **Mount of Olives** opposite Jerusalem, to which Jesus and the disciples retreat after the Last Supper. In the Gethsemane episode (14:28–52), Mark places a dual emphasis on Jesus' fulfilling predictions in the Hebrew Bible (14:26–31, 39) and on his personal anguish. By juxtaposing these two elements, Mark demonstrates that, while the Crucifixion will take place as God long ago planned (and revealed in Scripture), Jesus' part in the drama of salvation demands heroic effort. While the disciples sleep, Jesus faces the hard reality of his impending torture, experiencing "grief" and "horror and dismay." To Mark, his hero—emotionally ravaged and physically defenseless—provides the model for all believers whose loyalty is tested. Although Jesus prays that God will spare him the humiliation and pain he dreads, he forces his own will into harmony with God's. Mark reports that, even during this cruel testing of the heavenly Father–Son of Man relationship, Jesus addresses the Deity as *Abba,* an Aramaic term expressing a child's trusting intimacy with the parent (14:32–41).

Jesus' Hearing Before Caiaphas Mark's skill as a storyteller—and interpreter of the events he narrates—is demonstrated in the artful way he organizes his account of Jesus' Passion. Peter's testing (14:37–38) and denial that he even knows Jesus (15:65–72) provide the frame for and ironic parallel to Jesus' trial before the Sanhedrin, the Jewish council headed by **Caiaphas,** the High Priest. When Peter fulfills Jesus' prediction about denying him, the disciple's failure serves a double purpose: confirming Jesus' prophetic gifts and strengthening readers' confidence in Jesus' ability to fulfill other prophecies, including those of his resurrection (14:28) and reappearance as the glorified Son of Man (14:62).

Mark contrasts Peter's fearful denial with Jesus' courageous declaration to the Sanhedrin that he is indeed the Messiah and the appointed agent of God's future judgment (14:62). The only Gospel writer to show Jesus explicitly accepting a messianic identity at his trial, Mark may do so to highlight his theme that Jesus' messiahship is revealed primarily through humility and service, a denial of self that also effects humanity's salvation (10:45). Like the author of Hebrews, Mark sees Jesus' divine Sonship earned and perfected through suffering and death (Heb. 2:9–11; 5:7–10).

Pilate's Condemnation of Jesus At daybreak on Friday, the "whole council held a consultation" (15:1)—perhaps implying that the night meeting had been illegal and therefore lacked authority to condemn Jesus—and sends the accused to **Pontius Pilate,** the Roman prefect (governor) who was in Jerusalem to maintain order during Passover week. Uninterested in the Sanhedrin's charge that Jesus is a blasphemer, Pilate focuses on Jesus' reputed political crime, seditiously claiming to be the Jewish king. After remarking that it is Pilate himself who has stated the claim, Jesus refuses to answer further questions. Because Mark re-creates almost the entire Passion story in the context of Old Testament prophecies, it is difficult to know if Jesus' silence represents his actual behavior or the author's reliance on Isaiah 53, where Israel's suffering servant does not respond to his accusers (Isa. 53:7).

As Mark describes the proceedings, Pilate is extremely reluctant to condemn Jesus and does so only after the priestly hierarchy pressures him to act. Whereas the Markan Pilate maneuvers to spare Jesus' life, the historical Pilate (prefect of Judea from 26 to 36 CE), whom Josephus describes, rarely hesitated to slaughter troublesome Jews (cf. *Antiquities* 18.3.1–2; *The Jewish War* 2.9.4). When a mob demands that not Jesus but a convicted terrorist named **Barabbas** be freed, Pilate is pictured as having no choice but to release Barabbas (the first person to benefit from Jesus' sacrifice) and order the Galilean's crucifixion.

Jesus' Crucifixion Stripped, flogged, mocked, and crowned with thorns, Jesus is apparently unable to carry the crossbeam of his cross, so Roman soldiers impress a bystander, **Simon of Cyrene,** to carry it for him (15:16–21). Taken to **Golgotha** (Place of the Skull) outside Jerusalem, Jesus is crucified between two criminals (traditionally called "thieves" but probably brigands similar to those who formed the Zealot party in Mark's day). According to Pilate's order, his cross bears a statement of the political offense for which he is executed: aspiring to be the Jewish king—a cruelly ironic revelation of his true identity (15:22–32).

Mark's description of the Crucifixion is almost unendurably bleak (see Figure 7.8). To bystanders, who mock him for his assumed pretensions to kingly authority, Jesus—nailed to the cross—appears powerless and defeated (15:29–30). As Mark so darkly paints it, the scene is a tragic paradox: Despite the seeming triumph of religious and political forces allied against him, Jesus is neither guilty nor a failure. The failure lies in humanity's collective inability to recognize the sufferer's inestimable value, to see in him God's hand at work. To emphasize the spiritual blindness of Jesus' tormenters, Mark states that a midday darkness envelops the earth (15:33).

Unlike Luke or John, who show Jesus dying with serene confidence (see Box 10.7), Mark focuses only on Jesus' isolation and abandonment, making his last words (in Aramaic) a cry of despair: *"Eli, Eli, lema sabachthani?"*—"My God, my God, why hast thou forsaken me?" (15:34). In placing this question—a direct quotation of Psalm 22:1—on Jesus' lips, the author may echo a memory of Jesus' last words. Mark's main purpose, however, is probably to create a paradigm for Christians facing a similar fate and to show that out of human malice the divine goal is accomplished. From the author's perspective, there is an enormous disparity between what witnesses to the Crucifixion think is happening and the saving work that God actually achieves through Jesus' death. In Mark's eschatological vision, the horror of Jesus' agony is transformed by God's intervention to raise his son in glory.

Jesus' Burial

Although some scholars believe that Mark's wealth of concrete detail indicates that he drew on a well-developed oral form of the Passion story for his Gospel, others think that the narrative of Jesus' last week is basically a Markan composition. In contrast to the geographical vagueness of much of his Galilean narrative, the author's Passion account is full of the names of specific places and participants, from Gethsemane, to Pilate's courtyard, to Golgotha. As in all four Gospels, **Mary of Magdala** provides the key human link connecting Jesus' death and burial and the subsequent discovery that his grave is empty (15:40–41, 47; 16:1). **Joseph of Arimathea,** a mysterious figure introduced suddenly into the narrative, serves a single function: to transfer Jesus' body from Roman control to that of the dead man's disciples. Acquainted with Pilate, a member of the Sanhedrin and yet a covert supporter of Jesus' ministry, he bridges the two opposing worlds of Jesus' enemies and friends. Not only does Joseph obtain official permission to remove Jesus' body from the cross—otherwise, it would routinely

FIGURE 7.8 *The Small Crucifixion.* Painted on wood by Matthias Grünewald (c. 1470–1528), this small version of Jesus' tortured death heightens the sense of the sufferer's physical pain and grief. Although his emphasis on Jesus' agony reflects Mark's account, Grünewald follows John's Gospel in showing Jesus' mother and the beloved disciple (as well as another Mary) present at the cross.

be consigned to an anonymous mass grave—but he also provides a secure place of entombment, a rock-hewn sepulcher that he seals by rolling a large, flat stone across the entrance (15:42–47).

Postlude: The Empty Tomb

Because the Jewish Sabbath begins at sundown on Friday, the day of Jesus' execution, the female disciples cannot prepare the corpse for interment until Sunday morning. Arriving at dawn, the women find the entrance stone already rolled back and the crypt empty except for the presence of a young man dressed in white. (Is he the same unidentified youth who fled naked from Gethsemane in 14:50–51?)

Mark's scene at the vacant tomb recalls themes recurring throughout his Gospel. Like the male disciples who could not understand Jesus' allusion to resurrection (9:9–10), the women are bewildered, unable to accept the youth's revelation that Jesus is "risen." Fleeing in terror, the women say "nothing to anybody" about what they have heard (16:8), leaving readers in suspense, wondering how the "good news" of Jesus' resurrection was ever proclaimed. The Gospel thus concludes with a frightened silence, eschewing any account of Jesus' post resurrection appearances (16:8).

Mark's Challenge to the Reader

Some interpreters suggest that the double failure of Jesus' disciples—the Eleven who desert him in Gethsemane and the Galilean women too paralyzed by fear to proclaim the good news of his resurrection—is intended to challenge the reader. If all Jesus' closest followers fail him, who but the readers, who now know conclusively that God has acted through their crucified Lord, can testify confidently that he is both Israel's Messiah and universal king (see Tolbert in "Recommended Reading")?

Mark's Inconclusiveness: Resurrection or Parousia?

Other commentators propose that Mark's belief in the nearness of Jesus' Parousia may explain why the risen Jesus does not manifest himself in the earliest Gospel. The mysterious youth in white tells the women how to find Jesus—the risen Lord has already started a posthumous journey "to Galilee," where Peter and the other disciples "will see him" (16:6–7). Some scholars think that Mark, convinced that the political and social chaos of the Jewish Revolt will soon climax in Jesus' return, refers not to a resurrection phenomenon but to the Parousia. Forty years after the Crucifixion, Mark's community may believe that their wandering through the wilderness is almost over: They are about to follow Jesus across Jordan into "Galilee," his promised kingdom.

Mark's inconclusiveness, his insistence on leaving his story open-ended, must have seemed as unsatisfactory to later Christian scribes as it does to many readers today. For perhaps that reason, Mark's Gospel has been heavily edited, with two different conclusions added at different times. All the oldest manuscripts of Mark end with the line stressing the women's terrified refusal to obey the young man's instruction to carry the Resurrection message to Peter. In time, however, some editors appended post resurrection accounts to their copies of Mark, making his Gospel more consistent with Matthew and Luke (Mark 16:8b and 16:9–20).

Summary

Christianity's first attempt to create a sequential account of Jesus' public ministry, arrest, and execution, Mark's Gospel includes relatively little of Jesus' teaching. Focusing on Jesus' actions—exorcisms, healings, and other miracles—the author presents his mighty works as evidence that God's kingdom has begun to rule, breaking up Satan's control over suffering humanity. Writing under the shadow of Roman persecution and the impending Roman destruction of Jerusalem, Mark presents Jesus as an eschatological Son of Man, who will soon reappear to judge all people.

Mark's ironic vision depicts Jesus as an unexpected and unwanted kind of Messiah who is predestined to be misunderstood, rejected, and crucified—a Messiah revealed only in suffering and death. God, however, uses humanity's blindness and inadequacy to provide a ransom sacrifice in his Son, saving humankind despite its attempts to resist him.

Questions for Review

1. According to tradition, who wrote the Gospel according to Mark? Why are modern scholars unable to verify that tradition? What themes in the Gospel suggest that it was composed after the Jewish Revolt against Rome had already begun?
2. Outline and summarize the major events in Jesus' public career, from his baptism by John and his Galilean ministry through his last week in Jerusalem. Specify the devices that Mark uses to connect the powerful miracle worker in Galilee with the seemingly powerless sacrificial victim in Jerusalem. Why does Mark devote so much space and detail to narrating the Passion story? Why does he have Jesus predict his own death three times?
3. Describe the three different categories Mark assigns the Son of Man concept. How is this concept related to earlier Jewish writings, such as the books of Ezekiel, Daniel, and 1 Enoch?
4. Define *parable*, and discuss Jesus' use of this literary form to illustrate his vision of God's kingdom. Why does Mark state that Jesus used parables to *prevent* people from understanding his message?
5. Explain a possible connection between the messianic secret concept and Mark's picture of the disciples as hopelessly inept and Jesus' opponents as mistakenly seeing him as the devil's agent. What devices does the author employ to convey his view that Jesus had to be misunderstood for him to fulfill God's plan?

Questions for Discussion and Reflection

1. How does the historical situation when Mark wrote help account for the author's portrait of Jesus as a suffering Messiah whose disciples must also expect to suffer? Would the wars, insurrections, and persecutions afflicting Mark's community have stimulated the author's sense of eschatological urgency?
2. Why does Mark paint so unflattering a picture of Jesus' Galilean family, neighbors, and disciples, all of whom fail to understand or support him? Do you think that the author is trying to disassociate Christianity from its Palestinian origins in favor of his Gentile church's understanding of Jesus' significance?
3. Do you think that Mark's emphasis on Jesus' exorcisms—his battle with cosmic evil—is an expression of the author's eschatology, his belief that in Jesus' activities God's kingdom has begun and the End is near? Explain your answer.
4. Discuss Mark's use of irony in his presentation of Jesus' story. List and discuss some incongruities between the spiritual reality that Jesus embodies and the way in which most people in the Markan narrative perceive him. In the literary world that Mark creates in his Gospel, how do appearance and reality conflict? How does Mark demonstrate that God achieves his purpose in Jesus even though political and religious authorities succeed in destroying him?
5. In your view, why does Mark end his Gospel so abruptly? Are there any clues in the Gospel that the author expects the Parousia to occur imminently? Are stories of Jesus' post resurrection appearances merely precursors of his return as eschatological judge?

Terms and Concepts to Remember

Abba	Eucharist
allegory	exorcism
Andrew	Galilee
apocalypse	Gethsemane
baptism	Golgotha
Barabbas	Holy Spirit
Bartholomew	Jairus
Caesarea Philippi	James
Caiaphas	John the Baptist
Capernaum	Joseph of Arimathea
Cephas	Judas Iscariot
Christ	kingdom of God
Christology	Last Supper
disciples	Mark
epiphany	Mary of Magdala
eschaton	Matthew

messianic secret
Mount of Olives
Nazareth
oracles
parable
Passion
Passover
Pella
Peter
Philip
Pontius Pilate
Sabbath
Sanhedrin (Great
    Council)
Satan

Sea of Galilee
Second Coming
    (Parousia)
simile
Simon of Cyrene
Simon Peter
Son of God
Son of Man
Thaddeus
Thomas
Transfiguration
Zebedee [sons of
    thunder
    (Boanerges)]
Zoroastrianism

Recommended Reading

Bryan, Christopher. *A Preface to Mark: Notes on the Gospel in Its Literary and Cultural Settings.* New York: Oxford University Press, 1993. Links Mark with the oral tradition.

Collins, Adela Yarbro. *Mark: A Commentary.* Minneapolis: Fortress Press, 2007. A detailed, verse-by-verse analysis of the Gospel, emphasizing the author's eschatological urgency.

France, R. T. *The Gospel of Mark. New International Greek Testament Commentary.* Grand Rapids, Mich.: Eerdmans, 2002. Analyzes Mark as a literary whole; for advanced students.

Harrington, Daniel J. *What Are They Saying About Mark?* New York: Paulist Press, 2005. An accessible survey of contemporary critical interpretations.

Henderson, Suzanne W. "Mark, Gospel According to." In M.D. Coogan, ed., *The Oxford Encyclopedia of the Books of the Bible*, Vol. 2, pp. 42–56. New York: Oxford University Press, 2011. Surveys Mark's version of Jesus' story, summarizing different critical interpretations.

Kelber, W. H. *Mark's Story of Jesus.* Philadelphia: Fortress Press, 1979. A penetrating but succinct analysis of Mark's rendition of Jesus' life.

———. *The Oral and the Written Gospel: The Hermeneutics of Speaking and Writing in the Synoptic Tradition, Mark, Paul, and Q.* Philadelphia: Fortress Press, 1983. A major scholarly study of Mark's place in the Jesus tradition.

Ladd, George Eldon. *A Theology of the New Testament.* Grand Rapids, Mich.: Eerdmans, 1974.

Levine, Amy-Jill, ed. *A Feminist Companion to Mark.* Feminist Companion to the New Testament and Early Christian Writings Series. Cleveland: Pilgrim Press, 2004. Essays reexamining the role of women in the earliest Gospel.

Marcus, Joel. *Mark 1–8* (The Anchor Yale Bible Commentaries). New Haven, CT: Yale University Press, 2002. An excellent resource, emphasizing the Jewish context.

———. *Mark 8–16* (The Anchor Yale Bible Commentaries). New Haven, CT: Yale University Press, 2009. Provides historical background and appropriate theological interpretation.

Minor, Mitzi. "Mark, Gospel of." In K. D. Sakenfeld, ed., *The New Interpreter's Dictionary of the Bible,* Vol. 3, pp. 798–811. Nashville: Abingdon Press, 2008. A concise analysis of the earliest narrative Gospel.

Perkins, Pheme. "The Gospel of Mark." In *The New Interpreter's Bible,* Vol. 8, pp. 509–733. Nashville: Abingdon Press, 1995. Complete Markan text with extensive commentary.

Tolbert, Mary Ann. "Mark." In Carol A. Newsom and S. H. Ringe, eds., *Women's Bible Commentary,* pp. 350–362. Louisville, Ky.: Westminster John Knox, 1998. A perceptive essay.

Wrede, William. *The Messianic Secret.* Translated by J. C. G. Greig. Cambridge: Clarke, 1971. A technical but crucial study of Mark's narrative methods.

CHAPTER 8

Matthew's Portrait of Jesus
A Teacher Greater Than Moses

*Do not suppose that I have come to abolish the Law and the prophets;
I did not come to abolish, but to complete.* Matthew 5:17

Key Topics/Themes Most scholars agree that Matthew's Gospel is an expanded edition of Mark, which the author frames with accounts of Jesus' birth (chs. 1 and 2) and post resurrection appearances (ch. 28). Although retaining Mark's general sequence of events, Matthew adds five blocks of teaching material, emphasizing Jesus as the inaugurator of a New Covenant (26:26–29) who definitively interprets the Mosaic Torah and who, by fulfilling specific prophecies in the Hebrew Bible, proves his identity as Israel's Messiah. Written a decade or two after the Roman destruction of Jerusalem, Matthew somewhat softens Mark's portrait of an eschatological Jesus, adding parables that imply a delay in the Parousia (Second Coming) (chs. 24 and 25), an interval of indefinite length devoted to the missionary work of the church (*ekklesia*). Matthew's principal discourses include the Sermon on the Mount (chs. 5–7), instructions to the Twelve (ch. 10), parables of the kingdom (ch. 13), instructions to the church (ch. 18), and warnings of Final Judgment (chs. 23–25).

Matthew's Relationship to the Hebrew Bible

If Mark was the first Gospel written, as most scholars believe, why does Matthew's Gospel stand first in the New Testament canon? The original compilers of the New Testament probably assigned Matthew the premier position for several reasons. It offers more extensive coverage of Jesus' teaching than any other Gospel, making it the church's major resource in instructing its members. In addition, Matthew's

Gospel was particularly important to early church leaders because it is the Gospel most explicitly concerned with the nature and function of the **church** (Greek, *ekklesia*). The only Gospel even to use the term *ekklesia,* Matthew devotes two full chapters (chs. 10 and 18) to providing specific guidance to the Christian community.

The placement of Matthew's Gospel at the opening of the New Testament is also thematically appropriate because it forms a strong connecting link with the Hebrew Bible (Old Testament), albeit in a Greek edition. Matthew

165

initiates his account with a genealogy that associates Jesus with the most prominent heroes of ancient Israel. Beginning with Abraham, progenitor of the Hebrew people, Matthew lists as Jesus' ancestors celebrated kings like David, Solomon, and Josiah. The manner in which Matthew presents his record of Jesus' ancestors is typical of his use of the Hebrew Bible. His purpose is not only to establish Jesus' messianic credentials—by right of descent from Abraham and David—but also to present Jesus' birth as the climax of Israelite history. He therefore arranges Jesus' family tree in three distinct segments, each representing a particular phase of the biblical story. From the time of Abraham, bearer of the covenant promises for land, nationhood, and universal blessing (Gen. 12:1–3; 22:18), to that of David, bearer of the covenant promise of an everlasting line of kings (2 Sam. 7:16), is fourteen generations. From the time of David, whose prosperous kingdom is the high point of Israel's history, to the Babylonian exile, the lowest ebb of Israelite fortunes, is another fourteen generations. From the time

of Babylonian captivity to the appearance of Jesus, who inherits all the promises made to Abraham and David, is also fourteen generations (Matt. 1:17). As fourteen generations intervened between Yahweh's vow to Abraham and the establishment of David's throne, so an equal span of time elapsed between the Babylonian overthrow of the Davidic line and the appearance of David's ultimate heir, the Messiah. Although the neatness of Matthew's numerical scheme conveys the author's sense of Jesus' crucial importance to the covenant people—and his view of the mathematically precise way in which God arranges Israel's history—closer examination of the genealogy raises some difficulties.

First, Matthew actually lists thirteen, not fourteen, generations between the Babylonian destruction of Jerusalem and Jesus' birth. Second, one of Matthew's sources for the period between David and the exile, 1 Chronicles 3:10–12, reveals the names of several Davidic kings (at least three generations) that he omitted from the list, presumably to fit his desired sequence of fourteen. Finally, at the end of his genealogy, Matthew unexpectedly states that the line of royal descent directly connects not with Jesus, but with Joseph, who the writer believes was not Jesus' biological father. Somewhat paradoxically, Matthew concludes his list by noting that Jesus' paternal grandfather is "Jacob [father] of Joseph, the husband of Mary, who gave birth to Jesus called Messiah" (Matt. 1:16). The Evangelist may assume that Joseph is Jesus' legal and social parent, and thus can transmit his Davidic legacy to a nonrelative, perhaps through adoption, even if he did not transmit it genetically.

Writing independently of Matthew, Luke compiled a strikingly different genealogy, which further clouds the issue of Jesus' Davidic ancestry (Luke 3:25–38). Using many names not on Matthew's list, Luke states that people "thought" that Jesus was Joseph's son and that his paternal grandfather was Heli (not Jacob, as Matthew has it). Almost since the two Gospel

The Gospel According to Matthew

Author: Traditionally Matthew (also called Levi), one of the Twelve. Because the writer uses Mark as his primary source, scholars believe it unlikely that he was an apostolic witness to the events he describes. The work is anonymous.

Date: The 80s CE, at least a decade after the destruction of Jerusalem, when tensions between postwar Jewish leaders and early Christians provoked bitter controversy. The author, a Greek-speaking Christian Jew, penned the most violent denunciations of his fellow Jews in the New Testament.

Place of composition: Probably Antioch in Syria, site of a large Jewish and Jewish-Christian community.

Sources: Mark, Q, and special Matthean material (M).

Audience: Greek-speaking Jewish Christians and Gentiles who were, at least partly, Torah observant.

genealogies were first published, Christians have sought to resolve their apparent disagreement, but although ingenious solutions have been proposed, none yet has been universally accepted. Whatever its historical credibility, the family tree with which Matthew begins his Gospel (and hence the New Testament itself) proclaims Jesus as the culminating figure in a long biblical tradition. As several scholars have observed, Matthew may have devised his genealogical pattern of fourteen for its messianic significance. Because Hebrew, like Greek and many other ancient languages, uses letters to signify numbers, each letter of the alphabet has a numerical value. In Hebrew, the three consonants making up David's name (DWD) total fourteen, which can function as the symbolic number of David's promised heir.

Although biblical genealogists uniformly recorded only the male line, linking fathers to sons, Matthew includes four female ancestors of Jesus—Tamar (1:3), Rahab (1:5), Ruth (1:5), and Bathsheba, "the wife of Uriah," who later became David's queen and the mother of King Solomon (1:6). Matthew's reasons for departing from biblical tradition are unclear, but scholars have found at least two factors that thematically bind these women together and that may have influenced the Evangelist's decision to list them as part of Jesus' heritage. Besides the fact that all four were Gentiles (Ruth was a Moabite, Tamar and Rahab Canaanites, and Bathsheba a Hittite), all four were also involved in irregular sexual activity. While Tamar posed as a prostitute to beguile her father-in-law into impregnating her (Gen. 38), Rahab actually plied the trade of a "harlot" in Canaanite Jericho (Josh. 2; 6). A young widow, Ruth seduced Boaz into marrying her (Ruth 1–4), and Bathsheba committed adultery with David, becoming his wife only after the king had arranged to have her husband Uriah slain in battle (2 Sam. 11–12; 1 Kings 1–2).

Matthew states that, when Joseph discovered that his future bride, Mary, was already expecting a child, he planned to divorce her secretly to spare her public dishonor. He accepts Mary as his wife only after he dreams of an angel informing him that she had "conceived this child" by the "Holy Spirit" (1:18–25). Although Matthew connects Jesus with Abraham and David explicitly through Joseph, he also specifies that Mary is the sole human parent (1:16). As Matthew arranged Jesus' forebears in groups of fourteen to express divine providence at work, so he underscores the presence of ancestresses (and their male partners) with questionable pasts to illustrate God's unexpected use of flawed humanity to accomplish his purpose.

Matthew's wish to connect Jesus with the Hebrew Bible goes far beyond genealogical concerns. More than any other Gospel writer, he presents Jesus' life in the context of biblical law and prophecy. Throughout the entire Gospel, Matthew underscores Jesus' fulfillment of ancient prophecies, repeatedly emphasizing the continuity between Jesus and the promises made to Israel, particularly to the royal dynasty of David. To demonstrate that Jesus' entire career, from conception to resurrection, was predicted centuries earlier by biblical writers from Moses to Malachi, Matthew quotes from, paraphrases, or alludes to the Hebrew Bible at least 60 times. (Some scholars have detected 140 or more allusions to the Hebrew Scriptures.) Nearly a dozen times, Matthew employs a literary formula that drives home the connection between prophecy and specific events in Jesus' life: "All this happened in order to fulfill what the Lord declared through the prophet," Matthew writes, then citing a biblical passage to support his contention (1:22–23; 2:15, 23; see Box 8.1).

Matthew takes great pains to show that Jesus both taught and fulfilled the principles of the Mosaic Law (5:17–20). For these and other reasons, Matthew is usually regarded as the "most Jewish" of the Gospels. At the same time, the author violently attacks the leaders of institutional Judaism, condemning the Pharisees and scribes with extreme bitterness (ch. 23).

BOX 8.1 **Representative Examples of Matthew's Use of the Septuagint (Greek) Version of the Hebrew Bible to Identify Jesus as the Promised Messiah**

MATTHEW

HEBREW BIBLE SOURCE

All this happened in order to fulfill what the Lord declared through the prophet. (Matt. 1:22)

1. The Virgin will conceive and bear a son, and he shall be called Emmanuel. (Matt. 1:22)

2. Bethlehem in the land of Judah, you are far from least in the eyes of the rulers of Judah; for out of you shall come a leader to be the shepherd of my people Israel. (Matt. 2:5–6)

3. So Joseph . . . went away . . . to Egypt, and there he stayed till Herod's death. This was to fulfill what the Lord had declared through the prophet: "I called my son out of Egypt." (Matt. 2:15)

4. Herod . . . gave orders for the massacre of all children in Bethlehem and its neighborhood, of the age of two years or less. . . . So the words spoken through Jeremiah the prophet were fulfilled: "A voice was heard in Rama, wailing and loud laments; it was Rachael weeping for her children, and refusing all consolation, because they were no more." (Matt. 2:16–18)

5. He shall be called a Nazarene. (Matt. 2:23)
   [This statement does not appear in the Hebrew Bible; it may be a misreading of Isaiah 11:1.]

6. When he heard that John had been arrested, Jesus withdrew to Galilee; and leaving Nazareth he went and settled at Capernaum on the Sea of Galilee, in the district of Zebulun and Naphtali. This was to fulfill the passage in the prophet Isaiah which tells of the land of Zebulun, the land of Naphtali, the Way of the Sea, the land beyond Jordan, heathen Galilee, and says:

   "The people that lived in darkness saw a great light:
   light dawned on the dwellers in the land of death's dark shadow." (Matt. 4:12–16)

7. And he drove the spirits out with a word and healed all who were sick, to fulfill the prophecy of Isaiah: "He took away our illnesses and lifted our diseases from us." (Matt. 8:16–17)

1. A young woman is with child, and she will bear a son and will call him Immanuel. (Isa. 7:14)

2. But you, Bethlehem in Ephrathah, small as you are to be among Judah's clans, out of you shall come forth a governor for Israel, one whose roots are far back in the past, in days gone by. (Mic. 5:2)

3. When Israel was a boy, I loved him;
   I called my son out of Egypt. (Hos. 11:1)
   [Hosea refers to the Exodus from Egypt, not a future Messiah.]

4. Hark, lamentation is heard in Ramah, and bitter weeping,
   Rachel weeping for her sons.
   She refuses to be comforted: they are no more.
   (Jer. 31:15)

5. Then a shoot shall grow from the stock of Jesse, and a branch [Hebrew, *nezer*] shall spring from his roots. (Isa. 11:1)

6. For, while the first invader has dealt lightly with the land of Zebulun and the land of Naphtali, the second has dealt heavily with Galilee of the Nations on the road beyond Jordan to the sea:

   The people who walked in darkness
   have seen a great light:
   light has dawned upon them,
   dwellers in a land as dark as death.
   (Isa. 9:1–2)

7. Yet on himself he bore our sufferings,
   our torments he endured,
   while we counted him smitten by God,
   struck down by disease and misery.
   (Isa. 53:4)

MATTHEW	**HEBREW BIBLE SOURCE**

All this happened in order to fulfill what the Lord declared through the prophet. (Matt. 1:22)

8. Jesus . . . gave strict injunctions that they were not to make him known. This was to fulfill Isaiah's prophecy:

> "Here is my servant, whom I have chosen,
> my beloved on whom my favour rests;
> I will put my spirit upon him,
> and he will proclaim judgment among the
>   nations.
> He will not strive, he will not shout,
> nor will his voice be heard in the streets.
> He will not snap off the broken reed,
> nor snuff out the smouldering wick,
> until he leads justice on to victory.
> In him the nations shall place their hope."
>   (Matt. 12:16–21)

9. In all his teaching to the crowds, Jesus spoke in parables; in fact, he never spoke to them without a parable. This was to fulfill the prophecy of Isaiah:

> "I will open my mouth in parables;
> I will utter things kept secret since the
>   world was made."   (Matt. 13:34–35)

10. Jesus instructs his disciples to bring him a donkey and her foal. "If any speaks to you, say 'Our Master needs them'; and he will let you take them at once." This was to fulfill the prophecy which says, "Tell the daughter of Zion, 'Here is your king, who comes to you riding on an ass, riding on the foal of a beast of burden.'" (Matt. 21:2–5) *[Matthew shows Jesus mounted on two beasts—the donkey and her foal. See Luke 19:29–36, where a single mount is mentioned.]*

11. *[Judas returns the bribe—"thirty silver pieces"—given him to betray Jesus.]*
. . . and in this way fulfillment was given to the saying of the prophet Jeremiah: "They took the thirty silver pieces, the price set on a man's head (for that was his price among the Israelites) and gave the money for the potter's field, so the Lord directed me." (Matt. 27:9–10)

---

8. Here is my servant, whom I uphold,
   my chosen one in whom I delight,
   I have bestowed my spirit upon him,
   and he will make justice shine on the nations.
   He will not call out or lift his voice high,
   Or make himself heard in the open street.
   He will not break a bruised reed,
   or snuff out a smouldering wick;
   he will make justice shine on every race,
   never faltering, never breaking down,
   he will plant justice on earth,
   while coasts and islands wait for his teaching.
       (Isa. 42:1–4)

9. Mark my teaching, O my people,
   listen to the words I am to speak.
   I will tell you a story with a meaning,
   I will expound the riddle of things past,
   things that we have heard and know,
   and our fathers have repeated to us.
       (Ps. 78:2—*not* in Isaiah)

10. Rejoice, rejoice, daughter of Zion,
    shout aloud, daughter of Jerusalem;
    for see, your king is coming to you,
    his cause won, his victory gained,
    humble and mounted on an ass,
    on a foal, the young of a she-ass.
        (Zech. 9:9)

11. *[Matthew is wrong in citing Jeremiah as the source of this passage, which, in the form he quotes it, does not appear in the Hebrew Bible. It is Zechariah who reports being paid "thirty shekels of silver," which he then donates to the Temple treasury:]*
So they weighed out as my wages thirty shekels of silver. Then the Lord said to me, "Throw it into the treasury—this is the lordly price [the standard price of a slave] at which I was valued by them." So I took the thirty shekels of silver and threw them into the treasury in the house of the Lord. *[Jeremiah does record investing in a field near Jerusalem (Jer. 32:6–15) and refers to visiting a potter's house (Jer. 18:1–3), but neither he nor Zechariah provides support for Matthew's claim of prophetic fulfillment.]*

Authorship, Purpose, Sources, and Organization

Who was the man so deeply interested in Jesus' practice of the Jewish religion and simultaneously so fierce in his denunciation of Jewish leaders? As in Mark's case, the author does not identify himself, suggesting to most historians that the Gospel originated and circulated anonymously. The tradition that the author is the "publican" or tax collector mentioned in Matthew 9:9–13 (and called "Levi" in Mark 2:14) dates from the late second century CE and cannot be verified. The main problem with accepting the apostle Matthew's authorship is that the writer relies heavily on Mark as a source. It is extremely unlikely that one of the original Twelve would have depended on the work of Mark, who was not an eyewitness to the events he describes.

The oldest apparent reference to the Gospel's authorship is that of Papias (c. 140 CE), whom Eusebius quotes: "Matthew compiled the Sayings [Greek, *logia*] in the Aramaic language, and everyone translated them as well as he could" (*History* 3:39:16). As many commentators have noted, the Sayings, or *logia,* are not the same as the "words" (Greek, *logoi*) of Jesus, nor are they the same as the Gospel of Matthew we have today. Whereas scholars once believed that Matthew's Gospel was first written in Aramaic by the apostle who was formerly a tax collector, modern analysts point out that there is no evidence of an earlier Aramaic version of the Gospel. Papias's use of *logia* may refer to an early collection of Jesus' sayings compiled by someone named Matthew, or it may allude to a list of messianic prophecies from the Hebrew Bible that a Christian scribe assembled to show that Jesus' life was foretold in Scripture. Most scholars do not believe that Papias's description applies to the canonical Gospel of Matthew.

Matthew and Judaism

The author remains unknown (we call him Matthew to avoid confusion), but scholarly analysis of his work enables us to gain some insight into his theological intentions and distinctive interests. Thoroughly versed in the Hebrew Bible, the writer is remarkably skilled at its exegesis (the explanation and critical interpretation of a literary text). Some scholars believe that he may have received scribal training, a professional discipline he utilizes to demonstrate to his fellow Jews that Jesus of Nazareth is the predicted Messiah. The author may refer to himself or to a "school" of early Christian interpreters of the Hebrew Scriptures when he states: "When, therefore, a teacher of the law [a scribe] has become a learner [a disciple] in the kingdom of Heaven, he is like a householder who can produce from his store both the new and the old" (13:52–53). Matthew effectively combines "the new" (Christian teaching) with "the old" (Judaism). To him, Jesus' teachings are the legitimate outgrowth of Torah study.

Recent scholarly investigations have demonstrated that several varieties of Jewish Christianity existed in the first-century church. The particular type to which Matthew belongs can only be inferred from examining relevant aspects of his Gospel. Some Jewish Christians demanded that all Gentile converts to the new faith keep the entire Mosaic Law or at least undergo circumcision (Acts 15:1–6; Gal. 6:11–16). Matthew does not mention circumcision, but he insists that the Mosaic Torah is binding on believers (5:17–20). In his view, Christians are to continue such Jewish practices as fasting (6:16–18), regular prayer (6:5–6), charitable giving (6:2), and formal sacrifices (5:23). His account also implies that Mosaic purity laws, forbidding certain foods, apply to his community. Matthew includes Mark's report of Jesus' controversy with the Pharisees over ritual hand washing but omits Mark's conclusion that Jesus declares all foods ceremonially clean (cf. 15:1–20 with Mark 7:1–23, especially 7:19).

Matthew depicts Jesus' personal religion as Torah Judaism, but he has no patience with Jewish leaders who disagree with his conclusions. He labels them "blind guides" and hypocrites (23:13–28). Despite his contempt for

Jewish opponents, however, Matthew retains his respect for Pharisaic teachings and urges the church to "pay attention to their words" (23:3).

Like the writers at Qumran, the Essene community of monklike scholars who withdrew from the world to await the final battle between good and evil, Matthew interprets the prophecies of the Hebrew Bible as applying exclusively to his group of believers, whom he regards as the true Israel. He also commonly presents Jesus' teaching as a kind of midrash on the Torah. A detailed exposition of the underlying meaning of a biblical text, a **midrash** includes interpretations of Scripture's legal rules for daily life (called **Halakah**) and explanations of nonlegal material (called **Haggadah**). At various points in his Gospel, Matthew shows Jesus providing halakic interpretations of the Torah (5:17–48), particularly on such legal matters as Sabbath observance and divorce (12:1–21; 19:3–12).

Matthew's Methods of Interpretation

Although contemporary scholars may flinch at the ideological way in which Matthew interprets ancient Scripture as specifically prophetic of Jesus, the Evangelist follows procedures that most Jewish scholars accepted in the first century CE. As David H. Stern reminds us, Jewish scribes and rabbis recognized "four basic modes" of biblical interpretation. The first mode (Hebrew, *P'shat,* "simple") analyzes a passage's literal meaning, taking into account both grammatical construction and historical context. In the second method (*Remez,* "hint"), rabbis examined individual words or phrases that offer clues to a significance not apparent in a literal reading. The third mode (*Drash* or *midrash,* "search") involves a particular reader's interpretation, a commonly figurative or allegorical response to the text that illuminates an individual's mind but may have little to do with the text's literal sense. The fourth approach (*Sod,* "secret") allows for a passage's "mystical or hidden meaning," perhaps suggested by individual letters or other minute details (see David H. Stern in "Recommended

Reading"). As we have seen, Matthew freely employs all four interpretative techniques when applying texts from his Greek edition of the Hebrew Bible to Jesus' biography.

Date and Place of Composition

The Gospel gives few clues to its precise time of origin, but Matthew apparently refers to Jerusalem's destruction as an accomplished fact (22:7). The author's hostility to the Jewish leadership and references to "their" synagogues (9:35; 10:17; 12:9; 13:54) may suggest that he wrote after the Christians already had been expelled from Jewish meeting places, a process that occurred at many different synagogues during the 80s and 90s CE.

The oldest citations from Matthew's Gospel appear in the letters of Ignatius, who was bishop of Antioch in Syria about 110–115 CE. Ignatius's reference and the unusual prominence given **Peter** in this Gospel (Matt. 16:16–19) suggest that it originated in Antioch, a city in which Peter had great influence (Gal. 2:11–14). Although we lack conclusive evidence, many scholars favor Antioch as the place of Matthew's composition.

Founded by Greek-speaking Jewish Christians in the late 30s CE, during the first generation of Christianity, the Antioch church was second only to that in Jerusalem (Acts 11:19–26; 15:2–35). The Antiochean congregation was also the stage on which two different wings of the early Christian community waged a vigorous battle over the status of Gentile converts. Whereas Paul advocated total equality for Gentiles, James (called "the Lord's brother") took a decidedly more conservative stance, insisting that Gentiles keep at least some Torah restrictions. Peter seems to have occupied a middle position between James and Paul, permitting Gentiles into the group but drawing the line at close association with them, particularly if they did not observe kosher food laws. Matthew's Gospel reflects his community's historical movement away from exclusively Jewish Christianity and toward a ministry that focuses on Gentiles. In chapter 10, the Matthean Jesus orders his disciples not to enter Gentile territories and to preach only to "the lost sheep of the house of Israel" (10:5–6). At the very end of his Gospel, however, Matthew pictures the risen Jesus issuing the **"great commission"**—to "make *all nations* my disciples" (28:19; emphasis added). Mediating between Torah-oriented traditions and a Hellenistic cosmopolitanism, Matthew produced a Gospel appropriate for his transitional generation, perhaps about 85 CE.

The Author's Purpose

In composing his Gospel, Matthew has several major objectives. Three of the most important are demonstrating Jesus' credentials as Israel's true Messiah; presenting Jesus as the supreme teacher and interpreter of the Mosaic Torah, the principles of which provide ethical guidance for Matthew's particular Jewish-Christian community; and instructing that community—the church—in the kind of correct belief and behavior that will ensure Jesus' approval when he returns.

Structure and Use of Sources

Matthew accomplishes his multiple purposes by assembling material from several different sources to construct his Gospel. Using Mark as his primary source, he incorporates about 90 percent of the earlier Gospel into his account. Into the Markan outline, Matthew inserts five large blocks of teaching material. Many ancient Jewish authors, consciously paralleling the Torah (the "five books of Moses"), arranged their works into fivefold divisions, as did the editors of the Psalms. The first of Matthew's five collections is the most famous, as well as the most commonly quoted—the Sermon on the Mount (chs. 5–7). The other four are instructions to the Twelve Apostles (ch. 10), parables on the kingdom (ch. 13), instructions to the church (Matthew's Christian community) (ch. 18), and warnings of the Final Judgment (chs. 23–25).

The Q Source Some of the material in these five sections is peculiar to Matthew, such as the parables involving weeds in a grain field (13:24–30)

and the unforgiving debtor (18:23–35). Other parts are similar or virtually identical to material found in Luke but not in Mark. Scholars believe that Matthew and Luke, independently of each other, drew much of their shared teaching from the now-lost Q (*Quelle* [source]) document (see above). Containing a wide variety of sayings attributed to Jesus, including kingdom parables, instructions to the disciples, and (at least in its final edition) prophecies of impending judgment, the Q document hypothesis works well in accounting for the source of Jesus' sayings absent in Mark but present in both Matthew and Luke (see Box 6.3).

The M Source In addition to Mark and Q (assuming its historicity), Matthew uses material found only in his Gospel. Scholars designate this material unique to Matthew as **M** (Matthean). M includes numerous sayings and parables, such as the stories about the vineyard laborers (20:1–16) and many of the kingdom pronouncements in chapter 13 (13:24–30, 44–45, 47–52). Finally, Matthew frames his story of Jesus with a narrative of Jesus' birth and infancy (1:18–2:23) and a concluding account of two post resurrection appearances, the first to women near Jerusalem and the second to the "eleven disciples" in Galilee (28:8–20).

Matthew's Editing of Mark

Before considering passages found only in Matthew, we can learn something of the author's intent by examining the way in which he edits and revises Markan material (see Box 8.2). Although he generally follows Mark's chronology, Matthew characteristically condenses and shortens Mark's narrative. In fact, Matthew generally summarizes and abbreviates Mark's account, commonly correcting Mark's grammar or awkward phrasing. In the story of the epileptic boy, Matthew severely abridges Mark's version, recounting the episode in a mere five verses (17:14–18) compared with Mark's sixteen (Mark 9:14–29). Matthew is also significantly briefer in his telling of Jesus' healing of Peter's mother-in-law (8:14–15; Mark 1:29–31), the

BOX 8.2 Examples of Matthew's Editing of Markan Material*

JESUS' BAPTISM

Mark: It happened at this time that Jesus came from Nazareth in Galilee

and was baptized in the Jordan by John. At the moment when he came up out of the water, he saw the heavens torn open and the Spirit, like a dove, descending upon him. And a voice spoke from heaven: "Thou art my Son, my Beloved; on thee my favour rests." (Mark 1:9–11)

Matthew: Then Jesus arrived at the Jordan from Galilee, and came to John to be baptized by him. **John tried to dissuade him, "Do you come to me?" he said. "I need rather to be baptized by you." Jesus replied, "Let it be so for the present; we do well to conform in this way with all that God requires." John then allowed him to come.** After baptism Jesus came up out of the water at once, and at that moment heaven opened; he saw the Spirit of God descending like a dove to alight upon him; and a voice from heaven was heard saying, "**This is my Son,** my Beloved, on whom my favour rests." (Matt. 3:13–17)

In comparing the two accounts of Jesus' baptism, the reader will note that Matthew inserts a speech by John into the Markan narrative. Recognizing Jesus as "mightier" than himself, John is reluctant to baptize him. By giving John this speech, Matthew is able to stress Jesus' superiority to the Baptist. Matthew also changes the nature of Jesus' *experience of the "Spirit" after his baptism. In Mark, the heavenly voice is addressed directly to Jesus and apparently represents Jesus' own private mystical experience of divine sonship at the event. Matthew changes the "thou art," intended for Jesus' ears, to "this is," making the divine voice a public declaration audible to by-standers.*

JESUS' RECEPTION BY HIS NEIGHBORS IN HIS HOMETOWN OF NAZARETH

Mark: He left that place and went to his home town accompanied by his disciples. When the Sabbath came he began to teach in the synagogue; and the large congregation who heard him were amazed and said,
"Where does he get it from?", and, "What wisdom is this that has been given him?", and, "How does he work such miracles? Is not this the carpenter, the son of Mary, the brother of James and Joseph and Judas and Simon? And are not his sisters here with us?"
So they [turned against] him. Jesus said to them, "A prophet will always be held in honour except in his home town, and among his kinsmen and family." He could work no miracle there, except that he put his hands on a few sick people and healed them; and he was taken aback by their want of faith. (Mark 6:1–6)

Matthew: Jesus left that place, and came to his home town, where he taught the people in their synagogue.

In amazement they asked,
"Where does he get this wisdom from, and these miraculous powers? **Is he not the carpenter's son? Is not his mother called Mary,** his brothers James, Joseph, Simon, and Judas? And are not all his sisters here with us? Where then has he got all this from?" So they [turned against] him, and this led him to say, "A prophet will always be held in honour, except in his home town, and in his own family." And **he did not work many miracles there: such was their want of faith.** (Matt. 13:54–58)

*Matthew's chief editorial changes are printed in boldface type.

In editing Mark's account of Jesus' unsatisfactory re-union with his former neighbors in Nazareth, Matthew reproduces most of his source but makes some significant changes and deletions. He omits Mark's reference to the Sabbath, as well as Mark's brief list of Jesus' "few" deeds there and Jesus' apparent surprise at his fellow towns-men's refusal to recognize or trust in his powers. Matthew also substitutes the phrase "the carpenter's son" for Mark's "the son of Mary," with its implication of Jesus' illegitimacy. In both accounts, the Nazareans' familiar-ity with Jesus' background and family (naming four "brothers" and referring to two or more "sisters") is enough to make them skeptical of Jesus' claims to special wisdom or authority.

JESUS' STILLING OF A STORM

Mark: [Immediately after miraculously feeding the multitudes who had gathered to hear him preach, Jesus sends the disciples by boat across the Sea of Galilee to Bethsaida.] After taking leave of them [the crowds], he went up the hill to pray. It was now late and the boat was already well out on the water, while he was alone on the land. Somewhere between three and six in the morning, seeing them laboring at the oars against a head wind, he came toward them, walking on the lake. He was going to pass by them; but when they saw him walking on the lake, they thought it was a ghost and cried out; for they all saw him and were terrified.

But at once he spoke to them: "Take heart! It is I; do not be afraid." Then he climbed into the boat with them, and the wind dropped. At this they were utterly astonished, for they had not under-stood the incident of the loaves; their minds were closed. (Mark 6:45–52)

Matthew: As soon as they had finished, he made the disciples embark and cross to the other side [of the Sea of Galilee] ahead of him, while he dismissed the crowd; then he went up the hill by himself to pray. It had grown late, and he was there alone. The boat was already some distance from the shore, bat-tling a head wind and a rough sea. Between three and six in the morning he came towards them, walking across the lake. When the disciples saw him walking on the lake they were so shaken that they cried out in terror: "It is a ghost!" But at once Jesus spoke to them: "Take heart! It is I; do not be afraid."

Peter called to him: "Lord, if it is you, tell me to come to you over the water." "Come," said Jesus. Peter got down out of the boat and walked over the water towards Jesus. But when he saw the strength of the gale he was afraid; and beginning to sink, he cried, "Save me, Lord!" Jesus at once reached out and caught hold of him. "Why did you hesitate?" he said. "How little faith you have!" Then they climbed into the boat; and the wind dropped. **And the men in the boat fell at his feet, exclaiming "You must be the Son of God."** (Matt. 14:22–33)

Besides adding the episode involving Peter's impetuous attempt to imitate Jesus' power over nature, Matthew radically changes the disciples' reaction to their Master's miraculous control of the sea, symbol of primal chaos. Whereas the Markan disciples fail to perceive Jesus' di-vinity in his ability to subdue wind and storm—Mark says that "their minds were closed"—the Matthean disci-ples immediately recognize Jesus as "Son of God." Matthew's editorial changes reflect not only his promo-tion of Peter's importance (see Matt. 16:13–19) but also his tendency to picture the disciples as better role models than Mark had portrayed them.

Gerasene demoniac (8:28–34; Mark 5:1–20), and the resuscitation of Jairus's daughter and the curing of the woman with a hemorrhage (9:18–26; Mark 5:21–43). In abbreviating Mark's version of events, Matthew typically omits much physical detail, as well as Jesus' emotional responses to the situation.

Emphasis on the Miraculous and Supernatural At the same time that he shortens Mark's description of Jesus' miracles, Matthew heightens the miraculous element, stressing that Jesus effected instant cures (9:22; 15:28; 17:18). In recounting Jesus' unfriendly reception in Nazareth, Matthew changes Mark's observation that Jesus "could work no miracle there" (Mark 6:5) to the declaration that "he did not work many miracles there," eliminating the implication that the human Jesus could be weakened by others' unbelief (13:58) (see Box 8.2). He similarly omits Mark's definition of John's baptism as a rite "in token of repentance, for the forgiveness of sins" (3:2, 6, 11; Mark 1:4). Mark's exact phrase, "for the forgiveness of sins," does appear in Matthew, but it is transferred to the Matthean Jesus' explanation of the ceremonial wine at the Last Supper (26:26–28). The author may have effected this transposition to make sure his readers understood that "forgiveness of sin" comes not from John's baptism but from Jesus' expiatory death.

Matthew's edition of the Passion narrative also intensifies the supernatural element. In Gethsemane, the Matthean Jesus reminds his persecutors that he has the power to call up thousands of angels to help him (26:53), a claim absent from Mark. Matthew's Christ allows himself to be arrested only to fulfill Scripture (26:54).

Matthew also revises Mark's crucifixion account, inserting several miracles to highlight the event's cosmic significance. To Mark's plague of darkness and the rending of the Temple curtain, Matthew adds a violent earthquake, severe enough to open graves and permit suddenly resuscitated **"saints"** (holy persons) to rise and walk the streets of Jerusalem (27:50–53). (This mysterious raising of saints is not mentioned elsewhere in the New Testament but probably appears here to express Matthew's conviction that Jesus' death makes possible the resurrection of the faithful.) Matthew introduces yet another earthquake into his description of the first Easter morning, stating that the women disciples arrive at Jesus' tomb in time to see a divine being descend and roll away the stone blocking the tomb entrance. Mark's linen-clad youth becomes an angel before whom the Roman guards quake in terror (28:1–4). What Mark's account implies, Matthew's typically makes explicit, ensuring that the reader will not miss the hand of God in these happenings. Nor does Matthew leave the Galilean women wondering and frightened at the empty sepulcher. Instead of being too terrified to report what they have seen, in Matthew's version the women joyously rush away to inform the disciples (28:8; Mark 16:8). In this retelling, the women set the right example by immediately proclaiming the good news of Jesus' triumph over death (28:19).

Organization of Matthew's Gospel

Because of the complex nature of the Matthean composition and the skill with which the author has interwoven Mark's narrative with Jesus' discourses (from Q and M), it is difficult to reduce Matthew to a clear-cut outline. Separating the book into convenient divisions and subdivisions in conventional outline form tends to distort and oversimplify its interlocking themes. One can, however, identify some of the major parts that make up the Gospel whole.

The following gives a rough idea of Matthew's general structure:

1. Introduction to the Messiah: genealogy and infancy narratives (1:1–2:23)
2. The beginning of Jesus' proclamation: baptism by John; the temptation by Satan; inauguration of the Galilean ministry (3:1–4:25)
3. First major discourse: the Sermon on the Mount (5–7)
4. First narrative section: ten miracles (8:1–9:38)
5. Second major discourse: instructions to the Twelve Apostles (10)

6. Second narrative section: the Baptist's questions about Jesus; controversies with Jewish authorities (11:1–12:50)

7. Third major discourse: parables on the kingdom (13:1–52)

8. Third narrative section: from the rejection in Nazareth to the Transfiguration (13:53–17:27)

9. Fourth major discourse: instructions to the church (18)

10. Fourth narrative section: the Jerusalem ministry (19:1–22:46)

11. Fifth major discourse: warnings of Final Judgment (23–25)

12. Fifth and final narrative section: the Passion story and post resurrection appearances (26:1–28:20)

Except for the birth narratives and final post resurrection apparitions, even a minimal outline makes clear that Matthew tells essentially the same story that we find in Mark and Luke (see Box 6.1). Only by carefully scrutinizing Matthew's handling of his sources, the Hebrew Bible, Mark, M, and (presumably) Q can we appreciate the ways in which his Gospel is distinctive (see Boxes 8.3 and 8.4).

BOX 8.3 Representative Examples of Material Found Only in Matthew

A "Table of Descent" [genealogy] listing Jesus' ancestors (1:1–17)

Matthew's distinctive version of Jesus' miraculous conception and birth at Bethlehem (1:18–2:23)

Some parables, sayings, and miracles unique to Matthew:

The dumb demoniac (9:32–34)

Wheat and darnel [weeds] (13:24–30)

Buried treasure (13:44)

The pearl of "special value" (13:45)

Catching fish in a net (13:47–50)

A learner with treasures old and new (13:51–52)

Earthly rulers collecting taxes (17:25–26)

Finding a coin in a fish's mouth to pay Temple taxes (17:27)

The unforgiving debtor (18:23–35)

Equal wages for all vineyard laborers (20:1–16)

The two sons and obedience (21:28–32)

The improperly dressed wedding guest (22:11–14)

The wise and foolish virgins (25:1–13)

The judgment separating sheep from goats (25:31–46)

Judas and the chief priests (27:3–10)

The dream of Pilate's wife (27:19)

The resurrection of saints (27:52–53)

The Easter morning earthquake (28:2)

The chief priests' conspiracy to deny Jesus' resurrection (28:11–15)

BOX 8.4 New Characters Introduced in Matthew

Joseph, husband of Mary (1:16, 18–25; 2:13–14, 19–23)

Herod the Great, Roman-appointed king of Judea (ruled 40–4 BCE) (2:1–8, 16–19)

The Magi (astrologers or "wise men" from the east) (2:1–12)

Satan, the devil (as a speaking character) (4:1–11)

Two blind men (9:27–31)

A dumb demoniac (9:32–34)

Revised list of the Twelve (10:1–4)

The mother of James and John, sons of Zebedee (20:20–21)

Introduction to the Messiah: The Infancy Narrative

Except for Matthew and Luke, no New Testament writers refer even briefly to the circumstances of Jesus' birth. Nor do Matthew and Luke allude to Jesus' infancy in the main body of their Gospels. In both cases, the infancy narratives are self-contained units that act as detachable prefaces to the central narrative of Jesus' public ministry.

Matthew constructs his account (1:18–2:23) with phrases and incidents taken from a Greek edition of the Hebrew Bible. To him, the infant Messiah's appearance gives new meaning to ancient biblical texts, fulfilling prophecy in many unexpected ways. The child is born to a virgin made pregnant by the Holy Spirit (1:18–19). To the author, this fulfills a passage from Isaiah 7:14, which in Hebrew states that "a young woman is with child, and she will bear a son." Matthew, however, quotes not the original Hebrew-language version of the text, but an Old Greek translation in which "young woman" is rendered as *parthenos,* or "virgin." Historians believe that Isaiah's words originally referred to the birth of an heir to the then-reigning Davidic king, but Matthew sees them as forecasting the Messiah's unique manner of birth. Like other New Testament writers, Matthew reads the Hebrew Bible from an explicitly Christian viewpoint, consistently giving the Jewish Scriptures a Christological interpretation. By making almost the entire Hebrew Bible foreshadow the Christ event, Matthew transforms it retroactively into a Christian document.

Matthew's concern to anchor Jesus' entrance into life firmly in the context of Scripture fulfillment is evident in his account of the mysterious **Magi,** or "wise men" from the east who come to pay homage to the infant Jesus. Traditionally three in number (although Matthew does not say how many they were), the Magi were probably Babylonian or Persian astrologers who had studied the horoscope of Judah and concluded that it was then time for "the king of the Jews" to be born. Astrology was extremely popular with all classes of society in Greco-Roman times, and it was commonly believed that the appearance of unusual celestial bodies, such as comets or "falling stars," heralded the occurrence of major events on earth (Isa. 14:12–23; Job 38:23; Judg. 5:20).

Matthew's reference to the "star" that guides the Magi to Jesus' birthplace is puzzling. Modern scientists do not know what astronomical phenomenon Matthew has in mind, but a conjunction of the planets Jupiter and Saturn in the constellation Pisces (7 BCE) may have been seen as a divine "sign" or portent. (No other New Testament writer or contemporary historian alludes to the "star of Bethlehem.") Noting that the star "stops" to hover over Jesus' birthplace (2:10)—behavior impossible for a genuine celestial body—some commentators suggest that Matthew invites his readers to believe that an angel (traditionally likened to a star [Isa. 40:26; Rev. 12:4, 9]) actually directs the Magi.

In the Evangelist's account, the unnamed heavenly body leads the traveling astrologers to create a situation in which several biblical prophecies can be fulfilled. On reaching Jerusalem, the astrologers are brought before King Herod, who recognizes that their inquiry about a new Jewish king refers to the Messiah's birth in **Bethlehem,** King David's home city, foretold in Micah 5:2.

Herod's jealous attempt to kill the child (2:1–18) fulfills prophecy (Jer. 31:15), as does the holy family's flight into Egypt (Hos. 11:1). Matthew structures the entire episode to parallel the biblical story of Moses' infancy (Exod. 1:8–2:25). As the baby Moses survived the Egyptian pharaoh's murderous schemes, so the infant Jesus escapes another ruler's plot to kill God's chosen one. The analogy between the two figures is also intended to apply to Jesus' adult life. Like Moses, Jesus will be summoned from Egypt to deliver his people. Moses led Israel from Egyptian slavery to a covenant relationship with God; Jesus will free believers from sin and establish a New Covenant (2:13–15, 19–21; 19:27–29).

The Beginning of Jesus' Proclamation

Matthew gives no information about Jesus' life from the time of his family's settling in Nazareth (2:22–23) to the appearance of John the Baptist, a gap of approximately thirty years (Luke 3:1, 23). Although he starts his account of Jesus' adult career (3:1–4:25) at exactly the same point as Mark (1:1–13), Matthew edits Mark's baptism narrative to emphasize Jesus' superiority to John and to avoid any implication that Jesus needed forgiveness of previous sins (3:1–17). (See Figures 8.1 and 8.2 for two distinctly different interpretations of the young Jesus.)

The Temptation

Mark (1:12–13) briefly alludes to Satan's tempting Jesus, but Matthew expands the scene to include a dramatic dialogue between Jesus and the Evil One (4:1–11). Whether he is viewed as an objective reality or a metaphor signifying human failure to obey God, Matthew's Satan attempts to deflect Jesus from the true course of his messiahship.

As Matthew and Luke (4:1–13) present it, the confrontation with Satan serves to clarify Jesus' concept of his messianic role. Representing false notions of the Messiah, Satan prefaces his first two challenges with the phrase "If you are the Son of God," a mean-spirited attempt to capitalize on any doubts that the human Jesus may have experienced about his origins or his future authority as God's agent. The first temptation involves Jesus' personal hunger: Satan calls for Jesus to test the extent of his miraculous power by turning stones into bread, a ploy Jesus refutes by quoting the Torah principle that one lives spiritually on the word of God (Deut. 8:3). Some modern commentators have suggested that Jesus thereby rejects the temptation to undertake a messiahship exclusively focused on material good works, although he makes feeding the hungry and destitute an important part of his ministry.

The second temptation is a profound challenge to Jesus' consciousness of his own messianic identity. "If you are the Son of God," Satan demands, show that you can fulfill the terms of Psalm 91, a poem that unconditionally asserts that God will save from all harm the man he has chosen.

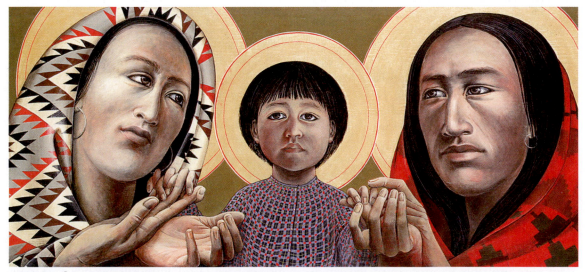

FIGURE 8.1 *The Holy Family.* In depicting Jesus, Mary, and Joseph as indigenous Americans, the twentieth-century painter Fr. John B. Giuliani emphasizes both the archetypal sacredness of the family and the tradition of spirituality attained by pre-Columbian peoples of North America.

The poem continues to reassure God's favorite that Yahweh will "lift him beyond danger" and "rescue him and bring him to honour" (Ps. 91:14–16). In Matthew's time, many Jews must have pointed out to Christians that Jesus' death on the cross was entirely contrary to the promises of divine protection given in this well-known psalm. In Matthew 4:6, the devil quotes this Scripture, and Jesus counters this "demonic" use of the Bible by citing the general Torah principle of not putting God to the test (Deut. 6:16).

In a third and final attempt to subvert Jesus' understanding of his messianic role, Satan offers him worldly power on a vastly grander scale than King David, the Messiah's prototype, had enjoyed. All Jesus must do in return is "pay homage" to Satan, a demand that Jesus recognizes as undermining the essence of Judaism's commitment to one God (Deut. 6:13). A thousand years earlier, David had gained his kingdom through war and bloodshed, a procedure that Jesus recognizes as unsuitable to the Messiah, who will not impose his rule by cruelty and violence. Satan is not to be "worshiped" by imitating his methods.

FIGURE 8.2 *The Good Shepherd.* This early Christian painting of Christ can be found on the ceiling of a crypt in the catacombs of Saint Priscilla in Rome. Note that the artist portrays Jesus in a pose that would be familiar to a Greco-Roman audience. Like earlier renditions of Apollo, the Greek god of prophecy, intellect, music, and shepherds, the youthful Jesus carries a lamb on his shoulders to demonstrate his concern for his human flock. Compare John 10:1–18, Matthew 18:12–14, and Luke 15:4–7.

For you the LORD [Yahweh] is a safe retreat;
you have made the Most High your refuge.
No disaster shall befall you,
no calamity shall come upon your home.
For he [Yahweh] has charged his angels
    to guard you wherever you go,
    to lift you on their hands
for fear you should strike your foot
against a stone.

(Ps. 91:9–12)

First Major Discourse: The Sermon on the Mount

In the temptation scene (4:1–11), Matthew shows Jesus repudiating some of the functions then popularly associated with the Messiah. In the **Sermon on the Mount** (chs. 5–7), Matthew demonstrates how radically different Jesus' concept of this messiahship is from the popular expectation of a conquering warrior-king. This long discourse, in which Jesus takes his seat on a Galilean hill, reminding the reader of Moses seated on Mount Sinai, is the New Testament's most extensive collection of Jesus' teachings. Matthew's "sermon" is not the record of a single historical speech by Jesus, but a compilation of Jesus' sayings from several different sources. Some of the same teachings appear in Luke's

Sermon on the Plain, the Third Gospel's equivalent version of the discourse (Luke 6:17–7:1). Matthew collects the sayings in one place (5:1–8:1); Luke scatters them throughout his Gospel narrative (see Chapter 9).

In Matthew's opening discourse, Jesus addresses both the undifferentiated "crowds" that gather to hear him and a much smaller group of disciples who sit at his feet. Challenging his audience to practice a "higher righteousness," exceeding even that of the most scrupulous Pharisees (5:20), he calls on them to express God-like love, radiating "light for all the world" (5:15–16, 43–48). Jesus begins by summoning those who will most benefit from his teaching—the needy, the unsatisfied, the grieving, and the persecuted—many of whom now seem permanently excluded from the "good things" God's world provides. In the sermon's first section, known as the **Beatitudes,** Matthew's Jesus pronounces a blessing on "those who know their need of God," "those who hunger and thirst to see right prevail," and "those who show mercy" (5:3, 6, 7). Because Luke's version of the Beatitudes applies Jesus' blessings to the literally poor and hungry (see Box 9.4), many scholars think that Matthew has modified the original import of these sayings by "spiritualizing" them.

For both Matthew and Luke, however, the Beatitudes express a radical reversal of the world's social values that will prevail in God's kingdom (which, in Matthew, is represented by the church). Whereas society presently exalts the rich, the powerful, and the successful, particularly military conquerors victorious in war, Jesus reverses these common value judgments, congratulating those who seek divine justice rather than material acquisitions, "those of a gentle spirit," and those who are "peacemakers." These are the citizens of God's dominion, who will inherit both the earth (5:5) and the "kingdom of Heaven" (5:3), people whom God calls his children (5:9).

Immediately after the Beatitudes and his designation of Christians as the "salt of the earth" and "light" to the world, Matthew emphasizes Jesus' crucial role as upholder and interpreter of the Mosaic Law. In a statement probably aimed at Pauline churches that did not observe Torah commandments (see Chapters 15 and 17)—and which appears only in Matthew's Gospel—the Matthean Jesus declares:

> Do not suppose that I have come to abolish the Law and the prophets; I did not come to abolish [as Paul maintains in Galatians], but to complete. I tell you this: so long as heaven and earth endure, not a letter, not a stroke, will disappear from the Law until all that must happen has happened.
>
> (5:17–18)

Aware that Paul's churches did not share a conviction that the Torah was eternally binding, Matthew concedes that nonobservant believers may still belong to the kingdom (the church), although they will rank significantly below Torah loyalists:

> If any man therefore sets aside even the least of the Law's demands, and teaches others to do the same, he will have the lowest place in the kingdom of Heaven, whereas anyone who keeps the Law, and teaches others so, will stand high in the kingdom of Heaven.
>
> (Matt. 5:19)

The Antitheses

For Matthew's Jewish Christian community, Jesus' teachings did not replace the Mosaic Law; they intensified it. Rather than serving as a refutation of Jewish tradition, Jesus' Torah pronouncements illustrate how his disciples should observe it, emphasizing the essential core of ethical meaning that lies behind each commandment. Immediately after his declaration of the Law's unchanging validity, Matthew introduces a set of Jesus' sayings, known as the **antitheses,** that are found only in his Gospel. Employing a rhetorical formula, Jesus makes an initial statement (the thesis), which he then follows with an apparently opposing idea (the antithesis). In this series, he appears to contrast biblical tradition with his own authoritative opinion; as scholars have pointed out, however, he does not contradict Torah rules, but rather interprets them to reveal the human motivation that often causes them to be broken:

> You have learned that our forefathers were told, "Do not commit murder: anyone who commits murder must be brought to judgment." But what I tell you is this: Anyone who nurses anger against his brother must be brought to judgment. If he abuses his brother, he must answer for it to the court; if he sneers at him he will have to answer for it in the fires of hell [Gehenna].
>
> (5:21–22)

Anger, the emotion triggering murderous aggression, must be rooted out, for if it leads to overt behavior, it will be punished by both human courts and divine judgment.

In another antithesis, Jesus looks beyond the literal application of a Torah command to seek a more effective way to obey the principle it embodies:

> You have learned that they [the biblical Israelites] were told, "Eye for eye, tooth for tooth." But what I tell you is this: Do not set yourself against the man who wrongs you. If someone slaps you on the right cheek, turn and offer him your left. If a man wants to sue you for your shirt, let him have your coat as well. If a man in authority makes you go one mile, go with him two.
>
> (5:38–41)

The **lex talionis,** or law of retaliation, that Jesus quotes before giving his three examples of recommended behavior is central to the Mosaic concept of justice and appears in three different Torah books (Exod. 21:23–25; Lev. 24:19–20; Deut. 19:21). Although it may seem harsh by today's standards, in ancient society the *lex talionis* served to limit excessive revenge: Simply receiving an injury did not entitle one to kill the offending party. In the world inhabited by the (generally poor and powerless) members of Jesus' audience (the "you" whom he addresses), however, retaliatory actions of any kind against those who exploited them automatically led to severe reprisals, including torture and death.

Recognizing that the law's intent was to curb violence, Jesus goes beyond its literal application to demand that his listeners give up their traditional right to retaliate in kind. Is Jesus, then, urging people to submit passively to those who wrong them?

Although many commentators have interpreted Jesus' emphasis on nonviolence as tantamount to accepting injustice, some interpreters, such as Walter Wink, suggest an alternative reading. Instead of advocating a "slave morality" that would make it easier for the strong to abuse the weak, Wink argues that Jesus was instructing his audience on how to deal with people who exercised power over them. Jesus' remark on slapping is directed to classes of people who customarily receive demeaning treatment: slaves who are struck by masters; wives, by their husbands; children, by their parents; or a conquered people, such as the Jews, by their Roman overlords. According to Wink, Jesus advised a simple technique by which mistreated people could react without violence and yet retain their human dignity. Because it was customary to strike a social inferior with the back of the right hand, turning the other cheek made it difficult for the aggressor to repeat the blow in the same way. (Hitting with the fist was supposedly ruled out, since it implied that one was striking an equal.)

Jesus' advice to a poor person whom a wealthy creditor sues in court similarly offers a means to shame the exploiter. When a creditor demands the outer garment (here translated as "shirt") to pay off a debt, the debtor should strip off the inner tunic ("coat") as well. Standing naked before the debt collector in full public view would, according to social standards of the era, have been more humiliating to the creditor than to his victim, who had dramatically illustrated the other's excessive avarice. Jesus' counsel to go an "extra mile" refers to the legal practice that entitled a Roman soldier to force a peasant to carry his pack for a mile—but no farther. By voluntarily carrying the pack beyond the legally stipulated distance, the carrier would place his oppressor in an awkward position, causing the soldier to exceed his legal mandate and thus blurring the distinction between the "man in authority" and the servant he had conscripted (see Wink in "Recommended Reading").

Other commentators suggest that Jesus' main objective was probably to discover and apply the essential precepts contained in the Mosaic tradition. Matthew's version of the "golden rule" most succinctly expresses this view: His Jesus states that treating others as one would like to be treated by them encapsulates the biblical message, succinctly embodying "the Law and the prophets" (7:12; cf. Luke 6:31). Similarly, after reciting the Torah injunctions to love God and neighbor wholeheartedly, Jesus states, "Everything in the Law and the prophets hangs on these two commandments" (22:34–40; cf. Mark 12:28–34).

In Matthew's final antithesis, Jesus expands on this fundamental perception, contrasting the command to love one's neighbor (Lev. 19:18) with the apparently common assumption that it is permissible to hate an enemy (5:43–48). Again, he demands a "higher righteousness" that will imitate God's own character, revealed in the daily operation of physical nature, where he lavishes his gifts equally on both deserving and undeserving people:

> But what I tell you is this: Love your enemies and pray for your persecutors; only so can you be children of your heavenly Father, who makes his sun rise on good and bad alike, and sends the rain on the honest and dishonest. If you love only those who love you, what reward can you expect? . . . There must be no limit to your goodness, as your heavenly Father's goodness knows no bounds.
>
> (5:44–48)

"Boundless" in loving generosity, the Father provides the supreme model for Jesus' disciples to emulate, refashioning them in his image. In seeking first the kingdom and God's "justice" (6:33), they personally "pass no judgment" on others, for judgmental attitudes blind people to their own defects (7:1–5). Instead, disciples must focus on the infinite graciousness of the Father, who endlessly "gives good things to those who ask him" (7:9–11).

Jesus' Authority

The sermon ends with Jesus' parable about the advantages of building one's life firmly on the rock of his teachings (7:24–27), after which, Matthew reports, the crowds "were astounded" because "unlike their own teachers he taught with a note of [his personal] authority" (7:28). Matthew's phrase "when Jesus had finished this discourse," or a variation thereof, marks the conclusion of each of the four other blocks of teaching material in his Gospel (11:1; 13:53; 19:1; 26:1).

First Narrative Section: Ten Miracles

In the first long narrative section of his Gospel (8:1–9:38), based largely on Mark, Matthew concentrates on depicting Jesus' miraculous healings and exorcisms. To Mark's account of the cleansing of a leper (Mark 1:40–45), Matthew adds the story of a **centurion,** the highest-ranking noncommissioned Roman army officer (8:5–13; see also Luke 7:1–10). Matthew connects this episode with references to the practice of converting Gentiles that existed in the author's own day. After expressing Jesus' astonishment that the Gentile soldier reveals a faith stronger than that of any Israelite, the author makes his point: Non-Jews like the centurion will come to feast with Abraham and the other patriarchs, and Jews, once the favored people, will be left outside. Throughout his Gospel, Matthew pictures the Christian community as the "true Israel," inheritors of the divine promise made to the ancient Israelites.

Second Major Discourse: Instructions to the Twelve Apostles

In his second major collection of ethical teachings, Matthew presents Jesus' instructions to the twelve chief disciples (listed by name in 10:2–4).

The author specifies that the Twelve are sent exclusively to Jews and forbidden to preach to Gentiles or Samaritans (10:5–6), an injunction found only in Matthew. (In contrast, both Luke and John show Jesus leading his disciples on a brief Samaritan campaign [Luke 9:52–56; John 4:3–42].) The Twelve are to preach the kingdom's imminent appearance, the same apocalyptic message that the author attributes to both the Baptist (3:2) and Jesus at the outset of his career (4:17). While healing the sick, cleansing lepers, and raising the dead—thus replicating Jesus' spectacular miracles—the disciples are to expect hostility and persecution. This extended warning (10:16–26) seems to apply to conditions that existed in the author's generation, rather than in the time of Jesus' Galilean ministry. Matthew's apparent practice of combining Jesus' remembered words with commentary relating them to later experiences of the Christian community is typical of all the Gospel writers.

A strong eschatological tone pervades the entire discourse. Followers are to be loyal at the time of testing because destruction in Gehenna awaits the unfaithful. The New Testament name for a geographical location, the **"Valley of Hinnom,"** Gehenna is commonly rendered as "hell" in English translations, although it is uncertain that the later Christian notion of a metaphysical place of punishment accurately expresses the original meaning of Gehenna (see Box 8.5). A site of human sacrifice in Old Testament times (Jer. 7:32; 1 Kings 11:7, etc.), the Valley of Hinnom later housed a garbage dump that was kept permanently burning, a literal place of annihilation for "both soul and body" (Matt. 10:28; 18:8; 25:30, 46, etc.).

Equally arresting is the statement that before the Twelve have completed their circuit of Palestine "the Son of Man will have come" (10:23). Writing more than half a century after the events he describes, Matthew surprisingly retains a prophecy that was not fulfilled, at least not in historical fact. The author's inclusion of this apocalyptic prediction indicates that he may not have understood it literally. Matthew may have regarded the "Son of Man" as already spiritually present in the missionary activity of the church. If so, this suggests that many of Matthew's other references to "the end of the age" and Jesus' Parousia (chs. 24 and 25) are also to be understood metaphorically.

Second Narrative Section: Questions and Controversies

Jesus and John the Baptist

Matthew opens his second extended narrative (11:1–12:50) by discussing the relationship of Jesus to John the Baptist, whose fate foreshadows that of Jesus. Locked in Herod Antipas's prison and doomed to imminent martyrdom, John writes to inquire if Jesus is really God's chosen one (11:2–3). The Baptist's question contrasts strangely with his earlier proclamation of Jesus' high status (3:11–15) and may reflect a later competition between the disciples of Jesus and John in Matthew's day.

Matthew uses the incident to place the two prophets' roles in perspective, highlighting Jesus' superiority. Without answering John's question directly, Jesus summarizes his miracles of healing that suggest God's presence in his work (11:4–6). Matthew then contrasts the function and style of the two men, emphasizing Jesus' far greater role. Although John is the "destined Elijah" whose return to earth was to inaugurate the time of Final Judgment, he does not share in the "kingdom." Perhaps because Matthew sees John operating independently of Jesus, he does not consider him a Christian. (Box 8.6 indicates the four Gospel authors' strikingly different views of John's role.)

John is a wild and solitary figure; Jesus is gregarious, friendly with Israel's outcasts, prostitutes, and "sinners." Enjoying food and wine with socially unrespectable people, Jesus provokes critics who accuse him of gluttony and overdrinking (11:7–19). In Matthew's evaluation, neither John nor Jesus, representing two very different approaches to the religious life, can win the fickle public's approval.

BOX 8.5 Matthew's Use of Hell: Some Biblical Concepts of the Afterlife

The term that many English-language Bibles translate as "hell" is **Gehenna** (*gē hinnōm*) (Matt. 5:22, 29–30; 10:28; 23:15, 33), which originally referred not to a place of posthumous torment but to a specific geographical location, a ravine near Jerusalem. A valley bordering Israel's capital city on the southwest, Gehenna was named for the "sons of Hinnom (*gē ben(e) hinnōm*)," the biblical designation of an ancient Canaanite group that occupied the site before King David captured it about 1000 BCE. Gehenna had an evil reputation as the place where humans were sacrificed and burned as offerings to false gods, a practice that Israelite prophets vehemently condemned (Jer. 7:31; 19:11; 32:35; cf. 2 Kings 23:10; 2 Chron. 28:3; 33:5).

In time, perhaps influenced by Persian ideas about afterlife punishments in fire, some Jewish writers made Hinnom's valley (Gehenna) the symbol of God's eschatological judgment, where the wicked would suffer after death (1 Enoch 26:4; 27:2–3). A potent image of alienation from God, the earthly Gehenna was eventually associated with mythical concepts of an Underworld "lake of fire," the future abode of unrepentant sinners (2 Esd. 7:36; Rev. 20).

SHEOL AND HADES

The concept of eternal punishment does not occur in the Hebrew Bible, which uses the term **Sheol** to designate a bleak subterranean region where the dead, good and bad alike, subsist only as impotent shadows. When Hellenistic Jewish scribes rendered the Bible into Greek, they used the word *Hades* to translate Sheol, bringing a whole new mythological association to the idea of posthumous existence. In ancient Greek myth,

Hades, named after the gloomy deity who ruled over it, was originally similar to the Hebrew Sheol—a dark place underground in which all the dead, regardless of individual merit, were indiscriminately housed (see Homer's *Odyssey*, book 11). By the Hellenistic period, however, Hades had become compartmentalized into separate regions: These included Elysium, a paradise for the virtuous, and Tartarus, a place of punishment for the wicked. Influenced by philosophers such as Pythagoras and Plato and by the Orphic mystery religions (see Chapter 4), Greek religious thought eventually posited a direct connection between people's behavior in this life and their destiny in the next: Good actions earned them bliss, whereas injustices brought fearful penalties.

HELL

Popular concepts of hell derive from a variety of sources extending back in time to the earliest Mesopotamian and Egyptian speculations about the terrors of the next world. Although the concept is absent from the Hebrew Bible and most of the New Testament, a few scattered references to it (primarily involving Gehenna or a fiery lake) appear in the Synoptic Gospels and the Book of Revelation, as well as some noncanonical Jewish and Christian books, such as 1 and 2 Enoch and the Apocalypse of Peter. In general, pre-Christian mythologies and other extrabiblical sources supply most of the frightening imagery for such celebrated literary works as Dante's *Inferno* and Milton's *Paradise Lost*, as well as the "hellfire" sermons of many Puritan divines and their modern successors. The word itself, not found in the Bible, commemorates Hel, the fierce Norse goddess who reigned over the netherworld.

Harsh Sayings

At the same time that he shows Jesus performing works of mercy and forgiveness (11:28–30),

Matthew also includes harsh sayings very similar to the denunciations and threats of divine judgment uttered by the Baptist. When the towns of Chorazin and Bethsaida fail to repent

BOX 8.6 **John the Baptist as the Eschatological Elijah Figure**

MATTHEW

He is the man of whom Scripture says, "Here is my herald, whom I send on ahead of you, and he will prepare your way before you." I tell you this: never has there appeared on earth a mother's son greater than John the Baptist, and yet the least in the kingdom of Heaven is greater than he.

Ever since the coming of John the Baptist the kingdom of Heaven has been subject to violence and violent men are seizing it. For all the prophets and the Law foretold things to come until John appeared, and John is the destined Elijah, if you will but accept it. If you have ears, then hear. (Matt. 11:10–14)

MARK

[Popular speculations about John's return to life after his beheading by Herod Antipas:]
Now King Herod heard of it [Jesus' miracles], for the fame of Jesus had spread; and people were saying, "John the Baptist has been raised to life, and that is why these miraculous powers are at work in him." Others said, "It is Elijah." (Mark 6:14–15)

LUKE

He is the man of whom Scripture says, "Here is my herald, whom I send on ahead of you, and he will prepare your way before you." I tell you, there is not a mother's son greater than John, and yet the least in the kingdom of God is greater than he. (Luke 7:27–28)

Until John, it was the Law and the prophets; since then, there is the good news of the kingdom of God, and everyone forces his way in. (Luke 16:16)

JOHN

This is the testimony which John gave when the Jews of Jerusalem sent a deputation of priests and Levites to ask him who he was. He confessed without reserve and avowed, "I am not the Messiah." "What then? are you Elijah?" "No," he replied. "Are you the prophet whom we await?" He answered "No."* "Then who are you?" they asked. "We must give an answer to those who sent us. What account do you give of yourself?" He answered in the words of the prophet Isaiah: "I am a voice crying aloud in the wilderness, 'Make the Lord's highway straight.'" (John 1:19–23)

*Note that John's Gospel denies the Baptist the roles of prophet and latter-day Elijah that the Synoptics accorded him.

after witnessing Jesus' miracles there, Jesus makes a sweeping statement that **Sodom,** which Yahweh destroyed by fire, would fare better on Judgment Day than they (11:20–24).

Castigating his opponents as poisonous snakes (12:33–37), Jesus seems to echo the ferocity of John's earlier diatribes (3:7–13; cf. Luke 3:7–9).

Third Major Discourse: Parables on the Kingdom

Matthew frames Jesus' third discourse with his version of Jesus' alienation from his family (12:46–50; Mark 3:31–35) and Jesus' rejection by the citizens of Nazareth (13:54–58; Mark 6:1–6). The author divides Jesus' parable teachings into two distinct episodes, the first public and the second private (13:10–23). Although only the Twelve are initiated into the secrets of God's rule, Matthew softens Mark's explanation of Jesus' reasons for using parables in public. Instead of employing figures of speech to prevent understanding (Mark 4:11–12), Matthew states that Jesus speaks metaphorically *because* most people have the wrong attitude and unconsciously shut their mental eyes and ears (13:11–15; Isa. 6:9–10). Matthew's version of the parable lesson explicitly states that the Twelve do understand and appreciate Jesus' teaching (13:16–17, 51–52), thus eliminating Mark's view of the disciples' chronic stupidity.

To Mark's original collection of kingdom parables, Matthew adds several comparisons in which the kingdom is likened to a buried treasure, a priceless pearl, a harvest of fish, and a field in which both grain and "darnel" (weeds) grow (13:24–30, 36–50). The last two introduce a distinctly Matthean concept: The kingdom (church) consists of a mixture of good and bad elements that will not be separated completely until the last day. The same theme reappears in Matthew's version of the parable about ungrateful guests (22:1–13; cf. Luke 14:16–23).

Third Narrative Section: From the Rejection in Nazareth to the Transfiguration

Revisions of Mark's Narrative

Matthew's third narrative section (13:53–17:27) slightly revises many incidents related in Mark's Gospel. Recounting Jesus' rejection by his fellow citizens of Nazareth, Matthew subtly modifies Mark's older account, calling Jesus "the carpenter's son" rather than the Markan "son of Mary" (Mark 6:3) and changing Mark's statement that Jesus "could work no miracle there" (Mark 6:5) to "did not work many miracles there" (13:54–58) (see Box 8.2).

With minor changes, Matthew generally follows Mark's account of the Baptist's execution, the miraculous feeding of 5,000 people, and the stilling of the Galilean storm (14:1–27; Mark 6:14–52). Matthew's editing of this part of the Markan narrative, however, entails a major change in Mark's order of events. The episode in which Jesus sends the Twelve on a missionary journey (Mark 6:7–13) does not appear in Matthew's third narrative section because he has already incorporated it into his version of Jesus' instructions to the Twelve (ch. 10). Matthew also revises other Markan passages dealing with the disciples. He embellishes Mark's account of Jesus' striding across the Sea of Galilee by adding that Peter also attempted to walk on water. More significantly, Matthew deletes Mark's reference to the disciples' "closed" minds, or "hard-heartedness," and replaces it with their positive recognition of Jesus as "Son of God" (14:28–33; Mark 6:52). He further modifies Mark's theme of the disciples' obtuseness by insisting that the Twelve fully comprehend the miracle of loaves and fishes (15:5–12; Mark 8:1–21). Most of these revisions to Mark's account—especially Matthew's deletion of Mark's criticisms of the Twelve—serve to enhance the disciples' role and reputation.

Describing Jesus' dispute with the Pharisees over ritual hand washing (taken from Mark 7:1–23), Matthew gives the debate a meaning significantly different from that in his Markan source. In Mark, the episode's climax is reached when the author interprets Jesus' words to mean that all foods are clean, including those the Torah forbids Jews to eat (7:19). Believing that dietary laws remain in effect, Matthew drops Mark's climactic interpretation (15:1–11).

Peter and the Church

One of Matthew's most celebrated additions to Mark's narrative appears in his version of Peter's recognition of Jesus' identity (16:13–29). Matthew's Peter not only acknowledges Jesus as the Messiah but also identifies him as the Son of God (an element absent in Mark). Jesus' declaration that Peter is the rock upon which Jesus will build his church appears only in Matthew, as does the promise to award Peter spiritual powers that are honored in heaven and on earth. Matthew's Jesus, however, makes no provision for the transmission of ecclesiastical authority to Peter's successors.

Despite his singling Peter out as foremost among the **apostles** ("ones sent out [by Jesus]"), Matthew retains Mark's tradition that Peter fundamentally misunderstands the nature of Jesus' messiahship. When Peter attempts to dissuade Jesus from a decision that will lead to his death in Jerusalem, Jesus again ironically addresses the apostle as "Satan" (16:21–23).

Fourth Major Discourse: Instructions to the Church

In chapter 18, Matthew assembles disparate sayings of Jesus and applies them to the Christian community of the writer's generation. Taken together, chapters 10 and 18 form a rudimentary instruction manual for the early church. The author skillfully combines numerous small literary units to achieve his intended effect. A brief glimpse of the disciples' squabbling for power (18:1–2) introduces opposing images of a powerless child and a drowning man (18:2–7), which are quickly followed by pictures of self-blinding and the flames of Gehenna (18:8–9). The variety of literary forms gathered here makes the author's prescription for an ideal Christian community intensely vivid. The writer's devices include hyperbole (exaggeration for rhetorical effect), parable (the lost sheep and the unforgiving debtor [18:12–14, 23–35]), advice on supervising troublesome people (18:15–17), prophetic promises (18:10, 18–20), and direct commands (18:22). In Matthew's view of the church, service, humility, and endless forgiveness are the measure of leadership. Practicing the spirit of Torah mercy, the church is the earthly expression of divine rule (18:23–35), a visible manifestation of the kingdom.

In regulating the community, Matthew gives the individual "congregation" the right to exclude or ostracize disobedient members (18:15–17). During later centuries, this power of excommunication was to become a formidable weapon in controlling both belief and behavior. The same authority accorded Peter in Jesus' famous "keys of the kingdom" speech (16:16–20) is also given to individual congregation leaders (18:18).

Fourth Narrative Section: The Jerusalem Ministry

In this long narrative sequence (19:1–22:46), Matthew arranges several dialogues between Jesus and his opponents, interspersed with incidents on the journey south from Galilee to Jerusalem. The section opens with "some Pharisees" challenging Jesus on the matter of divorce. In Mark's version of the encounter, Jesus revokes the Torah provisions for divorce and forbids remarriage (Mark 10:1–12). Matthew modifies the prohibition, stating that "unchastity" or sexual unfaithfulness provides grounds for lawful divorce (19:3–9). He also adds a discussion with the disciples in which Jesus mentions several reasons for not marrying, including a commitment to remain single for "the kingdom" (19:10–12).

Discipleship and Suffering

After the third prediction of Jesus' impending death in Jerusalem (20:17–19), Matthew again emphasizes that suffering must precede the disciples' heavenly reward, as it does Jesus'. In Mark, the sons of Zebedee, James and John, directly ask Jesus for positions of honor in his kingdom, presumably to satisfy personal ambition (Mark 10:35–40). In Matthew's version of the episode, it is the apostles' mother who makes the request on their behalf (20:20–21). (Jesus had already promised his followers that he would share his heavenly rule with them [19:27–29].) The prediction that the two sons of Zebedee will follow their leader to a martyr's death indicates that Matthew wrote after both apostles had died (20:23). According to Acts (12:1–2), James was beheaded by **Herod Agrippa I,** who reigned as king of Judea 41–44 CE. It may be that John was also executed at about that time.

Entrance into Jerusalem

Matthew prepares his readers for the significance of Jesus' Jerusalem experience by prefacing his account with a miracle found only in his Gospel. After Jesus restores sight to two blind men, they immediately become his followers—in contrast to the "blind" guides of Jerusalem (20:29–34). The author's determination to show that Jesus' actions match biblical prophecy in every detail causes him to create a somewhat bizarre picture of his hero's entrance into the holy city. Matthew quotes Zechariah's prophecy about the Messiah's arrival in full and inserts an additional phrase from Isaiah. However, he apparently misunderstands Zechariah's poetic use of parallelism. In Zechariah's poetic structure, "the foal of a beast of burden" on which the Messiah rides is parallel to and synonymous with the prophet's reference to "an ass" (Zech. 9:9; Isa. 62:11). To make Jesus' action precisely fit his concept of the prophecy, Matthew has Jesus mount not one but two animals simultaneously, "the donkey and her foal," for his triumphant ride into Jerusalem (21:1–11).

In his account of Jesus' Jerusalem ministry, Matthew generally adheres to Mark's narrative, although he adds some new material and edits Mark, usually to enhance his portrait of Jesus. After driving the moneychangers from the Temple, Jesus heals some blind men and cripples (21:14), miracles absent in Mark. During this brief period, Jesus is repeatedly hailed as

"Son of David," one of Matthew's chief designations for his hero (1:1; 20:30; 21:9, 16). Matthew reproduces many of the Markan debates between Jesus and Jewish Torah experts on matters such as payment of taxes to Rome (22:16–22), the resurrection (22:23–33), and the law of love (22:34–40). However, he significantly edits Mark's report on Jesus' encounter with a friendly Torah instructor (Mark 12:28–34). Whereas Mark states that this congenial exchange prevented further attacks on Jesus, Matthew transfers Mark's comment to the conclusion of Jesus' remarks about the Messiah as David's "son" (22:46; Mark 12:35). Matthew has only harsh words for the Jerusalem authorities and declines to show Jesus on good terms with rival Jewish teachers.

The Church as the True Israel

While studying Matthew's account of Jesus' last days, readers will discover that most of the author's changes and additions to Mark serve to express his extreme hostility toward Jewish leaders. In the author's bitter view, prostitutes and criminals stand a better chance of winning divine approval than do the Temple priests, Pharisees, or their associates (21:31).

The three parables that Matthew inserts into the Markan narrative serve to condemn the Jewish establishment. In the parable of the two sons, the disobedient youth represents Jewish leaders (21:28–32). In a second parable, the "wicked tenants" who kill a landlord's son are the Jerusalem officials who reject Jesus (21:42–46). To Matthew, the vineyard owner's transfer of his estate to more deserving tenants means that God now regards the church as his covenant people.

Matthew replays the same theme in the parable featuring guests who ungratefully ignore their invitations to a wedding party (the messianic banquet). Matthew's statement that the outraged host then burns down the ingrates' city probably refers to the Romans' burning Jerusalem in 70 CE. As in the wicked tenant parable, newcomers replace the formerly chosen group—the Jewish Christian church becomes the true Israel (22:1–10).

Fifth Major Discourse: Warnings of Final Judgment

Hostility Toward the Jewish Establishment

This fifth and final block of teaching material summarizes the Matthean Jesus' adverse judgment on Jerusalem, particularly its Temple and religious hierarchy (chs. 23–25). It opens with a blistering denunciation of the **scribes and Pharisees**—professional transmitters and interpreters of the law—upon whom Jesus is pictured as heaping **"seven woes,"** perhaps corresponding to the curses on a disobedient Israel listed in Deuteronomy 28. According to Matthew, Jesus blames the Pharisees and their associates for every guilty act—every drop of innocent blood poured out—in Israel's entire history. He condemns the religious leadership to suffer for their generation's collective wrongdoing, as well as that of their distant ancestors.

Matthew implies that the Roman devastation of Jerusalem in 70 CE, an event that occurred during the author's lifetime, is tangible proof of God's wrath toward Israel (23:35–36). Matthew intensifies this theme in his version of Jesus' trial before Pilate (ch. 27); only in Matthew does a Jerusalem crowd, demanding the Messiah's crucifixion, hysterically invite the Deity to avenge Jesus' blood upon them and their children (27:25). Matthew further revises Mark's Passion narrative by adding that Pilate, symbol of imperial Rome, washed his hands of responsibility for Jesus' death—even while ordering Jesus' execution (27:24). All four Gospel writers shift the blame from the Roman government to the Jewish leadership, but only Matthew extends responsibility to the Jews' as-yet-unborn descendants.

Many commentators find an ethical paradox in Matthew's vindictive attitude toward his fellow Jews who did not accept Jesus as the national Messiah. Earlier in his Gospel, Matthew presents Jesus as repudiating the *lex talionis* (5:38–40), stressing instead the necessity of practicing infinite forgiveness (6:12, 14–16; 18:21–35) and exercising mercy (5:7). In dealing with his church's opponents, however, Matthew judges without compassion, apparently regarding Jewish rejection of his Messiah as falling beyond the tolerable limits of charity. The author, in effect, reintroduces the old law of retaliation that Jesus himself rejected. Historically, the consequences of New Testament writers attributing collective guilt to the Jewish people helped fuel the waves of anti-Semitism that repeatedly swept through the Western world for centuries afterward. Throughout Europe, Jews were indiscriminately persecuted as "Christ-killers," often with the blessing of ecclesiastical authorities.

Since the Holocaust of World War II, when Nazi Germany led a campaign of genocide against European Jews, killing approximately 6 million men, women, and children, a number of church leaders—Catholic, Protestant, and Greek Orthodox—have publicly condemned the practice of anti-Semitism. In 1974, the Roman Catholic Church officially reminded Christendom that modern Jews are not responsible for Jesus' crucifixion.

To place Matthew's negative verdict on the first-century Jewish establishment in historical perspective, we must remember that he condemns only the Jerusalem leadership, not Judaism itself. Despite his dislike of Pharisaic customs, the author agrees with Pharisaic teaching. He reminds his readers to "pay attention to their words" and "do what they tell you," for they occupy "the seat of Moses" and their teachings are authoritative (23:1–3).

The Fall of Jerusalem and the Parousia

Signs of the Times The second part of Jesus' fifth discourse is based largely on Mark 13, the prediction of Jerusalem's impending destruction. Whereas Mark states that the disciples asked only about when the Temple would fall (Mark 13:1–4), Matthew expands the disciples' question to include an eschatological inquiry into Jesus' Second Coming (the **Parousia**) and the "end of the age," the close of human history as we know it (24:1–3). Jesus' reply is a good illustration of how first-century Jewish eschatology was incorporated into the Christian tradition.

Matthew's presentation of the "signal" or "signs" leading to Jesus' return is a complex mixture of first-century historical events, such as the Jewish War, and prophetic images from the Hebrew Bible, particularly Daniel, Joel, Zechariah, and the pseudepigraphical 1 Enoch. All three Synoptic writers link the Jewish Revolt against Rome (66–73 CE) with supernatural portents of End time and Jesus' reappearance. Mark, the first to make this association of events, seems to have written at a time when the revolt had already begun (note the "battles" and "wars" in 13:7–8) and Jerusalem was about to fall. These cataclysmic events he called "the birth pangs of the new age." Both Matthew and Luke follow Mark's lead and connect these political upheavals with persecution of believers, perhaps allusions to Nero's cruel treatment of Roman Christians (c. 64–65 CE) or Zealot violence against Jewish Christians who refused to support the revolt. The Synoptic authors concur that attacks on the church, then a tiny minority of the Greco-Roman population, are of critical importance. The sufferings of the Christian community will bring God's vengeance on all humanity.

Matthew follows Mark in referring to the mysterious "abomination of desolation" as a warning to flee Judea (24:15), perhaps echoing a tradition that Jewish Christians had escaped destruction by leaving the holy city and seeking refuge in Pella, east of Jordan (see Box 7.6). In his version of Mark's eschatological prediction, however, Luke omits the "abomination" sign and substitutes an allusion to Roman armies besieging Jerusalem (Luke 21:20–24).

Both Mark and Matthew are aware that in the white heat of eschatological expectation there were "many" false reports of the Messiah's return (Mark 13:21–23; Matt. 24:23–27). Some Christians must have experienced crushing disappointment when their prophets' "inspired" predictions of Jesus' reappearance failed to materialize. Thus, both Evangelists caution that even "the Son" does not know the exact date of the Parousia (Mark 13:32; Matt. 24:36). Matthew adds that when the Son does return, his coming will be unmistakable in its universality, "like lightning from the east, flashing as far as the west" (24:27).

Matthew preserves the "double vision" nature of the Parousia found in Mark. Jesus' supernatural coming will be preceded by unmistakable "signs" that it is near (24:21–22, 29–35); at the same time, he will come without warning and when least expected (24:42–44). Although contradictory, both concepts apparently existed concurrently in the early church, which was deeply influenced by eschatological thinking.

Although the author of Revelation connects End time with cosmic catastrophe, other New Testament writers (perhaps aware of the repeated failure of attempts to calculate the date of the Parousia) state that the Son's return is essentially unheralded (1 Thess. 5:1–5; 2 Peter 3:10).

Matthew probably wrote almost two decades after Mark's Gospel was composed, but he retains the Markan tradition that persons who knew Jesus would live to see his predictions come true (24:34; Mark 13:30). To Matthew, the Roman annihilation of the Jewish state, which coincided with the emergence of the Christian church as an entity distinct from Judaism, may essentially have fulfilled Jesus' words, or at least an important part of his prophecy. From the writer's perspective, the "New Age" had already dawned with Jerusalem's fall and the church's new role in future human history (28:19–20).

Parables of Jesus' Return Chapters 24 and 25 contain three parables and a prophetic vision of Jesus' unannounced Parousia. Whatever their original meaning to Jesus, in Matthew they serve to illustrate believers' obligation to await faithfully and patiently their absent Lord's return. The first parable contrasts two servants, one of whom abuses his fellow employees until the master suddenly reappears to execute him (24:45–51)—a clear warning to church members to treat others honorably. The parable about a delayed bridegroom similarly contrasts two kinds of believers: those who are alert and prepared for the wedding event and those who are not. Because the "bridegroom" is "late in coming," Matthew implies that Christians must reconcile themselves to a delay in the Parousia (25:1–13).

The parable of the talents, in which a master's servants invest huge sums of money for him, probably had a quite different meaning before Matthew used it as a warning illustration of Jesus' delayed return. The master in the parable is a "hard man" who reaps what he does not sow and who inspires terror in his servants. In the context of Jesus' original telling, he was most likely an absentee landowner who amassed enormous profits from his slaves' labor and who punished them severely if they failed to make him enough money. For Matthew, Jesus' parable dramatizing the Palestinian aristocracy's economic exploitation translates into a reminder that the master's servants (transformed into Christian workers) must be productive while awaiting the Parousia, increasing Jesus' treasure (recruiting new members for the church) (25:14–30).

The fourth and final judgment parable concerns not only the church but also "the nations." The term *nations* refers primarily to Gentiles living without the Mosaic Law, but it may be intended to include all humanity—Jews, Christians, and those belonging to other world religions as well. In the parable about separating worthy "sheep" and unworthy "goats," all are judged exclusively on their behavior toward Jesus' "little ones," Matthew's favored term for Christian disciples (25:31–46) (see Figure 8.3).

FIGURE 8.3   *Christ Separating Sheep from Goats.* This early-sixth-century mosaic illustrates Matthew's parable of eschatological judgment (Matt. 25:31–46). At his Parousia (Second Coming), an enthroned Jesus, flanked by two angels, divides all humanity into two mutually exclusive groups. The sheep are gathered in the favored position at Jesus' right hand, whereas the goats, at Jesus' left, are condemned to outer darkness for their failure to help others.

Matthew's eschatological vision makes charitable acts, rather than "correct" religious doctrines, the standard in distinguishing good people from bad. In such passages, Matthew reflects the ancient Israelite prophets, who regarded service to the poor and unfortunate as acts of worship to God. The Book of James, which defines true religion as essentially humanitarian service to others (James 1:27), espouses a similar view.

The Author's Purpose in the Judgment Parables
By adding the four parables of judgment to his expansion of Mark 13 and by linking them to "the kingdom" (25:1, 14), Matthew shifts the apocalyptic emphasis from expectations about the Parousia to the function and duties of the church. Matthew links the parables of the alert householder, the trustworthy servant, and the talents with Jesus' predictions of the *eschaton*. In contrast, Luke, who uses the same parables, places them among the general teachings of Jesus' pre-Jerusalem ministry (cf. Matt. 24:43–44 with Luke 12:39–40; Matt. 24:45–51 with Luke 12:42–46; and Matt. 25:14–30 with Luke 19:12–27).

Fifth and Final Narrative Section: The Passion Story and Resurrection

Matthew retells the story of Jesus' last two days on earth (Thursday and Friday of Holy Week) with the same grave and solemn tone we find in Mark. To the Gospel writers, Jesus of Nazareth's suffering, death, and resurrection are not only the most important events in world history but also the crucial turning point in humanity's relation to God. Although Matthew's Passion narrative (26:1–28:20) closely follows Mark's sequence of events, he adds a few new details, probably drawn from the oral tradition of his community. The treachery of Judas Iscariot is emphasized and linked to the fulfillment of a passage in Jeremiah, although the relevant text actually appears in Zechariah (Matt. 26:14–15, 20–25, 47–50; 27:3–10; Jer. 32:6–13; Zech. 11:12–13). The theme of a warning dream, used frequently in the birth story, is reintroduced when Pilate's wife, frightened by a dream about Jesus, urges her husband to "have nothing to do with that innocent man" (27:19).

Miraculous Signs

To emphasize that the very foundations of the world are shaken by the supreme crime of crucifying God's son, Matthew reports that an earthquake accompanies Jesus' last moment and triggers a resurrection of the dead (27:50–53), an eschatological phenomenon usually associated with the Final Judgment. Although the author presumably includes the incident to show that Jesus' death opens the way for humanity's rebirth, neither he nor any other New Testament writer explains what eventually happens to the reanimated corpses that leave their graves and parade through Jerusalem.

The Centurion's Reaction

Whereas Mark reports that only one Roman soldier recognizes Jesus as God's son, Matthew states that both the centurion and his men confess Jesus' divinity (27:54). Perhaps Matthew's change of a single man's exclamation to that of a whole group expresses his belief that numerous Gentiles will acknowledge Jesus as Lord.

The Empty Tomb

Despite some significant differences, all three Synoptic Gospels agree fairly closely in their account of Jesus' burial and the women's discovery of the empty tomb. Matthew, however, adds details about some Pharisees persuading Pilate to dispatch Roman soldiers to guard Jesus' tomb. According to Matthew, the Pharisees are aware of Jesus' promise to rise from the grave "on the third day" and so arrange for a Roman guard to prevent the disciples from stealing the body and creating the false impression that Jesus still lives. In Matthew's account, the Romans guarding the tomb on Sunday morning actually see an angel descend from heaven, a sight that paralyzes them with terror. (See Chapter 20 for a discussion of the noncanonical Gospel of Peter, which describes Jesus' actual resurrection.)

The Plot to Discredit the Resurrection

After the women discover the empty gravesite and then encounter Jesus himself, some guards report what has happened to the Jerusalem priests. According to Matthew, the Sadducean priests then plot to undermine Christian claims that Jesus has risen by bribing the soldiers to say that the disciples secretly removed and hid Jesus' corpse (27:62–66; 28:11–15).

Matthew implies that the Jews of his day used the soldiers' false testimony to refute Christian preaching about the Resurrection. However, his counterargument that the Roman soldiers had admitted falling asleep while on duty is not convincing. Severe punishment, including torture and death, awaited any Roman soldier found thus derelict. In 79 CE, only a few years before Matthew wrote, soldiers guarding the gates of Pompeii preferred being buried alive during the cataclysmic eruption of Mount Vesuvius to facing the consequences of leaving their posts without permission. Some commentators believe that a rumor about the possible theft of Jesus' body may have circulated, but probably not for the reasons that Matthew gives. (For a different view, see Wright in "Recommended Reading.")

Post Resurrection Appearances and the Great Commission

In Mark's Gospel, Jesus promises that after his death he will reappear to the disciples in Galilee (Mark 14:28; 16:7). After recording the women's dawn encounter with the risen Lord, Matthew then reports that Jesus also appeared to the Eleven at a prearranged mountain site in Galilee. Matthew observes that some disciples had doubts about their seeing Jesus, as if mistrusting the evidence of their own senses. The author seems to imply that absolute proof of an event so contrary to ordinary human experience is impossible.

Even though some disciples doubt, all presumably accept the final command of the One whose teachings are vindicated by his resurrection to life: They, and the community of faith they represent, are to make new disciples throughout the Gentile world (28:16–20). This commission to recruit followers from "all nations" further expresses Matthew's theme that the church has much work to do before Jesus returns. It implies that the author's tiny community had only begun what was to be a vast undertaking—a labor extending into the far-distant future.

Summary

In composing a new edition of Jesus' life, Matthew provides his community with a comprehensive survey of Jesus' teaching. The unknown author, who may have lived in Antioch or some other part of Syria in the 80s CE, was a Jewish Christian who used scribal techniques to place Jesus' life and death in the context of ancient Jewish prophecy. Writing to demonstrate that Jesus of Nazareth is the expected Messiah foretold in the Hebrew Bible, Matthew repeatedly quotes or alludes to specific biblical passages that he interprets as being fulfilled in Jesus' career.

The author's concurrent emphasis on scriptural fulfillment and on Jesus' authoritative reinterpretation of the Mosaic Torah (Matt. 5–7) suggests that his work is directed primarily to an audience that sees itself, at least in part, still bound by Torah regulations. Jesus' comments on such matters as Sabbath observance (12:1–14) and divorce (19:3–12) can be seen as examples of Halakah characteristic of first-century Palestinian rabbinic teaching.

By incorporating a large body of teaching material into Mark's narrative framework, Matthew balances Mark's emphasis on Jesus' deeds—miracles of healing and exorcism—with a counterstress on the ethical content of Jesus' preaching. Instructions to the original disciples (chs. 10 and 18) are applied to conditions in the Christian community of Matthew's day.

Matthew retains the apocalyptic themes found in Mark, but he significantly modifies them. He links the eschatological "kingdom" to missionary activities of the early church, a visible manifestation of divine rule. Matthew's Gospel typically shifts the burden of meaning from speculations about the *eschaton* to necessary activities of the church during the interim between Jesus' resurrection and the Parousia. Thus, Matthew expands Mark's prediction of Jerusalem's destruction to include parables illustrating the duties and obligations of Jesus' "servant," the church (cf. Mark 13 and Matt. 24–25). The shift from eschatological speculation to concern for the indefinitely extended work of the church will be even more evident in Luke-Acts.

By framing Mark's account of Jesus' ministry and Passion with narratives of the Savior's birth and resurrection, Matthew emphasizes the divinely directed, supernatural character of Jesus' life. In Matthew, Jesus becomes the Son of God at conception and is the inheritor of all the ancient promises to Israel. He is the "son" of Abraham, heir to the Davidic throne, successor to the authoritative seat of Moses, and the embodiment of divine Wisdom. A guidebook providing instruction and discipline for the community of faith, Matthew's Gospel became the church's premier source of wise counsel to the faithful.

Questions for Review

1. Even if Mark's Gospel is an older work, what features of Matthew's Gospel can account for its standing first in the New Testament canon? How does Matthew connect his account with the Hebrew Bible?
2. Why do scholars believe it unlikely that one of the Twelve wrote Matthew's Gospel? From the content of the Gospel, what can we infer about its author and the time and place of its composition?
3. In his apparent use of Mark, Q, and other sources unique to his account, how does Matthew reveal some of his special interests and purposes? To underscore his individual

themes, what kinds of changes does he make in editing Mark's account?
4. In adding five blocks of teaching material to Mark's framework, how does Matthew emphasize Jesus' role as an interpreter of the Mosaic Torah? How does Matthew present Jesus' teachings as the standard and guide of the Christian community?
5. In what ways does Matthew follow standards of his day in interpreting the Hebrew Bible? How does the author's emphasis on the supernatural affect his portrait of Jesus?
6. Although he emphasizes that Jesus' personal religion is Torah Judaism, Matthew also presents his hero as founder of the church (*ekklesia*). How "Jewish" and Torah abiding did Matthew intend the church to be?
7. In editing and expanding Mark's prophecy of Jerusalem's fall and the *eschaton,* Matthew interpolates several parables of judgment. How do these parables function to stretch the time of the End into the far-distant future?

Questions for Discussion and Reflection

1. Highlighting Jesus' kingdom message, Matthew devotes long sections to presenting a "kingdom ethic," which involves ending the cycle of retaliation and returning good for evil. If practiced fully today, would Jesus' teaching about giving up all possessions and peacefully submitting to unfair treatment change modern society for the better?

Can Jesus' policy of turning the other cheek be applied to relations among nations, or does it apply to individual relationships only? Did Jesus intend his ethic for a future ideal time, for dedicated members of the church, or for this imperfect world? Do you think that he expected everyone eventually to follow the principles in the Sermon on the Mount and thus bring about God's rule on earth?
2. With his frequent allusions to Gehenna's fires and a place of "outer darkness" where there is "wailing and grinding of teeth," Matthew makes more references to sinners' punishment in the afterlife than any other Gospel writer. As shown in chapters 10 and 18, he also seems more interested in maintaining church order and exercising control over church members than do

the other Evangelists. Do you see any connection between these two concerns? Historically, does a religious institution attain greater power if it promotes the belief that it alone offers the means of escaping eternal torment? How large a role does fear of damnation play in eliciting obedience to ecclesiastical authority?

Terms and Concepts to Remember

antitheses	M (Matthew's special
apostle	source)
Beatitudes	Magi
Bethlehem	midrash
centurion	Parousia
church	Peter
ekklesia	saints
Gehenna	scribes and Pharisees
great commission	Sermon on the Mount
Haggadah	seven woes
Halakah	Sheol
Herod Agrippa I	Sodom
lex talionis (the law of	Valley of Hinnom
retaliation)	

Recommended Reading

Boring, M. Engene. "The Gospel of Matthew." In *The New Interpreter's Bible*, Vol. 8, pp. 89–105. Nashville: Abingdon Press, 1995. Extensive scholarly commentary on the origin, purpose, and text of Matthew.

Brown, Michael J. "Matthew, Gospel of." In K. D. Sakenfeld, ed., *The New Interpreter's Dictionary of the Bible*, Vol. 3, pp. 839–852. Nashville: Abington Press, 2008. A scholarly analysis of the Gospel's probable origins, structure, and theological content.

Brown, R. E. *The Birth of the Messiah: A Commentary on the Infancy Narratives in Matthew and Luke*, 2nd ed. New York: Doubleday, 1993. A thorough analysis of traditions surrounding Jesus' birth.

———. *The Death of the Messiah*, Vols. 1 and 2. New York: Anchor/Doubleday, 1994. An exhaustive analysis of the Gospel accounts of Jesus' arrest, trial, and execution by a leading Roman Catholic scholar.

Bryan, Christopher. *The Resurrection of the Messiah*. New York: Oxford University Press, 2011. Examines earliest recoverable beliefs about the nature of Jesus' resurrection.

Carter, Warren. *Matthew: Storyteller, Interpreter, Evangelist*, 2nd ed. Peabody, Mass.: Hendrickson, 2004. Analyzes Matthew's implied original audience in Antioch to explain the Jewish-Christian tensions in his Gospel.

Clarke, Howard. *The Gospel of Matthew and Its Readers: A Historical Introduction to the First Gospel*. Bloomington: Indiana University Press, 2003. A commentary focusing on Christian ethics.

Kingsbury, J. D. *Matthew as Story*. Philadelphia: Fortress Press, 1986. A more advanced analysis of the Gospel.

Meier, John P. "Matthew, Gospel of." In D. N. Freedman, ed., *The Anchor Bible Dictionary*, Vol. 4, pp. 622–641. New York: Doubleday, 1992. A lucid survey of important scholarship on the origin and purpose of Matthew's Gospel.

Miller, Robert J. *Born Divine: The Births of Jesus and Other Sons of God*. Santa Rosa, Calif.: Polebridge Press, 2003. Places the Gospel infancy stories firmly in the context of other Greco-Roman tales of miraculous births.

Overman, J. A. *Matthew's Gospel and Formative Judaism: The Social World of the Matthean Community*. Minneapolis: Fortress Press, 1991. Examines the social and religious milieu of the Jewish-Christian group that produced Matthew.

Peabody, David; Cope, Lama; and McNicol, Allan J. *One Gospel from Two: Mark's Use of Matthew and Luke: A Demonstration of the Research Team of the International Institute for Gospel Studies*. Harrisburg, Penn.: Trinity Press International, 2002. Argues that Mark is an abridgment of the two other Synoptics.

Runesson, Anders. "Matthew, Gospel According to." In M. D. Coogan, ed., *The Oxford Encyclopedia of the Books of the Bible*, Vol. 2, pp. 59–78. New York: Oxford University Press, 2011. Examines the Gospel's structure and theological purpose.

Senior, D. P. *What Are They Saying About Matthew?* Revised and Expanded Edition. New York: Paulist Press, 1995. A survey of critical approaches to interpreting Matthew.

Sim, David. *The Gospel of Matthew and Christian Judaism: The History and Social Setting of the Matthean Community*. Edinburgh: T and T Clark, 1998. Argues for an exclusively Christian Jewish environment as the Gospel's source.

Stern, David H. *Jewish New Testament Commentary*. Clarksville, Md.: Jewish New Testament Publications, Inc., 1992. An important contribution to recognizing the Jewish cultural context of the early Christian writings.

Talbert, Charles H. *Matthew*. Grand Rapids, Mich.: Baker Academic, 2010. Examines the Gospel's cultural environment and the author's theological concerns.

Wink, Walter. *The Powers That Be: Theology for a New Millennium.* New York: Galilee/Doubleday, 1998. Includes a chapter, "Jesus' Third Way" (between the extremes of violence and passivity), that perceptively interprets Matthew's Sermon on the Mount.

Wright, N. T. *The Resurrection of the Son of God* (Christian Origins and the Question of God, Vol. 3). Minneapolis: Augsburg Fortress Press, 2003. Probably the most cogently argued work defending the historicity of Jesus' physical resurrection.

CHAPTER 9

Luke's Portrait of Jesus
A Savior for "All Nations"

But [Jesus] said, "In the world kings lord it over their subjects; and those in authority are called 'Benefactors.' Not so with you: on the contrary, the highest among you must bear himself like the youngest, the chief of you like a servant. . . . Here I am among you like a servant." Luke 22:25–27

Key Topics/Themes The first part of a two-volume work (Luke-Acts), Luke's Gospel presents Jesus' career not only as history's most crucial event but also as the opening stage of an indefinitely extended historical process that continues in the life of the church (Acts 1–28). Writing for a Greco-Roman audience, Luke emphasizes that Jesus and his disciples, working under the Holy Spirit, are innocent of any crime against Rome and that their religion is a universal faith intended for all people. The parables unique to Luke's Gospel depict the unexpected ways in which God's approaching kingdom overturns the normal social order and reverses conventional beliefs. After a formal preface and extended nativity account (chs. 1 and 2), Luke generally follows Mark's order in narrating the Galilean ministry (chs. 3–9); he then inserts a large body of teaching material, the "greater interpolation" (9:51–18:14), supposedly given on the journey to Jerusalem, returning to Mark for his narration of the Jerusalem ministry and Passion story (18:31–23:56). Luke's final chapter reports post resurrection appearances in or near Jerusalem (ch. 24).

The author of Luke-Acts is unique among New Testament writers, manifesting a breadth of historical vision comparable to that shown in the sweeping narrative of Israel's history from the conquest of Canaan to the first destruction of the Jewish state (the Hebrew Bible books of Joshua through 2 Kings). Like the final editors of Israel's historical books (sixth century BCE), the writer of Luke-Acts lived at a time when Jerusalem and its Temple lay in ruins and Jews were enslaved to Gentiles. Babylon had demolished Solomon's Temple in 587 BCE, and Rome (labeled the new Babylon in Revelation) had obliterated its successor in 70 CE. In both of these national disasters, the people of Israel lost their sanctuary, priesthood, and homeland. Both catastrophes raised similar questions about God's loyalty to his covenant people. In the bleak decades after 587 BCE, the authors of Psalm 89 and of Lamentations questioned their God's faithfulness to his promises, while the author of Job demanded that Yahweh, the Lord of history, justify his permitting the righteous and innocent to suffer as if they were guilty of unpardonable crimes.

Israel and the Church: Luke's Theology of History

About thirty years before Luke compiled his accounts of Jesus and the early church, Paul had insisted that his fellow Jews were still God's covenant people: "They are Israelites: they were made God's sons; theirs is the splendour of the divine presence, theirs the covenants, the law, the temple worship, and the promises" (Rom. 9:4). Paul was executed several years before the cataclysm of 70 CE; we do not know how he would have interpreted the event to other Jews. Luke, however, who was thoroughly acquainted with God's promises to Israel, attempted to place the Jews' seemingly inexplicable fate in historical and theological perspective. As L. T. Johnson notes in his essay on Luke-Acts (see "Recommended Reading"), Luke's two-volume narrative functions in part as a **theodicy,** a literary work that tries to reconcile beliefs about divine goodness with the irrefutable fact that evil and undeserved suffering permeate human experience.

As he indicates in his formal preface to the Gospel, Luke has pondered long over "the whole course of these events" and is determined to provide "a connected narrative" that will give readers "authentic knowledge" (1:3–4) about the interlocking stories of Judaism and nascent Christianity. Luke's wish to convey "authentic" information (a reliable meaning) through *kathexes* (proper sequential order) in writing his account suggests his moral purpose: Luke-Acts will demonstrate that God did indeed fulfill his promises to Israel before giving his new revelation to the Gentiles. Assured that God has been faithful to Israel, Gentiles can now rely on his promises made through the church, a renewed Israel that includes both Jews and Greeks.

Luke thus begins his double volume—in length Luke-Acts makes up a full third of the New Testament—with a narrative about the conception of John the Baptist. As Luke presents John's nativity, the future baptizer of Jesus is the culminating prophetic figure in Israel's history. The author makes John's parents resemble **Abraham**

The Gospel According to Luke

Author: Traditionally Luke, a traveling companion of Paul, not an eyewitness to Jesus' ministry. Because the writer, who also composed the Book of Acts, rarely shows Paul promoting his distinctive ideas and never mentions Paul's letters, scholars think it unlikely that he was an intimate of the apostle. Luke-Acts is anonymous.

Date: About 85–90 CE, significantly after the destruction of Jerusalem and the church's transformation into a primarily Gentile movement.

Place of composition: Unknown. Suggestions range from Antioch to Ephesus.

Sources: Mark, Q, and special Lukan material (L).

Audience: Gentile Christians dispersed throughout the Roman Empire. The person to whom both Luke and Acts are dedicated, Theophilus, may have been a Greco-Roman government official, or, because his name means "beloved [or lover] of God," he may be a symbol for the Gentile church.

and **Sarah** in Genesis: Like their biblical prototypes, the Baptist's parents, **Zechariah** and **Elizabeth,** are aged and childless—until an angel appears to announce that the hitherto barren wife will conceive a son destined to be an agent of God's plan for humanity. As the son of Abraham and Sarah—**Isaac**—is the precious "seed" through whom the promised benefits to Israel will flow, so John is the connecting link between Israel's past and the future blessings bestowed by Jesus. John will fill the prophesied role of a returned **Elijah,** messenger of a New Covenant and precursor of Jesus (1:5–21). Because John's father, Zechariah, is a priest who devotedly officiates at the Temple— the location of Zechariah's angelic visitation— the Baptist's heritage is firmly planted at the exact center of Israel's religious tradition.

Midway through his Gospel, Luke makes John's transitional function explicit: "Until John, it was the Law and the prophets; since then there is the good news of the kingdom of God, and everyone forces his way in" (16:16). As the last of Israel's long line of prophets, John represents the First Covenant (Torah and prophets). As the figure who introduces the new era of God's kingdom, John's successor— Jesus of Nazareth—stands at the precise center of time, the pivot on which world history turns. Beginning his ministry with John's baptism, the Lukan Jesus completes it with extensive post resurrection appearances in which he interprets the Hebrew Bible as a christological prophecy, declaring that "everything written about me in the Law of Moses and in the prophets and psalms . . . [is now] fulfilled" (Luke 24:36–53). Jesus then commands his disciples to recruit followers from "all nations," creating a multi-cultural Gentile community (24:47; Acts 1:8).

In Luke's view, God *has* kept his biblical promises to Israel; the divine advantages that formerly were Israel's exclusive privilege can now be extended to others as well. Accordingly, Luke ends his account of the early church with Paul's declaration that "this salvation of God has been sent to the Gentiles; the Gentiles will *listen*" (Acts 28:28; emphasis added). It is significant that Paul is in Rome, the Gentile center of imperial power, when he asserts that henceforth he and his fellow missionaries will focus their efforts on Gentiles.

After showing Paul preaching "without [legal] restraint" in Rome, Luke abruptly ends his account. He does not continue the story with Paul's execution for sedition or Jerusalem's destruction, twin blows to the church that effectively eliminated both the chief missionary to the Gentiles and the original Jewish nerve center of Christianity. For Luke's purpose, it is enough to imply that Christianity metaphorically has outgrown its Jewish roots and has been transplanted abroad in order to thrive on Gentile soil.

Luke-Acts thus traces the course of a new world religion from its inception in a Bethlehem stable to its (hoped-for) status as a legitimate faith of the Roman Empire. By making Jesus' life the central act of a three-part drama that begins with Israel and continues with the Christian church, Luke offers a philosophy of history vital to Christianity's later understanding of its mission. Instead of bringing the world to an apocalyptic end, Jesus' career is a new beginning that establishes a heightened awareness of God's intentions for all humanity. The Lukan Jesus' triumph over death is closely tied to the disciples' job of evangelizing the world

(24:44–53; Acts 1:1–8). In revising Mark's Gospel (Luke's principal source), the author creatively modifies the Markan expectation of an immediate End to show that Jesus' essential work is continued by the believing community. Acts portrays the disciples entering a new historical epoch, the age of the church, and thereby extends the new faith's operations indefinitely into the future. Acts concludes, not by drawing attention to the Parousia, but by recounting Paul's resolve to concentrate on ministering to Gentiles (28:27–28).

The Author and His Sources

Dedication to Theophilus

Luke addresses his Gospel to **Theophilus,** the otherwise unknown person to whom he also dedicates his sequel, the Book of Acts (1:1; Acts 1:1). Bearing a Greek name meaning "lover of God," Theophilus—whom Luke calls "your Excellency"—may have been a Greek or Roman official, perhaps an affluent patron who underwrote Luke's composition and publication.

Authorship and Date

The most important early reference to the author of Luke-Acts confirms that, like Mark, he was not an eyewitness to the events he narrates. In the Muratorian list of New Testament books (usually dated at about 200 CE, although some recent scholarly studies place it in the fourth century), a note identifies the author of this Gospel as **Luke,** "the beloved" physician who accompanied Paul on some of the apostle's missionary journeys. The note also states that Luke did not know Jesus. In the late second century CE, Irenaeus, a bishop of Lyon in Gaul (modern France), also referred to the author as a companion of Paul's, presumably the same Luke named in several Pauline letters (Col. 4:14; Philem. 24; 2 Tim. 4:11). If the author of Luke-Acts is Paul's friend, it explains the "we" passages in Acts in which the narration changes from the third to the first person in describing certain episodes; presumably, he was a participant in these events (Acts 16:10–17; 20:5–15; 21:1–18; 27:1–28:16). Some commentators also argue for Lukan authorship on the basis of the writer's vocabulary, which includes a number of medical terms appropriate for a physician. Other scholars, however, point out that the writer uses medical terms no more expertly than he employs legal or maritime terminology.

The author nowhere identifies himself, either in the Gospel or in Acts. His depiction of Paul's character and teaching, moreover, does not always coincide with what Paul reveals of himself in his letters. To many contemporary scholars, these facts indicate that the author could not have known the apostle well. Perhaps the most telling argument against Luke's authorship is that the writer shows no knowledge of Paul's letters. Not only does he never refer to Paul's writing, but he alludes to none of Paul's characteristic teachings in any of the Pauline speeches contained in Acts. At the same time, critics who uphold Lukan authorship point out that the physician associated with Paul for only brief periods and wrote long after Paul's death, when the theological issues argued in Paul's letters were no longer as immediate or controversial as they had been. Luke's concern in Acts is not to reopen theological disputes but to smooth over differences that divided the early church and depict apostles and missionaries united in spreading the faith. Although many experts regard the writer of Luke-Acts as anonymous, others retain the traditional assumption that the historical Luke is the author.

Although the author's identity is not conclusively established, for convenience we refer to him as Luke. Based on his interest in a Gentile audience and his facility with the Greek language (he has the largest vocabulary and most polished style of any Evangelist), the writer may have been a Gentile, perhaps the only non-Jewish biblical writer.

According to most scholars, Luke-Acts was written after 70 CE, when Jerusalem was destroyed by the Roman armies under General (and later, Emperor) Titus. In his version of Jesus' prediction of the holy city's fall (paralleling Mark 13

and Matt. 24), Luke reveals detailed knowledge of the Roman siege:

> But when you see Jerusalem encircled by armies, then you may be sure that her destruction is near. Then you who are in Judea must take to the hills; those that are in the city itself must leave it . . . because this is the time of retribution. . . . For there will be great distress in the land and a terrible judgment upon this people. They will fall at the sword's point; they will be carried captive into all countries; and Jerusalem will be trampled down by foreigners until their day has run its course.
>
> (21:20–24)

In this passage, Luke substitutes a description of Jerusalem's siege for the cryptic "sign" (the "abomination of desolation") that Mark and Matthew allude to at this point in their accounts (see Mark 13:13–19; Matt. 24:15–22). Luke also refers specifically to the Roman method of encircling a besieged town, a military technique used in the 70 CE assault on Jerusalem:

> Your enemies will set up siege-works against you; they will encircle you and hem you in at every point; they will bring you to the ground, you and your children within your walls, and not leave you one stone standing on another.
>
> (19:43–44)

It would appear, then, that the Gospel was written at some point after the Jewish War of 66–73 CE and before about 90 CE, when publication made Paul's letters accessible to Christian readers. Many scholars place Luke-Acts in the mid-to-late 80s CE and favor Ephesus, a Greek-speaking city in Asia Minor with a relatively large Christian population, as the place of composition.

Luke's Use of Sources

As a Christian living two or three generations after Jesus' time, Luke must rely on other persons' information, including orally transmitted recollections about Jesus and traditional Christian preaching. Besides using memories of "eyewitnesses" and later missionary accounts, the author depends on his own research skills—the labor he expends going "over the whole course of these events in detail" (1:1–4).

Luke is aware that "many" others before him produced Gospels (1:1). His resolve to create yet another suggests that he was not satisfied with his predecessors' efforts. As Matthew did, he chooses Mark as his primary source, but he omits several large units of Markan material (such as Mark 6:45–8:26 and 9:41–10:12), perhaps to make room for his own special additions. Adapting Mark to his creative purpose, Luke sometimes rearranges the sequence of individual incidents to emphasize his particular themes. Whereas Mark placed Jesus' rejection at Nazareth midway through the Galilean campaign, Luke sets it at the beginning (4:16–30). Adding that the Nazarenes attempted to kill Jesus to Mark's account, he uses the incident to foreshadow his hero's later death in Jerusalem (see Box 9.1).

In addition, Luke frames Mark's central account of Jesus' adult career with his own unique stories of Jesus' infancy (chs. 1 and 2) and resurrection (ch. 24). Luke further modifies the earlier Gospel by adding two extensive sequences of teaching material to Mark's narrative. The first section inserted into the Markan framework—called the **"lesser interpolation"** (6:20–8:3)—includes Luke's version of the Sermon on the Mount, which the author transfers to level ground. Known as the **Sermon on the Plain** (6:20–49), this collection of Jesus' sayings is apparently drawn from the same source that Matthew used, the hypothetical Q (*Quelle,* "source") document. Instead of assembling Q material into long speeches as Matthew does, however, Luke scatters these sayings throughout his Gospel. Scholars believe that he observes Q's original order more closely than Matthew.

Luke's second major insertion into the Markan narrative, called the **"greater interpolation,"** is nearly ten chapters long (9:51–18:14). A miscellaneous compilation of Jesus' parables and pronouncements, this collection supposedly represents Jesus' teaching on the road from Galilee to Jerusalem. It is composed almost exclusively of Q material and Luke's special source, which scholars call **L (Lukan).** After this interpolation section, during which all narrative action stops, Luke returns to Mark's account at 18:15 and then reproduces an edited version of the Passion story.

Like the other Synoptic writers, Luke presents Jesus' life in terms of images and themes from the Hebrew Bible, which thus constitutes another of the author's sources. In Luke's presentation, some of Jesus' miracles, such as his resuscitating a widow's dead son, are told in such a way that they closely resemble similar miracles in the Hebrew Scriptures. Jesus' deeds clearly echo those of the prophets Elijah and Elisha (1 Kings 17–19; 2 Kings 1–6). Luke introduces the Elijah–Elisha theme early in the Gospel (4:23–28), indicating that for him these ancient men of God were prototypes of the Messiah.

Although he shares material from Mark, Q, and the Hebrew Bible with Matthew, Luke gives his "connected narrative" a special quality by including many of Jesus' words that occur only in his Gospel (the L source). Only in Luke do we find such celebrated parables as those of the prodigal son (15:11–32), the lost coin (15:8–10), the persistent widow, the good Samaritan (10:29–32), and Lazarus and the rich man (16:19–31) (see Box 9.2). These and other parables embody consistent themes, typically highlighting life's unexpected reversals and/or God's gracious forgiveness of wrongdoers.

Despite the inclusion of some of Jesus' "hard sayings" about the rigors of discipleship, Luke's special material tends to picture a gentle and loving Jesus, a concerned shepherd who tenderly cares for his flock (the community of believers). Luke has been accused of "sentimentalizing" Jesus' message; however, the author's concern for oppressed people—the poor, social outcasts, women—is genuine and lends his Gospel a distinctively humane and gracious ambience.

Some Typical Lukan Themes

Luke makes his Gospel a distinctive creation by sounding many themes important to the self-identity and purpose of the Christian community for which he writes. Many readers find Luke's account especially appealing because it portrays Jesus taking a personal interest in women, the poor, social outcasts, and other powerless persons. In general, Luke portrays Jesus as a model of compassion who willingly forgives

BOX 9.1 Luke's Editing and Restructuring of Mark

Luke generally follows Mark's narrative sequence, though he uses less of Mark's Gospel (about 35 percent) than Matthew. Besides omitting large sections of Mark (Mark 6:45–8:26 and 9:41–10:12), Luke also typically deletes Markan passages that might reflect unfavorably on Jesus' family or disciples. Consistent with his exaltation of Mary in the birth stories (1:26, 56; 2:1, 39), he omits Mark's story of Jesus' "mother and brothers" trying to interfere in his ministry (Mark 3:21, 33, 34) and rewrites the Markan Jesus' statement about not being respected by his "family and kinsmen" (cf. Mark 6:4; Luke 4:22, 24). Several of Luke's representative changes to his Markan source—apparently made for thematic or theological reasons—are given below.

JESUS' BAPTISM

Mark: It happened at this time that Jesus came from Nazareth in Galilee and was baptized in the Jordan by John. (1:9)

Luke: During a general baptism of the people, when Jesus too had been baptized, heaven opened and the Holy Spirit descended. (Luke 3:21)

[Luke deletes Mark's statement that John baptized Jesus, perhaps to avoid any implication that the Baptist was Jesus' superior.]

JESUS AS SERVANT

Mark: "You know that in the world the recognized rulers lord it over their subjects, and their great men make them feel the weight of authority. That is not the way with you; among you, whoever wants to be great must be your servant, and whoever wants to be first must be the willing slave of all. For even the Son of Man did not come to be served but to serve, and to give up his life as a ransom for many." (Mark 10:42–45)

Luke: "In the world, kings lord it over their subjects; and those in authority are called their country's 'Benefactors.' Not so with you: on the contrary, the highest among you must bear himself like the youngest, the chief of you like a servant. For who is greater—the one who sits at table or the servant who waits on him? Surely the one who sits at table. Yet here am I among you like a servant." (Luke 22:25–27)

[Luke changes the setting of Jesus' words from the road to Jerusalem to the scene of the Last Supper and omits the Markan declaration that Jesus' death is a "ransom for many," perhaps suggesting that he viewed Jesus' death as an act of heroic service rather as a sacrifice that "ransoms"

humanity. In Acts, where Luke consistently depicts Jesus' followers as imitating his example of service, the author briefly cites Isaiah's "suffering servant" passage (Isa. 53:7–8), but excludes any reference to vicarious atonement (Acts 8:30–35).]

AT THE CROSS

Mark: Then Jesus gave a loud cry and died . . . And when the centurion who was standing opposite him saw how he died, he said, "Truly this man was a son of God." (Mark 15:37, 39)

Luke: Then Jesus gave a loud cry and said, "Father, into thy hands I commit my spirit"; and with these words he died. The centurion saw it all, and gave praise to God. "Beyond all doubt," he said, "this man was innocent." (Luke 23:46–47)

[Instead of perceiving Jesus as worthy of divine honor, as in Mark, the Lukan centurion declares that Jesus is legally *innocent of treason against Rome, a theme prominent in Acts' description of the disciples' trials before Roman law courts.]*

SEEKING THE RISEN JESUS

Mark: "Nevertheless, after I am raised again I will go on before you into Galilee." (14:28)

Luke: The risen Jesus instructs the disciples: "I am sending upon you my Father's promised gift [the Holy Spirit], so stay here in this city [Jerusalem] until you are armed with the power from above." (24:49)

[At the empty tomb, a youth "wearing a white robe" instructs the frightened women disciples to "give this message to his disciples and Peter: 'He is going on before you into Galilee, and there you will see him, as he told you'" (16:7).]

[Whereas Mark directs the disciples to find their risen Lord in Galilee (as does Matthew 28:7, 10, 16–17), Luke insists that they remain in Jerusalem, where all the Lukan post resurrection appearances take place and where the Holy Spirit anoints the early church (Acts 1:8–2:47).]

BOX 9.2 Representative Examples of Material Found Only in Luke

A formal preface and statement of purpose (1:1–4)

A narrative about the parents of John the Baptist (1:5–25, 57–80)

Luke's distinctive story of Jesus' conception and birth (1:26–56; 2:1–40)

Jesus' childhood visit to the Jerusalem Temple (2:41–52)

A distinctive Lukan genealogy (3:23–38)

The Scripture reading in the Nazareth synagogue and subsequent attempt to kill Jesus (4:16–30)

Jesus' hearing before Herod Antipas (23:6–12)

The sympathetic criminal (23:39–43)

Jesus' post resurrection appearances on the road to Emmaus (24:13–35)

Some parables, sayings, and miracles unique to Luke:
  Raising the son of a Nain widow (7:11–17)
  Two forgiven debtors (7:41–43)

Satan falling like lightning from heaven (10:18)

The good Samaritan (10:29–37)

The rich and foolish materialist (12:13–21)

The unproductive fig tree (13:6–9)

Healing a crippled woman on the Sabbath (13:10–17)

A distinctive version of the kingdom banquet (14:12–24)

The parable of the lost coin (15:8–10)

The prodigal (spendthrift) son (15:11–32)

The dishonest manager (16:1–13)

Lazarus and the rich man (16:19–31)

The Pharisee and the tax collector (18:9–14)

---

sinners, comforts the downtrodden, and heals the afflicted. Luke's Jesus is particularly attentive to issues of social and economic justice. In numerous parables unique to his Gospel, Luke demonstrates that Jesus' kingdom ethic demands a radical change in society's present social and religious values. Some major themes that strongly color Luke's portrait of Jesus are described next.

The Holy Spirit Luke is convinced that Jesus' career and the growth of Christianity are not historical accidents, but the direct result of God's will, which is expressed through the Holy Spirit. Luke uses this term more than Mark and Matthew combined (fourteen times). It is by the Spirit that Jesus is conceived and by which he is anointed after baptism. The Spirit leads him into the wilderness (4:1) and empowers his ministry in Galilee (4:14). The Spirit is conferred through prayer (11:13), and at death, the Lukan Jesus commits his "spirit" to God (23:46).

The Holy Spirit reappears with overwhelming power in Acts 2 when, like a "strong driving wind," it rushes upon the 120 disciples gathered in Jerusalem to observe **Pentecost.** Possession by the Spirit confirms God's acceptance of Gentiles into the church (Acts 11:15–18). To Luke, it is the Spirit that is responsible for the faith's rapid expansion throughout the Roman Empire. Like Paul, Luke sees the Christian community as charismatic, Spirit led, and Spirit empowered.

Prayer Another of Luke's principal interests is Jesus' and the disciples' use of prayer. Luke's infancy narrative is full of prayers and hymns of praise by virtually all the adult participants. In his account of John's baptizing campaign, the Holy Spirit descends upon Jesus not at his baptism, as in Mark, but afterward while Jesus is at prayer (3:21). Similarly, Jesus chooses the disciples after prayer (6:12) and prays before he asks them who he is (9:18). The Transfiguration occurs "while he is praying" (9:29). Jesus' instructions on prayer are also more extensive than in other Gospels (11:1–13; 18:1–14). The Lukan emphasis on prayer carries over into Acts, in which the heroes of the early church are frequently shown praying (Acts 1:14, 24–26; 8:15; 10:1–16).

Jesus' Concern for Women From the beginning of his account, Luke makes it clear that women play an indispensable part in fulfilling the divine plan. Elizabeth, Zechariah's wife, is chosen to produce and raise Israel's final prophet, the one who prepares the way for Jesus. Her cousin

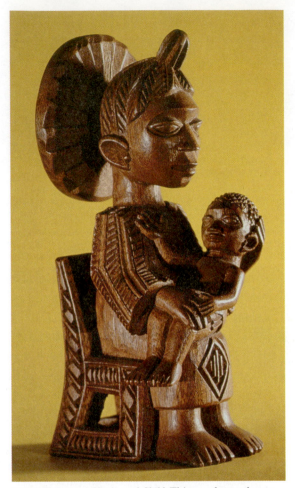

FIGURE 9.1 *Virgin and Child.* This wooden sculpture from Africa shows the infant Jesus with Mary, a rendition illustrating the archetypal image of mother and child, nurturer and bearer of new life, as well as an image of black holiness.

Mary responds affirmatively to the Holy Spirit, conceiving and nurturing the world-savior (see Figure 9.1). During his adult ministry, Jesus accepts many female disciples, praising those who, like **Mary,** the sister of **Martha,** abandon domestic chores to take their places among the male followers—a privilege Jesus declares "will not be taken from [them]" (10:38–42) (see Figure 9.2). Galilean women not only follow Jesus on the path to Jerusalem but also financially support him and his male companions (8:2–3).

FIGURE 9.2 *The Holy Family.* The unknown years of Jesus' boyhood are given a Japanese setting in this twentieth-century painting on silk. Shouldering his share of the family's work, the young Jesus carries wood to help Joseph, his carpenter father, while Mary, his mother, is busy at her spinning wheel. The themes of productive labor, mutual assistance, and familial harmony dominate the domestic scene in Nazareth, providing a contrast to the adult Jesus' later rejection of family ties and obligations (Mark 3).

As in Mark, it is these Galilean women who provide the human link between Jesus' death and resurrection, witnessing the Crucifixion and receiving first the news that he is risen (23:49; 23:55–24:11).

Jesus' Affinity with the Unrespectable Closely linked to Jesus' concern for women, who were largely powerless in both Jewish and Greco-Roman society, is his affinity for many similarly vulnerable people on the margins of society. "A friend of tax-gatherers and sinners" (7:34), the Lukan Jesus openly accepts social outcasts, including "immoral" women, such as an apparently notorious woman who crashes a Pharisee's dinner party and seats herself next to Jesus, bathing his feet with her tears, much to his host's indignation (7:37–50). Luke alone preserves one of Jesus' most provocative stories, in which the central character is an ungrateful son who consorts with prostitutes and sinks to groveling with swine—but whom his father loves unconditionally (15:11–32). In Luke, Jesus not only conducts a brief ministry in **Samaria** (traditionally viewed as a center of religious impurity [9:52–56]) but also makes a **Samaritan** the embodiment of neighborly love (10:30–37).

Accused of being "a glutton and a drinker," Jesus personally welcomes "tax-gatherers and other bad characters" to dine with him, refusing to distinguish between deserving and undeserving guests (7:29–34; 15:1–2). In Luke's version of the great banquet, the host's doors are thrown open indiscriminately to "the poor, the crippled, the lame, and the blind," people incapable of reciprocating hospitality (14:12–24). To Luke, it is not the "poor in spirit" who gain divine blessing, but simply "the poor," the economically deprived for whom productive citizens typically show little sympathy (cf. 6:20–21 and 6:24–25).

Christianity as a Universal Faith The author designs Luke-Acts to show that, through Jesus and his successors, God directs human history to achieve humanity's redemption. Luke's theory of salvation history has a universalist aspect: From its inception, Christianity is a religion intended for "all nations," especially those peoples who have hitherto lived without Israel's Law and prophets. As **Simeon** prophesies over the infant Jesus, the child is destined to become "a revelation to the heathen [Gentiles]" (2:32). Luke's emphasis on Jesus' universality also appears in his genealogy, which, like that in Matthew, traces Jesus' descent through Joseph (Luke 3:23). Unlike Matthew, however, who lists Jesus' ancestors back to Abraham, "father of the Jews," Luke takes Jesus' family tree all the way back to the first human, Adam, whom he calls "son of God" (Luke 3:23–38). By linking Jesus with Adam, the one created in God's "image" and "likeness," Luke presents Jesus as savior of the whole human race. Whereas Matthew emphasizes Jesus' heritage as Jewish Messiah, Luke shows him as the heir of Adam, from whom all of humanity is descended. In Acts, therefore, the risen Christ's final words commission his followers to bear witness about him from Jerusalem "to the ends of the earth" (Acts 1:8), conveying his message to all of Adam's children.

Christianity as a Lawful Religion Besides presenting Christianity as a universal faith, Luke works to show that it is a peaceful and lawful religion. Both the Gospel and its sequel, the Book of Acts, function as an **apology** (*apologia*), a form of literature written to defend or explain a particular viewpoint or way of life. In reporting Jesus' trial before the Roman magistrate and Paul's similar

hearings before various other Roman officials, Luke is careful to mention that in each case the accused is innocent of any real crime. Although Pilate condemns Jesus for claiming to be "king of the Jews," an act of sedition against Rome, in Luke's Gospel, Pilate also affirms Jesus' innocence, explicitly stating that he finds the prisoner "guilty of no capital offence" (23:22). In Acts, Luke creates parallels to Jesus' trial in which the apostles and others are similarly declared innocent of subversion. Convinced that Christianity is destined to spread throughout the empire, Luke wishes to demonstrate that it is no threat to the peace or stability of the Roman government.

The Importance of Jerusalem More than any other Gospel author, Luke links crucial events in Jesus' life with Jerusalem and the Temple. He is the only Evangelist to associate Jesus' infancy and childhood with visits to the Temple and the only one to place *all* of Jesus' post resurrection appearances in or near Jerusalem. Jerusalem is the place where his Gospel account begins (1:8–22), where Jesus' parents take their eight-day-old son for circumcision (2:31–39), and where the twelve-year-old Jesus astonishes "teachers" in the Temple with the profundity of his questions (2:41–51).

Near the conclusion of his ministry, the adult Jesus "set his face to go to Jerusalem," the city where he would endure a fatal confrontation with priestly and Roman authorities (9:51). As the Lukan Jesus insists, "It is impossible for a prophet to be killed outside of Jerusalem"—a statement that occurs only in Luke (13:33).

In Mark, the youth at Jesus' empty tomb directs the bewildered female disciples to seek their risen Lord "in Galilee" (Mark 16:7), an order that Matthew says the male disciples eventually obeyed (Matt. 28:16–20). In contrast, the Lukan Jesus commands his followers to remain in Jerusalem (24:49), where they will receive the Holy Spirit. Luke's insistence that Jerusalem and its environs—not Galilee—were the sites of all Jesus' appearances after his resurrection expresses his view that Jerusalem and the Temple were central to God's plan. For Luke, not only is Jerusalem the place where Jesus dies, is buried,

BOX 9.3 New Characters Introduced in Luke

Elizabeth and the priest Zechariah, parents of the Baptist (1:5–25, 39–79)

Gabriel, the angel who announces Jesus' virginal conception (1:26–38)

Augustus, emperor of Rome (2:1–2)

Simeon, who foretells Jesus' messiahship (2:25–35)

Anna, an aged prophetess (2:36–38)

The widow of Nain (7:11–16)

The unidentified sinful woman whom Jesus forgives (7:36–50)

The sisters Mary and Martha (10:38–39)

Zacchaeus, the wealthy tax collector (19:1–10)

Herod Antipas, as one of Jesus' judges (22:7–12; also 9:7–9)

Cleopas and an unidentified disciple (24:13–35)

rises from the tomb, appears to his followers, and ascends to heaven, it is also the sacred ground on which the Christian church is founded. In Luke's theology of history, God thus fulfills his ancient promises to Israel, focusing his divine power on the holy city where King David once reigned and where David's ultimate heir inaugurates an everlasting kingdom.

Jesus as Savior Finally, Luke also presents Jesus in a guise that his Greek and Roman readers will understand. Matthew had labored to prove from the Hebrew Bible that Jesus was the Davidic Messiah. In the account of Jesus' infancy, Luke also sounds the theme of prophetic fulfillment. But he is aware as well that his Gentile audience is not primarily interested in a Jewish Messiah, a figure traditionally associated with Jewish nationalism. Although Mark and Matthew had declared their hero "Son of God," Luke further universalizes Jesus' appeal by declaring him "Savior" (1:69; 2:11; Acts 3:13–15). He is the only Synoptic writer to do so. Luke's term (the Greek *sōter*) was used widely in the Greco-Roman world and was applied to gods, demigods, and human rulers alike. Hellenistic peoples commonly worshiped savior deities in numerous mystery cults and hailed emperors by the title "god and savior" for the material benefits, such as health, peace, and prosperity, that they conferred (see the discussion of the emperor cult in Chapter 5). For Luke, Jesus is the **Savior** of repentant humanity, one who delivers believers from the consequences of sin, as the

judges of ancient Israel "saved" or delivered their people from military oppressors. (The NEB translators therefore use the English noun *deliverer* for *sōter* in Luke [1:24, 69; 2:11].)

Organization of Luke's Gospel

A simple outline of Luke's structure follows:

1. Formal preface (1:1–4)
2. Infancy narratives of the Baptist and Jesus (1:5–2:52)
3. Prelude to Jesus' ministry: baptism, genealogy, and temptation (3:1–4:13)
4. Jesus' Galilean ministry (4:14–9:50)
5. Luke's travel narrative: Jesus' teachings on the journey to Jerusalem (the "greater interpolation" [9:51–18:14])
6. The Jerusalem ministry: Jesus' challenge to the holy city (18:31–21:38)
7. The final conflict and Passion story (22:1–23:56)
8. Epilogue: post resurrection appearances in the vicinity of Jerusalem (24:1–53)

In examining Luke's work, we focus primarily on material found only in his Gospel, especially the narrative sections and parables that illustrate distinctively Lukan themes (see Box 9.3 for new characters introduced in Luke). Because we have already discussed the preface, we begin with one of the most familiar and best-loved stories in the entire Bible—the account of Jesus' conception and birth.

Infancy Narratives of the Baptist and Jesus

We do not know Luke's source for his infancy narratives (1:5–2:52), but he apparently drew on a tradition that differed in many details from Matthew's account. The two writers agree that Jesus was born in Bethlehem to **Mary,** a virgin, and **Joseph,** a descendant of David (see Figure 9.3). Apart from that, however, the two Evangelists relate events in strikingly different manners.

In composing his parallel infancy narratives, Luke adopts a consciously biblical style, writing in the old-fashioned Greek of the Septuagint Bible. The effect is akin to that of reading the birth stories in the archaic language of the King James Version and most of the rest of the Gospel in more contemporary English. Luke's purpose here, however, is more than merely stylistic: He is echoing the ancient Scriptures, both by his style and by extensive quotations from the Hebrew prophets, because what he relates in these passages is the climactic turn of history: "Until John, it was the Law and the prophets, since then there is the good news of the kingdom" (16:16). Whereas the Baptist will serve as the capstone of Israel's ancient prophetic tradition, in Jesus, God will both fulfill his promises to Israel and begin the climactic process of human salvation.

FIGURE 9.3 *Our Lady of Colombia.* In this conception of Mary and the infant Jesus, the artist pictures the Madonna as an archetypal image of abundance and fertility, giving her a crown to depict her queenly status and surrounding her with flowers to suggest her association with natural fecundity. This twentieth-century rendition of the Virgin by F. Botero of Colombia effectively demonstrates her thematic connection with nurturing goddesses of pre-Christian antiquity.

The Birth of John the Baptist

In depicting John's aged parents, Elizabeth and Zechariah, Luke highlights their exemplary piety and devotion to the letter of Israel's religion. Described as "upright and devout, blamelessly observing all the commandments and ordinances of the [Torah]" (1:6), Zechariah and Elizabeth represent the best in Judaism.

Luke is the only New Testament writer to state that the respective mothers of John and Jesus are blood relatives (1:36). The later adult association between John and Jesus is thus foreshadowed by their physical kinship, their mothers' friendship, and the similar circumstances of their births.

The Role of Mary

Luke interweaves the two nativity accounts, juxtaposing **Gabriel**'s visit to Mary (1:26–38) (the **Annunciation**) with Mary's visit to her cousin Elizabeth, a meeting that causes the unborn John to stir in his mother's womb at the approach of the newly conceived Jesus. As Mary had been made pregnant by the Holy Spirit, so Elizabeth at their encounter is empowered by the Spirit to prophesy concerning the superiority of Mary's child. This emphasis on women's role in the divine purpose (note also the prophetess Anna in 2:36–38) is a typical Lukan concern. Also significant is Luke's hint about Mary's family background. Because Elizabeth is "of priestly descent," which means that she belongs to the tribe of Levi, it seems probable that Mary also belongs to the Levitical clan rather than the Davidic tribe of Judah. Like that of Matthew, Luke's genealogy traces Jesus' Davidic ancestry through Joseph (1:5; 3:23–24).

In relating the two infancy stories, Luke subtly indicates the relative importance of the two children. He dates John's birth in King Herod's reign (1:5). In contrast, when introducing Jesus' nativity, the author relates the event not to a Judean king, but to a Roman emperor, Augustus Caesar (2:1). Luke thus places Jesus in a worldwide (as opposed to a local Jewish) context, suggesting both the universal scope of Jesus' significance and the babe's ultimate destiny to rule all humanity.

For Luke, Jesus' humble arrival on earth shows that God is henceforth actively intervening in Roman society. A Lukan angel proclaims "good news" that contrasts markedly with Rome's imperial propaganda. Although Augustus, divine "son" of the deified Caesar, reigned "throughout the Roman world," the real "deliverer [savior]" is the infant lying "in a manger" (2:1–14). (For a discussion of the Roman emperor cult, see Chapter 5.)

In telling of Jesus' circumcision and Mary's ritual purification (2:21–24), Luke emphasizes another theme important to his picture of Jesus' Jewish background: Not only relatives like Elizabeth and Zechariah but also Jesus' immediate family observe the Mosaic Law scrupulously. His parents obey every Torah command (2:39), including making a yearly pilgrimage to the Jerusalem Temple for Passover (2:41–43). The author's own view is that most of the Torah's provisions no longer bind Christians (Acts 15), but he wishes to emphasize that from birth Jesus fulfilled all Torah requirements.

Luke's Use of Hymns

Throughout the infancy stories of Jesus and the Baptist, Luke follows the Greco-Roman biographer's practice of inserting speeches that illustrate themes vital to the writer's view of his subject. The long poem uttered by Zechariah—known by its Latin name, the **Benedictus** (1:67–79)—combines scriptural quotations with typically Lukan views about Jesus' significance. The same is true of the priest Simeon's prayer, the **Nunc Dimittis** (2:29–32), and ensuing prophecy (2:23–25). Some of the speeches ascribed to characters in the nativity accounts may be rewritten songs and prayers first used in Christian worship services. These liturgical pieces include the angel Gabriel's announcement to Mary that she will bear a son, the Ave Maria (1:28–33), and Mary's exulting prayer, the **Magnificat** (1:46–55). Mary's hymn closely resembles a passage from the Hebrew Bible, the prayer Hannah recites when an angel foretells the birth of her son, Samuel (1 Sam. 2:1–10). In its present form, this hymn may be as much a composition of the early church, conceived as an appropriate biblical response to the angel's visit, as a memory of Mary's literal words. Nonetheless, Luke implies that Jesus' mother may have been a source of this tradition, noting that she reflected deeply on the unusual circumstances surrounding her son's birth (2:19; see also 2:51).

Luke includes the only tradition about Jesus' boyhood contained in the New Testament, an anecdote about the twelve-year-old boy's visit to the Temple in which he impresses some learned scribes with the acuteness of his questions and understanding (2:41–52). The statement that Jesus "advanced in wisdom and in favor with God and men" (2:52) almost exactly reproduces the Old Testament description of young Samuel (1 Sam. 2:26) and is probably a conventional observation rather than a historically precise evaluation of Jesus' youthful character. For Luke, this Temple episode serves primarily to anticipate Jesus' later ministry at the Jerusalem sanctuary.

Jesus' Galilean Ministry

Jesus' Rejection in Nazareth

After describing John's baptism campaign and Jesus' temptation by Satan (3–4:13), Luke introduces Jesus' public career in a way that significantly revises Mark's order of events. Whereas Matthew closely follows Mark in placing Jesus' rejection in Nazareth after the Galilean campaign is already well under way (cf. Mark 6:1–6; Matt. 13:53–58), Luke transfers this episode almost to the beginning of Jesus' ministry (4:16–30). The Evangelist makes this change in his source not to provide a more factually accurate biography, but probably for the same reason that the author of John's Gospel switches his account of Jesus' assault on the Temple from the time of Jesus' final entry into Jerusalem (as all three Synoptics have it) to the

beginning of his career: He wants his readers to understand the event's thematic or theological meaning. (See Chapter 10 for a discussion of John's probable motives in repositioning the Temple incident.)

In this highly dramatic scene of conflict between Jesus and the residents of his hometown, Luke extensively rewrites Mark's account. Besides eliminating Mark's implication that Jesus' family failed to recognize his worth and inserting a quotation from Isaiah that expresses Luke's view of Jesus' prophetic role, the author creates a speech for Jesus that outrages the people of Nazareth. Taking full authorial advantage of his first opportunity to show the adult Jesus interacting with his contemporaries, Luke uses the occasion of Jesus' visit to the Nazareth synagogue to give readers a thematic preview of his entire two-volume work. By adding that Jesus' former neighbors try to kill him (an element absent in Mark and Matthew, who merely report that Nazareth's residents showed him little respect), Luke foreshadows Jesus' later rejection and death in Jerusalem. By having Jesus deliver a sermon in which two of Israel's greatest prophets, Elijah and Elisha, perform their most spectacular miracles to benefit Gentiles, not native Israelites, Luke anticipates the church's future mission to Gentile nations, developments he will narrate in the Book of Acts.

Even more important to Luke is his vision of Jesus' essential calling, which he evokes in the quotation from Isaiah: Jesus is empowered by the same divine Spirit that motivated Israel's prophets, and he will pursue the same kind of work they did, offering aid and comfort to people suffering the harsh realities of economic and political oppression, explicitly "the poor" and downtrodden. Restoring vision to persons metaphorically imprisoned or blind and helping "broken victims go free," Jesus proclaims God's favor to those whom society typically ignores or exploits. Characteristically, Luke omits Isaiah's reference to divine "vengeance" (Isa. 61:1–2; 58:6). Luke's implicit critique of the Roman status quo, then, includes neither the threat of armed rebellion nor a promise of divine retribution.

Luke's Version of Jesus' Teaching

For the next two chapters (4:31–6:11), Luke reproduces much of the Markan narrative dealing with Jesus' miracles of healing and exorcism. Despite violent opposition in Nazareth, Jesus draws large crowds, healing many and preaching in numerous Galilean synagogues. Luke transposes the Markan order, however, placing Jesus' calling of the Twelve after the Nazareth episode (6:12–19). This transposition serves as an introduction to Jesus' first public discourse, the Sermon on the Plain (6:20–49). The Sermon begins a long section (called the "lesser interpolation") in which the author interweaves material shared with Matthew (presumably from Q) with material that appears only in his own Gospel (6:20–8:3).

Luke's Sermon on the Plain Resembling an abbreviated version of Matthew's Sermon on the Mount (see Box 9.4 and Figure 9.4), the Lukan discourse begins with briefer forms of four Beatitudes, all of which are in the second person and hence directed at "you" (the audience/reader). Matthew had phrased the Beatitudes in the third person ("they") and presented them as blessings on people who possessed the right spiritual nature, such as "those who hunger and thirst to see right prevail" (Matt. 5:6). In contrast, Luke "materializes" the Beatitudes, bluntly referring to physical hunger: "How blest are you who now go hungry; your hunger shall be satisfied" (6:21). His "poor" are the financially destitute, the powerless who are to receive the "kingdom of God."

Luke follows the Beatitudes with a list of "woes" ("alas for you") in which the "rich" and "well-fed" are cursed with future loss and hunger. Persons happy with the present Roman social order are destined to regret their former complacency (6:24–26). This harsh judgment on people whom society generally considers fortunate occurs only in Luke and represents one of Luke's special convictions: The kingdom will bring a radical reversal of presently accepted values and expectations. The author does not specify his objections to the wealthy as a class, but in material exclusive to his Gospel, he repeatedly attacks the rich, predicting that their present affluence and luxury will be exchanged for misery.

Reversals of Status for Rich and Poor In pleading the cause of the poor against the rich, Luke also includes his special rendering of Jesus' command to love one's enemies (6:32–36; cf. Matt. 5:43–48). One must practice giving unselfishly because such behavior reflects the nature and purpose of God, who treats even the wicked with kindness (6:32–36). As the Lukan parables typically illustrate unexpected reversals of status between the rich and poor, so do they teach generosity and compassion—qualities that to Luke are literally divine (6:35–36).

To Luke, Jesus provides the model of compassionate behavior. When Christ raises a widow's son from the dead (7:11–17), the miracle expresses the twin Lukan themes of God's special love for the poor and unfortunate (especially women) and Jesus' role as Lord of the resurrection. (Luke imparts a particularly awe-inspiring quality to this scene, highlighting Jesus' empathy for the grieving mother.) By including this episode (unique to his Gospel), the author reminds his readers of the joy they will experience when Jesus appears again to restore life to all.

The Importance of Women Luke commonly uses Jesus' interaction with women to reveal his concept of Jesus' character, emphasizing his hero's combination of authority and tenderness. After providing ultimate comfort to the grieving widow at Nain, Jesus reveals similar compassion for a prostitute, to whom he imparts another form of new life. All four Gospels contain an incident in which a woman anoints Jesus with oil or some other costly ointment (Mark 14:3–9; Matt. 26:6–13; John 12:1–8). In Luke (7:36–50), however, the anointing does not anticipate preparation for Jesus' burial, as it does in the other Gospels, but is an act of intense love on the unnamed woman's part. Set in the house of a Pharisee where Jesus is dining, the Lukan

BOX 9.4 **Comparison of the Beatitudes in Matthew and Luke**

MATTHEW

How blest are these who know their
       need of God [the "poor in spirit"];
   the kingdom of Heaven is theirs.
How blest are those of a gentle spirit;
       they shall have the earth for
   their possession.
How blest are those who hunger and
       thirst to see right prevail;
   they shall be satisfied.
How blest are those who show mercy;
       mercy shall be shown to them.
How blest are those whose hearts
       are pure;
   they shall see God.
How blest are the peacemakers;
       God shall call them his [children].
How blest are those who have suffered
       persecution for the cause of right;
   the kingdom of Heaven is theirs.

   How blest you are, when you suffer insults and
persecution and every kind of calumny for my
sake. Accept it with gladness and exultation, for
you have a rich reward in heaven; in the same
way they persecuted the prophets before you.
(Matt. 5:3–12)

LUKE

How blest are you who are in need ["you poor"];
       the kingdom of God is yours.

How blest are you who now go hungry;
       your hunger shall be satisfied.

   How blest you are when men hate you, when
they outlaw you and insult you, and ban your very
name as infamous, because of the Son of Man.
On that day be glad and dance for joy; for assur-
edly you have a rich reward in heaven; in just the
same way did their fathers treat the prophets.

                [The "Woes"]
But alas for you who are rich; you have had your
       time of happiness.
Alas for you who are well-fed now; you shall go
       hungry.
Alas for you who laugh now; you shall mourn and
       weep.
Alas for you when all speak well of you; just so
       did their fathers treat the false prophets.
(Luke 6:20–26)

version focuses on the woman's overwhelming emotion and on the typically Lukan theme of compassion and forgiveness. To Luke, the "immoral" woman's love proves that "her many sins have been forgiven."

In John, the woman is identified as Mary, sister of Martha and Lazarus, but there is no hint of her possessing a lurid past. It would appear that Jesus' emotional encounter with a woman who lavished expensive unguents upon

him impressed onlookers enough to remember and transmit it orally to the early Christian community, but—as in the case of many other of Jesus' actions and sayings—the precise context of the event was forgotten. Each Gospel writer provides his own explanatory frame for the incident (cf. Luke 7:36–50; Mark 14:3–9; Matt. 26:6–13; John 12:1–8).

Fittingly, the first extensive interpolation of Lukan material concludes with a summary of the

FIGURE 9.4 Traditional site of the Sermon on the Mount. According to tradition, it was on this hill overlooking the Sea of Galilee that Jesus delivered his most famous discourse, the teachings compiled in Matthew 5–7. The Gospel of Luke, however, states that Jesus spoke to his Galilean audience on "level ground" (Luke 6:17).

part women play in Jesus' ministry. Accompanying him are numerous female disciples, Galilean women whom he had healed and who now support him and the male disciples "out of their own resources" (8:1–3).

Luke's Travel Narrative: Jesus' Teachings on the Journey to Jerusalem

Luke begins this long section (9:51–18:14) with Jesus' firm resolution to head toward Jerusalem, a distance of about sixty miles, and the final conflict that will culminate in his death and resurrection. Although ostensibly the record of a

journey from Galilee to Judea, this part of the Gospel (traditionally known as the "greater interpolation") contains little action or sense of forward movement. Emphasizing Jesus' teaching, it is largely a miscellaneous collection of brief anecdotes, sayings, and parables. Here the author intermixes Q material with that of his individual source (L), including most of the parables unique to his Gospel.

At the beginning of this section, Luke records two incidents that preview later developments in Acts. On his way south to Jerusalem, Jesus passes through Samaria, carrying his message to several villages. In Matthew (10:5–6), Jesus expressly forbids a mission to the Samaritans, bitterly hated by Jews for their interpretation of the Mosaic Law. Luke, however, shows Jesus forbidding the disciples to punish an inhospitable Samaritan town and conducting a short campaign there (9:52–56).

Along with the celebrated story of the "good Samaritan," this episode anticipates the later Christian mission to Samaria described in Acts 8. Jesus' sending forth seventy-two disciples to evangelize the countryside (10:1–16) similarly prefigures the future recruiting of Gentiles. In Jewish terminology, the number seventy or seventy-two represented the sum total of non-Jewish nations. As the Twelve sent to proselytize Israel probably symbolize the traditional twelve Israelite tribes (9:1–6), so the activity of the seventy-two foreshadows Christian expansion among Gentiles of the Roman Empire.

Luke's Jesus experiences a moment of ecstatic triumph when the seventy-two return from conducting a series of successful exorcisms. Possessed by the Spirit, he perceives the reality behind his disciples' victory over evil. In a mystical vision, Jesus sees Satan, like a bolt of lightning, hurled from heaven. Through the disciples' actions, Satan's influence is in decline (although he returns to corrupt Judas in 22:23).

In this context of defeating evil through good works, Jesus thanks God that his uneducated followers understand God's purpose better than the intellectual elite. In this passage, Luke expresses ideas that are more common in John's Gospel: Only Christ knows the divine nature, and only he can reveal it to those whom he chooses (10:17–24; cf. Matthew's version of this prayer in Matt. 11:25–27).

The Parable of the Good Samaritan

Luke is aware, however, that "the learned and wise" are not always incapable of religious insight. In 10:25–28, a Torah expert defines the essence of the Mosaic Law in the twin commands to love God (Deut. 6:5) and neighbor (Lev. 19:18). Confirming the expert's perception, Jesus replies that, in loving thus, the man "will live." In this episode, Luke provides a good example of the way in which he adapts Markan material to his theological purpose. Mark places this dialogue with the Torah instructor in the Jerusalem

Temple and emphasizes Jesus' approval of the speaker's view that the "law of love" is the epitome of Judaism (Mark 12:28–31). Luke changes the site of this encounter from the Temple to an unidentified place on the road to Jerusalem and uses it to introduce his parable of the good Samaritan. The author creates a transition to the parable by having the instructor ask Jesus to explain what the Torah means by "neighbor."

Instead of answering directly, Jesus responds in typical rabbinic fashion: He tells a story. The questioner must discover his neighbor's identity in Jesus' depiction of a specific human situation. In analyzing the tale of the good Samaritan (10:29–35), most students will find that it not only follows Luke's customary theme of the unexpected but also introduces several rather thorny problems.

Ethical Complexities Jesus' original audience would have seen enormous ethical complexities in this parable. The priest and **Levite** face a real dilemma: When they find the robbers' victim, they do not know whether the man is alive or dead. If they so much as touch a corpse, the Torah declares them ritually unclean, and they will be unable to fulfill their Temple duties. In this case, keeping the Law means ignoring the claim of a person in need. The priest's decision to remain faithful to Torah requirements necessitates his failure to help.

By making a Samaritan the moral hero of his story, Jesus further complicates the issue. In Jewish eyes, the Samaritans, who claimed guardianship of the Mosaic Law, were corrupters of the Torah from whom nothing good could be expected. (Note that a Samaritan village had refused Jesus hospitality because he was making a pilgrimage to Jerusalem, site of the Temple cult that the Samaritans despised [9:52–56].) Finally, Jesus' tale underscores a typical Lukan reversal: The religious outsider, whom the righteous hold in contempt, is the person who obeys the Torah's essential meaning—to act as God's agent by giving help to persons in need.

When Jesus asks the Torah expert which person in the tale behaves as a neighbor, the expert apparently cannot bring himself to utter the hated term *Samaritan*. Instead, he vaguely identifies the hero as "the one who showed [the victim] kindness." Jesus' directive to behave as the Samaritan does—in contrast to the priest and the Levite—contains a distinctly subversive element. When the Samaritan helps a Jew (the victim had been traveling from Jerusalem), he boldly overlooks ethnic and sectarian differences in order to aid a religious "enemy."

By constructing this particular scenario, Jesus forces the Torah instructor (and Luke, his reader) to recognize that a "neighbor" does not necessarily belong to one's own racial or religious group but can be any person who demonstrates generosity and human kindness. (From the orthodox view, the Samaritan belongs to a "false" religion; he is not only a foreigner but a "heretic" as well.) An even more subversive note is sounded when the parable implies that the priest's and Levite's faithful adherence to biblical rules is the barrier that prevents them from observing religion's essential component, which the Torah expert had correctly defined as the love of God and neighbor.

Mary and Martha

Luke follows the Samaritan parable with a brief anecdote about Jesus' visit at the house of two sisters, Mary and Martha (10:38–42). In its own way, this episode draws a similar distinction between strict adherence to duty and a sensitivity to "higher" opportunities. The Lukan Jesus commends Mary for abandoning her traditional woman's role and joining the men to hear his teaching. The learning experience will be hers to possess forever.

Instructions on Prayer

Luke places a greater emphasis on prayer than any other Synoptic author. Although his version of the Lord's Prayer is much shorter than Matthew's, he heightens its significance by adding several parables that extol the value of persistence. Petitioning God is implicitly compared to pestering a friend until he grants what is asked (11:5–10). The same theme reappears in the parable of the importunate or "pushy" widow (18:1–8) who seeks justice from a cynical and corrupt judge. An unworthy representative of his profession, the judge cares nothing about God or public opinion—but he finally grants the widow's petition because she refuses to give him any peace until he acts. If even an unresponsive friend and unscrupulous judge can be hounded into helping someone, how much more is God likely to reward people who do not give up talking to him (18:7–8)?

Luke contrasts two different kinds of prayers in his parable of the Pharisee and a **"publican"** (officially licensed tax-gatherer for Rome) (18:9–14). In Jesus' day, the term *tax-gatherer* was a synonym for *sinner,* one who betrayed his Jewish countrymen by hiring himself out to the Romans and making a living by extorting money and goods from an already-oppressed people. The parable contrasts the Pharisee's consciousness of religious worth with the tax collector's confession of his failings. In Luke's reversal of ordinary expectations, it is the honest outcast—not necessarily the conventionally good person—who wins God's approval.

Luke's Views on Riches and Poverty

More than any other Gospel writer, Luke emphasizes forsaking worldly ambition for the spiritual riches of the kingdom. The Lukan Jesus assures his followers that, if God provides for nature's birds and flowers, he will care for Christians. He urges his disciples to sell their possessions, give to the poor, and thus earn "heavenly treasures" (12:22–34).

Luke's strong antimaterialism and apparent bias against the rich is partly the result of his conviction that God's judgment may occur at any time. The rich fool dies before he can enjoy his life's work (12:13–21), but Christians may face judgment even before death. The Master may return without warning at any time (12:35–40). Rather than accumulating wealth, believers must share with the poor and with social outcasts

(14:12–14). Luke also emphasizes that the deformed and unattractive, rejects and have-nots of society, must be the Christian's primary concern in attaining Jesus' favorable verdict (14:15–24).

Lazarus and the Rich Man

Reversals in the Afterlife   The Lukan Jesus makes absolute demands upon his disciples: None can belong to him without giving away everything he owns (14:33). In his parable of Lazarus and the rich man, Luke dramatizes the danger of hanging onto great wealth until death parts the owner from his possessions (16:19–31). Appearing only in Luke's Gospel, this metaphor of the afterlife embodies typically Lukan concepts. It shows a rich man experiencing all the posthumous misery that Jesus had predicted for the world's comfortable and satisfied people (6:24–26) and a poor beggar enjoying all the rewards that Jesus had promised to the hungry and outcast (6:20–21). Demonstrating Luke's usual theme of reversal, the parable shows the two men exchanging their relative positions in the next world.

In recounting Jesus' only parable that deals with the contrasting fates of individuals after death, Luke employs ideas typical of first-century Hellenistic Judaism. The author's picture of Lazarus in paradise and the rich man in fiery torment is duplicated in Josephus's contemporary description of Hades (the Underworld).

Significantly, Luke charges the rich man with no crime and assigns the beggar no virtue. To the author, current social conditions—the existence of hopeless poverty and sickness alongside the "magnificence" and luxury of the affluent—apparently will undergo a radical change when God rules the world completely. The only fault of which the rich man is implicitly guilty is his toleration of the extreme contrast between his own abundance and the miserable state of the poor. For Luke, it seems to be enough. The author's ideal social order is the commune that the disciples establish following Pentecost, an economic arrangement in which the well-to-do sell their possessions, share them with the poor, and hold "everything in common" (Acts 2:42–47).

Luke modifies his severe criticism of great wealth, however, by including Mark's story of Jesus' advice to a rich man. (He returns to the Markan narrative again in 18:15.) If wealth disqualifies one from the kingdom, who can hope to please God? Jesus' enigmatic reply—all things are possible with God (18:18–27)—leads to the concept of divine compensation. Persons who sacrifice family or home to seek the kingdom will be repaid both now (presumably referring to the spiritual riches they enjoy in church fellowship) and in the future with eternal life (18:28–30).

Jesus' Love of the Unhappy and the Outcast

All the Gospel authors agree that Jesus sought the company of "tax-gatherers and sinners," a catchall phrase referring to the great mass of people in ancient Palestine who were socially and religiously unacceptable because they did not or could not keep the Torah's requirements. This "unrespectable" group stood in contrast to the Sadducees, the Pharisees, the scribes, and others who conscientiously observed all Torah regulations in their daily lives. In the Synoptic Gospels, Jesus ignores the principle of contamination by association. He eats, drinks, and otherwise intimately mixes with a wide variety of persons commonly viewed as both morally and ritually "unclean." At one moment we find him dining in the homes of socially honored Pharisees (7:36–50) and at the next enjoying the hospitality of social pariahs like **Simon** the leper (Matt. 26:6–13) and Zacchaeus the tax collector (19:1–10). Jesus' habitual associations lead some of his contemporaries to regard him as a pleasure-loving drunkard (7:34). According to Luke, Jesus answers such criticism by creating parables that illustrate God's unfailing concern for persons the "righteous" dismiss as worthless (see Box 9.5).

Parables of Joy at Finding What Was Lost

One of the ethical highlights of the entire New Testament, Luke 15 contains three parables dramatizing the joy humans experience when

BOX 9.5 The Parable of the Great Banquet: Three Authorial Interpretations

Three Gospels—the canonical Matthew and Luke and the apocryphal Thomas—preserve three strikingly different versions of a parable in which guests who are first invited to a great dinner party fail to respond and are unexpectedly replaced by strangers recruited from the streets. Each of the three versions is distinguished by the distinctive concerns of the individual Gospel writer.

MATTHEW

Then Jesus spoke to them again in parables: "The kingdom of Heaven is like this. There was a king who prepared a feast for his son's wedding; but when he sent his servants to summon the guests he had invited, they would not come. He sent others again, telling them to say to the guests, 'See now! I have prepared this feast for you. I have had my bullocks and fatted beasts slaughtered; everything is ready; come to the wedding at once.' But they took no notice; one went off to his farm, another to his business, and the others seized the servants, attacked them brutally, and killed them. The king was furious; he sent troops to kill those murderers and set their town on fire. Then he said to his servants, 'The wedding-feast is ready; but the guests I invited did not deserve the honour. Go out to the main thoroughfares, and invite everyone you can find to the wedding.' The servants went out into the streets, and collected all they could find, good and bad alike. So the hall was packed with guests.

"When the king came in to see the company at the table, he observed one man who was not dressed for a wedding. 'My friend,' said the king, 'how do you come to be here without your wedding clothes?' He had nothing to say. The king then said to his attendants, 'Bind him hand and foot; turn him out into the dark, the place of wailing and grinding of teeth.' For though many are invited, few are chosen."

(Matt. 22:1–14)

LUKE

One of the company, after hearing all this, said to him, "Happy the man who shall sit at the feast in the kingdom of God!" Jesus answered, "A man was giving a big dinner party and had sent out many invitations. At dinner-time he sent his servant with a message for his guests, 'Please come, everything is now ready.' They began one and all to excuse themselves. The first said, 'I have bought a piece of land and I must go and look over it; please accept my apologies.' The second said, 'I have bought five yoke of oxen, and I am on my way to try them out; please accept my apologies.' The next said, 'I have just got married and for that reason I cannot come.' When the servant came back he reported this to his master. The master of the house was angry and said to him, 'Go out quickly into the streets and alleys of the town, and bring me in the poor, the crippled, the blind, and the lame.' The servant said, 'Sir, your orders have been carried out and there is still room.' The master replied, 'Go out on to the highways and along the hedgerows and make them come in; I want my house to be full. I tell you that not one of those who were invited shall taste my banquet.'"

(Luke 14:15–24)

THOMAS

Jesus said, "A person was receiving guests. When he had prepared the dinner, he sent his slave to invite the guests. The slave went to the first and said to that one, 'My master invites you.' That one said, 'Some merchants owe me money; they are coming to me tonight. I have to go and give them instructions. Please excuse me from dinner.' The slave went to another and said to that one, 'My master has invited you.' That one said to the slave, 'I have bought a house, and I have been called away for a day. I shall have no time.' The slave went to another and said to that one, 'My master invites you.' That one said to the slave, 'My friend is to be married, and I am to arrange the banquet. I shall not be able to come. Please excuse me from dinner.' The slave went to another and said to that one, 'My master invites you.' That one said to the slave, 'I have bought an estate, and I am going to collect the rent. I shall not be able to come. Please excuse me.' The slave returned and said to his master, 'Those whom you invited to dinner have asked to be excused.' The master said to his slave, 'Go out on the streets and bring back whomever you find to have dinner.'

"Buyers and merchants [will] not enter the places of my Father."

(G. Thom. 64)

(continued)

BOX 9.5 **continued**

In Matthew's version of the parable, a king issues invitations to a sumptuous wedding feast for his son. Not only are the ruler's supposed friends indifferent to his hospitality, but some kill the servants who invited them. Furious, the ruler then dispatches armies to destroy those who murdered his emissaries and "burn their city." The king's overreaction to his spurned generosity is even more extreme when one of the rabble brought in to replace the ungrateful guests shows up without the proper festal garments, a social faux pas for which he is tied up and thrown into a frighteningly "dark" prison.

Setting the parable in the narrative context of Jesus' rejection by the Jerusalem authorities, Matthew transforms it into a historical allegory of God's relationship with Israel. When the covenant people reject the invitation to his son's (Jesus') messianic banquet, God's anger results in the Roman destruction of Jerusalem and the replacement of his former people by a new crowd that includes "good and bad alike," the Matthean religious community. The divine host's arbitrary rejection of the improperly dressed guest—who could not reasonably have been expected to be carrying a set of formal attire when he was suddenly dragged to a stranger's wedding—may derive from another (otherwise lost) parable. The supernatural darkness to which the fashion felon is consigned is one of Matthew's characteristic images.

Luke introduces the parable as simply a "big dinner party" given by an ordinary (but presumably rich) host whose prospective guests all turn down his last-minute invitation. The three guests' stated excuses for not attending are entirely reasonable: All are busily engaged in life's ordinary pursuits, tending to their farms, their animals, and their marriages. The spurned host then invites a typically Lukan category of guests—the poor, crippled, lame,

and blind, precisely the kind of commonly devalued people that Jesus had already instructed his followers to include in their feasts (cf. Luke 14:12–14). As Matthew had turned a parable involving ungrateful guests into a polemic against the Jerusalem establishment and a justification for Jerusalem's destruction, so Luke makes it into a plea for the social outcasts—those who can't repay one's hospitality—whose cause he espouses throughout his Gospel.

Whereas most traditional folk narratives feature a set of three actions, as does Luke's story of three rejected invitations in his version of the parable, that contained in Thomas breaks the usual pattern by including four guests and their reasons for not attending. All four invited guests are people of property, homeowners, landlords, and financiers—members of the economically successful class of whom most early Christian writers are profoundly suspicious. Thomas's bias is clearly apparent in the parable's final line: The commercial class—"buyers and merchants"—are not God's kind of people.

In its three variations, the banquet parable has one consistent theme: The host has everything ready and, without warning his chosen guests in advance, suddenly demands that they drop everything and come to enjoy his good things. When, busily employed elsewhere, they fail to appreciate his offer, the disappointed host unexpectedly opens his house to people who could not previously consider themselves eligible—loiterers in the marketplace, social pariahs, and anybody else who had no better place to go. Despite the Gospel writers' editorial revisions, themes characteristic of Jesus' authentic parables, including God's incalculable ways of intervening in human lives and the reversals of normal expectations his appeals create, are embedded in the "sweet unreasonableness" of this tale.

they recover something precious they had thought forever lost.

The Lost Sheep The parable of the lost sheep (also in Matt. 18:10–14) recounts a shepherd's

delight in finding a stray animal. In Luke's version, the focus is on the celebration that follows the shepherd's find: "friends and neighbors" are called together to rejoice with him (15:1–7).

The Lost Coin A second parable (15:8–10) invites us to observe the behavior of a woman who loses one of her ten silver coins. She lights her lamp (an extravagant gesture for the poor) and sweeps out her entire house, looking in every corner, until she finds the coin. Then, like the shepherd, she summons "friends and neighbors" to celebrate her find. Although Luke sees these two parables as allegories symbolizing heavenly joy over a "lost" sinner's repentance (15:7, 10), they also reveal Jesus' characteristic tendency to observe and describe unusual human behavior. Both the shepherd and the woman exhibit the intense concentration on a single action—searching for lost property—that exemplifies Jesus' demand to seek God's rule first, to the exclusion of all else (6:22; Matt. 6:33). For the Lukan Jesus, they also demonstrate the appropriate response to recovering a valued object—a spontaneous celebration in which others are invited to participate.

The Prodigal Son One of the most emotionally moving passages in the Bible, the parable of the prodigal son might better be called the story of the forgiving father, for the climax of the narrative focuses on the latter's attitude toward his two very different sons. Besides squandering his inheritance "with his women" (15:30), the younger son violates the most basic standards of Judaism, reducing himself to the level of an animal groveling in a Gentile's pigpen. Listing the young man's progressively degrading actions, Jesus describes a person who is utterly insensitive to his religious heritage and as "undeserving" as a human being can be. Even his decision to return to his father's estate is based on an unworthy desire to improve his diet.

Yet the parable's main focus is not on the youth's unworthiness, but on the father's love. Notice that when the prodigal (spendthrift) is still "a long way off," his father sees him and, forgetting his dignity, rushes to meet the returning son. Note, too, that the father expresses no anger at his son's shameful behavior, demands no admission of wrongdoing, and inflicts no punishment. Ignoring the youth's contrite request to be hired as a servant, the parent instead orders a lavish celebration in his honor.

The conversation between the father and his older son, who understandably complains about the partiality shown to his sibling, makes the parable's theme even clearer. Acknowledging the older child's superior claim to his favor, the father attempts to explain the unlimited quality of his affection (15:11–32). The father's nature is to love unconditionally, making no distinction between the deserving and the undeserving recipients of his care. The parable expresses the same view of the divine Parent, who "is kind to the ungrateful and wicked," that Luke pictured in his Sermon on the Plain (6:35–36).

Like many of Jesus' authentic parables, this tale ends with an essential question unanswered: How will the older brother, smarting with natural resentment at the prodigal's unmerited reward, respond to his father's implied invitation to join the family revel? As Luke views the issue, Jesus' call to sinners was remarkably successful; it is the conventionally religious who too often fail to value an invitation to the messianic banquet.

The Parable of the Dishonest Steward

Not only do Luke's parables surprise us by turning accepted values upside down, consigning the fortunate rich to torment and celebrating the good fortune of the undeserving, but they can also puzzle us. Luke follows the parable of the prodigal son with a mind-boggling story of a dishonest and conniving businessman who cheats his employer and is commended for it (16:1–9).

Teaching none of the conventional principles of honesty or decent behavior, this parable makes most readers distinctly uncomfortable. Like the prodigal son, the steward violates the trust placed in him and defrauds his benefactor. Yet, like the prodigal, he is rewarded by the very person whom he has wronged. This unexpected twist upsets our basic notions of justice and fair play, just as the prodigal's elder brother was upset by having no distinction drawn between his own moral propriety and his younger brother's outrageous misbehavior. The meaning Luke attaches to this strange parable—worldly people like the steward are more clever than the unworldly—does not explain the moral paradox. We must ask: In what context, in response to what situation, did Jesus first tell this story? Is it simply another example of the unexpected, or is it a paradigm of the bewilderingly unacceptable that must happen when the kingdom breaks into our familiar and convention-ridden lives? Clearly, Luke's readers are asked to rethink ideas and assumptions previously taken for granted.

The Jerusalem Ministry: Jesus' Challenge to the Holy City

In revising Mark's account of the Jerusalem ministry (see Figure 9.5), Luke subtly mutes Mark's apocalyptic urgency and reinterprets Jesus' kingdom teaching to indicate that many eschatological hopes have already been realized (18:31–21:38). While he preserves elements of traditional **apocalypticism**—urging believers to be constantly alert and prepared for the *eschaton*—Luke also distances the final consummation, placing it at some unknown time in the future. Aware that many of Jesus' original followers assumed that his ministry would culminate in God's government being established on earth, Luke reports that "because he [Jesus] was now close to Jerusalem . . . they thought the reign of God might dawn at any moment" (19:11), an expectation that persisted in the early church (Acts 1:6–7). Luke counters this belief with a parable explaining that their Master must go away "on a long journey" before he returns as "king" (19:12–27). (Matthew also uses this parable of the "talents," in which slaves invest money for their absent owner, for the same purpose of explaining the delayed Parousia.)

FIGURE 9.5   Bust of the emperor Tiberius (ruled 14–37 CE). According to Luke, Jesus was "about thirty years old" when he began his Galilean campaign during the fifteenth year of Tiberius's reign (c. 27–29 CE) (Luke 3:1, 23). In Acts, Luke notes that Jesus is "a rival king" (Acts 17:8).

Luke's Modifications of Apocalyptic Expectation

Luke deftly intermingles Markan prophecies about the appearance of the Son of Man with passages from Q and his own special material, suggesting that the kingdom is, in some sense, a present reality in the presence and miraculous deeds of Jesus. When the Pharisees accuse Jesus of exorcising demons by the power of "Beelzebub [Satan]," he answers, "If it is by the finger of God that I drive out the devils, then be sure the kingdom of God has already come upon you" (11:20; cf. Matt. 12:28). The Lukan Jesus equates his disciples' success in expelling demons with Satan's fall from heaven (10:18–20), a sign that evil has been overthrown and that God's rule has begun. In another saying unique to Luke, Jesus tells the Pharisees: "You cannot tell by observation when the kingdom of God comes. There will be no saying, 'Look, here it is!' or 'there it is!'; for in fact the kingdom of God is among you [or in your midst]" (17:20–21).

While Luke implies that in Jesus' healing work the kingdom now reigns, the author also includes statements that emphasize the unexpectedness and unpredictability of the End. Readers are told not to believe premature reports of Jesus' return, for the world will continue its ordinary way until the Parousia suddenly occurs. Although (in this tradition) arriving without signs, it is as unmistakable as "the lightning flash that lights up the earth from end to end" (17:30). While retaining the Markan Jesus' promise that some of his contemporaries "will not taste death before they have seen the kingdom of God," Luke omits the phrase "already come in power" (9:27; cf. Mark 9:1). For Luke, the mystical glory of Jesus' Transfiguration, which immediately follows this declaration, reveals his divine kingship.

The Fall of Jerusalem and the Parousia

In his edited version of Mark 13, the prophecy of Jerusalem's destruction, Luke distinguishes between the historical event, which he knows took place in the recent past, and the Parousia, which belongs to an indefinite future (21:5–36). The author replaces Mark's cryptic allusion to the "abomination of desolation" (cf. Mark 13:14; Matt. 24:15) with practical advice that warned Christians to flee the city when Roman armies begin their siege (21:20–24). In Luke's modified apocalypse, a period of unknown length will intervene between Jerusalem's fall in 70 CE and the Parousia. The holy city "will be trampled down by foreigners until their day has run its course" (21:24). In Luke's view, this interim of "foreign" domination allows the Christian church to grow and expand throughout the Roman Empire, the subject of his Book of Acts (see Chapter 12).

Luke's editing of Mark 13 indicates that the author divides apocalyptic time into two distinct stages. The first stage involves the Jewish Revolt and Jerusalem's fall; the second involves the Parousia. To describe the second phase, Luke invokes mythic and astronomical language to characterize events: Cosmic phenomena, such as "portents in sun, moon and stars," will herald the Son of Man's reappearance. Although he had previously stated that there will be no convincing "sign" of the End (17:21), Luke nonetheless cites Mark's simile of the fig tree. As the budding tree shows summer is near, so the occurrence of prophesied events proves that the "kingdom" is imminent. Luke also reproduces Mark's confident assertion that "the present generation will live to see it all" (21:32). In its revised context, however, the promise that a single generation would witness the death throes of history probably applies only to those who observe the celestial "portents" that immediately precede the Son's arrival. Luke's muted eschatology does not require that Jesus' contemporaries who heard his teaching and/or witnessed Jerusalem's destruction be the same group living when the Parousia takes place.

Luke does suggest, however, that the astronomical phenomena he predicts may have already occurred. In Acts 2, the author describes the Holy Spirit's descent on Jesus' disciples gathered in Jerusalem, a descent symbolized by rushing winds and tongues of fire. Interpreting this spiritual baptism of the church at Pentecost as a fulfillment of apocalyptic prophecy, Peter is represented as quoting from the Book of Joel, the source of many of the cosmic images Luke employed (Luke 21:25–28):

> No, this [the Pentecost event] is what the prophet spoke of: God says, "This will happen in the last days: I will pour out my spirit upon everyone. . . . And I will show portents in the sky above, and signs on the earth below— blood and fire and drifting smoke. The sun

shall be turned to darkness and the moon to blood, before that great, resplendent day, the day of the Lord shall come. And then every one who invokes the name of the Lord shall be saved."

(Acts 2:16–21)

For the Lukan Peter, Joel's metaphors of divine action were fulfilled when the same Spirit that had guided Jesus infused his church, opening the way to salvation for Jew and Gentile alike. After describing Peter's speech, Luke rarely again mentions apocalyptic images or expectations, nor does he show Peter, James, Stephen, Paul (contrary to Paul's own letters), or any other Christian leader preaching Jesus' imminent return. Did he believe that the figurative language of apocalypse is fulfilled primarily in symbolic events of great spiritual significance, such as the birth of the church and the establishment of a community that lived by Jesus' kingdom ethic? (For a discussion of the "realized eschatology"—a belief that events usually associated with the End have already been fulfilled in Jesus' spiritual presence among his followers—that Luke at times seems to anticipate, see Chapter 10, "John's Reinterpretation of Jesus.")

The Final Conflict and Passion Story

Luke's Interpretation of the Passion

Although Luke's account of Jesus' last days in Jerusalem roughly parallels that of Mark (14:1–16:8), it differs in enough details to suggest that Luke may have used another source as well. In this section (22:1–23:56), Luke underscores a theme that will also dominate Acts: Jesus, like his followers after him, is innocent of any sedition against Rome. More than any other Gospel writer, Luke represents Pilate as testifying to Jesus' political innocence, repeatedly declaring that the accused is not guilty of a "capital offence."

Only when pressured by a Jerusalem mob does Pilate consent to Jesus' crucifixion.

Besides insisting on Jesus' innocence, Luke edits the Markan narrative (or another tradition parallel to that contained in Mark) to present his own theology of the cross. Mark had stated that Jesus' death was sacrificial: His life is given "as a ransom for many" (Mark 10:45). In the Lukan equivalent of this passage (placed in the setting of the Last Supper), Jesus merely says that he comes to serve (cf. Mark 10:42–45; Luke 22:24–27). Unlike some other New Testament writers, Luke does not see Jesus' Passion as a mystical atonement for human sin. Instead, Jesus appears "like a servant," providing an example for others to imitate, the first in a line of Christian models that includes Peter, Stephen, Paul, and their companions in the Book of Acts.

The Last Supper

Mark's report of the Last Supper (Mark 14:17–25) closely parallels that found in Paul's first letter to the Corinthians (1 Cor. 11:23–26). Luke's version introduces several variations: In the Lukan ceremony, the wine cup is passed first and then the unleavened bread. The author may present this different order in the ritual because he wants to avoid giving Jesus' statement about drinking wine again in the kingdom the apocalyptic meaning that Mark gives it. Luke also omits the words interpreting the wine as Jesus' blood, avoiding any suggestion that Jesus sheds his blood to ransom humanity from sin or that he gives his blood to establish a New Covenant. In Luke, Jesus' only interpretative comment relates the bread (Eucharist) to his "body" (22:17–20). The author also inverts Mark's order by having Jesus announce Judas's betrayal after the ritual meal, implying that the traitor was present and participated in the communion ceremony.

Jesus' Final Ordeal

In his report of Jesus' arrest, trials, and crucifixion, Luke makes several more inversions of the

Markan order and adds new material to emphasize his characteristic themes. Softening Mark's harsh view of the disciples' collective failure, Luke states that they fell asleep in Gethsemane because they were "worn out by grief" (22:45–46). In this scene, the author contrasts Jesus' physical anguish with the spiritual help he receives from prayer. (The assertion that Jesus "sweats blood" may be a later scribal interpolation.) After asking the Father to spare him, Jesus perceives "an angel from heaven bringing him strength," after which he prays even more fervently. In this crisis, Jesus demonstrates the function of prayer for those among the Lukan community who suffer similar testing and persecution (22:39–44).

In describing Jesus' hearing before the Sanhedrin, Luke makes several changes in the Markan sequence of events. In Mark, the High Priest questions Jesus, Jesus is then physically abused, and Peter denies knowing him (Mark 14:55–72). Luke places Peter's denial first, the beating second, and the priest's interrogation third (22:63–71). Instead of announcing his identity as Messiah, as in Mark, the Lukan Jesus makes only an ambiguous statement that may or may not be an admission. Luke also rephrases Jesus' allusion to the "Son of Man" to show that with Jesus' ministry the Son's reign has already begun (22:67–71).

Herod Antipas In Luke, the Sanhedrin can produce no witnesses and cannot support charges of blasphemy. Its members bring Jesus to Pilate strictly on political terms: The accused "subverts" the Jewish nation, opposes paying taxes to the Roman government, and claims to be the Messiah, a political role. When Pilate, eager to rid himself of this troublesome case, learns that Jesus is a Galilean, and therefore under the jurisdiction of Herod Antipas, he sends the prisoner to be tried by Herod, who is in Jerusalem for the Passover (23:6–12). Found only in Luke, the Herod episode serves to reinforce Luke's picture of an innocent Jesus. Pilate remarks that neither he nor Herod can find

anything in Jesus' case to support the Jews' charge of "subversion" (23:13–15).

Twice Luke's Pilate declares that the prisoner "has done nothing to deserve death" (23:15) and is legally "guilty of [no] capital offence" (23:22). The Roman prefect, whom other contemporary historians depict as a ruthless tyrant contemptuous of Jewish public opinion, is here only a weak pawn manipulated by a fanatical group of his Jewish subjects.

Last Words on the Cross In recounting Jesus' crucifixion, Luke provides several "last words" that illustrate important Lukan themes. Only in this Gospel do we find Jesus' prayer to forgive his executioners because they do not understand the meaning of their actions (23:34). Because Luke regards both Jews and Romans as acting in "ignorance" (see Acts 2:17), this request to pardon his tormentors encompasses all parties involved in Jesus' death. Besides illustrating Jesus' heroic capacity to forgive, this prayer shows Luke's hero vindicating his teaching that a victim must love his enemy (6:27–38) and end the cycle of hatred and retaliation that perpetuates evil in the world. To Luke, the manner of Jesus' death represents the supreme parable of reversal, forgiveness, and completion.

Even in personal suffering, the Lukan Jesus thinks not of himself, but of others. Carrying his cross on the road to **Calvary,** he comforts the women who weep for him (23:26–31). He similarly consoles the man crucified next to him, promising him an immediate reward in **paradise** (23:43), perhaps because this fellow sufferer has recognized Jesus' political innocence (23:41). The Messiah's final words are to the Father whose Spirit he had received following baptism (3:21; 4:1, 14) and to whom in death he commits his own spirit (23:46–47).

Except for the symbolic darkness accompanying the Crucifixion (23:44–45), Luke mentions no natural phenomenon comparable to the great earthquake that Matthew describes. Consequently, the Roman centurion does not recognize in Jesus a supernatural being, "a son of God," as in Mark and Matthew (Mark 15:39; Matt. 27:54). The centurion's remark refers not to Jesus' divinity, but to the political injustice of his execution. "Beyond all doubt," he says, "this man was innocent" (23:47). This account of Jesus' death dramatizes two major Lukan themes: Jesus, rather than being a sacrifice for sin, is an example of compassion and forgiveness for all to emulate; he is also, like his followers, innocent of any crime against Rome.

Like Matthew, Luke generally follows Mark's order through Jesus' burial and the women's discovery of the empty tomb. Omitting any Matthean reference to supernatural phenomena such as an Easter morning earthquake or the appearance of an angel that blinds the Roman guards, Luke diverges from Mark only in that the women report what they have seen to the Eleven, who do not believe them (23:49–24:11). (No Gospel writer except Mark has the women keep silent about their observation.)

Epilogue: Post Resurrection Appearances in the Vicinity of Jerusalem

Because early editions of Mark contain no resurrection narrative, it is not surprising that Matthew and Luke, who generally adhere to Mark's order through the discovery of the empty sepulcher, differ widely in their reports of Jesus' post resurrection appearances. Consistent with his emphasis on Jerusalem, Luke omits the Markan tradition that Jesus would reappear in Galilee (Mark 16:7; Matt. 28:7, 16–20) and places all the disciples' experiences of the risen Jesus in or near Jerusalem.

In concluding his Gospel, the author creates two detailed accounts of Jesus' posthumous teaching that serve to connect Jesus' story with that of the community of believers for whom Luke writes. The risen Jesus' words are not a final farewell, but a preparation for what follows in Luke's second volume, the Book of Acts. Because Luke wishes to show that Jesus' presence and power continue unabated in the work of the early church, he describes Jesus' last instructions in terms that directly relate to the ongoing practices of the church. For Luke, the disciples' original experience of their risen Lord is qualitatively the same spiritually renewing experience that believers continue to enjoy in their charismatic community. Even after ascending to heaven, Jesus remains present in the church's characteristic activities: sharing sacramental meals, studying Scripture, and feeding the poor.

In narrating Jesus' first appearance, on the road to **Emmaus** (a few miles from Jerusalem), Luke emphasizes the glorified Lord's relationship to followers left behind on earth. The two disciples, Cleopas and an unnamed companion (perhaps a woman), who encounter Jesus do not recognize him until they dine together. Only in breaking bread—symbolic of the Christian communion ritual—is Jesus' living presence discerned.

In Luke's second post resurrection account, the disciples are discussing Jesus when he suddenly appears in their midst, asking to be fed— it has been more than three days since the Last Supper, and he is hungry. The Lukan disciples' offering Jesus a piece of cooked fish makes several points: Their job is to care for the poor and hungry whom Jesus had also served; they have fellowship with Jesus in communal dining; and they are assured that the figure standing before them is real—he eats material food—and not a hallucination. By insisting on Jesus' physicality, Luke also firmly links the heavenly Christ and the human Jesus—they are one and the same.

Perhaps most important for Luke's understanding of the way in which Jesus remains alive and present is the author's emphasis on studying the Hebrew Bible in order to discover the true significance of Jesus' career. At Emmaus, Jesus explains "the passages which referred to himself in every part of the scriptures" (24:27), thus setting his listeners' "hearts on fire" (24:32). In Jerusalem, he repeats these lessons in biblical exegesis, interpreting the Torah, Prophets, and Writings as Christological prophecies (24:44), an innovative practice that enabled Christians to recognize Jesus in the Mosaic revelation. Luke also connects these post resurrection teachings with the church's task: Jesus' death and resurrection, foretold in Scripture, are not history's final act but the beginning of a worldwide movement. The disciples are to remain together in Jerusalem until Jesus sends the Holy Spirit, which will empower them to proclaim God's new dispensation to "all nations" (24:46–49; fulfilled in Acts 1–2).

Summary

The author of the Gospel traditionally ascribed to Luke, traveling companion of the apostle Paul, wrote primarily for a Gentile audience. His portrait of Jesus reveals a world *sōter* (savior or deliverer), conceived by the Holy Spirit, who launches a new era in God's plan for human salvation. As John the Baptist represents the culmination of Israel's role in the divine plan, so Jesus—healing, teaching, and banishing evil—inaugurates the reign of God, the "kingdom," among humanity.

Emphasizing God's compassion and willingness to forgive all, the Lukan Jesus provides a powerful example for his followers to imitate in service, charity, and good works. An ethical model for Jews and Gentiles alike, Jesus establishes a Spirit-led movement that provides a religion of salvation for all people. The eschatological belief that the Son of Man would return "soon" after his resurrection from the dead is replaced with Luke's concept of the disciples' role in carrying on Jesus' work "to the ends of the earth," a commission that extends the time of the End indefinitely into the future. In the meantime, a law-abiding and peaceful church will convey its message of a Savior for all nations throughout the Roman Empire—and beyond.

Questions for Review

1. Describe some of Luke's major themes and concerns. How do parables that appear only in Luke's Gospel, such as Lazarus and the rich man and the prodigal son, illustrate typically Lukan ideas?
2. Describe the roles that women play in Luke's account. Which women, absent in Mark and Matthew, appear in Luke's version of Jesus' ministry? What qualities of Jesus does their presence elicit?
3. Evaluate the evidence for and against the tradition that Luke, Paul's traveling companion, wrote the Gospel bearing his name. Because the author was aware that "many" other accounts of Jesus' life and work had already been composed, why did he—who was not an eyewitness to the events he describes—decide to write a new Gospel? Does the fact that the writer added the Book of Acts as a sequel to his Gospel narrative suggest something about his purpose?
4. In the Greco-Roman world, historians and biographers often composed long speeches to illustrate their characters' ideas, ethical qualities, and responses to critical events. Do you find any evidence that Luke uses this method in the Gospel and/or Acts?
5. Show some of the specific ways that Luke's version of Jesus' arrest, trial, and execution reflects an awareness of the political realities with which the Christian community had to deal. How does Luke take pains to show that Jesus is innocent of sedition against Rome?

Questions for Discussion and Reflection

1. Much of the material that appears only in Luke's Gospel highlights Jesus' concern for women, the poor, and social outcasts. The parables unique to his account—such as the prodigal son, the good Samaritan, and Lazarus and the rich man—emphasize unexpected reversals of society's accepted norms. What view of Jesus' character and teaching do you think Luke wishes to promote?
2. Compare Matthew's Sermon on the Mount (Matt. 5–7) with Luke's similar Sermon on the Plain (6:20–49). When Luke's version of a saying differs from Matthew's, which of the two do you think is probably closer to Jesus' own

words? Do the different versions of the same saying—such as Jesus' blessing of the poor— also illustrate the individual Gospel writer's distinctive viewpoint?

3. Luke's Gospel emphasizes such themes as prayer, the activity of the Holy Spirit, the kingdom's reversal of normal expectations, the rejection of wealth and other material ambitions, Jesus' compassion, and the divine joy in human redemption. How do these themes relate to the author's belief that Jesus' ministry completes the purpose of Israel's revelation and begins a "new age" leading to the kingdom?

4. Luke consistently shows Jesus gravitating toward economically and politically powerless persons, including women, social outcasts, and the poor. Do you think that the Lukan Jesus' concern for socially marginal and "unrespectable" people— such as prostitutes, notorious sinners, and tax collectors who collaborated with the "evil empire" of Rome—is sufficiently recognized or honored by today's political and religious leaders? Can someone be a Christian and *not* follow Jesus' example of siding with the poor and oppressed? Explain your answer.

5. In editing Mark's prophecy of Jerusalem's fall and Jesus' Second Coming, how does Luke modify his predecessor's emphasis on the nearness of End time? Are Luke's changes to Mark's apocalyptic viewpoint consistent with his writing a second book about the purpose and goals of the early Christian church (the Book of Acts)?

Terms and Concepts to Remember

Abraham	Levite
Annunciation	L (Lukan) source
apocalypticisim	Luke
apology	Magnificat
Benedictus	Martha
Calvary	Mary
Elijah	Nunc Dimittis
Elizabeth and	paradise
Zechariah	Pentecost
Emmaus	publican
Gabriel	Samaria
"greater interpolation"	Samaritan
Issac	Sarah
Joseph	Savior (*sōter*)
"lesser interpolation"	Sermon on the Plain
Simeon	theodicy
Simon	Theophilus

Recommended Reading

Borgman, Paul C. *The Way According to Luke: Hearing the Whole Story of Luke-Acts.* Grand Rapids, Mich.: Eerdmans, 2006. Offers a competent literary analysis of the two-volume work.

Carroll, John T. "Luke, Gospel of." In K. D. Sakenfeld, ed., *The New Interpreter's Dictionary of the Bible*, Vol. 3, pp. 720–734. Nashville: Abingdon Press, 2008. Surveys questions of authorship, circumstances of composition, theological issues, and recent history of critical interpretation.

Fitzmyer, J. A., ed. *The Gospel According to Luke*, Vols. 1 and 2 of the Anchor Bible. Garden City, N.Y.: Doubleday, 1981, 1985.

Johnson, Luke Timothy. "Luke-Acts, Book of." In D. N. Freedman, ed., *The Anchor Bible Dictionary*, Vol. 4, pp. 403–420. New York: Doubleday, 1992. A lucid analysis of Luke's concept of divine justice both to Israel and to the church.

Johnson, Luke Timothy, and Harrington, Daniel J. *The Gospel of Luke.* Sacra Pagina Series. Collegeville, Minn.: Liturgical Press, 2006. A scholarly commentary.

Karris, Robert J. "The Gospel According to Luke." In R. E. Brown et al., eds., *The New Jerome Biblical Commentary*, pp. 675–721. Englewood Cliffs, N.J.: Prentice-Hall, 1990. Provides detailed commentary on Lukan accounts.

Patterson, Stephen. "Luke, Gospel According to." In M. D. Coogan, ed., *The Oxford Encyclopedia of the Books of the Bible*, Vol. 1, pp. 587–600. New York: Oxford University, Press, 2011. Offers clear discussion of the Gospel's compositional history, sources, and current critical interpretation.

Powell, M. A. *What Are They Saying About Luke?* New York: Paulist Press, 1989. A good place to begin a study of current scholarship on Luke's Gospel.

Schaberg, Jane. "Luke." In Carol Newsom and Sharon Ringe, eds., *Women's Bible Commentary*, pp. 363–380. Louisville, Ky.: Westminster John Knox, 1998. A thoughtful analysis of Luke's treatment of his women characters, concluding that despite his sensitivity to their condition, he espouses typically Greco-Roman male attitudes.

Schüssler Fiorenza, Elisabeth. *In Memory of Her: A Feminist Theological Reconstruction of Christian Origins.* New York: Crossroads/Herder & Herder, 1983 (reprint 1994). An important contribution to understanding women's roles in the formation of early Christianity.

Shillington, V. George. *An Introduction to the Study of Luke-Acts.* Edinburgh: T and T Clark International, 2007. A concise survey of different critical approaches to studying Luke's narratives.

Talbert, Charles H. *Reading Luke: A Literary and Theological Commentary,* rev. ed. Macon, Ga.: Smyth & Helwys, 2002. An informative study of Luke's historical sweep.

Tannehill, Robert. *Abingdon New Testament Commentary: Luke.* Nashville: Abingdon Press, 1996. Offers helpful historical/cultural context for Luke's writings.

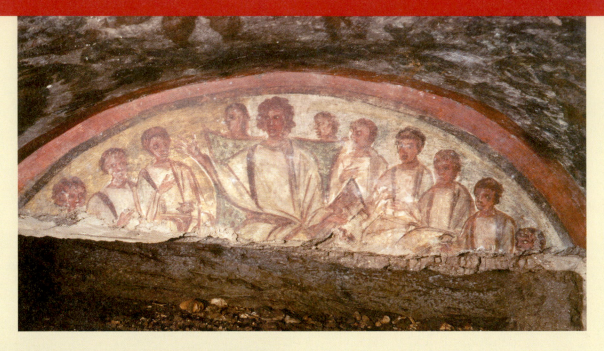

Early Christian artists commonly emphasized Jesus' relevance to their lives by portraying him dressed as a contemporary, but they also envisioned him in a variety of ways, ranging from a clean-shaven youth to a mature, bearded figure. A fresco in the Catacomb of Saint Domitilla in Rome (*above*) shows Jesus and the apostles as beardless, with short hair, and wearing white linen tunics in the Greco-Roman fashion. By contrast, the image of Jesus on the famous Shroud of Turin (*detail left*), a burial cloth in which Jesus' crucified body was allegedly wrapped, shows a bearded figure with long hair in what may have been the style of Palestinian-Jewish men of the early first century CE. Although carbon 14 dating of a swath from the shroud in 1988 indicated that it was woven in about the fourteenth century CE, recent chemical tests of other parts of the shroud suggest that it is actually much older. (The cloth sample dated in 1988 reportedly was taken from a medieval-era patch used to repair the shroud after it was damaged by fire.)

In a mosaic from the mid-third century CE (*above*), a Christian artist portrays Christ as the sun-god Apollo, thereby expressing the glorified Jesus' cosmic importance. As the "light of the world," Christ replaces Greco-Roman solar deities and now shines "like the sun in full strength" (Rev. 1:16). Sixth-century mosaics in Ravenna depict scenes from Jesus' ministry: (*left*) A youthful Jesus summons the brothers Peter and Andrew to leave their fishing boat and follow him. (*below*) A mature, bearded Jesus (with halo) and his disciples are dressed in a style characteristic of the late eastern Roman (Byzantine) period.

(*top*) As a disciple looks on, Jesus expels demons from a man and casts them into swine at Gergesa. (*middle*) On his fatal journey to Jerusalem, a beardless Jesus touches the eyes of a blind man to restore his sight. (*bottom left*) Judas kisses Jesus in the garden of Gethsemane, identifying him to the guards who have come to arrest him, as Peter draws his sword to cut off the ear of Malchus, slave of the High Priest (John 18:10, 26). (*bottom right*) In a post resurrection appearance found only in John's Gospel, the risen Jesus allows a skeptical Thomas to touch his wounds, leading to Thomas's recognition of Jesus as "my Lord and my God." ◼

CHAPTER 10

John's Reinterpretation of Jesus
Divine Wisdom Made Flesh

He who has faith in me will do what I am doing; and he will do greater things still. . . .
Your Advocate [Paraclete], the Holy Spirit . . . will teach you everything,
and will call to mind all that I have told you. John 14:12, 26

Key Topics/Themes In John's Gospel, the order of events and the portrayal of Jesus and his teaching are strikingly different from those in the Synoptic accounts. Whereas the Synoptics depict Jesus as an eschatological healer-exorcist whose teachings deal primarily with Torah reinterpretation, John describes Jesus as an embodiment of heavenly Wisdom who performs no exorcisms and whose message centers on his own divine nature. In John, Jesus is the human form of God's celestial Word, the cosmic expression of divine Wisdom by which God created the universe. As the Word incarnate (made flesh), Jesus reveals otherwise unknowable truths about God's being and purpose. To John, Jesus' crucifixion is not a humiliating ordeal (as Mark characterizes it), but a glorification that frees Jesus to return to heaven. Although John's Gospel alludes briefly to Jesus' future return, it contains no prophecies of the Second Coming comparable to those found in the Synoptics. Instead of emphasizing the Parousia, it argues that the risen Christ is eternally present in the invisible form of a surrogate—the Paraclete, or Holy Spirit, which continues to inspire and direct the believing community.

From the moment we read the opening lines of John's Gospel—"When all things began, the Word already was. The Word dwelt with God, and what God was, the Word was" (1:1)—we realize that we have entered a world of thought strikingly different from that of the Synoptic Gospels. "Word," which John uses to denote the state of Jesus' preexistence in heaven before he came to earth, translates the Greek term *Logos*. A philosophical concept with a long pre-Christian history, **Logos** can mean anything from a divine utterance to the principle of cosmic reason that orders and governs the universe. To John, it is the infinite wisdom of God personified, the ultimate consummation of Israel's long wisdom tradition (see below).

Identifying his hero with the Greek Logos concept is only the first of John's many astonishing innovations in retelling Jesus' story. While the three Synoptics give generally similar accounts of their subject's life, John creates a portrait of Jesus that differs in both outline and content from the other Gospels. Ninety percent of John's material appears exclusively in his

231

The Gospel According to John

Author: Traditionally, John, son of Zebedee and brother of James, one of the Twelve. The writer, who does not identify himself, states that this version of Jesus' life is based on testimony of an unnamed "Beloved Disciple." Scholars classify the work as anonymous.

Date: Between about 95 and 100 CE, after some Christians were expelled from Jewish synagogues. Small fragments of the Gospel found in Egypt, dating from the first half of the second century CE, are the oldest surviving part of the New Testament.

Place of composition: Unknown. The Gospel may have evolved at a number of different sites as the Johannine community moved from a Jewish-Palestinian to a Gentile environment.

Sources: A compilation of Jesus' miraculous acts, the hypothetical Signs Gospel; Greek and Jewish traditions involving heavenly Wisdom; and the oral teachings of an unidentified "Beloved Disciple."

Audience: Communities influenced by a uniquely high Christology, including belief in Jesus' prehuman existence as Cosmic Wisdom (the Logos), as well as a proto-Gnostic group.

account and has no parallel in the Synoptics. The Fourth Gospel offers a different chronology of Jesus' ministry, a different order of events, a different teaching, and a distinctly different teacher. Instead of Mark's humble carpenter-prophet, John presents a divine hero whose supernatural glory radiates through every speech he makes and every miracle he performs. John's Jesus is a being of light even while walking the earth.

Writing perhaps thirty years after Mark had invented the Gospel form, the author of the Fourth Gospel is aware that, even after the destruction of Jerusalem and its Temple in 70 CE, the End did not come and Jesus did not return. He is also aware that, despite its disappointment in the delayed Parousia, the Christian movement had not only survived the tribulations of the Jewish wars and government persecutions, but had grown vigorously and expanded throughout the Roman Empire. Inspired by the **Paraclete**—which he defines as "the Spirit of truth" (John 14:16; 15:26)—the fourth Evangelist boldly reinterprets Jesus' theological significance, emphasizing what Jesus accomplished at his first coming and spotlighting his cosmic stature.

Unlike the Synoptic writers, John gives little indication that Jesus was remembered as an apocalyptic prophet who announced God's dawning kingdom and who expelled demons to show that Satan no longer controlled humanity. In John, Jesus does not predict Jerusalem's fall, prophesy about his return to earth, or perform a single exorcism. Instead, John portrays Jesus as effectively disclosing his "glory" during his earthly ministry. When the divine Logos became human as the man Jesus, his disciples could already see "his glory, such glory as befits the Father's only Son, full of grace and truth" (John 1:14). For John, the Crucifixion itself reveals Jesus' "hour of glory" and it is Jesus' death and return to heaven, his place of origin, which allows him to reveal the "power and glory" that Mark had ascribed to the Second Coming (Mark 13:26; cf. John 1:14; 12:27–33; 17:5, 22, 24).

In creating a portrait of Jesus so different from those in the Synoptic Gospels, John freely confesses that his purpose is not biographical but theological: His account was written "in order that you may hold the faith that Jesus is the Christ, the Son of God, and that through this faith you may possess life by his name" (20:31). This declaration follows the Gospel's climactic scene—a post resurrection appearance in which the reality of Jesus' living presence conquers the doubts of his most skeptical follower, Thomas. Confronted with a sudden manifestation of the risen Jesus, Thomas acknowledges him as "My Lord and my God"—a confession of faith that the reader is intended to echo.

Authorship

Since the late second century CE, the Gospel of John (commonly labeled the Fourth Gospel to distinguish it from the Synoptics) has been attributed to the apostle John, son of Zebedee and brother of James. In the Synoptics, John and James are Galilean fishermen and, along with Peter, form an inner circle of Jesus' most intimate followers. The most prominent of the Twelve, the three are present when Jesus raises Jairus's daughter (Mark 5:37), at the Transfiguration (Mark 9:2), and in the garden of Gethsemane when Jesus is arrested (Mark 14:33). Jesus nicknames John and his brother "Boanerges," meaning "sons of thunder," perhaps for their aggressive temperaments, as when they ask Jesus to send fire to consume a Samaritan village (Luke 9:54) or demand first place in his kingdom (Mark 10:35–40). Writing in the mid-50s CE, Paul describes John as one of the three "pillars" in the Jerusalem church (Gal. 2:6–10) during its formative period.

According to one church tradition, John eventually settled in Ephesus, where he lived to an exceptionally old age, writing his Gospel, three letters, and the Book of Revelation. These five works are known collectively as the "Johannine literature."

The tradition ascribing authorship to the son of Zebedee is relatively late. Before about 180 CE, church writers do not mention the Gospel's existence. After that date, some leading churchmen accept it as John's composition, although others doubt its authenticity. Some even suggest that it was the work of Cerinthus, a Gnostic teacher.

One church leader, Clement of Alexandria, states what became the official view of John's origin. Clement (c. 200 CE) recognized the salient differences between the Synoptics and John and noted that after the other Evangelists had preserved the "facts of history" John then wrote "a spiritual Gospel." Both traditionalists and modern critics agree with Clement on two counts: that John's Gospel was the last one written and that it profoundly "spiritualizes" Jesus.

Problems with the Traditional Theory

Most contemporary scholars doubt that the apostle John wrote the document bearing his name. Most scholars are also skeptical that the same author wrote all of the Johannine literature (see Chapter 18 for a discussion of the letters of John and Chapter 19 on the authorship of Revelation). The Gospel itself does not mention the author's identity, stating instead that it is based on the testimony of an anonymous disciple "whom Jesus loved" (21:20–24). Tradition identifies this "Beloved Disciple" with John (whose name does not appear in the Gospel), but scholars can find no evidence to substantiate this claim. Jesus predicted that John would suffer a death similar to his (Mark 10:39), whereas the Gospel implies that its author, unlike Peter, James, and John, did not die a martyr's death (21:20–22). Many historians think it likely that Herod Agrippa executed the apostle John along with his brother James about 41–43 CE (Acts 12:1–3).

Some critics propose that another John, prominent in the church at Ephesus about 100 CE, is the author. Except that he was called "John the Elder" (presbyter), we know nothing that would connect him with the Johannine writings. Lacking definite confirmation of traditional authorship, scholars regard the work as anonymous. For convenience, we refer to the author as John.

The Beloved Disciple

Although the Gospel text does not identify its author, editorial notes added to the final chapter associate him with the unnamed Beloved Disciple, suggesting that at the very least this disciple's teachings are the Gospel's primary source (21:23–24). Whether or not this anonymous personage was a historical character, he is certainly an idealized figure, achieving an intimacy and emotional rapport with Jesus unmatched by that with Peter or the other disciples. In the Gospel, he does not appear (at least as the one "Jesus loved") until the final night of Jesus' life, when we find him at the Last Supper, lying against his friend's chest (13:23). (The Twelve dined in the Greco-Roman fashion, reclining two-by-two on benches set around the table.)

Designed to represent the Johannine community's special knowledge of Christ, the Beloved Disciple is invariably presented in competition with Peter, who may represent the larger apostolic church from which the disciple's exclusive group is somewhat distanced. At the Last Supper, the Beloved Disciple is Peter's intermediary, transmitting to Jesus Peter's question about Judas's betrayal (13:21–29). Acquainted with the High Priest, he has access to Pilate's court, thus gaining Peter's admittance to the hearing, where Peter denies knowing Jesus (18:15–18). The only male disciple at the cross, he receives Jesus' charge to care for Mary, becoming her "son" and hence Jesus' "brother" as well (19:26–27).

Outrunning Peter to the empty tomb on Easter morning, he arrives there first and is the first to believe that Jesus is risen (20:2–10). In a boat fishing with Peter on the Sea of Galilee, the disciple is the first to recognize the resurrected Jesus standing on the shore, identifying him to Peter (21:4–7). Peter, future "pillar" of the Jerusalem church, is commissioned to "feed" (or spiritually nourish) Jesus' "sheep" (his future followers), but Jesus has a special prophecy for the Beloved Disciple's future: He may live until the Master returns (21:20–22).

This brief allusion to the Beloved Disciple's surviving until Jesus' return is one of only two explicit references to the Parousia in John's Gospel. The single reference to Jesus' coming again in the main body of the Gospel appears in John 14:3, where it is placed in the context of Jesus' receiving the disciples into their everlasting home, perhaps at the hour of their deaths. In John 21, which scholars believe is an epilogue to the Gospel and by a writer or editor different from that of the main narrative, the author states that Jesus' words about the Beloved Disciple had been misunderstood "in the brotherhood," the community that produced the Gospel. "But in fact Jesus did not say that he would not die," the editor points out, "he only said, 'If it should be my will that he wait until I come, what is it to you?'" (21:23). By the time the epilogue was written, the Beloved Disciple had apparently already died, suggesting that even the longest-lived followers who had personally known Jesus had by then passed from the scene. Does the writer mean to imply that expectations of Jesus' return during the lifetimes of some original followers was a misapprehension, a mistaken interpretation of Jesus' teaching?

Instead of emphasizing Jesus' return to earth, John's Gospel underscores Jesus' return to heaven, his place of origin. At the Last Supper Jesus promises the disciples: "I will not leave you bereft; I am coming back to you," coming not visibly at the Parousia, but in the unseen form of the Paraclete, which Jesus describes as "your Advocate, the Holy Spirit, whom the Father will send in my name" (14:26). Explaining the necessity of his return to heaven, Jesus tells the disciples: "It is for your good that I am leaving you. If I do not go, your Advocate [the Paraclete] will not come, whereas if I go, I will send him to you" (16:7). Not the Parousia, but the Paraclete, the Spirit that assures Jesus' continuing presence among believers, will reveal Jesus' "glory" and invisibly express God's will in human society (16:8-15).

One disciple clearly articulates Jesus' intent in thus revising expectations of his Second Coming: "You mean to disclose yourself to us alone and not to the world?" (14:22). In the Johannine view, Jesus has already returned spiritually to dwell within believers sanctified by love, and perhaps will not manifest himself visibly to "the world" at a Parousia (14:10–29).

Place and Date of Composition

Despite its use of Hellenistic terms and ideas, recent studies indicate that John's Gospel is deeply rooted in Palestinian tradition. It shows a greater familiarity with Palestinian geography than the Synoptics and reveals close connections with first-century Palestinian Judaisms, particularly concepts prevailing in the Essene community at Qumran. Study of the Dead Sea Scrolls from Qumran reveals many parallels between Essene ideas and those prevailing in the Johannine community. Essene writers and the author of John use a remarkably similar vocabulary to express the same kind of ethical dualism, dividing the world into two opposing groups of people: those who walk in the *light* (symbolizing truth and goodness) and those who walk in *darkness* (symbolizing deceit and evil). In comparing John with the Dead Sea Scroll known as the *Rule of the Community,* scholars find not only an almost identical use of distinctive terms but also a comparable worldview according to which the universe is a battleground of polar opposites. In this dualistic cosmos, the devil (synonymous with "liar") and his "spirit of error" oppose Jesus' "spirit of truth" (cf. John 8:44; 12:35; 14:17; 15:26 with *Rule of the Community* 1QS 3.13, 17–21).

The Qumran and Johannine communities are also alike in that each is apparently based on the teachings of a spiritually enlightened founder. As the mysterious Teacher of Righteousness had earlier brought the light of true understanding to the Essenes, so the Johannine Jesus—"the light of the world"—came to illuminate humanity's mental and spiritual darkness.

Although the unidentified Essene teacher receives nothing comparable to the exaltation the Johannine writer accords Jesus, the two groups display similar attitudes, regarding themselves as specially chosen to fulfill the divine will. Both the Dead Sea Scrolls and the Johannine writings claim exclusive knowledge of God denied to outsiders and both view their respective groups, tiny as they were, as the *only* guardians of light and truth in a fatally benighted world.

Before the Dead Sea Scrolls were discovered, many scholars believed that John's Gospel—with its seemingly Platonic dualism and use of Greek philosophical terms such as *Logos*—originated in a Hellenistic environment, perhaps in Ephesus, the traditional home of the apostle John in his old age. A wealthy seaport and capital of the Roman province of Asia (western Turkey), **Ephesus** was a crossroads of Greek and Near Eastern ideas. With a large colony of Jews, it was a center for Paul's missionary work, as well as the base of a John-the-Baptist sect (Acts 19:1–7). If the Gospel was composed in an area where the Baptist was regarded as Jesus' superior, it would account for the writer's severe limitation of the Baptist's role in the messianic drama, reducing his function to that of a mere "voice" bearing witness to Jesus (1:6–9, 19–28). The many

similarities between Essene and Johannine thought, however, now incline many scholars to fix the Gospel's place of composition (at least its first edition) in Palestine or Syria.

Some critics once thought that John's Gospel was composed late in the second century, when Christian authors first mention it. However, tiny manuscript fragments of John discovered in the Egyptian desert have been dated to about 125 to 150 CE, making them the oldest surviving part of a New Testament book. Allowing time for the Gospel to have circulated abroad as far as Egypt, the work could not have originated much later than about 100 CE. The Gospel's references to believers' being expelled from Jewish synagogues (9:22, 34–35)—an extended process that began about 85 or 90 CE—suggest that the decisive break between church and synagogue was already in effect when it was written. Hence, the Gospel is usually dated to between about 95 and 100 CE.

Relation to the Synoptic Gospels

Despite some verbal parallels to Mark (cf. John 6:7 and Mark 6:37; John 12:27–28 and Mark 14:34–36), most scholars do not think that the author of John's Gospel drew on the earlier Gospels. A few scholars, however, such as Thomas Brodie (see "Recommended Reading"), argue that the author created his account by appropriating material from the Synoptics and thoroughly transforming it. After carefully analyzing John's presumed reworking of his sources (primarily Mark, Matthew, Ephesians, and the Mosaic Torah), Brodie concludes that John's Gospel is basically a theological reinterpretation of previously existing traditions about Jesus' life and meaning. Instead of deriving from a marginal Christian group, the supposedly independent Johannine community, John's narrative actually represents mainstream Christianity.

The enormous differences between the Synoptics and the Fourth Gospel, however, persuade most scholars that John's vision of Jesus does not derive from the older canonical Gospels

BOX 10.1   **Representative Examples of Material Found Only in John**

Concept of the Logos: Before coming to earth, Jesus preexisted in heaven, where he was God's mediator in creating the universe (1:1–18).

Miracle at Cana: Jesus changes water into wine (the first "sign") (2:1–12).

Principle of spiritual rebirth: the conversation with Nicodemus (3:1–21; see also 7:50–52; 19:39).

Conversation with the Samaritan woman (4:1–42).

Jesus healing the invalid at Jerusalem's Sheep Pool (5:1–47).

The "I am" sayings: Jesus speaks as divine Wisdom revealed from above, equating himself with objects or concepts of great symbolic value, such as "the bread of life" (6:22–66) and "the resurrection and the life" (11:25).

Cure of the man born blind: debate between church and synagogue (9:1–41).

The raising of Lazarus (the seventh "sign") (11:1–12:11).

A different tradition of the Last Supper: washing the disciples' feet (13:1–20) and delivering the farewell discourses (13:31–17:26).

Resurrection appearances in or near Jerusalem to Mary Magdalene and the disciples, including Thomas (20:1–29).

Resurrection appearances in Galilee to Peter and to the Beloved Disciple (21:1–23).

(see Boxes 10.1 and 10.2). Concentrating on Jesus as a heavenly revealer of ultimate truth, John does not present his hero in Synoptic terms. Most of the material that appears in the Synoptics does not appear in John; conversely, most of John's contents are not even alluded to in the Synoptic Gospels.

A dozen representative differences between John and the Synoptics follow, along with brief suggestions about the author's possible reasons for not including characteristic Synoptic material:

1. John has no birth story or reference to Jesus' virginal conception, perhaps because he sees Christ as the eternal Word (Logos) who "became flesh" (1:14) as the man Jesus of Nazareth. John's doctrine of the **Incarnation** (the spiritual Logos becoming physically human) makes the manner of Jesus' human conception irrelevant.

2. John contains no record of Jesus' baptism by John, emphasizing Jesus' independence of and superiority to the Baptist. Besides denying the Baptist an Elijah role, the author shows Jesus conducting his own baptism campaign, thus competing with the Baptist (3:22–23; 4:1).

3. John includes no period of contemplation in the Judean wilderness or temptation by Satan. His Jesus possesses a vital unity with the Father that makes worldly temptation impossible.

4. John never mentions Jesus' exorcisms, which play so large a role in Mark's and Matthew's reports of his ministry. Instead, Jesus himself is accused of "having a demon" (7:20; 8:46–52; 10:19–20).

5. Although he recounts some friction between Jesus and his brothers (7:1–6), John does not reproduce the Markan tradition that Jesus' family thought he was mentally unbalanced or that his neighbors in Nazareth viewed him as nothing extraordinary (Mark 3:20–21, 31–35; 6:1–6). In John, Jesus meets considerable opposition, but he is always too commanding and powerful a figure to be ignored or devalued.

6. John presents Jesus' teaching in a form radically different from that of the Synoptics. Both Mark and Matthew state that Jesus "never" taught without using parables

BOX 10.2 Characters Introduced or Given New Emphasis in John

Andrew, Peter's brother, as a speaking character (1:40–42, 44; 6:8–9; 12:20–22)

Philip, one of the Twelve (1:43–49; 6:5–7; 12:20–22; 14:8–11)

Nathanael, one of the Twelve (1:45–51)

Mary as a participant in Jesus' ministry (2:1–5) and at the cross (19:25–27)

Nicodemus, a leading Pharisee (3:1–12; 7:50–52; 19:39)

A Samaritan woman (4:7–42)

The woman taken in adultery (8:3–11; an appendix to John in the NEB)

A man born blind (9:1–38)

Lazarus, brother of Mary and Martha (11:1–44; 12:1–11)

An unidentified disciple whom "Jesus loved" (13:23–26; 18:15–16; 19:26–27; 20:2–10; 21:7, 20–24)

Annas, father-in-law of Caiaphas, the High Priest (18:12–14, 19–24)

(Mark 4:34; Matt. 13:34), but John does not record a single parable of the Synoptic type (involving homely images of agricultural or domestic life). Instead of brief aphorisms and vivid comparisons, the Johannine Jesus conducts long dialogues with figures like Nicodemus and delivers philosophical speeches in which Jesus' own nature is typically the subject of discussion. In John, he speaks both publicly and privately in this manner, in Galilee as well as in Jerusalem. The Synoptic Jesus almost never speaks as he does everywhere in John; the Johannine Jesus almost never speaks as he does throughout the Synoptics.

John stands alone in his adaptation of Jesus' teaching, decisively outvoted four to one by the other Evangelists and their respective sources. Not only Mark but also Q and the special material in Matthew (M) and Luke (L) agree that Jesus taught chiefly in aphorisms and parables.

7. John includes none of Jesus' reinterpretations of the Mosaic Law, the main topic of Jesus' Synoptic discourses. Instead of the many ethical directives about not divorcing, keeping the Sabbath, ending the law of retaliation, and forgiving enemies that we find in Mark, Matthew, and Luke, John records only one "new commandment"—to love. In both the Gospel and the Epistles, this is Jesus' single explicit directive; in the Johannine community, mutual love among "friends" is the sole distinguishing mark of true discipleship (13:34–35; 15:9–17).

8. Conspicuously absent from John's Gospel is any prediction of Jerusalem's fall, a concern that dominated the Synopticists' imaginations (Mark 13; Matt. 24–25; Luke 21). Viewing events a full generation after the Jewish Revolt, the Johannine author effectively disassociates Jesus from the apocalyptic hopes that many early Christians had linked to Jerusalem's destruction (see below).

9. Instead of apocalyptic prophecies of Jesus' Second Coming (Mark 13; Matthew 24–25; and Luke 21), John's Gospel focuses on two vital concepts: Jesus has already completed his role as Israel's Messiah and he is already present in the believing community. For John, the Paraclete, the **Holy Spirit** that serves as Christians' Helper, Comforter, or Advocate (14:25–26; 16:7–15) and that inspires the Johannine fellowship, is Jesus' surrogate, marking his invisible presence. To this Evangelist, Jesus' first coming means that believers have life *now* (5:21–26; 11:25–27) and that divine judgment is a current reality, not merely a

future event (3:18; cf. 9:39; 12:31). Scholars find in John a **realized eschatology,** a belief that events usually associated with the *eschaton* (world's End), such as divine judgment and the awarding of eternal life, are even now realized or fulfilled by Jesus' spiritual presence among believers. For John, the earthly career of Jesus, followed by the infusion of his Spirit into the disciples (20:22–23), has already accomplished God's purpose in sending the Messiah. For the Johannine community, in his hour of "glory" (crucifixion), Jesus had essentially finished his work (19:30). Just as John's doctrine of the Incarnation made the concept of a virgin conception theoretically unnecessary, so his view of the Paraclete effectively mutes the expectation of the Parousia.

10. Although he represents the sacramental bread and wine as life-giving symbols, John does not preserve a communion ritual or the institution of a New Covenant between Jesus and his followers at the Last Supper. Stating that the meal took place a day before Passover, John substitutes Jesus' act of humble service—washing the disciples' feet—for the Eucharist (13:1–16).

11. As his Jesus cannot be tempted, so John's Christ undergoes no agony before his arrest in the garden of Gethsemane. Unfailingly poised and confident, Jesus experiences his painful death as a glorification, his raising on the cross symbolizing his imminent ascension to heaven. Instead of Mark's cry of despair, in John, Jesus dies with a declaration that he has "accomplished" his life's purpose (19:30).

12. Finally, it must be emphasized that John's many differences from the Synoptics are not simply the result of the author's trying to "fill in" the gaps in his predecessors' Gospels. By carefully examining John's account, we see that he does not write to supplement earlier narratives about Jesus; rather, both his omissions and his inclusions are determined almost exclusively by

the writer's special theological convictions (20:30–31; 21:25). From his opening hymn praising the eternal Word to Jesus' promised reascension to heaven, every part of the Gospel is calculated to illustrate Jesus' glory as God's fullest revelation of his own ineffable Being.

Differences in the Chronology and Order of Events

Although John's essential story resembles the Synoptic version of Jesus' life—a public ministry featuring healings and other miracles followed by official rejection, arrest, crucifixion, and resurrection—the Fourth Gospel presents important differences in the chronology and order of events. Significant ways in which John's narrative sequence differs from the Synoptic order include the following:

1. The Synoptics show Jesus working mainly in Galilee and coming south to Judea only during his last days. In contrast, John has Jesus traveling back and forth between Galilee and Jerusalem throughout the duration of his ministry.

2. The Synoptics place Jesus' assault on the Temple at the end of his career, making it the incident that consolidates official hostility toward him; John sets it at the beginning (2:13–21).

3. The Synoptics agree that Jesus began his mission after John the Baptist's imprisonment, but John states that their missions overlapped (3:22–4:3).

4. The earlier Gospels mention only one Passover and imply that Jesus' career lasted only about a year; John refers to three Passovers (2:13; 6:4; 11:55), thus giving the ministry a duration of about three years.

5. Unlike the Synoptics, which present the Last Supper as a Passover celebration, John states that Jesus' final meal with the disciples occurred the evening before Passover and that the Crucifixion took place on Nisan 14, the day of preparation when paschal lambs were

being sacrificed (13:1, 29; 18:28; 19:14). Many historians believe that John's chronology is the more accurate, for it is improbable that Jesus' arrest, trial, and execution took place on Nisan 15, the most sacred time of the Passover observance.

Scholars also note, however, that John's probable reason for his dating of the Crucifixion is more theological than historical. Because he identifies Jesus as the "Lamb of God" at the beginning of his Gospel (1:29), it is thematically appropriate for John to coordinate the time of Jesus' death with the ritual slaying of the paschal lambs (prescribed in Exod. 12:3–10; cf. Isa. 53:7–12).

John's Purpose and Method

As an author, John states that his goal is to elicit belief in his community's distinctively **high Christology,** an emphasis on Jesus' divinity (17:3–5; 20:30–31), but other purposes also can be inferred from his text. Like the other Evangelists, John writes partly to defend his community against hostile criticism, particularly from Jewish leaders. Unlike the Synoptic authors, however, John does not generally differentiate among his Jewish opponents; instead of identifying them as scribes, Pharisees, or Sadducees, he generally lumps them all together simply as "the Jews"—as if his fellow countrymen belonged to a group from which he is entirely disassociated. Scholars believe that John's blanket condemnation of "the Jews" echoes the bitterness that developed in the decades following 70 CE, when the church and the synagogue became increasingly divided. Reflecting a social situation comparable to that in Matthew's Gospel, John indicates that his group—perhaps because of their increasingly vocal claims that Jesus is equal to God—has been banished from fellowship in the synagogue. The expulsion was evidently traumatic for John, who responds by retrojecting the event back to the time of Jesus and insisting that his group is spiritually superior to their synagogue critics

(cf. John 3:9–11 and 9:13–35). Nonetheless, the Evangelist states that "salvation comes" "from the Jews" (4:22).

The Work of the Paraclete: Jesus and Believers Are "One"

John's Double Vision Many commentators have noted that John's Gospel portrays Jesus not as a figure of the recent historical past, but as an immortal being who still inhabits the author's community. In John's narrative, Jesus' ministry and the similar activities of his later followers—the Johannine "brotherhood"—merge into an almost seamless whole. To articulate his vision that Christ and the members of his own group are "one" (17:12), John employs a double vision, creating in his Gospel a two-level drama in which Jesus of the past and believers of the present perform the same Spirit-directed work.

John is able to blend past and present in Jesus' biography through the operation of the Paraclete, a distinctively Johannine concept introduced in Jesus' farewell speeches at the Last Supper (chs. 14–17). This long section presents Jesus explaining precisely why he must leave his disciples on earth while he dies and ascends to heaven. His death is not a permanent loss, for he returns to the Father only in order to empower his disciples with the Paraclete, the Holy Spirit, which acts as his invisible self among them (14:12–26). Functioning as a manifestation of the post resurrection Jesus, the Paraclete guides the Johannine community to interpret Jesus' teachings as no other group could: "It will teach you everything, and will call to mind all that I have told you" (16:26). This Spirit, Jesus' own double, allows the author to portray Christ in his full theological splendor. It also enables John's group not only to continue Jesus' miraculous works, but even to surpass his deeds. He who has faith, Jesus promises, "will do what I am doing; and he will do greater things still because I am going to the Father. Indeed, anything you ask in my name I will do" (14:12–14). In this vow—found only in

John—the writer finds his key to understanding the continuity between the Master and his later disciples.

John's singular method of telling Jesus' story becomes especially clear in chapter 9. In narrating Jesus' restoration of sight to a man born blind, John skillfully melds traditions of Jesus' healing miracles with the works that members of his community currently perform. John's narrative can equate the two parties—Jesus and his later disciples—because the same Paraclete operates through both. An awareness of John's method, conflating past and present, will help readers understand the historical forces at work in this episode. After Jesus cures the man's lifelong blindness, a series of confrontations and arguments ensue between the man, his parents, and officials of the local synagogue. The Jewish officials' interrogation of the man replicates circumstances prevailing not in Jesus' day but in the writer's own time. Explicit references to the expulsion of Jesus' followers from the synagogue (9:22, 34)—a process that began well after Jesus' death, during the last decades of the first century CE—are sure indicators of John's two-level approach.

John employs a comparable blending of past and present in Jesus' dialogue with the Pharisee Nicodemus (3:1–21). Jesus' pretended astonishment that Nicodemus—depicted as one of Israel's most famous teachers—does not understand or experience the power of the Holy Spirit motivating the author's community could not have taken place in Jesus' lifetime. But it accords well with what we know of much later debates between Jewish authorities and the author's group, which proclaimed the Paraclete's role in their lives. Using the first-person plural "we" to signify the whole believing community, John affirms that his brotherhood intimately knows the Spirit's creative force, whereas "you" (the unbelievers) stubbornly refuse to credit the Johannine testimony (3:9–11). Readers will also note that in this dialogue Jesus speaks as if he has already returned to heaven (3:13), another indicator

that this passage reflects a perspective that developed long after the incident supposedly took place.

Apparent Stages in the Composition of John

Evidence of Editing In his extended meditations on Jesus' cosmic stature and their Lord's ongoing relationship with the Johannine group, the author/redactor apparently modified his Gospel text from time to time, not always smoothing over his editorial changes. Recognized "seams" in John's narrative include passages in chapter 8, where Jesus first addresses "Jews who had believed him" (8:31) but then suddenly accuses his supposedly friendly audience of planning to "kill [him]" (8:37). In chapter 11, the narrator identifies Mary, the sister of Martha and Lazarus, as "the woman who anointed the Lord with ointment" (11:2), but doesn't actually show her performing this action until the next chapter (12:2–8).

The most obvious disconnections appear during Jesus' farewell speeches at the Last Supper. Partway through the present form of the discourse, Jesus states that he will "not talk much longer with you [the disciples]" and then orders them to stand "up" and "go forward," as if he has finished his conversation with them (14:31). Yet his farewell oration continues for another three chapters (15:1–17:26). Only in John 18 does Jesus actually leave the room and "cross the Kedron ravine" to the garden of Gethsemane (18:1).

The editorial expansions of Jesus' last discourse result in further disjunctions. When Jesus first mentions his imminent departure (for heaven), Peter asks where he is going (13:33–36), a question that Thomas later repeats (14:5). Yet in John 16, Jesus states that "None of you asks me 'Where are you going?'" (16:5). Thus Jesus seems to have forgotten the disciples' earlier inquiries. For the Johannine Evangelist, however, the material in these added chapters—featuring the activity of the Paraclete, the necessity of communal love, and the "oneness" of Jesus and his friends—was too significant to leave out. Guided by the Paraclete, John was moved to include these ongoing communications from the risen Jesus as if his Lord had delivered them on the night before his death.

Relation to Gnostic Ideas In addition to refuting Jewish critics offended by the Johannine community's proclamation of Jesus' divinity (viewed as an attack on Jewish monotheism) and its claim to spiritual superiority, John appears to defend his view of Jesus' nature against incipient Gnostic influences. **Gnosticism** was a complex religious/philosophical movement that developed into Christianity's first major challenge to what later became official church teaching. Whereas the church eventually espoused a doctrine that declared Jesus both fully human and fully divine, many Gnostics tended to focus on Jesus as pure spirit, free of human weakness (see Box 18.3). Although Gnosticism took many forms, it typically held a dualistic view of the cosmos. This dualism saw the universe as two mutually exclusive realms: The invisible world of spirit is eternal, pure, and good, whereas the physical world is inherently evil, the creation of a deeply flawed deity, whom some Gnostics identified with Yahweh. According to Gnostic belief, human beings gain salvation only through special knowledge (*gnosis*), imparted to a chosen elite through communion with spiritual beings. A divine redeemer (presumably Christ) descends from the spirit realm to transmit saving knowledge to persons whose souls are sufficiently disciplined to escape the body's earthly desires. Transcending the material world's false reality, the soul can then perceive the eternal truths of the spirit world.

A sometimes baffling mixture of elements from Greek philosophies and mystery cults, as well as aspects of Judaism and Christianity, Gnosticism embraced a variety of ideas about Christ. One branch of Gnosticism, called **Docetism** (a name taken from the Greek verb "to seem"), argued that Christ, being good, could not also be human; he only *seemed* to have a physical body. The Docetists contended that, as God's true Son, Christ was wholly spiritual, ascending to heaven while leaving another's body on the cross (see discussion of the Johannine Letters in Chapter 18).

Although he sometimes uses Gnostic terms, John—despite his doctrine of Jesus' heavenly origins and divinity—avoids Gnosticism's extremism by insisting on Jesus' physical humanity (1:14). Even after the Resurrection, Jesus displays fleshly wounds and consumes ordinary food (20:24–29; 21:9–15). To show that Jesus was a mortal man who truly died, John eliminates from his Passion story Mark's tradition that Simon of Cyrene carried Jesus' cross (lest the reader think that Simon might have been substituted for Jesus at the Crucifixion). John also adds an incident in which a Roman soldier pierces Jesus' side with a spear, confirming his physical vulnerability and mortality (19:34–37).

Despite its conviction that the divine Logos "became flesh" (1:14), John's Gospel was popular in many Gnostic circles (which may account for its relatively slow acceptance by the church at large). Besides the metaphysical concepts of Christ's preexistence and his inherent divinity, John contains other statements that accord with Gnostic ideas. To *know* the "true God" and his Son is to gain "eternal life" (17:3); the assertion that "the spirit alone gives life; the flesh is of no avail" (6:63); and the teaching that only spiritual rebirth can grant immortality—all found only in John—are classic Gnostic beliefs. Considering John's emphasis on Jesus' spiritual invincibility and God-like stature, it is not surprising that the first commentaries written on John were by Gnostic Christians—or that some church leaders suspected that the author himself was a Gnostic!

Organization of John's Gospel

John's Gospel is framed by a prologue (1:1–51) and an epilogue (21:1–25). The main narrative (chs. 2–20) divides naturally into two long sections: an account of Jesus' miracles and public teachings (chs. 2–11) and an extended Passion story focusing on Jesus' private speeches to the disciples (chs. 12–20). Because John regards Jesus' miracles as "signs"—direct evidence of his hero's supernatural power—the first section is commonly known as the **Book of Signs.** Many scholars believe that the author uses a previously compiled collection of Jesus' miraculous works as a primary source (see below). Because it presents Christ's death as a "glorious" fulfillment of the divine will, some commentators call the second part the **Book of Glory.**

The Gospel can be outlined as follows:

1. Prologue: hymn to the Logos; testimony of the Baptist; call of the disciples (1:1–51)
2. The Book of Signs (2:1–11:57)
   a. The miracle at Cana
   b. The cleansing of the Temple
   c. The dialogue with Nicodemus on spiritual rebirth
   d. The conversation with the Samaritan woman
   e. Five more miraculous signs in Jerusalem and Galilee; Jesus' discourses witnessing to his divine nature
   f. The resuscitation of Lazarus (the seventh sign)
3. The Book of Glory (12:1–20:31)
   a. The plot against Jesus
   b. The Last Supper and farewell discourses
   c. The Passion story
   d. The empty tomb and post resurrection appearances to Mary Magdalene, Peter, and the Beloved Disciple
4. Epilogue: post resurrection appearances in Galilee; parting words to Peter and the Beloved Disciple (21:1–25)

Hymn to the Word (Logos)

John's opening hymn to the Word introduces several concepts vital to his portrait of Christ. The phrase "when all things began" recalls the Genesis creation account when God's word of command—"Let there be light"—illuminated a previously dark universe. In John's view, the prehuman Christ is the creative Word (divine Wisdom, cosmic Reason) whom God uses to bring heaven and earth into existence. "With God at the beginning," the Word is an integral part of the Supreme Being—"what God was, the Word was" (1:1–5).

John's supreme irony is that the very world that the Word created rejects him, preferring spiritual "darkness" to the "light" he imparts. Nonetheless, the Word "became flesh"—the man Jesus—and temporarily lived among humans, allowing them to witness his "glory, such glory as befits the Father's only Son" (1:10–14).

Greek and Jewish Background

As noted previously, *Logos* (Word) is a Greek philosophical term, but John blends it with a parallel Hebrew tradition about divine Wisdom that existed before the world began. According to the Book of Proverbs (8:22–31), Wisdom (depicted as a gracious young woman) was Yahweh's companion when he created the universe, transforming the original dark **chaos** into a realm of order and light. As Yahweh's darling, she not only was his intimate helper in the creative process but also became God's channel of communication with humanity. As Israel's wisdom tradition developed in Hellenistic times, Wisdom was seen as both Yahweh's agent of creation and the being who reveals the divine mind to the faithful (Ecclus. 24; Wisd. of Sol. 6:12–9:18).

In the Greek philosophical tradition, Logos is also a divine concept, the principle of cosmic Reason that gives order and coherence to the otherwise chaotic world, making it accessible to human intellect. The Logos concept had circulated among Greek thinkers since the time of the philosopher Heraclitus (born c. 540 BCE). In John's day, *Logos* was a popular Stoic term, commonly viewed as synonymous with the divine intelligence that created and sustained the universe.

These analogous Greek and Hebrew ideas converge in the writings of **Philo Judaeus,** a Hellenistic-Jewish scholar living in Alexandria during the first century CE. A pious Jew profoundly influenced by Greek rationality, Philo attempted to reconcile Hellenistic logic with the revelation contained in the Hebrew Bible. Philo used the Hebrew concept of Wisdom as the creative intermediary between the transcendent Creator and the material creation. However, he employed the

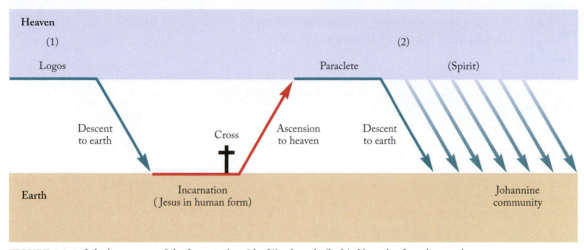

FIGURE 10.1 John's concept of the Incarnation (the Word made flesh). Note that Jesus' ascension to heaven (return to his place of spiritual origin) is followed by a descent of the Paraclete, Jesus' Spirit—an invisible surrogate that inspires the Johannine brotherhood. Whereas Jesus' human presence on earth was brief, John implies that the Paraclete abides permanently within the believing community.

Greek term *Logos* to designate Wisdom's role and function. (Philo may have preferred *Logos* because it is masculine in Greek, whereas Wisdom [*Sophia*] is feminine.) Philo's interpretation can be illustrated by an allegorical reading of Genesis 1, in which God's first act is to speak—to create the Word (Logos)—by which power the **cosmos** is born.

In identifying the prehuman Christ with Philo's Logos, John equates Jesus with the loftiest philosophical ideal of his age. His Christ is thus superior to every other heavenly or earthly being, all of whom owe their creation to him. John's Jesus not only speaks the word of God but is the Word incarnate. From the author's perspective, Jesus' human career is merely a brief interlude, a temporary descent to earth preceded and followed by eternal life above (3:13). (Compare John's Logos doctrine with similar ideas discussed in Phil. 2 and Col. 1–2; see also Figure 10.1.)

Jesus and Divine Wisdom

After the prologue, John does not again refer explicitly to Jesus as the Word. He does, however, repeatedly link his hero to the concept of **divine Wisdom,** a personification of God's creative

intelligence (see Box 10.3). In the Hebrew Bible, Wisdom is both the means by which God creates and the channel through whom he communicates to humankind. Hebrew Bible writers characteristically picture Wisdom speaking in the first person, using the phrase "I am" and then defining her activities as God's agent. John casts many of Jesus' speeches in exactly the same form, beginning with a declaration "I am" and then typically equating himself with a term of great religious significance. Wisdom's speeches clearly anticipate John's concept of Jesus' cosmic stature:

> The Lord created me the beginning of his
> works,
> before all else that he made, long ago.
> Alone, I was fashioned in times long past,
> at the beginning, long before earth itself.
> (Prov. 8:22–23)

Identifying Wisdom with God's verbal command to create light (Gen. 1:3), the author of Ecclesiasticus represents her as saying:

> I am the word which was spoken by the
> Most High; . . .
> Before time began he created me,
> and I shall remain for ever. . . .
> (Ecclus. 24:3, 9)

BOX 10.3 Wisdom Speeches in the Hebrew Bible and the Apocrypha as Models for the Johannine Jesus

Wisdom searches the streets for those willing to
   receive her:
Hear how Wisdom lifts her voice
and Understanding cries out.
She stands at the cross-roads, . . .
beside the gate, at the entrance to the city. . . .
"Men, it is to you I call,
I appeal to every man: . . .
Listen! For I will speak clearly,
you will have plain speech from me;
for I speak nothing but the truth. . . .
I am Wisdom, I bestow shrewdness
and show the way to knowledge and prudence. . . .

I have force, I also have ability;
understanding and power are mine.
Through me kings are sovereign
and governors make just laws . . .
from me all rulers on earth derive their nobility.
Those who love me I love,
and those who search for me find me.

. . .

The Lord created me the beginning of his works,
before all else that he made, long ago.
Alone, I was fashioned in times long past,
at the beginning, long before earth itself.
When there was yet no ocean I was born. . . .
When he set the heavens in their place I was there,
when he girdled the ocean with the horizon,
when he fixed the canopy of clouds overhead
and set the springs of ocean firm in their place. . . .
Then I was at his side each day, his darling and delight,
playing in his presence continually,
playing on the earth, when he had finished it,
while my delight was in mankind. . . .
Happy is the man who keeps to my ways,
happy the man who listens to me, . . .
for he who finds me finds life
and wins favor from [Yahweh],
while he who finds me not, hurts himself
and all who hate me are in love with death."

(Prov. 8:1–7, 12–17, 22–36)

Hear the praise of Wisdom from her own mouth, . . .
in the presence of the heavenly host:

"I am the word [Logos] which was spoken by the
   Most High:
it was I who covered the earth like a mist.
My dwelling-place was in high heaven;
my throne was in a pillar of cloud. . . ."
Then the Creator decreed where I should dwell.
He said, "Make your home in Jacob;
find your heritage in Israel." . . .
"Before time began he created me,
and I shall remain for ever. . . .
I took root among the people whom the Lord had
   honoured
by choosing to be his special possession. . . .
Come to me, you who desire me,
and eat your fill of my fruit. . . .
Whoever feeds on me will be hungry for more,
and whoever drinks from me will thirst for more."

(Ecclus. 24:1–12, 18–21)

For in wisdom there is a spirit intelligent and holy,
unique in its kind, yet made up of many parts, subtle,
free-moving, lucid, spotless, clear, invulnerable,
loving what is good, . . . kindly towards men, . . . all-
powerful, all-surveying, and permeating all intelligent,
pure, and delicate spirits. . . . She is the brightness
that streams from everlasting light, the flawless mirror
of the active power of God and the image of his goodness. She is one, yet can do everything; herself unchanging, she makes all things new, age after age she
enters into holy souls, and makes them God's friends
and prophets, for nothing is more acceptable to God
but the man who makes his home with wisdom.

She is initiated into the knowledge that belongs
to God and she decides for him what he shall do. . . .
Through her I shall have immortality, and shall
leave an undying memory to those who come after
me. I shall rule over my peoples, and nations will
become my subjects.

Send her forth from the holy heavens, and from
thy glorious throne bid her come down, so that she
may labour at my side and I may learn what pleases
thee. For she knows and understands all things, and
will guide me presently in all I do, and guard me in
her glory. So shall my life's work be acceptable, and
I shall judge thy people justly, and be worthy of my
father's throne.

(Wisd. of Sol. 7:22–28; 8:4, 13; 9:10–12)

BOX 10.4 Isis and the "I Am" Statements in John

Yahweh's declaration of being as the eternal "I AM" in Exodus 3 and Lady Wisdom's assertion of her cosmic role in Proverbs 8 and the deuterocanonical books of Wisdom and Ecclesiasticus provide a biblical model for John's "I am" speeches. In Hellenistic culture, the closest parallel to these Johannine statements occurs in hymns honoring Isis, an Egyptian mother goddess who, in John's time, was recognized as a universal deity throughout the Greco-Roman world. One text from the first or second century CE pictures **Isis** asserting her divine preeminence:

I am Isis, the mistress of every land . . .
I gave and ordained laws for men, which no one is
    able to change . . .
I am she who findeth fruit for men . . .

I divided the earth from the heaven.
I showed the paths of the stars,
I ordered the course of the sun and the moon . . .
I made strong the right . . .
I broke down the governments of tyrants.
I made an end to murders . . .
I ordained that the true should be thought
    good . . .
With me the right prevails. . . .

Although the exact form of the Johannine declarations "I am the . . ." does not occur in this hymn, it does appear in another fragmentary Isis text, where she affirms her eternity: "I am the deity that had no beginning . . . I am the truth, I am the creator and the destroyer." (Compare John 14:6, where Jesus says, "I am the way, the truth, and the life.")

Sent by God to live among his people, Israel, Wisdom invites all to seek her favor:

Come to me, you who desire me,
and eat your fill of my fruit; . . .
Whoever feeds on me will be hungry for more,
and whoever drinks from me will thirst for
    more.
(Ecclus. 24:19, 21–22;)

Whereas Wisdom stimulates a thirst for knowledge, the Johannine Jesus fully satisfies it:

. . . whoever drinks the water that I shall
give him will never suffer thirst any more.
The water that I shall give him will be an inner spring always welling up for eternal life.
(John 4:14)

Jesus and Yahweh

Jesus' "I Am" Pronouncements Besides associating Jesus with the Hebrew principle of eternal Wisdom, John's "I am" speeches also express an important aspect of his Christology. They echo Yahweh's declaration of being to Moses at the burning bush (Exod. 3:14), in which God reveals his sacred personal name. In the Hebrew Bible, only Yahweh speaks of himself (the "I AM") in this manner. Hence, Jesus' reiterated "I am . . . the bread of life" (6:35), "the good shepherd" (10:11), "the resurrection and the life" (11:25), or "the way," "the truth," and "the life" (14:6) express his unity with God, the eternal "I AM" (see Box 10.4).

John attributes much of "the Jews'" hostility toward Jesus to their reaction against his apparent claims to divinity. When Jesus refers publicly to his prehuman existence, declaring that "before Abraham was born, I am," his outraged audience in the Temple attempts to stone him for blasphemy (8:56–59). Most scholars doubt that Jesus really made such assertions. In John's double-vision approach, the attempted stoning represents Jewish leaders' response to the preaching of John's group, which made extraordinary claims about Jesus' divine nature.

Role of the Baptist

Readers will notice that John repeatedly interrupts his Logos hymn to compare the Baptist unfavorably to Jesus. Insisting on the Baptist's inferiority, the author has him bear witness against himself: He is neither a prophet nor the Elijah figure, but only "a voice" whose sole function is to announce Jesus. Thus, the Baptist bears witness to seeing the Holy Spirit descend upon Jesus, a phenomenon that Mark reports as Jesus' inward or private experience of his calling (Mark 1:10–11) (see Box 8.6).

Contrary to the Markan tradition of a hidden Messiah whose identity is only gradually revealed, John has the Baptist immediately hail Jesus as the "Lamb of God . . . who takes away the sin of the world." In John, Jesus is recognized as "God's Chosen One" right from the start (1:6–9, 19–36).

 ## The Book of Signs

John structures his account of Jesus' public ministry around seven signs—miracles that illustrate Jesus' supernatural power—to demonstrate his hero's divinity. The Johannine emphasis on signs contrasts emphatically with the Markan Jesus' categorical refusal to give *any* miraculous proof of his identity: "no sign shall be given to this generation" (Mark 8:11–12; cf. Matt. 12:38–40).

Many scholars believe that in composing his narrative the Johannine author used an older document, known as the Signs Gospel. According to this theory, the **Signs Gospel** was a straightforward narrative that depicted Jesus' performing (probably seven) wondrous deeds calculated to show that he was the Messiah (see Box 10.5). Some scholars think that the Signs Gospel was the first written account of Jesus' public ministry, composed about the same time as Q, the similarly hypothetical collection of Jesus' sayings. Presumably compiled by a group of Jewish Christians about 50–60 CE, it served as the narrative framework for the present Gospel of John. Advocates of this theory believe that the Johannine author merely inserted his elaborate dialogues and lengthy speeches into the Signs Gospel, usually without deleting or changing much of the original wording. Scholars

therefore were able to attempt a reconstruction of the text of the earlier Gospel that was John's principal source. Although the Signs Gospel has not survived as an independent account, it seems to be preserved embedded in the canonical Gospel of John (see R. T. Fortna in "Recommended Reading").

The Miracle at Cana

The first Johannine sign occurs at the Galilean town of Cana (not mentioned in the Synoptics), where Jesus, attending a wedding with his disciples and his mother, changes water into wine. Although the transformation of water into wine has no parallel in any other Gospel, the miracle—reminiscent of festivals honoring Dionysus, the Greco-Roman god of wine—is consistent with Synoptic traditions that depict Jesus' propensity toward eating and drinking with all kinds of people (Luke 7:33–35, etc.). John's narrative of the Cana event similarly highlights Jesus' paradoxical combination of ethical leadership with almost outrageous behavior, acting in a way that seems to invite excess. When informed that the host's supply of wine has run out, indicating that the wedding guests are probably already intoxicated, Jesus adds to the party's merriment by providing an additional 180 gallons of a vintage superior to that which the guests have already consumed. In John's view, Jesus' offering the means for celebrants to continue imbibing "good wine" reveals "his glory" and causes the disciples to "believe in him" (2:11), as if confirming his qualifications to host the promised messianic banquet. Presented as Jesus' initial "sign" that God is present in his actions, this joyous celebration of life, symbolized not only by the marriage ceremony but also by the shared enjoyment of a divinely bestowed beverage, foreshadows a more solemn celebration described at the end of John's narrative—that of Jesus' "glorious" death on the cross. Using the images of water and wine—and the blood these liquids symbolize—the author thematically links the beginning of Jesus' ministry at Cana with its culmination at Golgotha, where a Roman soldier

BOX 10.5 The Signs Gospel

Many scholars believe that the author of John's Gospel used as one of his sources an earlier narrative that emphasized Jesus' miracles. Because John's Gospel presents these miracles as "signs" revealing Jesus' glory, scholars have labeled this hypothetical source the Signs Gospel, claiming that it would have contained the following miraculous deeds (listed here in the order found in the Gospel of John):

1. Turning water into wine at Cana (in Galilee, 2:1–11)
2. Healing an official's son (in Galilee, 2:12a; 4:46b–54)

3. Healing a crippled man (in Jerusalem, 5:2–9)
4. Feeding 5,000 people (in Galilee, 6:1–15)
5. Walking on water (in Galilee, 6:16–25)
6. Restoring sight to a blind man (in Jerusalem, 9:1–8)
7. Raising Lazarus from the dead (near Jerusalem, 11:1–45)

Some scholars also think that the disciples' huge catch of fish (21:1–14) was originally a Galilean miracle that the Gospel's final editor incorporated into his appended account of Jesus' post resurrection appearances.

---

thrusts his spear into Jesus' body, releasing a flow of "blood and water" (19:34). Underscoring the connection between these two framing incidents, John has Jesus' mother present at both Cana and the Crucifixion, the only two occasions on which she appears in his Gospel (cf. 2:1–11; 19:25–27).

Assault on the Temple

Reversing the Synoptic order, John shows Jesus driving moneychangers from the Temple during a Passover at the outset of his ministry. For John, the episode's significance is Jesus' superiority to the Jerusalem sanctuary. The Temple is no longer sacred because the Holy Spirit now dwells in Jesus' person rather than in the shrine King Herod constructed. Jesus' physical body may be destroyed, but unlike the Herodian edifice, he will rise again as proof that God's Spirit imbues him (2:13–25).

Dialogue with Nicodemus

Jesus' conversation with **Nicodemus,** a Pharisee and member of the Jewish Council (Sanhedrin), typifies John's method of presenting Jesus' teaching (3:1–21). In most of the Johannine dialogues, Jesus uses a figure of speech or metaphor that the person with whom he is speaking almost comically misinterprets, usually taking Jesus' words literally. John then has Jesus explain his figurative meaning, commonly launching a long monologue in which Jesus discourses on his metaphysical nature and unique relationship with the Father.

Thus, when Jesus remarks that unless one is "born over again"—or, in an alternative translation, "born from above"—he cannot "see the kingdom of God," Nicodemus mistakenly thinks he refers to reemerging from the womb. Jesus then explains that he means rebirth "from water and spirit," referring to the spiritual renewal that accompanies Christian baptism. Found only in John, this doctrine of becoming "born again" resembles beliefs characteristic of Gnosticism and Greek mystery religions. In both cults, converts undergo initiation rites, commonly involving purification by water, to achieve the soul's new birth on a higher plane of existence, leading eventually to immortality. In the case of being "born from above," initiates experience the Gnostic truth that their souls (or true selves) are of heavenly origin and hence intrinsically divine and eternal.

Perhaps aware of non-Christian parallels to this teaching, the author stresses that Jesus is uniquely qualified to reveal spiritual truths. He is intimately acquainted with the unseen world because heaven is his natural environment, the home to which he will return when "lifted up [on the cross]" (3:12–15).

In perhaps the most famous passage of the New Testament, Jesus states his purpose in coming to earth. God so intensely loves the world that he sends his Son, not to condemn it, but to save it, awakening in humanity a faith that gives "eternal life." Believers pass the test for eternal life through their attraction to Jesus' "light," while others judge themselves by preferring the world's "darkness" (3:16–21). Here, John's attitude toward the world is positive, although elsewhere he expresses an ambiguous attitude toward its mixed potential for good and evil. Representing Jesus' ministry and crucifixion as the world's time of judgment (12:31), he declares that Christians are "strangers in the world" (17:16).

Despite acknowledging the world's capacity to believe (17:21, 23), the author shows Jesus telling Pontius Pilate that his "kingdom does not belong to this world"—at least not the kind of system that Pilate and the Roman Empire represent (18:36).

Conversation with the Samaritan Woman

Luke emphasizes Jesus' positive relationships with women, who are numbered among his most faithful disciples. John further explores Jesus' characteristic openness to women, with whom he converses freely, teaching them on the same level as his male followers. As in Luke, John shows Jesus ignoring the rigid social conventions that segregate the sexes, even to the point of speaking intimately with prostitutes and others of questionable reputation.

Astonishing the disciples with his violation of the social code (4:27), Jesus publicly discusses fine points of theology with a Samaritan woman who gives him water to drink at Jacob's well. Recalling the deep hostility then existing between Jews and Samaritans, we understand the woman's surprise at Jesus' willingness to associate with her (see Chapter 3 for a description of the Samaritans and Chapter 9 for Luke's parable of the "good Samaritan," a phrase most Jews would regard as a contradiction in terms). She assumes that he is a prophet and seizes the opportunity to learn from him (see Figure 10.2).

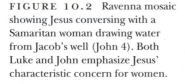

FIGURE 10.2 Ravenna mosaic showing Jesus conversing with a Samaritan woman drawing water from Jacob's well (John 4). Both Luke and John emphasize Jesus' characteristic concern for women.

As Jesus later instructs Martha in the mysteries of the Resurrection (11:17–27), so he reveals to the Samaritan woman that he is the "living water" that satisfies humanity's spiritual thirst. Disclosing that neither the Jerusalem Temple nor the Samaritans' rival shrine at Mount Gerizim is the only right place to worship, Jesus teaches her that "spirit and truth" transcend the claims of any earthly sanctuary.

John uses this episode to illustrate several provocative ideas. Although the woman's situation is ambiguous (she has had five husbands and now lives with a man to whom she is not married), Jesus selects her to fill an important role. She is not only the first non-Jew to whom he reveals that he is the Christ (4:25–26) but also the means by which "many Samaritans" become believers (4:39). The woman's rush to inform her fellow villagers about Jesus anticipates Mary Magdalene's later role as prophet to the male disciples when she brings the news that their crucified Lord still lives (20:1–2, 10–18) (see Box 10.6).

The Woman Taken in Adultery

Because it does not appear in the oldest New Testament manuscripts, editors of the New English Bible relegate the story of the adulterous woman (8:1–11) to an appendix following chapter 21. In some manuscripts, the incident shows up in Luke, where it well suits the Lukan theme of forgiveness. The episode in which Pharisees demand that Jesus judge a woman "caught in the very act" of illicit sex was apparently a well-known tradition that had difficulty finding a home in the canonical Gospels, perhaps because many early Christians found it shocking.

Asked to endorse the Torah rule that prescribed death by stoning for adulterers (Lev. 20:10; Deut. 22:20–21), Jesus turns the responsibility for deciding the woman's fate back on her accusers. Only the person who is "faultless" (without sin) is qualified to enforce the legal penalty. Forcing those who would judge her to examine their own consciences, Jesus finds that the assembled crowd melts away, leaving him alone with the accused. He neither condemns nor imposes penance on the woman, merely instructing her not to "sin again." Neither blamed nor lectured, she is left to ponder the meaning of her rescue. Whether this episode belongs in John or not, it is consistent with Jesus' nonjudgmental attitude toward individual "sinners" in all four Gospels.

Further Signs and Miracles

Jesus' second sign is his curing a nobleman's dying son in Cana (4:46–54). His third is his healing a crippled man at the Sheep Pool in Jerusalem, a controversial act because it occurs on the Sabbath (5:1–15; see Figure 10.3). Criticism directed at Jesus' alleged Sabbath breaking provides the opportunity for an extended discourse on his special relation to the Father. In John's view, God's work (sustaining the universe) continues unceasingly and provides a model that the Son imitates in ministering to God's human creation (5:16–17).

When accused of claiming "equality with God," Jesus clarifies the nature of his authority. The Son initiates "nothing" on his own; he can only imitate the Father. As God creates life, so the Son grants "eternal life" to those trusting him. In Jesus' ministry, the long-hoped-for resurrection to immortality is already a reality (5:18–26). Emphasizing his dependence on the Father who sent him, Jesus states that he acts as he is told, dutifully obeying a superior intelligence (5:30). Those who reject him also misread the Hebrew Bible that anticipated God's ministry through him. If his critics really understood the Torah (including the Sabbath's true meaning), they would believe him (5:31–47).

John's presentation of the next two signs parallels the Synoptic tradition, but they are followed by a typically Johannine speech in which the author significantly reinterprets their meaning. The miraculous feeding of 5,000 people (the fourth sign) is the only miracle that appears in all four Gospels (6:1–12; Mark 6:30–44; Matt. 14:13–21; Luke 9:10–17). As in Mark, the miracle is immediately followed by Jesus' walking on water (John's fifth sign) (6:16–21; Mark 6:47–51).

BOX 10.6 The Role of Women in John's Gospel

Most striking in John's Gospel is the way he employs women characters to advance crucial theological ideas. In Jesus' conversation with a Samaritan woman—the longest dialogue between Jesus and a single individual in any canonical Gospel (4:7–26)—the Evangelist shows Jesus relating to the woman at Jacob's well on both a religious and a personal level. When Jesus mentions that she has had five husbands and is not married to her present male companion, he does not necessarily imply that the woman has misbehaved; she may have been widowed repeatedly or legally divorced through no fault of her own. After perceiving that Jesus is an authentic "prophet," the woman asks about the correct place to worship God, a major controversy then dividing Jews and Samaritans. Her question elicits Jesus' reply that geographical location is no longer significant, for now people "must worship in spirit and in truth," a spiritualized form of honoring God that can be accomplished anywhere. The woman's eager response is to affirm the Messiah's future coming and his promised revelation of "everything," which in turn is the catalyst for Jesus' statement that he is the Christ, the Johannine account's first such admission to a non-Jew.

Immediately, the woman abandons her waterjar and dashes back to town, her testimony inspiring neighbors to invite Jesus to stay with them. As a result of the woman's speech, many Samaritans listen to Jesus and become believers, declaring him "the Savior of the world." Although most villagers believe because of their direct experience of Jesus, it is the woman's initial perception of Jesus' identity that makes possible their faith (4:3–42).

In the story of Lazarus, the Evangelist uses Jesus' conversations with Lazarus's sister Martha to move from a general expectation that resurrection will occur "on the last day" to a realization that in Jesus' presence people rise from the dead *now*. When

Martha learns that Jesus is "on his way" to their town of Bethany, she seizes the initiative by traveling alone to meet him. Still on the road to Bethany, Jesus and Martha discuss the concept of resurrection, leading to his climactic revelation: "I am the resurrection and I am life . . . no one who is alive and has faith shall ever die." Even before the resuscitation of her brother, Martha professes her absolute trust in Jesus, whom she recognizes as "the Son of God" (11:20–27). Even so, the practical Martha later reminds Jesus that if he removes the stone blocking the entrance to Lazarus's tomb, "there will be a stench" from her brother's decaying corpse (11:38–41).

At a dinner party celebrating Lazarus's return to life, his sister Mary demonstrates a faith that equals that of Martha when she anoints Jesus' feet with an expensive perfume, symbolically preparing him for burial and, with the perfume's fragrance filling her house, banishing memories of physical decay. She alone of Jesus' friends seems to understand the fact of his imminent death. When she tenderly dries Jesus' feet "with her hair," Mary's humility anticipates Jesus' later action in washing and drying the disciples' feet at the Last Supper (12:1–8; cf. 13:3–17).

In the Johannine vision, women continue to play indispensable roles to the Gospel's conclusion. As if to emphasize her importance as the first witness of Jesus' resurrection, John shows Mary Magdalene acting alone when she visits Jesus' tomb the first Easter morning. (The Synoptic tradition has Mary accompanied by other Galilean women.) After informing Peter and the Beloved Disciple that Jesus' tomb is empty, she remains alone at the crypt, conversing first with angels and then with the risen Jesus, who instructs her to convey his message to the disciples. Mary Magdalene thus precedes the male disciples in proclaiming that Christ is risen, an appointed prophet who bears the original "good news" to Peter and the others (20:1–16).

FIGURE 10.3 Excavations at the Sheep Pool in Jerusalem. John's Gospel mentions two bathing pools, sites that pilgrims to Jerusalem possibly used for ritual washing before they approached the Temple precincts. The Sheep Pool, where Jesus healed a paralyzed man (John 5:2–15), was discovered in the late nineteenth century, but the Siloam Pool to which Jesus directed a man born blind (9:11) was not found until 2002. Both archaeological discoveries show that the author was intimately familiar with the Jerusalem of pre-70 CE.

The scene in which Jesus identifies himself with life-giving bread probably reflects the situation in John's day, when his community argued bitterly with other Jews about the Christian communion ritual. Jesus asserts that the only way to gain eternal life is to eat his flesh and drink his blood. Many persons, including some of his disciples, take offense at what seems to them an absurd recommendation of cannibalism. John's church apparently taught that the sacramental bread and communion wine literally became Jesus' body and blood (6:25–65), in a process of **transubstantiation.** Even centuries after John's time, numerous outsiders

charged that Christians practiced bloodthirsty rites, including cannibalism, during their secret meetings.

Jesus' sixth sign—bestowing sight to a blind man (9:1–41)—illustrates John's theme that Christ is "the light of the world" (8:12). His gift of sight dispels the darkness that afflicted the man and reflects Jesus' identity as the Word that originally brought light out of dark chaos at the world's creation (Gen. 1:1–5). As mentioned previously, this lengthy episode probably mingles traditions about Jesus' healings with similar miraculous cures performed by Christian prophets in John's church. The dialogue in the synagogue that follows the miracle illustrates the tension that prevailed between church and synagogue in John's day.

The Raising of Lazarus

The seventh and most spectacular miracle—raising Lazarus from the dead (11:1–44)—demonstrates another Johannine conviction, that Jesus literally possesses power over life and death. Concluding the Book of Signs, the narrative of Lazarus's miraculous resuscitation also functions to connect Jesus' good works with his arrest and crucifixion. As John relates it, Jesus' ability to revive a man who has been dead for four days is the act that consolidates Jewish opposition to him and leads directly to his death (11:45–53).

Although no other canonical Gospel mentions the Lazarus episode, some scholars suggest that John may have drawn upon the oral traditions behind Luke's parable of Lazarus and the rich man, which illustrates the starkly differing fates of two newly deceased men in the afterlife (Luke 16:19–31; see Chapter 9). Luke is also the only other Gospel author to mention Jesus' friends Mary and Martha, although unlike John he gives no indication that they had a brother named Lazarus (Luke 10:38–42).

Whatever the historical foundation of the Lazarus incident, John uses it to prove that Jesus is Lord of the Resurrection. In a climactic "I am" speech, Jesus declares, "I am the resurrection and I am life. If a man has faith in me, even though he die, he shall come to life; and no one who is alive and has faith shall ever die" (11:25). In dramatic fulfillment of his claims, Jesus orders Lazarus to rise from his tomb, showing all witnesses that the eschatological hope of life comes through Jesus now (11:1–44).

In John's account, the raising of Lazarus serves multiple literary and theological purposes. As a turning point in the Gospel narrative, it has the same function as the assault on the Temple in the Synoptics: The incident provokes hostility toward Jesus and ignites a fatal conspiracy leading to his execution. As the episode linking the Book of Signs with the Book of Glory (the story of Jesus' Passion), the Lazarus account operates as a preview of Jesus' own death and resurrection. Like Lazarus, Jesus will be entombed in a cave from which a great stone—signifying death's finality—will be rolled away as he rises to immortal life. In the Johannine narrative, Martha's confession of faith in Jesus' divine Sonship—made just before Lazarus's resuscitation—anticipates Thomas's more complete recognition of the risen Jesus' true divinity (11:27; 20:28).

The raising of Lazarus is also a perfect demonstration of John's realized eschatology. Events traditionally assigned to the *eschaton,* such as the dead obeying a divine summons to exit from their graves, now occur during Jesus' ministry. "As the Father raises the dead and gives them life, so the Son gives life to men," Jesus had earlier declared (5:21), adding that those who trust him *already* possess "eternal life, and [do] not come up for judgment, but [have] already passed from death to life" (5:24). For the Johannine writer, "the time is already here, when the dead shall hear the voice of the Son of God, and all who hear shall come to life" (5:25). In John's view, the life-imparting final resurrection is currently taking place among believers: "No one," Jesus assures Martha, "who is alive and has faith shall ever die" (11:26). In thus reinterpreting the timing and nature of resurrection, the author transfers fulfillment of eschatological prophecies about eternal life from the indefinite future—the End of the world—to the concrete here and now.

In grim contrast to the joyous belief that greets Jesus' life-giving miracle, John shows some Jerusalem leaders plotting Jesus' death. Jesus' opponents fear that if the Jewish people accept his messiahship (making him "king of the Jews") their response will incite the Romans to destroy their state and place of worship. (This passage refers to the Roman destruction of Jerusalem in 70 CE.) Caiaphas, the High Priest, proposes that eliminating Jesus will spare the nation that ordeal. Caiaphas's remark— that "it is more to your interest that one man should die for the people, than that the whole nation should be destroyed"—is deeply ironic. While justifying the plot to kill Jesus, the High Priest unwittingly expresses the Christian belief that Jesus' death redeems the world (11:47–53).

John's Book of Signs is bracketed by miracles that Jesus performs at two of life's milestone events—a wedding and a funeral. In his first public "sign" of divine power, at Cana, Jesus transforms water into a beverage of intoxicating joy, extending and intensifying a marriage celebration. In his culminating miracle, at Bethany, Jesus brings life to a dead man, transmuting grief into gladness, an eschatological triumph that he and his friends then celebrate at yet another dinner party (12:1–2).

The Book of Glory

The second section of John's Gospel— commonly labeled the Book of Glory (chs. 12–20)—may be based on a Passion narrative that had already been added to the primitive Signs Gospel when John incorporated the older work into his expanded account. If scholars are correct in assuming John's use of an earlier document, the Johannine author thoroughly transformed his source, radically reinterpreting the meaning of Jesus' last days. Connecting the Book of Glory with the miraculous signs previously reported, John opens this section by showing Jesus at dinner with friends, celebrating

Lazarus's return to life. The festive scene features several important themes, looking back to Jesus' feeding of the multitudes and the resuscitation of Lazarus and looking forward to the Last Supper and Jesus' own death. Even while rejoicing in one man's escape from the tomb, the dinner guests are forewarned of their leader's imminent death when Lazarus's sister Mary anoints Jesus' feet with expensive perfume. Christ approves her prophetic action as preparing his body for burial, for his hour of "glory" is near at hand.

Whether following different sources or reworking the older Synoptic tradition, John pictures Jesus' final days in a way that transforms the Messiah's betrayal and suffering into a glorious triumph. After his messianic entry into Jerusalem (John adds the detail of the crowds' waving palm branches that gives Palm Sunday its name) (12:12–19), Jesus foretells his death in terms resembling Mark's description of the agony in Gethsemane (14:32–36) but reinterpreted to highlight the Crucifixion's saving purpose: "Now my soul is in turmoil, and what am I to say? Father, save me from this hour. No, it was for this that I came to this hour. Father, glorify thy name" (12:27–28). When a celestial voice affirms that God is glorified in Christ's actions, Jesus interprets his "lifting up" (crucifixion) as God's predestined means of drawing all people to him, a process of human salvation that cannot occur without his death (12:28–33).

The Last Supper and Farewell Discourses

Perhaps because he has already presented his view of Jesus as the "heavenly bread" that gives life to those who partake of it (6:26–58), John's account of the Last Supper contains no reference to Jesus' distributing the ceremonial bread and wine (the Eucharist). Instead, John's narrative dramatizes a concept found also in Luke's Gospel—that Jesus comes "like a servant" (Luke 22:27). Given the author's view that Christ shares the nature of the omnipotent Creator (1:1), Jesus' taking the role of a domestic slave, washing his disciples' travel-stained feet, is

extremely significant. The Master's humility both demonstrates God's loving care for the faithful and sets an example of humble service for the Johannine community (13:3–17).

After Judas Iscariot leaves the group to betray his Master (a treachery that John believes is predestined), Jesus delivers a series of farewell speeches intended to make clear the way in which his ministry reveals the Father and to place Jesus' inevitable death in proper perspective. Summarizing the divine purpose fulfilled in his life, Jesus gives the "new commandment" of love that distinguishes his people from the rest of the world (13:34–35). Christ's ultimate "act of love" is surrendering his life for his friends' benefit (15:11–14). The Johannine Jesus' directive to love fellow believers, however, contrasts with the Synoptic Jesus' command to love even "enemies" and other outsiders (cf. Matt. 5:44; Luke 6:27).

With his example of love opening the true "way" to the Father, the Johannine Jesus faces death as a transfiguring experience. In John's view, Jesus' death and return to heaven will permit believers to experience life with God (14:1–6) and simultaneously will allow God to live with them (14:23). Because the divine Parent dwells in him, Christ can reveal God fully—to see Jesus in his true meaning is to see the Father (14:7–11). John insists on Jesus' unique relationship to God—he and the Father "are one," but it is a unity of spirit and purpose that also characterizes the disciples (17:12, 20–21). Despite his close identification with the Deity, John's Jesus does not claim unequivocal equality with God. He simply states that "the Father is greater than I" (14:28).

The Paraclete (Holy Spirit)

With John's emphasis on the disciples' mystic union with Christ (15:5–10; 17:12, 20–22) and the superiority of the unseen spirit to mere physical existence (6:63), it is not surprising that he presents a view of Jesus' return that differs strikingly from that in the Synoptics. Instead of an eager anticipation of the Second Coming (as in

Mark 13, Matt. 24–25, or Luke 21), John teaches that Jesus is already present, inspiring the faithful. Brief allusions to Christ's reappearance after death (14:3) are fulfilled when he sends the disciples the Paraclete. The Paraclete, variously translated as "Advocate," "Helper," "Counselor," or "Comforter," is synonymous with "the Spirit of Truth" (14:17) and "the Holy Spirit" (14:26). Although unbelieving humanity will see Jesus no more, he remains eternally with the faithful (14:16–26). An invisible counterpart to Jesus, the Paraclete enables the disciples to understand the true significance of Jesus' teaching (16:1–15). By implication, the Paraclete also empowers the author to create a Gospel that fully portrays the glory of Jesus' first advent.

By its presence in the Johannine community's preaching, the Paraclete serves to judge the world's unbelief. Affirming that Jesus is present simultaneously with the Father and with believers, the Paraclete also witnesses to the invincibility of good, resisting the spiritual darkness that claimed Jesus' physical life and now threatens his followers.

In John's view, Jesus imparts the promised Advocate (Paraclete) at his resurrection, merely by breathing on the disciples and saying, "Receive the Holy Spirit" (20:21–23). The risen Lord's action recalls the creation scene in Genesis 2 when Yahweh breathes into Adam's nostrils "the breath of life," making him an animate being or "living creature." As John's Gospel begins with the Word creating the universe (1:1–5), so it closes with the Word breathing the pure spirit of life into his renewed human creation.

John's Interpretation of the Passion

Crucifixion as Glorification

John's Passion narrative is pervasively shaped by the author's high Christology and his wish to shift responsibility for Jesus' death to his Jewish opponents. The author of Mark's Gospel had already wrestled with the problem of reconciling his portrait of Jesus as a powerful miracle worker in Galilee with the fact of Jesus' apparent helplessness before his enemies in Jerusalem (see Chapter 7). After depicting Jesus as a figure of virtually irresistible force throughout his Gospel, John faces an even greater problem in explaining how this incarnation of divine Wisdom became his adversaries' mortal victim. John resolves the potential dilemma by affirming the paradox inherent in Jesus' circumstance: Even in Jerusalem, Jesus retains his superhuman power but voluntarily declines to use it in order to fulfill scriptural predictions that God's Son must die to save others.

No Agony in Gethsemane John's description of events in Gethsemane differs sharply from the Synoptic tradition. Whereas Mark's Jesus throws himself on the ground in an agony of dread, begging to be spared a painful and public humiliation (Mark 14:32–36), John's Jesus remains calmly standing while the soldiers who come to arrest him are hurled to the ground. When the Temple police ask Jesus to identify himself, he replies, "I am he," a revelation of divinity that causes them to collapse in a heap (18:4–8). The last of Jesus' "I am" statements, this declaration echoes John's earlier association of Jesus and Yahweh, the divine "I AM" (John 8:58; cf. Exod. 3:8–16), a claim to equality with God that incites an attempt to stone Jesus for blasphemy. For John, enemies plotting Jesus' downfall only *seem* to be in charge: As Jesus had explained, he alone makes the decision to give up his life (10:17–18). Pilate, the representative of Roman imperial power, is explicitly informed that his role as judge is only illusory (19:9–10).

Instead of fleeing in terror as they do in the Synoptics, the Johannine disciples are simply dismissed by their Master, who prevents their arrest to fulfill Scripture—the Messiah will lose no one entrusted to him. The author then interweaves the story of Peter's denial with his unique account of Jesus' interrogation before **Annas,** father-in-law of the High Priest Caiaphas (18:8–17). Unlike the Synoptics, John does not show Jesus being formally tried before the full Sanhedrin, but only having an informal hearing at the High Priest's private residence.

An Innocent Pilate It is in his version of Jesus' appearance before Pontius Pilate that John most explicitly mirrors his community's estrangement from the Jewish community. Only John states that Pharisees, as well as Temple priests, are involved in Jesus' indictment before the Roman governor. Presenting events in a strangely implausible way, John shows a frightened and harried Pilate dashing back and forth between a Jewish crowd outside his palace and the accused prisoner inside. (John states that Jewish priests could not enter a Gentile's quarters because such contact would make them ritually unclean for the upcoming Passover.) In his desire to foster good relations with Rome, Luke had depicted a Pilate technically innocent of arranging Jesus' death (Luke 23:1–25), but John goes even further. His Pilate is literally run ragged shuttling between accommodation of the priests who demand Jesus' execution and his sympathetic support of the "king" whom they wish to kill (18:28–19:16). In John's account, Pilate makes no fewer than *eight* attempts to persuade Jesus' priestly accusers (John inaccurately labels them collectively as "Jews") that Jesus is guilty of no crime (cf. 18:31, 38–39; 19:4–6, 12, 14–16). Only after the crowd threatens to accuse Pilate himself of sedition against Rome for championing Jesus' cause (19:12) and insists that their nation has no ruler but the Roman emperor (19:15–16) does Pilate reluctantly submit and turn Jesus over for execution. John also has Pilate symbolically vindicate Jesus' claim to be the rightful Jewish king by refusing to revise a public notice of the crime for which Jesus was crucified (19:19–22).

The Crucifixion: Water and Blood John's picture of the **Crucifixion** includes a number of his distinctive concerns. The Johannine Jesus carries his crossbeam all the way to Golgotha, thus precluding any Gnostic or other claim that someone else, such as Simon of Cyrene or even Judas, died in his stead (19:17). In an incident recounted nowhere else, John has a Roman soldier thrust his lance into Jesus' side, initiating a torrent of blood and water. This wounding not only confirms Jesus' physical death (lest one think that he only seemed to perish) but also provides typical Johannine symbols of sacramental wine (blood) and truth (water and spirit), emblems that nourish the community of faith (cf. 4:10–14; 6:53–58; 7:37–39).

Besides the small group of Galilean women who witness the Crucifixion in the Synoptic tradition, John adds the figures of Jesus' mother and the Beloved Disciple. Mary (who is never named in this Gospel) apparently fills a symbolic function: Appearing only twice—at the joyous wedding in Cana, where water is turned into wine, and at the cross, where water and blood flow from Jesus—Mary may signify the believing community that benefits from the sacramental emblems of shed blood and crucified body. Only in John's account does Jesus place her (the church) under the care of the Beloved Disciple, the one who personally testifies to the significance of Jesus' sacrificial death (19:25–27). (See Box 10.7 for a comparison of Gospel accounts of Jesus' last words.) By designating the Beloved Disciple as Mary's honorary son, John also makes him Jesus' brother, in effect Jesus' successor as leader of the Johannine community (see Figure 10.4).

Post Resurrection Appearances in Jerusalem

Although John apparently follows the same tradition that Luke used, placing Jesus' post resurrection appearances in and around Jerusalem (instead of Galilee as in Mark and Matthew), he modifies the story to illustrate his characteristic themes. On the first Easter Sunday, Mary

BOX 10.7 Jesus' Last Words: A Summary of the Evangelists' Beliefs About Him

Jesus' final utterances, compiled from the four different Gospel accounts of his crucifixion, are traditionally known as the "seven last words on the cross." Whereas Mark and Matthew agree that Jesus is almost entirely silent during his agony, crying out only once—in Aramaic—to ask why God has deserted him, Luke and John ascribe several short speeches to their dying hero, showing him in full control of his final hours. The particular statements that each Evangelist has Jesus voice represent that author's individual understanding of Jesus' nature and the meaning of his death.

MARK (15:34)

Eli, Eli, lema sabachthani?

(My God, my God, why have you forsaken me?)

MATTHEW (27:46)

Eli, Eli, lema sabachthani?

(My God, my God, why have you forsaken me?)

LUKE (23:34, 43, 46)

Father, forgive them [Roman executioners]; they do not know what they are doing.

Truly I tell you: today you [the sympathetic felon next to him] will be with me in Paradise.

Father, into your hands I commit my spirit.

JOHN (19:26–27, 28, 30)

Mother, there is your son. . . . There is your mother [placing Mary (the church) in the future care of the Beloved Disciple (the Johannine community)].

I am thirsty [to fulfill Scripture].

It is accomplished!

Writing to a vulnerable group then undergoing hardship and suffering, Mark devotes much of his Gospel to a bleak description of Jesus' Passion, emphasizing that, if God permitted his son to endure pain and humiliation, the disciples may expect no better fate. Jesus' cry of despair anticipates his persecuted followers' sense of similarly being abandoned by God. Although Matthew modifies the Passion story to underscore its fulfillment of biblical prophecy, he retains Mark's emphasis on Jesus' solitary and extreme anguish.

Luke, who presents Jesus as a model of self-sacrificing service to others, thoroughly edits the Passion narrative to highlight Jesus' innocence of any crime against Rome and to illustrate the themes of forgiveness and spirituality that color his portrait of Jesus. Contrary to Mark's account, in which Jesus appears almost numb with shock at his brutal treatment, Luke's Jesus is neither silent nor despairing: He speaks repeatedly and confidently, as if he were already enthroned as eschatological judge. He pardons his Roman tormentors, absolving them of responsibility for his execution, and comforts the felon crucified next to him, granting him a posthumous reward in paradise. Because Luke presents Jesus as led by the Holy Spirit throughout his earthly ministry, it is thematically appropriate for him to show, at the end, Jesus calmly relinquishing his own spirit to God.

Consistent with his picture of Jesus as fully aware of his divine nature, including his prehuman existence in heaven, John paints a Jesus absolutely untroubled by doubt or dejection. Acting out the purpose for which he descended to earth, John's Jesus remains in complete charge of his destiny, allowing soldiers to capture him only to fulfill the divine will (John 18:4–9). The Johannine Jesus thus undergoes no agony in Gethsemane or despair on the cross. In contrast to Mark's picture of lonely abandonment, John shows Jesus accompanied by his mother and his favorite disciple, whose future lives together he arranges. When he says he thirsts, it is not because he experiences ordinary human suffering, but only to fulfill prophecy. His moment of death is simultaneously his "hour of glory," when he can announce that he has accomplished all the Father sent him to do. In his serene omniscience, the Johannine Jesus seems altogether a different being from Mark's disconsolate Son of Man.

FIGURE 10.4 *Crucifixion.* A modern Japanese artist offers a highly stylized interpretation of Jesus' crucifixion. Two figures, possibly representing Jesus' mother and the Beloved Disciple, kneel in adoration of the incarnate Word of God.

Magdalene is alone when she discovers that Jesus' corpse has vanished from Joseph of Arimathea's garden tomb where it had been placed late the previous Friday. Prophet of her Lord's resurrection, she is the first to report the empty tomb and the first to see the risen Jesus, announcing these glad tidings to the male disciples (20:1–2, 10–18).

Following Jesus' Sunday evening appearance to the disciples, infusing them with the Holy Spirit, he appears again to "doubting Thomas," vanquishing his skepticism. (The Beloved Disciple, an example to others, believes that Jesus lives even before physical proof is offered, illustrating the Johannine community's cultivation of faith [20:8–9, 26–29].) His "light" having "overcome" the world's spiritual darkness, Jesus also conquers death. His resurrection is the final victorious "sign" toward which all his earlier miracles pointed.

Epilogue: Post Resurrection Appearances in Galilee

Most scholars believe that the Fourth Gospel originally ended at 20:31 with the author's stated purpose of inspiring faith. Chapter 21, which records traditions about Jesus' posthumous appearances in Galilee, seems to be the work of an editor, who may have prepared the Gospel manuscript for publication. This redactor also emphasizes the complementary roles of Peter, leader of the Twelve, and the unidentified "disciple whom Jesus loved."

When Jesus appears to share an early-morning breakfast of bread and fish (again demonstrating that the risen Christ is not a ghost or other disembodied spirit), he questions Peter about the depth of his love. Using three different Greek verbs for "love," Jesus emphasizes that love for him means feeding his "lambs." Thus, Peter and the church are to provide spiritual and other care for future believers, the "other sheep" (10:16), including Gentiles, who will soon join the apostolic fold (21:4–17).

After Peter has been given the opportunity to redeem his relationship with Christ—three times asserting his love to counterbalance his three previous denials of Jesus (18:16–18, 27)—Peter asks about the future of the Beloved Disciple (21:20–21). When Jesus indicates that this disciple, unlike Peter, will not suffer martyrdom but may remain alive "until I come," the editor states that the Johannine "brotherhood" mistakenly took Jesus' statement "to mean that the disciple would not die." By the time the epilogue was written, however, it is evident that the disciple had died, contrary to the expectations of the community founded on that disciple's "testimony" (21:22–24). In this brief dialogue—in which the passage of time has clarified the meaning of Jesus' words—the redactor seems to abandon the earlier notion that the Parousia would occur during the lifetimes of at least some original followers.

The epilogue concludes with the editor's musing on the large number of oral traditions surrounding Jesus. If his entire career were to be recorded in detail, the "whole world" could not contain "the vast number of books that would be produced" (21:25).

The Letters of John

Several years after John's Gospel was published, another member of the Johannine community wrote three documents—1, 2, and 3 John—that describe later developments within the Johannine group. Because these documents address problems troubling the later church, they are discussed in their canonical order, among the **catholic** (general) **epistles** (see Chapter 18).

Summary

Although John's Gospel may have originated on the fringes of the Christian community (it shows traces of an Essene-like sectarianism and proto-Gnostic influences), it eventually provided mainstream Christianity with concepts crucial to its theological development. Doctrines of Christ's prehuman existence as God's eternal Word (the Logos), his descent from heaven, his incarnation as the man Jesus, his apparent equality with God, and his continuing presence among believers in the form of the Paraclete, the Spirit of Truth—all absent from the Synoptic Gospels—profoundly influenced the church's later declaration that Jesus and God are one.

Writing perhaps thirty years after Mark, John also offers believers a plausible means to cope with disappointment in Jesus' failure to return during the lifetimes of his original followers. The Synoptic writers, in effect, had divided Jesus' messiahship into two contrasting parts: a ministry in the recent past as a sacrificial servant and a future Second Coming (the Parousia) as the glorious Son of Man. With his doctrine of realized eschatology, John effectively addresses this troubling issue: The Johannine Jesus accomplishes everything for the Messiah's success in a single earthly coming. Whereas Mark vividly anticipated the "Son of Man coming in the

clouds with great power and glory" (Mark 13:16), John testifies that Jesus' "glory" has already appeared: "we [members of the Johannine community] saw his glory, such glory as befits the Father's only son, full of grace and truth" (John 1:14; cf. 13:31–32).

When the Johannine Jesus speaks his last words on the cross—"It is accomplished" (John 19:30)—the implications are hugely significant. In his ministry and crucifixion, Jesus has completed his messianic tasks, including those traditionally assigned to the *eschaton*—divine judgment, spiritual regeneration, resurrection, and the giving of full knowledge to the faithful.

John's vision does not emphasize Jesus' imminent return because the Johannine Christ had already achieved his disciples' redemption and, in the guise of the Paraclete, is eternally present with them. Believers, Jesus insisted, have already experienced a favorable judgment, passing "from death to life" (John 5:24–25); they will never die (John 11:26).

Matthew's Gospel concludes with Jesus' promise that he will be with his disciples "to the end of time" (Matt. 28:20). Luke also frames his resurrection accounts to suggest that Jesus remains present in such Christian practices as Bible study and communal meals (Luke 24). But only John portrays the advent of the Paraclete as if "he" were Jesus' double (15:26–27), fulfilling believers' desire for a continuing presence. At the Last Supper, the Johannine Jesus emphasizes the importance of his return to heaven, not his return to earth: "If I do not go [back to heaven] your Advocate [the Paraclete] will not come, whereas if I go, I will send him to you. When he comes, he will confute the world and show where wrong and right and judgment lie. He will convict them [unbelievers] of wrong, by their refusal to believe in me; he will convince them that right is on my side, by showing that I go to the Father when I pass from your sight; and he will convince them of divine judgment, by showing that the Prince of this world [the devil] stands condemned" (16:7–11; cf. 14:10–26). That Spirit is given when the risen Jesus "breathes" it into his disciples (20:22). Basking in the presence of the Paraclete, Jesus' surrogate self, the Johannine community directly experiences the eschatological judgment that vindicates their faith and defeats evil.

Besides helping resolve the problem of a delayed Second Coming, John's Gospel also succeeds in giving Jesus cosmic stature, portraying a figure so exalted that he reigns with God: No prophet, lawgiver, angel, or other heavenly being possesses his relationship to (or equality with) God (8:58; 14:09). More than any single book in the New Testament, this Gospel lays the foundations for later theological interpretations of Christ's nature and function. In post–New Testament times, theologians came to see Christ as the Second Person in the **Trinity** (a term that does not appear in canonical Scripture), co-equal, consubstantial, and co-eternal with the Father. Although the Johannine writings do not articulate so formal a dogma, historically John's high Christology profoundly influenced official Christianity's eventual understanding of its Master.

Questions for Review

1. Evaluate the arguments for and against the apostle John's responsibility for the Gospel traditionally attributed to him. Describe the role of the Beloved Disciple and his relationship to the Fourth Gospel.
2. Describe some of the major differences between the Gospel of John and the Synoptic Gospels. Compare Jesus' manner of speaking and use of parables in Mark with his long philosophical discourses in John. In Jesus' Johannine speeches, how was the author influenced by the form of Wisdom's speeches in Proverbs, Ecclesiasticus, and the Wisdom of Solomon?
3. In presenting Jesus as a spiritual redeemer descended from heaven, John reflects or parallels some ideas later expressed in Gnosticism. In what specific ways does John's Gospel resemble— or differ from—Gnostic teachings? How does the author's presentation "rescue" Jesus from the Gnostic claims? How does John indicate that Jesus is *both* divine and human?
4. John's Gospel contains almost no traditional apocalyptic teaching and has no prediction of Jesus' Second Coming comparable to that in the Synoptics. How does John's teaching about the Advocate, or Paraclete, deal with the problem of Jesus' delayed return? Remember that John was written almost seventy years after Jesus' death.

5. Name several of the seven "signs" or miracles that Jesus performs to demonstrate his divinity. How does the raising of Lazarus lead to Jesus' death?
6. What is the purpose of Jesus' "I am" speeches? What do they reveal about him?

Questions for Discussion and Reflection

1. The "brotherhood," or Christian community, that produced John's Gospel preserved traditions about Jesus that roughly paralleled but significantly differed from those on which the Synoptic Gospels are based. Why do you suppose the Johannine community so strongly identified Jesus with the divine Wisdom that God used to create the universe (Prov. 8)? How does John's introductory hymn to the Logos (Word) express the author's view of Jesus' prehuman existence and divine nature?
2. More than any other New Testament book, the Gospel of John has influenced subsequent Christian thought about Jesus' divinity. What specific Johannine teachings do you think most contributed to the conception of the Trinity—the doctrine that defines the Christian God as embodying the triune Being: Father, Son, and Holy Spirit?
3. In discussing the idea that the heavenly being (Logos) who became the human Jesus had no beginning but dwelt in eternity with the Father, interpret such diverse Johannine statements as "the Father and I are one" and "the Father is greater than I am."
4. Explain Jesus' meaning when he says, "He who has seen me has seen the Father." Is Jesus like God or is God like Jesus? Describe the specific qualities, traits, and behavior patterns by which the Johannine Jesus reveals the heavenly Father. Discuss the role of divine/human love in John's portrait of divinity. Why does John emphasize the practice of showing love only among members of his Christian community (John 13:34–35) and not among strangers and enemies as Jesus commands in the Sermon on the Mount (Matt. 5:43–48)?
5. The idea that Jesus is divine—to be identified with the God of the Hebrew Bible—is perhaps the chief source of division between monotheistic Jews and orthodox Christians. Is Jesus'

"full divinity" a major preoccupation of the Synoptic writers? How does John's claim of Jesus' virtual godhood work to separate today's Jews and Christians?

Terms and Concepts to Remember

Annas	Incarnation
Book of Glory	Isis
Book of Signs	Logos (Word)
catholic epistles	Nicodemus
chaos	Paraclete (the
cosmos	Advocate)
Crucifixion	Philo Judaeus
Docetism	realized eschatology
Ephesus	Signs Gospel
Gnosticism	transubstantiation
high Christology	Trinity
Holy Spirit	Wisdom (Prov. 8)

Recommended Reading

Anderson, Paul. *The Christology of the Fourth Gospel: Its Unity and Disunity in the Light of John 6. (With a New Introduction, Outlines, and Epilogue)*. Eugene, Ore.; Cascade Books, 2010. Interprets John's Christology not as a Gnostic-redeemer myth, but as based on Deuteronomy 18, with Jesus as the prophet greater than Moses.

_____. *The Riddles of the Fourth Gospel: An Introduction to John*. Minneapolis: Fortress Press, 2011. Argues for the potential historicity of many distinctly Johannine themes and events, and explores the Gospel's relationship to the Synoptic traditions.

Baltz, Frederick W. *Lazarus and the Fourth Gospel Community*. Lewiston, N.Y.: Mellen Biblical Press, 1995. Presents evidence that Lazarus was the Beloved Disciple, whom the author identifies with the historical figure Eleazar, son of Boethus, whose sisters, Miriam and Martha, appear briefly in rabbinical literature.

Brodie, Thomas L. *The Quest for the Origin of John's Gospel: A Source-Oriented Approach*. New York: Oxford University Press, 1993. Argues that John composed his Gospel by theologically transforming the Synoptic accounts.

Brown, R. E. *The Community of the Beloved Disciple*. New York: Paulist Press, 1979. A readable and insightful study of the Christian group that produced the Gospel and the Letters of John.

Conway, Colleen M. "John, Gospel of." In K. D. Sakenfeld, ed., *The New Interpreter's Dictionary of the Bible,* Vol. 3, pp. 356–370. Nashville: Abingdon Press, 2008. Surveys distinctive qualities of the Gospel's portrait of Jesus, including its socioeconomic setting and unique emphasis on Jesus' divinity.

Dodd, C. H. *Historical Tradition in the Fourth Gospel*. Cambridge: Cambridge University Press, 1963.

_____. *The Interpretation of the Fourth Gospel*. Cambridge: Cambridge University Press, 1965.

Fortna, R. T. *The Fourth Gospel and Its Predecessor: From Narrative Source to Present Gospel*. Philadelphia: Fortress Press, 1988. The definitive analysis of the hypothetical Signs source underlying John's Gospel.

Hedrick, Pamela. "John, Gospel According to." In M. D. Coogan, ed., *The Oxford Encyclopedia of the Books of the Bible*, Vol. 1, pp. 457–472. New York: Oxford University Press, 2011. Highlights John's distinctive theology and later influence on church doctrine.

Keener, Craig S. *The Gospel of John: A Commentary*. Peabody, Mass.: Hendrickson, 2004. An extensive and detailed investigation of John's social and historical setting, for more advanced students.

Kysar, Robert. "John, the Gospel of." In D. N. Freedman, ed., *The Anchor Bible Dictionary,* Vol. 3, pp. 912–931. New York: Doubleday, 1992. A thoughtful review of Johannine literature and scholarship.

_____. *John, the Maverick Gospel*. Atlanta: John Knox Press, 1976. An influential study of the Fourth Gospel.

_____. *Voyages with John: Charting the Fourth Gospel*. Waco, Tex.: Baylor University Press, 2006. An effort by major Johannine scholars to trace evolving academic interpretations of John through the twentieth and early twenty-first centuries.

Martyn, J. L. *History and Theology in the Fourth Gospel,* 2nd ed. Nashville: Abingdon Press, 1979. A brilliant interpretation of John's method of composition that focuses on John 9.

Perkins, Pheme. "The Gospel According to John." In R. E. Brown et al., eds., *The New Jerome Biblical Commentary,* pp. 942–985. Englewood Cliffs, N.J.: Prentice-Hall, 1990. An insightful commentary on the Gospel.

Sloyan, Gerard S. *What Are They Saying About John?,* rev. ed. New York: Paulist Press, 2006. An accessible introduction to contemporary scholarship on John's Gospel.

CHAPTER 11

The Continuing Quest for the Historical Jesus

"Who do [people] say I am?"
Jesus questions his disciples. Mark 8:28

Key Topics/Themes Because the Evangelists present Jesus' life almost exclusively in theological terms, and non-Christian first-century writers refer only briefly to his existence, scholars face a formidable challenge in trying to distinguish the Jesus of history from the Christ of faith. In their ongoing quest to recover the historical Jesus, scholars have developed criteria by which they hope to evaluate the authenticity of the words and actions the early church ascribed to Jesus. Although most scholars generally agree on a methodology for screening traditions to find Jesus' authentic voice, they have reached strikingly different conclusions about his essential teachings and self-identity, particularly on the issue of his eschatology.

After reading the four canonical narratives of Jesus' ministry—not to mention the many noncanonical accounts, such as the Gospel of Peter and the Gospel of Thomas—students may wonder who the "real" Jesus of Nazareth was. Almost from the moment that an oral gospel of the risen Jesus was first proclaimed among Palestinian Jews about 30 CE, believers have tried to "capture" the man and his message, typically interpreting them from a biblical and/or Greco-Roman perspective.

The Christ of Theology and the Jesus of History

The first person to commit his views on Jesus to writing—years before the earliest canonical Gospel appeared—was a Hellenistic Jew named Paul, a man brought into the Christian fold by his vision of the post resurrection Jesus. Although Paul may have known little about the living Jesus (and his letters rarely refer to Jesus' teaching), he was convinced that he knew the "real" Jesus intimately, the cosmic Christ whose sacrificial death removed the barrier of the Mosaic Law that separated Jews and Gentiles and thus opened the way for Gentiles to become "justified" before God through their faith in Jesus' redemptive power (see Chapters 13–15). Although it was a minority opinion at the time he wrote (c. 50–62 CE), Paul's concept of Jesus' supreme importance for humanity's salvation has influenced virtually every interpretation of Jesus' life since. Even John's uniquely "high" Christology, which portrays Jesus as the eternal Word, an incarnation of divine Wisdom, may represent a natural development of themes and ideas initially explored in Paul's letters.

261

Showing little interest in Jesus' earthly career, except for his death, Pauline Christology emphasizes Jesus' posthumous divinity, his exaltation in heaven, and superiority to all others (Phil. 2:9–11). According to Colossians (written either by Paul or by a disciple pursuing the implications of his thought), Jesus is "the image of the invisible God," in whom "the complete being of the Godhead dwells embodied" (Col. 1:15–20; 2:9–10). In both Colossians and the prologue to John's Gospel, Jesus' existence predates that of the universe, of which he is the source. As both the agent and the ultimate goal of creation, he so fully reveals God's purpose that John represents him as saying that "anyone who has seen me has seen the Father" (John 14:9).

As the worship of Jesus gradually replaced the older Greco-Roman religions throughout the Mediterranean region, the church placed ever greater emphasis on Jesus' divine nature and unity with the Father. Assembling in Asia Minor at the town of Nicaea in 325 CE, church leaders rejected the idea that Jesus was ever entirely human or that there had been a time when he did not exist, declaring that he was not merely Son of God, but God himself, the Second Person in the Trinity (see Figure 11.1). Although fierce debates over the issue of Jesus' precise relationship to the Father and the Holy Spirit continued to divide Christians long after the conference at Nicaea, a formal statement of orthodox Christian doctrine, the Nicene Creed, eventually emerged.

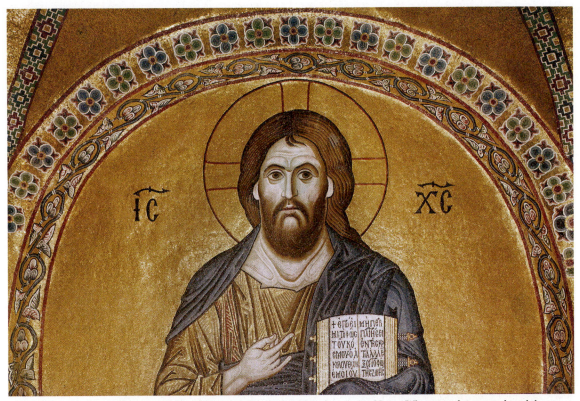

FIGURE 11.1 *Christ Pantokrator* (Christ "All-Powerful")—a theological portrait of Jesus. When translators produced the Septuagint (the Greek edition of the Hebrew Bible), they rendered the Hebrew phrase *El Shaddai* (God Almighty) as *Pantokrator,* a term reserved for Yahweh alone. Except for one use in Paul's letters (2 Cor. 6:18), *Pantokrator* appears only in Revelation (nine times), where it seems to refer to God. After the fourth century however, when the doctrine of the Trinity was affirmed at the Nicaea church council, Christian artists began to depict Jesus as *Pantokrator,* emphasizing his divinity and equality with the Father. Typical of Greek Orthodox icons, this mosaic appears in the narthex of Monastery Church, Hosios, Loukas, Greece.

Regularly recited by hundreds of millions of believers throughout Christendom as a definitive declaration of faith, the creed's repeated insistence on Jesus' absolute equality with God reflects the intense doctrinal controversy in which it historically originated:

> We believe in one Lord, Jesus Christ,
> the only Son of God,
> *eternally begotten of the Father,*
> *God from God, Light from Light,*
> *true God from true God,*
> *begotten, not made,*
> *of one Being with the Father.*
> Through him all things were made.
> For us and for our salvation
> he came down from heaven;
> by the power of the Holy Spirit
> he became incarnate from the virgin Mary,
>   and was made man. (emphasis added)

As many commentators have observed, the Nicene Creed's intense focus on Jesus' godhood leaves a vacuum at the center: It says nothing about what Jesus himself believed or what he taught others.

Although they wrote more than two centuries before the council at Nicaea, the Gospel authors were almost equally concerned about Jesus' theological function—the role he played not only during his earthly life but also after his resurrection and ascension to heaven, where he now stands at God's right hand. Regarding Jesus as qualitatively different from every other human being, the Evangelists emphasize his supernatural status, commonly shaping their narratives and reports of Jesus' teaching to illustrate his unique nature. Although most scholars believe that the Synoptic Gospels, as well as the Gospel of Thomas, incorporate many authentic traditions about Jesus' words and deeds, they face the challenge of separating reliable history from theological overlay.

In searching for the historical Jesus, it is important to distinguish scholarly goals from those of theology. Whereas theologians are concerned with Jesus' cosmic meaning, a dimension of spirit informed by faith, historians can examine only the material world, evaluating evidence to judge its plausibility in terms of ordinary human experience; the spiritual and supernatural lie beyond the reach of scientific inquiry. Gospel reports of events that by definition occur outside life's normal historical processes—such as Jesus' miraculous ability to control a storm, walk on water, or rise from the dead—cannot be investigated in themselves, but only as a phenomenon of belief among early Christians. Historians have no means of "proving" that the Resurrection did (or did not) occur; they can merely study the reported behavior of believers who were convinced that it did happen. Scientific analysis cannot deal with Jesus conceived as divinity but must approach the living man only as a legitimate object of historical research, leaving to theologians the task of interpreting the paradox of Jesus as both completely human and fully divine.

Aware that Gospel authors are more theologians than biographers interested in factual reporting, students often ask if it is possible to find the authentic man amid the sometimes conflicting sayings and deeds that the Evangelists attribute to their hero. Are there any "unbiased" historical sources that give us reliable information about the human Jesus?

Early Historical References to Jesus

Although Christians wrote much about Jesus during the last third of the first century CE, writers of the larger Greco-Roman world apparently ignored him, if they were even aware of his existence. It is not until the early second century that a few Roman authors refer—very briefly—to Jesus or his followers. Tacitus, a Roman senator and historian, is one of the earliest non-Christian writers to mention Christianity, and he seems to have based his report largely on secondhand evidence. His single allusion to Jesus merely states that Jesus "had been executed in Tiberius's reign by the governor of Judaea,

Pontius Pilate"(*Annals* 15.44). Tacitus's statements about Jesus and his followers are incidental to the historian's main purpose—illustrating the cruelty and corruption of Nero, who tried to blame the Christians for a great fire that consumed much of Rome about 64 CE:

> Nero had self-acknowledged Christians arrested. Then, on their information, large numbers of others were condemned—not so much for incendiarism as for their anti-social tendencies. Their deaths were made farcical. Dressed in wild animals' skins, they were torn to pieces by dogs, or crucified, or made into torches to be ignited after dark as substitutes for daylight. . . . Despite their guilt as Christians, and the ruthless punishment it deserved, the victims were pitied. For it was felt that they were being sacrificed to one man's brutality rather than to the national interest.
>
> (*Annals* 15.44)

Nero's persecution, which was apparently confined to the imperial capital, represents the Roman government's first official recognition of the new faith. That even an enlightened author such as Tacitus could regard Christians as so "notoriously depraved" that they deserved the death penalty indicates the extent to which Rome's ruling classes misunderstood the Jesus movement. Given first-century officialdom's ignorance of early Christian beliefs, it is likely that few educated non-Christians were in a position to know the facts of Jesus' life and teachings.

Suetonius, a Roman historian writing in the early second century CE, records that even before Nero, the emperor **Claudius** (reigned 41–54 CE) had expelled the Jews from Rome because of trouble arising from "Chrestus" (probably a variant spelling of Tacitus's "Christus" [the Greek *Christos,* or Christ]) (*Twelve Caesars* 25). The alleged "constant rioting" that Claudius punished about 49 CE may have resulted from conflicts between Roman Jews and Jewish-Christian missionaries who brought their

innovative religion from Palestine. (The author of Acts refers to Claudius's expulsion of Jews, including Priscilla and Aquila, who met Paul in Corinth about 50 CE [Acts 18:2].)

Pliny the Younger, who governed the Roman province of **Bithynia** (north-central Turkey) from about 111 to 115 CE, wrote to the emperor **Trajan** for advice about dealing with Christians who refused to participate in "emperor worship," a public ritual then popularly regarded as much an expression of patriotism as one of religious commitment. Pliny's letter notes that Christians gathered to "partake of a meal [probably the Eucharist or Holy Communion]" and to sing "a hymn to Christ, as if to a god" (*Letters* 97), adding that cities, villages, and even the rural districts had been "thoroughly infected" by the "seditious" cult.

With one exception, no Jewish writer of the first or early second century alludes to either Jesus or the movement named for him. The exception is Flavius Josephus, a first-century contemporary of the Gospel writers, who wrote two major historical works interpreting his people's customs for a Greco-Roman audience. A controversial figure, Josephus at first participated in the Jewish Revolt against Rome (66–73 CE) but later went over to the Roman side, becoming an interpreter for General (later, Emperor) Titus. Because most of his fellow Jews regarded Josephus as a traitor, the Jewish community did not preserve his writings. For Christians, however, Josephus's *Antiquities of the Jews*, which covered Israel's history from creation to the revolt, and the *Jewish Wars* [against Rome], to which he was an eyewitness, were invaluable resources. Although he does not mention Jesus in his *Wars,* Josephus refers to Jesus twice in *Antiquities*. Because Josephus was copied exclusively by Christian scribes (and perhaps added to in transmission), scholars are cautious about accepting the first passage about Jesus at face value. Stripped of phrases that scholars believe to be later Christian interpolations, Josephus's comments may have run as follows:

> Now there was about this time [the administration of Pontius Pilate (26–36 CE)], Jesus, a wise man, . . . a doer of wonderful works, a teacher of such men as receive the truth with pleasure. He drew over to him . . . many of the Jews, . . . and when Pilate, . . . had condemned him to the cross, those that loved him at the first . . . [believed] that he appeared to them alive again the third day. . . . [A]nd the tribe of Christians, so named from him, are not extinct at this day.
>
> (*Antiquities* 18.3.3)

Josephus's second reference deplores the illegal execution of James, "the brother of Jesus, who was called Christ" (*Antiquities* 20.9.1). Although from a later date, allusions to Jesus in the Talmud, which condemns him for practicing sorcery and "for leading Israel astray," similarly attest to Jesus' historicity.

Whereas Jewish and Greco-Roman authors' cursory allusions to Jesus tend to confirm his martyrdom under Pilate and posthumous influence, they offer almost no information with which to construct a biography. Virtually everything we can learn about Jesus derives from the New Testament and a few other Christian documents, such as the Gospel of Thomas. Because no nonbeliever has left behind a comprehensive account of Jesus' life to use as a check against what the Evangelists claimed about him, we are forced to rely almost entirely on the testimony of Christian partisans.

The Current Quest for the "Real" Jesus

Since the dawn of the "Age of Enlightenment" in early eighteenth-century Europe, scholars have systematically labored to recover the Jesus of history. Perhaps the most influential of these studies was published in **Albert Schweitzer**'s *Quest for the Historical Jesus* (1906). Building on the research of his German predecessors, Schweitzer's book presents a thoroughly apocalyptic Jesus, a first-century prophet convinced that he is God's chosen instrument to announce the impending consummation of history. Burning with eschatological zeal, he demands that followers abandon all earthly ties and work with him to hasten the arrival of God's kingdom, which will overturn the present satanic world order and usher in the New Age. Jesus' driving goal is to establish the prophetic conditions that will lead to a supernaturally inspired chain of events culminating in his cosmic reign as the Son of Man. When Jesus' early expectations do not materialize (Matt. 10:22–23), he marches to Jerusalem, confident that he can compel the kingdom's appearance through his voluntary death, the final "tribulation" leading to God's direct imposition of his sovereignty. The anticipated divine intervention does not occur, however, and Jesus is crushed by the system he defies.

Schweitzer's reading of Jesus as a devoted but misguided apocalyptist made Christianity's core figure seem irrelevant to the modern worldview. No matter how sincere, a prophet whose eschatological predictions had been disproved by the world's stubborn failure to end had little to say to twentieth-century thinkers accustomed to scientific rationalism.

Since Schweitzer's time, the international scholarly community has been deeply divided on the issue of the historical Jesus' actions and teachings. During recent decades, the majority of scholars seem to have split into two opposing camps. One group argues, as had Schweitzer, that Jesus was an apocalyptist preaching the imminent arrival of God's kingdom; his historical role and teachings are therefore best understood in terms of first-century Jewish eschatology. In contrast, another group, including scholars like Marcus Borg and John Dominic Crossan, contends that Jesus was essentially a Jewish Wisdom teacher whose followers, misunderstanding his figurative language, later misinterpreted him apocalyptically. Although these two groups have reached extremely different conclusions, they generally agree on the scholarly methodologies to be used in attempting to recover Jesus' historical identity.

Some Criteria for Testing the Authenticity of Jesus' Words and Deeds

Orality

The first challenge facing scholars is to distinguish between the historical Jesus' actual sayings and those attributed to him in the written sources. Recognizing that Jesus' original teaching was entirely oral and that it was transmitted only by word of mouth for several decades before being written down, scholars have devised a test that respects the implications of this orality. To be remembered and quoted repeatedly, Jesus' words must have been both memorable and relatively brief. Statements likely to qualify as genuine will be vivid and attention-getting.

Examples of concise, highly quotable sayings include Jesus' declaration that "the Sabbath was made for the sake of man and not man for the Sabbath: therefore the Son of Man is sovereign even over the Sabbath" (Mark 2:27–28; cf. Matt. 12:1–8; Luke 6:1–5). Equally terse are the advice to pay Caesar (the government) his due but to give God what belongs to God (found in both Mark 12:17 and G. Thom. 100) and the wry observation that prophets are honored everywhere except on their home turf and/or among their relations (Mark 6:4; Matt. 13:15; John 4:44; G. Thom. 33).

Form

The distinctive literary form in which Jesus casts his sayings also offers a clue to their probable historicity. In both the Synoptic Gospels and Thomas, Jesus' most characteristic forms of speech are aphorisms and parables that draw on familiar religious, domestic, and agricultural practices in rural Palestine. Jesus' frequent use of **aphorisms**—terse, snappy pronouncements that typically overturned conventional wisdom—forced people to think about the world in new ways. "It is not what goes into a person that defiles," he said, "but what comes out" (Mark 7:15, Scholars Version)—an almost scatological criticism of biblical dietary laws. Although they resemble proverbs in form, Jesus' aphorisms are typically nonproverbial in rejecting commonsensical assumptions, such as his declaration "It's easier for a camel to squeeze through a needle's eye than for a wealthy person to get into God's domain" (Mark 10:25, SV). Such statements would not only elicit a double take among Jesus' peasant listeners, most of whom probably envied the rich, but also reverse traditional assurances that wealth is a divine blessing (Prov. 6:6–11; 10:15; 24:30–34; Job 42:12; Deut. 28:1–14).

Utilizing such rhetorical devices as hyperbole, humor, surprise, and paradox, Jesus' genuine aphorisms tend to shock with their audacity or to provoke with their reversal of social norms. Such aphorisms include the recommendation to take a "plank" out of one's eye (Matt. 7:3–5; Luke 6:41–42; Thom. 26), to be sly as a snake and simple as a dove (Matt. 10:16; Thom. 39), and to rob a strong man (Mark 3:27; Matt. 12:29; Luke 11:21–22; Thom. 35).

Using the homeliest of images, Jesus' authentic parables compare God's "domain" or kingdom to familiar settings and actions of everyday peasant life, typically stressing quiet processes of growth or almost imperceptible change. Unlike the well-known apocalyptic vision in Daniel, in which the kingdom literally crashes into the earth, violently shattering and replacing other nations (Dan. 2:44), Jesus' metaphors commonly emphasize a slow or hidden development. God's impending rule is thus likened to the sowing of seeds (Mark 4:3–8; Matt. 13:3–8; Luke 8:5–8a; Thom. 9), the sprouting of a mustard plant (Mark 4:30–32; Matt. 13:31–32; Luke 13:18–19; Thom. 20), and a woman baking bread, in which leaven gradually transforms the dough (Matt 13:33; Luke 13:20–21; Thom. 96).

Dissimilarity

The criterion of dissimilarity holds that a saying is likely to be authentic if it differs significantly from *both* first-century Jewish attitudes or practices and those of the later Hellenistic church.

Jesus' use of the Aramaic word *Abba* (an informal term for "father") (Mark 14:36; Luke 11:2) differs from the church's more formal way of addressing the Deity (Matt. 6:9) and probably represents Jesus' personal style. Luke's Gospel preserves some of Jesus' most distinctive teaching, containing numerous parables that defy conventional thought and overturn ordinary expectations. These include provocative stories involving an irresponsible and ungrateful son (Luke 15:11–32), a despised Samaritan who is a moral hero (Luke 16:1–8a), a lazy and unjust judge (Luke 18:1–8), and a righteous Pharisee who is outclassed by a sinful tax collector (Luke 18:9–14a).

The obvious weakness in the dissimilarity criterion is that many of Jesus' characteristic teachings, including his emphasis on love, were shared by other Palestinian teachers of his day (Mark 12:28–34). In fact, historians find Judean parallels to virtually all of Jesus' ethical pronouncements. Many scholars now believe that Jesus is best understood when seen operating in his first-century Palestinian-Jewish milieu. Recent studies have shown that Jesus has much in common with the Essenes and Pharisees, in both the content and the parabolic style of his teachings (see Chilton's *Rabbi Jesus* in "Recommended Reading").

The Embarrassment Factor

Some scholars believe that certain traditions about Jesus that the early church apparently found awkward or problematic—such as the reputed irregularity of Jesus' birth, his baptism by John for "remission of sins," his proclivity for associating with notorious sinners, and (above all) his shameful execution by a Roman governor—are likely authentic. Traditions that church apologists found embarrassing or difficult to explain caused too much general discomfort for believers to have added them as accretions to Jesus' story. This criterion of discomfort is particularly helpful in evaluating the plausibility of Jesus' actions, including his inability to win over most of his contemporaries and his controversial behavior in the Temple.

Potentially embarrassing traditions about Jesus include his baptism by John (Mark 1), his family's belief that he behaved irrationally (Mark 3:21, 31–35), his inability to heal those who do not trust him (Mark 6:5), his alleged reputation as a drunkard and a glutton who cultivated bad company (Matt. 11:16–19; Luke 7:31–35), his refusal to be called good (Mark 10:18; changed in Matt. 19:16–17), and the brutal fact of his crucifixion as a threat to the Roman government. (For a partial list of sayings that many scholars believe form an authentic core of Jesus' teachings, see Box 11.1.)

Multiple Attestation

With this standard for determining reliable material, scholars consider the variety of different sources in which a particular statement or teaching occurs. If a saying appears in Mark, the Q document, and the Gospel of Thomas—all of which are presumed to be independent of one another—it is likely to be genuine. Jesus' emphasis on the kingdom of God appears to be confirmed by its frequent appearance in all three of these sources. (The specific form or interpretation of an individual kingdom pericope, however, is open to question. Each Christian writer or editor tends to modify individual sayings when incorporating them into a written text.) The criterion of multiple attestation also affirms several other traditions, including Jesus' interest in women, the poor, and social outcasts such as lepers, tax collectors, prostitutes, and other "sinners." The tradition that Jesus performed healings, emphasized Wisdom precepts, and challenged both religious and political authority structures is also multiply attested.

Examples of material found in different sources, such as Mark, Q, and/or Thomas, include the parable of the dinner party (Matt. 22:1–14; Luke 14:16–24; Thom. 64); the perplexing command to hate one's relatives (Matt. 10:37; Luke 14:26; Thom. 55 and 101); asking, seeking, and finding (Matt. 7:7–8; Luke 11:9–10; Thom. 2 and 94); new wine and old wineskins (Mark 2:22; Luke 5:37–38; Thom. 47); and blessing the hungry (Matt. 5:6; Luke 6:21a; Thom. 69).

BOX 11.1 The Authentic Voice of Jesus

These are a few of the approximately one hundred sayings that meet the Jesus Seminar's criteria for genuineness (all quotations are from the Scholars Version). Many scholars also regard some of Jesus' eschatological pronouncements as authentic.

Love your enemies. . . . God causes the sun to rise on both the bad and the good, and sends rain on both the just and the unjust. Tell me, if you love those who love you, why should you be commended for that? Even the [tax] collectors do that. (Matt. 5:44–46)

Congratulations, you poor! God's domain belongs to you.
  Congratulations, you hungry! You will have a feast.
  Congratulations, you who weep now! You will laugh. (Luke 6:20–21)

When someone strikes you on the cheek, offer the other as well. When someone takes away your coat, don't prevent that person from taking your shirt along with it. . . . Give to everyone who begs from you. (Luke 6:29–30)

Forgive, and you'll be forgiven. (Luke 6:37b)

Foxes have dens, and birds of the sky have nests; but the son of Adam has nowhere to rest his head. (Luke 9:58)

You won't be able to observe the coming of God's imperial rule. People are not going to be able to say, "Look, here it is!" or "Over there!" On the contrary, God's imperial rule is right here in your presence. (Luke 17:20–21)

Every government divided against itself is devastated, and a house divided against a house falls. If Satan is divided against himself—since you claim that I drive out demons in Beelzebub's name—how will his domain endure? If I drive out demons in Beelzebub's name, in whose name do your own people drive (them) out? In that case, they will be your judges. But if by God's finger I drive out demons, then for you God's imperial rule has arrived. (Luke 11:17–20)

What does Heaven's imperial rule remind me of? It is like leaven which a woman took and concealed in fifty pounds of flour until it was all leavened. (Luke 13:20–21)

To what should we compare God's imperial rule, or what parable should we use for it? Consider the mustard seed: When it is sown on the ground, though it is the smallest of all the seeds on the earth, yet when it is sown, it comes up, and becomes the biggest of all garden plants, and produces branches, so that the birds of the sky can nest in its shade. (Mark 4:30–32)

Heaven's imperial rule is like treasure hidden in a field: when someone finds it, that person covers it up again, and out of sheer joy goes and sells every last possession and buys that field. Again, Heaven's imperial rule is like some trader looking for beautiful pearls. When that merchant finds one priceless pearl, he sells everything he owns and buys it. (Matt. 13:44–45)

That's why I tell you: don't fret about life—what you're going to eat—or about your body—what you're going to wear. Remember, there is more to living than food and clothing. Think about the crows: they don't plant or harvest, they don't have storerooms or barns. Yet God feeds them. You're worth a lot more than the birds! . . . Think about how the lilies grow: they don't slave and they never spin. Yet let me tell you, even Solomon at the height of his glory was never decked out like one of these. If God dresses up the grass in the field, which is here today and tomorrow is tossed into an oven, it is surely more likely (God cares for) you, you who don't take anything for granted. (Luke 12:22–28)

So I tell you, ask—it'll be given to you; seek—you'll find; knock—it'll be opened for you. Rest assured: everyone who asks receives; everyone who seeks finds; and for the one who knocks it is opened. (Luke 11:9–10)

No man can be a slave to two masters. No doubt that slave will either hate one and love the other, or be devoted to one and disdain the other. You can't be enslaved to both God and a bank account. (Matt. 6:24; Luke 16:13)

There was a rich man whose fields produced a bumper crop. "What do I do now?" he asked himself, "since I don't have any place to store my crops. I know," he said, "I'll tear down my barns and build larger ones so I can store all my grain and my goods. Then I'll say to myself, 'You have plenty put away for years to come. Take it easy, eat, drink, enjoy yourself.'" But God said to him, "You fool! This very night your life will be demanded back from you. All this stuff you've collected—whose will it be now?" (Luke 12:16–20)

Coherence

The standard of coherence allows the scholar to regard material as potentially authentic if it resembles material already established by the criteria of orality, distinctiveness, and multiple attestation. If a saying or action is consistent with themes and concepts generally recognized as genuine, it, too, may be accepted.

Emphasizing a broader approach to the historical Jesus quest, Dale Allison suggests that instead of focusing primarily on the authenticity of individual sayings or actions, scholars should supplement this atomizing procedure by looking for consistent patterns that appear again and again in the Synoptic Gospels. Combining the principles of multiple attestation and coherence, Allison asks us to recognize that the Synoptic accounts generally agree in their portrayal of the kind of man Jesus was, consistently demonstrating his characteristic behaviors and manner of teaching. For all their incorporation of legendary material and authorial modifications of the tradition, the first three Evangelists repeatedly show Jesus as both a wisdom teacher and an apocalyptic prophet, a coherent portrait found in all relevant sources, including Mark, Q, and the special Matthean and Lukan materials. If we look for this broad consistency, Allison states, we are more likely to encounter a historically plausible Jesus.

Although generally agreeing on the techniques by which Jesus' sayings and deeds can be tested for historical plausibility, today's scholars have arrived at enormously disparate views of who Jesus really was. The process that began with the earliest Gospel writers' efforts to portray Jesus according to their differing visions of his significance continues unabated today. Whereas the Evangelists' main goal was to interpret Jesus theologically for the authors' believing community (cf. John 20:31), contemporary historians attempt a more objective approach. Even so, as many scholars have rightly cautioned, pure objectivity is rarely achieved; the picture that one tries to paint of Jesus typically says more about the painter than it does about the subject. Almost all efforts to reconstruct Jesus' personal character and motivation tend to be projections of qualities that the individual researcher consciously or unconsciously accepts as valuable. Students and scholars alike generally assume that Jesus, when found, will be relevant to contemporary needs and expectations. Most persons still reject the possibility that Jesus was too limited by his exclusively religious preoccupations as a first-century Jew to have anything meaningful to say to our largely secular and technological society.

A Nonapocalyptic Wisdom Teacher

Because Jesus' most characteristic speech forms—the parable and the aphorism—contain little apocalyptic material, many scholars have become increasingly skeptical that Jesus was a prophet of eschatological doom. Among numerous other passages regarded as inauthentic, these scholars almost unanimously dismiss the long apocalyptic prophecies about Jesus' Second Coming (Mark 13; Matt. 24; Luke 21) as largely the composition of the Evangelists. The lengthy Johannine meditations on Jesus' divine nature are similarly judged to reflect the Christology of the author's own community, not the speech of the historical Jesus. Neither the Synoptics' eschatological predictions nor John's metaphysical discourses correlate with Jesus' known forms of speech, which were characterized by brevity and images from daily life.

Researchers associated with the Jesus Seminar, a group of largely North American scholars, have published two valuable study aids, *The Five Gospels: The Search for the Authentic Words of Jesus* (1993) and *The Acts of Jesus: What Did Jesus Really Do?* (1998). Extensively annotated, these works provide detailed arguments for accepting or rejecting the authenticity of each saying in the four canonical Gospels, as well as in the Gospel of Thomas. Although the Seminar participants regard only about 20 percent of the Gospel sayings as authentic, they generally agree that during Jesus' lifetime he was known both as a healer and an exorcist, as well as a teacher of unconventional wisdom. Printing in red or pink the actions and statements of Jesus judged likely to be historical, these volumes portray Jesus as a compassionate sage deeply concerned with social justice—particularly for the poor and downtrodden—and with each person's intimate relationship with God.

In stripping away the Synoptic Gospels' eschatological overlay and the Johannine Gospel's high Christology, these scholars discover a nonapocalyptic Jesus. According to this view, Jesus was primarily a sage and a healer ministering to the politically powerless, a portrayal, they argue, inherently more credible than the Synoptics' prophet of eschatological judgment or John's divine Word descended from heaven. For some critics, discovering Jesus as a wisdom teacher, even a kind of Hellenistic-Jewish-Cynic philosopher, removes the embarrassment of regarding him as an apocalyptist whose promise to return (within his disciples' lifetimes) as the eschatological Son of Man was not kept.

An Apocalyptic Jesus

Other scholars doubt that rescuing a historical figure from his eschatological misconceptions is a reputable criterion for scholarship. Many scholars point out that, if Jesus did not advocate an eschatological viewpoint, it is extremely difficult, if not impossible, to fit him into his historical environment. There is general scholarly agreement that Jesus' immediate predecessor, John the Baptist, warned Judah of an impending divine visitation and that Jesus' most influential interpreter, the apostle Paul, eagerly anticipated Jesus' imminent return as eschatological judge (see Chapters 13 and 14). With Jesus' career closely bracketed by two such proponents of the approaching *eschaton,* advocates of a noneschatological Jesus face a formidable challenge in explaining the continuity

(or lack of it) in the sequence from John to Jesus to Paul.

Because of widespread public interest in searching for the historical Jesus, in recent years a veritable flood of new books on the subject has occurred; many of these are concisely summarized in David B. Gowler's helpful survey of the scholarly quest. Scholars who opt for a noneschatological Jesus who did *not* expect the world to end in his own day include Marcus Borg, who sensitively explores Jesus' ethical teachings and his concept of the divine–human relationship. In two important studies, John Dominic Crossan presents Jesus as a social revolutionary and champion of social justice whom Roman tyranny crushed.

Although the issue of whether the historical Jesus was primarily a wisdom teacher or an apocalyptist (or a mixture of both) is likely to remain unresolved for the foreseeable future, many studies of Jesus published during the twenty-first century argue strongly that he was a proponent of Jewish eschatology. In her biography of Jesus, Paula Fredriksen marshals impressive evidence to place Jesus firmly in his Jewish context as an apocalyptic preacher. In Fredriksen's reading, Jesus is a Torah-observant Palestinian Jew who shared John the Baptist's sense of impending eschatological crisis and preached that the kingdom of God would arrive during his final Passover week in Jerusalem, a seditious message for which Pilate executed him. Bart D. Ehrman subtitles his book *Apocalyptic Prophet of the New Millennium;* like Fredriksen, he seems to regard Mark's portrayal of Jesus as an eschatological preacher who expected the Son of Man's imminent appearance as generally reliable. Dale C. Allison also emphasizes Jesus' apocalyptic expectation that God would set up the long-awaited kingdom during Jesus' lifetime. These scholars, as well as many others, believe that the Synoptic tradition provides conclusive evidence that Jesus was motivated by the same kind of apocalyptic hope that inspired both the Baptist and Paul. However, as Schweitzer devastatingly pointed out a century ago, all three were wrong; the kingdom did not come. (See the works by Allison, Borg, Crossan, Ehrman, and Fredriksen in "Recommended Reading.")

In addition to the books already mentioned, students pursuing the issue of Jesus' historical identity will find several other works helpful, including recent volumes by E. P. Sanders and Gerd Theissen and Annette Merz, the latter a comprehensive review of contemporary Jesus research. John P. Meier's *A Marginal Jew: Rethinking the Historical Jesus,* of which four out of a projected five volumes have been published, exhaustively investigates the sociocultural world in which Jesus grew up, as well as his distinctive kingdom teachings. Ekkehard W. Stegemann and Wolfgang Stegemann provide a useful sociopolitical study of the first-century Jesus movement, which also examines in detail the economic environment in which Jesus and his early followers lived. Of recent works, particularly valuable is *The Historical Jesus in Context,* which examines historical inscriptions and other archaeological artifacts to position Jesus and his immediate followers in both their Jewish and their Greco-Roman environments (see "Recommended Reading").

Jesus and the Restoration of Israel

In an attempt to transcend the debate about whether Jesus was an apocalyptic or nonapocalyptic figure, several scholars have recently placed even greater emphasis on his social and historical context. How would impoverished Galilean villagers have responded to Jesus' message of the kingdom? Would they have viewed it as an implicit criticism of Roman imperial rule, particularly the system's exploitation of rural laborers through heavy taxation and unavoidable debt? Scholars such as Richard Horsley see Jesus in the tradition of Israelite prophecy, a teacher who worked for Israel's renewal and the establishment of economic and social justice. Inspired by the disparity between the covenant ideal and the present reality of Roman rule through client kings and aristocratic landowners, Jesus sought to reinterpret the Mosaic heritage in a way that would achieve God's intentions for his people. Selecting twelve disciples as a symbol of Jewish restoration, he led a movement that inevitably clashed with the Jerusalem leaders who benefited from Roman control (see Horsley in "Recommended Reading").

Taking Jesus' fatal relationship with the Roman Empire a step further, Reza Aslan's new study, *Zealot,* portrays Jesus as a passionate nationalist committed to evicting the Roman occupation from the land God had promised to Israel. Because the Romans executed Jesus by crucifixion—a penalty Aslan argues was reserved for rebels, bandits, and persons judged guilty of treason—he concludes that Jesus must have resembled other troublemakers whom the Romans had similarly eliminated, such as Judas the Galilean and Simon of Perea. (For a discussion of "Messianic Claimants Before and After Jesus," see Chapter 3.) In Aslan's reconstruction, Jesus did claim to be Israel's Messiah and therefore a king, a political aspiration the Romans would regard as treasonous—a direct threat to the emperor's legitimacy.

Although most scholars do not view Jesus as a forerunner of the extreme Zealot party, which, as Aslan states, did not formally coalesce until about 68 CE during the Jewish war with Rome, his biography is helpful in its detailed description of social, religious, and political currents running through Galilee in Jesus' day. Aslan's vivid depiction of the Temple cult—with its hundreds of daily animal sacrifices—and his astute speculations about Jesus' reasons for violently attacking the sanctuary's priestly administration (in collusion with Rome) make *Zealot* a valuable contribution to excavating the historical Jesus.

It is said that each new generation re-creates the great figures of the past according to its own values and aspirations. For this reason, scholars urge us to avoid retrojecting our present ideals on a Jesus who lived at a time and in a place qualitatively different from our own, making him appear too congenial to twenty-first-century tastes. However, scholarly portraits of a Jesus who was deluded and doomed by his eschatological obsessions may not satisfy most New Testament readers. Among other considerations, the man embodied in the Gospels seems far too profound and insightful to attempt forcing an egocentric and literalist eschatology into historical fulfillment. In the Jesus-as-apocalyptist view, he is entirely the product of his own time. But the opposing theory of a noneschatological Jesus, a benign wisdom teacher committed to helping the oppressed, creates a Jesus who is suspiciously compatible with the modern academic temperament.

To scholars who see Jesus as having promoted a **realized eschatology,** Jesus' challenge to discern that God's kingdom reigns now—if people can get over their spiritual blindness and recognize its transcendent power—is intellectually attractive. Perpetuating the Johannine doctrine of cultivating eternal life in the present, this view has the advantage of presenting a Jesus who transcends his ancient Palestinian milieu to speak directly to contemporary experience. Most scholars, however, advise us to beware of discovering a Jesus who appears too acceptable by today's standards. No matter how much Jesus may have differed from his peers, the historical person was a first-century rural Jew and, in many ways, would undoubtedly seem disturbingly alien to twenty-first-century sensibilities.

Some General Agreements About the Historical Jesus

Although scholars have not reached a consensus about Jesus' primary teachings, many do agree on the general outline of his life. The Gospel traditions contain numerous data about Jesus that are relatively "theology-free," particularly biographical information that is not cited as a fulfillment of biblical prophecy or a promulgation of Christological doctrine. We may accept the tradition, then, that Jesus was born late in the reign of Herod the Great (between 6 and 4 BCE); that he was raised in

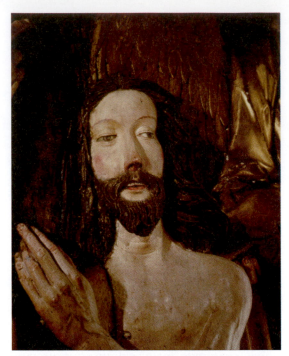

FIGURE 11.2 *The Baptism of Christ.* In this late-fifteenth-century wood carving, an anonymous sculptor imaginatively re-creates Jesus' ecstatic expression as he receives baptism from John. Showing Jesus as a bearded youth with thick, flowing hair, the artist suggests the overwhelming effect of the Holy Spirit that descends upon the young Nazarene, perhaps awakening him to a new awareness of his divine Sonship.

Nazareth (which is not mentioned in the Hebrew Bible); that he was the presumed son of Joseph, a carpenter, and his wife, Mary; and that he had brothers (or close relatives) named James (a future leader of the Jerusalem church), Joseph, Simon, and Judas (Jude), and an unknown number of sisters (or stepsisters) (Mark 6; Matt. 13:55). If Jesus and his putative father were carpenters (or some other kind of artisan), it probably means that the family had lost its hereditary land, which reduced them to a social status below that of Galilee's landowning peasants.

When "about thirty years old" (Luke 3:1), Jesus came to John the Baptist for baptism in the river Jordan (c. 27 or 29 CE, depending on how one calculates Luke's "fifteenth year of the emperor Tiberius") (see Figure 11.2). Mark's report that John baptized Jesus "in token of repentance for the forgiveness of sins" (Mark 1:4) is not an event that the early church would have invented. Because official doctrine held that Jesus was "sinless" and superior to the Baptist, Mark's baptismal story could not have emerged unless there was a firm tradition that Jesus had indeed submitted to John's ministrations. Some scholars think it likely that Jesus was, for an indefinite period, a disciple of the Baptist and did not begin his own ministry until after Herod Antipas had arrested and beheaded the prophet. Although it is impossible to confirm this theory, apparently Jesus held the Baptist in the highest regard, perhaps regarding him as a mentor.

Following his baptism and perhaps an interlude of solitary meditation, Jesus began proclaiming a distinctive variation on the Baptist's message—the kingdom of God is near (or perhaps already present). In Jesus' proclamation, God's burgeoning rule reversed ordinary social values and encompassed people who were typically devalued by "respectable" society. The Synoptic tradition consistently shows Jesus as an active friend of the poor and outcast, going out of his way to share meals with known "sinners" and other disreputable people. Jesus' penchant for unsavory associations—along with his reputation as "a glutton and a drinker"—passes the credibility test because no believer would invent such tales (Matt. 10:18–19; Luke 15:1–3; 7:33–8:3). Some commentators have even suggested that Jesus' parable of the prodigal son—which features a young man who squanders his inheritance in riotous living, much to the dismay of his disapproving brother—may hint at a situation in Jesus' own life before he underwent John's cleansing baptism.

Although anything said about Jesus before his association with the Baptist is necessarily conjectural, the twin traditions of his public repentance and his unfailing sympathy for social pariahs suggest that he knew this class of people well (and may once have been counted among them). His family's objections to Jesus' suddenly embarking on a controversial ministry and his neighbors' doubts about his newfound prophetic claims (Mark 3:20–21, 31–35; 6:1–6) also suggest that Jesus' early life was qualitatively different from his later career. The antifamily sentiments Jesus repeatedly expressed—including the "hard sayings" about hating father and mother and leaving "the dead to bury their dead"—emphasize a sharp break with his former connections and way of life.

Whereas Jesus' Nazarene acquaintances had defined (and thereby limited) him in terms of his occupation and blood ties—he was merely "Mary's son," "the carpenter"—Jesus seems to have attained a radically new identity: He called God *Abba* (Father). This divine-Parent/human-child relationship appears to underlie some of his most distinctive pronouncements, such as his injunction to be as giving and gracious to other mortals as God is to all his children, regardless of their merits (Matt. 5:44–48). The paradoxical command to "Love your enemies!" is practicable because God perceives human "enemies" as potential allies and friends.

Jesus' invitation to share in the divine relationship seems to have been remarkably inclusive: He breaks bread with Pharisees, lepers, tax collectors, slaves, women, and children (who, in the Greco-Roman world, were at the bottom of the social hierarchy). While raising their spirits, he also shows concern for their bodies: *All* the traditions agree that Jesus was a healer. How Jesus accomplished his healings and exorcisms is not known, but the people he helped were convinced that he had changed them for the better, not least by validating their intrinsic worth and accepting some of them among his disciples. Issuing witty, provocative statements that challenged widely accepted values and attitudes, baiting religious authorities, and imparting a sense of physical and spiritual health to persons desperately in need of curative attention, Jesus, whether he wished to or not, could not help attracting followers.

Pursuing an itinerant life of deliberately chosen poverty and wandering randomly throughout Galilee from village to village, Jesus inevitably drew around him a mixed group of Galilean fishermen, farmers, women, and other ordinary working people. In parables and other figures of speech, he illustrated the desirability of living in God's kingdom—or perceiving the reality of divine rule, despite the oppression of secular authority, in the worlds of nature and human society. Although the Synoptic writers imply that the Galilean campaign lasted about a year, John's Gospel may be right in stating that it extended over at least three years and included several visits to Jerusalem.

While attracting throngs of mostly powerless admirers, Jesus also aroused powerful enemies. His apparent habit of relying on his own authority to pronounce on religious observances, such as Sabbath keeping—so different from the rabbinic tradition of citing the honored view of one's predecessors—irritated some and outraged others. Whereas many disciples were probably delighted with Jesus' authoritative dismissal of some purity laws and criticism of the Temple's priestly administration, some influential Sadducean officials in Jerusalem were undoubtedly suspicious of his motives. The priestly leadership may have regarded him as a blasphemer and a potential threat to the delicate balance between Roman rule and Jewish welfare.

Jesus' healings, his preaching about God's kingdom, and his drawing of large, unruly crowds may have inspired some persons who particularly hated Roman occupation of the Holy Land to speculate that he was Israel's Messiah—the promised deliverer who would rid them of Gentile domination. John's report that a crowd wanted to proclaim him "[a Davidic] king" (John 6:15) and Luke's observation that as Jesus approached Jerusalem to celebrate Passover there his disciples "thought the reign of God might dawn at any moment" (Luke 19:11) may echo actual historical conditions. Although most scholars do not think that Jesus presented himself as Israel's Messiah, some of his followers may have viewed him as the one prophesied to restore David's monarchy (see Box 11.2). If such claims were being circulated

on Jesus' behalf, it would explain Pilate's action in executing Jesus on the charge of treason, pretending to be "king of the Jews." To the Roman prefect, Jesus was merely another messianic (royal) claimant, such as those who led popular uprisings after Herod the Great's death (see Chapter 3).

Jesus' crucifixion under Pilate, which Tacitus and other non-Christian historians confirm, was not the kind of death—public, shameful, and associated with slaves and criminals—believers would fabricate for their leader. In the considered opinion of many Jews, the fact that Jesus was crucified meant that he could *not* have been the Messiah: No passage in the Hebrew Bible even hinted that the Messiah would die, let alone be executed as a felon by Gentile agents. (Proof texts that Christians later cited, such as the suffering servant poem in Isaiah 53 or Psalm 22, to explain Jesus' death are not specifically messianic prophecies.) Paul candidly describes the awkward fact of Jesus "nailed to the cross" as a "scandal"—a "stumbling block to Jews" and "sheer folly" to the Greeks (1 Cor. 1:23, 18). The humiliating fact of Jesus' crucifixion—so contrary to scriptural expectations—was probably the chief obstacle that kept most Jews from taking Christian preaching about him seriously. Some scholars believe that the first narrative about Jesus' miracles (and perhaps including his Passion)—the hypothetical Signs Gospel presumably later incorporated into John's Gospel—was composed to demonstrate that Jesus *was* Israel's Anointed One and that he was killed only because people refused to believe in his wondrous deeds (see Chapter 10).

Wisdom and the Kingdom of God

In contrast to Mark and Matthew, who were apparently inspired by the disaster that befell Judea in 70 CE, the authors of John and Thomas show that it was possible to follow a Jesus who was fundamentally an exponent of divine

BOX 11.2 Developing Views of Jesus as the "Son of God"

Individual New Testament writers preserve different stages of a Christian concept that apparently developed over time—the conviction that Jesus was the "Son of God." As the passages discussed below indicate, Jesus' divine Sonship was interpreted in various ways. To understand the Christian authors' evolving views, we must start where they did, with the Hebrew Bible.

1. *Son by royal coronation.* According to the covenant made with David's royal dynasty, the kings of Israel—Yahweh's anointed ones or "messiahs"—enjoyed a special relationship with their God, comparable to that of a son with his father. Speaking of David's heirs, Yahweh promises, "I will be his father, and he shall be my son. . . . My love will never be withdrawn" (2 Sam. 7:14–15). Psalm 2, sung at the enthroning of one of David's descendants, expresses a similar view of the filial bond between king and God. Yahweh tells his "anointed" ruler (messiah): "You are my son . . . this day [the date of his crowning] I become your father" (Ps. 2:7). Thus, the Davidic king's coronation was simultaneously the time of his becoming God's "son" by adoption.

2. *Son by resurrection.* The oldest recorded Christian interpretation of Jesus' Sonship— Paul's letter to the Romans (mid-50s CE)— states that Jesus "was declared Son of God by a mighty act in that he rose from the dead" (Rom. 1:3). In this passage, Paul follows Israel's ancient tradition that David's ultimate heir—the Messiah—would also in some sense become God's Son. As Paul expresses the concept, Jesus receives Sonship at his resurrection, the Deity's miraculous confirmation of his messianic worthiness. The author of Acts preserves a similar view, representing Peter shortly after the Resurrection as saying that, by exalting Jesus to his "right hand," "God has made this Jesus . . . both Lord and Messiah" (Acts 2:36). The oldest layer of preserved tradition suggests that the first Christians saw

Jesus, like Israel's anointed kings, becoming God's Son by adoption, a reward conferred at his resurrection and ascension to heaven.

3. *Son by intimacy with God.* The early church's identification of Jesus as a divine Son was undoubtedly stimulated by Jesus' practice of addressing God as *Abba,* an Aramaic term children used to express intimacy with their male parent (Mark 14:36; Luke 11:2). Closer to "daddy" than the more formal "father," *Abba* suggests Jesus' sense of personal closeness to the Deity. Paul attests to his church's continued use of the word (Rom. 8:15; Gal. 4:6).

4. *Son by adoption at baptism.* If Mark's Gospel (c. 66–70 CE) were our only Gospel, we might conclude that Jesus was designated God's Son at his baptism (Mark 1:11), apparently through adoption and anointment by the Holy Spirit. In Mark, the demons recognize Jesus' relationship to God (3:11–12), but no human being acknowledges it until he has proven his faithfulness unto death (15:39). Jesus' final act of filial devotion affirms his divine Sonship (an idea also expressed in Hebrews [2:20; 5:7–9]).

5. *Son by conception.* Adding infancy narratives to their accounts of Jesus' life, Matthew and Luke (mid-80s CE) push the beginning of Jesus' Sonship back in time, to the moment of his conception (Matt. 1:10; Luke 2:26–35). Matthew and Luke interpret Yahweh's promise to become as a father to the Davidic "son" (2 Sam. 7; Ps. 2) as meaning more than mere adoption; they see the Heavenly Voice at Jesus' baptism as simply confirming the biological fact of divine parentage.

6. *Son as creative Word.* Eschewing traditions of Jesus' virginal conception, John's Gospel, the last one written (c. 95–100 CE), declares that Jesus existed as God's Son long before he came to earth, even before the universe came into being (John 1:1–18). A variation of the concept appearing in Colossians (1:15–20; 2:9–10), John's doctrine of Jesus' eternal deity and Sonship ultimately became the Christian standard of belief.

Wisdom rather than a purveyor of eschatological judgment. The Johannine writer rarely mentions the kingdom as an integral part of Jesus' teaching, but he may convey a significant historical truth when he makes the nature of Jesus' personal kingship the crucial issue on which Pilate's execution of Jesus hinges (John 18:33–19:22). During the confrontation with Pilate, the Johannine Jesus states that his kingdom is not of this world—that it is not political—but he fails to define either his government or his own kingly role (John 18:36).

John nonetheless gives his readers a relatively clear idea of what Jesus' kingdom involves. From the outset of his Gospel, the author identifies Jesus with the eternal Word, the expression of immortal Wisdom by and through which God created the universe (John 1:1–18; Prov. 8:22–36). In his person, Jesus reveals and shares with others the vital Wisdom by which God rules and communicates his will. As noted in Chapter 10, John firmly links Jesus with Israel's **wisdom literature,** the teachings of which associate the wise person with God's *basileia*—heavenly kingship.

The deuterocanonical Wisdom of Solomon expresses the affinity between Wisdom and divine kingship that may have influenced John's view of Jesus:

> For she [Wisdom] ranges [the earth] in
> search of those who are worthy of her; . . .
> The true beginning of wisdom is the desire
> to learn, and a concern for learning means
> the keeping of her laws; to keep her laws is
> a warrant of immortality; and immortality
> brings a man near to God. Thus the desire
> of wisdom leads to kingly stature [a *basileia*].
>
> (Wisd. of Sol. 6:16–20)

Notice that learning and keeping God's wise laws, the principles by which he orders the cosmos, lead to eternal life and make the obedient possessor of Wisdom a king.

Wisdom also reveals the kingdom of God: "She [Wisdom] guided him [Jacob, the embodiment of Israel] on straight paths; she showed him the **basileia tou theou** [literally, the kingdom or sovereignty of God]" (Wisd. of Sol. 10:10). In Israel's wisdom writings, Wisdom (Sophia, a personification of God's primary attribute) imparts knowledge, divine favor, and immortal life (Prov. 2:1–10; Job 28:12–23; Ecclus. 24; Wisd. of Sol. 8:4, 13). She discloses secrets of the unseen world to those who seek her, satisfying their intellectual and spiritual thirst (Wisd. of Sol. 7:17–29). The references to Jesus' unveiling the "secret" or "mystery of the kingdom of God" in Mark (4:11) may preserve a parallel to the Johannine tradition that Jesus' teaching focuses not on the eschatological but on Wisdom's revelation of previously hidden cosmic truths.

According to this view of Jesus' kingdom message, Jesus teaches that followers must come under God's rule by imitating and participating in the divine *basileia*. As noted previously, *basileia* implies kingly autonomy, freedom, and self-determination—living one's life as the master of one's situation. The Johannine Jesus tells his followers that he has already "conquered the world" (John 16:33). The self-confidence or "authority" with which Jesus habitually teaches may derive from his profound sense of possessing the celestial Wisdom that sets people free (Matt. 7:28–29; Mark 1:22; John 8:22). At liberty to proclaim his personal views on the Torah, he inevitably antagonizes many rival teachers of the Law. As a sage through whom Wisdom speaks, he is also free to recognize his own kingship—the *basileia* that Wisdom imparts (Wisd. of Sol. 6:17–20; 10:10). If Jesus publicly equated his wisdom teaching with kingship, the connection may have inspired Pilate's suspicion. As governor for Rome, Pilate could tolerate no Jew claiming to be a king of any kind.

The Johannine Jesus informs his disciples that he fully reveals the Father, the supreme reality with whom he—and they—enjoy a life-giving unity (John 17:1–8, 20–23). Spiritual union with the Deity confers a power upon Jesus' disciples that will enable them to accomplish greater deeds than he (John 14:10–14). The arrival of the Paraclete, or Spirit of Truth, endows believers with additional heaven-sent Wisdom and allows them to continue imitating

Jesus' example of kingly rulership. Indeed, the Paraclete manifests the same power of *basileia* that characterizes Jesus (John 16:7–15). Initiated into the mystery of divinity and empowered by the Spirit, the Johannine disciple possesses a kingdom authority resembling that of Jesus himself (John 14:12–21).

Summary

Given the diverse theological backgrounds and varying degrees of personal skepticism in today's scholarly community, it seems unlikely that widespread agreement about Jesus' exact teachings will soon be reached. Some scholars point out that intense eschatological expectations, particularly in first-century Palestine, were not incompatible with wisdom teaching. From this perspective, Jesus may have been both a sage and a relatively traditional eschatological prophet in the manner of John the Baptist. If this view is correct, there would be a direct line from the Baptist, to Jesus' Synoptic proclamation, to Paul's fervent expectations of Christ's swift return. A number of scholars, however, question whether the historical Jesus resembled either the Baptist or Paul in worldview or ideas about God's intentions. Some commentators believe that Paul's eschatological bent may be partly a carryover from his Pharisaic heritage and partly a result of his assumption that Jesus' resurrection signaled the beginning of End time, an idea that may derive from Daniel's apocalypse (Dan. 12:1–3).

Scholars in large part agree that the historical Jesus taught about God's kingdom (whatever his precise meaning by the phrase), but many question the belief that he taught about himself. Although he seems to have perceived the world and his mission from the vantage point of someone who holds a peculiarly close relationship to God, he may not have called himself Christ, Son of God, or the Holy One of Israel. All these honorific titles, scholars suggest, were bestowed on him posthumously by a community that—in retrospect—recognized him as Israel's Messiah and God's chief agent, the means by which the Deity reconciles humanity to himself. In telling Jesus' story so that readers could understand his

true significance, it was natural for the Gospel writers to apply titles such as Christ and Son of God to the historical figure. In the Evangelists' view, they could not write the truth about who Jesus was unless they presented him in the light of his resurrection and glorification. The Galilean prophet and teacher who had challenged the world's norms in the name of a radical egalitarianism for all God's children was—by his continuing life in the believing community—vindicated as divine, the Wisdom and love of God made flesh.

Questions for Review

1. Define the problem confronting scholars in their quest to find the historical Jesus. In what ways do the four Gospel writers' theological portraits of Jesus make it difficult to determine exactly what the man Jesus said and did? Besides the Gospels, which were written by believers in Jesus' unique divinity, what other first-century sources do we have that might help illuminate his life?

2. When did the modern quest to discover the "real" Jesus begin? Describe the picture of an "apocalyptic" Jesus that Albert Schweitzer drew in his famous *Quest of the Historical Jesus*. What different conclusions about Jesus' teachings have some contemporary scholars drawn? How do scholars who view Jesus as an apocalyptist portray his teachings?

3. Summarize some of the criteria scholars use to screen for authenticity the Gospel sayings ascribed to Jesus, including the tests of orality, distinctiveness, dissimilarity, and awkwardness (the "embarrassment" factor). What standards can we use to distinguish between what Jesus himself taught and what the believing community may have attributed to him later?

4. Describe some areas in which scholars generally agree about the historical Jesus.

5. Moving from the earliest to the latest canonical statements about Jesus as the "Son of God," summarize evolving New Testament views about Jesus' relation to the Father. How did Jesus' use of the term *Abba*, the concept that Davidic kings became God's sons by adoption at the time of their coronation and anointment, and Paul's implication that Jesus became "Son of God" at his resurrection and ascension

to heaven contribute to the idea of Jesus' divinity? Describe the important differences between the way Mark introduces Jesus' Sonship and John's doctrine of preexistence and incarnation.

Questions for Discussion and Reflection

1. How can we reconstruct a coherent picture of Jesus and his teaching using the source materials currently available? What sources do you regard as most trustworthy, as most likely to represent Jesus as he might have been rather than as he appeared to the believing community that worshiped him?

2. Do we possess any sure means of finding out what Jesus actually thought about himself and his purpose? In reading the four Gospels, do you detect any clues that reliably indicate the nature of Jesus' own self-awareness? Explain your answer.

3. Contrast the Synoptic portrait of Jesus as an apocalyptic exorcist and preacher with John's portrayal of him as a revealer of heavenly Wisdom. How would you distinguish Mark's idea of Jesus' kingdom from John's concept of Jesus' kingship?

4. The communities that produced the Synoptic Gospels clearly had very different traditions about Jesus from those treasured in the group that created John's Gospel. How do you account for such divergent views about Jesus' nature and teaching in two roughly contemporaneous Christian communities?

5. Contemporary scholars have not been content simply to accept traditional portraits of Jesus promoted in many church circles. Instead, using techniques of historical analysis, they attempt to construct a "theology-free" portrait of Jesus that seems rationally plausible. Is this scholarly quest helpful in understanding the "real Jesus," or does it have harmful effects? Explain your answer.

Terms and Concepts to Remember

aphorisms	realized eschatology
basileia tou theou	Trajan
(kingdom of God)	Wisdom and
Bithynia	*basileia*
Claudius	Wisdom literature

Recommended Reading

Allison, Dale C., Jr. *Constructing Jesus: Memory, Imagination, and History.* Grand Rapids, Mich.: Baker Academic, 2010. Places Jesus firmly in his first-century-CE Galilean religious context, and concludes that Jesus saw himself as both Messiah and chief actor in an imminent eschatological drama.

———. "Jesus Christ." In K. D. Sakenfeld, ed., *The New Interpreter's Dictionary of the Bible*, Vol. 3, pp. 261–293. Nashville: Abingdon Press, 2008. A concise but thorough analysis of the scholarly quest for the historical Jesus.

Aslan, Reza. *Zealot: The Life and Times of Jesus of Nazareth.* New York: Random House, 2013. Presents Jesus as a Jewish nationalist whom the Romans executed for treason.

Borg, Marcus J. *Jesus: Uncovering the Life, Teachings, and Relevance of a Religious Revolutionary.* San Francisco: HarperSanFrancisco, 2006. A thoughtful review of the historical Jesus and his relevance for today.

Charlesworth, James H. *The Historical Jesus: An Essential Guide.* Nashville: Abingdon Press, 2008. A concise survey of current scholarly attempts to recover the historical Jesus, emphasizing a rigorous methodology.

Chilton, Bruce. *Rabbi Jesus: An Intimate Biography.* New York: Doubleday, 2000. Places Jesus' life and teachings within their first-century Jewish context.

Crossan, John Dominic. *The Historical Jesus: The Life of a Mediterranean Peasant.* San Francisco: HarperSanFrancisco, 1991. A distinctive scholarly interpretation of Jesus as a sage advocating radical social egalitarianism.

———. *Jesus: A Revolutionary Biography.* San Francisco: HarperSanFrancisco, 1994. A distillation of Crossan's earlier book for the general reader.

Eddy, Paul R., and Boyd, Gregory A. *The Jesus Legend: A Case for the Historical Reliability of the Synoptic Jesus Tradition.* Grand Rapids, Mich.: Baker Academic, 2007. Argues for the historical authenticity of the Synoptic portrayals of Jesus.

Ehrman, Bart. *Did Jesus Exist?: The Historical Argument for Jesus of Nazareth.* San Francisco: HarperOne, 2013. Contrary to claims that Jesus is a figure of myth, this examination of the evidence concludes that Jesus was a historical person.

———. *Jesus: Apocalyptic Prophet of the New Millennium.* New York: Oxford University Press, 1999. Stresses Jesus' eschatological expectation of God's kingdom.

Fredriksen, Paula. *Jesus of Nazareth, King of the Jews: A Jewish Life and the Emergence of Christianity.* New York: Knopf, 1999. Places Jesus firmly in the context of apocalyptic Judaism.

Freyne, Sean. *Jesus, A Jewish Galilean: A New Reading of the Jesus Story.* Edinburgh: T and T Clark, 2004. A detailed study placing Jesus in his historical Galilean environment.

Funk, Robert W.; Hoover, Roy W.; and the Jesus Seminar. *The Five Gospels: The Search for the Authentic Words of Jesus.* A Polebridge Press Book. New York: Macmillan, 1993. Features a highly colloquial translation of the canonical Gospels and Thomas, with Jesus' authentic words printed in red or pink, doubtful sayings in gray, and speeches ascribed to him by tradition or Gospel authors in black.

Funk, Robert W., and the Jesus Seminar. *The Acts of Jesus: What Did Jesus Really Do?* San Francisco: HarperSanFrancisco, 1998. A radical evaluation of Jesus' historical actions that portrays him as a healer, exorcist, and wisdom teacher who associated with social outcasts.

Gowler, David B. *What Are They Saying About the Historical Jesus?* Mahwah, N.J.: Paulist Press, 2007. A lucid survey of current scholarly attempts to recover the Jesus of history.

Horsley, Richard. *The Prophet Jesus and the Renewal of Israel: Moving Beyond a Diversionary Debate.* Grand Rapids, Mich.: William B. Eerdmans, 2012. Argues that Jesus saw himself primarily as God's prophetic agent of Israel's restoration—a threat to the Temple high priests and the Roman imperial order.

Jeremias, Joachim. *Parables of Jesus,* 2nd ed. (Reprint). New York: Prentice-Hall, 1972. Still a required starting point for interpreting Jesus' parables.

Johnson, Luke T. *The Real Jesus: The Misguided Quest for the Historical Jesus and the Truth of the Traditional Gospels.* San Francisco: HarperOne, 1997. Challenges the Jesus Seminar's methodology without providing a persuasive alternative.

Levine, Amy-Jill. *The Misunderstood Jew: The Church and the Scandal of the Jewish Jesus.* San Francisco: HarperOne, 2006. A study by a feminist scholar who firmly places Jesus in his native Jewish cultural environment.

Levine, Amy-Jill; Allison, Dale C.; and Crossan, D. C., eds. *The Historical Jesus in Context.* Princeton Readings in Religions. Princeton, N.J.: Princeton University Press, 2006. A collection of scholary essays placing Jesus in the historical and archaeological milieu of the Greco-Roman world.

Meier, John P. *A Marginal Jew: Rethinking the Historical Jesus,* Vols. 1–4. New York: Doubleday, 1991 (Vol. 1), 1994 (Vol. 2), 2001 (Vol. 3), 2009 (Vol. 4). The first four volumes of a projected multivolume biography by an eminent New Testament scholar, the most comprehensive study to date.

Patterson, Stephen J., and Robinson, James M. *The Fifth Gospel: The Gospel of Thomas Comes of Age.* Philadelphia: Trinity Press International, 2000. Includes a new translation and interpretative commentary.

Sanders, E. P. *The Historical Figure of Jesus.* New York: Viking Press, 1994. A readable work of solid scholarship.

———. *Jesus and Judaism.* Philadelphia: Fortress Press, 1985. A scholarly and highly readable evaluation of the Gospel traditions about Jesus and his message, particularly about the kingdom and its original meaning in the context of Palestinian Judaisms.

Schweitzer, Albert. *The Quest of the Historical Jesus: A Critical Study of Its Progress from Reimarus to Wrede.* New York: Macmillan, 1961. A monumental work; originally published in 1906, but still an influential scholarly search for the real figure of history.

Sheehan, Thomas. *The First Coming: How the Kingdom of God Became Christianity.* New York: Random House, 1986. A scholar's careful and innovative account of historical and theological developments that transformed the Jesus of history into the Christ of faith.

Stegemann, Ekkehard W., and Stegemann, Wolfgang. *The Jesus Movement: A Social History of Its First Century.* Minneapolis: Fortress Press, 1999. A detailed survey of first-century Mediterranean society in general and Palestinian Judaism in particular.

Theissen, Gerd, and Merz, Annette. *The Historical Jesus: A Comprehensive Guide.* Minneapolis: Fortress Press, 1998. A detailed review of contemporary Jesus scholarship.

Van Voorst, Robert E. *Jesus Outside the New Testament: An Introduction to the Ancient Evidence.* Grand Rapids, Mich.: Eerdmans, 2000. Examines all known ancient noncanonical references to Jesus.

Whealey, Alice. *Josephus on Jesus: The Testimonium Flavianum Controversy from Late Antiquity to Modern Time.* New York: Lang, 2003. Evaluates the authenticity of Josephus's references to Jesus.

Wright, N. T. *The Original Jesus.* Grand Rapids, Mich.: Eerdmans, 1996. A conventional evaluation of the historical Jesus.

PART FOUR

An Account of the Early Church

The two scenes painted on this early-sixth-century codex illustrate themes prominent in the two-volume work of Luke-Acts (*left*). The upper scene shows Jesus' trial before Pilate, the Roman prefect of Judea; similar encounters with Roman magistrates occur throughout Acts, presenting court hearings in which the author repeatedly demonstrates that Christians pose no legal threat to governmental authorities. In the lower scene, Judas Iscariot first returns the thirty pieces of silver he received for betraying Jesus and then hangs himself; two different versions of Judas's death appear in Acts 1 and Matthew 27.

On his travels through the urban centers of Greece and Asia Minor, Paul and his missionary companions met a wide range of ethnic and cultural groups. These two Roman portrait busts (*below*), both depicting citizens of Ephesus, where Paul stayed at least two years, illustrate some of the diverse expressions that Paul's Gospel may have evoked in his Ephesian audience.

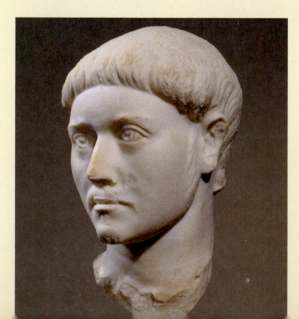

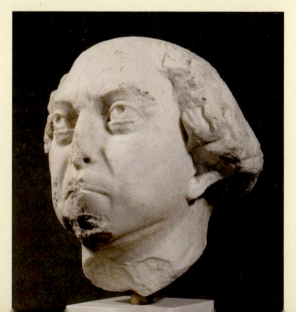

The partly reconstructed facade of this Ephesus library was erected in honor of Tiberius Julius Celsus (*right*), governor of the province of Asia after 117 CE. Although built after Paul's day, this elegant structure typifies the kind of sophisticated architecture that characterized the city of Ephesus.

Crowning the Athenian Acropolis, the Parthenon (*below*), a marble temple dedicated to Athene Parthenos (the Virgin), dominates the city's skyline today as it did when Paul debated Stoic philosophers in its shadow almost 2,000 years ago. Completed in 438 BCE, in Christian times the edifice was rededicated to Mary the Virgin (Maria Parthenos). ■

Designed to bring spring water from Mount Carmel to Caesarea Maritima, this aqueduct (*left*), with its massive stone arches, is typical of the city's monumental architecture. A thriving Mediterranean seaport that served as the headquarters for Roman administration of Judea (*middle*), Caesarea figures prominently in Acts: Here Peter baptized Cornelius, a Roman centurion, who became the first Gentile Christian (10:1–48), and here Paul was imprisoned for two years under the governors Felix and Festus (23:33–27:1).

When sent from Caesarea to Rome to stand trial in the emperor Nero's court, Paul would have seen many brick buildings similar to this modern reconstruction of a large house and apartments in Ostia (second century CE) (*below*). ▪

CHAPTER 12

Luke's Account of the Early Church:
The Book of Acts

You will bear witness for me in Jerusalem, and all over Judaea and Samaria, and away to the ends of the earth. Jesus to the Jerusalem disciples, Acts 1:8

Key Topics/Themes In the Book of Acts, Luke continues his two-part narrative of Christian origins, depicting characters who, like Jesus, are models of Christian behavior and service. This theologically shaped account of the early church emphasizes many of the same themes that dominated Luke's Gospel. First, God's ancient promises to Israel through Abraham and Moses are fulfilled in the life and work of Jesus and his successors, who constitute a Spirit-blessed community, the true Israel. Second, emphasizing that "the new way (Christianity)" is a universal means of salvation encompassing all nations, Jewish and Gentile alike, Luke then shows biblical promises being fulfilled when the Jewish disciples are empowered by the Holy Spirit at Pentecost (2:1–47). Third, the author illustrates the step-by-step process by which divine promises were extended to non-Jewish peoples, beginning with campaigns in Samaria and Syria (8:1–12:25). The climactic events of this first section are the conversions of Paul, a Pharisee (ch. 9), and Cornelius, a Roman soldier, the first Gentile anointed by the Holy Spirit (chs. 10–11).

In the second part of Acts (chs. 13–28), Luke focuses almost exclusively on the travels of Paul, who leads a successful mission to Gentiles in Asia Minor and then carries the new religion into Europe, arriving in Rome about 60 CE. Arguing that Christianity is a natural extension of Judaism that offers no threat to the Roman state, Luke designs his narrative to demonstrate that the church's task is to create an international and ethnically diverse community, a work that extends indefinitely into the future (28:28).

The author of Luke-Acts clearly conceived of his two-volume work, a narrative of Jesus' ministry followed by an account of the early church, as integrally linked. Not only does Luke dedicate both volumes to the same patron, Theophilus, he also makes the final event in his Gospel, Jesus' **Ascension** to heaven, the first event described in the Book of Acts (cf. Luke 1:1; 24:50–53 and Acts 1:1–5, 10–11). In fact, one of Luke's major goals in Acts is to demonstrate a strong connection between what Jesus said and did and what his disciples later accomplish in his name. Directed by the same Holy Spirit that had empowered Jesus, his followers loyally carry on their

285

The Book of Acts

Author: Traditionally Luke, companion of Paul (see Chapter 9). The same person who wrote the Gospel ascribed to Luke, name unknown.

Date: About 90 CE.

Place of composition: Unknown, perhaps Antioch or Ephesus.

Audience: Addressed, like Luke's Gospel, to Theophilus, representing Gentile Christians scattered throughout the Roman Empire.

Master's work, performing similar healing miracles and giving humble service to others. Operating as part of God's plan to redeem humanity, both Jew and Gentile, the disciples now serve on a world stage, bearing their message about Jesus from Jerusalem to the heart of the Roman Empire.

The author (whom we call Luke) structures the Acts narrative to parallel what happened in his Gospel, emphasizing many of the same themes. As Jesus received God's Spirit while at prayer (Luke 3:21–22), so the Spirit descends on his praying followers (Acts 2:1–13). Jesus' healing of a lame man (Luke 5:17–26) is mirrored by Peter's almost identical miracle (Acts 3:1–10), as is Jesus' resuscitation of a widow's son (Luke 7:11–17) reflected in Peter's resuscitation of a deceased widow named Dorcas (Acts 9:36–43). Similarly, Peter's healing of Aeneas, a "man who had been bedridden with paralysis for eight years" (Acts 9:32–35), echoes Jesus' curing "a paralyzed man on a bed" (Luke 5:18–20).

Luke's emphasis on Jerusalem and the Temple, so prevalent in his Gospel (see the discussion of Lukan themes in Chapter 9), also dominates Acts, in which Paul and other characters repeatedly travel to and from Jerusalem. After receiving the Holy Spirit, the disciples frequently gather at the Jerusalem Temple, where Peter proclaims that "Israel's God has given the highest honor to his servant Jesus" by "[raising] him from the dead" (Acts 3:1–4:4), a program that closely parallels the Lukan Jesus' extensive teaching at the Temple (Luke 19:45–21:38, especially 19:47–48; 21:1–5, and 37–38).

Most important, Acts also underscores the Gospel theme that both Jesus and his followers are totally innocent of sedition against Rome. In Luke's account of Jesus' trials before Pilate and Herod Antipas, both the Roman governor and the Roman-appointed local ruler conclude that the accused has committed no crime (Luke 23:1–25), as do the brigand crucified next to Jesus (23:40–43) and the Roman centurion who witnesses his death, judging him "innocent" (23:47). As noted below, Acts reinforces Luke's argument that Christians are guiltless of breaking Roman law, a theme of blamelessness highlighted in the accounts of Paul's parallel trials before Roman governors and Herodian rulers (Acts 23:1–26:32).

While emphasizing that Christians are not political revolutionaries determined to overthrow the Roman government, Luke's narrative also shows that their "new way" in fact undermines many accepted standards of Greco-Roman life. In examining Luke's presentation of Christianity's effect on established social customs, scholars have recently pointed to its disruptive and destabilizing consequences. To cite only one example, most inhabitants of the Roman Empire were polytheists who worshiped a multitude of gods, gods whose patronage and state-supported worship were widely recognized as essential to the public welfare. When Christians declared that only Israel's God—of whom no statue or other image could be made—was worthy of worship, their message often sparked mass rioting. Particularly in describing Paul's visits to Ephesus and other Greek cities, Luke shows that Christian missionaries, while innocent of political sedition, demanded changes in their converts' way of life that subverted many traditional civic and social values (19:1–41). To defenders of social and civil convention, they were guilty of "turning the world upside down" (16:6, NRSV).

In composing his idealized account of Christian beginnings, Luke is highly selective in his use of the oral "traditions" and "eyewitness" reports on which Acts presumably is based (cf. Luke 1:1–4). Although he lists the names of the original eleven apostles (1:13), Luke tells us almost nothing about most of them. Instead, he concentrates on only a few figures, using them to represent crucial stages in early Christianity's swift transition from a Jewish to a Gentile movement. The apostle Peter, representing Palestinian Jewish Christianity and the original Jerusalem church, presides over the first half of Acts (chs. 1–12). Paul, exemplifying Hellenistic Christianity's mission to the Gentiles, dominates the second half (chs. 13–28). Except for brief references to James and John, the sons of Zebedee (3:1–4:22; 12:1–3; cf. Gal. 2:6–10), Luke rarely mentions Jesus' Galilean disciples or their activities. Whatever anecdotes about other apostles the author may have heard, he does not include them in his narrative; nor does he explain how some major churches, such as that at Rome, were founded. More significantly, although Paul is Luke's heroic exemplar of true Christianity, the author does not actually portray Paul as he reveals himself in his letters, omitting controversial Pauline ideas and even contradicting some of Paul's own versions of events (see Box 13.1).

In looking at maps depicting Paul's journeys (see Figures 12.2, 12.3, and 12.6), we see immediately that Luke is interested in only one trajectory of Christianity's geographical expansion—that which resulted in the founding of Pauline churches in Asia Minor and Greece and in Paul's preaching in Rome. Focusing exclusively on the northeastern Mediterranean region, Luke says nothing about other large areas where churches were concurrently being established, such as those in Egypt, Cyrene, and other locations in North Africa. According to tradition, the author of Mark's Gospel founded a church in Alexandria (Eusebius, *History* 2.16), where a major Christian center developed. Although we cannot be sure why Luke ignores the southern Mediterranean churches, his silence may result from a strong preference for Pauline Christianity, a branch of the faith that historically came to dominate the Western church.

In reading Acts, we must remember that Luke's account of early Christianity is as theologically oriented as his Gospel. Luke believes that the apostles and missionaries who brought "the new way" (9:2) to Greece and Rome were led by the same divine force that inspired Jesus. For Luke, the church preserves and maintains the same ethical and spiritual qualities that distinguished Jesus' career, making the "acts of the apostles" a continuation of the Gospel story.

The Divine Plan of Humanity's Salvation

The incidents from early Christianity that Luke chooses to include in Acts are arranged to express the author's overarching concern: the Spirit-directed growth of the church and its expansion westward from Palestine to Italy. In general, the narrative advances chronologically, showing the religion's incremental expansion into new geographical areas. Luke's organizing principle is stated in Acts 1:8, in which the risen Jesus gives the disciples his final command: They are to "bear witness" to him "in Jerusalem, and all over Judaea and Samaria, and away to the ends of the earth."

Acts thus begins in Jerusalem (chs. 1–7), records a mission to Samaria (ch. 8), gives a detailed account of Paul's three missionary journeys throughout Asia Minor and Greece, and concludes with Paul's arrival in Rome, the center of imperial power and perhaps representing "the ends of the earth" (chs. 13–28).

Luke's Major Theme: God's Spirit Operating in Human History

In tracing Christianity's course from its Palestinian roots to Gentile flowering, Luke illustrates the manner in which God has kept his biblical promises to Israel. Jesus and his Jewish followers are the fulfillment of Israel's prophetic goals, a demonstration of God's faithfulness that will re-assure Theophilus and other Gentiles who join their ranks. At the end of his Gospel and the beginning of Acts, Luke takes pains to remind readers of Israel's hopes for a Davidic king. The disciples approaching Jerusalem wonder if the kingdom is at last about to materialize (Luke 19:11), a question they reformulate to Jesus immediately before his ascension to heaven: "Lord, is this the time when you are to establish once again the sovereignty of Israel?" (Acts 1:6). Jesus' answer—that they must remain in Jerusalem to "receive power" from above and then evangelize the earth—implies a positive response to their question. In Luke's view, God indeed reestablishes his rule over true citizens of Israel, the Jewish disciples of Jesus who represent the covenant people. Although most people do not perceive it, God has accomplished the restoration of true Israel through the faithfulness of Jesus' Jewish followers.

Luke further highlights the theme of Israel's restoration when the Eleven elect a replacement for Judas Iscariot (who dies soon after betraying Jesus), thus re-creating a leadership of Twelve, symbolic of Israel's twelve tribes (1:23–26). Once this continuity between Israel and the Christian community has been affirmed, however, Luke never again refers to the replacement (Matthias) or to any of the Twelve except for Peter and (briefly) John. (James, John's brother, is mentioned only to record his beheading by Herod Agrippa I [12:2].) In Luke's thematic purpose, the Twelve are the Israelite foundation of the Christian church, a cornerstone on which Gentiles will build the superstructure.

At Pentecost, when the Lukan Peter states that God's eschatological promise of Israel's Spirit-anointing is fulfilled (2:14–36), 3,000 Jews join the Galilean disciples (2:37–41). Throughout both his Gospel and Acts, Luke is careful to distinguish the Jewish people, many of whom accept Jesus as the national Messiah, from the small group of their priestly leaders who had advocated Jesus' execution. Not only had the Jews as a whole—including their "rulers"—acted in ignorance of Jesus' identity, but it was also God's foreordained will that the Messiah *had* to suffer—no human action could have prevented it (3:17–24).

Peter's second Jerusalem speech emphasizes the Lukan theme that Jews remain "the heirs of the prophets" and "within the covenant" that God made with Abraham. Hence, God sent his "servant" and offered his "blessing" to them first, keeping the vow he had sworn to Israel's patriarchs and prophets (3:25–26). As Luke presents his history of salvation, Jerusalem and its Temple—where Pharisees and Jewish Christians worship side by side—are the focal point of God's redemptive acts for all humanity.

Even when traveling in Gentile territories, the Lukan Paul consistently offers his message first to members of the local synagogue, before proselytizing Syrians or Greeks. Although Paul repeatedly threatens to devote himself entirely to recruiting Gentile believers, he continues to minister to fellow Jews. At the end of Acts, however, Paul cites a portentous verse from Isaiah 6 about God's people being deaf and blind to his prophetic word. (This is the same passage that Mark had used to explain why Jesus spoke in parables—to *prevent* his hearers from understanding him [cf. Mark 4:10–12; Acts 28:23–27].) When an exasperated Paul declares that henceforth he will concentrate all his efforts on "the Gentiles" because "the Gentiles will listen" (28:28), he expresses an unforeseen twist of history. By the time Luke wrote the sequel to his Gospel, Christianity, originally a Jewish phenomenon, had become a faith dominated by Gentiles. In this paradoxical event, Luke saw God's will accomplished: the gathering of every ethnic and national group into a universal worshiping community.

Luke's Use of Speeches

Like other historians of his day, Luke ascribes long, elaborate speeches to his leading characters, such as Peter, Stephen, James, and Paul. But whoever the speaker, most of the speeches sound much alike in both style and thought. This similarity among Acts' many discourses, as well as the fact that they seem to reflect attitudes prevalent in the author's time rather than those of the historical figures he describes, suggests to most scholars that they are largely Luke's own compositions. In the absence of exact transcriptions of apostolic speeches, many of which were delivered amid noisy and unruly crowds, Luke apparently follows the standard practice of Greco-Roman authors by supplementing what was remembered with material of his own creation. Ancient historians and biographers like Thucydides, Livy, Tacitus, and Plutarch commonly enlivened their narratives with speeches put in the mouths of historical characters. The classical writer composed such discourses based on his conception of the speaker's character and major concerns at the time the speech was given. He was not expected to reproduce a particular speech exactly as it was delivered. Thucydides explains the historian's method clearly and briefly:

> I have found it difficult to remember the precise words used in the speeches which I listened to myself and my various informants have experienced the same difficulty; so my method has been, while keeping as closely as possible to the general sense of the words that were actually used, to make the speaker say what, in my opinion, was called for by each occasion.
>
> (*The Peloponnesian War I.22*)

In short, while attempting to reproduce the "general sense" of what people said, Thucydides created their speeches according to his understanding of what "was called for by the occasion." We cannot know the extent to which Luke's speeches reflect ideas expressed in generations before his time.

Organization of the Book of Acts

Luke arranges his narrative in ten major sections:

1. Prologue and account of the ascension (1:1–11)
2. Founding of the Jerusalem church (1:12–2:47)
3. The work of Peter and the apostles (3:1–5:42)
4. Persecution of the Hellenistic-Jewish Christians: the first missions (6:1–8:40)
5. Preparation for the Gentile mission: the conversions of Paul and Cornelius (9:1–12:25)
6. The first missionary journey of Barnabas and Paul: the Jerusalem conference (13:1–15:35)
7. Paul's second missionary journey: evangelizing Greece (16:1–18:21)
8. Paul's third missionary journey: revisiting Asia Minor and Greece (18:22–20:38)
9. Paul's arrest in Jerusalem and imprisonment in Caesarea (21:1–26:32)
10. Paul's journey to Rome and his preaching to Roman Jews (27:1–28:31)

Prologue and Account of the Ascension

In his introduction to Acts (1:1–11), Luke refers to the "first part" of his work (the Gospel) and then picks up where his earlier story of Jesus left off. Before ascending to heaven, the resurrected Jesus remains on earth for "forty days," a number that symbolizes the period of time required to accomplish a major religious undertaking. (Moses remained on Mount Sinai for forty days while receiving the Torah, and Jesus' wilderness temptation was of similar duration.)

Although his report of Jesus' post resurrection instruction is tantalizingly brief, Luke makes some major points. The risen Jesus offers fresh insights into the nature of his kingdom, which is not the political restoration of the Jewish state that the disciples had anticipated (Luke 19:11; Acts 1:3, 6–7). Contrary to apocalyptic expectations, God's rule expands gradually as the Christian message slowly permeates Greco-Roman society. The historical process must begin in Jerusalem, but the Spirit will empower believers to carry their faith throughout the earth (1:1–8).

Luke is the only New Testament writer to describe Jesus' ascent to the spirit world. He presents it as a quasi-physical movement skyward, culminating in Jesus' disappearance into the clouds (symbolic of the divine presence [Exod. 40:34–35; 1 Kings 8:10; Dan. 7:13]). Luke thus makes the peaceful ascension a prophetic model of Jesus' quiet return (the Parousia) (1:9–11).

Founding the Jerusalem Church

The Apostles

After describing **Matthias**'s election to replace Judas Iscariot as one of the Twelve—Luke's version of Judas's death differs sharply from Matthew's report (Matt. 27:5)—Luke outlines the qualifications for apostleship. According to Luke, an apostle must be a person who had physically accompanied Jesus during his entire ministry and had also witnessed his resurrection (1:21–22). Perhaps because Paul had not personally known Jesus, Luke almost never calls him an apostle, although Paul himself passionately fought to make others acknowledge his right to that title (Gal. 1). (See Box 12.1 for a list of Acts' "major milestones.")

The Holy Spirit at Pentecost

Luke presents the disciples' experience at **Pentecost** (a Jewish harvest festival held fifty days after Passover) in terms of prophetic fulfillment (2:1–47). The **Holy Spirit**'s descent upon a group of 120 disciples (a multiple of the Twelve) vindicates Jesus' promise to equip them with supernatural power (1:8; Luke 24:29), and it fulfills the prophet Joel's ancient prediction that God would someday infuse all kinds of people with his Spirit (Joel 2:28–32) (see Figure 12.1). Its presence symbolically rendered as wind and flame, the Spirit empowers the disciples to speak in tongues. This phenomenon of religious ecstasy, in which believers emit an outpouring of strange sounds (called *glossolalia*), came to characterize the early church and was generally regarded as a sign of God's presence (11:14–18; cf. Paul's discussion of "ecstatic speech" in 1 Cor. 14). According to Luke, the pentecostal miracle enabled recipients of the Spirit to converse in foreign languages they had previously been unable to speak, although some onlookers accuse the inspired disciples of being "drunk," implying they spoke unintelligibly (2:1–13; cf. 1 Cor. 14:2–25).

Peter, chief of the apostles, delivers Acts' first major speech to interpret the pentecostal experience (2:14–20). Peter's discourse illustrates several Lukan themes. The pentecostal Spirit is the phenomenon that Joel had foreseen as a sign of the last days. It is bestowed upon all believers, regardless of age or gender—women prophesy equally with men.

The Lukan Peter says that the Spirit-giving event is linked to "portents in the sky" and other astronomical displays foretold in Joel's prophecy. Interestingly, Luke represents Peter as equating the disciples' religious ecstasy with Joel's vision of cosmic upheaval, such as the sun's being darkened and the moon's turning to blood. (This interpretation of the astronomical "portents" as purely metaphorical suggests that the author's references to identical phenomena in Luke 21:25–28 may also be seen as symbolic language rather than as forecasts of literal events in future history.) Luke's main point, however, is that God has anointed his church, giving it the power to preach in every known tongue, the many languages of Pentecost representing the universality of the Christian mission.

Peter's long speech expresses another important Lukan theme: Jesus' death occurred "by the deliberate will and plan of God"—and was thus a theological necessity (2:23). God has vindicated his "servant" by raising him from the dead and placing him at God's "right hand" (the position of favor and power) in heaven. Linking this exaltation of Jesus with Davidic

BOX 12.1 Major Milestones in the Book of Acts

According to Acts' version of Christian origins, the new faith began at a particular moment in time—at the Jewish Feast of Pentecost, in Jerusalem, when the Holy Spirit descended upon a gathering of Jesus' Galilean disciples (Acts 2). In Luke's carefully structured presentation, Christianity's growth in adherents and geographical expansion is marked by significant milestones, crucial events at which Christianity enters into a new stage of development. Each step along the evolutionary path from a Palestinian Jewish sect to a largely Gentile faith preached throughout the Greco-Roman world is indicated by a representative episode, headlining the author's "good news" bulletins.

1. The Christian church is born in Jerusalem—the Holy Spirit anoints 120 disciples at Pentecost, followed by mass conversions to the new Jesus movement (2:1–47).
2. Peter performs the first miraculous cure "in Jesus' name" (3:1–10), continuing Jesus' work.
3. Stephen, a "Hellenist" Jew, becomes the first Christian martyr (6:8–7:60).
4. Another Hellenist, Philip, makes the first non-Jewish converts—a Samaritan sorcerer and an African eunuch (8:4–40).
5. Saul (Paul) of Tarsus, while fiercely persecuting "the way," is suddenly converted by a vision of the risen Jesus on the road to Damascus (9:1–30; cf. 22:6–11; 26:12–19).
6. Peter converts the Roman centurion Cornelius, who becomes the first non-Jew to receive the Holy Spirit (10:1–42).

7. Believers in Jesus are first called "Christians" in Antioch, Syria, which becomes the second major center of Christianity (11:19–26).
8. James, the son of Zebedee and brother of John, becomes the first member of the Twelve to suffer martyrdom (12:1–3).
9. Paul, following Barnabas, makes his first missionary journey from Antioch to Asia Minor (modern Turkey) (13:1–14:28), carrying Pauline Christianity to the Greek-speaking world.
10. The first church council, held at Jerusalem to discuss whether Gentile converts must observe Mosaic Law, decides in favor of admitting uncircumcised males, opening "the way" to all nationalities (15:1–35).
11. Carrying the faith from western Asia to Europe, Paul makes his first missionary tour of Greece, founding churches at Philippi, Thessalonica, and Corinth (16:9–18:23).
12. In Jerusalem, Paul is arrested by a Roman officer (21:15–22:29). After two years in a Caesarean prison, Paul appears before Governor Festus and Herod Agrippa II (25:6–32), fulfilling the risen Jesus' prediction that Paul will testify "before kings" (9:15).
13. Exercising his right as a Roman citizen, Paul is sent to Rome for trial. Under house arrest in Rome, Paul vows to focus exclusively on recruiting Gentiles (28:16–30).

themes from the Psalms, Peter declares that by resurrecting Jesus, God has made him "both Lord and Messiah." Because Luke believes that Jesus was Messiah during his lifetime, the author may here preserve a very early Christian belief that Jesus—the "man singled out by God"—became confirmed as Messiah only on his ascension to heavenly glory (2:22, 36; see Box 11.2).

The Jerusalem Commune

Repeating a theme prominent in his Gospel, the author connects the Spirit's presence with its recipients' subsequent way of life, particularly their social and economic arrangements. The overwhelming "sense of awe" that believers feel is translated into the work of creating an ideal community without rich or poor.

FIGURE 12.1 *The Descent of the Holy Spirit at Pentecost.*
In this painting by El Greco (1541–1614), like a rushing
wind and hovering tongues of flame, the Holy Spirit
anoints disciples gathered in an "upper room" in
Jerusalem. For the author of Acts, this event parallels the
Spirit's descent at Jesus' baptism, empowering the early
church to carry on Jesus' work.

Luke reports that the faithful sold their
possessions so that money and goods could be
distributed according to individual members'
needs. Holding "everything" "in common" (2:43–
45; 4:32–35), the Jerusalem community meets
Jesus' challenge to sacrifice material possessions
to attain true discipleship (Luke 18:18–30). As
a result of establishing the kingdom's economic
ethic as its standard, however, the Jerusalem
church apparently depended on financial help
from Gentile churches to sustain its ideal (Gal.
2:10; Rom. 15:25–28).

The Work of Peter and the Apostles

In the next section (3:1–5:42), Luke describes
the activities of Peter and some of his Jerusalem
associates. Peter's healing a crippled man by
invoking Jesus' authority (3:1–10) demonstrates that the disciples continue their leader's work. Presenting a second Petrine speech
(3:11–26), delivered in the Temple precincts,
Luke interprets the miracle's significance.
God wishes to reconcile Judaism with its infant daughter, the church. Jesus' resurrection,
to which Peter and his associates are living witnesses (2:32; 3:15), proves the validity of the
disciples' faith and provides an opportunity
for official Judaism to unite with the followers
of Jesus. Luke insists that the persons who
condemned Jesus did so "in ignorance." The
Jerusalem leaders acted blindly because God,
for his own mysterious reasons, had already
determined that his "servant" must die (3:13–18).
Perhaps because the Deity is the ultimate
cause of Jesus' death, he now offers forgiveness to those who unwittingly carried out his
will (3:17–19; Luke 23:24). As Luke portrays
the situation, at this critical moment in Jewish–
Christian relations, union of the two parties is
possible.

Part of Israel does unite with the Christian
fold. Luke rekindles the excitement of these

early days as he records large numbers of Jews flocking to join the disciples (4:4). In contrast to the people's enthusiastic response, Luke also shows the Jerusalem leadership hardening its position and attempting to halt the new movement.

In chapters 3–5, Luke heightens the sense of dramatic tension by presenting several direct confrontations between the apostles and the Jerusalem authorities. The author attributes much of the church's trouble to the Sadducees, whose priests control the Temple (4:1–6; 5:17–18). In contrast, many Pharisees tend to tolerate or even champion some Christian activities (5:34–40; 23:6–9). During Peter's second hearing before the Sanhedrin, the Pharisee **Gamaliel,** a famous first-century rabbinical scholar, is represented as a protector of the infant church.

Seeing "the new way" (9:2) as divinely supported, Luke shows that its growth cannot be stopped. After the High Priest (identified as Annas in 4:6) imprisons the apostles, celestial forces intervene to release them (5:17–26). Whether employing human agents like Gamaliel or angels from heaven, the Deity acts decisively to ensure the Jesus movement's survival and expansion.

Persecution of the Hellenistic-Jewish Christians: The First Missions

Even as the Sadducees attack it from without, the Christian community simultaneously experiences internal trouble (6:1–8:40). Strife breaks out between two different groups within the Jerusalem church. Although Luke only hints at the cause of this disagreement, he makes it clear that two distinct parties emerge: the **Hellenists,** who are Greek-speaking Jews of the Diaspora, and the "Hebrews," who are Aramaic-speaking Jews apparently native to Palestine.

Some historians believe that this division reflects first-century Judaism's prevailing social and religious distinction between Palestinian Jews and Jews from foreign countries who had more thoroughly adopted Greek ideas and customs.

Because he wishes to present the Jerusalem church as a model for later Christianity, Luke portrays the incipient conflict as being resolved by an orderly administrative process. Accordingly, the Twelve act unanimously to elect seven Greek-speaking disciples to represent the Hellenists (6:1–6).

Stephen: The First Christian Martyr

Although he implies that the seven leaders were elected to supervise the church's communal meals, Luke soon reveals that the seven were mainly proclaimers of the gospel. Because of his public preaching, the chief Hellenist, **Stephen,** becomes the focus of Saducean hostility. The priestly opposition accuses Stephen of attacking the Temple cult and subverting the Mosaic Torah, charges that also had been leveled against Jesus (6:8–15).

The account of Stephen's trial and public stoning effectively links the first part of Luke's history, centered in Jerusalem, with the second part, which records Christianity's expansion into non-Jewish territory. The author fashions Stephen's speech (7:2–53) as a Hellenist's severely critical indictment of Jerusalem's religious institutions. Stephen accuses the Temple leadership of "fighting against the Holy Spirit" (to Luke, the supreme offense), murdering the Messiah, and failing to keep the Torah (7:2–53). The episode concludes with typically Lukan themes: In prayer, the dying Stephen— the first Christian **martyr**—experiences a vision of heaven and, echoing Jesus' words on the cross, asks God to forgive his executioners (7:54–60).

The author juxtaposes Stephen's ecstatic vision with the introduction of "a young man named Saul" who guards the cloaks of those stoning the victim. Luke's contrast of the two men, each zealous in his faith, is deeply ironic. The young Saul will become Paul the apostle, Christianity's most famous missionary, and eventually suffer martyrdom himself. His appearance at this point in Luke's narrative connects the episode about Stephen, a Greek-educated Christian Jew, with Paul's mission to Greek-speaking Gentile nations, a development recorded in the second half of Acts.

Demonstrating that the church's enemies cannot seriously interfere with its progress, Luke states that the Saducean priests' efforts to block "the new way" have the opposite effect. The persecution that follows Stephen's execution drives the Greek-speaking Jewish Christians from Jerusalem, but this event only serves to spread the faith into receptive new areas. (Although the Hellenists are expelled from the holy city, the Aramaic-speaking disciples evidently are permitted to remain.) Contrary to their expectations, the priests' hostile action becomes the means by which Jesus' order to plant the faith in Judea and Samaria (1:8) is obeyed.

The Samaritan Mission

In his parable of the humane Samaritan, Luke (10:29–37) indicates Jesus' goodwill toward that despised group and anticipates Christianity's later growth in Samaria. In Acts, Luke portrays the Samaritan mission mainly through the work of a single figure, **Philip,** one of Stephen's fellow Hellenists. Focusing on two of Philip's new converts, the author illustrates the increasing ethnic (and ethical) diversity of the church as it takes in the mixed population living outside Judea. The first convert is **Simon Magus,** a notorious magician who later tries to buy Peter's gift of imparting the Holy Spirit, an attempt the apostle severely rebukes (8:4–24). In legends that developed after New Testament times, Simon became a sinister figure involved in black magic and the occult. According to some historians, he is the prototype of Faust, the medieval scholar

who—to gain forbidden knowledge—sells his soul to the devil.

The Simon Magus episode suggests the moral risks taken as the church absorbed potential troublemakers from the Hellenistic world; Philip's second major convert represents a significant breakthrough for the new religion. Occurring south of Jerusalem rather than in Samaria, Philip's conversion of an Ethiopian eunuch forms the climax of his career. According to the Mosaic Torah, a eunuch (a sexually mutilated male) was excluded from full Israelite citizenship. Despite the prejudice against him, however, this eunuch is a "God-fearer," a term Luke uses to denote a class of Gentiles who have adopted the Jewish religion without undergoing circumcision or observing all the dietary requirements.

Luke sets up the scene to illustrate several characteristic themes. The author shows Philip encountering the Ethiopian while he is reading a singularly appropriate passage from a Greek edition of the Hebrew Bible—Isaiah 53. This poem describes an anonymous servant of God who suffers unjustly and offers Philip the perfect opportunity to identify Isaiah's mysterious servant with Jesus, who, though innocent, endured comparable suffering. Throughout this section of Acts, Luke repeatedly refers to Jesus as a "servant" (3:13, 26; 4:27, 30), the only New Testament writer to do so (cf. Luke 22:26–27). Interestingly, Luke omits Isaiah's allusions to the "servant" bearing punishment for others' sins, probably because the author does not interpret Jesus' death as a ransom or vicarious atonement for sinful humanity (see Box 9.1).

In depicting the early church's missionary efforts, Luke emphasizes the Spirit's directing role. Evangelists like Philip (and later Paul) go exactly where and to whom the Holy Spirit guides them, moving almost erratically from place to place. After Philip baptizes the eunuch, we are told that "the Spirit snatched Philip away, and the eunuch saw no more of him . . ." (8:39).

Preparation for the Gentile Mission: The Recruitment of Paul and Cornelius

Paul's Vision of Jesus

As a literary artist, Luke skillfully prepares his readers for the historic transformation of Christianity from a movement within Judaism to an independent world religion. He does this by recording the recruitment of two different men whose acceptance of the new faith foreshadows the Gentile mission (9:1–12:25). The most dramatic event is the encounter of **Saul (Paul)** with the risen Lord on the road to **Damascus.** The author regards Paul's experience as crucial and gives no fewer than three separate accounts of the incident (9:3–8; 22:6–11; 26:12–19). Luke clothes the event in supernatural images—a blinding light and heavenly voice—although Paul's only surviving reports of what happened are much more subdued (cf. Gal. 1:12, 15–16; 1 Cor. 15:8–9).

In Luke's historical scheme, Paul becomes God's agent (9:15), explicitly chosen to bring "the new way" (as Greek-speaking Christians first called their faith) to non-Jewish nations. As a result of the mystical experience that transformed his view of Jesus, Paul now suffers the same kind of persecution he had inflicted on others. Luke recounts two separate plots on Paul's life, which he foils by escaping first from Damascus and then from Caesarea (9:24–30).

Peter's Call to Baptize a Gentile

Luke devotes two full chapters (10–11) to the episode involving **Cornelius,** a Roman military officer and the first Gentile Christian. To Luke, admitting uncircumcised Gentiles into the Christian fold represents one of the most important developments in religious history. The author's manner of telling the story reveals how crucial he believes the event to be. By this point in Luke-Acts, readers have probably realized that whenever Luke wishes to emphasize the significance of an event, he describes it in terms of supernatural phenomena. At both Jesus' birth (Luke 1–2) and that of the church at Pentecost (Acts 2), the invisible spirit realm directly impinges on the human world. (The Resurrection and the apostles' escape from death in prison are two other examples.) Thus, God sends visions and dreams to both Cornelius and Peter, instructing the apostle to baptize his first Gentile convert, an act symbolizing God's intent to make both Gentiles and Jews his own people.

Underscoring his view that the Spirit's presence validates a religious decision, Luke shows Cornelius and his entire household speaking in tongues exactly as the Jewish Christians had at Pentecost. As he had at the church's spiritual baptism, Peter again interprets the incident's religious meaning—the equal worth of Jews and Gentiles in God's sight (10:35–48). Peter's statement also clarifies the meaning of his dream: God declares all animal foods "clean" and acceptable, as well as the Gentiles who eat them. Dietary restrictions are no longer a barrier between Jew and non-Jew.

Typically Lukan concerns dominate the Cornelius–Peter narration. Both men receive their respective visions while at prayer. The Spirit arranges and guides the human participants in this momentous event, guiding Jew and Gentile alike. Readers will also note that Luke injects into his narrative words of the resurrected Jesus directing believers how to behave at moments crucial to the growing church. Speaking through trances or visions to Paul (9:4–6), Ananias (9:10–16), Cornelius (10:3–6), and Peter (10:10–16), the risen Lord continues to instruct his disciples (cf. Luke 24:25–27, 44–50). The intimate communication prevailing between the heavenly Lord and his people on earth expresses Luke's belief in the unbroken continuity between Jesus and his later followers.

Herod Agrippa

Luke concludes this section by describing the attack on the Jerusalem church's leadership by Herod Agrippa I. A grandson of Herod the Great, Herod Agrippa reigned briefly (41–44 CE) over a reunited Jewish state. Although the emperor Claudius, who had appointed him king, supported Herod's rule, the puppet ruler was unpopular among his Jewish subjects. Herod apparently cultivated support from the Sadducees by persecuting their opponents, including Christians. Luke states that he beheaded James, brother of John, and also imprisoned Peter. After recording Peter's miraculous escape from prison, the author dramatizes Herod's punishment. Hailed publicly as "a god" by a fawning crowd, the king is instantly afflicted with a loathsome and fatal disease "because he had usurped the honour due to God" (12:1–24). Herod's miserable death, like that of Judas, illustrates the fate of persons who oppose the Spirit.

FIGURE 12.2 Paul's first missionary journey. According to Acts, Paul made three major tours through the northeastern Mediterranean region. Although the account in Acts may oversimplify Paul's complex travel itineraries, it correctly shows him focusing his efforts on major urban centers in Asia Minor (modern Turkey).

The First Missionary Journey of Barnabas and Paul: The Jerusalem Conference (St. Martyr)

According to Acts 11, the initial persecution and scattering of Hellenistic-Jewish Christians eventually led to the formation of a mixed Jewish-Gentile church in Antioch, Syria. A prosperous city situated on the main trade and travel routes of the eastern Mediterranean, Antioch rapidly became the center for a hugely successful mission to the Gentiles (13:1–15:35). Paul and **Barnabas,** a Greek-speaking Jewish Christian from Cyprus, made the city their headquarters. It was here that followers of "the way" first were called Christians (11:22–26).

In Acts 13, Luke shows Barnabas and Paul leaving Antioch to begin their first missionary tour of Asia Minor (see Figure 12.2). According

to this account, the two made it their practice to preach first in Jewish synagogues and, when rejected there, to turn then to a Gentile audience (13:46–48; 18:6; 28:28). Luke's version of Paul's speech in Pisidian **Antioch** (in Asia Minor) shows little sensitivity to Paul's characteristic teaching on the saving power of Christ or his anticipation of an early Parousia. (Compare Acts' account with Paul's letters to the Thessalonians and Corinthians, discussed in Chapter 14.) Many scholars believe that the speeches in Acts reflect the Hellenistic preaching style typical of the author's own time, late in the first century CE.

Luke announces that Barnabas and Paul opened "the gates of faith to the Gentiles"

(14:27), but he is not above remarking on the religious gullibility of some Gentiles. When Paul and Barnabas are evangelizing in **Lystra,** a Roman colony in Asia Minor, they are mistaken for gods in human form. After Paul miraculously heals a crippled man, the populace decides that he must be **Mercury** (Hermes), messenger of the Olympian gods, and that Barnabas is Jupiter (Zeus), king of the immortals. The crowd's fickleness, however, matches its credulity. At one moment, the Lystrans are ready to offer sacrifices to Barnabas and Paul, but at the next—persuaded by some visiting Jews—they stone Paul and leave him for dead (14:8–30). Apparently indestructible, Paul recovers quickly and completes his missionary tour, returning to Syrian Antioch, his home base.

The First Church Conference

The great success that Barnabas and Paul have in converting large numbers of Gentiles brings the church to its first major crisis (15:1–25). In Antioch, many Jewish Christians insist that unless the new converts become circumcised they "[can] not be saved" (15:1). In Jerusalem, Christian Pharisees argue that Gentile converts "must be circumcised and told to keep the Law of Moses" (15:5). According to Genesis, circumcision is required of all Israelite males if they are to be part of the covenant community (Gen. 17:9–14). Because this ritual mark on the organ of procreation distinguishes Jews as heirs to Yahweh's promises to Abraham, Jewish Christians naturally see it as a prerequisite to entering the kingdom. In their opinion, foreigners must become Jews before they can be Christians. Paul and Barnabas oppose this notion with "fierce dissension and controversy" (15:2) (see Box 12.2).

The battle between advocates of the Mosaic Torah and Hellenistic-Jewish Christians like Barnabas and Paul gives Luke an opportunity to create a model, or paradigm, for dealing with such controversies in the church. By the time he wrote Acts, the issue had long been decided in favor of the Gentiles. Paul's advocacy

of "freedom" from the "bondage" of the Mosaic Torah had triumphed over the "circumcision party." Thus, Luke presents the controversy as considerably less intense than it actually was and simplifies the historical situation by picturing a peaceful and unanimous resolution of the problem.

The first church conference, held in Jerusalem about 49 CE to decide the circumcision issue, provides Luke's model of orderly procedure. Initiating the conference, Antioch sends delegates, including Barnabas and Paul, to Jerusalem, and the Jerusalem "apostles and elders" investigate the problem, permitting an extended debate between the two sides. Peter, representing Palestinian apostolic authority, delivers a speech reminding his fellow Jews that the Spirit had been given to the Gentile Cornelius just as it had been to Jewish Christians. Peter advises against laying the Torah "yoke" upon converts. The entire congregation then listens to Barnabas and Paul plead their case for the Gentiles.

According to Luke, James (Jesus' "brother" or kinsman), the person who later succeeds Peter as head of the Jerusalem church, essentially decides the issue. (See Box 12.3 for a history of the leadership in the early Jerusalem church.) Although Acts pictures James as a "moderate," accepting of Gentiles who do not observe Torah rules, Paul's letters paint him as a strongly conservative Jew advocating circumcision for all (Gal. 2). Luke presents James as using his prestige to influence the Jerusalem church to accept Gentiles without imposing Torah restrictions.

The Lukan James, however, does insist upon the observation of some Jewish dietary laws by Gentiles. James's stipulations seem based largely on Torah rules from Leviticus, according to which both Jews and foreigners living in Israel are forbidden to eat blood or meat that has not been drained of blood (Lev. 17–18). Recognizing that Gentiles are accustomed to a more sexually permissive culture than are Jews, James also forbids "fornication" or sexual misconduct (15:13–21). In James's

BOX 12.2 Circumcision, the Consumption of Blood, and the Inclusion of Gentiles

According to Acts 15, the first church conference was held in Jerusalem to decide what parts of the Mosaic Law Gentile converts had to obey to become members of the Christian community, which was then primarily Jewish. In Luke's account, Paul's argument that Gentile males did not need to become circumcised prevailed, with Peter and James, leaders of the Jerusalem church, agreeing. In order to enjoy full fellowship with Jewish Christians, however, it was stipulated, all converts had to observe four provisions of the Torah, which were addressed to both Israelites and foreign residents (15:19–21). Besides abstaining from sexual misconduct (such as various forms of incest listed in Lev. 18), Gentile Christians were also required to obey specified Mosaic dietary prohibitions, such as consuming blood or eating animals that had not been properly drained of blood (a kosher process described in Lev. 17). In addition, converts were not to consume the flesh of animals sacrificed to alien gods. Whereas Acts shows Paul accepting these restrictions, in his own version of the meeting, Paul declares that he yielded to no Torah demands (Gal. 1–2).

Although both Acts and Paul's letters agree that circumcision is not to be required of Gentile males, many Jewish Christians in Palestine and elsewhere probably thought that they had good scriptural reasons to insist on the requirement. According to the Book of Exodus, any foreigner or alien resident—whether enslaved or free—who wished to participate in the Passover feast had first to be circumcised (Exod. 12:43–45, 48–49). Because Exodus specifically states that "the same law shall apply to both the native born and to the alien who is living with you," Jewish Christians, believing that God's law is universal and unchanging, could argue that persons desiring to partake of the Lord's supper (communion), which derived from Jesus' final Passover meal (Mark 14:12–26; Matt. 26:17–30; Luke 22:14–38), must be circumcised in order to qualify for full participation. After all, God's decree that circumcision is the distinguishing mark of membership in the covenant community predates the giving of the Mosaic Law and is the physical expression of Yahweh's original promises to Abraham (Gen. 17).

---

speech, Luke shows a basic victory for one party (the Gentile side), accompanied by a compromise that is sensitive to the consciences of the losing sides.

The author completes his example of model church procedures by illustrating the manner in which James's recommendation is carried out. Themes of unity and cooperation dominate Luke's account: The "whole church" agrees to send "unanimously" elected delegates back to Antioch with a letter containing the Jerusalem church's directive. Characteristically, Luke notes that the decision of this precedent-setting conference is also "the decision of the Holy Spirit" (15:22–29). To the author, the church's deliberations reflect the divine will.

Paul's Independence of the Apostolic Church

Luke's description of Paul's cooperative relationship with the apostolic leadership in Jerusalem differs significantly from the account in Paul's letters. According to Luke, shortly after his conversion Paul went to Jerusalem, where he "tried to join the body of disciples there" but was rebuffed. After Barnabas took this zealous convert under his wing, however, Luke implies, Paul became an accepted member of Jerusalem's Christian community (9:26–30). In his own version of events, Paul categorically denies that he had early contact with the Jerusalem church or that his teaching about

BOX 12.3 Jesus' Family and the Jerusalem Church

In describing Jesus' return to Nazareth, Mark lists four of Jesus' "brothers" (or close kinsmen) by name: James, Joseph, Judas, and Simon, as well as at least two unidentified "sisters" (6:3). Mark's report that Jesus' "mother and his brothers" attempted to interfere with Jesus' ministry (3:21, 31–35) is consistent with the New Testament tradition that none of Jesus' family members followed him until after his resurrection. Paul cites James as one of the prominent individuals to whom Jesus made a post resurrection appearance (1 Cor. 15:7), which was undoubtedly the experience that made James a disciple. (Acts 1:14 states that Mary, Jesus' mother, and "his brothers" assembled with the Twelve in Jerusalem shortly after the Ascension; they were presumably also present at the community's Spirit-anointing at Pentecost.)

When Paul made his postconversion visit to Jerusalem (probably c. 35 CE), he found that "James the Lord's brother" was already an acknowledged leader of the Jerusalem church (Gal. 1:18–19). At the time of Paul's second Jerusalem visit (c. 49 CE), James was recognized as one of three "reputed pillars of our society" (along with the apostles Cephas [Peter] and John) (Gal. 2:6–10). After Peter and John had left Jerusalem, James assumed undisputed leadership of the mother church (Acts 15:13–21; 21:18–26).

The author of Acts does not record the executions of any of his leading missionary characters, including Peter and Paul (who were probably martyred in Rome under Nero). But the Jewish historian Josephus reports that James, "the brother of Jesus, who was called Christ," was illegally brought to trial by some Sadducees and stoned to death (c. 62 CE) (Josephus, *Antiquities* 20.9.1).

In *The History of the Church,* Eusebius reports that James, who "was called Christ's brother," was the first **bishop** (overseer) of Jerusalem and known to his fellow Jewish Christians as James the Righteous. He also records a version of James's death, but different from that given in Josephus. Quoting Clement,

a late-first-century writer, Eusebius states that James was hurled down from "the parapet [Temple walls?] and beaten to death with a fuller's club" (*History* 2.1, 23; 3.5, 11; 4.5, 22; 7.19).

According to another (unverifiable) tradition preserved in Eusebius, even after James's death, Jesus' relatives continued to play influential roles in the Jerusalem church. Shortly after the Romans destroyed Jerusalem (c. 70 CE), Eusebius says, "apostles and disciples of the Lord who were still alive" gathered together from different parts of the country, along with "kinsmen of the Lord, for most of them were still living." Their purpose was to appoint a successor to James who would preside over Christians in postwar Jerusalem. Eusebius states that Jesus' disciples and family members, forty years after his death, voted "unanimously" for Jesus' cousin, Symeon, to "occupy the throne" of the Jerusalem church. (Because Eusebius does not ordinarily refer to a bishop's "throne," the Jerusalem congregation may have accorded royal or Davidic status to Jesus' heirs.) Eusebius adds that Symeon was a son of Clopas (John 19:25), who was supposedly a brother of Joseph, Jesus' putative father (*History* 3.11).

According to Eusebius's source, an early church historian named Hegesippus, Symeon remained head of the Jerusalem church until persecutions under the emperor Trajan (ruled 98–117 CE), when, at age 120, he was tortured and crucified for being both a Davidic descendant and a Christian. Symeon was then succeeded by another Jewish Christian, Justus; Eusebius does not mention whether he, Jerusalem's third bishop, was also a member of Jesus' family (*History* 3.32, 35).

To his testimony about members of Jesus' family taking leadership roles in the early church, Eusebius adds an anecdote about the grandsons of Jude (Judas)—"the brother, humanly speaking, of the Savior." Again citing Hegesippus as his source, Eusebius states that the emperor Domitian (ruled 81–96 CE) ordered a search made for royal descendants of David who might push messianic claims to restore the Jewish throne. According to Hegesippus's account, when Jude's grandsons were brought before Domitian, the emperor dismissed them contemptuously when he found that they were poor peasants with work-worn, callused hands. After this close call with Roman authority (they were more fortunate than Symeon in Trajan's reign), the two apparently took a more active part in the Christian community, becoming church leaders (*History* 3.19–20). The lingering influence of James and Jude in the Christian tradition is evident in the two New Testament books ascribed to them (see Chapter 18).

Jesus owed anything to his apostolic predecessors. After describing his private "revelation" of the risen Jesus, Paul states, "without consulting any human being, without going up to Jerusalem to see those who were apostles before me, I went off at once to Arabia, and afterwards returned to Damascus" (Gal. 1:17). Three years later, Paul notes, he did make a trip to Jerusalem "to get to know Cephas [Peter]," but he did not confer "with any other of the apostles, except James, the Lord's brother" (Gal. 1:18–19). When Paul immediately adds, "What I write is plain truth; before God I am not lying" (Gal. 1:20), it is clear that he rejects any suggestion that he was ever under the influence or jurisdiction of the Jerusalem leadership.

Given Luke's policy of depicting Paul as an obedient churchman, willingly subject to apostolic decrees, it is not surprising that Acts' portrayal of the Jerusalem conference contrasts markedly with Paul's eyewitness report (Gal. 2:1–10). Whereas Acts shows the Gentile–Torah issue peacefully and unanimously settled, Paul declares that "not for one moment" did he compromise his position that Gentile Christians should live absolutely free of Torah "bondage." According to Galatians, Paul accepted no restrictions, whereas Acts states that he unhesitatingly agreed to James's four Torah prohibitions. In addition, Paul reveals an attitude toward eating meat sacrificed to Greco-Roman gods that differs from that ascribed to him in Acts (1 Cor. 8:8; 10:27).

Some historians believe that the apostolic decree involving dietary matters may have been issued at a later Jerusalem conference, one that Paul did not attend. In this view, Luke has combined the results of two separate meetings and reported them as a single event. Later in Acts, the author seems aware that Paul did not know about the Jerusalem church's decision regarding Torah-prohibited meats. During Paul's final Jerusalem visit, James is shown speaking about the dietary restrictions as if they were news to Paul (21:25).

Paul's Second Missionary Journey: Evangelizing Greece

Luke devotes the remainder of Acts to recounting Paul's missionary journeys and confrontations with Jewish and Roman authorities (see Figure 12.3). Emphasizing Christianity's acceptability to the Greco-Roman world, the author structures the book's second half to illustrate three basic themes: (1) The Spirit controls the church's growth, precisely instructing missionaries on where they may or may not travel (16:6–10); (2) when Christian preachers are not interfered with, Gentiles respond favorably to the "new way," which flourishes throughout Asia Minor and Greece; and (3) from its beginnings, Christianity is familiar to Roman officials, who invariably see it as no threat to the imperial government. As Luke tells the story, only ignorant mobs or envious Jewish leaders oppose the faith and incite Roman authorities to suppress it.

FIGURE 12.3 Paul's second missionary journey. As Acts depicts it, this journey brought Christianity to Europe, with new cells of Christians established in Philippi, Thessalonica, and Corinth. Note that Antioch in Syria is Paul's missionary headquarters.

At the same time, the narrator is candid about "the way's" potential disruptiveness, asking converts to abandon their worship of Greco-Roman gods and to cease their former participation in cults intimately associated with civic life. In his account of Christianity's expansion from Asia into Greece (16:1–18:2), Luke repeatedly describes the riots and other social upheavals that result from the missionaries' preaching. After quarreling with Barnabas (15: 36–40; cf. Gal. 2:13) and recruiting new companions, **Silas** and **Timothy,** Paul has a vision in which Macedonian Greeks appeal to him for help (16: 9–10). Accepting the vision as a divine command, Paul and his new partners cross into Macedonia, a Roman province in northern Greece. (At this point, the author begins to speak in the first-person plural; his use of "we" and "us" suggests either that he was an eyewitness to this part of Paul's journey or that he has incorporated another party's travel journal into his narrative.) In **Philippi,** where Paul establishes the first Christian church in Europe, an irate slaveholder accuses the missionaries of illegally

BOX 12.4 **The Christian Message's Disruptive Effect on Greco-Roman Society**

According to Paul's critics in Thessalonica, he and his fellow missionaries disturb the Roman peace: "They flout the Emperor's laws, and assert that there is a rival king, Jesus" (Acts 17:7). In the critics' view, the Christian message subverts both Roman custom and the legitimate authority of the emperor, promoting a ruler superior to Caesar. Although most scholars traditionally have emphasized the Book of Acts' conciliatory attitudes toward Rome, recent commentators have pointed out that the author presents Christianity as so radically different a way of life that it profoundly disrupts the ordinary norms of Greco-Roman society. Paul's accusers in Philippi, for example, complain that his group is "advocating customs which it is illegal for us Romans to adopt and follow" (16:21).

In Ephesus, "the Christian movement gave rise to a serious disturbance" when Paul's monotheistic preaching threatens the livelihood of artisans who manufacture replicas of the goddess Artemis (Diana) and of her temple. As the silversmith Demetrius correctly observes, "our high standard of living depends on this industry." If the general population accepts Paul's message, both the Ephesian tourist trade and the workers who depend on it will collapse (19:23–20:1). In addition, Paul's activities put several Ephesian exorcists out of work, inspiring many citizens to burn publicly their books of magic, a sacrifice worth "fifty thousand pieces of silver" (19:13–20). The narrative makes clear that accepting the Christian view may have negative economic consequences.

In Athens, Paul reproaches the inhabitants for their idolatry, implicitly condemning the entire pantheon of Greco-Roman gods and the civic order that supports them. If the Athenians turn to the invisible God of Israel and to the risen Lord who will soon judge the whole world, they must change not only their individual lives but also their entire social behavior. For the ancient world did not separate religion from the rest of life; the gods' worship was intimately interwoven with social ties and economic associations, with participation in civic and national festivals, rites, and offices. To become a Christian was to withdraw from what most people in the Roman Empire regarded as praiseworthy activities, manifestations of loyalty to the public order (see C. Kavin Rowe in "Recommended Reading").

trying to convert Romans to Judaism. Wrongfully flogged and imprisoned, Paul and Silas assert their legal rights as Roman citizens, who are protected from punishment without a trial. Luke uses this incident to show that (1) only personal malice causes Paul's arrest; (2) God protects his agents, in this case sending an earthquake to open their prison doors; and (3) Philippi's legal authorities have no case against Paul or his associates (see Box 12.4).

After establishing another church at Thessalonica, Paul moves southward to **Athens,** famous for its magnificent artwork and schools of philosophy (see Figures 12.4 and 12.5). A university city noteworthy for its celebration of free speech and tolerance of diverse ideas, Athens is the only place on Paul's itinerary where he is neither mobbed nor arrested. Instead, he is politely invited to speak at the **Areopagus,** an open-air court where speakers can express their views. In a celebrated speech, Paul identifies the Athenians' "unknown god" as the biblical Creator. Representing Paul as quoting two ancient Greek poets on the unity of humankind, Luke incorporates their insights into the Christian message. Upon Paul's allusion to Jesus' physical resurrection, however, the Athenians lose interest, perhaps because their philosophers commonly taught that the body has no part in a future immortal state. Only a few

FIGURE 12.4 A reconstruction of the Athenian Acropolis. According to Acts 17, Athenian philosophers invited Paul to explain his new religion at the Areopagus (Hill of Ares), a public forum located on a spur of the Acropolis. Named for Athene, goddess of wisdom, Athens was celebrated for encouraging freedom of thought and speech.

among Paul's audience are converted or baptized (17:16–34).

Paul enjoys much greater success in **Corinth,** a prosperous Greek seaport notorious for its materialism and houses of prostitution. Luke enables his readers to fix the approximate time of Paul's arrival—the early 50s CE—by his reference to two secular events that coincided with the apostle's visit. Luke notes that two Jewish Christians, **Aquila** and **Priscilla,** were in Corinth following the emperor Claudius's decree expelling all Jews from the capital. Claudius issued this edict about 49 CE. The author also mentions that **Gallio** was then **proconsul** (governor) of Achaia, the Greek province in which Corinth is located. Archaeologists excavating the Greek sanctuary of Delphi found

an inscription there that enables them to place Gallio's term between about 51 and 53 CE. This find is extremely important because it gives us one of the few relatively precise dates in Paul's career.

As in the episode at Philippi, Luke presents Paul's Corinthian visit as another illustration of his major themes—the new religion is both Spirit-directed and lawful, albeit disruptive of many social norms. In a night vision, the Lord directs Paul to remain in Corinth despite persecution. When Paul is arrested and brought before Gallio, the governor dismisses Jewish charges against the missionary as irrelevant to Roman law. Legally exonerated, Paul and his companions continue their work unhindered (18:1–17).

FIGURE 12.5 The Stoa of Attalus in Athens. A roofed colonnade donated to the city of Athens by King Attalus II of Pergamum in the second century BCE, the Stoa (rebuilt in the twentieth century) originally offered shelter for meetings and discussions, such as the debates with Athenian philosophers that Paul is said to have held when he first visited Athens (Acts 17). The Acropolis rises in the background.

Paul's Third Missionary Journey: Revisiting Asia Minor and Greece

In depicting Paul's third missionary journey (18:21–20:38), in which the apostle revisits churches he had founded in Asia Minor and Greece (see Figure 12.6), Luke concentrates on Paul's activities in Ephesus (see Figure 12.7). A thriving port city on the west coast of Asia Minor (modern Turkey), Ephesus had an ethnically mixed population and a great variety of religious cults. Luke demonstrates the social and religious complexity of this cosmopolitan center by having his hero encounter a wide diversity of religionists there, both Jewish and Gentile.

The author hints that even Christianity in Ephesus differs from that found elsewhere, being influenced by Jewish followers of John the Baptist. Luke records two separate incidents in which members of a Baptist-Christian group are apparently brought into line with Pauline doctrine. The first involves the eloquent **Apollos,** an educated Jew from Alexandria, who delivers persuasive sermons about Jesus—but knows "only John's baptism." Hearing him in the Ephesus synagogue, Priscilla and Aquila "take him in hand," presumably bringing his ideas into harmony with Paul's teaching. After Apollos departs for Corinth (see 1 Cor. 1), Paul finds another group of Ephesian Christians observing "John's baptism." On their being rebaptized in Jesus' name, the converts receive the Holy

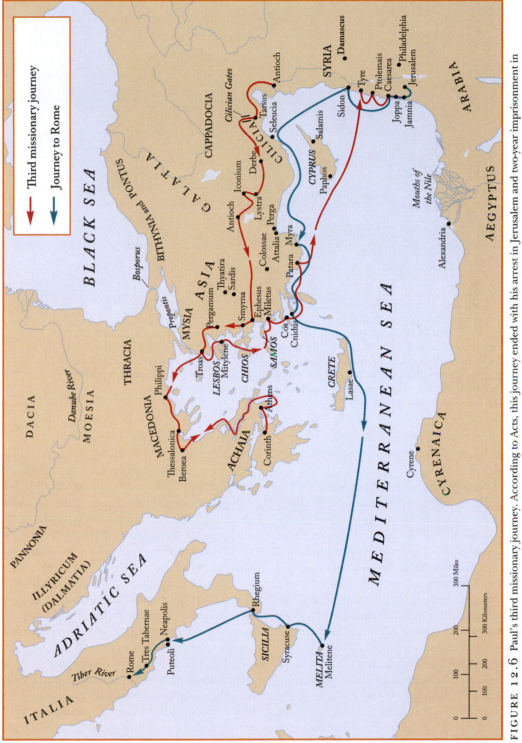

FIGURE 12.6 Paul's third missionary journey. According to Acts, this journey ended with his arrest in Jerusalem and two-year imprisonment in Caesarea. The bottom line shows the route of Paul's sea voyage to Rome, where he was taken to be tried in the imperial courts.

FIGURE 12.7 The amphitheater at Ephesus. A wealthy Greco-Roman seaport in Asia Minor (western Turkey), Ephesus was the site of one of the Seven Wonders of the Ancient World, the lavish marble Temple of Artemis (the Roman Diana). According to Acts 19, Ephesian silversmiths staged a riot in the amphitheater when Paul's Christian message threatened to subvert the worship of Artemis—and the prosperity of the silversmiths, who profited from selling miniature silver replicas of the goddess's statue and shrine to tourists.

Spirit, confirming the superiority of Jesus to his forerunner.

Luke further illustrates Christianity's superiority by contrasting Paul's astonishing ability to heal with the inability of some Jewish competitors. The apostle's spiritual power is so great that articles of clothing that had touched his skin are used to heal the sick and cast out "evil spirits." In contrast, seven Jewish exorcists trying to expel demons by invoking Jesus' authority fail ignominiously. Defying the exorcists, the possessed man strips all seven and throws them naked from his house (19:11–17).

Ephesus's greatest pride was its enormous temple dedicated to **Artemis** (the Roman Diana), one of the Seven Wonders of the Ancient World (see Figure 12.8). Although bearing a Greek name, the Ephesian Artemis was a mother goddess closely related to other Near Eastern fertility

deities such as Cybele and Ashtoreth. Paul's success in converting Ephesians brings him into conflict with the goddess's worshipers. Jewish-Christian monotheism, proclaiming the existence of only one God, threatens to hurt the business of Ephesian silversmiths who make their living selling replicas of Artemis and her shrine. (See Box 12.4).

Duplicating the trial scene at Corinth, Luke states that Ephesian officials find the missionary innocent of disturbing the city's peace. Once again, attempts to harm the disciples backfire against the persecutors (19:23–41).

Luke frames Paul's adventures in Ephesus with intimations of the apostle's final journey—to Rome. As Luke had pictured Jesus turning his face resolutely toward Jerusalem and the death that awaited him there (Luke 9:51), so the author shows Paul determined to complete

FIGURE 12.8 The cult statue of Artemis (Diana) at Ephesus. Although the Greeks honored Artemis as the virgin patron of wildlife and the hunt, Ephesian sculptors depicted her as a Near Eastern fertility goddess, decorating her torso with images of breasts, eggs, or perhaps the testicles of bulls that were sacrificed on her altar. The Roman Diana was also identified with the feminine symbol of the moon.

his last tour and head for the imperial capital (19:21–22). After revisiting Greece (20:1–16), Paul calls for the Ephesian church leaders to meet him in Miletus, an ancient Greek city on the west coast of Asia Minor. There, Paul delivers a farewell speech, predicting his imminent imprisonment and implying a coming martyrdom. In this speech, Luke emphasizes holding to the apostolic teaching that Paul represents and resisting heresy (20:17–38).

Paul's Arrest in Jerusalem and Imprisonment in Caesarea

In this section, Luke foreshadows Paul's death, although he never explicitly refers to it (21:1–26:32). On his way to Jerusalem, presumably to deliver the money collected from the Pauline churches for the "poor" of Jerusalem's Christian commune, Paul encounters a prophet who foretells the apostle's fatal "binding" (arrest) there. Highlighting the resemblance between Jesus and his later followers, Luke shows Paul expressing his willingness to die in Jerusalem. (Compare Paul's misgivings about the fatal return to Jerusalem in Romans 15:22–33.)

Ironically, the apostle to the Gentiles seals his fate by cooperating with the Palestinian-Jewish Christians of Jerusalem. When Paul bows to James's influence and agrees to undergo purification rites in the Temple to prove his faithfulness to Torah regulations, his presence in the sanctuary incites a riot. (Jews allegedly familiar with his preaching accuse Paul of bringing uncircumcised Gentiles into the Temple.) The Roman soldiers who intervene in the fray save Paul's life but also place him in protective custody (21:18–36). From this time until the end of his story, Luke's hero is a prisoner of Roman authorities.

Christianity and the State

Luke's intense focus on Paul's legal troubles, particularly his appearances before Roman magistrates, illustrates the author's overarching concern for Christianity's legal position in the Roman Empire. Devoting the last section of his narrative (21:27–28:31) to explaining the process by which Paul was brought to Rome for trial in the emperor's tribunal, Luke consistently shows Roman officials as favoring Paul and his innovative religion. A Roman army officer (later identified as Lysias) permits Paul to explain his mission to a Jerusalem crowd (21:37–22:21), in a speech where he gives a second version of his mystical experience on the road to Damascus. When Lysias discovers that Paul is a Roman citizen, a legal status that entitles him to protection from punishment without a trial, the commander personally escorts his prisoner to the Sanhedrin to answer charges Jewish leaders have brought against him.

In describing the Sanhedrin appearance, Luke again insists that Paul is a devout adherent of the Mosaic Law who does not hesitate to identify his cause with the Pharisee party. As in Peter's two hearings before the same council (4:1–22; 5:17–42), Paul's religious judges divide along party lines, with the Sadducees condemning him and the Pharisees lending their support (22:30–23:10).

Christians' Political Innocence

Paul's first formal hearing before a high Roman official, the governor **Antonius Felix,** takes place in Caesarea Maritima, a busy port city on the Mediterranean coast that served as headquarters for Roman governors of Judea. Paul's prosecutors are emissaries from the High Priest who accuse him of profaning the Jerusalem sanctuary and being a "ringleader of the sect of the **Nazarenes,**" an early name for Jesus of Nazareth's followers (24:1–9). In his defense, Paul insists that he observes "the written Law" (an assertion contradicted in his letters), that he has done nothing to desecrate the Temple, and that the "real issue" is whether God actually raised Jesus from the dead, thereby validating him as the Jewish Messiah (24:10–21). For two years, Paul then languishes in captivity while the corrupt Felix vainly awaits an expected bribe (24:26–27). (It appears that none of the Christian leaders in either Jerusalem or Antioch attempt to secure Paul's release.)

After **Porcius Festus** succeeds Felix as Roman governor, Paul is granted a second hearing, at which the new magistrate also absolves him of any illegal activity (25:25; 26:30–32). In one of Hellenistic literature's most dramatic courtroom scenes, Luke shows Paul facing not only Festus, the Roman emperor's personal representative, but also rulers of Herod's line. King Julius Agrippa II, son of Herod Agrippa I, who had beheaded the apostle James (12:1–2), attends the session with his sister (and mistress) Bernice. Because Festus is married to Drusilla, another of King Agrippa's sisters, the apostle confronts a ruling family in which the might of Rome and the prestige of Jewish royalty are combined. Luke thus shows Paul fulfilling Jesus' earlier prophecy that Paul would testify "before kings" and the "people of Israel" (9:15).

Paul's long speech before Festus (26:1–29) is a vivid summary of his career as depicted in Acts, including a third account describing his "heavenly" vision of the risen Jesus. This discourse corresponds more closely to Paul's own account of his conversion (Gal. 1:1, 15–17) than do Acts' two earlier versions. But the author still represents Paul as operating under Mosaic Law—asserting "nothing beyond what was foretold by the prophets and by Moses." In the author's view, Christianity is in full agreement and continuity with true Judaism: Jews have no cause to condemn it as a perversion of their Mosaic heritage.

Luke's main emphasis, however, is on his hero's complete innocence. Echoing Pilate's opinion of Jesus, Festus admits that Paul is guilty of "nothing that deserves death or imprisonment." Agrippa drives home the point: Paul could have been released a free man if "he had not appealed to the Emperor" (26:30–32). In Luke's presentation of the early church to Greco-Roman readers, the author makes clear that missionaries like Paul are prosecuted in Roman courts only because of officials' misunderstanding or the malice of their false accusers.

Simultaneously, however, Luke also makes clear that the Christian proclamation is a potentially destabilizing force in Greco-Roman society. The author must maintain a precarious balance between his argument that Christianity is no political threat to the empire and his frank admission of Jesus' spiritual superiority to the emperor (17:7). Luke's many examples of socioreligious and legal challenges to the faith lead to an unavoidable conclusion: the profound changes that "the way" brings cause "trouble all over the world" (17:6), a headache to even the best-intentioned Roman officials.

Paul's Journey to Rome and His Preaching to Roman Jews

Luke begins his final section—Paul's sea journey to Rome—with an exciting account of a shipwreck (27:1–28:31). Told in the first person, this description of a Roman cargo ship disintegrating amid high winds and pounding waves reads like an eyewitness experience. (We do not know whether the author uses the diary of a participant in this passage or simply employs the first-person "we" as a literary device to heighten the immediacy of his narrative.) As always in Acts, the incident is included for its theological meaning. Although Paul is a prisoner perhaps destined for conviction and death, he comforts his Roman captors during the storm, assuring them that Jesus destines him (and them) to arrive safely in Rome. As Paul had prophesied, all aboard—crew, military officers, and prisoner—survive the ordeal unscathed, swimming ashore at the island of Malta (27:6–44).

Luke concludes his selective account of the early church with Paul's arrival in Rome, where the apostle, although under house arrest, enjoys considerable freedom, receiving visitors

and preaching openly. The author does not reveal Paul's ultimate fate. One tradition states that, after remaining in the capital for two years, Paul was released and carried out his planned missionary trip to Spain (Rom. 15:24). Many historians, however, believe that Paul's first Roman imprisonment led to his execution, perhaps about 62 CE, following the emperor Nero's order to impose the death penalty on anyone who spoke or behaved in a way that appeared to undermine his supreme authority. Other scholars date Paul's death at about 64 or 65 CE, when Nero first persecuted Christians as a group. According to a brief reference in 1 Clement (c. 96 CE), both Peter and Paul were martyred during Nero's persecution.

Some critics suggest that Luke, deeply concerned with Christianity's legal status in the Roman Empire, deliberately omits any mention that Paul and Peter, like Jesus, were tried and executed for treason against Rome. This unfortunate outcome for the religion's two leading proponents runs counter to the author's insistence that Christianity is a lawful faith innocent of any sedition against the state, despite its problematic social consequences.

Many scholars contend that Acts ends abruptly, not because Luke wants to avoid political facts that do not fit his theme, but because he regards Paul's evangelizing in Rome as the fulfillment of his purpose in writing. Luke's conclusion well illustrates his principal historical-theological interest: Paul resolves to focus his message on receptive Gentiles, shifting his primary attention from Jews to a Greco-Roman audience. Luke sees the church's future in the teeming millions of Gentiles throughout Rome's vast empire, a vision confirmed by later history.

As a believer who infers religious meaning from historical events, Luke completes his picture of early Christianity with a sketch of Paul—representing the church's mission to all nations—vigorously proclaiming his vision of God ruling through Jesus. To Luke, Paul's activity symbolizes the divinely commanded business of the church that must continue into the distant future. Rather than end his account with a reaffirmation of Jesus' eschatological return (the Parousia), Luke looks to a future in which the "kingdom" can be preached "openly and without hindrance," attaining a recognized legal position in the world. In sharp contrast to the historical Paul's belief in an imminent Parousia (so different from Acts' portrayal of him), Luke sees the world, not as a wicked place to be destroyed, but as the arena in which God effects humanity's salvation.

Acts' ending thus echoes Jesus' departing words to the disciples recorded at the book's beginning. Believers are not "to know about dates or times" (eschatological speculations about the world's End) because such knowledge belongs exclusively to "the Father" and has been "set within his own control." Instead, Christians are to carry the "good news" of Jesus "to the ends of the earth" (1:7–8). With Paul's arrival in Rome, the work is well begun. Its completion Luke entrusts to his readers.

Summary

A continuation of Luke's Gospel, Acts is a theologically oriented account of the early Christian church. Focusing principally on two representative leaders of the faith, Peter and Paul, it traces the church's growth from exclusively Jewish origins in Jerusalem to its dissemination throughout the northeastern Roman Empire. The church's rapid expansion from a Jewish nucleus to an international community composed of many different ethnic groups brings major problems of adjustment, particularly the issue of requiring Gentiles to observe the Jewish Torah.

In many respects, the Book of Acts is an apology (an explanation or defense) for Christianity. Luke's interpretation of Christian origins defends the "new way" as the legitimate outgrowth of Judaism and a lawful faith intended for citizens of the Roman Empire. Luke emphasizes that there is no necessary or inherent conflict between Christianity and the Jewish religion that gave it birth or the Roman state in which it finds

its natural environment. As in his Gospel, he minimizes early expectations of an imminent Parousia and emphasizes the church's objective to expand indefinitely into the distant future. Eager to find accommodation with the imperial government, the author offers no criticism of Roman officials but invariably depicts them as fair-minded and competent. He attributes Roman suspicion of the faith to the ill will of envious opponents. While placing Roman magistrates in a favorable light, however, Luke also describes socially disruptive responses to the Christian message, which include riots in Greek cities such as Ephesus, Philippi, and Thessalonica, where preaching of the Christian message is correctly interpreted as a threat not only to Judaism but also to Greco-Roman customs and religious practices. As if walking a tightrope between an implicit appeal for Roman officialdom to tolerate the Jesus movement and an admission that the Christian proclamation is inherently destabilizing to Greco-Roman society, the author nonetheless insists that "the new way" can coexist with the imperial government. Historically, Luke's argument of coexistence helped pave the way for Rome's eventual adoption of Christianity as the empire's official religion, a triumph foreshadowed by Paul's preaching in the capital "without [legal] hindrance."

Questions for Review

1. A sequel to Luke's Gospel, the Book of Acts continues the story of Christian origins. Which of the same themes that appear in the Gospel are also found in Acts? Compare the account of Jesus' trial before Pilate with that of Paul before Pilate's successors, Felix and Festus.

2. How does Luke organize his account of Christianity's birth and growth? Identify the leaders of the Jerusalem church and the missionaries who first helped carry "the new way" into the larger world beyond the Jewish capital.

3. In recording the events of Pentecost, how does Luke emphasize his theme that Christianity is a universal religion—led by the Holy Spirit and destined for peoples of all nations? In the author's view, what ancient Hebrew prophecy is fulfilled by the Spirit's descent upon the first disciples?

4. In what ways does the Jerusalem commune put into operation the social and economic principles enunciated in Luke's Gospel? How does the early church "equalize" wealth and poverty?

5. Summarize the events that led to the expansion of "the way" from Jerusalem into Judea and Samaria. Describe the roles of Stephen and Philip in this process.

6. The conversions of an Ethiopian eunuch and a Roman centurion are milestones in Christianity's transformation from a Jewish sect into an international religion in which Gentiles dominate. Explain how this process of ethnic change led to problems in the early church. According to Acts 15, how is the problem resolved at the first church conference in Jerusalem?

7. Describe the roles played by Barnabas and his partner, Paul (formerly Saul) of Tarsus. Summarize the results of Paul's three missionary journeys into Gentile territories. What sequence of events leads to Paul's arrest and imprisonment in Caesarea and Rome?

Questions for Discussion and Reflection

1. By adding a history of nascent Christianity to his Gospel narrative, how does Luke deemphasize apocalyptic hopes of Jesus' early return? What future does Paul's arrival in Rome forecast for church–state relations? In what ways does Luke-Acts show early Christians cultivating a positive relationship with Roman officials? Why does Luke not narrate the martyrdoms of Peter and Paul?

2. In contrast to the author of Revelation, Luke includes no denunciations of the Roman Empire or predictions of its cataclysmic fall. Given Luke's universalism and concern for social justice, how do you think he envisions Christianity's goals and obligations in its ongoing role in secular society? Does Luke see God's kingdom manifested in the application of Christian principles to social and political institutions? Explain why or why not.

Terms and Concepts to Remember

Antioch	Aquila
Antonius Felix	Areopagus
Apollos	Artemis
Ascension	Matthias
Athens	Mercury
Barnabas	Nazarenes
bishop	Paul
Corinth	Pentecost
Cornelius	Philip
Damascus	Philippi
Gallio	Porcius Festus
Gamaliel	proconsul
glossolalia	Silas
Hellenists	Simon Magus
Holy Spirit	Stephen
Lystra	Timothy
martyr	

Recommended Reading*

Arlandson, James M. *Women, Class, and Society in Early Christianity: Models from Luke-Acts.* Peabody, Mass.: Hendrickson, 1997. Applies social theory to the role of women in ancient society and the church.

Dillon, Richard J. "Acts of the Apostles." In R. E. Brown et al., eds., *The New Jerome Biblical Commentary,* pp. 722–767. Englewood Cliffs, N.J.: Prentice-Hall, 1990. A thorough introductory study.

Dunn, James D. G. *The Acts of the Apostles.* Narrative Commentary Series. Philadelphia: Trinity Press International, 1997. Examines the nature of history writing in the first century CE and Acts' narrative structure.

Gaventa, Beverly R. "Acts of the Apostles." In *The New Interpreter's Dictionary of the Bible,* Vol. 1, pp. 33–47. Nashville: Abingdon Press, 2006. A helpful survey of current critical approaches to interpreting Acts, including theological concerns.

Levine, Amy-Jill, and Blickenstaff, Marianne, eds. *A Feminist Companion to the Acts of the Apostles.* Feminist Companion to the New Testament and Early Christian Writings. Cleveland: Pilgrim Press, 2005. Essays exploring women's roles in Acts and the early church.

Matthews, Christopher R. "Acts of the Apostles," in M.D. Coogan, ed., *The Oxford Encyclopedia of the Books of the Bible,* Vol. 1, pp. 11–26. New York: Oxford University Press, 2011. Describes the book's narrative structure and the author's theological purpose.

_____

*See also the "Recommended Reading" for Luke's Gospel (Chapter 9).

Powell, M. A. *What Are They Saying About Acts?* New York: Paulist Press, 1991. A helpful review of influential scholarship on Acts.

Rowe, C. Kavin. *World Upside Down: Reading Acts in the Greco-Roman Age.* New York: Oxford University Press, 2010. Offers a close analysis of Acts' presentation of Christianity's disruptive effect on Greco-Roman society.

Theissen, Gerd. *The Sociology of Early Palestinian Christianity.* Philadelphia: Fortress Press, 1978.

Wall, Robert W. "The Acts of the Apostles." In *The New Interpreter's Bible,* Vol. 10, pp. 3–368. Nashville: Abingdon Press, 2002. Offers extensive historical and literary analysis.

Wilken, R. L. *The Christians as the Romans Saw Them.* New Haven, Conn.: Yale University Press, 1984. A careful analysis of the social, religious, and political conflicts between early Christians and their Roman critics.

PART FIVE

Paul and the Pauline Tradition

In this ancient Christian mosaic portrait of Paul (*left*), the apostle stares directly at the viewer, the intensity of his gaze suggesting a passionate commitment to his mission. Although no one knows what any New Testament figure looked like, later Christian artists commonly depicted Paul as physically unimpressive.

This street scene in Herculaneum (*below*), an excavated Roman town on the Bay of Naples buried by an eruption of Vesuvius in 79 CE, features modest structures with small apartments above shops on the ground floor. Such buildings probably resemble the kind in which Paul set up the tent-making or leather goods business by which he supported himself while on his missionary tours.

Like most Roman dwellings, Herculaneum's stone houses (*above*) have few windows facing the street but enclose an inner courtyard (atrium), open to the sky, around which Roman family life centered.

Although some scholars disagree, many think that this wooden cabinet (*right*), with the imprint of a cross on a white stucco panel above, was a Christian shrine or place of prayer, indicating a Christian presence in Herculaneum well before 79 CE. En route to Rome in the early 60s CE, Paul came ashore at nearby Puteoli, where there was already a group of believers to greet him (Acts 28:13–15). ■

CHAPTER 13

Paul

Apostle to the Nations

I am a free man . . . but I have made myself every man's servant. . . . To the Jews I became like a
Jew, to win Jews. . . . To win Gentiles . . . I made myself like one of them. Indeed, I have become
everything in turn to men of every sort, so that in one way or another I may save some.
Paul to the church at Corinth, 1 Corinthians 9:19–22

Key Topics/Themes Paul is second only to Jesus in his contribution to the development of Christianity. Although Paul apparently never knew the living Jesus and once persecuted his disciples, he experienced an *apokalypsis* (revelation) of the risen Christ that transformed his life. Becoming a missionary to the Gentiles, Paul created and disseminated a view of Jesus' cosmic significance that profoundly shaped the future course of Christian thought. A former Pharisee rigorously educated in Torah interpretation, Paul reinterprets selected parts of the Hebrew Bible to defend his thesis that faith in Jesus' saving power replaced Torah obedience as the means of reconciling human beings to God.

Paul, former Pharisee and persecutor of the church who later spearheaded Christianity's mission to the Gentiles, dominates the second half of Acts. To an incalculable degree, he also dominates the later history of Christian thought. His letters, which form the third unit of the New Testament, represent the new religion's first—and in important ways most lasting—attempt to interpret the meaning of Jesus' "scandalous" death and its significance to human salvation. Paul's startling view is that Jesus' crucifixion introduced a radically different relationship between God and all humanity—Gentiles as well as Jews. Paul's declaration that faith in Christ made all believers heirs to God's covenant promises transformed the Jesus movement from a purely Jewish phenomenon into, ultimately, a new world religion. In his letters to the Romans and Galatians, Paul outlined a theology of redemption through faith that has become central to Christianity's self-understanding. Later theologians as diverse as the Roman church father Augustine (354–430) and Martin Luther (1483–1546), the German monk who sparked the Protestant Reformation, derived many of their doctrines from Paul's letters.

Many historians have remarked that there is perhaps more of Paul than Jesus in official Christianity. Even Mark, the earliest story of Jesus' life, bears the imprint of Pauline ideas in its bias toward Gentile believers, account of the Last Supper, and theology of the cross. Some commentators accuse Paul, who did not know the historical Jesus, of largely ignoring Christ's original proclamation—God's active role in individual human lives—in favor of promulgating a mystery cult *about* Jesus. Certainly, Paul almost never cites Jesus' kingdom teaching and instead emphasizes his own personal experience of the risen Christ, which he interprets in cosmic and mystical terms.

In contrast to Jesus, who apparently wrote nothing, Paul speaks directly to us through his letters, permitting us to compare what he says about himself with what later writers, such as Luke, say about him. Paul's position in the canon is unique: He is the only historical personage who is both a major character in a New Testament book and the author of New Testament books himself. Church tradition ascribes no fewer than thirteen canonical letters to Paul, in total length nearly one-third of the New Testament. Most scholars regard only seven as genuinely Pauline, but the presence of other works attributed to him shows in what high esteem he was held. His ideas and personality so captured the imagination of later Christian writers that they paid tribute to the great apostle by writing in his name and perpetuating his teachings.

Seeking the Historical Paul

As a Christian thinker, Paul never forgets his Jewishness. Although he fights to free Christianity from the "bondage" of Torah observance, Paul consistently stresses the continuity between Judaism and the new religion. For him, as for Matthew, Christianity is revealed through Jesus' ministry but shaped and largely defined by the Hebrew Bible. Throughout his letters, Paul quotes selected parts of the Hebrew Scriptures (primarily from the Greek Septuagint edition) to support the validity of his particular gospel. Despite Paul's ambivalent attitude toward the Mosaic Torah, much of the Hebrew biblical tradition retains its teaching authority for him.

Although our most reliable source for Paul's life is his letters, they do not offer enough information to compile a viable biography. The letters are silent on such matters as his birthplace, parentage, education, and other essentials of his preconversion history, as well as on the later sequence of his travels as a Christian missionary. Because it relates directly to his postconversion battles with his fellow Jews, however, Paul does provide some data about his Jewish heritage. Describing himself as a circumcised "Hebrew born and bred" from the Israelite tribe of Benjamin (Phil. 3:5–6), Paul states that as a "practicing Jew" he outstripped his Jewish contemporaries in strict observance of "the traditions of [his] ancestors" (Gal. 1:13–14). A member of the Pharisee party, he obeyed the Torah completely. "In legal rectitude"—keeping the Torah commandments—Paul judges himself "faultless" (Phil. 3:6).

The Historical Reliability of Acts

Acts supplies much information about Paul not contained in his letters, but most scholars urge great caution about accepting Acts at face value. A great deal of the material in the letters is difficult to reconcile with Acts' narrative sequence. Where discrepancies occur, scholars prefer Paul's firsthand version of events. The author of Acts investigated various sources to compile his account of Christianity's beginnings (Luke 1:1–4), but he appears to have worked with inadequate documentation in recording Paul's career. As noted in Chapters 9 and 12, the author seems unaware of Paul's voluminous correspondence, his insistent claims to apostleship, and his distinctive teaching. Acts says virtually nothing about Paul's essential gospel—that people are saved, not by obedience to Torah commands, but by faith in Christ. More to the point, the writer of Acts is concerned primarily with outlining a precise scheme of history into which he fits his characters as it seems appropriate.

BOX 13.1 Some Differences Between Acts and Paul's Letters

ACTS	PAUL'S LETTERS
Is named Saul and raised in Tarsus	Is not mentioned (but was born to the tribe of Benjamin, whose first king was Saul [Phil. 3:5])
Studies under Rabbi Gamaliel	Is not mentioned
Belongs to the Pharisee party	Is confirmed in Philippians 3:6
Persecutes Christians	Is mentioned several times
Experiences a vision of Jesus on the road to Damascus	Receives a "revelation" of Jesus (Gal. 1:12, 16)
Following his call, goes immediately to Damascus, where he preaches in synagogues	Goes to "Arabia" for an unspecified period (Gal. 1:17)
Is initially shunned by the Jerusalem disciples but is later introduced to the apostles (9:26–30)	Does not go to Jerusalem until three years after his return from "Arabia," and meets only Peter and James (Gal. 1:17–20)
Receives the Holy Spirit after **Ananias** baptizes and lays hands upon him	Asserts that he owes his apostolic gospel and commission to no one; never refers to his baptism (Gal. 1:11–12, 16–17)
Attends an apostolic conference on his third Jerusalem visit	Attends the conference on his second Jerusalem visit (Gal. 2:1–10)
Agrees to impose Torah dietary restrictions on Gentile converts	Refuses to accept any legal restrictions (Gal. 2:5)
Agrees to forbid eating meat sacrificed to idols	Regards eating such meat as nondefiling (1 Cor. 8; 10:27; Rom. 14:13–15:6)

In some cases, Acts provides biographical details that Paul never mentions, such as his birth in Tarsus, capital city of Cilicia (in modern southeastern Turkey), and the claim that Paul's family possessed Roman citizenship. These and similar traditions—such as Paul's originally being named Saul, his studying at the feet of Rabbi Gamaliel (the leading Pharisee scholar of his day), and his supporting himself by tent making—are never referred to in the Pauline letters, so we have no way of verifying their historical accuracy.

Other statements in Acts seem to contradict Paul's direct testimony (see Box 13.1), particularly the chronological order of events following his decisive confrontation with the risen Jesus. With Acts' reliability in question and Paul's biographical disclosures so few, scholars are unable to reconstruct anything resembling a satisfactory

life of Christianity's Apostle to the Gentiles. We do not know when he was born, how his family gained Roman citizenship (if Acts is correct on this point), whether he was once married, where or when he wrote many of his letters, and under what precise circumstances he died. These and other missing facts are partly compensated for, however, in the brilliant revelation of thought and personality that his letters impart.

Paul's Radical Change

In both Acts and the letters, Paul's life can be divided into two contrasting parts. During his early career, Paul was a devout Pharisee who "savagely" persecuted the first Christians. During his later years, he was a Christian missionary who successfully implanted the new religion in non-Jewish territories and established the first churches of Europe. The event that changed Paul from a persecutor of Christians into a tireless promoter of the faith was, in his words, a "revelation [*apokalypsis*] of Jesus Christ" (Gal. 1:12). Acts depicts the "revelation" as a blinding vision of the risen Messiah on the road to Damascus, emphasizing its importance by narrating it fully three times (Acts 9:1–9; 22:3–11; 26:12–19). Paul's briefer allusions to the experience speak simply of being called by God's "grace" (Gal. 1:15) to an "abnormal birth" and of witnessing a post resurrection appearance of Jesus (1 Cor. 9:1; 15:8–9).

Many scholars prefer to speak of Paul's encounter with Christ as a "call," rather than a religious "conversion." Some recent commentators, however, suggest that Paul's sudden change from a zealous opponent to a devoted champion of the Jesus movement is best understood as a change in his relationship with his divine patron, the God of Israel. Carefully analyzing Paul's accounts of his experience, Zeba Crook argues persuasively that they reflect the pervasive patron–client structure of Roman society and that Paul saw himself as the loyal client of his divine benefactor. The model on which most Roman social and political relationships were based, the Roman patronage system created a social network that was virtually all-encompassing. In this arrangement, a wealthy or politically powerful patron conferred "benefactions" or benefits on his social dependent, the client. This process commonly involved a patron's representative, an intermediary who acted as broker to the client (cf. Luke 22:25 and the discussion of Roman patronage in Chapter 5). In the religious sphere, the same arrangement prevailed, with a particular god bestowing blessings, both material and spiritual, on his client, the god's worshiper. For Paul, the "revelation [*apokalypsis*]" he received from Jesus was an unexpected recognition that henceforth all divine benefactions came through Christ, God's son and intermediary.

Subscribing to universally recognized Roman custom, Paul displayed gratitude to his divine patron through loyal service, thereby increasing his patron's honor and public reputation. Obligated to his all-powerful benefactor, Paul redirected his abundant energies to proclaiming God's gracious gifts through Christ. As he explained to the Corinthians, Paul feels compelled to preach the gospel because he is "discharging a trust," his public obligation to the God who commissioned him (1 Cor. 9:16–18). Like other converts in the ancient world, Paul regards his preconversion state as deeply inferior to his present status; he dismisses his previous religious "assets" as "so much garbage" because in the glorified Jesus he has gained benefits of incomparable value (Phil. 3:7–9; see Crook in "Recommended Reading").

If Paul saw his calling in terms of the Roman patron–client relationship, he also drew on other contemporary Roman practices to express his central message about Jesus. In choosing the word *evangelion* (good news) to summarize the content of his preaching, Paul adopted a term that the imperial government was already using to praise the emperor's policies and accomplishments, such as his establishment of empirewide peace. By appropriating "gospel" or "good news" for the proclamation of Jesus' lordship, Paul and the Gospel authors who came after him presented the Greco-Roman world with a new option for supreme ruler. (*Evangelion* also appears in the Greek edition of Isaiah 61:1, where the prophet states he has been sent to "bring good news to the oppressed," a passage that would affirm Paul's use of the term.)

In an even more targeted reference to imperial customs, Paul uses the word *parousia* (presence, coming, or arrival) to denote Jesus' anticipated return to earth, when he would visibly subject all nations and peoples to his rule. When the emperor made a *parousia* or public appearance at some city, it was a major social and political event that was expected to involve virtually the entire population of that city. Hailing the emperor as *soter* (deliverer or savior), the whole populace typically acclaimed his godlike persona. For Paul, these imperial displays were mere shadows of future realities, when *the* Parousia occurred (see the discussion of 1 Thessalonians in Chapter 14).

FIGURE 13.1 The earliest known portrait of Paul. Recently discovered in the Catacomb of Saint Thecla in the Vatican, this image of Paul probably dates from the early fourth century CE. Following the era's artistic conventions in depicting the Apostle to the Gentiles, the painter gives him a distinctively thin face, small eyes, furrowed brow, and pointed beard. Paul's legendary mentorship of Saint Thecla is discussed in Chapter 20.

Eager to honor his divine patron and spread the word of Jesus' imminent reappearance (see below), Paul did not spare himself either discomfort or danger. His physical stamina—even today duplicating his travel itinerary would exhaust most people—is matched by the strength of his loyalty. Paul's letters reveal their author's rhetorical intensity, ranging from paternal tenderness to biting sarcasm. In one letter, he insults his readers' intelligence and suggests that some of their advisers castrate themselves (Gal. 3:1; 5:12). In other letters, he reacts to criticism with threats, wild boasting, and wounding anger (2 Cor. 10–13). In still others, he expresses profound affection and gentle tact (1 Cor. 13; Phil. 1:3–9; 2:1–4; 4:2–3) (see Figure 13.1).

Paul's conviction that Jesus had privately revealed to him the one true gospel (Gal. 1–2) isolated the apostle from many fellow believers. Acts and the letters agree that Paul quarreled with many of his intimate companions (Acts 15:37–39; Gal. 2:11–14), as well as with entire groups (Gal.; 2 Cor. 10–13). This sense of a unique vision, one not shared by most other Christians, may have shaped Paul's admitted preference for preaching in territories where no Christian had preceded him. The more distant his missionary field from competing missionaries, the better it suited him. Paul's desire to impress his individual gospel on new converts may have influenced his ambition to work in areas as far removed from established churches as possible (Rom. 15:20–23).

Dating Paul's Career

In his letter to the Galatians, Paul briefly summarizes his career up to the time of writing, giving us a few clues on which to base a rough chronology of his life. After the decisive "revelation" of Jesus, "without going up to Jerusalem" to consult the Twelve, Paul went immediately to "Arabia" (probably an area east of the Jordan River), staying there for an unspecified time before returning to Damascus. Only after "three years" had passed did he travel to Jerusalem "to get to know Cephas" (Peter's Aramaic name). Staying precisely two weeks with Peter (Paul evidently counted the days), he visited no other "Apostle" except "James the Lord's brother." Paul insists on this point because he wants to emphasize his complete independence of the Jerusalem leadership: "What I write is plain truth; before God I am not lying" (Gal. 1:16–20).

After making Peter's acquaintance, Paul went north to Syria, allowing another fourteen years to elapse before he again visited Jerusalem. The occasion for this second visit was almost certainly the church conference described in Acts 15, a meeting of delegates from Antioch with the Jerusalem congregation to discuss whether Gentile Christians must become circumcised or

FIGURE 13.2 *The Apostle Paul.* This somber portrait by Rembrandt (1606–1669) shows Paul in a deeply reflective mood and evokes the apostle's consciousness of the enormous burden he bears—the task of serving his divine patron by communicating his unique vision of Christ to the Gentiles. In his letters, Paul expresses a wide variety of moods—joy, anger, bitter sarcasm—but Rembrandt captures here the sense of melancholy and isolation that typically characterizes this great missionary.

follow other provisions of the Mosaic Law. Paul remembers the gathering as less formal than Acts depicts it, emphasizing his private conversations with the three "pillars" of the Jerusalem leadership—Peter, John, and Jesus' kinsman James (see Box 12.3). Observing that **Titus,** a Greek youth accompanying him, was not required to become circumcised, Paul declares that the three Jerusalem "pillars" recognized the legitimacy of his peculiar "gospel" proclaiming freedom from the Torah's "bondage." The Jerusalem leaders shake hands on this agreement and endorse Paul as the recognized missionary to the Gentiles, as Peter is to the Jews (Gal. 2:1–10) (see Figure 13.2).

Paul's account indicates that approximately seventeen years (or about fifteen when calculated by the Hebrew method) passed between the time of his initial vision and the conference held in Jerusalem. If the Jerusalem conference took place about 49 CE, as many historians believe, then Paul must have become a Christian about 32 or (possibly) 34 CE, shortly after Jesus' crucifixion.

Two allusions to historical figures help us fix other dates in Paul's life. The first is a reference to King Aretas, whose commissioner forced Paul to escape from Damascus by being lowered down the city wall in a basket (2 Cor. 11:32–33). Aretas IV ruled the powerful Arab kingdom of Nabatea (located south and east of Palestine) between about 9 and 39 CE. Fixing the time of Aretas's reign confirms the assumption that Paul was already an active Christian missionary during the same decade that witnessed Jesus' death.

According to the second historical reference (Acts 18:11), Gallio was the Roman governor of Greece during the period of Paul's Corinthian visit. Because Gallio's administration took place between about 51 and 53 CE and because Paul had been in Corinth for about eighteen months when he was brought before the governor, Paul probably arrived in that city about 49 or 50 CE. Additional evidence tends to confirm that date. Acts refers to the emperor Claudius's expulsion of Jews from Rome, a decree enacted about 49 CE. Two Jewish Christians, Aquila and Prisca (Priscilla), had recently moved from Rome to Corinth when Paul arrived in the city (Acts 18:1–2).

Paul's Letters

The Genuine Letters

New Testament historians generally agree that Paul became a Christian in the mid-30s CE and that he traveled extensively as a missionary during the 40s and 50s CE, arriving in Rome about the year 60. Scholarly agreement disappears, however, in attempting to date Paul's letters or even establish the exact order in which he wrote them.

The majority of scholars accept seven letters as authentically Pauline. Virtually all scholars regard Romans, 1 and 2 Corinthians, Galatians, Philippians, 1 Thessalonians, and Philemon as Paul's own writing. Some also accept 2 Thessalonians and Colossians. But the majority doubt that Ephesians is genuine and are certain that three—Titus and 1 and 2 Timothy—were composed by a Pauline disciple after the apostle's death. Almost no reputable scholar believes that Hebrews, which is a sermon rather than a letter, is a Pauline composition (see Box 13.2).

The Order of Composition

Although scholars debate the exact order in which Paul composed his letters, they generally agree that 1 Thessalonians was written first (c. 50 CE) and is thus the oldest known Christian writing. If Paul also wrote 2 Thessalonians, it dates from about 50 CE as well. The two Corinthian letters are usually placed in the mid-50s, and the more theologically mature letters, such as Romans and Philippians, are dated later. Four letters—Colossians, Philemon, Philippians, and possibly Ephesians—were reputedly composed while Paul was imprisoned and thus are known as the "captivity letters." Unfortunately, Paul does not reveal in the letters where he was jailed, so we do not know whether he wrote them from Ephesus, Caesarea, or Rome, all cities in which he presumably suffered imprisonment. The canonical letters (others have been lost) were probably all written during a relatively brief span of time, the decade between about 50 and 60 CE.

Paul's Use of the Letter Form

Paul is aware that his letters are persuasive documents. He consciously uses letters as substitutes for his own presence, making them an effective means of influencing people and

BOX 13.2 Paul's Letters: Authentic, Disputed, and Pseudonymous

Paul's genuine letters, composed between about 50 and 62 CE, form the oldest surviving Christian literature. In the decades after Paul's death, his influence became so great that different Christian groups apparently competed for the role of authoritative interpreter of his teaching. Following the Hellenistic-Jewish practice of pseudonymity (writing in the name of an honored religious authority of the past, such as Moses or one of the prophets), some Christian authors composed letters in Paul's name, using their understanding of the Pauline heritage to address problems of their own day. Whereas Paul's genuine letters invariably deal with specific problems besetting individual congregations (and presume a relatively informal church structure), pseudonymous letters such as 1 and 2 Timothy and Titus (the pastoral epistles) typically deal with such issues as maintaining the doctrinal purity of apostolic traditions and presume a much more structured church administration (see Chapter 17).

LETTERS BY PAUL	LETTERS POSSIBLY NOT BY PAUL	LETTERS DEFINITELY NOT BY PAUL
1 Thessalonians (c. 50 CE) 1 and 2 Corinthians Galatians Romans Philemon Philippians	2 Thessalonians Colossians	Ephesians 1 and 2 Timothy Titus Hebrews (Even in early Christianity, most churchmen did not believe that Hebrews was Paul's work.)

events from a distance. Although he gives directions on a wide variety of matters, his primary object is to correct his recipients' beliefs and to discipline their behavior. His letters are also potent weapons for shooting down opposition to his teaching.

Writing to the Corinthians, Paul states that his critics contrast his "weighty and powerful" letters with his unimpressive physical appearance and ineffectiveness as a speaker (2 Cor. 10:9–11). The apostle may exaggerate his defects for rhetorical effect, but he is right about his letters. From the time they were first written, they have exerted enormous influence on Christian thought and conduct.

Paul writes letters so effectively that he makes this literary category the standard medium of communication for many later Christian writers. The large majority of New Testament authors imitate Paul by conveying their ideas in letter form. Twenty-one of the twenty-seven canonical books are (at least theoretically) letters. Even the writer of Revelation uses this form to transmit Jesus' message to the seven churches of Asia Minor (Rev. 2–3).

Hellenistic Letters

In general, Paul follows the accepted Hellenistic literary form in his correspondence, modifying it somewhat to express his peculiarly Christian interests. Much Greco-Roman correspondence, both personal and business, has survived from early Christian times, allowing us to compare Paul's letters with those of other Hellenistic writers.

The Hellenistic letter writer typically begins with a prescript, identifying the writer and the reader, and a greeting, wishing good fortune to the reader and commonly invoking the blessing of a god. Paul varies this formula by mentioning the Christian allegiance of the writer and recipients, substituting "grace" and "peace" for the customary greetings, and frequently including an associate's name in the salutation. He also elaborates on the Hellenistic custom by giving praise, thanks, or prayers for the welfare of his recipients. A typical example of Paul's modification of the Hellenistic greeting appears in the opening of 1 Thessalonians:

> From Paul, Silvanus, and Timothy to the congregation of Thessalonians who belong to God the Father and the Lord Jesus Christ. Grace to you and peace.
>
> (1 Thess. 1:1)

Paul also modifies his letters' prescripts according to his attitude toward the church he is addressing. His letter to his trusted friends at Philippi opens with an effusive outpouring of affection and praise for the Philippians (Phil. 1:1–11). In contrast, when he writes to the churches in Galatia, he is furious with the recipients and includes no warm or approving salutation (Gal. 1:1–5).

After stating the letter's principal message, the Hellenistic writer closes with additional acknowledgments, typically including greetings from other people and sometimes adding a request that the recipient(s) convey the sender's greetings to mutual acquaintances. Paul often expands this custom to include a summary statement of faith and a benediction, as well as a list of fellow Christians to be greeted (Rom. 16; 1 Cor. 16:10–21; Col. 4:7–18).

The Role of Dictation

As was customary in Greco-Roman correspondence, Paul apparently dictated all his letters to a secretary or scribe, occasionally adding a signature or a few other words in his own hand. In antiquity, secretaries ordinarily did not record the precise words of those dictating but, instead, paraphrased the gist of what was said (Rom. 16:21–22; Gal. 6:11; Col. 4:18; Philem. 19; 2 Thess. 3:17), a practice that helps explain the spontaneous quality of Pauline letters.

The Circumstances of Writing

Most of Paul's letters were composed under the pressure of dealing with an emergency in a given church. With the exception of Romans, which is addressed to a congregation that he had not yet visited, every Pauline letter is directed to a particular group, and most of the groups are personally known by the writer. In virtually every case, the recipients are experiencing some form of crisis, of either belief or behavior, which the author tries to resolve.

Paul's main concern is always pastoral; he deals with individual problems caused by church members' teaching or conduct. In counseling these small groups of infant Christians, Paul typically invokes theological arguments or examples to reinforce his advice. Because Paul's letters are *occasional*—dealing with a specific occasion, issue, or crisis—scholars caution that they do not represent a complete or systematic exposition of Paul's beliefs. Paul's theological statements appear primarily to support the counsel he applies to particular situations at a given congregation. In his first letter to the Thessalonians, he outlines his beliefs about the future resurrection of persons who die before the Parousia takes place only because some believers at Thessalonica were worried that the Christian dead would miss out on their reward (1 Thess. 4:13–5:11). When writing to the church at Corinth, he passes on the traditions he had received about the Last Supper primarily because some Corinthians were behaving improperly at the celebration (1 Cor. 11:17–34). If there had been no misconduct, Paul would have had no occasion to mention the tradition, and we would have been deprived of one of the few passages in which Paul cites a teaching from Jesus. In no letter, with the partial exception of Romans, does Paul set out a comprehensive statement of his theology. The occasional nature of his correspondence means that we have only partial glimpses of Pauline doctrines.

Paul's Characteristic Theology

As the author of 2 Peter cautioned, Paul's letters "contain some obscure passages" that are easy to misinterpret (2 Pet. 3:16). Pauline thought can be subtle and complex, making it difficult even for scholars familiar with his language and historical-social context to achieve a consensus about his views on many important topics. In studying Paul's letters, it helps to keep in mind that his theology was not static but grew and developed over time. Although Paul states that he received his distinctive gospel from a revelation of Christ (Gal. 1:11–12), he does not claim that it arrived complete and unchanging. In fact, Paul's ideas and approaches to different topics seem to change from letter to letter as he wrestles with new problems that beset his congregations. Because his letters deal with ever-changing situations, as well as his recipients' sometimes unanticipated reactions to his statements, we cannot expect them to be entirely consistent. His negative judgment of the Mosaic Torah in Galatians, for example, contrasts markedly with his more positive pronouncements on the law in Romans (see Chapter 15).

Paul's relationship to God, Christ, and the unseen spirit world was dynamic and creative. Because he had experienced divine intervention in his personal life and afterward continued to receive mystical visions (2 Cor. 12:1–10), Paul could speak progressively about God's intentions for humanity and the imminent transformation of believers at the End of history. In surveying some characteristic Pauline theological assumptions or principles, it is important to recognize that the following summations represent a composite view of the apostle's teachings. He did not arrive at them all at once, nor does he usually expound his characteristic beliefs in a single letter.

Mysticism and Eschatology

Understanding Paul's writings means recognizing his sense of the spiritual power that inspired his apostolic career. Paul bases his authority as a Christian leader and the validity of his distinctive gospel on an *apokalypsis,* a private revelation of the post resurrection Jesus (Gal. 1:11–12, 15–17). His personal knowledge of Christ, which he insists he received as a direct heavenly communication and not from any apostolic predecessor, informs Paul that the glorified Jesus now exists in two separate but related dimensions: the macrocosm (great world) of God's spiritual domain and the microcosm (little world) of human consciousness. This **dualism,** characteristic of apocalyptic thought (see Chapter 19), expresses Paul's conviction that Christ possesses both an objective and a subjective reality. Christ is at once a cosmic figure who will soon return to judge the world and a being who also mysteriously dwells within the individual believer. The tension between the transcendent and the immanent Christ, one who is simultaneously universal and yet intimately experienced by the faithful, appears in almost every letter Paul wrote.

Paul's mysticism—his powerful sense of union with an invisible spiritual reality—is an important component of his worldview. Indeed, some scholars suggest that, even before his ecstatic encounter with Christ, Paul may have belonged to an apocalyptic brand of Pharisaism that included mystical beliefs and practices. In 2 Corinthians, he writes of being "caught up as far as the third heaven . . . into paradise," where he "heard words so secret that human lips may not repeat them" (2 Cor. 12:1–4) (see Box 14.2). These "visions and revelations granted by the Lord," which undoubtedly played their part in sustaining Paul through the many dangers and hardships he endured, may not have occurred as often as he would have liked. He adds that to prevent him "from being unduly elated by the magnificence of such revelations" he was given "a sharp physical pain," perhaps to remind him that even sporadic experiences of the infinite could not allow him to escape his finite humanity (2 Cor. 12:7–8).

Paul may have been familiar with the noncanonical Book of 1 Enoch, which describes **Enoch**'s vision of God's heavenly throne—or at least the tradition surrounding it—for he clearly shares its aspiration for mystical oneness with the divine. Paul also shares Enoch's apocalyptic viewpoint. His conviction that the Messiah's appearance has inaugurated the End of time permeates his thought and underlies much of his ethical teaching. Paul's advice on marriage, divorce, slavery, celibacy, and human behavior in general is largely shaped by his expectation of an imminent Final Judgment. In his oldest surviving letter, he states that he expects to witness the Parousia: "We who are left alive until the Lord comes . . . [will be] caught up in the clouds to meet the Lord in the air" (1 Thess. 4:15–17).

In 1 Corinthians, his expectation to live until the End is equally certain; hence, he advises his correspondents that "the time we live in will not last long. While it lasts, married men should be as if they had no wives; . . . buyers must not count on keeping what they buy, nor those who use the world's wealth. . . . For the whole frame of this world is passing away" (1 Cor. 7:29–31). Eagerly anticipating the *eschaton,* he also tells the Corinthians, "Listen! I will unfold a mystery: we shall not all die, but we shall all be changed in a flash, in the twinkling of an eye, at the last trumpet-call. For the trumpet will sound, and the dead will rise immortal, and we [the living] shall be changed" (1 Cor. 15:51–52).

Like many Jewish apocalyptists of the first century, Paul sees human history as divided into two qualitatively different ages, or periods of time. The present evil age will soon be replaced by a New Age, a new creation, in which God will reign completely (Gal. 6:14; 1 Cor. 15:20–28; 2 Cor. 5:17). Because the Messiah has not only arrived but also died and risen from the dead—his resurrection a guarantee that the End has already begun—Paul believes that the eschatological consummation of history is at hand. Paul's letters thus burn with special urgency

because he believes that his day marks the crucial transition period between the two ages. "For upon us," he wrote, "the fulfillment [end] of the ages [the present age and that to come] has come" (1 Cor. 10:11). God will soon "rescue us [believers] from this present age of wickedness" and establish his direct rule over a renewed creation (Gal. 1:4). Those about to be judged, especially members of his infant churches, must therefore prepare for the impending visitation, pursuing lives of unblemished virtue. The following summaries of Paul's principal ideas offer a brief survey of his thought; his distinctive concepts are developed more fully in discussions of the individual letters (Chapters 14–16).

The Centrality and Preeminence of Jesus

Absolutely central to Paul's thought is his conviction that, in Jesus, God achieves the world's salvation. Although Paul rarely refers to Jesus' earthly ministry or teachings, he may have known more of Jesus' life than he reveals in his letters. He quotes or cites Jesus' sayings only when they are directly pertinent to regulating his correspondents' behavior (cf. 1 Cor. 11 and 15). Paul's chief concern is with the heavenly Christ whom he sees in three roles: (1) as God's revealed Wisdom (1 Cor. 1–4), (2) as the divine Lord through whom God rules (Phil. 2:11; Rom. 10:9; 1 Cor. 15:24–28), and (3) as the means by whom God's Spirit dwells in believers (Rom. 8; 14:17). The operation of the Spirit, God's active force denoting his presence and effecting his will in the world, characterizes all of Paul's churches.

Christ and Humanity

In contrasting Christ with the symbol of earthly humanity, **Adam** (in Genesis, God's first human creation), Paul emphasizes the vast change Jesus' activity has effected for the human race. Prior to Jesus' coming, humans existed in Adam's perishable image, victims of sin and death (Rom. 5:12–21). In contrast, believers now "in Christ" (imbued with his spirit) will also share in the glorified Christ's life-giving nature (1 Cor. 15:21–24, 45–49): "As in Adam all men die, so in Christ all will be brought to life."

The Faithful as Christ's Body

Using a corporate image to identify the believing community as the earthly manifestation of the exalted Christ, Paul states that the faithful collectively are Christ's "body" (1 Cor. 10:16–18; 12:12–30; Rom. 12). As a people defined and influenced by the Spirit, the church functions in union with Christ so fully that it reveals his visible form. Because Paul's concept of the body is so central to his thought, we will discuss it more fully in Chapter 14.

Christ as Liberator from Sin, Torah, and Death

In Paul's view, all human beings are negatively influenced by sin's power and hence are alienated from the perfect God (Rom. 7). Sin's invariable consequence is death, a condition of the defective humanity we share with Adam (Rom. 5:12–21). By defining both the nature of and the punishment for sin, the Torah increased its power, revealing the universality of sin and condemning all sinners—the entire human race (Rom. 1–3).

Christ's total obedience to the Father and his selfless death on the cross, taking unto himself the Torah's penalty for sin, liberates those persons accepting him (living fully under his power) from sin, death, and the Torah's curses (Gal. 3–5; Rom. 3–7). For Paul, "freedom in Christ" means deliverance from the old order of sin and punishment, including the Torah's power to condemn. (For a fuller discussion of sin and of Christ's role in conquering it, see Chapter 15.)

Christ's Universal Sufficiency

To Paul, Jesus' sacrificial death and God's exaltation of Christ as the agent by whom God rules and imparts his Spirit constitute a total change in the relationship between God and humanity. Christ is the final and complete means of canceling the powers of sin and destruction. Because Christ is now all-sufficient in reconciling humanity to God, neither "angelic powers" nor the Torah any longer play a decisive role in achieving human salvation.

Justification by Faith

Historically, one of Paul's most influential concepts was his understanding of the moral logic by which a perfectly righteous God can accept or "justify" human beings whose unrighteous behavior makes them veritable "slaves" to sin. Does God, who sits as Judge over the universe, compromise his ethical standards by granting salvation to sinful humans? Paul's personal experience of divine mercy, expressed through an *apokalypsis* (revelation) of Jesus, convinced him that in Christ he has been justified or "made right" before God. His divine patron or benefactor had revealed that he henceforth related to humankind exclusively through Jesus. Jesus, moreover, while living under Mosaic Law, had demonstrated perfect faith in God, making him the exemplar and intermediary for all who have faith. This conviction—that faith in Christ delivered him from sin more effectively than had obedience to the Mosaic Law—placed Paul on a collision course with his native Judaism, as well as with many Jewish Christians who saw no reason to abandon their Mosaic heritage. For Jewish Christians of the first century CE (probably including Jesus' "brother" James), to accept Jesus as Israel's Messiah (Christ) was to follow the same Torah obligations that Jesus had.

For observant Jews, the Law provided a God-given—and fully adequate—means of atoning for sin and maintaining a right relationship with the Deity. Mosaic Law prescribes detailed rituals by which genuinely repentant sinners can express their desire to make peace with God. (As many scholars have noted, Torah statutes involving "sin offerings" and other sacrifices to effect forgiveness presuppose that petitioners have already experienced appropriate sorrow and remorse for their errors.) Both personal contrition and sacrificial rites were part of the biblical arrangement for restoring harmony between Israel's God and his worshipers.

Although Paul claims that "by the law's standard of righteousness [he had been] without fault" (Phil. 3:6), at some point after his encounter with the risen Jesus he came to believe that the Mosaic Covenant was no longer the means by which God reconciled sinful humanity to himself. In two of his most theologically important letters, Galatians and Romans, Paul argues that the Law serves only to expose the universal reality of human sin, which it justly condemns. By his sacrificial death on the cross, however, Jesus paid for *everyone* the Law's penalty for human sin, effectively canceling the Law's authority. Through spiritual union with Christ, who is now God's sole instrument of human redemption, believers share in the benefits of Jesus' self-sacrifice and freely receive the divine favor that grants them eternal life. For Paul, the Law can no longer confer forgiveness, a function that in God's new arrangement belongs exclusively to Christ. In Paul's view, it is God's *grace*—his undeserved kindness and mercy—that opens the way to salvation for Jews and Gentiles alike, graciously assigning them the capacity to accept and believe in Jesus. Believers are thus justified before God only through their faith—complete trust—in Jesus' power to save those with whom he is spiritually united. (For further discussion of Paul's ideas about faith in Christ replacing works of Torah, see Chapter 15.)

During the sixteenth century CE, European Christians were bitterly divided over the interpretation of Paul's doctrine of justification by faith. Martin Luther, the Protestant reformer, held that it is through faith alone that believers are saved, whereas the Catholic Church maintained that salvation also comes through deeds, particularly observance of such sacraments as baptism, confession, and absolution. It was not until the close of the twentieth century that Catholics and Protestants reached an accord on Paul's teaching. In 1999, on the 482nd anniversary of Luther's posting his protests against church practices on the door of Castle Church in Wittenberg, Germany—an act that ignited the Protestant Reformation—leaders of the Catholic and Lutheran churches signed a historic agreement stating that faith is essential to salvation. According to this joint Catholic–Lutheran declaration, "By grace alone, in faith in Christ's saving work and not because of any merit on our part, we are adopted by God and receive the Holy Spirit, who renews our hearts while equipping and calling us to good works."

The Importance of Women in Early Christianity

Did the Historical Paul Judge Women Negatively?

More than any other New Testament writer, in recent decades, Paul has drawn scathing criticism for his apparent inconsistency regarding the role of women in the Christian community. Given that both Jewish and Greco-Roman society of his day typically relegated women to subservient positions in which their lives were rigidly controlled by fathers, husbands, or other male kinsmen, some of Paul's pronouncements appear surprisingly positive. In Galatians, he sweeps away both class and gender distinctions, declaring that for people baptized "into union" with Christ, "There is no such thing as Jew and Greek, slave and freeman, male and female; for you are all one person in Christ Jesus" (Gal. 3:28). Writing to the Corinthians, he recognizes that women, like men, serve the congregation by offering prayers and delivering prophecies (1 Cor. 11:4–5). He also notes that some women, such as his friend Phoebe, hold responsible office in the church (Rom. 16:1–5). Besides describing two women in Philippi, Euodia and Syntyche, as his "fellow workers" in spreading the gospel (Phil. 4:2–3), Paul also refers to a Roman woman, Junia (Junias), as "eminent among the apostles"

(Rom. 16:7). Writing to the congregation at Rome, Paul sends individual greetings to twice as many men as women, but he singles out for special commendation twice as many women, such as Junia and Mary (otherwise unknown), as men (Rom. 16).

Throughout most of Christian history, however, it is Paul's seemingly negative attitude toward women's roles that church leaders have traditionally accepted as the norm. Later in the same letter in which he affirms women as prophets, Paul apparently forbids them to "address the meeting":

> They have no license to speak, but should keep their place as the law directs. If there is something they want to know, they can ask their own husbands at home. It is a shocking thing that a woman should address the congregation.
>
> (1 Cor. 14:34–35)

In 1 Timothy, the writer appears to relegate women to perpetual passivity, silence, and submission:

> A woman must be a learner, listening quietly and with due submission. I do not permit a woman to be a teacher, nor must woman domineer over man; she should be quiet.
>
> (1 Tim. 2:11–12)

The author's scriptural justification for denying all women the authority to teach others derives from his interpretation of the second of two different accounts in Genesis about humanity's creation. Whereas the first version states that "male and female" came into being simultaneously, both in the divine "image" (Gen. 1:26–27), the second, which the writer selects to support his argument, awards Adam (the first male) priority in time and importance. In the author's view, Eve (the first female) is implicitly inferior to Adam because she was formed "afterwards" (1 Tim. 2:13; cf. Gen. 2: 18–25). However, 1 Timothy's most damaging charge against Eve (and, hence, all her daughters) is her alleged susceptibility to deceit: "It was not Adam who[m] [the serpent] deceived; it was the woman, who, yielding to

deception, fell into sin" (1 Tim. 2:14; cf. Gen. 3). In a stroke, the ultimate responsibility for humanity's disobedience of and alienation from God is thus placed on Eve, whose credulity and irresponsibility manifestly exclude her entire sex from positions of trust in the Christian fellowship. Yet, as the writer concedes, nature accords women one clear means of redemption: They can be "saved through motherhood"—bearing children.

The insulting estimate of women's innate character found in 1 Timothy is but one reason a large majority of scholars agree that this document—along with 2 Timothy and Titus (known as the pastoral epistles)—did not originate with Paul (see the discussion of pseudonymous authorship in Chapter 17). Many scholars also suspect that the passage in 1 Corinthians 14 denying women the right to speak before the congregation was not originally part of Paul's letter, but that later copyists inserted it into the manuscript to make it harmonize with the (non-Pauline) restrictions that the author of 1 Timothy imposed. The verses forbidding women's public participation in church services (1 Cor. 14:34–35), in fact, interrupt Paul's general train of thought and may be taken as scribal interpolations.

Some scholars who accept Pauline authorship of these controversial passages, however, also urge readers not to view them as universal prescriptions permanently limiting women's roles. C. S. Keener, for example, emphasizes the occasional nature of Paul's letters, noting that most of Paul's directives concern particular crises then affecting his churches and that his recommendations may be limited to resolving specific situations then troubling individual congregations. First Timothy's restrictions on women's public speaking may apply primarily to women who have not yet been fully instructed in the Christian message and who must learn quietly at home before they can legitimately contribute to congregational discussions (see Keener in "Recommended Reading"). (Many women in the early church took vows of perpetual virginity, leading lives of celibacy that allowed them relative freedom from patriarchal oppression; see the Acts of Paul and Thecla, a celibate woman disciple whom Paul authorized to teach others [see Chapter 20].)

The Gospel Traditions

In considering the legitimate participation of women in church leadership, many scholars recommend viewing Paul's letters in the larger context of the entire New Testament canon. Virtually all components of the Jesus tradition—from Mark, to John, to Luke's special material—highlight the crucial role that women play in Jesus' ministry. Both Mark and Luke state that women accompanied Jesus throughout his Galilean campaign, some supporting his work by acting as patrons who contributed financially (Mark 15:40–41; Luke 8:1–3). Mark and John also show Jesus, contrary to prevailing custom, engaging in public conversations with "foreign" women (unaccompanied by male protectors) who assert their right to benefit from his healing gifts and his spiritual insights, including a Syro-Phoenician woman (Mark 7:24–30) and a frequently married Samaritan woman with whom he discusses the fine points of acceptable worship (John 4:1–42). In Luke's special tradition, Jesus also commends Mary, the sister of Martha, for abandoning her traditional household duties to gather with his male disciples, noting that what she learns "shall not be taken away from her" (Luke 10:38–42).

Whereas all of Jesus' twelve principal male disciples precipitately abandon him at his arrest, a group of Galilean women loyally follow him to the cross, where they witness his death and then observe the location of his burial. In all four Gospels, it is these Galilean women (in John, Mary Magdalene alone) who discover the empty tomb; in three of the four accounts (Mark's narrative concludes at the vacant sepulcher), it is also the female disciples who first proclaim Jesus' resurrection,

although the male followers initially discount their testimony (Matt. 28:1–10; Luke 23:55–24:11; John 20:1–3, 10–18).

Following Jesus' resurrection and ascension, as Christianity spread through the Greco-Roman world, women continued to assume important functions that helped the new faith grow. According to Acts, when Paul traveled through Macedonia to the town of Philippi, he met there a wealthy woman, Lydia, "a dealer in purple fabric from the city of Thyatiria," who not only responded enthusiastically to his preaching but also "insisted" that he and his fellow missionaries stay at her house. Possessing a house large enough to accommodate meetings of local Christians, Lydia in effect became the patron of the Philippian congregation, with which Paul had an exceptionally warm and affectionate relationship (Acts 16:12–16, 40; cf. Phil. 1). Prisca (Priscilla) and her husband, Aquila—in both Acts and Paul's letters, she is usually mentioned first, perhaps indicating her prominence in the Christian movement—serve as Paul's co-workers in Corinth, and Ephesus, where the two instruct Apollos, an "eloquent" Jewish Christian from Alexandria, in correct Christian teaching (Acts 18:2, 18, 26; Rom. 16:3; 1 Cor. 16:19; cf. 2 Tim. 4:19).

Although the New Testament evidence does not suggest that the mid-first-century CE witnessed a "golden age" of gender equality and mutuality in the Christian community, it does confirm that some women, in some locations, assumed leading roles as teachers, prophets, and missionary workers. The question then arises: If Jesus included women among his closest disciples, and Paul endorsed several women, such as Phoebe and Prisca, as Christian "co-workers," how did the later church eventually come to reject the leadership of all women—no matter how intellectually gifted, well versed in Scripture, or prominent in charitable works—in favor of exclusively male domination?

Several scholars suggest that the gradual shrinking of women's roles in the church may have corresponded to a historical change in the kinds of places in which believers assembled. During Paul's career, Christians gathered only in private houses—no separate church buildings then existed. Because only comparatively well-to-do homeowners had dwellings large enough to hold even a few dozen people, the host and/or hostess probably took a leading role in presiding over meetings in his or her home. If a congregation met at the home of a wealthy widow—one no longer under a husband's control—it is likely that she participated actively in worship services, praying, prophesying, and instructing others (1 Cor. 11:5), as Lydia presumably did when believers assembled at her home (Acts 16:13–15, 40).

As congregations grew, attracting larger numbers of qualified men, however, the prominence of women householders who hosted gatherings gradually declined. The shift from meeting in private accommodations, traditionally run by women, to assembling in larger edifices in the public sphere, where men dominated, had an inevitable effect on the composition of church leadership. The change in meeting place from the domestic to the public arena was reinforced by two other concurrent trends: By the second and third centuries CE, the Christian community was no longer living in the fervent apocalyptic hope that had characterized its beginnings. As expectations that God would soon bring history to an end diminished, Jesus' kingdom ethic—in which "many who are first will be last and the last first" (Mark 10:31)—also had less impact. Early believers, eagerly awaiting the Parousia, could form a subculture in which the kingdom values prevailed, incorporating the least and "last" of society's members, including women, slaves, and other socially marginalized people, into full community participation (Gal. 3:28). But after belief in an imminent divine intervention waned and the church accepted an indefinitely delayed Parousia, the church increasingly adapted itself to the customs and assumptions of the larger Greco-Roman world.

The adaptation seems to have included almost wholesale acceptance of Roman society's view of male–female relationships, a patriarchal view that the author of 1 Timothy seems uncritically to endorse.

In the Roman social structure, men achieved status—and positions of public honor—by exercising power over other men, whether economic, political, social, or military. While men universally controlled all public activities and institutions, women, regarded as physically weaker and less capable, were confined to the domestic realm. Given Roman society's universal approval of masculine dominance, if a free man had joined a Christian congregation supervised by a woman, it seems likely that he would have been publicly shamed, forfeiting his claim to honor. In light of Roman mores, it is not surprising that the church, desiring as many converts as possible, chose to model its leadership structure in a way that Roman males would find acceptable. As many feminist scholars have observed, however, Western society has experienced such radical changes since the Enlightenment that the Christian community is now free to construct more inclusive models of leadership, creating an environment of humane mutuality that does not depend on the social and gender assumptions of antiquity.

The Supremacy of Love

In writing the Corinthian church about the "spiritual gifts" bestowed upon Christians, both men and women, Paul ranks the practice of **love** (Greek, *agapē*) as chief among them (1 Cor. 13:1–14:1).

As scholars have recently observed, however, we should not assume that Paul's use of *agapē* (which occurs 116 times as a noun and 143 times as a verb in the New Testament) necessarily corresponds to our twenty-first-century ideas about love. Shaped by contemporary psychology, we tend to regard love as a subjective emotion, a feeling of warm affection for someone. By contrast, Paul describes *agapē* not as an emotional state but as a loyal commitment to others' welfare, which is expressed in *action* that benefits others. For Paul, *agapē* is probably equivalent to the Hebrew Bible's use of *hesed,* a term commonly translated as "loving kindness" or "steadfast love." *Hesed* is expressed in terms of unwavering loyalty to God and to fellow members of the covenant community, a concept that Jesus emphasizes when he cites the Bible's two most important commandments: love of God (Deut. 6:4–5) and love of neighbor (Lev. 19:18). In this declaration, Jesus implicitly invokes biblical love as the basis of the divine–human relationship (Mark 12:28–34). On the divine level, God expresses covenant loyalty through faithfulness to his promises; in the human sphere, love and loyalty are inseparable from active service. As Paul informs the Galatians: "The only thing that counts is faith active in love," faith that reveals itself through compassionate deeds (Gal. 5:6).

In judging *agapē* as the supreme spiritual gift, Paul underscores the fact that love shows itself primarily through right behavior, the kinds of actions that help others and please God. In the world of human interactions, love can also mean avoiding hurtful behaviors: "love is never selfish, not quick to take offense"; above all, it "keeps no score of wrongs" (1 Cor. 13:4–6). Like God, its source, love is eternal: It has "no limit" and "will never come to an end" (13:7–8). The single divinely acceptable motivator of human conduct, its absence robs all other virtues of ethical meaning: Even the "**faith** strong enough to move mountains" and the knowledge of "every hidden truth" are love's inferiors. "If I have no love," Paul declares, "I am nothing" (1 Cor. 13:2–3). Without *agapē,* all Paul's labors are in vain.

Paul does not echo Jesus' radical directive to "love your enemies" (Matt. 5:44), but generally concentrates on cultivating love within the Christian fold: "let us work for the good of all, especially members of the household of the faith" (Gal. 6:10). In this near-exclusive emphasis on the Christian fellowship, Paul anticipates the Johannine tradition, where the identifying quality of Jesus' followers is their expression of love for one another, without a comparable statement of concern for persons outside their group (John 13:34–35). Nonetheless, in formulating the New Testament's most compelling articulation of human love in action, Paul bequeathed a legacy to the Christian church—and the world—that retains a potential to transform human lives.

Summary

In the New Testament canon, Paul's letters are listed roughly according to their length. Letters to churches, such as Romans, appear first, and those to individuals, such as Philemon, appear last. In this text, we discuss the letters in the general order of their composition, beginning with 1 Thessalonians and concluding with later works like Philippians and Philemon.

A sensitivity to Paul's eschatological hope and his mystical experience of Christ may make it easier for readers to appreciate Paul's ideas. Despite the difficulty of understanding some passages (2 Pet. 3:15–16), the rewards of entering the brilliant world of Pauline thought are well worth the effort.

Questions for Review

1. Summarize Paul's biography, from his career as a zealous Pharisee to his work as a missionary among Gentile populations in Macedonia and Greece. In what respects does the biographical information contained in Acts differ from that found in Paul's letters?
2. How did Paul's experience of a revelation (*apokalypsis*) of the risen Jesus change his life and affect his religious outlook?

Questions for Discussion and Reflection

1. Discuss some of the topics and themes that dominate Paul's letters, including his apocalyptic outlook and his views on faith, righteousness, justification, and the saving power of Christ.

2. In the twenty-first-century church, Paul's attitude toward women arouses considerable debate. Briefly outline the historic roles women played in early Christianity, including the Gospel narratives about Jesus' women disciples and Paul's recognition of Phoebe, Prisca, and other "co-workers." How did meeting in house churches facilitate women's leadership positions and how did the church eventually adopt typically Greco-Roman restrictions on women's participation in church affairs? Do the social assumptions of antiquity necessarily determine women's position today?

Terms and Concepts to Remember

Adam	faith
Ananias	love (*agapē*)
dualism	Titus
Enoch	Torah

Recommended Reading

Crook, Zeba A. *Reconceptualizing Conversion: Patronage, Loyalty, and Conversion in the Religions of the Ancient Mediterranean.* New York: Walter de Gruyter, 2004. A detailed analysis of Paul's use of the Roman patron–client system to express his relationship to God and Christ.

Dunn, James P. G. *The Theology of Paul the Apostle.* Grand Rapids, Mich.: Eerdmans, 1998. An authoritative discussion of Paul's major ideas and beliefs about God's actions in Christ.

Engberg-Pedersen, Troels. *Cosmology and Self in the Apostle Paul: The Material Spirit.* New York: Oxford University Press, 2010.

————. *Paul and the Stoics.* Louisville, Ky.: Westminster John Knox, 2000. Both works minutely dissect the letters to infer Paul's worldview, the latter to reveal the extent of Stoic influence on Paul's thought and rhetoric.

Fitzmyer, Joseph. *Paul and His Theology,* 2nd ed. Englewood Cliffs, N.J.: Prentice-Hall, 1989. A brief but careful introduction to Paul's central teachings.

Hawthorne, Gerald F.; Martin, Ralph P.; and Reid, D. G., eds. *Dictionary of Paul and His Letters.* Downers Grove, Ill.: InterVarsity Press, 1993. Argues for authenticity of all letters traditionally ascribed to Paul, including the pastorals.

Holmberg, B. *Paul and Power.* Philadelphia: Fortress Press, 1980. An incisive study of the social forces at work in the Pauline communities and of Paul's difficult relationships with other apostolic leaders.

Keener, C. S. "Man and Woman." In G. F. Hawthorne and R. P. Martin, eds., *Dictionary of Paul and His Letters.* Downers Grove, Ill.: InterVarsity Press, 1993, pp. 583–592. Argues that the Pauline corpus does not advocate women's exclusion from church offices.

Levine, Amy-Jill, ed. *A Feminist Companion to Paul.* Cleveland: Pilgrim, 2004. Ten scholarly essays analyzing Paul's writings on women in their original social/cultural context.

Malina, Bruce J., and Pilch, John J. *Social Science Commentary on the Letters of Paul.* Minneapolis: Fortress Press, 2006. Offers important insights into Paul's thinking by interpreting his letters in light of Greco-Roman ideas and social practices.

Polaski, Sandra Heck. *A Feminist Introduction to Paul.* St. Louis: Chalice Press, 2005. Perceptively surveys diverse interpretations of Paul, offering feminist insights into his thought.

Richards, E. Randolph. *Paul and First-Century Letter Writing: Secretaries, Composition, and Collection.* Downers Grove, Ill.: InterVarsity Press, 2004. Places Paul's letters in the sociohistorical context of Hellenistic correspondence.

Roetzel, Calvin J. "Paul, the Apostle." In K. D. Sakenfeld, ed., *The New Interpreter's Bible,* Vol. 4, pp. 404–421. Nashville: Abingdon Press, 2009. Offers a tentative chronology of Paul's ministry and a survey of his developing theology in the letters.

Sanders, E. P. *Paul, the Law, and the Jewish People.* Philadelphia: Fortress Press, 1983. An excellent exploration of Paul's Jewish heritage.

————. *Paul: A Very Short Introduction.* New York: Oxford University Press, 1991. A remarkably concise and incisive survey of Paul's thought and theology.

Segal, Alan F. *Paul the Convert: The Apostolate and Apostasy of Saul the Pharisee.* New Haven, Conn., and London: Yale University Press, 1990. Examines Paul's views of the Christ event in the light of his Jewish heritage.

Soards, Marion L. *The Apostle Paul: An Introduction to His Writings and Teaching.* Mahwah, N.J.: Paulist Press, 1987. A clearly written introduction to Paul's thought, emphasizing his eschatology.

Theissen, Gerd. *The Social Setting of Pauline Christianity.* Philadelphia: Fortress Press, 1982. A study of the social dynamics operating in the church at Corinth; one of the most illuminating studies of primitive Christianity.

Witherup, Ronald D. *101 Questions and Answers of Paul.* New York: Paulist Press, 2003. A good introduction to Paul's life and theological preoccupations.

Zetterholm, Magnus. "Paul, Letters of." In M. D. Coogan, ed., *The Oxford Encyclopedia of the Books of the Bible,* Vol. 2, pp. 127–138. New York: Oxford University Press, 2011. Surveys first Paul's authentic letters and then the disputed and pseudonymous works, emphasizing his evolving theology.

Unity, Freedom, and Christ's Return
Paul's Letters to Thessalonica and Corinth

*The time we live in will not last long. . . . For the whole frame
of this world is passing away.* 1 Corinthians 7:29, 31

Key Topics/Themes The dominant theme of Paul's letters to Thessalonica and Corinth is that the *eschaton* is near: Paul expects to witness Jesus' return and the resurrection of the dead in his lifetime (1 Thess. 4:13–18). However, believers must not waste time speculating about the projected date of the Parousia (1 Thess. 5:1–3).

Paul's letters to Corinth are aimed at healing serious divisions in the newly founded church there. Paul urges members to give up their destructive competitiveness and work toward unity of belief and purpose. Their cooperation is essential because the remaining time is so short. His most important topics include (1) differences between human and divinely revealed wisdom (1:10–3:23), (2) Christian ethics and responsibilities (5:1–11:1), (3) behavior at the communion meal (11:17–34), valuing gifts of the Spirit (chs. 12–14), and (4) the resurrection of the dead (ch. 15).

A composite work composed of several letters or letter fragments, 2 Corinthians shows Paul defending his apostolic authority (2 Cor. 10–13); chapters 1–9, apparently written after chapters 10–13, describe his reconciliation with the church at Corinth.

Paul's early letters are dominated by his **eschatology.** Convinced that the Messiah's death and resurrection have inaugurated End time, Paul strives to achieve several related goals. Traveling from city to city, he establishes small cells of believers whom he calls to a "new life in Christ." He argues that Jesus' crucifixion has brought freedom from both Torah observance and the power of sin, and he emphasizes the necessity of leading an ethically pure life while awaiting Christ's return. In his letters to the young Greek churches at Thessalonica and Corinth, Paul underscores the nearness of the Parousia—the

Second Coming—an event that he believes to be imminent. Much of Paul's advice to these congregations is based on his desire that they achieve unity and purity before Christ reappears.

While he is attempting to keep believers faithful to the high ideals of Christian practice, Paul also finds himself battling opponents who question the correctness of his teaching and/or his apostolic authority. According to Luke, an apostle was one whom Jesus had personally called to follow him and who had witnessed the Resurrection (Acts 1:21–22). Not only had Paul not known the earthly Jesus; he had cruelly persecuted the disciples. Paul's sole claim to apostolic status was his private revelation of the risen Lord, a claim others repeatedly challenged. To achieve the goal of guiding his flock through End time, Paul must ensure that his apostolic credentials are fully recognized (1 Cor. 15:9–10; 2 Cor. 11:1–13:10).

To appreciate the urgency of Paul's first letters, we must approach them from the writer's historical perspective: The Messiah's coming spelled an end to the old world. The New Age—entailing the Final Judgment on all nations, a universal resurrection of the dead, and the ultimate fulfillment of God's purpose—was then in the process of materializing. Paul writes as a parent anxious that those in his care survive the apocalyptic ordeal just ahead and attain the saints' reward of eternal life.

First Letter to the Thessalonians

The oldest surviving Christian document, 1 Thessalonians preserves our earliest glimpse of how the new religion was established in Gentile territory. Capital of the Roman province of Macedonia, Thessalonica (now called Thessaloniki) (see Figure 14.1) was a bustling port city located on the Via Egnatia, the major highway linking Rome with the East. According to the Book of Acts, Paul spent only three weeks there, preaching mainly in the local synagogue to generally unreceptive Jews, who soon drove him out of town (17:1–18:5).

Paul's letter to the newly founded Thessalonian congregation, however, paints a different picture, making no reference to a synagogue ministry and implying that his converts were largely Gentile (1 Thess. 1:9). Probably written in Corinth about 50 CE, a scant twenty years after the Crucifixion, 1 Thessalonians is remarkable in showing how quickly essential Christian ideas had developed and how thoroughly apocalyptic Paul's message was. Referring to the Parousia in no fewer than six different passages, at least once in each of the letter's five brief chapters,

First Thessalonians

Author: Paul, missionary Apostle to the Gentiles.

Date: About 50 CE.

Place of composition: Probably Corinth.

Audience: Mostly Gentile members of a newly founded congregation in Thessalonica, Greece.

Paul makes the imminence of Jesus' return his central message (1:10; 2:19; 3:13; 4:13–18; 5:1–11).

The Thessalonians, he says, have become a shining example to other Greek churches because they have

> turned from idols to be servants of the true and living God, . . . to wait expectantly for his Son from heaven, whom he raised from the dead, Jesus our deliverer from the retribution to come.
>
> (1 Thess. 1:10)

This passage may, in fact, epitomize the principal themes of Paul's oral gospel, the *kerygma* he preached in urban marketplaces, shops, and private homes. In general content, it resembles the more elaborate proclamation that Luke placed on Paul's lips when he spoke to the Athenians (Acts 17: 22–31). Urging the Greeks to forsake lifeless idols for the "living God" of Judaism, Paul presents Jesus' resurrection from the dead as introducing history's climactic moment: his impending descent from heaven to rescue his followers from catastrophic divine judgment.

For Paul, the implications of the coming apocalypse are clear: The Thessalonians must reform their typically lenient Gentile attitudes toward sexual activity. They have already made progress in living "to please God," but they can do better, abstaining from "fornication," becoming "holy," living "quietly," and showing love to all (4:1–12).

Although the Thessalonians do not exhibit the kind of opposition Paul describes in letters to the Corinthians and Galatians, he devotes considerable space to self-justification, emphasizing how nurturing, altruistic, and hardworking he was when in their company (2:1–12). In particular, he emphasizes the fact that he remained financially independent of the people

FIGURE 14.1 Paul's churches. Paul established largely Gentile churches in the northeastern Mediterranean region at Philippi, Thessalonica, Beroea, and Corinth. Paul's teaching was also influential in the Asia Minor city of Ephesus, where he lived for at least two years. The sites of some other Christian centers are also given.

he taught, working "night and day" to be self-supporting (2:9). Some commentators have suggested that Paul set up a leather goods shop, where he preached to customers and passersby. The passage in which he suddenly departs from praising his healthy relationship with the Thessalonians to castigate his fellow Jews, referring to the "retribution" inflicted on them, may have been inserted by a later copyist after Rome's destruction of Jerusalem in 70 CE (2:13–16).

Chapter 2 concludes with an insight into the source of Paul's concern for the Thessalonians' good behavior: Their ethical purity will provide validation for him when "we stand before our Lord Jesus at his coming." If they maintain their righteous conduct until the Parousia, their loyalty to his teaching will be a "crown of pride" for him, showing that Paul has properly discharged his obligation to God, his patron and divine benefactor (2:19–20). Declaring that their faithfulness is no

less than "the breath of life" to him, Paul offers a fervent prayer that the Thessalonians remain "holy and faultless," acceptable to "our God and Father" at Jesus' return (3:7–13).

The Parousia and the Resurrection

Having demonstrated the importance—to both the congregation collectively and the apostle individually—of their leading ethically unblemished lives until the Parousia, Paul then previews events that will take place when Jesus reappears in glory. Apparently, some Thessalonians believed that Jesus' return would occur so swiftly that all persons converted to Christianity would live to see the Second Coming. That belief was shaken when some believers died before Jesus had reappeared. What would become of them? Had the dead missed their opportunity to join Christ in ruling over the world?

Paul explains that the recently dead are not lost but will share in the glory of Christ's return. To denote the exalted Jesus' arrival from heaven, Paul uses the term *Parousia,* a Greek word meaning "presence" or "coming" (the same word that the authors of the Synoptic Gospels later adopt to designate Jesus' return to earth [see Chapters 7–9]). In employing this word, Paul refers to an impressive public ceremony with which his audience in Thessalonica would have been familiar—the actions accompanying the formal entrance of a Roman emperor or other high official into some provincial city. As the visiting dignitary approached the city gates, a trumpet blast announced his appearance, at which sound the inhabitants were expected to drop everything they were doing and rush outside the city walls to greet the important visitor. Gathering along the main roadway, the crowds then followed the official as he moved into the city. Paul's vision of Jesus' imminent Parousia, his coming in supernatural glory, not only draws on this common Roman political spectacle but also shows that he fully expects to be alive when Jesus reappears:

> [W]e who are left alive until the Lord comes shall not forestall those who have died; because at the word of command, at the sound of the archangel's voice and God's trumpet call, the Lord himself will descend from heaven; first the Christian dead will rise, then we who are left alive shall join them, caught up in clouds to meet the Lord in the air.
>
> (1 Thess. 4:15–17)

Jesus' followers, in joyous acclamation, will then accompany their Master—humanity's true king—as he revisits the earth to begin his active rule as Israel's Messiah. After his Parousia, Jesus at last will reign, not only over a redeemed Israel but over the entire cosmos. In thus likening Jesus' Parousia to an emperor's display of power, Paul implies that Christ is clearly superior to an earthly sovereign (see Malina and Pilch in "Recommended Reading").

Although he depicts Jesus' triumphant return by analogy to a Roman imperial custom,

Paul's allusion to a "trumpet" (Greek, *salpinx*) sounding probably also refers to trumpets used in Jewish worship, such as the playing of a "ram's horn" (Hebrew, *shophar*) announcing the Day of Atonement (Lev. 25:9; cf. Num. 10:2, 10). (In his description of the Parousia, Matthew mentions a similar eschatological trumpet call [Matt. 24:31].) Paul's immediate purpose, however, is to assure his Thessalonian friends that in both life and death the believer remains with Jesus (4:13–18). (Compare 1 Thessalonians with Paul's more elaborate discussion of the resurrection in 1 Corinthians 15, a passage in which he reaffirms his hope to be alive at Jesus' Parousia.)

On Not Calculating "Dates and Times"

Although he eagerly expects Jesus' reappearance "soon," Paul has no patience with those who try to predict the exact date of the Parousia. He discourages speculation and notes that calculating "dates and times" is futile because the world's final day will come as quietly as a thief at midnight. Emphasizing the unexpectedness of the Parousia, Paul declares that it will occur while men proclaim "peace and security" (a common political theme in Roman times, as well as today). Disaster will strike the nations suddenly, as labor pains strike a woman without warning (5:1–3).

In the Hebrew Bible, the "Day of the Lord" was the time of Yahweh's intervention into human history, his visitation of earth to judge all nations and to impose his universal rule (Amos 5:18; Joel 2:14–15). In Paul's apocalyptic vision, Jesus is the divinely appointed agent of *eschaton.* As the eschatological Judge, Jesus serves a double function: He brings punishment to the disobedient ("the terrors of judgment") but vindication and deliverance to the faithful. Paul's cosmic Jesus is paradoxical: He dies to save believers from the negative judgment that his return imposes on unregenerate humanity. Returning to his main theme, Paul concludes that "we, awake [living] or asleep [dead]" live in permanent association with Christ (5:4–11).

The Role of the Spirit

With anticipation of Jesus' speedy return a living reality, Paul reminds the Thessalonians that the Holy Spirit's visible activity among them is also evidence of the world's impending transformation. As noted in Acts, the Spirit motivating believers to prophesy, heal, or speak in tongues was taken as evidence of God's active presence. Thus, Paul tells his readers not to "stifle inspiration" or otherwise discourage believers from prophesying. Christian prophets, inspired by the Spirit, play a major role in Pauline churches, but Paul is aware that enthusiastic visionaries can cause trouble. Believers are to distinguish between "good" and "bad" inspirations, avoiding the latter, but they are not to inhibit charismatic behavior. Besides providing evidence that the End is near, the Spirit's presence also validates the Christian message (Joel 2:28–32; Acts 2:1–21; 1 Cor. 2:9–16; 12–14).

(A disputed letter, 2 Thessalonians is discussed in Chapter 17.)

First Corinthians

Author: Paul.

Date: Early 50s CE.

Place of composition: Ephesus.

Audience: Members of the newly established church at Corinth, Greece.

First Letter to the Corinthians

According to Acts (17:1–18:17), after establishing churches at Philippi, Thessalonica, and Beroea (all in northern Greece), Paul briefly visited Athens and then journeyed to Corinth, where he remained for a year and a half (c. 50–52 CE). Accompanied by Prisca (Priscilla) and Aquila, Jewish Christians exiled from Rome, he subsequently sailed to Ephesus, from which city he addressed several letters to the Corinthians. The first letter has been lost (1 Cor. 5:9), but the books presently numbered 1 and 2 Corinthians embody the most voluminous correspondence with any single church group in the New Testament. Whereas 1 Corinthians is a single document, scholars believe that 2 Corinthians is a patchwork of several Pauline letters or parts of letters written at different times that an editor later combined.

Paul's correspondence with the Corinthian church was not a one-way affair, for the Corinthians also wrote to the apostle (1 Cor. 7:1). Delegations from Corinth also kept Paul in touch with the group (1:11; 16:15–18; 2 Cor. 7:5–7, 13). Preserving a comprehensive picture of the diversity of ideas and behavior of a youthful Jewish and Gentile church, the Corinthian letters give us an unrivaled sociological study of early Christianity.

The City and Its People

The emperor Augustus made Corinth, the richest and most populous city in Greece, the Greek capital in 27 BCE (see Figure 14.2). In Paul's day, Corinth was famous for its prosperity, trade, and materialism. As a busy seaport, it was also notorious for its legions of prostitutes, who entertained sailors from every part of the Greco-Roman world. With Aphrodite—supreme goddess of love and fertility—as its patron deity, Corinth enjoyed a reputation for luxury and licentiousness remarkable even in pagan society. Given this libertine environment, it is not surprising that Paul devotes more space to setting forth principles of sexual ethics to the Corinthians than he does in letters to any other churches (1 Cor. 5:1–13; 7:1–40).

Recent sociological studies of early Christianity indicate that the Corinthian group may have been typical of Gentile churches in many parts of the Roman Empire. In the past, many historians thought that the first Christians largely belonged to the lower socioeconomic ranks of Greco-Roman society. Recent analyses of Paul's letters to Rome and Corinth, however, suggest that early Christians came from many different social classes and represented a veritable cross section of the Hellenistic world.

Paul's statement that "few" members of the Corinthian congregation were highborn, wealthy, or politically influential (1 Cor. 1:26–28) implies

FIGURE 14.2 View of Corinth. Once a prosperous commercial center, Corinth was dominated by the Acrocorinth, the steep hill in the background. After the Romans destroyed the original Greek city, it was refounded in 44 BCE as a Roman colony. As Paul's letters to the Corinthians demonstrate, however, it soon became a Greek-speaking urban center, of which Aphrodite, goddess of love, was the divine patron.

that some were. This inference is borne out by the fact that some Corinthian believers apparently held important positions in the city (see Figure 14.3). Acts identifies the Crispus whom Paul baptized (1 Cor. 1:14) as the leader of a local synagogue, a function ordinarily given to persons rich enough to maintain the building. Erastus, who also seems to have belonged to the Corinthian church, was the civic treasurer (Rom. 16:23).

A diverse assortment of Jews and Gentiles, slaves and landowners, rich and poor, educated and unlettered, the Corinthian group was apparently divided by class distinctions and educational differences, as well as by varieties of religious belief. Even in observing the communion ritual, members' consciousness of differences in wealth and social status threatened to splinter the membership (1 Cor. 11:17–34).

From Paul's responses to their attitudes and conduct, readers learn that the Corinthians individually promoted a wide range of ideas. Some

advocated a spiritual marriage in which sexual union played no part; others visited prostitutes. Some defrauded their fellow believers, causing victims to seek restitution in the public courts. Some, convinced of their Christian "freedom," not exist, dined at banquets in Greco-Roman temples and attended religious ceremonies there. Still others claimed a superior understanding of spiritual matters, viewed themselves as already living in the kingdom, denied the necessity of a bodily resurrection, or questioned Paul's right to dictate their behavior.

As the Corinthian correspondence shows, Paul faced the almost impossible challenge of bringing this divisive and quarrelsome group into a working harmony of belief and purpose. In reading Paul's letters to Corinth, remember that he is struggling to communicate his vision of union with Christ to an infant church that has apparently only begun to grasp the basic principles of Christian life.

FIGURE 14.3 Painting of a Roman couple. In this portrait uncovered at Pompeii (buried by an eruption of Mount Vesuvius in 79 CE), Terentius Neo and his wife proudly display the pen and wax tablets that advertise their literary skills. Similar young Roman couples of the professional classes undoubtedly were among the members of Paul's newly founded churches in Corinth and other Greco-Roman cities.

Topics of Concern

Paul's first extant letter to the group is distinguished by some of his most memorable writing. Two passages in particular, chapter 13 (on love) and chapter 15 (on resurrection), are highlights of Pauline thought and feeling. His praise of love (ch. 13) uses the Greek term *agapē,* "selfless love," as opposed to *eros,* the word denoting the sexual passion associated with Aphrodite. This may be an appropriate hint to those Corinthians sexually involved with persons other than their legal mates. Paul's mystic vision of attaining immortality (ch. 15) is the most extensive commentary on life after death in the New Testament. It also contains the earliest account of Jesus' post resurrection appearances.

Organization The first letter to the Corinthians divides into two main sections. In the first six chapters, Paul directly addresses his principal

objective—helping the church, split by rivalries and factions, attain the unity befitting a Christian congregation. Here, Paul shows the futility of false wisdom and human competitiveness and of attempts to demonstrate Christian freedom by violating the sexual conventions honored even by unbelievers. In the second half (chs. 7–15), he answers specific questions that the Corinthians addressed to him. These issues include marriage and divorce, the consumption of meat previously sacrificed to Greco-Roman gods, proper conduct during the **Lord's Supper,** and eschatology—the Final Judgment and resurrection of the dead.

Paul's Eschatological Urgency As in his letters to the Thessalonians, Paul structures his advice to the Corinthian church according to his eschatological convictions. The Parousia is imminent: The Corinthians "wait expectantly for our Lord Jesus to reveal himself," for he will keep them "firm to the end . . . on the Day of our Lord Jesus" (1:7–8). Like the Thessalonians, the recipients of Paul's Corinthian letters expect to experience the **Day of Judgment** soon, a belief that affects their entire way of life. Paul advises single people to remain unmarried; neither slaves nor free citizens are to change their status because "the time we live in will not last long." All emotions—from joy to grief—are only temporary, as are ordinary human pursuits. "Buyers must not count on keeping what they buy," because "the whole frame of this world is passing away" (7:29–31). Paul speaks here not of the philosopher's conventional wisdom—that the wise person shuns life's petty goals to pursue eternal truths—but of the *eschaton,* the End of the familiar world.

In anticipating the coming resurrection, Paul echoes his words in 1 Thessalonians 4: When Judgment's trumpet sounds, "we [Christians then living] shall not all die, but we shall all be changed in a flash, in the twinkling of an eye" (15:51–55). Such passages reveal that Paul, along with his contemporaries, expects to be alive when Christ returns to raise the dead.

The Necessity of Christian Unity

Paul's first objective is to halt the rivalries that divide the Corinthians. Without imposing a dogmatic conformity, he asks his readers to work together cooperatively for their mutual benefit (1:8–10). Like all early Christian congregations, that at Corinth met in a private house large enough to accommodate the entire group. Although membership was limited to perhaps 50–100 persons, the group was broken into several cliques. Some members placed undue importance on the particular leader who had converted or baptized them and competed with one another over the prestige of their respective mentors.

Avoiding Competitiveness and Cultivating Divine Wisdom A more serious cause of division may have been the members' unequal social and educational backgrounds. As in any group, modern or ancient, some individuals believed they were demonstrably superior to their neighbors. Examining chapter 1 carefully, readers will see that Paul's attack on false "wisdom" is really an attempt to discourage human competitiveness. In Paul's view, all believers are fundamentally equal: "For through faith you are all [children] of God in union with Christ Jesus. . . . There is no such thing as Jew and Greek, slave and freeman, male and female; for you are all one person in Christ Jesus" (Gal. 3:26, 28). This assumption underlies Paul's method of presenting the *kerygma*—the proclamation about Jesus. When he reminds the Corinthians that he taught them the message as simply as possible, he does so to show that the new faith is essentially incompatible with individual pride or competitiveness.

Paul's concurrent theme is that human "weakness" is the unexpected medium through which God reveals his strength. In contrast to the Roman soldiers who crucified him, Christ was weak. Paul is also weak in refusing to use the rhetorical embellishments with which Hellenistic teachers were expected to present their ideas. Thus, with almost brutal directness, he proclaims "Christ nailed to the cross" (1 Cor. 1:23; 2:1).

(Paul's relative lack of success debating philosophers in Athens just before coming to Corinth [Acts 17] may have influenced his decision to preach henceforth without any intellectual pretensions.)

Paul's weak and "foolish" proclamation of a crucified Messiah offends almost everyone. It is a major obstacle to Jews, who look for a victorious conqueror, not an executed criminal, and an absurdity to the Greeks, who seek rational explanations of the universe. To the believer, however, the paradox of a crucified Messiah represents God's omnipotent wisdom (1:22–24).

Paul's argument (1:17–2:5) is sometimes misused to justify an anti-intellectual approach to religion, in which reason and faith are treated as if they were mutually exclusive. The apostle's attack on "worldly wisdom" is not directed against human reason, however. It is aimed instead at individual Corinthians who boasted of possessing special insights that gave them a "deeper" understanding than that granted their fellow Christians. Such elitism led some persons to cultivate a false sense of superiority that devalued less educated believers, fragmenting the congregation into groups of the "wise" and the "foolish."

Paul seeks to place all believers on an equal footing and allow them no cause for intellectual competition. He reminds the Corinthians that human reason by itself is not sufficient to know God, but that God revealed his saving purpose through Christ as a free gift (1:21). No one merits or earns the Christian revelation, which comes through God's unforeseen grace, not through human effort. Because all are equally recipients of the divine benefits, no believer has the right to boast (1:21–31).

Paul does, however, teach a previously hidden wisdom to persons mature enough to appreciate it. This wisdom is God's revelation through the Spirit (Greek, *pneuma*) that now dwells in the Christian community. The hitherto unknown "mind" of God—the ultimate reality that philosophers make the object of their search—is unveiled through Christ (2:6–16). The divine mystery, although inaccessible to rational inquiry, is finally made clear in the weakness and obedient suffering of Christ, the means by which God reconciles humanity to himself.

The Limits of Christian Freedom Paul's doctrine of freedom from Torah restraints is easily abused when mistakenly interpreted as an excuse to ignore all ethical principles. As a result of some Corinthians' misuse of Christian freedom, Paul finds it necessary to impose limits on believers' individual liberty. Exercising his apostolic authority, Paul orders the Corinthians to excommunicate a Christian living openly with his stepmother. Apparently, the Corinthian church was proud of the man's bold use of freedom to live as he liked, though his incest scandalized even Greek society. Directing the congregation to evict the sinner from their midst, Paul establishes a policy that later becomes a powerful means of church control over individual members. In excommunication, the offender is denied all fellowship in the believing community and is left bereft of God as well. Although consigned "to Satan" (the devil-ruled world outside the church), the outcast remains a Christian destined for ultimate salvation on the Lord's Day (5:1–13).

Lawsuits Among Christians Claiming freedom "to do anything," some Corinthians bring lawsuits against fellow Christians in civil courts, allowing the unbelieving public to witness the internal divisions and ill will existing in the church. Paul orders that such disputes be settled within the Christian community. He also orders men who frequent prostitutes to end this practice. Answering the Corinthians' claim that physical appetites can be satisfied without damaging faith, Paul argues that Christians' bodies are temples of the Holy Spirit (God's *pneuma*) and must not be defiled by intercourse with prostitutes (6:1–20).

Answering Questions from the Congregation

Marriage, Divorce, and Celibacy In chapters 7–15, Paul responds to a letter from the Corinthians, answering their questions on several crucial topics. The first item concerns human sexuality (7:1–40), a subject in which the writer takes a distant but practical interest. Paul clearly prefers a single life without any kind of sexual involvement. He begins this section by declaring that "it is a good thing for a man to have nothing to do with women," and he closes by observing that women whose husbands have died are "better off" if they do not remarry. In both statements, Paul may be quoting some Corinthians who boasted of their superior self-control. Although he does not find marriage personally attractive, he is far from forbidding others to marry (7:2–9). He also emphasizes the mutual obligations of marriage, stating that husbands and wives are equally entitled to each other's sexual love. However, he pragmatically describes marriage as an inevitably painful experience that can interfere with a believer's religious commitment (7:28, 32–34).

Paul's general principle is that everyone should remain in whatever state—single or married, slave or free—he or she was in when first converted. Although aware of Jesus' command forbidding divorce, he concedes that a legal separation is acceptable when a non-Christian wishes to leave his or her Christian mate (7:10–24).

It is important to remember that Paul's advice, particularly on celibacy, is presented in the context of an imminent Parousia. The unmarried remain free "to wait upon the Lord without distraction." Freedom from sexual ties that bind one to the world is eminently practical because "the time we live in will not last long" (7:25–35). Paul regards singleness not as the prerequisite to a higher spiritual state but as a practical response to the eschatological crisis.

A Problem of Conscience In the next long section (8:1–11:1), Paul discusses a problem that ceased to be an issue over 1,600 years ago—eating meat that had previously been sacrificed in Greco-Roman temples. (The meat was then commonly sold in meat markets or cooked and served in public dining halls, which some of the Corinthian Christians frequented.) Although the social conditions that created the issue have long since disappeared, the principle that Paul articulates in this matter remains relevant to many believers.

Paul argues that, although Christians are completely free to do as they wish when their consciences are clear, they should remember that their behavior can be misinterpreted by other believers who do not think as they do. Some believers may interpret actions such as eating meat that had been given to "idols" as violating standards of religious purity. Paul rules in favor of the "weak" who have trouble distinguishing between abstract convictions and observable practices. Respecting a fellow Christian's sensitive conscience, the mature believer will forfeit his or her right to eat sacrificed meat—or, presumably, to engage in any other action that troubles the "weak" (8:1–13; 10:23–11:1).

Paul interrupts his argument to insert a vigorous defense of his apostolic authority (9:1–27) and give examples of ways in which he has sacrificed his personal freedoms to benefit others. The rights Paul has voluntarily given up suggest some significant differences between his style of life and that practiced by leaders of the Jerusalem church. Unlike Peter, Jesus' brothers, and the other apostles, he forfeits the privilege of taking a wife or accepting money for his missionary services. He even sacrifices his own inclinations and individuality, becoming "everything in turn to men of every sort" to save them. Paul asks the "strong" Corinthians to imitate his selfless example (9:3–23; 10:33–11:1).

Paul's demand to live largely for other people's benefit and to accommodate one's conduct to others' consciences raises important issues. Some commentators observe that, although Paul's argument protects the sensibilities of believers who are less free-thinking, it places the intellectually aware Christian at the mercy of overscrupulous or literal-minded believers. Followed explicitly, the apostle's counsel here seriously compromises his doctrine of Christian freedom.

Regulating Behavior in Church

Chapters 11–14 contain Paul's advice regulating behavior in church. The issues he addresses

include the participation of women, conduct during reenactments of the Last Supper, and the handling of charismatic "gifts," such as the Spirit-given ability to prophesy, heal, or speak in tongues.

The Role of Women in the Church In recent decades, Pauline regulations about women's roles in the church have been attacked as culture-bound and chauvinistic. Because we know so little of very early Christian practices, it is difficult to establish to what degree women originally shared in church leadership (see Chapter 13). Jesus numbered many women among his most loyal disciples, and Paul refers to several women as his "fellow workers" (Phil. 4:3). In the last chapter of Romans, in which Paul lists the missionary Prisca (Priscilla) ahead of her husband, Aquila, the apostle asks the recipients to support **Phoebe,** a presiding officer in the Cenchreae church, in discharging her administrative duties (Rom. 16:1–6).

In Corinthians, however, Paul seems to impose certain restrictions on women's participation in church services. His insistence that women cover their heads with veils (11:3–16) is open to a variety of interpretations. Is it the writer's concession to the existing Jewish and Greco-Roman custom of secluding women, an attempt to avoid offending patriarchal prejudices? If women unveil their physical attractiveness, does this distract male onlookers or even sexually tempt angels, such as those who "lusted" for mortal women before the Flood (Gen. 6:1–4)? Conversely, is the veil a symbol of women's religious authority, to be worn when prophesying before the congregation?

Paul's argument for relegating women to a subordinate position in church strikes many readers as labored and illogical. (Some scholars think that this passage [11:2–16] is the interpolation of a later editor, added to make Corinthians agree with the non-Pauline instruction in 1 Timothy 2:8–15.) Paul grants women an active role, praying and prophesying during worship, but he argues as well that the female is a secondary creation, made from man, who was

CHAPTER 14 UNITY, FREEDOM, AND CHRIST'S RETURN   **345**

created directly by God. The apostle uses the second version of human origins (Gen. 2) to support his view of a human sexual hierarchy, but he could as easily have cited the first creation account, in which male and female are created simultaneously, both in the "image of God" (Gen. 1:27). Given Paul's revelation that Christian equality transcends all distinctions among believers, including those of sex, class, and nationality (Gal. 3:28), many commentators see the writer's choice in a Genesis precedent as decidedly arbitrary.

The Communion Meal (the Lord's Supper, or Eucharist) Christianity's most solemn ritual, the reenactment of Jesus' last meal with his disciples, represents the mystic communion between the risen Lord and his followers. Meeting in private homes to commemorate the event, the Corinthians had turned the service into a riotous drinking party. Instead of a celebration of Christian unity, it had become another source of division. Wealthy participants came early and consumed all the delicacies of the communion meal before the working poor arrived, thus leaving their social inferiors hungry and humiliated (11:17–22).

Paul contrasts this misbehavior with the tradition coming directly from Jesus himself. Recording Jesus' sacramental distribution of bread and wine, he insists that the ceremony is to be decorously repeated in memory of Christ's death until he returns. This allusion to the nearness of Jesus' reappearance reminds the Corinthians of the seriousness with which they must observe the Last Supper ceremony (11:23–34).

Gifts of the Spirit Led by the Holy Spirit, the early Christian community was composed of many persons gifted with supernatural abilities. Some had the gift of prophecy; others were apostles, teachers, healers, miracle workers, or speakers in tongues. In Corinth, these individual gifts, and the rivalries among those possessing them, were yet another cause of division. Reminding them that one indivisible Spirit (*pneuma*) grants all these different abilities, Paul employs a

favorite metaphor in which he compares the church to the human body, with its many different parts. "Christ," Paul explains, "is like a single body with its many limbs and organs, which, many as they are, together make up one body" (12:12). Because they represent the visible form of Christ on earth, the congregational "body" must function harmoniously, showing due respect to each of its many parts. Apparently some Corinthians judged themselves to be analogous to the more "honorable" body parts, such as the head or eye, and despised the lower or more "unseemly parts"—thereby discriminating against humbler church members. Whereas the more educated or spiritually gifted leaders evidently dismissed the poor or "weak" members as unworthy, Paul insists that they are "indispensable." "The eye," he asserts, "cannot say to the hand, 'I do not need you'; nor the head to the feet, 'I do not need you.'" Everyone belonging to the people of God, whatever their position or function, must be treated honorably because all are part of Christ's "body." In fact, God gives "special honor to the humbler parts," the laboring hands and feet, elevating them to equality with the "strong" and "wise" (12:4–31).

The Hymn to Love (*Agapē*) Paul's famous discourse on **love (*agapē*)** is intimately linked to his call for congregational unity and mutual respect. In every letter, Paul is more concerned about behavior—how people live the gospel—than he is about subjective feeling. As noted in Paul's concept of love (*agapē*) in Chapter 13, biblical love does not refer primarily to an emotional state, but to active care and concern for others. Defining *agapē* as "the best way of all," Paul emphasizes its expression through action: Love is patient, kind, forgiving; it keeps no record of offenses. Its capacity for loyal devotion is infinite: "there is no limit to its faith, its hope, and its endurance." Love once given is never withdrawn. Whereas other spiritual gifts are only partial reflections of the divine reality and will be rendered obsolete in the perfect world to come, the supreme trio of Christian virtues—faith, hope, and love—endures forever (1 Cor. 13:1–13).

Speaking in Tongues (*Glossolalia*) Although he gives love top priority, Paul also acknowledges the value of other spiritual gifts, especially prophecy, which involves rational communication. "Ecstatic utterance"—speaking in tongues, or *glossolalia*—may be emotionally satisfying to the speaker, but it does not "build up" the congregation as do teaching and prophecy. Although he does not prohibit ecstatic utterance (Paul states that he is better at it than any Corinthian), the apostle ranks it as the least useful spiritual gift (14:1–40).

The Eschatological Hope: Bodily Resurrection of the Dead

Paul's last major topic—his eschatological vision of the resurrection (15:1–57)—is theologically the most important. Apparently, some Corinthians challenged Paul's teaching about the afterlife. One educated group may have questioned the necessity of a future bodily resurrection because, influenced by the popular philosophy of the day, they held negative views of the physical body, making the concept of a future "resurrection body" undesirable. Others may have denied Paul's concept of bodily resurrection because they shared the Greek philosophical view that a future existence is purely spiritual. According to Socrates, Plato, and many Stoic thinkers, death occurs when the immortal soul escapes from the perishable body. The soul does not need a body when it enters the invisible spirit realm. To believers in the soul's inherent immortality, Paul's Hebrew belief in the body's material resurrection was grotesque and irrelevant (cf. Acts 17:32).

The Historical Reality of Jesus' Resurrection To demonstrate that bodily resurrection is a reality, Paul calls on the Corinthians to remember that Jesus rose from the dead. Preserving the earliest tradition of Jesus' post resurrection appearances, Paul notes that the risen Lord appeared to as many as 500 believers at once, as well as to Paul (15:3–8; see Box 14.1). Paul uses his opponents' denial against them and argues that if

there is no resurrection, then Christ was not raised and Christians hope in vain. He trusts, not in the Greek philosophical notion of innate human immortality, but in the Jewish apocalyptic faith in God's ability to raise the faithful dead (Dan. 12:1–3). Without Christ's resurrection, Paul states, there is no afterlife, and of all people Christians are the most pitiable (15:12–19).

Paul now invokes two archetypal figures to illustrate the means by which human death and its opposite, eternal life, entered the world. Citing the Genesis creation account, Paul declares that the "first man," Adam (God's first earthly son), brought death to the human race, but Christ (Adam's "heavenly" counterpart, a new creation) brings life. The coming resurrection (and perhaps salvation as well) is universal: "as in Adam all men die, so in Christ all will be brought to life." The "first fruits" of the resurrection harvest, Christ will return to raise the obedient dead and defeat all enemies, including death itself. Noting that the Corinthians practice baptism of their dead (perhaps posthumously initiating them into the church), Paul argues that this ritual presupposes the resurrection's reality (15:29).

When the Corinthians ask how the dead are raised and "in what kind of body," Paul's answer, particularly his use of the term "spiritual body," merits close analysis. Traditionally, scholars have read Paul's discussion of the resurrection as invoking the classic duality between the physical body (Greek, *soma*) and the nonmaterial spirit (Greek, *pneuma*). An increasing number of scholars, however, have come to realize that, for Paul, as for most Greco-Roman thinkers, all forms of existence, including the spiritual, partake of matter. Spiritual beings—gods, stars, and angels—manifest a more refined, ethereal existence, but they were still thought to embody some form of matter, albeit infinitely superior to that of earthly organisms. As we shall see, Paul's concept of the "resurrection body" embraces this ancient philosophical consensus.

In persuading the Corinthians to share his understanding of the eschatological means by which God restores people to life, Paul first cites the example of a seed "that does not come to life

BOX 14.1 Resurrection Traditions in Paul and the Gospels

The oldest surviving account of Jesus' post resurrection appearances occurs in Paul's first letter to the Corinthians, which contains a tradition "handed on" to Paul from earlier Christians. None of the Gospels' resurrection narratives, written fifteen to forty years after the date of Paul's letter, refers to Jesus' manifestations to his kinsman James or to the "over 500 brothers" who simultaneously beheld him (cf. 1 Cor. 15:3–8).

PAUL (C. 54 CE)	MARK (C. 66–70 CE)	MATTHEW (C. 85 CE)	LUKE (C. 85–90 CE)	JOHN (C. 95–100 CE)
Jesus appears to Cephas (Peter) to "the Twelve" to "over 500" to James (Jesus' "brother") to "all the Apostles" to Paul (as an *apokalypsis,* or "revelation," Gal. 1:15–16)	No post resurrection account in original text (Two accounts were added later: Mark 16:8b and 16:9–19, in which Jesus appears first to Mary Magdalene, and then to the Eleven.)	No parallels Jesus appears to "the eleven disciples" (minus Judas Iscariot) "in Galilee"	Reference to "Simon [Peter]" to "the Eleven" (in Jerusalem) Jesus appears to "Cleopas" and an unnamed disciple on the road to Emmaus (near Jerusalem)	No parallels Jesus appears to Mary Magdalene (in Jerusalem) to "the disciples," particularly Thomas (in Jerusalem) to "the sons of Zebedee," Simon Peter, and the "Beloved Disciple" (in Galilee)

unless it has first died." As the seemingly dead seed bears little resemblance to the colorful flower that grows from it, so the resurrection body little resembles the deceased physical body that is "sown," buried in earth. Reasoning by analogy, Paul then observes that earth's different life forms—men, animals, birds, and fish—all have different kinds of "flesh." So, too, the "heavenly bodies"—sun, moon, and stars—are composed of a different—and superior—substance from that composing earthly creatures. By implication, resurrected bodies will not only differ from their present physical forms but will also, like the stars, show hierarchical degrees of difference. Presumably depending on their individual merits, the risen and transformed dead will reveal a wide range of "splendor," even as individual stars visibly differ in "brightness." Like Jesus, who "died" and "was buried" (15:4), yet who rose to eternal life, believers will undergo radical transformation: "Sown in the earth as a perishable thing," their bodies will be "raised in glory" because the "animal body" will be "raised as a spiritual [pneumatic] body," still material but wholly etherealized (15:35–44).

Returning to his contrast between "the first man, Adam" and "the last Adam [Christ]," Paul underscores the perishable nature of the first human creation, from whom we are all descended and with whom we share unavoidable mortality. When Paul describes Adam as "an animate being," he borrows the phrase from the Genesis creation account. Absolutely essential to Paul's thought here is the Hebrew Bible's concept of human nature: "God formed a man from the dust of the ground and breathed into his nostrils the breath of life. Thus the man became a living creature" (Gen. 2:7). The Hebrew word translated "living creature" is *nephesh,* the same term used to denote animals, or any other mortal creature that the divine breath has animated. When Genesis was translated into Greek, *nephesh* was rendered as *psyche,* the word that Plato and other Greek philosophers later employed to describe the "soul," the immortal part of humans that allegedly separates from the body at death and then enters into the divine realm. Contrary to the Greek duality of immortal soul housed in a mortal body, however, the biblical view consistently portrays humans as a physical/spiritual unity—and fully mortal. In the biblical tradition, humans do not *have* a soul, they *are* a soul, whether called *nephesh* or *psyche.*

According to this line of thought, future life depends not on a person's intrinsic possession—an immortal soul—but entirely on the life-giving power of God. This is the view that Paul adopts when he argues that the *psyche* (soul) is as perishable as the *soma* (body) (cf. the reference to *soma psychikon* in 15:44). Adam, "the man made of dust," is the model of human mortality, the image of death that comes to all. By contrast, Christ, "the heavenly man," offers, through resurrection, the opportunity to be refashioned in his divine image. In describing what happens in the eschatological raising of the dead, Paul emphasizes that our mortal natures will be radically "changed": "This perishable being must be clothed with the imperishable, and what is mortal must be clothed with immortality" (15:53).

Although he concedes that "flesh and blood can never possess the kingdom of God," Paul insists that the mortal components of human existence will be utterly transformed at the eschatological consummation, as if absorbed into a "spiritual [pneumatic] body." In his letter to the Romans, Paul explicitly attributes this change to the Spirit (*pneuma*) of God, which is already effecting inward changes in the Christian's present life. "If the Spirit of him who raised Jesus from the dead dwells within you," Paul states, "then the God who raised Jesus from the dead will also give new life to your mortal bodies through his indwelling Spirit" (Rom. 8:11; see also Paul's discussion of pneumatic transformations currently at work within believers in 2 Cor. 4:16–5:10).

In Paul's view, it is not the Greek idea of an innately eternal soul that guarantees future life, but the omnipotence and graciousness of the God who first created humanity—the One upon whom all depend for eschatological *re-creation* at the resurrection. Raised to a purified, exalted form of bodily existence, the resurrection body affirms not only the goodness of God's material creation but also the universality of his reign. Following the resurrection, when God has subjected the world to Christ, Paul declares, "then the Son himself will also be made subordinate to God who made all things subject to him" (15:25–28). The purpose of Christ's climactic submission to the Father is clearly stated in the new Scholars Version of Paul's letters: "so that God may be the one who rules everything everywhere" (15:28). (For this new edition of Paul's authentic letters, see Dewey et al. in "Recommended Reading.") Paul says little about the "intermediate state," the interval between a believer's death and the future time of resurrection, but elsewhere he implies that believers will posthumously "be with Christ" (Phil. 1:23–24), perhaps enjoying the "paradise" to which the Lukan Jesus refers (Luke 23:43).

For Paul, however, resurrection is not a vague hope for the distant future, but the promise of imminent bodily transformation. As Jesus' rising from the dead took place in the recent historical past, so his return to earth will occur in the near future. Similarly, Jesus' rising is the "first fruits" of an impending global "harvest" in which the faithful dead will be restored to life and living Christians will be instantly and gloriously transformed. "Listen!" Paul commands the Corinthians, "I will unfold a mystery: we shall not all die, but we [the living believers] shall all be changed in a flash, in the twinkling of an eye, at the last trumpet-call" (15:51–52). Paul fully expects to be alive to hear that final trumpet blast announcing Jesus' Parousia (cf. 1 Thess. 4:15–18). (For helpful analyses of Paul's concept of resurrection, see Martin, Engberg-Pedersen, and Wright in "Recommended Reading.")

Closing Remarks Retreating abruptly from his cosmic vision of human destiny to take up mundane themes again, Paul reminds the Corinthians of their previous agreement to help the Jerusalem church. They are to contribute money every Sunday, an obligation Paul had assumed when visiting the Jerusalem leadership (Gal. 2). The letter ends with Paul's invocation of Jesus' speedy return—"*Marana tha*" ("Come, O Lord")—an Aramaic prayer dating from the first generation of Palestinian Christians.

Second Letter to the Corinthians

Whereas 1 Corinthians is a unified document, 2 Corinthians seems to be a compendium of several letters or letter fragments written at different times and reflecting radically different situations in the Corinthian church. Even casual readers will note the contrast between the harsh, sarcastic tone of chapters 10–13 and the generally friendlier, more conciliatory tone of the earlier chapters. In the opinion of many scholars, chapters 10–13 represent the "painful letter" alluded to in 2 Corinthians 2:3–4, making this part necessarily older than chapters 1–9. Some authorities find as many as six or more remnants of different letters in 2 Corinthians, but for our purposes, we concentrate on the work's two main divisions (chs. 10–13 and 1–9), taking them in the order in which scholars believe they were composed.

Underlying the writing of 2 Corinthians is a dramatic conflict between Paul and the church he had founded. After he had dispatched 1 Corinthians, several events took place that strained his relationship with the church almost to the breaking point. New opponents, whom Paul satirizes as "superlative apostles" (11:5), infiltrated the congregation and rapidly gained positions of influence. Paul then made a brief, "painful" visit to Corinth, only to suffer a public humiliation there (2:1–5; 7:12). His visit a failure, he returned to Ephesus, where he wrote the Corinthians a severe reprimand, part of which is preserved in chapters 10–13. Having carried the

Second Corinthians

Author: Paul.

Date: Mid-50s CE.

Place of composition: The "severe letter" was probably sent from Ephesus, and the letter of reconciliation from Macedonia.

Audience: The congregation at Corinth, Greece.

"severe" letter to Corinth, Titus then rejoins Paul in Macedonia, bringing the good news that the Corinthians are sorry for their behavior and now support the apostle (7:5–7). Paul subsequently writes a joyful letter of reconciliation, included in chapters 1–9. Although this reconstruction of events is speculative, it accounts for the sequence of alienation, hostility, and reconciliation found in this composite document.

Although a scholarly majority holds that the document known as 2 Corinthians is a composite work, other commentators point out that we have no manuscript evidence indicating that it is a patchwork of letter fragments. Some proposals that divide the letter into as many as six or eight different missives may be criticized as overly ingenious. As in many scholarly debates, a theory that makes good sense to one investigator is not necessarily convincing to others. Some critics argue that the letter's abrupt changes of subject and tone can be explained by assuming that Paul dictated it over a period of days or weeks, during which time his attitude toward the Corinthians fluctuated considerably. Most commentators, however, do not find this argument persuasive.

The "Severe" Letter: Paul's Defense of His Apostolic Authority

In the last three chapters of 2 Corinthians, Paul writes a passionate, almost brutal defense of his apostolic authority. A masterpiece of savage irony, chapters 10–13 show Paul boasting "as a fool," using every device of rhetoric to demolish his opponents' pretensions to superiority. We don't know the precise identity of these opponents, except that they were Jewish Christians whom Paul accuses of proclaiming "another

Jesus" and imparting a "spirit" different from that introduced by his "gospel." The label "superlative apostles" suggests that these critics enjoyed considerable authority, perhaps as representatives from the Jerusalem church.

Whoever they were, the "superlative apostles" had succeeded in undermining many Corinthians' belief in Paul's individual teaching and trust in his personal integrity. Pointing to Paul's refusal to accept payment for his apostolic services (perhaps implying that he knew he was not entitled to it), his critics seriously questioned his credentials as a Christian leader. When he fights back, Paul is defending both himself (hence the many autobiographical references) and the truth of the gospel he proclaims. In some passages, Paul sounds almost desperately afraid that the church for which he has labored so hard will be lost to him.

Although Paul's bitter sarcasm may offend some readers, we must realize that this unattractive quality is the flip side of his intense commitment to the Corinthians' welfare. Behind the writer's "bragging" and threats (10:2–6; 11:16–21; 13:3, 10) lies the sting of unrequited affection. The nature of loyal love that Paul had so confidently defined in his earlier letter (1 Cor. 13) is now profoundly tested.

The Nature of Apostleship and the Christian Ministry   Whereas in 1 Corinthians Paul deals with ethical and doctrinal issues, in 2 Corinthians he struggles to define the qualities and motives that validate his leadership and authority. His main purpose in boasting "as a fool" (11:1–12:13) is personally to demonstrate that true apostleship does not depend on external qualities like race or circumcision or the strength to browbeat other believers. Paradoxically, it depends on the leader's "weakness"—his complete dependence on God, who empowers him to endure all kinds of hardship to proclaim the saving message. Outwardly "weak" but inwardly strong, Paul willingly suffers dangers, discomforts, humiliations, and unceasing toil—daily proof of selfless devotion—for the sake of a church that now openly doubts his motives (11:16–33).

It is not certain that the "superlative apostles" (11:5) are the same opponents as the "sham apostles" (11:13) whom Paul accuses of being Satan's agents (11:12–15). Whatever their identity, they apparently based their authority at least in part on supernatural visions and revelations. Paul responds by telling of a believer, caught up to "the third heaven," who experienced divine secrets too sacred to reveal (see Box 14.2). Disclosing that the mystic is himself, Paul states that to keep from becoming overelated by such mystical experiences he was given a counterbalancing physical defect. This unspecified "thorn in the flesh" ties Paul firmly to his earthly frame and grounds him in the human "weakness" through which God reveals spiritual power (12:1–13; 13:3–4).

Paul implores the Corinthians to reform so that his planned third visit will be a joyous occasion rather than an exercise in harsh discipline. He closes the letter with a final appeal to the congregation to practice unity and "live in peace" (13:1–14).

The Letter of Reconciliation

Although scholars discern as many as five or more separate letter fragments in this section, we discuss chapters 1–9 here as a single document. The opening chapters (1:1–2:13) contrast sharply with the angry defensiveness of chapters 10–13 and show a "happy" writer reconciled to the Corinthians. The unnamed opponent who had publicly humiliated Paul on his second visit has been punished and so must be forgiven (2:5–11). Titus's welcome news that the Corinthians are now on Paul's side (7:5–16) may belong to this section of the letter, misplaced in its present position by a later copyist.

Paul's Real Credentials   Despite the reconciliation, the Corinthian church is still troubled by Paul's rivals, whom he denounces as mere "hawkers" (salespersons) of God's word (2:17). Although he is more controlled than in chapters 10–13, his exasperation is still evident when he asks if he must begin all over again proving his apostolic credentials (3:1). Placing the

BOX 14.2 Paul's Ascent to the "Third Heaven"

In listing his apostolic qualifications—which include mystical visions and other spiritual gifts—Paul "boasts" that he was "caught up as far as the third heaven . . . into paradise," where he "heard words so sacred that human lips may not repeat them" (2 Cor. 12:1–4). Paul's reference to the "third heaven" indicates that he, like many of his Hellenistic-Jewish contemporaries, envisioned the spirit realm as a vertical hierarchy of successive levels. Some Jewish mystics of Paul's day postulated that heaven contained three levels, in which case Paul, "whether in the body or out of it" (the expression he uses to denote his altered state of consciousness), attained the topmost level. Other visionaries, however, conceived of seven celestial stages, with the ultimate spiritual reality—God's throne room—at the pinnacle (hence the expression "to be in seventh heaven") (see Figure 14.4). Still other traditions assumed as many as ten levels of heaven.

Because Paul does not specifically mention how many different levels he believes heaven encompasses, interpreters have long debated the significance of his having visited the "third heaven."

His reference to "paradise," which some contemporaries conceived as the temporary habitation of blessed souls awaiting resurrection (cf. Luke 23:43; Josephus, *Discourse on Hades*), suggests that it was not the locus of the divine throne. Given that Paul cites his mystical experience in the context of his quarrel with the Corinthians, in which he argues that God uses human "weakness" in order to show divine strength, it may be that in 2 Corinthians 12, Paul is actually confessing the limitations of his spiritual striving. Along with the "magnificence of [these] revelations," he was given a counterbalancing "physical pain" that severely limited the extent of his ecstatic experiences. Presuming that the Corinthians had heard of realms higher than "paradise," Paul's account of his heavenly ascent may have served to emphasize that, despite his apostolic rank, he—like his fellow believers—must await the Parousia for complete spiritual fulfillment; only then will the faithful behold divinity "face to face" (1 Cor. 13:12). (For a detailed examination of Paul's report of his ascent, see Gooder in "Recommended Reading.")

responsibility for recognizing true apostolic leadership squarely on the Corinthians, the writer reminds them that they are his living letters of recommendation. Echoing Jeremiah 31:31, Paul contrasts the Mosaic Covenant, inscribed on stone tablets, with the New Covenant, written on human hearts. Inhabited by the Holy Spirit, the Christian reflects God's image with a splendor exceeding that of Moses (3:2–18).

Nurturing a Spiritual Body Paul pursues his theme of the indwelling Spirit and further develops ideas about the future life that he had previously outlined in discussing resurrection (1 Cor. 15). In the earlier letter, Paul wrote that the believer will become instantly transformed—receive an incorruptible "spiritual body"—at Christ's return. He said nothing about the

Christian's state of being or consciousness during the interim period between death and the future resurrection. In the present letter (4:16–5:10), Paul seems to imply that believers are already developing a spiritual body that will clothe them at the moment of death.

Paul appears to state that God has prepared for each Christian an eternal form, a "heavenly habitation," that endows the bearer with immortality. Yearning to avoid human death, he envisions receiving that heavenly form now, putting it on like a garment over the physical body, "so that our mortal part may be absorbed into life immortal." The presence of the Spirit, he concludes, is visible evidence that God intends this process of spiritual transformation to take place during the current lifetime (5:1–5). United with Christ, the believer thus becomes a new creation (5:11–17).

FIGURE 14.4 The Ptolemaic Universe. Ptolemy (c. 100–178 CE), a Greek astronomer and mathematician, posited a geocentric theory of the universe, in which the planets and stars rotated around a stationary earth. In Paul's day, most Hellenistic mystics accepted a similar concept, a system in which the orbits of planets and stars represented successive levels of a heavenly hierarchy (see Box 14.2). In this seventeenth-century drawing of the Ptolemaic cosmos, at least seven stages of heaven appear.

The spiritual renewal is God's plan for reconciling humankind to himself. As Christ's ambassador, Paul advances the work of reconciliation; his sufferings are an expression of loyal service to his divine benefactor (5:18–6:13). Imploring the Corinthians to return his loyalty, Paul ends his defense of the apostolic purpose with a not-altogether-convincing expression of confidence in their reliability (7:2–16). (Many scholars believe that 6:14–7:1, which interrupts Paul's flow of thought, either belongs to a separate letter or is a non-Pauline fragment that somehow was interpolated into 2 Corinthians. Because of its striking resemblance to Essene literature, some critics suggest that this passage, with its reference to "Belial [the devil]," originated in Qumran.)

Chapters 8 and 9 seem to repeat each other and may once have been separate missives before an editor combined them at the end of Paul's reconciliation letter. Both concern the collections for the Jerusalem church, a duty that had been allowed to lapse during the hostilities between the apostle and his competitors. Highlighting Titus's key role, Paul emphasizes the generosity of Macedonia's churches, an example the Corinthians are expected to imitate. He reminds prospective donors that "God loves a cheerful giver" (9:7).

Summary

Paul's letters to the early Greek churches at Thessalonica and Corinth reveal that the first Christians held widely diverging opinions about the content and practice of their new religion. In 1 Thessalonians, Paul struggles to correct misconceptions about the fate of believers who die before the Parousia. In 1 Corinthians, he urges the congregation to overcome rivalries and unite as a single body for the spiritual welfare of all believers. The passionate arguments with which Paul defends his right to lead and teach (especially 2 Cor. 10–13) are reminders that God operates through human instruments who, like Paul, are "weak" and dependent on divine power. The key to understanding the urgency of Paul's plea for unity in belief and behavior is his assumption that his generation stands at the turning point between two ages. The history of evil is nearly finished; Christ will soon return to establish the New Age, in which God rules all.

Questions for Review

1. Which passages in 1 Thessalonians and 1 Corinthians indicate that Paul believed the End to be very near?
2. When Paul advises believers about choosing between marriage and the single life, to what extent does his expectation that ordinary history will soon end affect his counsel? What eschatological assumptions underlie his view of the world?
3. What kinds of wisdom does Paul discuss in 1 Corinthians 1–3?
4. Why do some Corinthians disagree with Paul's belief in the future resurrection of the body? Explain the difference between the notion of having an inherently immortal soul and the concept of receiving eternal life through resurrection, by the power of Christ's Spirit (*pneuma*) that dwells in the believer? How does Paul link Jesus' resurrection to the Christian hope of an afterlife?
5. In 2 Corinthians 10–13, what arguments do Paul's Corinthian opponents use against him? Why does he respond by boasting "as a fool"? Why are his mystical experiences important to the Corinthians?

Questions for Discussion and Reflection

1. If Paul was wrong about the occurrence of the Parousia during his lifetime, to what extent does that mistaken view affect readers' confidence in his teachings?
2. After reading 1 Corinthians 7 and 11, discuss Paul's views on human sexuality and the relative status of men and women. On what tradition does Paul base his opinion of women's roles in the church? How have Paul's attitudes influenced modern policies on the ordination of women for the ministry?
3. In 2 Corinthians 1–9, the Corinthian majority apparently decided to accept Paul and his individual gospel on the apostle's own terms. Which of Paul's threats or arguments do you think most influenced the church to become reconciled with its founder?

Terms and Concepts to Remember

Day of Judgment
eschatology
glossolalia
Lord's Supper
love (*agapē*) (1 Corinthians 13)
Parousia (1 Thessalonians)
Phoebe

Recommended Reading

1 Thessalonians

Ascough, Richard S. "Thessalonians, First Letter to the." In K. D. Sakenfeld, ed., *The New Interpreter's Dictionary of the Bible*, Vol. 5, pp. 569–574. Nashville: Abingdon Press, 2009. A concise analysis, including the Parousia theme and Paul's rhetorical devices.

Bridges, Linda M. "1 Thessalonians." In M. D. Coogan, ed., *The Oxford Encyclopedia of the Books of the Bible*, Vol. 2, pp. 406–410. New York: Oxford University Press, 2011. Focuses on the recipients' social setting, their manual labor, and the absence of women.

Malherbe, Abraham J. *The Letters to the Thessalonians: A New Translation with Introduction and Commentary.* Anchor Bible, Vol. 32B. New York: Doubleday, 2000. Argues that 2 Thessalonians is genuinely Pauline, but was sent to a different house church in Thessalonica.

Malina, Bruce J., and Pilch, John J. *Social Science Commentary on the Letters of Paul.* Minneapolis: Fortress Press, 2006. Offers important insights into the cultural content of Paul's thought, including his comparison of Jesus' return to a Roman leader's parousia.

1 and 2 Corinthians

Capes, David B. "1 Corinthians." In M. D. Coogan, ed., *The Oxford Encyclopedia of the Books of the Bible*, Vol. 1, pp. 139–148. New York: Oxford University Press, 2011. Offers a chapter-by-chapter analysis of Paul's ideas to correct the recipients' faith and behavior.

Dewey, Arthur J.; Hoover, Roy W.; McGaughy, L. C.; and Schmidt, Daryl D. *The Authentic Letters of Paul: A New Reading of Paul's Letters and Meaning.* The Scholars Version. Salem, Ore.: Polebridge Press, 2010.

Ehrensperger, Kathy. *That We May Be Mutually Encouraged: Feminism and the New Perspective in Pauline Studies.* London: T and T Clark, 2004. Examines Paul's "theology of mutuality" in human relationships.

Engberg-Pedersen, Troels. *Cosmology and Self in the Apostle Paul: The Material Spirit.* New York: Oxford University Press, 2010. A detailed examination of Stoic influences on Paul's worldview, including his concept of material spirit.

Gooder, Paula. *Only the Third Heaven? 2 Corinthians 12:1–10 and Heavenly Ascent.* London: T and T Clark, 2006. Reviews the literature of heavenly ascents and places Paul's account in the context of human weakness and divine strength, presenting it as one more example of failure and demonstrating the need for God's grace.

Goulder, Michael J. *Early Christian Conflict in Corinth: Paul and the Followers of Peter.* Peabody, Mass.: Hendrickson, 2000. Argues that the chief source of division in Corinth resulted from infighting between disciples of Peter and Paul.

Hays, Richard B. *Interpretation: First Corinthians.* Louisville, Ky.: Westminster John Knox Press, 1997. Examines Paul's theological response to socioeconomic problems at Corinth.

Levine, Amy-Jill, and Blickenstaff, Marianne, eds. *A Feminist Companion to Paul's Authentic Writings.* London: T and T Clark, 2004. A collection of essays examining Paul's views on such topics as gender, sexuality, marriage, and the physical body.

Martin, Dale B. *The Corinthian Body.* New Haven: Yale University Press, 1995. A groundbreaking study on Paul's concept of the materiality of the resurrected "spiritual body" and on his attitude toward the physical body and human sexuality.

Maschmeier, Jens-Christian. "2 Corinthians." In M. D. Coogan, ed., *The Oxford Encyclopedia of the Books of the Bible,* Vol. 1, pp. 148–158. New York: Oxford University Press, 2011. Discusses scholarly theories about the letter's composite nature, emphasizing Paul's defense of his apostolic status.

Meeks, Wayne. *The First Urban Christians: The Social World of the Apostle Paul,* 2nd ed. New Haven, Conn.: Yale University Press, 2003. An insightful investigation into the cultural environment and socioeconomic background of the earliest Christians.

Schütz, J. H., ed. *The Social Setting of Pauline Christianity.* Philadelphia: Fortress Press, 1982.

Soards, Marian J.; Sampley, Paul; and Wright, N. T., eds. *Romans–First Corinthians.* The New Interpreters Bible, Vol. 10. Nashville: Abingdon Press, 2000. Includes critical analysis of Pauline letters.

Talbert, C. H. *Reading Corinthians: A Literary and Theological Commentary on 1 and 2 Corinthians.* New York: Crossroads, 1987.

Theissen, Gerd. *The Social Setting of Pauline Christianity: Essays on Corinth.* Edited, translated, and with an introduction by J. H. Schütz. Philadelphia: Fortress Press, 1982.

Thiselton, Anthony C. "Corinthians, First Letter to." In K. D. Sakenfeld, ed., *The New Interpreter's Dictionary of the Bible,* Vol. 1, pp. 735–744. Nashville: Abingdon Press, 2006. An informative introduction to the letter's contents and theology.

Towner, Philip. "Corinthians, Second Letter to." In K. D. Sakenfeld, ed., *The New Interpreter's Dictionary of the Bible,* Vol. 1, pp. 744–751. Nashville: Abingdon Press, 2006. Examines date and place of composition, major themes, and theological significance.

Wright, N. T. *Surprised by Hope: Rethinking Heaven, the Resurrection, and the Mission of the Church.* San Francisco: HarperOne, 2008. Explains that Christian hope is not for a heavenly destiny but for bodily resurrection to a renewed earthly creation.

CHAPTER 15

Freedom from Law and Justification by Faith
Galatians and Romans

For through faith you are all [children] of God in union with Christ Jesus. . . .
There is no such thing as Jew and Greek, slave and freeman, male and female;
for you are all one person in Christ Jesus. Galatians 3:26, 28

Key Topics/Themes In his letters to the Galatians and the Romans, Paul defines Christianity's relationship to Judaism. He uses the Hebrew Bible to demonstrate that faith was always God's primary means of reconciling humanity to himself. God's revelation (*apokalypsis*) of Jesus frees believers from the "bondage" of Torah observance.

Paul argues in Romans that all humanity imitates Adam's disobedience and is therefore enslaved to sin and alienated from God. The "holy" and "just" Law of the Torah serves only to increase an awareness of human imperfection and to condemn the lawbreaker. Thus, obedience to the Torah cannot rescue people from sin's consequence—death—or unite them with the Deity. Only the heavenly benefactor's undeserved love expressed through Christ and accepted through faith can reconcile humanity with the Creator.

The Jewish lack of faith in Jesus as the divinely appointed agent of redemption is only temporary, a historical necessity that allows believing Gentiles also to become God's people.

Galatians and Romans are two of Paul's most important letters, for in these he spells out his distinctive vision of freedom from the Mosaic Torah and justification by faith in Christ. An angry declaration of Christianity's independence from Torah obligations, Galatians argues that obedience to Torah commandments cannot justify the believer before God. Only trust (faith) in God's gracious willingness to redeem humanity through Christ can now win divine approval and obtain salvation for the individual.

This uniquely Pauline gospel revolutionized the development of Christianity. By sweeping away all Torah requirements, including circumcision and dietary restrictions, Paul opened the church wide to Gentile converts. Uncircumcised former adherents of Greco-Roman religions were now granted full equality with Jewish Christians. Although the process was only beginning in Paul's day, the influx of Gentiles would soon overwhelm the originally Jewish church, making it an international community with members belonging to every known ethnic

Galatians

Author: Paul.

Date: About 56 CE.

Place of composition: Perhaps Ephesus or Corinth.

Audience: The "churches of Galatia," perhaps southern Galatia, a Roman province containing the towns of Lystra, Iconium, and Derbe.

Occasion or purpose: To refute opponents who advocated circumcision and to demonstrate that Jew and Gentile are equally saved by faith in Jesus' redemptive power.

group. This swift transformation would not have been possible without Paul's radical insistence on the abandonment of all Mosaic observances, which for centuries had separated Jew from Gentile.

An Angry Letter to the "Stupid" Galatians

Perhaps written at about the same time he was battling the "superlative apostles" of Corinth (2 Cor. 10–13), Paul's Galatian letter contains a similarly impassioned defense of his apostolic authority and teaching. It seems that almost everywhere Paul founded new churches troublemakers infiltrated the congregation, asserting that Christians must keep at least some provisions of the Mosaic Law. Influenced either by representatives from the Jerusalem church or by a wish to combine Jewish practices with elements of pre-Christian religions, the Galatians had abandoned Paul's gospel (1:6) and now required all male converts to undergo circumcision (5:2–3; 6:12–13), the physical sign of belonging to God's covenant community (Gen. 17).

The Recipients

The identity of the Galatian churches Paul addresses is uncertain. In Paul's time, two different geographical areas could be designated "Galatia." The first was a territory in north-central Asia Minor inhabited by descendants of Celtic tribes that had invaded the region during the third to first centuries BCE. Brief references

to Galatia in Acts (16:6; 18:23) suggest that Paul may have traveled there, but this is not certain.

The other possibility, as some historians suggest, is that Paul was writing to Christians in the Roman province of **Galatia.** The southern portion of this province included the cities of Iconium, Lystra, and Derbe, places where the apostle had established churches (Acts 14). If the "southern Galatia" theory is correct, it helps to explain the presence of "Judaizers" (those persons advocating circumcision), for the Roman province was much closer to Jewish-Christian centers at Antioch and at Jerusalem than was the northern, Celtic territory (see Figure 15.1).

The Identity of Paul's Opponents

Some commentators identify Paul's opponents as emissaries of the Jerusalem church, such as those apparently sent by James to inspect the congregation at Antioch (2:12). It seems improbable, however, that Jewish Christians from Jerusalem would have been unaware that requiring circumcision also meant keeping the entire Torah (5:2–3). Paul's opponents appear to combine aspects of Greco-Roman cult worship, such as honoring cosmic spirits and observing religious festival days (4:9–10), with selected Torah requirements (6:12–14). This **syncretism**—mixing together aspects of two or more different religions to create a new doctrine—suggests that the opponents are Galatian Gentiles. In Paul's view, their attempt to infuse Jewish and pagan elements into Christianity misses the point of the Christ event.

Purpose and Contents

Writing from Corinth or Ephesus about 56 CE, Paul has a twofold purpose: (1) to prove that he is a true apostle, possessing rights equal to those of the Jerusalem "pillars" (chs. 1–2), and (2) to demonstrate the validity of his gospel that Christian faith replaces works of Mosaic Law, including circumcision. The letter can be divided into five parts:

1. A biographical defense of Paul's autonomy and his relationship with the Jerusalem leadership (1:1–2:14)
2. Paul's unique gospel: justification through faith (2:15–3:29)

FIGURE 15.1 Potential locations of Paul's Galatian churches. The identity of Paul's Galatians is uncertain. The letter may have been directed to churches in the north-central plateau region of Asia Minor (near present-day Ankara, Turkey) or to churches in the southern coastal area of east-central Asia Minor (also in modern Turkey). Many scholars believe that the Galatians were Christians living in Iconium, Lystra, Derbe, and other nearby cities that Paul had visited on his first missionary journey.

3. The adoption of Christians as heirs of Abraham and children of God (4:1–31)
4. The consequences and obligations of Christian freedom from the Mosaic Law (5:1–6:10)
5. A final summary of Paul's argument (6:11–18)

Paul's Freedom from Institutional Authority

Largely dispensing with his usual greetings and thanksgiving, Paul opens the letter with a vigorous defense of his personal autonomy. His apostolic rank derives not from ordination or "human appointment" but directly from Israel's God, his divine patron (1:1–5). Similarly, his message does not depend on information learned from earlier Christians but is a direct "revelation of Jesus Christ" (1:12). Because he regards his gospel of faith as a divine communication, Paul sees no need to consult other church leaders about the correctness of his policies (1:15–17).

Unlike in Acts, in Galatians Paul presents himself as essentially independent of the parent church at Jerusalem. Nevertheless, he apparently recognizes the desirability of having his work among the Gentiles endorsed by the Palestinian Christian leadership. His visit with the Jerusalem "pillars"—Peter (Cephas), John, and James—is probably the same conference described in Acts 15. According to Paul, the pillars (a term he uses somewhat ironically) agree to recognize the legitimacy of his Gentile mission. Imposing no Torah restrictions on Gentile converts, the Jerusalem trio ask only that Paul's congregations contribute financially to the mother church, a charitable project Paul gladly undertakes (2:1–10; cf. Paul's appeals for donations in 2 Cor. 8–9 and Rom. 15).

After the Jerusalem conference, Paul meets Peter again at Antioch, a meeting that shows how far the Jewish–Gentile issue is from being resolved. Paul charges that Jesus' premier disciple is still ambivalent about associating with uncircumcised believers. When James sends emissaries to see if Antiochean Christians are properly observing Mosaic dietary laws, Peter stops sharing in communal meals with Gentiles. Apparently, Peter fears James's disapproval. Although Paul denounces Peter's action as hypocrisy, claiming that Peter privately does not keep Torah regulations, we cannot be sure of Peter's motives. He may have wished not to offend more conservative Jewish believers and behaved as he did out of respect for others' consciences, a policy Paul himself advocates (1 Cor. 8:1–13).

Justification by Faith

Paul's strangely negative attitude toward the Mosaic Law has puzzled many Jewish scholars. Why does a Pharisee trained to regard the Torah as God's revelation of ultimate Wisdom so vehemently reject this divine guide to righteous living? Is it because of a personal consciousness that (for him) the Law no longer has power to justify his existence before God? In both Galatians and Romans, Paul closely examines his sense of a relationship to his divine benefactor, attempting to show how the experience of Christ achieves for him what the Law failed to do—assure him of God's love and acceptance.

Replacing Law with Faith Using a legal metaphor to interpret the Crucifixion, Paul states that Jesus' voluntary death pays the Torah's penalty for all lawbreakers (3:13–14). Thus, Paul can say figuratively, that "through the law I died to law." He escaped the punishments of the Torah through a mystical identification with the sacrificial Messiah. Vicariously experiencing Jesus' crucifixion, Paul now shares in Christ's new life, which enables him to receive God's grace as never before (2:17–21).

Paul also appeals to the Galatians' personal experience of Christ, reminding them that they received the Spirit only when they believed his gospel, not when they obeyed the Law (3:1–5). If they think that they can be judged righteous by obeying the Torah, then there was no purpose or meaning to Christ's death (2:21). Paul reinforces his argument in the rabbinic tradition by finding a precedent in the Hebrew Bible that anticipates his formula of "faith equals righteousness." Paul notes that Abraham's "faith" in God's call "was counted to him as righteousness" (Gen. 15:6). Therefore, Paul reasons, persons who exercise faith today are Abraham's spiritual children, heirs to the promise that God will "bless," or justify, Gentile nations through faith (3:6–10). Faith, not obedience to the Law, is the key to divine approval.

In support of his appeal to biblical authority, Paul finds only one additional relevant text, Habakkuk 2:4: "he shall gain life who is justified through faith." Paul interprets the Habakkuk text as prophetic of the messianic era and contrasts its emphasis on faith with the Law's focus on action (3:11–12). The faith Habakkuk promised comes to the lawless Gentiles because Christ, suffering a criminal's execution, accepted the Law's "curse" on unlawful people and allowed them to become reconciled to God (3:13–14).

The Role of the Mosaic Torah in Human Salvation If, as Paul repeatedly asserts, the Mosaic Torah cannot really help anyone, why was it given? Paul's answer is that the Torah is a temporary device intended to teach humans that they are unavoidably lawbreakers, sinners whose most conscientious efforts cannot earn divine favor. Using an analogy from Roman society, Paul compares the Law to a tutor—a man appointed to guide and protect youths until they attain legal adulthood. Like a tutor imposing discipline, the Law makes its adherents aware of their moral inadequacy and their need for a power beyond themselves to achieve righteousness. That power is Christ. Having served its purpose of preparing Abraham's children for Christ, the Torah is now obsolete and irrelevant (3:19–25).

The Equality of All Believers Paul denies the Law's power to condemn and separate Jew from Gentile and asserts the absolute equality of all believers, regardless of their nationality, social class, or sex. Among God's children, "there is no such thing as Jew and Greek, slave and freeman, male and female," because all are "one person in Christ Jesus" (3:26–28).

All Believers as Heirs of Abraham Because Jesus purchased Christians' freedom from slavery to the Torah's yoke, all are now God's adopted heirs. As such, they are entitled to claim the Deity as *Abba* ("father" or "daddy") and to receive the Abrahamic promises. Paul underscores the contrast between the Christian community and Judaism by interpreting the Genesis story of Abraham's two wives as an allegory, a narrative in which the characters symbolize some higher truth. Hagar, Abraham's Egyptian slave girl, is earthly Jerusalem, controlled by Rome. Sarah, the patriarch's free wife, symbolizes the "heavenly Jerusalem," the spiritual church whose members are also free (4:21–31).

Responsibilities of Freedom What does freedom from Torah regulations mean? Aware that some Galatians used their liberty as an excuse to indulge any desire or appetite (a practice called **antinomianism**), Paul interprets his doctrine as freedom to practice neighborly love without external restrictions. Somewhat paradoxically, Paul quotes from the Torah to define the limits of Christians' freedom from Torah restrictions. Citing Leviticus 19:18, he asserts that "the whole law can be summed up in a single commandment: 'Love your neighbor as yourself'" (Gal. 5:13–14; cf. Mark 12:31). For Paul, "the harvest of the Spirit is love," which has the power not only to transcend Torah regulations but also to safeguard believers from the potential excesses of freedom. Exercising "faith active in love" (5:6), the Galatians will not indulge humanity's "lower nature"; love keeps them from all abuses and errors that the Torah prohibits. Practicing love promotes the kindness and mutual support that makes the congregation thrive spiritually (5:13–6:2).

Paul's exasperation with the Galatians' failure to understand that Jesus' death and resurrection are God's complete and all-sufficient means of human salvation inspires his most brutal insult. With savage irony, he suggests that persons who insist on circumcision finish the job by emasculating themselves (5:7–12). Paul's remark may refer to an infamous practice among male adherents of the goddess Cybele, some of whom mutilated themselves in a religious frenzy. This oblique allusion to a pagan cult also implies that Paul's opponents were Galatian syncretists.

In closing his letter, Paul seizes the pen from his secretary to write a final appeal to the Galatians in his own hand. Accusing his opponents of practicing circumcision only to escape persecution, presumably from Torah-abiding Jews, Paul summarizes his position: Torah obedience is meaningless because it implies that God's revelation through Jesus is not sufficient. Contrary to his opponents' limited view, Paul asserts that Jesus alone makes possible the new creation that unites humanity with its Creator. Paul's closing words are as abrupt and self-directed as his opening complaint (1:6): "In future let no one make trouble for me" (6:11–17).

Recent Scholarly Evaluations of Paul's Interpretation of Judaism

A scholarly debate about Paul's interpretation of first-century-CE Judaism that began in the 1970s has persisted into the twenty-first century, with many scholars advocating a "new perspective" on Paul's seemingly negative attitude toward Torah-observant Judaism, the religion in which he was raised. Before this ongoing reevaluation of Paul's thought, many commentators contrasted a "legalistic" Judaism—dominated by scrupulous law-keeping and the consequent fear of divine punishment—against a Pauline gospel of divine grace and redemption. Scholars such as E. P. Sanders and James Dunn have argued that this traditional view is too simplistic, pointing out that the Judaism of Paul's day not only was extremely diverse—making it

In contrasting our dark present age with the future light of divine rule, Paul states that now "we see only puzzling reflections in a mirror, but then we shall see face to face" (1 Cor. 13:12). To many students of Paul's work, recent critical interpretations of his thought offer no less than a major paradigm shift in our understanding of the apostle's worldview. In reevaluating Paul's attitude toward Judaism, for example, scholars increasingly view it from a "new perspective," rejecting earlier conclusions that Paul had dismissed the Mosaic Torah as "legalistic," in contrast to the dynamic exercise of "faith in Christ." Citing passages that many earlier critics largely ignored, current scholarship emphasizes Paul's vision of the law as "holy and just and good" (Rom. 7:12; cf. 3:31). Taking this argument further, Douglas Campbell has proposed an even

more radical reconsideration of Paul's doctrine of justification. Focusing on Romans, Campbell insists that the letter should be read through the lens of chapters 5 through 8, which emphasize the positive effects of God's unconditional love, rather than through the first four chapters describing humanity's dire predicament, the traditional approach. (See works by Campbell, Sanders, Westerholm, Wright, and Yinger in "Recommended Reading.")

Another scholarly trend sees Paul as a political as well as a religious activist, a Christian missionary who established a network of new communities practicing egalitarian ideals that opposed the materialistic goals of Greco-Roman society, particularly the coerciveness and economic exploitations of the Roman imperial system. (See Horsley and Crossan and Reed in "Recommended Reading.")

---

impossible to lump all branches indiscriminately together—but also embraced a number of components, such as many Jewish teachers' emphasis on God's mercy and grace, that also characterized Christianity.

Some commentators have suggested that Paul addresses his criticism of Judaism only to Gentiles, who, as people born outside the Mosaic Covenant, do not need to follow Torah regulations. By demonstrating the same kind of faith that Abraham manifested, however, non-Jews also become Abraham's spiritual descendants, recipients of the "blessing" that God promised eventually to extend to all nations (Gen. 12:3; 15:6). According to this theory, Christian Jews, who *are* born into the covenant community, presumably may continue to practice their ancestral customs, which they can rightly view as an act of faith in Christ (who also kept Torah). This proposal has the advantage of exonerating Paul from a doctrine that some see as anti-Semitic and of acknowledging that all, both Jew and Gentile, are "made righteous" by faith in Christ, but the scholarly community generally has not found this argument persuasive.

Although scholars generally agree that interpreting Paul's theology in terms of an uncritical opposition between "faith" and "works of the law" misrepresents his gospel, there is still no consensus on the exact meaning of his complex ideas about the interrelationship of Judaism and its offspring, Christianity. Despite the continuing controversy, many scholars welcome the "new perspective's" insights into Pauline thought, which may result in a clearer understanding about the nature of membership in the covenant and the people of God (see Box 15.1).

Letter to the Romans

Galatians was dictated in the white heat of exasperation; Romans is a more calmly reasoned presentation of Paul's doctrine of salvation through faith. This letter is generally regarded as the apostle's most systematic expression of his theology. In it, Paul thoughtfully explores an issue central to all world religions: how to bridge the moral gap between God and humanity, how to

Romans

Author: Paul.

Date: About 57–58 CE.

Audience: The house churches at Rome.

Place of composition: Corinth.

Occasion or purpose: To give a careful explanation of his "gospel to the Gentiles," particularly the doctrine of justification by faith and the place of both Jews and Gentiles in the divine plan for human redemption.

reconcile imperfect, sinful humanity to a pure and righteous Deity. As a Jew, Paul is painfully aware of the immense disparity between the actions of mortals and the immaculate holiness of Israel's God, whose justice cannot tolerate human error or wrongdoing. Yet Paul sees these irreconcilable differences between humanity and God as overcome in Christ, the Son who closes the gulf between perfect Father and imperfect children. In Paul's vision of reconciliation, God himself takes the initiative by re-creating a deeply flawed humanity in his own transcendent image.

Purpose, Place, and Time of Composition

Unlike other Pauline letters, Romans is addressed to a congregation the writer has neither founded nor previously visited. In form, the work resembles a theological essay or sermon rather than an ordinary letter, lacking the kind of specific problem-solving advice that characterizes most of Paul's correspondence. Some commentators regard Romans as a circular letter, a document intended to explain Pauline teachings to various Christian groups who may at that time have held distorted views of the apostle's position on controversial subjects.

Many scholars view chapter 16, which contains greetings to twenty-six different persons, as a separate missive. If it is, it originally served as a letter of recommendation for **Phoebe,** who probably conveyed Paul's letter to Rome and was perhaps commissioned to prepare for his impending visit to the capital. Paul describes Phoebe as **deacon** ("minister" or "servant") of the church at

Cencreae, the eastern port of Corinth, a term he also uses to describe his own ministry and that of other male leaders (1 Cor. 3:5). As host of the congregation that met in her house, Phoebe acted as "patron [*prostates*]" to the group, including Paul (16:1–2). The apostle's greetings to Prisca (Pricilla) and her husband, Aquila, indicates that the couple so instrumental to him in Corinth (1 Cor. 16:19; cf. Acts 18:18, 26) had returned to Rome. Although the present chapter 16 likely originated as a separate missive asking the Romans to assist Phoebe "in any business in which she may need your help," a later editor appended it to the main body of Paul's letter.

Although Paul may have intended the document we call Romans to circulate through many different churches, at the time of writing, he has compelling personal reasons to open communications with Rome. As 2 Corinthians 10–13 and Galatians reveal, Paul's churches in the northeastern Mediterranean region were rife with divisions and rebellion against his authority. Perhaps in hope of leaving this strife behind, Paul intends to move westward to Spain. He frankly confesses that he prefers to work in territories where no Christian has preceded him (Rom. 15:19–24; 1 Cor. 3:10–15; 2 Cor. 10:15–16). Paul writes not only to enlist Roman support for his Spanish mission (15:24) but also to ensure that his doctrines are understood and endorsed by the prestigious church at Rome, center of the imperial government and capital of the civilized world. He assures the Romans that he intends only to pass through their city (see Figure 15.2), lest they fear a lengthy visit from so controversial a figure.

Before journeying to Rome, however, Paul plans to take the money collected from his churches in Greece to the Jerusalem headquarters. He feels some anxiety about the trip to Judea, stronghold of his Jewish and Jewish-Christian opponents, and may have composed Romans as a means of marshaling the most effective arguments for his stand on the relationship between Judaism and Christianity (15:26–32). Chapters 9–11 contain his most extensive analysis of the parent religion's role in the divine plan. As Acts indicates, Paul's

FIGURE 15.2 Streetside restaurant in Ostia. Remarkably well preserved, this restaurant in Ostia, the seaport of Rome, offered convenient meals to busy passersby. Such "fast food" establishments were common in Roman cities and a familiar sight to Paul and other early Christians.

premonition of future trouble was fully justified by his subsequent arrest in Jerusalem and imprisonment in Caesarea (Acts 21–26). The letter was probably sent from Corinth about 57–58 CE.

Organization

The longest and most complex of Paul's letters, Romans can be divided into nine thematically related parts:

1. Introduction (1:1–15)
2. Statement of theme (1:16–17) and exploration of both Gentile and Jewish predicaments: God's wrath directed at all humanity because all people are guilty of deliberate error (1:18–3:31)
3. Abraham as the model of faith (4:1–25)
4. Faith in Christ ensuring deliverance from sin and death (5:1–7:25)
5. Renewed life in the Spirit (8:1–39)
6. The causes and results of Israel's disbelief (9:1–11:36)
7. Behavior in the church and the world (12:1–15:13)
8. Paul's future plans and greetings (15:14–33)
9. Appendix: a letter recommending Phoebe, a woman serving as deacon of the Cenchreae church (16:1–27)

Introduction

Paul opens the letter with an affirmation of his apostleship as the result of God's direct call, again implicitly denying that he owes his authority to any human ordination. Chosen for a special role, Paul is divinely commissioned to achieve both faith and obedience among all people. As Apostle or divinely appointed envoy to the Gentiles, he now plans to bring his gospel (*evangelion*) to Rome (1:1–15).

In defining his message as *evangelion* ("good news"), Paul implicitly identifies it as an alternative to Roman imperialistic propaganda, official government pronouncements about the "glad tidings" of the emperor's accomplishments. (See the discussion of imperial *evangelion* in Chapter 5.) Whereas the emperor was widely credited with establishing world peace and prosperity, in this letter Paul will present Jesus— "who was declared Son of God by a mighty act in that he rose from the dead" (1:4; cf. Acts 2:36)— as the real source of universal blessings. "Gracious favor and peace," Paul states, come from "God our great Benefactor and from our lord Jesus the Anointed" (1:7, Scholars Version).

Eager to convince the Roman congregations that his distinctive "gospel [*evangelion*]" is correct, Paul announces the same grand theme of salvation "through faith" that he had used in his earlier letter to the Galatians. "God's way of righting wrong," he insists, is "a way that starts from faith and ends in faith." He then cites the same passage from Habakkuk that he had quoted in Galatians: "He shall gain life who is justified through faith" (Rom. 1:17; cf. Gal. 3:11; Hab. 2:4). Or, as the Scholars Version renders it: "'The one who decides to live on the basis of confidence in God is the one who gets it right.'" The Greek term that Paul uses here, *pistis,* is usually translated as "faith," but has a broader connotation of "trust," a deep confidence in God's reliability, such as that which Abraham displayed when God summoned him to a new life (see below). For Paul, such confidence in God is the foundation on which the divine–human relationship must be built.

The Gentiles' Idolatry and Its Consequences

In the first part of Romans, Paul surveys the causes and consequences of humanity's present alienation from God, turning first to the Gentiles,

the "nations" outside a covenant bond with God. Like other Jewish moralists of his day, Paul sees the Gentiles' moral errors as resulting from their polytheism and idolatry. In Paul's eyes, the Creator's glory is unmistakably revealed in the natural world, making idol-worship inexcusable. Describing the Gentiles' religious and moral failures, Paul reflects ideas from Hellenistic-Jewish literature, as well as the concepts of "natural" and "unnatural" from the philosophies of Aristotle and the Stoics. Paul also adopts a popular Jewish view that the Gentiles deliberately "bartered away the true God for [a lie]" (1:25). Although Genesis, a narrative of human origins, says nothing about the beginning of polytheism, some noncanonical works, such as the Book of Jubilees, anticipate Paul's view that, at a particular point in history, the Gentiles deliberately abandoned a pure monotheism to pursue a multiplicity of false gods. They are thus guilty of "exchanging the splendor of immortal God for an image shaped like [human or animal forms]" (1:23). Because they fell into idolatry, worshiping images instead of true divinity, God abandoned them to the "shameful passions" of erotic desire. Throughout this section, Paul echoes the Wisdom of Solomon, a book of the Apocrypha, which was probably written only a few decades before his birth. According to Wisdom's theory of human history, "The idea of making idols was the beginning of fornication, and the invention of them was the corruption of life" (Wisd. 14:12; cf. 14:11–31).

Paul's controversial opinion about same-sex love affairs (1:26–27), common in the Greco-Roman world, was probably determined by the prohibitions against them in Leviticus (18:22; 20:13), but Paul's attempt to validate this Torah ordinance is based on his assumptions about the history of religion. Paul assumes that monotheism originally prevailed in human society, only to be followed by the proliferation of polytheism, spawning an idolatry that fatally corrupted the human mind. Twenty-first-century historians and anthropologists, however, find no evidence to support this Hellenistic-Jewish hypothesis, on which Paul grounds his condemnation of same-sex attraction. As scholars have discovered, belief in a single universal God, such as that characterizing postexilic stages of Israelite religion, is a late historical development. Today's readers, including many ethicists and psychologists, may similarly be puzzled by Paul's assumed link between idolatry and homosexual behavior, a connection prevalent in the first-century CE Jewish milieu but not verifiable by the standards of contemporary science. (For an exploration of this topic, see Michael Coogan and Dale Martin in "Recommended Reading.")

Jews Are Also Alienated from God When Paul turns from describing Gentile errors to addressing his fellow Jews, he does not accuse them of idolatry, though he judges them "equally guilty." Although God provided Jews with the Torah to guide them in righteousness, a fact that gives them an initial advantage over the Gentile nations, they have not, Paul asserts, lived up to the Law's high standards. As a result, Jews have not achieved justification before God any more than Gentiles have. Paul reiterates his argument to the Galatians that the Torah fails to effect a right relationship between God and the lawkeeper; it serves only to make one conscious of sin (2:17–3:20).

All humanity, then, both Jew and Gentile, is in the same sinking boat, incapable of saving itself. No one can earn through his or her own efforts the right to enjoy divine approval. Paul now goes on to show how God—whose just nature does not permit him to absolve the unjust sinner—works to rescue undeserving humanity (3:21–31).

Abraham as the Model of One "Justified" by Faith

Paul realizes that, if his doctrine is to convince Jewish Christians, it must find support in the Hebrew Bible. He therefore argues that God's plan of rescuing sinners through faith began with Abraham, foremost ancestor of the Jewish people. As in Galatians, he cites Genesis 15:6: Abraham's faith in God "was counted to him as righteousness." For Paul, the fact that God

pronounced Abraham "righteous" while the patriarch was still uncircumcised has enormous implications for the uncircumcised Gentiles, providing a prophetic model of God's plan to save all peoples through faith. In achieving justification by placing his trust in God, Abraham is not only the father of his Jewish descendants but also "the father of all who have faith when uncircumcised, so that righteousness is 'counted' to them" (4:3–11). Therefore, Gentiles who imitate Abraham's example—trusting that God will do what he has promised—are also heirs of the divine promises given in Genesis. Without compromising his impartiality, God succeeds in justifying both Jew and Gentile, encompassing previously distinct groups in an act of redemptive grace. As Abraham proved his confidence in God by obediently responding to Yahweh's voice, so must the faithful now respond to God's new summons through Christ (4:15–25). "Justified through faith" in Jesus' sacrificial death, a demonstration of divine love, believers are now reconciled to God (5:1–11).

In using Abraham's example to support his thesis that people are "justified by faith quite apart from success in keeping the law" (3:28; cf. 4:1–25), Paul selects only one verse (Gen. 15:6) from the thirteen chapters that Genesis devotes to Abraham's story. Another New Testament letter—traditionally ascribed to James, Jesus' Torah-keeping "brother"—cites a different part of the Genesis narrative to argue that it was not Abraham's trust in itself but his faith expressed *in action* that pleased God. Insisting that "faith divorced from deeds is barren," the author of James interprets Abraham's significance as that of a person who demonstrates his faith through his deeds, such as (almost) offering his son Isaac as a human sacrifice. Only by translating his trust into action, James declares, did Abraham prove "the integrity of his faith." Tellingly, James then cites the same Genesis verse that Paul had evoked to illustrate the sufficiency of faith alone, but, by placing Genesis 15:6 in the broader context of Abraham's actions, James interprets the passage quite differently (James 2:14–26). Although most

BOX 15.2 Differing New Testament Views on Torah Keeping

Paul's "gospel"—that Gentiles may become full-fledged members of the Christian community without having to keep Torah ordinances—so completely won the day that later generations of Christians have taken it for granted. By the end of the first century CE, Gentile converts numerically dominated the church, relegating Torah-keeping Jewish Christians to a small minority. Although the writings of Torah-observant Christians were not included in the New Testament canon, occasional voices of dissent from the Pauline position appear in Christian Scripture. The author of Matthew's Gospel, for example, argues that Israel's Messiah "did not come to abolish the Law [Torah]" and that it remains binding on Jesus' followers:

> If any man therefore sets aside even the least of the Law's demands, and teaches others to do the same [as Paul did], he will have the lowest place in the kingdom of Heaven, whereas anyone who

keeps the Law, and teaches others so [as did Paul's opponents], will stand high in the kingdom of Heaven. (Matt. 5:19)

In describing Jesus' future judgment on those claiming to follow him, the Gospel writer is even more severe:

> Not everyone who calls me, "Lord, Lord," will enter the kingdom of Heaven, but only those who do the will of my heavenly Father [who commanded Israel to obey his laws]. . . . Then I [Jesus as eschatological judge] will tell them [the condemned] to their faces, "I never knew you; out of my sight, you and your wicked ways." (Matt. 7:21–23)

The phrase here translated "wicked ways" is more accurately rendered "subverters of the Law," as in the Scholars Version. According to Matthew, Jesus will thus condemn Christians who fail to imitate his example in observing Torah regulations. Paul, of course, would disagree.

commentators believe that James is merely correcting a later misinterpretation of Paul's doctrine of faith, and not necessarily contradicting it, his conclusion that people are "justified by deeds and not by faith in itself" (2:25) does not precisely accord with the Pauline equation of faith and righteousness (see Chapter 18). (For another New Testament author's view on the "works of the law," see Box 15.2.)

Faith in Christ Ensuring Deliverance from Sin and Death

The Roles of Adam and Christ At the outset of his letter (1:5), Paul declares that he tried to bring the whole world to a state of obedient faith. In chapter 5, he outlines a theory of history in which God uses these two qualities—obedience and faith—to achieve human salvation. God's intervention into human affairs became necessary when the first human, Adam (whose name means "humankind"), disobeyed the Creator. Through this act, Adam alienated not only

himself but all his descendants from their Maker (see Box 15.3). Like some other Jewish teachers of the first century CE, Paul interprets the Genesis story of Adam's disobedience as a tragic **Fall** from grace, a cosmic disaster that introduces sin and death into the world. (Paul's word for "sin"—*hamartia*—is a Greek archery term that means "missing the mark" or "falling short of a desired goal." Aristotle used the same term to denote the "fatal flaw" of the tragic hero in Greek drama. *Hamartia* commonly refers to an error of judgment rather than an act of inborn human wickedness.) In Paul's moral scheme, the entire human race fails to hit the target of reunion with God, thus condemning itself to death—permanent separation from the Source of life.

Obedience to the Torah cannot *save* because the Law merely defines errors and assigns legal penalties. It is God himself who overcomes the hopelessness of the human predicament. He does this by sending his Son, whose perfect obedience and sacrificial death provide a saving

BOX 15.3   Paul's Views on the Origin of Sin and Death

In Romans 5, Paul attributes the existence of sin and death to the first man's deliberate disobedience of a divine command, that which prohibited Adam and Eve from eating the fruit of the tree of knowledge (Rom. 5:12–23; cf. Gen. 3). According to orthodox interpretations of Paul's thought, particularly Augustine's doctrine of original sin, the first couple's error resulted in a death sentence not only for them but also for their descendants, all of whom are born under divine condemnation. In scrutinizing Genesis 3, however, readers will notice that most of the terms commonly used to describe the tale of Adam's and Eve's alienation from Yahweh are entirely absent. The Genesis narrator makes no reference to sin, evil, rebellion, disobedience, punishment, damnation, or a fall from grace—all are interpretative terms supplied by later theologians. The narrator, moreover, does not present the talking serpent who persuades Eve to taste the forbidden fruit as "bad," but only as "subtle" or "shrewd." Interestingly, after Genesis 3, no writer in the canonical Hebrew Bible (Tanakh) ever again refers to this Genesis episode or accords it any theological significance.

It was not until shortly before Paul's day that Hellenistic-Jewish writers began to reinterpret the events related in Genesis 3. During the first century BCE, a Hellenistic Jew in Alexandria, Egypt, composed the Wisdom of Solomon, a book that integrated Greek philosophy with the Hebraic biblical tradition. (Excluded from the Tanakh, the Wisdom of Solomon was part of the Septuagint Apocrypha and is included in Catholic and Orthodox editions of the Old Testament.) According to this source, the devil was responsible for introducing death into human experience: "God created man for immortality, and made him the image of his own eternal self; it was the devil's spite that brought death into the world" (Wisd. of Sol. 2:23–24). Other extrabiblical traditions that it was the devil, speaking through the serpent, who tempted Eve to sin were eventually incorporated into the noncanonical Life of Adam and Eve, a Hellenistic work that imaginatively dramatizes Satan's role in corrupting the first humans. Whether directly influenced by this work or by the oral traditions underlying it, Paul evidently adopts the book's Hellenistic view that Adam and Eve are the sources of sin and death (Rom. 5:12–21; 2 Cor. 11:3; cf. 1 Tim. 2:4). (A Jewish apocalyptic work, 2 Esdras [c. 100 CE], also explores the concept of original sin; see Chapter 19.)

---

counterweight to Adam's sin. As all Adam's children share his mortal punishment, so all will share the reward of Christ's resurrection to life. It is the believer's trust in the saving power of Christ that makes him or her "righteous," enabling the just Deity to accept persons trustfully responding to his call (5:12–21).

Several scholars have proposed that, in a few crucial passages, Paul's use of the phrase "faith *in* Christ" (*pistis Christou*) should be translated as the "faith *of* Christ," referring to the faithfulness that Jesus displayed in loyally serving God to the end (Rom. 3:22, 25–26; cf. Gal. 2:16; 3:22). In this view, Christian faith can be interpreted as a willingness to imitate the perfect trust in God

that Jesus showed in submitting to a shameful death on the cross. A model of selfless devotion and confidence in divine mercy, Jesus' human life acquired cosmic significance when the Deity accepted his faithfulness as a means of validating or redeeming the human race. A majority of commentators, however, seem to endorse the traditional view that belief or trust *in* Christ correctly expresses Paul's concept. (For a perceptive treatment of this issue, see Dunn in "Recommended Reading.")

Some later theologians used Romans 5 to formulate a doctrine of **original sin,** which states that all human beings inherit an unavoidable tendency to do wrong and are innately corrupt.

From Augustine to Calvin, such theologians had a deeply pessimistic view of human nature, in some cases regarding the majority of people as inherently depraved and justly damned.

Paul, however, emphasizes the joyful aspects of God's reconciliation to humanity. It is the Deity who initiates the process, and God's "grace"—his gracious will to love and to give life—far exceeds the measure of human failings. So powerful is God's determination to redeem humankind, Paul implies, that he may ultimately save all people:

> It follows, then, that as the issue of one misdeed was the condemnation for all [people], so the issue of one just act is acquittal and life for all [people]. For as through the disobedience of the one man [Adam] the many were made sinners, so through the obedience of the one man [Christ] the many will be made righteous.
>
> (Rom. 5:18–19; see Paul's similar declaration in 1 Cor. 15:21–23)

This passage, in which Paul optimistically seems to envision a universally redeemed humanity, must be balanced against his more negative evaluation of human sinfulness in Romans 8. In this chapter, he contrasts two different ways of life that produce opposite results. Those who submit to their "lower nature" make themselves God's enemies and earn "death"; those united with Christ, however, live on a higher plane, "the level of the spirit," which produces "life and peace" (Rom. 8:5–13).

A Distortion of Paul's Teaching on Freedom In chapter 6, Paul seems to be refuting misconceptions of his doctrine on Christian freedom. As in Galatia, some persons were apparently acting as if liberty from the Law entitled them to behave irresponsibly. In some cases, they concluded that "sinning" was good because it allowed God's grace more opportunity to show itself. Paul reminds such dissidents that sin is a cruel tyrant who pays wages of death. In contrast, Christ treats his servants like a generous benefactor, bestowing the gift of everlasting life (6:1–23).

The Law's Holiness and Human Perversity

Paul makes one final attempt to place the Torah in the context of salvation history and to account for its failure to produce human righteousness. In Galatians, Paul describes the Law harshly, referring to it as slavery, bondage, and death. Writing more temperately in Romans, he judges the Law "holy and just and good" (7:12). If it is, why does it not serve to justify its practitioners?

In this case, Paul answers that the fault lies not in the Torah but in human nature. The Torah is "spiritual," but human beings are "unspiritual" and enslaved by sin. Throughout this long passage (7:7–25), Paul uses the first person, as if he were analyzing his own nature and then projecting his self-admitted defects onto the rest of humanity. His rhetorical "I," however, should probably be read "we"—for he means to describe human nature collectively. Laws not only define crimes, he asserts, but create an awareness of lawbreaking that does not exist in their absence. Thus, the Torah makes sin come alive in the human consciousness (7:7–11).

Speaking as if sin were an animate force inside himself, Paul articulates the classic statement of ethical frustration—the opposition between the "good" he wishes to do and the "wrong" he actually performs. As he confronts the huge gap between his conscious will and his imperfect actions, Paul can only conclude that it is not the real "he" who produces the moral failure, but rather the "sin that lodges in me" (7:14–20). For Paul, "sin" is not only autonomous but a personification of supernatural forces profoundly hostile to humankind.

With his higher reason delighting in the Torah but his lower nature fighting against it, he finds that he incurs the Law's punishment—death. He bursts with the desire to attain God's approval but always "misses the mark." In agony over his fate, he seeks some power to rescue him from an unsatisfying existence that ends only in death (7:21–25). Paul may be accused of attributing his personal sense of moral imperfection to everyone else, but his despairing self-examination illustrates why he believes that the Law is unable to deliver one from the lethal attributes of imperfect human nature (8:3).

Renewed Life in the Spirit

Paul then tries to show how God accomplishes his rescue mission through Christ (8:1–39). By sharing humanity's imperfect nature and dying "as a sacrifice for sin," Christ transfers the Torah's penalties to sin itself, condemning it and not the human nature in which it exists (8:3–4). Because Christ's Spirit now dwells within believers, sin no longer exerts its former control, and new life can flourish in each Christian's body. Thus, Christians escape their imperfection, having put it to death with Christ on the cross. No longer sin's slaves, they become God's children, joint heirs with Christ (8:5–17).

Universal Renewal Paul uses mystical language to describe not only human nature but also the cosmos itself struggling to be set free from the chains of mortality. During this period of cosmic renewal, the whole universe wails as if in childbirth. Believers now hope for a saving rebirth, but that reality is still ahead. Ultimately, they will be fully reshaped in the Son's image, the pattern of a new humanity reconciled to God (8:18–30).

Doxology Paul concludes this section of his letter with a memorable **doxology.** It is a moving hymn of praise to the God who has lovingly provided the means for humanity to transcend its weakness and attain "the liberty and splendour" of God's children. In this brilliant credo, Paul declares his absolute confidence that no suffering or power, human or supernatural, can separate the believer from God's love (8:31–39).

The Causes and Results of Israel's Disbelief

Now that he has explained his position on the Law and the means by which God arranges human salvation, Paul explores the difficult question of Israel's rejection of its Messiah. How does it happen that the people to whom God granted his covenants, Torah, Temple, and promises failed to recognize Jesus as the Christ? First, Paul argues that God never intended all Israelites to receive his promises; they were meant for only a faithful remnant, represented in Paul's day by Jewish Christians (9:1–9). (But does Paul's theory of a "faithful remnant" fully agree with other parts of his argument?)

Second, Paul tries to show that Israel's present unbelief is part of God's long-range plan to redeem all of humanity. In a long discourse sprinkled with loose paraphrases of passages from the Hebrew Bible, Paul makes several important assumptions about God's nature and the manner in which the Deity controls human destiny. He first assumes that because God's will is irresistible, humans' freedom of choice is severely limited. Citing the Exodus story, Paul reminds his readers that Yahweh manipulated the Egyptian king in order to demonstrate his divine strength (Exod. 9:15–16). He argues that God's omnipotence entitles him to show favor or cruelty to whomever he pleases. Paul compares the Deity's arbitrariness to that of a potter who can assign one clay pot an honorable use and smash another if it displeases him. Implying that might makes right, Paul declares that no human being can justly challenge the supreme Potter's authority to favor one person and not another (9:10–21; 10:7–10).

Paul's assumption is that the Creator predetermines the human ability to believe or disbelieve, thus foreordaining an individual's eternal destiny. This assumption troubles many believers for its apparent repudiation of free will, although some have embraced it. Later theologians such as Augustine and Calvin formulated a doctrine of **predestination,** in which God—before the world's creation—decreed everyone's fate, selecting a few for salvation and relegating the majority to damnation.

Paul, however, emphasizes the positive aspect of God's apparent intervention into the human decision-making process. In God's long-range plan, Jewish refusal to recognize Jesus as the Messiah allows Gentiles to receive the Gospel;

thus, nations previously ignorant of God can become part of his covenant people and thereby, through faith, receive redemption. In a famous analogy, Paul likens Gentile believers to branches from a wild olive tree that have been grafted onto the cultivated olive trunk, which signifies Israel. If some of the old branches from the domesticated tree had not been lopped off, there would have been no room for the new (11:16–18). For humanity's universal benefit, God has taken advantage of Israel's unresponsiveness to produce a greater good.

Paul also states that the creation of churches in which Greeks and Romans now worship Israel's God will incite a healthy envy among Jews, kindling a desire to share the churches' spiritual favor. Furthermore, Israel's disbelief is only temporary. When all Gentiles become believers, then the original branches will be regrafted onto God's olive tree and "the whole of Israel will be saved" (11:19–27).

Paul does not explain why both Israelites and Gentiles could not have been saved simultaneously, but he remains absolutely certain that the Jews are still God's chosen people. Writing before Rome destroyed the Jewish state in 70 CE, Paul does not predict divine vengeance upon Israel. He affirms instead that God's own integrity ensures that he will honor his promises to the covenant community. Some later Christian writers argue that God disowned Israel, replacing it with the Christian church. In contrast, Paul's witness confirms Israel's continuing role in the divinely ordered drama of human salvation (11:1–36).

Behavior in the Church and the World

Paul's ethical instruction (chs. 12–15) is closely tied to his sense of apocalyptic urgency. Because the New Age is about to dawn, believers must conduct themselves with special care, not only in their personal lives but also in their behavior toward the imperial powers that govern society at large.

Cooperation with Government Authority Paul's advice that "every person must submit to the supreme authorities" was written before his imprisonment and prosecution at Rome. We do not know if his counsel would be the same after his experience in the emperor Nero's court, but in chapter 13 he recommends a program of obedience and cooperation with government officials. Echoing the Stoic view that the state exists to maintain public order and to punish wrongdoing, Paul argues as if the Roman Empire were a "divine institutios"—an opinion contrasting with his earlier view that the present world is ruled by demonic forces (2 Cor. 4:4).

Although he emphasizes the Christian's duty to pay taxes and submit to legally constituted authority, Paul does not consider the ethical problem of a citizen's duty to resist the state's illegal or exploitative acts. Nor does he urge believers to change the present social system, probably because it will soon end. Immediately following his message of submission to the state (13:1–10), Paul reminds his Roman correspondents that their rescue from the present evil age is rapidly approaching: "It is time for you to wake out of sleep, for deliverance is nearer to us now that it was when first we believed. It is far on in the night; day [of the Parousia] is near" (13:11). Paul's apparent toleration of human slavery in his brief letter to **Philemon** may also stem from his conviction that Jesus will soon take over world rule, ending all imperial abuses (see Chapter 16).

Rome as Anti-Christ Paul implies that voluntary cooperation with Rome will benefit Christians; he could not know that he soon would be among the first victims of a state-sponsored persecution of his faith (see Figure 15.3). Following the emperor Nero's execution of many Roman believers (c. 64–65 CE) and the threat of more persecution under Domitian (81–96 CE), some New Testament authors came to regard the state as Satan's earthly instrument to destroy God's people. After the Jerusalem Temple was razed in 70 CE, Rome became the new Babylon in the eyes of many Christians. The author of Revelation pictures Rome as a beast and predicts its fall as a cause of universal rejoicing

FIGURE 15.3 Fourth-century Roman lime relief depicting the apostles Peter and Paul. Because early church traditions assert that both apostles were executed in Rome during Nero's reign, their images are commonly paired. Paul's letter to the Galatians indicates that their historical relationship was not so close (Gal. 2:11–13).

(Rev. 17–19). At the time Paul wrote, however, the adversarial relationship between church and state was still in the future (see the photo essay preceding Chapter 19, "The Tension Between Caesar and Christ").

Summary

Romans is the most comprehensive statement of Paul's teaching. In it, Paul wrestles with the problems of humanity's estrangement from God and God's response to human need. Arguing that Torah observance cannot justify one to the righteous God, Paul states that in Christ the Deity creates a new humanity, a new beginning. Through Christ, all persons of faith can become God's children and benefit from the promises made to Abraham.

God's ultimate plan is to defeat sin and reconcile all humanity—ironically, first Gentiles and then Jews—to himself. Because the time remaining is so short, believers must submit to existing governments and lead blameless lives.

Questions for Review

1. As Paul describes it in Romans 1–3, how is all humanity trapped in a hopeless predicament? How has God acted to rescue people from the power of sin and death?
2. Define what Paul means by such terms as *righteousness*, *justification*, and *faith*. According to Paul's evaluation of the Torah in Galatians and Romans, why are Torah observances such as circumcision irrelevant to God's action through Christ?
3. In both Galatians and Romans, Paul cites excerpts from Genesis 15 and Habakkuk 2 to prove that God always intended faith to be the means by which humanity was to be "justified." Compare Paul's interpretation of Abraham's example with that given by James (2:14–26). In what ways does James disagree with Paul's explanation of the Genesis text?

Questions for Discussion and Reflection

1. Some commentators have argued that Paul misunderstands the purpose of Torah obedience. They claim that most Jewish teachers of his day did not present Torah observance as a means of salvation and that Paul's contrast between "works" and "faith" misrepresents first-century Judaism. From your reading of Galatians and Romans, how would you explain Paul's position?

2. What aspects of Paul's teaching in Galatians or Romans are most influenced—hence limited—by his particular historical/social circumstances? If Paul were alive today, would a knowledge of modern anthropology and biological evolution cause him to change his presentation of the Adam–Christ parallel? How could Paul's notion of inherited Adamic sin be translated into an understanding of humanity's biological heritage in which humans retain genetic traits of more "primitive" ancestors?

3. How do you think Paul's ideas about submission to governmental authority should be modified to reflect post-Enlightenment principles of freedom and individual rights? If Paul had survived Nero's persecutions, would he have revised his advice in Romans 13?

4. Why does Paul, who believed that Mosaic Law had been superseded by divine grace and faith in Christ, base his condemnation of homosexuality on a Torah statute (Lev. 18:22; 20:13)? How do you think Paul's views on same-sex love need to be reinterpreted?

Terms and Concepts to Remember

Abraham	original sin
Adam	Philemon
antinomianism	Phoebe
circumcision	predestination
deacon	Roman Empire
doxology	syncretism
Fall, the	Torah
Galatia	

Recommended Reading

Galatians

Braxton, Brad R. *No Longer Slaves: Galatians and African American Experience.* Collegeville, Minn.: Liturgical Press, 2002. Explores the implications of Paul's emphasis on uniting different races in Christ for the African American community.

Dunn, James D. G. *Epistle to the Galatians.* Peabody, Mass.: Hendrickson, 1993. Discusses Pauline themes of faith and justification.

Koperski, Veronica. *What Are They Saying About Paul and the Law?* Mahwah, N.J.: Paulist Press, 2001. Essays on current interpretations of Paul's views on the Torah.

Martyn, J. Louis. *Galatians.* Anchor Bible Series. New York: Doubleday, 1997. A new translation and commentary.

Riches, John. "Galatians." In M. D. Coogan, ed. *The Oxford Encyclopedia of the Books of the Bible,* Vol. 1, pp. 311–315. New York: Oxford University Press, 2011. Emphasizes Paul's historic break with the past and its historical reinterpretations.

Soards, Marion. "Galatians, Letter to." In K. D. Sakenfeld, ed., *The New Interpreter's Dictionary of the Bible,* Vol. 2, pp. 508–514. Nashville: Abingdon Press, 2007. A helpful introduction.

Wiley, Tatha. *Paul and the Gentile Women: Reframing Galatians.* New York: Continuum International, 2005. Examines the effect of Paul's gospel on women believers.

Romans

Campbell, Douglas A. *The Deliverance of God: An Apocalyptic Rereading of Justification in Paul.* Grand Rapids: Eerdmans, 2009. Much more detailed than most books listed in this text, it reinterprets Romans as a statement of divine grace and unconditional love.

Coogan, Michael. *God and Sex: What the Bible Really Says.* New York: Twelve, 2010. Lucidly surveys differing biblical attitudes toward various sexual relationships, including marriage and homoeroticism.

Crossan, John Dominic, and Reed, Jonathan L. *In Search of Paul: How Jesus' Apostle Opposed Rome's Empire with God's Kingdom,* reprint edition. San Francisco: HarperOne, 2005. A scholarly analysis of Roman culture that emphasizes the political dimension of Paul's mission.

Dunn, James D. G. "Faith, Faithfulness." In K. D. Sakenfeld, ed., *The New Interpreter's Dictionary of the Bible,* Vol. 2, pp. 407–423. Nashville: Abingdon Press, 2007. Offers important insights on Paul's gospel of salvation through faith.

———. *The Theology of Paul the Apostle.* Grand Rapids, Mich.: Eerdmans, 1998. Thorough exposition of Paul's thought, using Romans as his most important theological statement.

Ehrensperger, Kathy. *That We May Be Mutually Encouraged: Feminism and the New Perspective in Pauline Studies.* New York: T and T Clark International, 2004.

Eisenbaum, Pamela. *Paul Was Not a Christian: The Original Message of a Misunderstood Apostle.* San Francisco: HarperOne, 2010. Argues that Paul continued to see himself as a Jew who promulgated Israel's Messiah.

Elliott, Neil. "Romans." In M. D. Coogan, ed., *The Oxford Encyclopedia of the Books of the Bible,* Vol. 2, pp. 271–279. New York: Oxford University Press, 2011. Offers a variety of traditional and innovative interpretations of Paul's arguments on Christ and Judaism, including nontheological views.

Fitzmyer, Joseph A. *Romans.* The Anchor Bible, Vol. 33. New York: Doubleday, 1993. A new translation with extensive commentary.

Gorman, Michael J. *Apostle of the Crucified Lord: A Theological Introduction to Paul and His Letters.* Grand Rapids, Mich.: Eerdmans, 2004. Explores Paul's doctrine of justification by faith.

Horsley, Richard, ed. *Paul and the Imperial Roman Order.* New York: Bloomsbury T & T Clark, 2004. Collection of cutting-edge essays on the political aspects of Pauline thought.

Martin, Dale B. *Sex and the Single Savior: Gender and Sexuality in Biblical Interpretation.* Louisville, Ky.: Westminster John Knox, 2006. Includes a careful analysis of Paul's views on sexuality, passion, and marriage.

Moo, Douglas. "Romans, Letter to the." In K. D. Sakenfeld, ed., *The New Interpreter's Dictionary of the Bible,* Vol. 4, pp. 841–852. Nashville: Abingdon Press, 2009. Examines the letter's historical background, purpose, and theological contents.

Sanders, E. P. *Paul and Palestinian Judaism.* Philadelphia: Fortress Press, 1978. An important scholarly study of Paul's relationship to rabbinic Judaism.

———. *Paul, the Law and the Jewish People.* Philadelphia: Fortress Press, 1983.

Soards, M. J.; Sampley, J. P.; and Wright, N. T., eds. *Romans–First Corinthians, The New Interpreter's Bible,* Vol. 10. Nashville: Abingdon Press, 2000. Provides extensive commentary.

Watson, Francis. *Paul, Judaism, and the Gentiles: Beyond the New Perspective,* rev. ed. Grand Rapids, Mich.: Eerdmans, 2007. A perceptive sociological approach.

Westerholm, Stephen. *Perspectives Old and New on Paul: The "Lutheran" Paul and His Critics.* Grand Rapids, Mich.: Eerdmans, 2004. A thorough review of recent Pauline scholarship on the relationship of Jewish law and Christian faith.

Witherington, Ben, III, and Hyatt, Darlene. *Paul's Letter to the Romans: A Socio-Rhetorical Commentary.* Grand Rapids, Mich.: Eerdmans, 2004.

Wright, N. T. *Justification: God's Plan and Paul's Vision.* Downers Grove, Ill.: InterVarsity Press, 2009. Argues that through the "faithfulness of Christ" God gathers believers into his covenant with Abraham.

———. *Paul: In Fresh Perspective.* Minneapolis: Fortress Press, 2006. Approaches Paul's doctrine of justification in the context of first-century Jewish theology. For more advanced students.

Yinger, Kent L. *The New Perspective on Paul: An Introduction.* Eugene, Ore.: Wipf and Stock Pub, 2011. A lucid and balanced exposition on scholars' recent interpretations of Paul's attitude toward Mosaic law and Christian faith.

CHAPTER 16

Letters from Prison

Philippians and Philemon

He [Jesus] did not think to snatch at equality with God, but made himself nothing, assuming the nature of a slave. Philippians 2:6–7

Key Topics/Themes Although it contains some sharp criticism of his opponents, Paul's letter to the Philippian church reveals an unusual warmth and friendliness in general. Urging cooperation for the mutual benefit of all believers, Paul cites an early hymn that depicts Jesus as the opposite of Adam—a humbly obedient son whose self-emptying leads to his heavenly exaltation.

The apostle's only surviving personal letter, Philemon shows Paul accepting the Greco-Roman institution of slavery while simultaneously emphasizing that Christians of all social classes are intimately related in love.

According to an early church tradition, Paul wrote four canonical letters while imprisoned in Rome—Ephesians, Philippians, Colossians, and Philemon. Known as the "captivity letters," they were long believed to represent the apostle's most mature reflections on such topics as the divine nature of Christ (Phil. 2:5–11; Col. 1:13–20; 2:9–15) and the mystic unity of the church (Eph. 1–5).

Rigorous scholarly analysis of the four works, however, has raised serious questions about the time and place of their composition, as well as the authorship of two of them. All leading scholars accept Philippians and Philemon as genuinely Pauline, but many (perhaps more than half) challenge Paul's authorship of Colossians. Even more deny that he wrote Ephesians, a work that differs in content, tone, and style from the apostle's accepted letters.

Because so many scholars question Paul's responsibility for Colossians, we discuss it among the disputed letters in Chapter 17. (For scholarly arguments defending or denying Pauline authorship of these works, see the "Recommended Reading" at the end of Chapter 17.)

Place of Origin

Scholars pose various objections to the traditional belief that Paul wrote Philippians and the other letters while under house arrest in Rome (Acts 28). In the apostles' day, traveling the almost 800 miles between Rome and **Philippi,** located in northeastern Greece, took as long as ten months (see Figure 16.1). Philippians implies that Paul's friends

FIGURE 16.1 Potential sites where Paul wrote his "prison letters." Paul may have written these letters in Rome (in the far west on this map), in Ephesus (on the coast of present-day Turkey), or in Caesarea (in the far eastern Mediterranean). Note that Ephesus is much closer to Philippi than either of the other two cities.

made four journeys between Philippi and his place of imprisonment and that a fifth trip was planned (Phil. 2:25–26). Some scholars consider the distance separating these two cities too great to travel so frequently. They propose Ephesus, a city where Paul spent three years (Acts 20:31) and that is only about ten days' travel time from Philippi, as the place of origin. Philippians' references to the Praetorian Guard, the Roman emperor's personal militia (1:13), and "the imperial establishment" (4:22) do not necessarily mean that the letter originated in Rome. Ancient inscriptions recently discovered in Ephesus show that members of the Praetorian Guard and other imperial officials were stationed in the Roman province of Asia, where Ephesus and Colossae are located.

Although many scholars support the "Ephesian theory," others suggest that Paul wrote from Caesarea, where he was imprisoned

for two years (Acts 23–25). Still other critics point out that we lack proof that Paul was actually jailed in Ephesus; they also claim that the difficulties in traveling between Macedonia and Rome have been overstated. Where Paul was imprisoned remains an open question, although many commentators still uphold the traditional view that Paul's prison letters emanate from the Roman capital (see Figure 16.2).

Letter to the Philippians

Paul enjoyed an unusually warm and affectionate relationship with Christians at Philippi. He and Timothy had established the church during their first tour of Greece (Acts 16:11–40), and he maintained an intimate communication

FIGURE 16.2 *St. Paul in Prison.* In this painting by Rembrandt (1606–1669), Paul sits in his murky cell, composing letters to inspire faith and hope in the membership of his tiny, scattered churches. Notice that the light from the cell's barred window seems to emanate from Paul himself, surrounding his head like a halo and glowing from the pages of the manuscripts he holds.

with the Philippians, who were the only group from whom he would accept financial support (4:15–16). In welcome contrast to the "boasting" and threats that characterize the letters to Corinth and Galatia, Philippians contains no impassioned defense of his authority, undoubtedly because his friends in Philippi did not question it. The author instead exposes a more kindly and loving aspect of his personality.

Like all genuinely Pauline letters, Philippians reveals the author's quick changes of mood, ranging from a personal meditation on the meaning of his impending death to a brief but savage attack on his opponents. The letter features so many abrupt changes of subject and shifts in tone that many analysts believe it to be, like 2 Corinthians, a composite work, containing parts of three or four different missives.

Philippians

Author: Paul.

Audience: Congregation at Philippi in north-eastern Greece.

Date and place of composition: About 56 CE if from Ephesus, 61–62 if from Rome, or 58–60 if from Caesarea (dating depends on the location of Paul's imprisonment).

Occasion or purpose: To express his friendship with the Philippians and to thank them for their monetary support.

According to this theory, the note thanking the Philippians for their financial help (4:10–20 or 23) was composed first, followed by a letter warning the church about potential troublemakers (partially preserved in 1:1–3:1a and 4:2–9). A third letter bitterly attacks advocates of circumcision (3:1b–4:1). The letter may be a single composition, however, for Paul commonly leaps from topic to topic, registering different emotional responses to different problems in the course of a single letter.

Philippians is important not only for the insight it permits into Paul's volatile character but also for the clues it gives to early Christian beliefs about Jesus' nature. The key passage appears in Philippians 2:5–11, in which Paul seems to quote an early Christian hymn celebrating Jesus' humble obedience and subsequent exaltation.

Organization

Philippians covers a variety of topics, but it can be divided into six relatively brief units:

1. Salutation and thanksgiving (1:1–11)
2. Paul's meditation on his imprisonment (1:12–30)
3. An exhortation to humility, in imitation of Christ's example (2:1–18)
4. The recommendation of Timothy and Epaphroditus (2:19–3:1a)
5. An attack on advocates of circumcision and an exhortation to live harmoniously, in imitation of Paul (3:1b–4:9)
6. A note of thanks for financial help (4:10–23)

The Significance of Paul's Imprisonment

After affectionately greeting the Philippians (1:1–11), Paul explores the significance of his prison experience and courageously underscores its positive effects. Apparently widely talked about, his case gives other believers the opportunity to witness publicly for Christ. At the same time, not all of Paul's fellow Christians support him; they use his imprisonment as a means of stirring up new troubles for the prisoner. Paul does not identify those Christians whose personal jealousies complicate his already difficult situation, but they may have been connected with the "advocates of circumcision" denounced in chapter 3. In Acts' narration of Paul's arrest, imprisonment in Caesarea, and transportation to Rome under armed guard, the Jerusalem church leadership is conspicuously absent from his defense. Perhaps those who shared James's adherence to Torah obligations were in some degree pleased to see Paul and his questionable views under legal restraint.

Paul's attitude toward his troublesome rivals is far milder than it is in Galatians. Determined to find positive results even in his opponents' activities, Paul adopts a stoic detachment and concludes that their motives, whether sincere or hypocritical, are finally irrelevant: They successfully proclaim the Christian message (1:12–18).

As he contemplates the possibility of his execution, Paul is torn between wishing to live for his friends' sake and wishing to "depart and be with Christ," thereby attaining a posthumous union with his Lord while awaiting resurrection (see 1 Cor. 15). Paul places himself on a par with his beloved Philippians when he states that they run the same race as he to win life's ultimate prize (1:19–30). Despite his ceaseless efforts, Paul remains aware of his imperfection and explicitly states that he is not yet certain of victory (3:10–14).

The Hymn to Christ

Chapter 2 contains the letter's most important theological concept. Urging the Philippians to place others' welfare before their own, Paul cites

Jesus' behavior as the supreme example of humble service to others. To encourage his readers to emulate the same self-denying attitude that Jesus displayed, he recites a hymn that illustrates his intent. The rhythmic and poetic qualities of this work, as well as the absence of typically Pauline ideas and vocabulary, suggest that it is a pre-Pauline composition. The first stanza reads as follows:

> Who though he was in the form of God,
> Did not count equality with God
> A thing to be grasped,
> But emptied himself,
> Taking the form of a servant,
> Being born in the likeness of men.
>
> And being found in human form
> He humbled himself
> And became obedient unto death.
>
> (2:6–8, Revised Standard Version)

The hymn's second stanza (2:9–11) describes how God rewards Jesus' selfless obedience by granting him universal lordship, elevating him to heaven, thereby glorifying "God, the Father."

In this famous passage, which has been translated in various ways to highlight different theories about Christ's divinity, Jesus' relation to the Father is ambiguously stated. Since the fourth century CE, when the church officially adopted the doctrine of the Trinity, it has commonly been assumed that the hymn refers to Jesus' prehuman existence and affirms the Son's co-eternity and co-equality with the Father. (See Box 16.1 for different ways of translating Philippians 2.)

Remembering Paul's explicit subordination of Jesus to God in 1 Corinthians (15:24–28), many readers will be cautious about attributing post–New Testament ideas to the apostle. A growing number of scholars believe that Paul employs the hymn in order implicitly to contrast two "sons" of God—Adam (Luke 3:38) and Jesus. (The Adam–Christ contrast figures prominently in 1 Corinthians 15:21–23, 45–49, and in Romans 5:12–19.) The mention of "form" (Greek, *morphe*) refers to the divine image that both Adam and Jesus reflect (Gen. 1:26–28). But whereas Adam tried to seize God-like status (Gen. 3:5), Jesus takes the form of a slave. Instead of rebelling against the Creator, he is fully obedient unto death.

Finally, Adam's disobedience brings shame and death, but Jesus' total obedience brings glory and exaltation. Jesus' self-emptying earns him the fullness of God's reward, the bestowal of "the name above all names," to whom all creation submits. In accordance with his usual method of using theology to impart behavioral instruction, Paul implicitly compares the reward given to Jesus for his humility with that in store for humbly obedient Christians. Now shining like "stars in a dark world," they will inherit a future life similar to that which Jesus now enjoys (2:14–18). (For a lucid discussion of the Adam–Christ contrast, see Dewey et al. in "Recommended Reading.")

Recommendations of Timothy and Epaphroditus

The references to Timothy and Epaphroditus, two of his favorite companions, suggest Paul's warm capacity for friendship. **Timothy,** whose name appears as courtesy coauthor of this letter (1:1), is one of Paul's most reliable associates. Unlike Barnabas and John Mark, with whom Paul quarreled, Timothy (who is half Jewish and half Greek) shares Paul's positive attitude toward Gentile converts. In the apostle's absence, Paul trusts him to act as he would (2:19–24).

Epaphroditus, whom the Philippians had sent to assist Paul in prison, has apparently touched Paul by the depth of his personal devotion. Epaphroditus's dangerous illness, which delayed his return to Philippi, may have resulted from his helping the prisoner. Paul implies his gratitude when urging the Philippians to give Epaphroditus an appreciative welcome home (2:25–3:1a).

Paul's concern for individual believers in Philippi is also apparent in his personal message for two estranged women, Euodia and Syntyche. Pleading with sensitivity and tact for their reconciliation, he ranks the two women as co-workers who share his efforts to promote the gospel (4:2–3).

BOX 16.1   Comparative Translations of the Hymn in Philippians 2

Unlike the two other great monotheistic religions, Judaism and Islam, Christianity traditionally expresses its ideas and insights in formal doctrines. During the first three or four centuries CE, Christian teachers were bitterly divided on the precise way to define Jesus' divine nature and his relationship to God. Whereas some Christians argued that Jesus was subordinate to the Father, others insisted that he was co-equal and co-eternal with God. The view that Jesus and God were the same Being eventually prevailed and was formulated in the concept of the Trinity, a doctrine articulated in the famous Nicene Creed.

Throughout the long controversy, both sides cited Paul's letter to the church at Philippi to support their conflicting arguments. In the second chapter of Philippians, Paul apparently quotes a pre-Pauline Christian hymn praising Jesus' example of humble obedience to the Father, a willing submission to the divine will that led to his death and posthumous exaltation. Understanding exactly what the hymn states about Jesus' relation to God—whether in a prehuman heavenly existence he was "equal to God"—depends largely on how one interprets a crucial Greek verb, which translators render in a variety of ways, giving different theological meanings to the text. The King James Version provides a traditional wording consistent with the orthodox belief that Jesus is the Second Person of the Trinity, whereas most modern translations reflect the ambiguity of the passage. (To avoid repetition, the second stanza is omitted in several examples. The key phrases for theological interpretation are placed in italics.)

PHILIPPIANS 2:5–11
KING JAMES VERSION

Let this mind be in you, which was also in Christ Jesus: *who, being in the form of God, thought it not robbery to be equal with God:* but made himself of no reputation, and took upon him the form of a servant, and was made in the likeness of men: and being found in fashion as a man, he humbled himself, and became obedient unto death, even the death of the cross. Wherefore God also hath highly exalted him, and given him a name which is above every name: that at the name of Jesus every knee should bow, of *things* in heaven, and *things* in earth, and *things* under the earth; and *that* every tongue should confess that Jesus Christ *is* Lord, to the glory of God the Father.

NEW AMERICAN BIBLE

Your attitude must be that of Christ.
Though he was in the form of God,
   he did not deem equality with God
   something to be grasped at.
Rather, he emptied himself
   and took the form of a slave,
   being born in the likeness of men.

He was known to be of human estate,
   and it was thus that he humbled himself,
   obediently accepting even death,
   death on a cross!

Because of this,
   God highly exalted him
   and bestowed on him the name
   above every other name,

Attacking Advocates of Circumcision

In chapter 3, flashes of Paul's old fire give his words a keen edge. This section (3:1b–20), which is thought to have originated as a separate memorandum, attacks Judaizers who insist on circumcising Gentile converts. Denouncing circumcision as "mutilation," he contemptuously dismisses his opponents as "dogs"—the common Jewish tag for the uncircumcised.

Paul provides valuable autobiographical information when he cites his ethnic qualifications—superior to those of his enemies—to evaluate the advantages of being a Jew. Despite his exemplary credentials—and his scrupulousness in keeping the Torah regulations—he discounts his Jewish heritage as "garbage." All human advantages are worthless when compared to the new life God gives in Christ (3:1–11).

So that at Jesus' name
  every knee must bend
  in the heavens, on the earth,
  and under the earth,
  and every tongue proclaim
  to the glory of God the Father:
  Jesus Christ Is Lord!

but made himself nothing,
  taking the very nature of a servant,
  being made in human likeness.
And being found in appearance as a man,
  he humbled himself
  and became obedient to death—even death on
  a cross! . . .

NEW REVISED STANDARD VERSION

Let the same mind be in you that was in Christ Jesus,
  who, *though he was in the form of God,*
  did not regard equality with God
  as something to be exploited,
but emptied himself, taking the form of a slave,
  being born in human likeness.
And being found in human form,
  he humbled himself
  and became obedient to the point of death—
  even death on a cross.

REVISED ENGLISH BIBLE

Take to heart among yourselves what you find in
Christ Jesus: *He was in the form of God; yet he laid no*
claim to equality with God, but made himself nothing, assuming the form of a slave. Bearing the human likeness, sharing the human lot, he
humbled himself, and was obedient, even to the
point of death, death on a cross! . . .

NEW INTERNATIONAL VERSION

Your attitude should be the same as that of Christ
  Jesus:
  Who, being in very nature God,
    did not consider equality with God something to be
    grasped,

NEW JERUSALEM BIBLE

Make your own the mind of Christ Jesus:
  Who, being in the form of God,
  did not count equality with God
  something to be grasped.

But he emptied himself,
taking the form of a slave,
becoming as human beings are;

and being in every way like a human being,
he was humbler yet,
even to accepting death, death on a cross. . . .

SCHOLAR'S VERSION

[You should] think in the same way that the
  Anointed Jesus did, who
although he was born in the image of God,
  did not regard "being like God"
  as something to use for his own advantage,
  but rid himself of such vain pretension
  and accepted a servant's lot.
Since he was born like all human beings
and proved to belong to humankind,
he recognized his true status
and became trustfully obedient all the way to death,
even to death by crucifixion.

Letter to Philemon

Consisting of a single chapter, Philemon is a
short letter dealing with a large topic—the relationship of Christian slaveholders to their
human property. Contemporary readers are typically shocked that Paul, who had proclaimed
the essential equality of all believers united in
Christ (Gal. 3:28), does not use this occasion to
denounce the institution of slavery as totally incompatible with Christian faith. Although Paul
does not condemn the practice of buying and
selling human beings—probably because he
believes that the Greco-Roman world order
will soon end—he does argue persuasively for
a new relationship between master and slave.
He asks the slave owner, **Philemon,** to accept

Philemon

Author: Paul.

Audience: Philemon's house church, probably at Colossae in western Asia Minor.

Date and place of composition: About 55–56 CE if from Ephesus, 61–63 if from Rome, or 58–60 if from Caesarea (dating depends on the location of Paul's imprisonment).

Occasion or purpose: To reconcile Philemon with one of his slaves, Onesimus, and perhaps to secure Onesimus's services for himself.

his runaway slave, **Onesimus,** as a "beloved brother," thereby establishing a new bond of kinship humanely linking Christian owners and their human chattel.

Unfortunately for enslaved persons, the divine intervention into human history that Paul expected to occur in his own day did not happen. Israel's Messiah did not reappear to overthrow unjust governments and set up a divinely empowered kingdom in which transformed believers would enjoy the full social and racial equality that Paul had envisioned. To the contrary, as late as the pre–Civil War United States (1860), Southern clergy and slaveholders continued to cite Paul's letter to Philemon as scriptural justification for their "peculiar institution" of legally sanctioned slave labor. The historical consequences of Paul's brief missive to his friend Philemon give this personal note an extraordinary importance (see Harrill in "Recommended Reading").

The Question of Slavery

In seeking out Paul's purpose in writing this letter, it is helpful to realize that it is addressed not only to Philemon but also to "Apphia our sister, and Archippus our comerade-in-arms, and the congregation at your house" in the town of Colossae (v. 2; because Philemon has only one chapter, all citations refer to verse numbers). Although the letter's main body (vv. 4–24) speaks directly to Philemon (the Greek pronoun "you" is singular throughout this section), the text was clearly intended to be read aloud to the whole congregation meeting in Philemon's house. (Apphia may have been the host's wife, and Archippus their son.)

Because the exact circumstances that prompted Paul to write his only surviving personal letter are not clear, scholars differ in their reconstruction of the situation involving Onesimus and his master. According to one plausible interpretation, Onesimus had stolen money or other property from Philemon. Somehow he then made his way from Colossae to Rome or Ephesus (if that is where Paul was imprisoned), where the apostle converted him to Christianity. Paul therefore speaks of Onesimus as "my child, whose father I have become" (by imparting to him the life-giving faith in Christ) (v. 10). Some recent commentators, however, think it highly unlikely that Onesimus happened to encounter Paul by pure chance. More likely, they suggest, Onesimus—after having displeased his master—deliberately set out to find Paul and enlist his aid in reconciling with Philemon, whom the apostle had earlier converted to the faith. According to widely accepted Roman legal practice, a third party could settle disputes between masters and slaves, and Paul may have filled that role. Punning on the meaning of Onesimus's Greek name ("useful"), Paul writes to Philemon that the slave was "once so little use to you, but now useful indeed, both to you and to me" (v. 11).

Although Onesimus had made himself almost indispensable to the imprisoned apostle, Paul—perhaps compelled by Roman law—decides to send the slave back to his master. Maintaining a fine balance between exercising his apostolic authority and appealing to the equality existing among all Christians, Paul asks Philemon to receive Onesimus back, treating him "no longer as a slave, but as more than a slave—as a dear brother, very dear indeed to me and how much dearer to you" (v. 16). We do not know if Paul is thereby requesting the master to free Onesimus, granting him legal and social status to match his Christian freedom, but the writer clearly underscores the slave's human value. Paul writes that Onesimus is "part of myself" and that Philemon should welcome him as he would the apostle himself (vv. 12, 17).

Paul also gives his guarantee to reimburse Philemon for any debt Onesimus may have incurred, or perhaps money he may have embezzled or stolen (vv. 18–20). Appealing to Philemon's reputation for showing love to his fellow Christians (vv. 4–6), Paul gently pressures the slave owner to be generous, anticipating that Philemon "will in fact do better than I ask" (vv. 20–21). Is Paul asking Philemon, in a not-too-subtle way, to free Onesimus in order for him to remain in Paul's service?

Having invoked his apostolic authority and addressed his letter so that it will be read before the entire congregation at Colossae (which will expect Philemon to live up to his saintly reputation and give Onesimus a loving welcome?), Paul adds a final element of persuasion at the letter's close. As if penning an afterthought, Paul says that he now expects to be freed from his prison and will pay Philemon a personal visit (v. 22), an apostolic parousia ensuring that his requests will be honored. He concludes with greetings from, among others, Mark and Luke, traditional authors of the two Gospels bearing their respective names.

Slavery in Context

Most readers today are deeply disappointed that Paul does not reject slavery outright as an intolerable evil. Instead, he advises slaves not to be "trouble[d]" about their status, advising them to remain in whatever social "condition" they had when they first became Christians (1 Cor. 7:17–24). Paul's reasons for accepting the slave–master arrangement even in Christian society probably derive from his expectation that Jesus would soon return.

But other factors also influenced Paul's lack of interest in abolishing slavery or reforming other unjust social customs. In its acceptance of slavery, the Hebrew Bible differs little from the Greco-Roman society in which Paul lived. The Torah does, however, distinguish between Gentile slaves captured in battle and native-born Israelites who sold themselves or their children to pay off financial debts. In a passage known as the "Book of the Covenant," Mosaic Law decrees that after six years' servitude a male Hebrew slave is to be set free. Any children born to him and one of his master's female slaves, however, are to remain the master's property. If at the end of six years' time the freed man wishes to remain with his wife and family, he must submit to a mutilation of his ear (the organ of obedience) and remain a slave for life (Exod. 21:2–6). This legal statute clearly favors slave owners' "rights."

Following Torah regulations—and the institutions of Greco-Roman society at large—New Testament writers neither condemn slavery nor predict its abolition. Only after the scientific Enlightenment of the eighteenth century CE was the persistence of slavery seen as inconsistent with the ethical principles of Christian freedom and with the innate worth of all humans as "images" of God. In American history, both pro- and antislavery parties used the New Testament to support their conflicting views. Slavery's proponents argued that biblical writers, including Paul, accepted the institution as a "natural" condition. Focusing on Paul's doctrines of freedom and Christian equality (Gal. 3:28), slavery's opponents eventually persuaded the Western world to grant a corresponding social and legal freedom to all people.

Paul's Lasting Influence

During his lifetime, Paul fought constantly to win other Christians' recognition that his gospel and claim to apostleship were legitimate. Even his own churches frequently challenged his authority and doubted his view that humans receive salvation through God's free gift, accepted in faith rather than through obedience to the biblical Torah. Ironically, in the decades following his death—as the church rapidly changed from a mostly Jewish to a largely Gentile institution—Paul was recognized as chief among the missionary apostles, and his doctrine became the basis for much of the church's theology.

FIGURE 16.3 Locations of the major churches at the end of Paul's ministry (c. 62 CE). Most of the tiny cells of Christians are at the eastern end of the Mediterranean (Palestine and Syria) or in Asia Minor (present-day Turkey). Paul established many of the churches in western Asia Minor, as well as the first churches in Greece (Philippi to Corinth). We do not know who founded the Italian churches, including the one in Rome. How or when Christianity was introduced to Egypt (Alexandria) or to other sites in Africa (Cyrene) is also unknown.

By the mid-second century, when the document known as 2 Peter was written, Paul's collected letters had assumed the authority of Scripture, at least in some Christian circles. At the same time, Paul's difficult ideas and sometimes ambiguous phrasing left his work open to a variety of interpretations. The author of 2 Peter denounces students of Paul who interpret Pauline thought in a way contrary to official church teaching:

> [Paul] wrote to you with his inspired wisdom.
> And so he does in all his other letters, . . .
> though they contain some obscure passages,
> which the ignorant and unstable misinterpret
> to their own ruin, as they do the other
> scriptures.
>
> (2 Pet. 3:16)

Now, as then, believers may find it easy to disagree on Paul's intentions in many "obscure passages."

Paul's Accomplishments

In a characteristic remark, Paul observes that he works harder than any other apostle to bring the Christian message to potential converts (2 Cor. 11:23). Even today, the enormous distances he traveled, by sea and on foot, would challenge the physical stamina of the most dedicated missionaries. He established Christian "colonies" throughout Syria, Asia Minor, Macedonia, and Greece and left behind an impressive network of churches (see Figure 16.3). These were interconnected by itinerant missionaries (many trained by Paul himself) and at least partly united by memories of Paul's preaching and his voluminous written legacy. As the author of Acts realized, Paul also made himself a formidable model for later believers to emulate.

Paul—Christianity's First Great Interpreter of Christ

In introducing Pauline thought (in Chapter 13), we listed some of the assumptions and personal experiences, such as his mystical encounter with the risen Christ, that helped shape Paul's distinctive ideas about God's changed relationship to humanity, Jew and Gentile alike. In assessing his legacy, we can briefly review several of Paul's most enduring contributions, teachings that have influenced the church for almost two millennia.

Although not a systematic thinker, Paul was the first to create a coherent theology about Jesus and is thus counted as Christianity's first theologian. In interpreting Jesus' career theologically—showing how God (*theos*) revealed his will through Jesus' death and resurrection—Paul laid the foundations on which later interpreters of the "Christ event" built. We have space here to summarize only a few of Paul's main ideas. The ones we select illustrate the general trend of his views on the nature of God and his purpose in using Jesus to reconcile the previously alienated human and divine components of the universe.

God As a "Hebrew born and bred" (Phil. 3:5), Paul is unquestionably a monotheist, recognizing the Jewish God as the entire world's sovereign and judge. Steeped in the Hebrew Bible's composite portrait of Yahweh, Paul regards God as embodying human traits on a superhuman scale. Both "severe" and "kind," he manifests his dual nature to humankind, alternately condemning or showing mercy according to his irresistible will. He is incomparably holy, just, and pure; his perfect justice does not allow full communion with imperfect, deliberately unjust, and otherwise sinful humanity. As supreme patron and benefactor, however, he sets in motion the process of reconciling an estranged human creation to himself.

The Role of Jesus Paul realized that his fellow Jews expected an undefeated Messiah and that Jesus' crucifixion was a major "stumbling block" to Jewish acceptance. He therefore formulated a theology of the cross. In Romans and Galatians, he interprets the Crucifixion as a redemptive act in which human "weakness"—Jesus' "shameful" death—is the means by which God bridges the great moral gulf between himself and humanity. Demonstrating absolute obedience to the divine will, Jesus sacrifices his life to satisfy God's justice and obtain forgiveness for others.

Justification By "justification" Paul means being "made righteous" or having a right standing or relationship with God. Keeping the Mosaic Torah cannot justify people because the Torah only serves to make them aware of lawbreaking, of committing "sin" (*hamartia*), of falling short of ethical perfection. When he died voluntarily, Jesus not only took on himself the Law's penalty for all sinners but also transferred just punishment to sin itself. He thus rid sin of its power to operate uncontrolled in what Paul calls our "fleshly" (physical) or "lower" nature (Rom. 1–4; 7–8).

Adam and Christ In Paul's view of human history, the earthly prototype—Adam—willfully disobeyed God, thus separating himself from life's source and bringing sin (error) and death to himself and all his descendants. In Jesus, God found Adam's moral opposite, a man of perfect obedience who achieved a right relationship with God and through his resurrection became God's Son (Rom. 1:4). Now the model of a renewed humanity reconciled to God, Jesus as Christ brings life to all who place their trust (faith) in him (Rom. 5; 1 Cor. 15), thereby imitating the loyalty or "faithfulness" of Jesus himself.

Salvation Through Faith The idea that humans are saved by their faith is one of Paul's most distinctive and revolutionary ideas. By "faith," Paul does not mean belief in a creed or a set of religious doctrines. For Paul, faith is a dynamic force that motivates a confidence and trust that Israel's God, humanity's great benefactor, willingly justifies believers through Christ, bringing even Gentiles into a covenant relationship with him. Whether it is the loyalty or "faithfulness *of* Christ," his perfect submission to the divine will, or believers' "faith *in* Christ['s]" saving power, Jesus is the cosmic agent who reconciles humankind to God. Because God, the divine patron, grants his rewards freely, a person can neither earn nor deserve them. Hence, the regulations of the Torah—including circumcision and food purity laws—are irrelevant.

God and Christ Although he calls the glorified Jesus "lord" (Greek, *kyrios*) and assigns him the highest possible status in God's plan for universal redemption, Paul remains a Jewish monotheist, always regarding the Son as subordinate to the Father (1 Cor. 15:24–28). Jesus refuses to attempt "equality with God" and is eternally the model of humble submission to the paternal will (Phil. 2:6–7). In some metaphysical sense, however, the Son is the agent by whom God created the universe, in whom "the complete being of the Godhead dwells embodied" and through whom the divine purpose is revealed (Col. 1–2). As human beings were originally created in God's "image" (Gen. 1:27), so Christ is that divine–human image perfected (Col. 1:15). (Even if not by Paul, these passages in Colossians express a Pauline **Christology.**)

Eschatology Because he believes that he is living at the very edge of the New Age that Jesus' advent introduced, Paul places much of his ethical instruction to the church in the context of End time. Jesus' resurrection and ascension to heaven now allow Christ's Spirit to dwell in each believer, giving him or her charismatic gifts of prophesying, healing, teaching, and speaking in or interpreting ecstatic language.

Paul regards these spiritual gifts as further evidence of the "last days" and urges believers to produce the Spirit's good fruits—steadfast loyalty and a grateful awareness that in Christ they attain a new nature. Thus, they are prepared for the "splendor" of the resurrection body they will receive at the Parousia.

Summary

This brief survey, concentrating on Paul's vision of God's plan to redeem humanity through Christ, does scant justice to the range and profundity of Pauline thought. The apostle's views on free will and predestination, Christian ethics, the church, human sexuality, and related matters merit fuller discussion than we can offer here.

Embattled in his own day, within two generations after his death Paul became a monument of orthodoxy (correct teaching) to many church leaders. The letters to Timothy and Titus, written in Paul's name by a later disciple, show in what high regard the apostle was held (see Chapter 17). After another 1,400 years had passed, Paul again became a center of controversy. During the Protestant Reformation, conflicting interpretations of the Pauline belief that human beings are saved by faith and not by works (including the performance of sacramental rituals) deeply divided Roman Catholics and Protestants. Today, Paul remains a stimulating, dynamic influence wherever the New Testament is read. Second only to Jesus in his lasting influence on Christendom, he is the prism through which Jesus' image is most commonly viewed.

Questions for Review

1. Why is it difficult to know exactly where Paul was imprisoned when he wrote to Philemon and the church at Philippi?
2. Although the hymn Paul cites in Philippians 2 is commonly interpreted as describing Jesus' prehuman existence, many commentators believe that it contains instead an implied contrast between Adam's disobedience and Jesus' humble obedience. Summarize the arguments for and against these differing interpretations.

3. Identify Philemon and Onesimus and their connection to Paul. Why do you think Paul does not condemn human slavery as an evil institution?

4. Summarize Paul's major contributions to Christian thought, including his beliefs about the *eschaton,* his teachings about the nature and function of Christ (Christology), and his doctrine of justification by faith.

Question for Discussion and Reflection

1. Like all historical figures, Paul is firmly linked to his particular time and place. On many issues, such as the restricted role of women and a hierarchical view of society, Paul reflects the accepted norms of his day. Writing as a former Pharisee who believed that the crucified Messiah would soon return to judge the world, bringing human history to an end, Paul often fails to address such important issues as the evils of slavery, widespread poverty, and governmental injustice. Do you think that if Paul were alive today—and fully aware of the past 1,900 years of human development—he would revise his opinions on such topics as master–slave relationships, celibacy, homosexuality, and unquestioning submission to governmental authorities? If they had followed Paul's advice in Romans 13, could the leaders of the American Revolution have framed the Declaration of Independence or broken free of British control?

Terms and Concepts to Remember

Christology	Philemon
Epaphroditus	Philippi
Onesimus	Timothy

Recommended Reading

Ascough, Richard S. "Philippians." In M. D. Coogan, ed., *The Oxford Encyclopedia of the Books of the Bible,* Vol. 2, pp. 167–170. New York: Oxford University Press, 2011. Includes scholarly speculations about where Paul was imprisoned and about the letter's composite nature.

Byrne, Brendan. "The Letter to the Philippians." In R. E. Brown et al., eds., *The New Jerome Biblical Commentary,* 2nd ed., pp. 791–797. Englewood Cliffs, N.J.: Prentice-Hall, 1990.

Dewey, Arthur J.; Hoover, Roy W.; McGaughy, Lane C.; and Schmidt, Daryl D., eds., "Paul's Correspondence to the Philippians." In *The Authentic Letters of Paul: A New Reading of Paul's Rhetoric and Meaning,* pp. 165–196. Salem, Ore.: Polebridge Press, 2010. Includes a perceptive reading of the Christ–Adam contrast in the famous hymn.

Fitzmyer, Joseph A. *The Letter to Philemon: A New Translation with Introduction and Commentary.* Anchor Bible. New York: Doubleday, 2000. A detailed analysis by a major scholar.

Harrill, J. Albert. "Philemon, Letter to." In K. D. Sakenfeld, ed., *The New Interpreter's Dictionary of the Bible,* Vol. 4, pp. 497–499. Nashville: Abingdon Press, 2009. Includes discussion of pre–Civil War U.S. Supreme Court decisions that cite Philemon to affirm the legality of racial slavery.

Holloway, Paul A. *Consolation in Philippians: Philosophical Sources and Rhetorical Strategies.* Albany, N.Y.: Cambridge University Press, 2007. Proposes that Paul uses Stoic ideas and rhetoric to "console" suffering believers through rational argument.

Knox, John. *Philemon Among the Letters of Paul,* rev. ed., New York: Abingdon Press, 1959. Develops Edgar Goodspeed's theory that about 90 CE a Paulinist—perhaps the former slave Onesimus, who may then have been bishop of Ephesus—collected Paul's letters and circulated them among the entire church.

Martin, R. P.; and Hawthorne, G. F. *Philippians,* rev. ed., World Biblical Commentary 43. Nashville: Thomas Nelson, 2004.

Saunders, Stanley P. "Philippians, Letter to." In K. D. Sakenfeld, ed., *The New Interpreter's Dictionary of the Bible,* Vol. 4, pp. 503–507. Nashville: Abingdon Press, 2009. A conventional description of the letter's contents.

Silva, Moises. *Philippians,* 2nd ed. Baker Exegetical Commentary on the New Testament. Grand Rapids, Mich.: Baker Academic, 2005.

Wright, N. T. *The Epistles of Paul to the Colossians and Philemon.* Tyndale New Testament Commentaries. Downers Grove, Ill.: InterVarsity Press Academic, 2007. Explores the slavery issue.

CHAPTER 17

Continuing the Pauline Tradition

2 Thessalonians, Colossians, Ephesians, and the Pastoral Epistles

*Stand firm . . . and hold fast to the traditions which you have
learned from us by word or letter.* 2 Thessalonians 2:15

*Keep before you an outline of the sound teaching which you heard from me. . . .
Guard the treasure [apostolic tradition] put into our charge.* 2 Timothy 1:13–14

Key Topics/Themes Paul's continuing influence on the church was so great after his death that various Pauline disciples composed letters in his name and spirit, claiming his authority to settle new issues besetting the Christian community. Whereas a minority of scholars defend Pauline authorship of 2 Thessalonians and Colossians, a large majority are certain that he did not write Ephesians, 1 or 2 Timothy, or Titus.

Repeating themes from Paul's genuine letter to the Thessalonians, 2 Thessalonians reinterprets Paul's original eschatology, asserting that a number of traditional apocalyptic "signs" must precede the *eschaton*.

In Colossians, a close Pauline disciple emphasizes Jesus' identification with the cosmic power and wisdom by and for which the universe was created. The divine "secret" is revealed as Christ's Spirit dwelling in the believer. A deutero-Pauline composition, Ephesians contains ideas similar to those in Colossians, revising and updating Pauline concepts about God's universal plan of salvation for both Jews and Gentiles and about believers' spiritual warfare with supernatural evil.

Writing to Timothy and Titus as symbols of a new generation of Christians, an anonymous disciple (known as the Pastor) warns his readers against false teachings (heresy). He urges them to adhere strictly to the original apostolic traditions, supported by the Hebrew Bible and the church.

Six canonical letters in which the author explicitly identifies himself as Paul, Apostle to the Gentiles, contain discrepancies that cause scholars to question their Pauline authorship. Two of the letters—2 Thessalonians and Colossians—are still vigorously disputed, with a large minority

championing their authenticity. But an overwhelming scholarly majority deny that Paul wrote the four others—Ephesians, 1 and 2 Timothy, and Titus. The latter three are called the **pastoral epistles** because the writer—as a pastor or shepherd—offers guidance and advice to his flock, the church.

According to tradition, Paul wrote 2 Thessalonians shortly after his first letter to believers at Thessalonica, and Ephesians and Colossians while imprisoned in Rome. After being released, he traveled to Crete, only to be thrown again in prison a second time (2 Tim.). During this second and final incarceration, the apostle supposedly composed these farewell letters to his trusted associates, Timothy and Titus, young men who represent a new generation of Christian leadership.

Since the eighteenth century, however, scholars have increasingly doubted Paul's responsibility for either Ephesians or the pastorals. More recently, they have also suspected that both 2 Thessalonians and Colossians are the work of later authors who adopted Paul's persona. Detailed analyses of four of the six documents—Ephesians and the pastorals—strongly indicate that they were composed significantly after Paul's time.

The Problem of Pseudonymity

The author of 2 Thessalonians tells his readers not to become overly excited if they receive a letter falsely bearing Paul's name, indicating that the practice of circulating forged documents purportedly by apostolic writers had already begun (2 Thess. 2:1–3). Known as **pseudonymity,** the practice of creating new works in the name of a famous deceased author was widespread in both Hellenistic Judaism and early Christianity. From about 200 BCE to 200 CE, Jewish writers produced a host of books ascribed to such revered biblical figures as Daniel, Enoch, Noah, David, Solomon, Isaiah, Ezra, and Moses. Some pseudonymous works, such as the Book of Daniel, were accepted into the Hebrew Bible canon; others, such as 1 Enoch (quoted as scripture in the canonical letter of Jude), were not. Still others, including the Wisdom of Solomon, Baruch, and the apocalyptic 2 Esdras, were regarded as deuterocanonical, part of the Old Testament's "second canon."

Disputed and Pseudonymous Letters

Authorship, date, and place of composition of the disputed and pseudonymous letters are unknown. If 2 Thessalonians and Colossians are by Paul, the former was written about 50 CE and the latter perhaps a decade later. Ephesians, which incorporates ideas from some genuine Pauline letters, may have originated about 90 CE. The pastoral epistles were probably composed during the early decades of the second century CE by a Pauline disciple eager to use the apostle's legacy to enforce church tradition and organizational structure.

Most scholars today view several books in the New Testament as pseudonymous, the productions of unknown Christians who adopted the Jewish literary convention of writing under an assumed identity. Scholars question the authenticity of not only six of the Pauline letters but also of the seven **catholic epistles,** documents ascribed to the "pillars" of the Jerusalem church whom Paul mentions in Galatians: James, John, and Peter, as well as the letter of Jude, James's putative brother (Gal. 2:9; see Chapter 18). In wrestling with the problem of pseudonymity in the early church, many scholars assume that pseudonymous authors wrote not to deceive but to perpetuate the thoughts of an apostle, to address later situations in the Christian community as they believed Peter or Paul would have if he were still alive. According to a common view, twenty-first century principles about the integrity of authorship were irrelevant in the Jewish and Greco-Roman worlds. In this view, ancient society tended to tolerate the practice of pseudonymity, a custom in which disciples of great thinkers were free to compose works in their respective masters' names.

Other scholars strongly disagree, pointing out that what little evidence we have of the early church's recorded attitude toward pseudonymous writing does not support the notion that it was tolerated. When a short missive purporting to be Paul's third letter to the Corinthians appeared, probably in the latter half of the second century CE, a few Christian groups apparently accepted it. By insisting that the resurrection was a bodily phenomenon, 3 Corinthians was useful in combating the Gnostics, who denigrated all forms of material existence. The church as a whole, however, denounced the work as a forgery and removed from office the bishop who confessed to writing it. Tertullian, a church leader of the late second and early third centuries CE, claimed that the author of the spurious Acts of Paul and Thecla, when discovered, was similarly stripped of his position. (See the discussion of the Paul and Thecla narrative in Chapter 20.) Whereas some scholars believe that no work suspected of being pseudonymous would have been admitted to the canon, others argue that in the late first century and early decades of the second, documents attributed to Paul or other apostles—provided that they were theologically consistent with a celebrated leader's known ideas—could be assimilated into Christian Scripture.

How believers react to the claim that a number of books in the New Testament were written by someone other than their ostensible authors typically depends on a reader's concept of biblical authority. For some people, the proposal that unknown Christians falsely assumed Paul's identity is ethically unacceptable on the grounds that such forgeries could not become part of the Bible. Other believers may ask if the value of a disputed or pseudonymous book is based on its traditional link to the "apostolic" generation. Is it "apostolic" authorship only that justifies a document's place in the New Testament canon? Or is it a book's ethical and theological content that makes it valuable, regardless of who wrote it? Perhaps most important, if a particular writing is a forgery—a work falsely claiming Paul, Peter, or James as its author—does that authorial deception invalidate its message, especially if its contents are useful to the Christian life? (See Bart Ehrman in "Recommended Reading.")

We can only speculate about the motives that inspired pseudonymous Christian writers, but some may have wished to obtain a respectful hearing for their views that only a letter by Paul, Peter, or James could command. Some Pauline disciples, perhaps even some who were listed as coauthors in the genuine letters, may have wished, after Paul's death, to address problems as they believed Paul would have. The fact that the historical Paul usually employed a secretary or amanuensis to whom he dictated his thoughts—and that in the ancient world an amanuensis supposedly rephrased dictation in his own style—further complicates the problem of authorship. Scholars defending the authenticity of disputed letters, such as 2 Thessalonians, Colossians, or 1 Peter, tend to emphasize the roles that different secretaries played in shaping these documents. Other critics suggest that pseudonymous authors may have incorporated fragments of otherwise unknown letters that Paul or Peter actually composed. As the readings for this chapter and the next indicate, scholarly speculation about plausible theories of authorship, genuine and pseudonymous, abounds. In studying the literature dubiously attributed to Paul or fellow leaders of the early church, readers will exercise their own judgments about authenticity. Whatever their degree of skepticism, they may conclude that Colossians is worthy of the apostle or that, if Paul wrote the Pastorals, they are a disappointing end to a brilliant writing career.

Second Letter to the Thessalonians

An increasing number of scholars are skeptical about the genuineness of 2 Thessalonians. If Paul actually composed it, why does he repeat—almost verbatim—so much of what he had already just written to the same recipients? More seriously, why does the author present an eschatology so different from that presented in the first letter? In 1 Thessalonians, the Parousia will occur stealthily, "like a thief in the night." In 2 Thessalonians, a number of apocalyptic "signs" will first advertise its arrival. The interposing of these mysterious events between the writer's time and that of the Parousia has the effect of placing the *eschaton* further into the future—unlike in 1 Thessalonians, where the End is extremely close.

Scholars defending Pauline authorship advance several theories to explain the writer's apparent change of attitude toward the Parousia. In the first letter, Paul underscores the tension between the shortness of time the world has left and the necessity of believers' vigilance and ethical purity as they await the Second Coming. In the second missive, Paul writes to correct the Thessalonians' misconceptions about or misuses of his earlier emphasis on the nearness of End time.

If Paul is in fact the author, he probably wrote 2 Thessalonians within a few months of his earlier letter. Some converts, claiming that "the Day of the Lord is already here" (2:2), were upsetting others with their otherworldly enthusiasms. In their state of apocalyptic fervor, some even scorned everyday occupations and refused to work or support themselves. It is possible that the visionary Spirit of prophecy that Paul encouraged the Thessalonians to cultivate (1 Thess. 5:19–22) had come back to haunt him. Empowered by private revelations, a few Christian prophets may have interpreted the Spirit's presence—made possible by Jesus' resurrection and ascension to heaven—as a mystical fulfillment of the Parousia. According to this belief in presently realized eschatology, the Lord's Day is now. Paul, however, consistently emphasizes that Jesus' resurrection and the Spirit's coming are only the first stage in God's plan of cosmic renewal. God's purpose can be completed only at the apocalyptic End of history.

Placing the Second Coming in Perspective

In 2 Thessalonians, Paul (or some other writer building on his thought) takes on the difficult task of urging Christians to be ever alert and prepared for the Lord's return and at the same time to remember that certain events must take place before the Second Coming can occur. The writer achieves this delicate balance partly by insisting on a rational and practical approach to life during the unknown interim between his writing and the Parousia.

In introducing his apocalyptic theme, the author invokes a vivid image of the Final Judgment to imprint its imminent reality on his readers' consciousness. He paraphrases images from the Hebrew prophets to imply that persons now persecuting Christians will soon suffer God's wrath. Christ will be revealed from heaven amid blazing fire, overthrowing those who disobey Jesus' gospel or fail to honor the one God (1:1–12).

Having assured the Thessalonians that their present opponents will be punished at Jesus' return, Paul (or a disciple) now admonishes them not to assume that the punishment will happen immediately. Believers are not to run wild over some visionary's claim that the End is already here. Individual prophetic revelations declaring that Jesus is now invisibly present were apparently strengthened when a letter—supposedly from Paul—conveyed the same or a similar message. (This pseudo-Pauline letter reveals that the practice of composing letters in Paul's name began very early in Christian history.) Speculations founded on private revelations or forged letters, the apostle points out, are doomed to disappoint those who fall for them (2:1–3).

Traditional (Non-Pauline?) Signs of the End

As mentioned previously, one of the strongest arguments against Paul's authorship of 2 Thessalonians is the letter's presentation of eschatological events that presage the End. Although the writer argues for the Parousia's imminence (1:6–10), he also insists that the final day cannot arrive until certain developments characteristic of Jewish apocalyptic thought have occurred. At this point, 2 Thessalonians reverts to the cryptic and veiled language of apocalyptic discourse, referring to mysterious personages and events that may have been understood by the letter's recipients but that are largely incomprehensible to contemporary readers. The End cannot come before the final rebellion against God's rule, when evil is revealed in human form as a demonic enemy who desecrates the Temple and claims divinity for himself. In this passage, Paul's terminology resembles that contained in the Book of Daniel, an apocalyptic work denouncing Antiochus IV, a Greek-Syrian king who polluted the Jerusalem Temple and tried to destroy the Jewish religion (see Chapter 5).

Some commentators suggest that Paul regards the Roman emperor, whose near-absolute power gave him virtually unlimited potential for inflicting evil on humankind, as a latter-day counterpart of Antiochus. Paul's explicitly stated view of the Roman government, however, is positive (Rom. 13), so readers must look elsewhere to identify the doomed figure.

Reminding the Thessalonians that he had previously informed them orally of these apocalyptic developments, Paul states that the mysterious enemy's identity will not be disclosed until the appointed time. This is an allusion to the typically apocalyptic belief that all history is predestined: Events cannot occur before their divinely predetermined hour. Evil forces are already at work, however, secretly gathering strength until the unidentified "Restrainer" disappears, allowing the evil personage to reveal himself.

Apocalyptic Dualism In this passage, the writer paints a typically apocalyptic worldview, a moral dualism in which the opposing powers of good and evil have their respective agents at work on earth. The enemy figure is Satan's agent; his opposite is Christ. As Jesus is God's representative working in human history, so the wicked rebel is the devil's tool. Operating on a cosmic scope, the conflict between good and evil culminates in Christ's victory over his enemy, who has deceived the mass of humanity into believing the "lie." (This is, perhaps, the false belief that any being other than God is the source of humanity's ultimate welfare.) An evil parody of

the Messiah, the unnamed satanic dupe functions as an **anti-Christ** (2:3–12).

The writer's language is specific enough to arouse speculation about the identities of the enigmatic "wicked man" and the "Restrainer" who at the time of writing kept the anti-Christ in check. It is also vague enough to preclude connecting any known historical figures with these eschatological roles. In typical apocalyptic fashion, the figures are mythic archetypes that belong to a realm beyond the reach of historical investigation.

A Disputed Letter to the Colossians

If Paul is the author of Colossians, as a large minority of scholars believe, he had not yet visited the city when he wrote this theologically important letter. A small town in the Roman province of Asia, **Colossae** was located about 100 miles east of Ephesus, the provincial capital (see Figure 16.1). **Epaphras,** one of Paul's missionary associates, had apparently founded the church a short time prior to Paul's writing (1:7).

If genuine, Colossians was probably composed at about the same time as Philemon, to which it is closely related. In both letters, Paul writes from prison, including his friend Timothy in the salutation (1:1) and adding greetings from many of the same persons—such as Onesimus, Archippus, Aristarchus, Epaphras, Mark, and Luke—cited in the earlier missive (4:9–18). If Philemon's was the house church at Colossae, it is strange that Paul does not mention him, but his absence from the letter does not discredit Pauline authorship.

Purpose and Organization

Although it was not one of his churches, Paul (or one of his later disciples) writes to the Colossae congregation to correct some false teachings prevalent there. These beliefs apparently involved cults that gave undue honor to angels or other invisible spirits inhabiting the universe. Some Colossians may have attempted to worship beings that the angels themselves worshiped. Paul refutes these "hollow and delusive" notions by emphasizing Christ's uniqueness and supremacy. Christ alone is the channel to spiritual reality; lesser spirit beings are merely his "captives."

The author's purpose is to make sure that the Colossians clearly recognize who Christ really is. He emphasizes two principal themes: (1) Christ is supreme because God's power now manifested in him was the same power that created the entire universe, including those invisible entities the false teachers mistakenly worship; and (2) when they realize Christ's supremacy and experience his indwelling Spirit, the Colossians are initiated into his mystery cult, voluntarily harmonizing their lives with the cosmic unity he embodies.

Christ—The Source of Cosmic Unity

In the opinion of some analysts, both the complex nature of the false teachings, which seem to blend Greco-Roman and marginally Jewish ideas into a Gnostic synthesis, and the **Christology** of Colossians seem too "advanced" for the letter to have originated in Paul's day. Other critics point out that, if the letter was written late in Paul's career to meet a situation significantly different from others he had earlier encountered, it could well have stimulated the apostle to produce a more fully developed expression of his views about Christ's nature and function.

Jesus as the Mediator of Creation As in the second chapter of Philippians, the author seems to adapt an older Christian hymn to illustrate his vision of the exalted Jesus' cosmic role:

> He is the image of the invisible god, the first-born of all creation;
> for in him all things were created, in heaven and on earth, visible and invisible, whether thrones or dominions or principalities or authorities,

all things were created through him and for him.

> He is before all things, and in him all things hold together.
> He is the head of the body, the church;
> He is the beginning, the first-born from the dead, that in everything he might be preeminent.

> For in him all the fullness of God was pleased to dwell,
> and through him to reconcile to himself all things, whether on earth or in heaven,
> making peace by the blood of his cross.

(1:15–20, Revised Standard Version)

Like the prologue to John's Gospel, this beautiful poem is modeled on biblical and Hellenistic-Jewish concepts of divine Wisdom (Prov. 8:22–31; Ecclus. 24:1–22; see also the discussion of John's usage of Logos [Word] in Chapter 10). Hellenistic Jews had created a rich lore of speculative thought in which God's chief attribute, his infinite Wisdom, is the source of all creation and the means by which he communicates his purpose to humanity. Many historians believe that early Christian thinkers adopted these ready-made wisdom traditions and applied them to Jesus.

Like Philippians 2, the Colossians hymn is traditionally seen as proclaiming Jesus' heavenly preexistence and his personal role as mediator in creation. More recently, many scholars—recognizing the hymn's use of wisdom language—view it as a declaration that the same divine Presence and Power that created the Cosmos now operates in the glorified Christ. The personified Wisdom whom God employed as his agent in fashioning the universe is now fully revealed in Christ, the agent through whom God redeems his human creation.

The phrase "image [*eikon*] of the invisible God" (1:15) may correspond to the phrase "form [*morphes*] of God" that Paul used in Philippians (2:6). In both cases, the term echoes the words of Genesis 1, in which God creates the first human beings in his own "image" (Gen. 1:26–27). (The writer describes the Colossians as also bearing the divine "image" [3:10].) Rather than asserting that the prehuman Jesus was literally present at creation, the hymn may affirm that he is the ultimate goal toward which God's world trends.

Whatever Christology he advances, the writer's main purpose is to demonstrate Christ's present superiority to all rival cosmic beings. The "thrones, sovereignties, authorities and powers" mentioned (1:16) probably represent the Jewish hierarchy of angels. Christ's perfect obedience, vindicating God's image in humanity, and his ascension to heaven have rendered these lesser beings irrelevant and powerless. By his triumph, Christ leads them captive as a Roman emperor leads a public procession of conquered enemies (2:9–15).

Moving from Christ's supremacy to his own role in the divine plan, Paul states that his task is to deliver God's message of reconciliation. He is the agent chosen to reveal the divine "secret hidden for long ages"—the glorified Christ dwelling in the believer, spiritually reuniting the Christian with God. Christians thus form Christ's visible body, here identified with the church (1:21–2:8).

The Mystical Initiation into Christ Employing the rather obscure language of Greek mystery religions (see Chapter 4), Paul compares the Christian's baptism to a vicarious experience of Christ's death and resurrection (2:12, 20; 3:1). It is also the Christian equivalent of circumcision, the ritual sign that identifies one as belonging to God's people, and the rite of initiation into Christ's "body" (2:12–14). Raised to new life, initiated believers are liberated from religious obligations sponsored by those lesser spirits who transmitted the Torah revelation to Moses.

Empowered by Christ's Spirit, the Colossians should not be intimidated by self-styled authorities who mortify the body and piously forbid partaking of certain food and drink, for Christ's death ended all such legal discriminations. Although the author declares the equality of all believers, regardless of nationality or social class, he omits the unity of the sexes that Paul included in Galatians 3:28 (2:20–3:11). As with many Greco-Roman mystery cults, initiation into Christ is a union of social and religious equality.

Obligations of Initiation Consistent with Paul's custom, the author concludes by underlining the ethical implications of his theology. Because Christians experience the indwelling Christ, they must live exceptionally pure and upright lives. The list of vices (3:5–9) and virtues (3:12–25) is typical of other Hellenistic teachers of ethics, but the writer adds a distinctively Christian note: Believers behave well because they are being re-created in Christ's nature and "image" (3:10).

Letter to the Ephesians

The Case of Ephesians

Whereas Paul's authorship of Colossians is seriously doubted, the claim that he wrote Ephesians is widely denied. Although it closely resembles Colossians (the style and theology of which also seem untypical of Paul), Ephesians differs from the undisputed Pauline letters in (1) vocabulary (containing over ninety words not found elsewhere in Paul's writings), (2) literary style (written in extremely long, convoluted sentences, in contrast to Paul's usually direct, forceful statements), and (3) theology (lacking typically Pauline doctrines such as justification by faith and the nearness of Christ's return).

Despite its similarity to Colossians (75 of Ephesians' 155 verses parallel passages in Colossians), it presents a different view of the sacred "secret" or "mystery" revealed in Christ. In Colossians, God's long-kept secret is Christ's mystical union with his followers (Col. 1:27), but in Ephesians, it is the union of Jew and Gentile in one church (Eph. 3:6).

More than any other disputed letter (except those to Timothy and Titus), Ephesians seems to reflect a time in church history significantly later than Paul's day. References to "Apostles and prophets" as the church's foundation imply that these figures belong to the past, not the author's generation (2:20; 3:5). The Gentiles' equality in Christian fellowship is no longer a controversial issue but an accomplished fact; this strongly suggests that the letter originated after the church membership had become largely non-Jewish (2:11–22). Judaizing interlopers no longer question Paul's stand on circumcision, again indicating that the work was composed after Jerusalem's destruction had largely eliminated the influence of the Jewish parent church.

When Paul uses the term "church" (*ekklesia*), he always refers to a single congregation (Gal. 1:2; 1 Cor. 11:16; 16:19, etc.). In contrast, Ephesians' author speaks of the "church" collectively, a universal institution encompassing all individual groups. This view of the church as a worldwide entity also points to a time after the apostolic period.

The cumulative evidence convinces most scholars that Ephesians is a deutero-Pauline document, a secondary work composed in Paul's name by an admirer thoroughly steeped in the apostle's thought and theology. The close parallels to Colossians, as well as phrases taken from Romans, Philemon, and other letters, indicate that unlike the author of Acts, this unknown writer was familiar with the Pauline correspondence. Some scholars propose that Ephesians was written as a kind of "cover letter" or essay to accompany an early collection of Paul's letters. Ephesians, then, can be seen as a tribute to Paul, summarizing some of his ideas and updating others to fit the changing needs of a largely Gentile and cosmopolitan church.

The phrase "in Ephesus" (1:1), identifying the recipients, does not appear in any of the oldest manuscripts. That fact, plus the absence of any specific issue or problem being addressed, reinforces the notion that Ephesians was intended to circulate among several churches in Asia Minor.

Date and Organization

If the letter to the Ephesians is by Paul, it probably originated from his Roman prison (60–64 CE). But if it is by a later Pauline disciple, as almost all scholars believe, Ephesians likely was written about the time Paul's letters first circulated as a unit, perhaps about 90 CE.

Ephesians' diverse contents can be subsumed under two major headings:

1. God's plan of salvation through the unified body of the church (1:3–3:21)
2. Instructions for living in the world while united to Christ (4:1–6:20)

Despite its long and sometimes awkward sentence structures (rephrased into shorter units in most English translations), Ephesians is a masterpiece of devotional literature. Unlike Paul's undisputed letters, it has a quiet and meditative tone, with no temperamental outbursts or attacks on the writer's enemies. Although it imitates the letter form by including a brief salutation (1:1–2) and a final greeting (6:21–24), Ephesians is really a highly sophisticated tract.

God's Plan of Salvation Through the United Body of Christ

Ephesians' main theme is the union of all creation with Christ, manifested on earth by the church's international unity (1:10–14). Echoing Romans' concept of predestination, the author states that before the world's foundation God selected Christ's future "children" (composing the church) to be redeemed by Jesus' blood, a sacrifice through which the chosen ones' sins are forgiven.

According to his preordained plan, God has placed Christ as head of the church, which is his body. The Spirit of Christ now fills the church as fully as God dwells in Christ (1:22–23). This mystical union of the human and divine is God's unforeseen gift, his grace that saves those who trust him (2:1–10).

BOX 17.1   Have Believers Already Experienced Resurrection to New Life?

Two of the letters whose Pauline authorship is disputed—Colossians and Ephesians—seem to accord believers a higher spiritual status than Paul gives them. In writing to the Corinthians, Paul had chastised those recipients—presumably, those who claimed superior "wisdom" (1 Cor. 1:18–3:23; 4:6–5:20)—who boasted that they had already "come into [their] kingdom" (1 Cor. 4:8–9). In repudiating those who behaved as if they had already attained guarantees of immortal life, Paul makes clear that Christians' attainment of spiritual validation and resurrection to immortality is still to come; it is tantalizingly near, but not yet (1 Cor. 15; cf. Rom. 6:4).

In Colossians, however, the writer appears to have adopted the "wise" Corinthians' viewpoint: "For in baptism also you were raised to life with him through your faith in the active power of God who raised him from the dead" (2:12).

Believers are now "alive with Christ" (2:13). Ephesians makes an even more startling claim about believers' state of being: "God . . . brought us to life with Christ even when we were dead in our sins; . . . and in union with Christ Jesus he raised us up and enthroned us with him in the heavenly realm" (Eph. 2:4–7). In such passages affirming believers' present spiritual exaltation—a celestial enthronement in which they already rule with Christ—these (post-Pauline?) writers approach the realized eschatology of John's Gospel. Muting Paul's apocalyptic hope for an imminent Parousia, Colossians and Ephesians resemble John's nonapocalyptic conviction: "anyone who . . . puts his trust in him who sent me has hold of eternal life . . . [and] has already passed from death to life." In fact, that "time" of transformation "is already here" (John 5:24–25; cf. 11:24–26).

Few New Testament writers can rival the author of Ephesians in his enthusiastic portrayal of the spiritual bounty that Christians enjoy. The "Father" not only "gives [us] the spiritual powers of wisdom and vision" by which we can come to know the divine nature but also provides believers with "the entire fullness of God" (2:17–18, 22–23). Those trusting in God can therefore draw upon the sustaining forces of the entire universe, the "vast . . . resources of [God's] power" (2:19). (For a discussion of believers' spiritually exalted status, see Box 17.1.)

The Sacred Secret—the Union of Jews and Gentiles in One Church God's long-hidden secret is that Gentiles, previously under divine condemnation, can now share in the biblical promises made to Israel. This divine purpose to unite Jew and Gentile in equal grace is the special message that Paul is commissioned to preach (3:1–21). (It is significant that the writer assumes a general acceptance of the Gentile-dominated church, a condition that did not exist in Paul's day.)

Instructions for Living in the World

Ephesians' last three chapters are devoted to instructions on living properly in the world while remaining united to Christ. Combining ideas from Philippians 2 and Colossians 1, the author reinterprets the concept of Jesus' descent from and reascension to the spirit realm whereby he made lesser spirits his prisoners and filled the universe with his presence. The author may also allude to Jesus' descent into the Underworld, a mythical exploit that appears in 1 Peter (3:19–20) (see Box 18.2).

Advancing Paul's conviction that the Christian revelation requires the highest ethical conduct, Ephesians contrasts Greco-Roman

FIGURE 17.1 Bas-relief of Roman soldiers. The Book of Ephesians' famous description of a Christian's spiritual defenses against evil is based on the armor and other military equipment used by Roman soldiers (Eph. 6:13–17).

must remain similarly alert for Christ's sudden reappearance. Ephesians discards the eschatological context of Paul's metaphor, however, and instead presents an ongoing battle between good and evil with no end in sight. In the genuine Pauline letters, the apostle foresees evil demolished at Christ's Second Coming. The Ephesian writer, in contrast, paints a picture of cosmic conflict reminiscent of Zoroastrianism—the Persian religion in which the world is viewed as a battlefield between invisible forces of light and dark, good and evil.

In Zoroastrian terms, the Ephesian Paul describes two levels of "cosmic powers"—the earthly rulers of the present dark age and the invisible forces of evil in heaven (6:10–12). Like Mark, the author apparently senses the reality of an evil so powerful that mere human wickedness cannot explain it. (For an insightful interpretation of the "powers" as entrenched social attitudes and practices that resist God's Spirit, see Wink in "Recommended Reading.") Instead of despairing, however, he rejoices that God provides ammunition with which successfully to defeat even supernatural evil. According to the author, each article of God's armor is a Christian virtue; cultivated together, qualities like truth and faith offer full protection from the devil's worst attacks (6:13–19).

Rich in spiritual insight, Ephesians is a creative summary of some major Pauline concepts. Even if not by Paul, it is nevertheless a significant celebration of Christian ideals, an achievement worthy of the great apostle himself.

vices with Christian virtues and urges believers to transform their personalities to fit God's new creation (4:17–5:20). Home life is to be as reverent and orderly as behavior in church. Although he insists on a domestic hierarchy—"man is the head of the woman, just as Christ . . . is head of the church"—the writer reminds husbands to love their wives and thus to honor them as a treasured equivalent of the self (5:21–6:9). Ephesians endorses the rigid social and domestic hierarchy of Greco-Roman society but makes the system more humane by insisting that Christian love apply to all public and private relationships.

Heavenly Armor In Ephesians' most famous passage, the Pauline analogy of Christians armed like Roman soldiers is vividly elaborated (see Figure 17.1). In 1 Thessalonians (5:8), Paul urges believers to imitate armed sentries who stay awake on guard duty, for Christians

The Pastorals: Letters to Timothy and Titus

In the opinion of most scholars, the case against Paul's connection with the pastorals is overwhelming. Besides the fact that they do not appear in early lists of Paul's canonical works, the pastorals seem to reflect conditions that prevailed long after Paul's day, perhaps as late as the first half of the second century CE. Lacking Paul's characteristic ideas about faith and the Spirit, they are also un-Pauline in their flat prose style and different vocabulary (containing 306 words not found in Paul's unquestioned letters). Furthermore, the pastorals assume a church organization far more developed than that current in the apostle's time.

Known for convenience as "the **Pastor**," the same Pauline disciple is the author of all three pastoral letters. He views Paul's teaching as the norm or standard for all Christians and writes primarily to combat false teachings, urging the church to reject any deviations from the apostolic heritage. An examination of the Pastor's interpretation of Pauline thought shows that he does not always use terms in the same way as his master, nor is he as vigorous and creative a thinker. Writing to preserve an inherited tradition and bolster the authority of an increasingly well-organized church, he tends to view Christian faith as a set of static doctrines rather than as the ecstatic experience of Christ that Paul knew.

Letters to Timothy

The first two pastorals are addressed to Timothy, the son of a Jewish mother and a Greek father (Acts 16:1), who served as Paul's missionary companion and trusted friend (1 Cor. 4:17; 16:10). According to Acts and Paul's authentic letters, Timothy was an important contributor to Paul's missionary campaigns in Greece and Asia Minor, a cofounder of churches in Macedonia, and later a diplomatic emissary to Philippi, Thessalonica, and Corinth. In listing him as coauthor of as many as six different letters, Paul (and perhaps also disciples who followed him) affirms Timothy's vital role in the expansion of Pauline Christianity (1 Thess. 1:1; 2 Thess. 1:1; 2 Cor. 1:1; Phil. 1:1; Philem. 1:1; Col. 1:1).

In the pastorals, however, Timothy is less a historical character than a literary symbol, representative of a new generation of believers to whom the task of preserving apostolic

truths is entrusted. Youthful (postapostolic) Christians must take on the job of defending "wholesome doctrine" against devilish heresies (1 Tim. 4:2, 11–12).

1 Timothy

Organization   The first letter to Timothy does not present us with a smooth progression of thought, so it makes sense to examine it in terms of topics rather than the somewhat haphazard sequence in which the author presents his material:

1. Timothy's duty to repress false teachings
2. Church order: the qualifications of bishops, deacons, and elders
3. The roles of women and slaves

Attacks on False Teachings (Heresies)   As inheritor of the true faith, Timothy is to combat church members' wrong ideas (1:3). Because the Pastor, unlike Paul, does not offer a rational criticism of his opponents' errors, we do not know the exact nature of the beliefs being attacked. Some commentators suggest that the false teachers practiced an early form of Gnosticism, a cult of secret "knowledge" mentioned in 6:20, but the letter reveals too little about the heresies involved to confirm this theory.

Because the author describes the deviants as teaching "the moral law" and being wrongly preoccupied with "interminable myths and genealogies" (1:3–4, 7–9), many critics suppose that some form of Hellenistic Judaism is under attack. Practicing an extreme asceticism (severe self-discipline of the physical appetites), these persons forbid marriage and abstain from various foods (4:1–3). Gnostic practices took diverse forms, ranging from the kind of self-denial mentioned here to the libertine behavior Paul rebuked in Corinth, Galatia, and elsewhere. Timothy (and the pastorship he represents) must correct such misguided austerity by transmitting the correct Pauline teachings (4:11), thereby saving both himself and those who obey his orders (4:16).

Qualifications for Church Offices Invoking Paul's authority, the Pastor is eager to preserve sound doctrine through a stable church organization. His list of qualifications for **bishops** (overseers), **deacons** (assistants), and elders (the religiously mature leadership) implies a hierarchy of church offices much more rigidly stratified than was the case in Paul's day. Paul once used the terms "bishop" and "deacon" (Phil. 1:1), but presumably as designating areas of service rather than the specific ecclesiastical offices enumerated here. Although the author says that church officials must demonstrate all the virtues typical of Hellenistic ethical philosophy (3:2–23), he says nothing about their intellectual qualifications or possession of the Spirit. Rather than the spiritual gifts that Paul advocates, the Pastor's standards for church offices are merely hallmarks of social respectability. The Pastor's list of requirements for leadership in an increasingly institutionalized community indicates the distance his church has moved from early Christian origins. The historical Jesus, an unmarried itinerant prophet who stirred controversy and public criticism even in his hometown, would seem to be excluded from holding an official position in the Pastor's church. Nor would Paul himself—by choice unmarried and a lightning rod for in-church dissension, a catalyst for public riots, and a frequently arrested and imprisoned disturber of the peace—qualify as the Pastor's version of a responsible church leader (cf. 2 Cor. 10–13).

The Pastor regards the institution of the church—rather than the Spirit of Christ dwelling in believers—as "the pillar and bulwark of the truth" (3:15). In the writer's time, an organization administered by right-thinking leaders replaces the dynamic and charismatic fellowship of the Pauline congregations.

The Church Hierarchy In 1 Timothy, the church membership reflects the social order of the larger Greco-Roman society external to it. Bishops, deacons, and elders govern a mixed group composed of different social classes, including heads of households, masters, slaves, wives, widows, and children, all of whom are commanded to submit to their respective superiors.

Women Whereas Paul recognizes women as prophets and speakers (1 Cor. 11:5), the Pastor does not permit women to teach because the first woman, Eve, was weak-minded and tempted her husband to sin (2:8–15) (see Chapter 13). The detailed instruction on women's dress and conduct in 1 Timothy probably applies to public worship and parallels the restricted position assigned women in Greco-Roman society. A reflection of then-current social customs, it is not logically defensible or a timeless prescription limiting women's participation in Christian life.

In his discussion of the church's treatment of widows, the Pastor distinguishes between "true" widows who demonstrate their worth by good deeds and women who are unqualified for that status because of their youth or inappropriate conduct. Following Jewish law (Exod. 22:22; Deut. 24: 17–24), the church early assumed responsibilities for supporting destitute widows (Acts 6:1), but the author stipulates that widows must be sixty years old before they can qualify for financial assistance. Relatives must support underage widows (5:3–16). The author seems uninterested in the fate of young widows who have no family to help them.

As Christians are to pray for government rulers (2:1–3), so slaves are to recognize their duties to masters and obey them (6:1–2). Yet the rich and powerful are reminded to share their wealth (6: 17–19). Those ambitious to acquire riches are told that a passion for money is the cause of much evil, a source of grief and lost faith (6:9–10).

The letter ends with an admonishment to Timothy to guard the apostolic legacy given him. Anyone who disagrees with the Pastor's updated interpretation of Paul's doctrine is "a pompous ignoramus" (6:3).

2 Timothy

Of the three pastorals, 2 Timothy most closely resembles Paul's genuine letters. Although the letter is similarly concerned with refuting false teachings, its tone is more intimate and personal. Especially poignant are several passages in which the author depicts himself as abandoned by former associates and languishing alone in prison except for the companionship of Luke (1:15; 4:9–11, 16). Although these and other flashes of Paul's characteristic vigor and emotional fire (see 4:6–8, 17–18) lead some scholars to speculate that the work contains fragments of otherwise lost Pauline letters, such theories are not widely accepted.

The part of 2 Timothy with the best claim to Pauline authorship is the section ending the letter (4:6–22), in which the writer emulates the fluctuations between lofty thoughts and mundane practicalities so typical of the apostle. In the first part, he compares himself to a runner winning the athlete's coveted prize—not the Greek competitor's laurel crown, but a "garland of righteousness" justifying him on God's Judgment Day (4:6–8). Switching abruptly to practical matters, the author asks the recipient to remember to bring his books when he comes. In another quick change of subject, he complains that during his court hearing nobody appeared in his defense and that the testimony of one "Alexander the coppersmith" seriously damaged his case. Then, in a seemingly contradictory about face, the writer states that he has (metaphorically) escaped the "lion's jaws" and expects to be kept safe until the Parousia (4:13–18).

Although such rapid changes of subject and shifts from gloom to optimism characterize Paul's genuine correspondence, most scholars believe that the entire document is the Pastor's work. The more vivid passages are simply the writer's most successful homage to the apostle's memory.

In describing the false teachings within the church that he identifies as signs of the last days, the Pastor reveals that he is using Paul to predict conditions that characterize the writer's own time. During the world's last days (3:1), hypocrites insinuate their way into Christians' homes, corrupting their occupants. These pretenders typically prey upon women because, in the Pastor's insulting opinion, even when eager to learn, women lack the ability to understand true doctrine (3:6–8). Instead of the false teachings' being punished at the Second Coming, the Pastor implies, the mere passage of time will expose their errors (3:9).

As in 1 Timothy, the Pastor does not refute the heretics with logical argument but merely calls them names and lists their vices (3:1–6, 13; 4:3–4), duplicating the catalogues of misbehavior common in Hellenistic philosophical schools. Even believers do not adhere to healthy beliefs but, instead, tolerate leaders who flatter them with what they want to hear.

Whereas the church is the stronghold of faith in 1 Timothy, in 2 Timothy the Hebrew Bible is the standard of religious orthodoxy (correct teaching), confounding error and directing believers to salvation. Scripture also provides the mental discipline necessary to equip the believer for right action (3:15–17).

Concluding with his memorable picture of the apostle courageously facing martyrdom, the Pastor graciously includes all the faithful in Christ's promised deliverance. Not only Paul but all who trust in Jesus' imminent return will win the victor's crown at the Parousia (4:6–8).

Letter to Titus

Although it is the shortest of the pastorals, Titus has the longest salutation, a fulsome recapitulation of Paul's credentials and the recipient's significance (1:1–4). This highly formal introduction would be inappropriate in a personal letter from Paul to his friend, but it is understandable as the Pastor's way of officially transmitting Paul's authoritative instruction to an apostolic successor.

Titus The historical Titus, a Greek youth whom Paul refused to have circumcised (Gal. 2), accompanied the apostle on his missionary tours of Greece, acting as Paul's emissary to reconcile the rebellious Corinthians (Gal. 2:1, 3, 10; 2 Cor. 8:6, 16–23). Like the "Timothy" of the other pastorals, however, "Titus" also represents the postapostolic church leadership, the prototype of those preserving the Pauline traditions. Consequently, the commission of "Titus" is to establish an orthodox and qualified ministry. The letter's chief purpose is to outline the requirements and some of the duties of church elders and bishops.

Organization Titus can be divided into two main sections:

1. Qualifications for the Christian ministry
2. Christian behavior in an ungodly world

Qualifications for the Christian Ministry The writer states that he left "Titus" in Crete, an ancient island center of Greek civilization, to install church assistants (elders) in every town (1:5). Such persons must be eminently respectable married men who keep their children under strict parental control (1:6). Besides possessing these domestic credentials, bishops (church supervisors) must also have a reputation for devotion, self-control, and hospitality (1:7–8). Again, the writer says nothing about the leaders' mental or charismatic gifts, so highly valued in the Pauline churches (2 Cor. 11–14).

One of the bishop's primary functions is to guard the received religion, adhering to established beliefs and correcting dissenters (1:7–9). Titus is the only book in the New Testament that uses the term **heretic** (3:10), which at the time of writing (early to mid-second century) probably meant a person who held opinions contrary to those of emerging church authority. Such dissenters are to be warned twice and then ignored (excluded from the church?) if they fail to change their ways (3:10–11).

Christian Behavior in an Ungodly World The Pastor reminds his readers that because they are Christians in a nonbelieving world they must live exemplary lives of obedience and submission to governmental authorities (3:1). Men and women, old and young, slaves and masters—all are to behave in a way that publicly reflects well on their religion (2:1–10). Christians must preserve an ethically pure community while awaiting Christ's return (2:13–14).

In a moving passage, the author contrasts the negative personality traits that many believers had before their conversion with the grace and hope for eternal life that they now possess (3:3–8). In counsel similar to that in the letter of James, he urges believers to show their faith in admirable and useful deeds and to refrain from "foolish speculations, genealogies, quarrels, and controversies over the Law" (3:9–10).

The Pastor's Contribution

Although compared to Paul's the Pastor's style is generally weak and colorless (except for some passages in 2 Tim.), the Pastor successfully promotes Paul's continuing authority in the church. His insistence that Paul's teaching, as he understood it, be followed and that church leaders actively employ apostolic doctrines to refute false teachers helped to ensure that the international Christian community would build its future on an apostolic foundation.

Although the Pastor values continuity, he does not seem to show an equal regard for continuing the individual revelations and ecstatic experiences of Christ's Spirit that characterized the Pauline churches. Regarding the "laying on of hands" as the correct means of conferring authority (2 Tim. 1:6), he would probably not welcome another like Paul who insisted that his private experience of Jesus— not ordination by his predecessors—validated his calling. Using Scripture, inherited doctrines, and the institutional church as guarantors of orthodoxy, the Pastor sees the Christian revelation as already complete, a static legacy from the past. He ignores Paul's injunction not to "stifle inspiration" or prophetic speech

(1 Thess. 5:19–20); his intense conservatism allows little room for future enlightenment.

Summary

Although it may shock modern sensibilities, innumerable ancient writers—Jewish, Greco-Roman, and Christian—practiced pseudonymity, composing books under the names of famous dead authors. In the decades following Paul's demise, several groups of Christians apparently contended for the right to claim the Pauline legacy and to use his posthumous authority to settle later church problems. Two letters, 2 Thessalonians and Colossians—seem to be much closer to genuine Pauline thought than Ephesians or the Pastorals, which emphasize the kind of church offices and institutional structure that evolved after his day.

Questions for Review

1. Define the term *pseudonymity* and explain its practice among Hellenistic-Jewish and early Christian writers. Which books of the New Testament do many scholars think are pseudonymous?
2. In what specific ways concerning Jesus' return does 2 Thessalonians differ from Paul's first letter to the Thessalonians? What elements in the second letter make scholars suspect that it was written after Paul's day? Describe the conventional apocalyptic "signs" that the writer says must occur before the End.
3. Summarize the arguments for and against Paul's authorship of Colossians.
4. What factors cause scholars to doubt Paul's authorship of Ephesians? In this document, how are Christ and the church related? What does their union imply for believers? What is the significance of the author's emphasizing warfare with unseen spirits rather than the Parousia?
5. Describe the evidence that persuades most scholars that the pastorals were written by a later churchman. In what specific concerns do the pastorals reflect church organization and administration that are different from those existing in Paul's time? Why are these letters so concerned about holding to tradition and combating "heresy"?

Questions for Discussion and Reflection

1. Analyze the similarities between the two Christian hymns quoted respectively in Philippians 2 and Colossians 1. Compare the view that humanity bears God's image (Gen. 1:27) with the similar language applied to Jesus (Col. 1:15). In what ways does the Colossians hymn apply the concepts of Israel's Wisdom tradition to Jesus?
2. Discuss the Pastor's views on women, children, and slaves. How does his prescription for internal church order reflect the hierarchical organization of the contemporary Greco-Roman society? What similarities and differences do you see between the character and behavior of Jesus and the Pastor's list of qualifications for church leaders? Would the historical Jesus, an unmarried itinerant prophet, have met the Pastor's standards for qualifying for church leadership? Would Paul himself?
3. The pastoral epistles show the extent to which the dynamic and spirit-led fellowship of early Christian communities (30s–50s CE) has developed into a more rigidly structured church organization with an administrative hierarchy of offices and leaders (c. 90 CE and later). In your opinion, what advantages did the church gain by adopting the hierarchical structures of Roman society? What losses came with this organizational shift?

Terms and Concepts to Remember

anti-Christ	Epaphras
bishop	heresy
catholic epistles	pastoral epistles
Christology	pseudonymity
Colossae	Timothy
deacon	Titus

Recommended Reading

2 Thessalonians

Ascough, Richard S. "Thessalonians, Second Letter to." In K. D. Sakenfeld, ed., *The New Interpreter's Dictionary of the Bible*, Vol. 5, pp. 574–579. Nashville: Abingdon Press, 2009. Surveys arguments for and against the letter's authenticity.

Malherbe, Abraham J. *The Letters to the Thessalonians: A New Translation with Introduction and Commentary*.

Anchor Bible, Vol. 32b. New York: Doubleday, 2000. Defends Pauline authorship of 2 Thessalonians.

Von Dehsen, Christian D. "2 Thessalonians." In M. D. Coogan, ed., *The Oxford Encyclopedia of the Books of the Bible*, Vol. 2, pp. 410–414. New York: Oxford University Press, 2011. Reviews arguments for and against authenticity, concluding that there is no scholarly consensus.

Colossians

Barth, Markus, and Blanke, Helmut. *Colossians*. Anchor Bible. Garden City, N.Y.: Doubleday, 1995. A scholarly translation and analysis.

Dunn, James D. G. "Colossians, Letter to." In K. D. Sakenfeld, ed., *The New Interpreter's Dictionary of the Bible*, Vol. 1, pp. 702–706. Nashville, Tenn.: Abingdon Press, 2006. A concise analysis of the work, suggesting the possibility of Pauline authorship.

———. *The Epistles to the Colossians and to Philemon: A Commentary on the Greek Text*. Grand Rapids, Mich.: Eerdmans, 1996. For advanced students.

O'Brien, P. T. *Colossians, Philemon*. Word Biblical Commentary 44. Waco, Tex.: Word Books, 1982. Defends Pauline authorship of Colossians; includes the author's translation.

Schweizer, Eduard. *The Letter to the Colossians: A Commentary*. Minneapolis: Augsburg, 1982. Less technical than the work by O'Brien; suggests that Timothy played a role in writing Colossians.

Ephesians

Barth, Markus, ed. and trans. *Ephesians*. Vols. 34 and 34a of the Anchor Bible. Garden City, N.Y.: Doubleday, 1974. An extensive commentary that defends Pauline authorship.

Bruce, F. F. *The Epistles to the Colossians, to Philemon, and to the Ephesians*. New International Commentary on the New Testament. Grand Rapids, Mich.: Eerdmans, 1984.

Furnish, V. P. "Ephesians, Epistle to the." In D. N. Freedman, ed., *The Anchor Bible Dictionary*, Vol. 2, pp. 535–542. New York: Doubleday, 1992.

Goodspeed, E. J. *The Meaning of Ephesians*. Chicago: University of Chicago Press, 1933. An older but perceptive study arguing that Ephesians was written as a cover letter for the first collected edition of Paul's correspondence.

O'Brien, P. T. *The Letter to the Ephesians*. Pillar New Testament Commentary. Grand Rapids, Mich.: Eerdmans, 1999. An insightful analysis of the letter's spiritual significance.

Turner, Max. "Ephesians, Letter to the." In K. D. Sakenfeld, ed., *The New Interpreter's Dictionary of the Bible*, Vol. 2, pp. 269–276. Nashville, Tenn.: Abingdon Press, 2007. An informative survey of the book's major themes.

Wink, Walter. *The Powers That Be: Theology for a New Millennium*. New York: Galilee Doubleday, 1998. Interprets traditional biblical imagery about supernatural forces—angels and demons—as social/cultural assumptions and practices that inhibit God's rule in human society.

The Pastorals

D'Angelo, Mary Rose. "Timothy, First and Second Letters to." In K. D. Sakenfeld, ed., *The New Interpreter's Dictionary of the Bible*, Vol. 5, pp. 602–605. Nashville: Abingdon Press, 2009. Takes no stand on authorship, emphasizing instead the letters' contents, including their misogyny and attitude toward slavery.

Fiore, Benjamin. "1 Timothy," "2 Timothy," and "Titus." In M. D. Coogan, ed., *The Oxford Encyclopedia of the Books of the Bible*, Vol. 2, pp. 422–430. New York: Oxford University Press, 2011. Offers a survey of the letters' contents, concluding that all three are pseudonymous.

Johnson, L. T. *The First and Second Letters to Timothy: A New Translation with Introduction and Commentary*. Anchor Bible. Garden City, N.Y.: Doubleday, 2001. A strongly traditionalist interpretation, advocating Pauline authorship of the pastorals.

Levine, Amy-Jill, and Blickenstaff, Marianne, eds. *Feminist Companion to Paul: Deutero-Pauline Writings*. Feminist Companion to the New Testament and Early Christian Writings. Sheffield, England: Sheffield Academic Press, 2004.

Quinn, J. D., ed., and trans. *1 and 2 Timothy and Titus*. Vol. 35 of the Anchor Bible. Garden City, N.Y.: Doubleday, 1976. A translation with commentary.

———. "Timothy and Titus, Epistles to." In D. N. Freedman, ed., *The Anchor Bible Dictionary*, Vol. 6, pp. 560–571. New York: Doubleday, 1992.

Pseudonymity

Ehrman, Bart. *Forged: Writing in the Name of God—Why the Bible's Authors Are Not Who We Think They Are*. San Francisco: HarperOne, 2011. Argues forcefully that many New Testament books are deliberate forgeries that successfully deceived the Christian community.

———. *Forgery and Counterforgery: The Use of Literary Deceit in Early Christian Polemics*. New York: Oxford University Press, 2013. Marshals detailed evidence to support the thesis that "the most distinctive feature of early Christian literature is the degree to which it was forged."

PART SIX

General Letters and
Some Visions of End Time

CHAPTER 18

General Letters on Faith and Behavior
Hebrews and the Catholic Epistles

The kind of religion which is without stain or fault . . . is this: to go to the help of orphans and widows in their distress and keep oneself untarnished by the world. James 1:27

Love cancels innumerable sins. 1 Peter 4:8 (cf. James 5:20)

Key Topics/Themes Addressed to believers scattered throughout the world, Hebrews and the other general epistles make the point that God's revelation through Jesus is final and complete. The very image of God's nature, Jesus now serves in heaven as an eternal High Priest and mediator for humanity (Hebrews).

Believers must therefore adhere to a high standard of conduct, maintaining a true understanding of Jesus' Incarnation (1 John), practicing charitable acts (James), setting examples of ethical behavior for the world (1 Peter), and keeping alive their hope of the Second Coming (2 Peter).

Sandwiched between the theologically powerful Pauline letters and the mystifying symbolism of the Book of Revelation is a second collection of New Testament letters or letterlike documents—the Book of Hebrews and the seven **catholic** (general) **epistles.** Although commonly less emphasized in many contemporary church services, these eight documents provide an important counterweight to the historical dominance of Paul's thought, demonstrating that other voices in the early Christian community offered somewhat different but equally acceptable interpretations of Jesus' theological significance and of instruction in the Christian way of life. The fact

that most documents in this section contain some element of the letter form—though few are true letters—suggests that their authors consciously imitated the literary genre that Paul had so effectively employed. The widespread influence of Paul's "weighty and powerful" correspondence (2 Cor. 10:10) apparently inspired the authors of Hebrews and the catholic epistles (or perhaps later editors) to frame their messages with letterlike greetings and/or a complimentary close (cf. Heb. 13:17–25). Unlike Paul's genuine letters, however, those in this unit of the canon are not addressed to individual congregations but are directed to the believing community as a whole.

Hebrews and the Catholic Epistles

Although some scholars argue that 1 Peter was written by the historical Peter, and James and Jude by Jesus' kinsmen, most scholars believe that this entire section of the New Testament is pseudonymous. In general, we do not know when or where these documents originated or, in most cases, to whom they were sent. A possible exception to this rule, the Teaching (Didache) of the Twelve Apostles (see Chapter 20) may have been compiled in Syria about 100 CE and is thus probably older than the documents ascribed to Peter or Jude.

Paul is also indirectly responsible for the canonical order in which editors eventually arranged the seven catholic epistles. In Galatians 2:9, he had briefly referred to the three "pillars" of the Jerusalem church as James (whom he identifies as "the Lord's brother"); Jesus' chief apostle "Cephas," also called Peter; and John, who with his brother, another James, was part of Jesus' inner circle (cf. Mark 3:16–17; 9:2). Hence, the epistles appear in this sequence: James; 1 and 2 Peter; 1, 2, and 3 John; and Jude (who identifies himself as "the brother of James"). Although called "epistles" (another term for letters), these short works encompass a wide variety of literary categories, ranging from wisdom literature (James) to theological essays (1 John).

🏛 Authors and Dates

Most of the catholic writings are linked not only by their attribution to leaders of the original Jerusalem church but also by the fact that collectively they are the last writings to be accepted into the New Testament canon. As late as the fourth century, Eusebius classified several as "doubtful" and noted that many churches did not accept them (*History* 3.3; 3.24.1; 3.24.18; 3.25.4; 3.39.6). Church writers do not even mention most of these epistles until almost 200 CE, and Jude, James, 2 Peter, and 3 John are typically absent from early lists of canonical books (see Chapter 2).

Near the end of the second century, the church began to associate many previously anonymous works with Jesus' apostles and their companions. This seems to have been the case with the catholic epistles, which scholars believe to include the latest-written documents in the New Testament.

Primary Concerns of the Late Canonical Authors

Writing in the late first century CE or early decades of the second, the authors of Hebrews and the catholic epistles address concerns that troubled the church in the generations following Paul's martyrdom. Whereas Paul's authentic letters, like the Gospel of Mark, glowed with eschatological urgency and warned of the imminent Parousia, the writers of this later period had to deal with diminishing hopes that Jesus would return soon. Roman imperial power had not—as the first generations of Christians so fervently hoped—come to an end. Virtually all the documents in this part of the canon repeatedly remind believers that Jesus' reappearance to judge the world—and them—is certain, but only one tackles the issue of the delayed Parousia head-on. The author of 2 Peter, which may be the last-written work to enter the New Testament canon, frankly acknowledges the problem, voicing the skeptics' complaints: "Where now is the promise of his coming? Our fathers have been laid to their rest, but still everything continues exactly as it has always been since the world began" (2 Pet. 3:4).

As generations of early Christians passed away, criticism of the core belief that Jesus would return to establish his kingdom during his original disciples' lifetime (cf. Mark 9:1; Matt. 24:34–35) may have perplexed many believers. Second Peter's response to such attacks asks us to remember the disparity between human sense of time and that of God, who dwells in eternity (3:1–15). Perhaps more important for the church's survival, virtually all the epistles' authors, including those of 1 and 2 Peter, affirm that the Parousia will indeed occur—and that Christians must behave as if Jesus will appear tomorrow to judge their conduct. Encouraging believers to practice a strict ethical code, the author of 1 John points to contemporary developments in his own community—the appearance of supposed "antichrists"—as proof that "the last hour" has already arrived (1 John 2:18). (This tendency to interpret events that affected their congregations as evidence of fulfilled eschatological prophecy characterizes most New Testament writers from Matthew to the author of 2 Peter.)

Because they lived in the indefinitely prolonged interim between Jesus' ascension to heaven and his return to earth, the authors of Hebrews and the epistles struggle to provide guidance that will enable their audiences to overcome a host of trials and temptations. Among the many problems that disturbed the churches' peace were issues that involved both secular and doctrinal difficulties. Living as monotheists who could not participate in the Greco-Roman world's numerous religious festivals or social associations, Christians frequently endured harsh criticism from their neighbors and even sporadic persecution by local magistrates. Although at this time persecution was more commonly social than governmental, the oppression and public disapproval were real and a source of ongoing concern (see the discussion of 1 Peter below).

While they faced hostility from the outside world, the geographically separated churches simultaneously wrestled with internal dissension. The Johannine communities were wracked with disputes over doctrine and behavior, as were the churches that Jude and 2 Peter addressed. Spirits of prophecy and interpretation that had characterized Paul's congregations now apparently inspired ideas that church leaders condemned as "false teachings," resulting in admonition similar to that in the pastorals (see Chapter 17). Even members' apathy threatened the churches' health, as Hebrews' author reveals when he urges believers not to "stay away from our meetings, as some do" (Heb. 10:25). In perusing the books of this unit, readers will discover that many of the perplexities that beset Christians at the turn of the first and second centuries remain with us today.

The Book of Hebrews

The Book of Hebrews was written by an early Christian scholar who was equally well acquainted with the Hebrew Bible and with Greek philosophy. Combining scriptural interpretation with philosophical concepts, the work challenges readers as does no other New Testament book except Revelation. With the warning that he offers "much that is difficult to explain" (5:11), the writer—who does not identify himself—presents a dualistic view of the universe in which earthly events and human institutions are seen as reflections of invisible heavenly realities. Employing a popular form of Platonic thought, he assumes the existence of two parallel worlds: the eternal and perfect realm of spirit above and the inferior, constantly changing world below. Alone among New Testament authors, he attempts to show how Christ's sacrificial death links the two opposing realms of perishable matter and eternal spirit. He is the only biblical writer to present Jesus as a heavenly priest who serves as an everlasting mediator between God and humanity.

Authorship and Date

Hebrews is an elaborate sermon—or series of interlocking sermons—rather than a letter, but it ends with a postscript recalling one of Paul's missives (13:17–25). Although some early Christians attributed the work to Paul, many others recognized that the theology, language, and style of Hebrews were distinctly un-Pauline. (The ending comments and reference to Timothy [13:23] do not fit the rest of the work and may have been appended by a later copyist or editor.) Various commentators have speculated that the author may have been Barnabas, Priscilla, or Paul's eloquent co-worker Apollos of Alexandria.

Such attempts to link Hebrews with some well-known figure associated with first-generation Pauline Christianity have proven futile. Most scholars agree with Origen, a church scholar prominent during the early third century, who remarked that the writer's identity is known only to God. The book's date and place of composition are also unknown. Various critics suggest Alexandria, Rome, Antioch, Corinth, or some equally cosmopolitan center as the city of origin, with the time of writing estimated as between about 80 and 110 CE.

The Writer's Methods of Interpretation

Whoever he was, the anonymous author was a master of rhetoric (the art of speaking or writing persuasively). He uses excellent Greek and also shows familiarity with Hellenistic-Jewish methods of scriptural analysis and interpretation. This suggests to many scholars that the writer may have lived in Alexandria, a metropolis where Greek-educated Jews like Philo Judaeus developed highly sophisticated ways of making ancient biblical texts relevant to Greco-Roman culture. As expounded by Philo and other Alexandrine scholars, the Hebrew Bible became much more than a mere repository of legal commandments or a record of past events. To Philo and the author of Hebrews, it is an allegory in which earthly events symbolize heavenly realities.

Hebrews' thesis is that, through Jesus, God gives his ultimate revelation of spiritual reality and that Jesus offers the sole means by which humans can find salvation. The author examines selected passages from the Hebrew Bible—principally Genesis 14:18–20 and Psalm 110:4—to demonstrate Christ's unique role in the universe. In his view, the biblical texts can be understood only in the light of Christ's death and ascension into heaven. He thus gives the Hebrew Bible a strictly Christological interpretation (**typology**), explaining biblical characters and Torah regulations as prophetic "types," or models that foreshadow Jesus' theological significance.

Of special importance to the author is the Genesis figure of **Melchizedek,** a mysterious king-priest of Canaanite Salem to whom the patriarch Abraham gave a tenth of the goods he had captured in war (Gen. 14:18–20). Melchizedek becomes a prototype or prophetic symbol of Jesus, whom the author regards as both a king (Davidic Messiah) and a priest (like Melchizedek). In the author's interpretation, Melchizedek's story serves to prefigure Jesus' priesthood.

Purpose and Organization

The book's title—"To the Hebrews"—is not part of the original text; it may have been added by an editor who assumed that the writer's interest in Jewish ritual implied that he wrote for Jewish Christians. The term may apply equally well to Gentile recipients, however, and probably refers to "spiritual Israel," the Christian church at large. Whatever the intended audience, Hebrews' purpose is to urge believers to hold fast to their faith, remembering their former loyalty during persecution (10:32–34) and avoiding the pitfalls of apathy or indifference.

After an introduction (1:1–4), Hebrews is arranged in three main sections:

1. Christ, the image of God, superior to all other human or heavenly beings (1:5–4:16)
2. The Torah's priestly regulations foreshadowing Jesus' role as a priest like Melchizedek (5:1–10:39)
3. Believers exhorted to emulate biblical examples and act on faith in Jesus' supremacy (11:1–13:16)

Christ's Superiority to All Other Beings

Emphasizing his theme of Christ's superiority to all others, the author begins Hebrews by contrasting earlier biblical revelations with that made in the last days through the person of Jesus. Whereas God formerly conveyed his message in fragmentary form through the Hebrew prophets, in Jesus he discloses a complete revelation of his essential nature and purpose. As in Colossians and John's Gospel, Jesus is the agent (or goal) of God's creative purpose and a perfect reflection of the divine being (1:1–4).

Echoing Paul's assertion that Jesus attained heavenly glory through obedient humility (Phil. 2), the author states that Jesus was perfected through suffering. As a perfectly obedient Son, he is greater than Moses, leading his followers, not to an earthly destination, but to God's celestial throne (3:1–4:16). Through him, God makes his complete and final revelation.

Christ—A Priest like Melchizedek

Asking his hearers to move beyond basic ideas and to advance in understanding (5:11–6:3), the author introduces his unparalleled interpretation of Jesus as an eternal High Priest, one foreshadowed by Melchizedek. To show that Christ's priesthood is superior to that of **Aaron,** Israel's first High Priest, and the Levites who assisted him at the **Tabernacle,** Hebrews cites the narrative about Abraham paying **tithes** to Melchizedek (14:18–20). Because Melchizedek blessed Abraham and accepted offerings from him, the writer argues, the king-priest of Salem was Abraham's superior. Furthermore, Abraham's descendants, the Levitical and Aaronic priests, also shared in the patriarch's homage to Melchizedek. Present in his ancestor's "loins" when Abraham honored Melchizedek, Aaron and all his priestly offspring also confessed their inferiority to Melchizedek (7:1–10). Melchizedek is thus acknowledged as the superior of Israel's Levitical priests by virtue of his priority in time.

The author now adds Psalm 110 to his explication of Genesis 14. He notes that Yahweh swore that his king, or "messiah," is both his son and an everlasting priest like Melchizedek (Ps. 110:4). Hebrews further argues that, because Genesis does not mention either ancestors or descendants for Melchizedek, the absence of human roots or connections implies that the king-priest is without either beginning or end—an eternal priest. The symbolic everlastingness of Melchizedek's priesthood is thus the prototype of Christ, who similarly remains a priest for all time (7:3, 21–24).

In biblical times, a priest's main function was to offer animal sacrifices to atone for the people's sins and to elicit God's forgiveness, a rite of **expiation** (appeasement of divine wrath). According to Hebrews, Jesus is both the priest and the sacrifice. His offering fulfills the reality of the Torah's required sacrifices, but it is superior to the old system because his life was perfected through suffering (5:8–9). Unlike the sacrifices offered at Israel's Tabernacle or Temple, which must be repeated endlessly to ensure divine approval, Jesus' sacrifice is made only once. It remains eternally effective and brings forgiveness and salvation to those accepting its efficacy (7:26–28).

Earthly Copy and Heavenly Reality

Hebrews employs the view that the universe is composed of two levels: a lower physical realm and a higher, unseen spirit world. The author envisions Israel's earthly ceremonies of sacrifice and worship as reflections, or copies, that parallel or correspond to invisible realities in heaven (8:5) (see Figure 18.1). He then cites the solemn ritual of the Day of Atonement, the one time of the year that the High Priest was permitted to enter the Tabernacle's innermost room, the Holy of Holies, where God's glory was believed to dwell. Interpreting the atonement ritual allegorically, the author states that the priest's annual entry into God's presence prophetically signified Christ's ascension to heaven itself. There, his life stands as an eternally powerful sacrifice, making humanity forever "at one" with God (8:1–6; 9:1–14).

Because his sacrifice surpasses those decreed under the old Mosaic Covenant, Jesus inaugurates a New Covenant with his shed blood. He acts as a permanent mediator, always pleading for humanity's forgiveness (7:24–25; 9:15–22). The writer repeatedly emphasizes that neither the Mosaic Tabernacle nor Herod's Temple in Jerusalem was intended to be permanent. Both sanctuaries are only copies of heavenly realities (9:23), mere "shadows, and no true image" of Christ's supreme priestly sacrifice (10:1).

Christ

Eternal Tabernacle

Altar of Christ's
perfect and eternal
sacrifice

God's
real
abode

Heaven
(Spirit World)

High Priest

Earthly Tabernacle

Altar of animal
sacrifice

God's Kavod
(Glory)

Earth
(Physical World)

FIGURE 18.1   The Book of Hebrews' theory of correspondences. According to this theory, reality exists in two separate but parallel dimensions—the spirit world (heaven) and the physical world (earth). Material objects and customs on earth are temporary replicas, or shadows, of eternal realities in heaven. The author's notion that Jesus' "perfect" sacrifice has rendered Jewish worship obsolete is clearly partisan and represents a claim that many scholars find highly unacceptable.

An Exhortation to Remain Faithful

In Hebrews' tenth chapter, the author narrows his focus to address directly a group within his community about whom he is particularly anxious. This group apparently included people who had formerly endured severe persecution but who now were tempted to abandon the Christian faith (10:32–34). For the author, leaving "the [revealed] truth" was tantamount to repudiating Christ's sacrifice and thus condemning oneself to face a "terrifying expectation of judgment and a fierce fire which will consume God's enemies" (10:26–30). "It is a terrible thing," he reminds his audience, "to fall into the hands of the living God" (10:31). The fact that he immediately follows this dire threat by assuring his readers that the Parousia will occur imminently suggests that the potential

deserters were persons disappointed in their apocalyptic hopes: "For 'soon, very soon' [in the words of Scripture], 'he who is to come will come; he will not delay'" (an unusual interpretation of Habakkuk 2:3, a text that does not involve either the first or second advent of a messiah) (10:27). In this and similar passages, the writer apparently fears that some members of his audience are suffering such a painful disillusionment about Christ's failure to return that they are prepared to forsake the church. The author's insistence that the Christian revelation is utterly final and his repeated warnings that persons who give up their faith also relinquish forever their hope of eternal life suggest that his purpose is to prevent **apostasy,** the renunciation of their previously held beliefs.

At this crucial point in his argument, the author offers the New Testament's only definition of faith, which he renders in Platonic terms as the "certain[ty] of realities that we do not see." This belief in God's invisible world, the existence of which he has argued for throughout his sermon, "gives substance to our hopes" (11:1). (Unlike Paul, who always associates faith with a living trust in Jesus' saving power, Hebrews' author defines faith with no explicit reference to Christ.) He then unfolds a panorama of prominent figures from the Hebrew Bible, from Abel and Enoch to Sarah, wife of Abraham, and Rahab, the Canaanite prostitute who hospitably sheltered Israelite spies. According to the writer, all of these ancient characters expressed their loyalty to God in a distant era when they had only a dim preview of heavenly realities. By contrast, today's believers now possess a complete understanding of God's plan: that the ancient faithful could not receive their reward except "in company with [present Christians]." The latter must therefore demonstrate an even higher level of trust in God and his promises (11:2–40). Christian faith must now include not only a recognition that Jesus invisibly reigns as everlasting king, priest, and intercessor but also total confidence in his eventual return in glory.

Evoking the metaphor of athletic competition, the author urges believers to compete the race they had previously entered, fixing their sights on Jesus' example of endurance, a loyal persistence that won him a position "at the right hand" of God's throne (12:1–2). Observing that none in his community had yet been required to shed their blood for Jesus' sake, the author encourages them not to fear future persecution, for, as legitimate children of God, the Father "disciplines" them (12:3–13).

As if to stiffen the resolve of would-be apostates, defectors from the church, the writer again reminds them of the contrast between the two covenants that God concluded with humankind. In the first, Moses mediated the agreement amid blazing fire, earthquakes, and other terrifying phenomena. Whereas inauguration of the first covenant took place on earthly Mount Sinai, the "new covenant" that Jesus mediates is established in the ultimate reality of heaven itself, where God is manifest in infinitely more awe-inspiring wonders. If God, who "is a devouring fire," levied the death penalty on disobedient Israelites at Sinai, how much more severely will he punish those who fail to keep faith in his supreme self-revelation (12:18–29).

Several scholars propose that Hebrews' target audience included Jewish Christians who may have considered returning to their ancestral religion, perhaps as a result of the unexpectedly long delay in the Parousia. The author's repeated declarations of Jesus' superiority to all biblical figures, both human leaders like Moses and the angelic beings who populate the heavenly court, would serve to remind this group that God now relates to humanity exclusively through Israel's Messiah, Jesus. His assertion that all the great heroes and heroines of faith in the Hebrew Bible looked forward to the reality now embodied in Christ similarly encourages believers, both Jewish and Gentile, to carry on the same great tradition as Israel's faithful leaders.

Urging believers to lead blameless lives of active good deeds, the author reminds them that Jesus Christ is "the same yesterday, today, and for ever." This is another powerful reason to regard this world, with its temptations and troubles, as a temporary trial resolved in the light of eternity (13:1–9). Christians have no permanent abode on earth but seek the unseen and perfect city above as their life's goal (13:14).

Judaism and Christianity

With its declaration that Jesus' sacrifice has rendered Israel's older system of sacrificial offerings unnecessary, Hebrews consistently argues for the superiority of Jesus as God's ultimate High Priest who now acts as sole intermediary between God and humanity. Some contemporary Christians have interpreted Hebrews' thesis to mean that the New Covenant that Christ initiated has *superseded* or replaced God's Old Covenant with Israel. In its extreme form, this notion of *supersessionism* claims that God, angry with Israel for rejecting his Messiah, has in turn repudiated his original covenant people and established the Christian church in their place, making it the New Israel. Historically, this notion of a rejected Israel and triumphant church has led to widespread Christian discrimination against and persecution of Jews, culminating in the Holocaust of the 1940s.

As we have seen, however, Hebrews' author does not advocate so irrevocable a disconnection between Judaism and Christianity. Although he, like Matthew, regards the Jewish Scriptures as a Christological resource, citing biblical texts that he believes foreshadow Christ's role as both holy priest and royal messiah, he also emphasizes the unbroken continuity between the Mosaic dispensation and that which Jesus concluded. In Romans, Paul had made clear that the New Covenant is God's extension of his special partnership with Israel to include Gentiles (Rom. 9–11). In Hebrews, the writer focuses instead on Jesus' fulfillment of biblical promises, arguing that even the priestly rituals of the Tabernacle were prophetic of Christ's cosmic significance. Regarding Jesus as the climax of God's purpose for Israel, the author sees not replacement but culmination.

James

Authorship

Addressing his work to "the Twelve Tribes dispersed throughout the world" (presumably "spiritual Israel," the international church), the author calls himself "James, a servant of God and the Lord Jesus Christ." He does not claim apostolic rank or mention a kinship with Jesus, but church tradition identifies him as the person whom Paul calls "James the Lord's brother" (Gal. 1:19), the principal leader of Palestinian Jewish Christianity between about 50 and 62 CE. He was a devout respecter of the Mosaic Torah and was known to his fellow Israelites as "James

the Righteous." Despite his high reputation among both Jews and Christians, however, he was illegally executed about 62 CE.

If the author is Jesus' brother (or close relative), it is strange that he rarely mentions Jesus and almost never refers to his teachings. As a man who had known Jesus all his life (Mark 6:3) and had seen the risen Lord (1 Cor. 15:7), he might be expected to use his personal acquaintance with Jesus to lend authority to his instructions. The fact that his writing contains virtually nothing about Jesus suggests that the author did not personally know him and consequently could not have been a member of Jesus' family (see Box 12.3). (For a defense of the author's relationship to Jesus, see Johnson in "Recommended Reading.")

Two qualities of this document offer general clues to its author's background. Besides being written in excellent Greek (not something a Galilean native was likely to be capable of), it repeatedly echoes Greek editions of the Hebrew Bible, especially the Book of Proverbs and later Hellenistic wisdom books like Ecclesiasticus and the Wisdom of Solomon. Both James's subject matter and his language reflect a deep interest in Greek-Jewish wisdom literature. This fact suggests that the author is a Hellenistic-Jewish Christian concerned about applying the principles of Israel's later sages to problems in his Christian circle. The writer may have lived in any Greek-speaking Jewish community in Syria, Palestine, Egypt, or Italy.

Form and Organization

Except for the brief opening salutation, the work bears no similarity to a letter. It is instead a collection of proverbs, commentaries, scriptural paraphrases, and moral advice. As a literary genre, James is the only New Testament document resembling the compilations of wise counsel found in the Hebrew Bible.

Lacking any principle of coherence, James leaps from topic to topic and then back again. The only unifying theme is the author's view of the purpose and function of religion (1:26–27), which he defines as typically Jewish good works, charitable practices that will save the soul and cancel a multitude of sins (5:19–20). Following the author's order, we examine several of his main interests:

1. The nature of trials and temptations (1:2–27)
2. Respect for the poor (2:1–13)
3. "Works," or good deeds, as the only measure of faith (2:14–26)
4. Control of speech (3:1–12)
5. Warnings against violent ambition and exploitation of the poor (4:1–5:6)

Recipients and Date

From the topics covered, this book seems directed at Jewish-Christian groups that had existed long enough to have developed a sense of class distinction within the church. Wealthy Christians snub poorer ones (2:1–9), fail to share their material possessions (2:14–26), engage in worldly competition (4:1–10), and exploit fellow believers of the laboring class (4:13–5:6). These socially stratified and economically divided communities suggest a time long after that of the impoverished Jerusalem commune described in Acts 2. Most scholars date the work in the late first century, considerably after the historical James's martyrdom in the early 60s.

Trials and Temptations

In this introductory section (1:2–27), James articulates a philosophy of human experience that puts his ethical advice in perspective. Dealing with the twin problems of external suffering and internal temptations to do wrong, the author offers insight into God's reasons for permitting evil to afflict even the faithful. "Trials" (presumably including persecutions) are potentially beneficial experiences because they allow the believer the opportunity to demonstrate faith and fortitude under pressure, thus strengthening character. To help Christians endure such trials, God grants insight to persons who pray for

it single-mindedly and never doubt that God will provide the understanding necessary to maintain faith.

Arguing that the Creator is not responsible for tests of faith or private temptations to sin, James declares that God, "untouched by evil," does not tempt anyone. Human temptation arises from within through the secret cultivation of forbidden desire that eventually inspires the act of "sin," which in turn breeds death (1:12–15). In contrast, God is the source of perfection (1:17) and the origin of life (1:12). In this miniature theodicy (defense of God's goodness despite the world's evil), the writer insists that God is not responsible for injustice or undeserved suffering. Society's evils result from purely human selfishness. If believers resist evil, God grants them the power to drive away even the devil (4:7–8).

The only New Testament writer to define religion, James describes it as the active practice of good works, an imitation of the divine benefactor who sets the example of generosity (1:16). The religion God approves is practical: helping "orphans and widows" and keeping "oneself untarnished by the world" (1:27). In James's two-part definition, the "orphans and widows" are Judaism's classic symbols of the defenseless who are God's special care, and "the world" represents a society that repudiates God. Thoroughly Jewish in its emphasis on merciful deeds, James's "true religion" cannot be formalized by doctrine, creed, or ritual (cf. Matt. 25:31–46).

Respect for the Poor

Addressing a social problem that plagues virtually every community, whether religious or secular, James denounces all social snobbery. Christians must make the poor feel as welcome in their midst as the rich and powerful (2:1–13). Noting that it is the wealthy who typically oppress the church, James reminds his audience that the poor will inherit "the kingdom" and that insulting them is an offense against God. Interestingly, the author does not use Jesus' teaching to emphasize God's gracious intent to reward those now poor but instead quotes from the Hebrew Bible. If believers do not love their fellow human beings (Lev. 19:18), they break all of God's laws, for to fail to keep one precept is to disobey the entire Torah (2:10).

Good Works as the Only Measure of Faith

In James's most famous passage (2:14–26), the author exposes the futility of persons who claim they have faith but do not follow the practical religion of good works. To James, belief that fails to inspire right action is "dead." Only "deeds"—serving the "orphans and widows" and others suffering comparable need—can demonstrate the reality of faith.

Many interpreters see this section as an attack on Paul's doctrine of salvation through faith (the apostle's rejection of "works" of Torah obedience in favor of trust in God's saving purpose in Christ; see the discussions of Galatians and Romans in Chapter 15). Like Paul, James cites the Genesis example of Abraham to prove his point, but he gives it a strikingly different interpretation. James asserts that it was Abraham's action—his willingness to sacrifice his son Isaac—that justified him. The writer's conclusion is distinctly un-Pauline: "a man is justified by deeds and not by faith in itself" (2:24). With its implication that one earns divine approval through hard work and service to others, this conclusion seems to contradict Paul's assertion that salvation comes only through God's grace, accepted on trust (faith) (see Gal. and Rom. 1–8).

James's conclusion that faith without action is as dead as a corpse without breath (2:26) may appear to repudiate Paul's primary teaching. Many scholars, however, regard it as a necessary corrective to a common misapplication of Pauline doctrine. It must be remembered that although Paul labored to the point of exhaustion serving others he did not see his "works" as the means God provided for his "justification." Martin Luther doubted the validity of James's argument, describing the work as "strawlike"

for its failure to recognize the primacy of divine grace. In its canonical function, however, James serves as a reminder to Christians that faith—which he apparently regards as a set of beliefs—must be expressed through diligent service to the poor and aid to the downtrodden.

Controlling the Tongue

Like earlier writers in the Hebrew wisdom tradition, James underscores the importance of self-control in speech (3:1–12; cf. Prov. 15:1–4, 26, 28; Ecclus. 5:11–6:1; 28:13–26). The tongue is a fire fed by the flames of hell (3:6), paradoxically both the instrument of divine praise and the organ of destructive gossip. Contrasting its abuses with spiritual wisdom, James emphasizes the constructive, peace-enhancing quality of the latter (3:13–18).

Warnings Against Ambition and Exploitation

True wisdom produces peace and harmony; James's recipients, in contrast, are divided by envy, ambition, and conflict. Their ambitious pursuit of unworthy goals makes them God's enemy (4:3–4). Boastful of their financial successes, they forget that their continued existence depends on God's patience and mercy. Christian merchants and landowners are the author's prime target in the New Testament's most incisive attack on the rich (4:13–5:4). Those whose wealth gives them power over their economic inferiors have exploited it shamelessly. Without conscience, wealthy employers have defrauded their workers, delaying payment of wages on which the laboring poor depend to live. Such injustice outrages the Creator, who views the luxury-loving exploiters as overfed animals ripe for slaughter (see Box 18.1).

Reminding his audience that the Lord will return (5:7), presumably to judge those who economically murder the defenseless (5:6), James ends his sermon on a positive note for any who have strayed from the right path. Sinners and others who are "sick," perhaps spiritually as

BOX 18.1 Biblical Views on Wealth

James's tirade against wealthy Christians may shock some readers, but it is consistent both with Jesus' pronouncements on riches in the Synoptic Gospels and with prophetic denunciations of economic greed in the Hebrew Bible. Part of the Bible's (sometimes) negative attitude toward wealth stems from a widespread belief in the ancient world that the supply of wealth was limited and that one person's acquisition of material goods must necessarily be at the expense of others. Thus the prophet Isaiah violently condemned entrepreneurs who ruthlessly acquired other people's property, perhaps foreclosing on loans during times of drought or famine:

> Shame on you! you who add house to house
>   and join field to field,
> until not an acre remains,
> and you are left to dwell alone in the land.
>   (Isa. 5:8)

Jesus' parables of the greedy "fool" who obsessively acquires possessions (Luke 12:16–20) and of the "rich man" who apparently ignores the starving poor (Luke 16:19–31) make the same point: Wealth that is unshared with the needy brings divine condemnation because "you cannot serve God and Money" (Luke 16:13). Specifically, James excoriates the rich who fail to pay living wages to their hired laborers. He also offers the eschatological key to interpreting the New Testament writers' attitude toward amassing wealth: "you have piled up wealth in an age that is near its close" (James 5:4). With the End at hand, the pursuit of riches is not only pointless but offensive to God. (For a contrasting view that presents material affluence as evidence of divine favor, see the list of secular blessings promised a faithful Israel in Deuteronomy 28:1–14; compare Proverbs 3:16; 10:22.)

---

well as physically, can hope for recovery. God's healing grace operates through congregational prayer for the afflicted. A good person's prayer has the power to rescue a sinner from death and to erase countless sins (5:13–20).

1 Peter

Like James, 1 Peter is ascribed to one of the three Jerusalem "pillars." The two works have other points in common as well, including similar convictions about proper Christian behavior and a shared belief that spiritual gifts like love and prayer can wipe out sin (James 5:20; 1 Pet. 4:8). Both also refer to social discrimination, and even persecution, against believers (James 1:2–8; 5:7–11; 1 Pet. 1:6–7; 4:12–19). A philosophy of peaceful submission and patience during trials and tests of faith characterizes both documents.

Authorship and Date

The majority of scholars also agree that 1 Peter resembles James in being pseudonymous, the work of a later Christian writing in Peter's name. This scholarly consensus is based on several factors, ranging from the elegant Greek style in which the epistle is composed to the particular social circumstances to which it alludes. As an Aramaic-speaking Galilean fisherman who had little formal education (Acts 4:13), the historical Peter seems unlikely to have produced the work's exceptionally fine Greek. Critics defending Peter's authorship note that the epistle was written "through Sylvanus [Silas]" (5:12), perhaps the same Sylvanus who accompanied Paul on some of his missionary journeys (Acts 15:22) and who presumably was skilled at preaching to Hellenistic audiences. According to the minority theory, Sylvanus acted as Peter's secretary, transforming his Aramaic dictation into sophisticated Greek.

Regarding the argument that Peter used an amanuensis as unverifiable, most scholars conclude that too many other factors combine to militate against a Petrine origin. If Peter—a member of Jesus' inner circle—was the author, why does he not reveal personal knowledge of Jesus' teachings, as an apostle would be expected to do? If Peter wrote the work shortly before he became a victim of Nero's persecution in Rome (mid-60s CE), as defenders of the work's genuineness maintain, why does he address the letter to churches in Asia Minor (1:1)? Historians can find no evidence that Nero's campaign against Christians extended into the provinces.

According to some interpreters, the epistle's references to believers' troubles (1:6) may mean nothing more than the social discrimination and hostility Roman society accorded many early Christians. Other commentators explain the "fiery ordeals" (4:12–13) as the public ill treatment of some Asia Minor believers under the emperor Domitian (c. 95 CE) or the more severe persecution under Trajan (c. 112 CE). According to 1 Peter, believers are punished merely for bearing Christ's name (4:14–16), a situation that does not seem to have characterized Nero's era but that does accord with the policies of his successors. Letters exchanged between the emperor Trajan and Pliny the Younger, his appointed governor of Bithynia, one of the provinces of Asia Minor to which 1 Peter is addressed, seem to reflect the same conditions the epistle describes (Pliny, *Letters* 97) (see Figure 18.2). For that reason, many scholars favor a date in the early second century for the epistle, though scholars do not yet fully agree.

A date after 70 CE is indicated by the author's greetings from "her who dwells in Babylon" (5:13). "Her" refers to the writer's church (2 John 1), and "Babylon" became the Christian code name for Rome after Titus destroyed Jerusalem, thus duplicating the Babylonian Empire's infamous desecration of the holy city (587 BCE). As an archetype of the ungodly nation, "Babylon" is also Revelation's symbol of Rome (Rev. 14:8; 18:2). Most critics

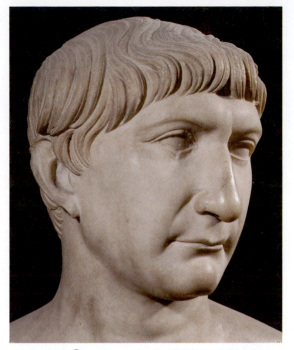

FIGURE 18.2 Bust of Trajan (98–117 CE). Under Trajan, the Roman Empire reached its greatest geographical extent, stretching from Britain in the northwest to Mesopotamia (Iraq) in the east. Pliny the Younger wrote to Trajan about the proper method of handling Christians. The emperor replied that he opposed anonymous accusations and ordered that accused persons who demonstrated their loyalty to the state by making traditional sacrifices should not be prosecuted.

assume that 1 Peter originated in the capital, the traditional site of Peter's martyrdom.

Purpose and Organization

Although Peter probably did not write this epistle, the early church recognized its ethical value by adopting it into the canon. The author's purpose is to encourage believers to hold fast to their integrity, as Christians like Peter did in Nero's time, and to promote Christian ethics. He urges the faithful to live so blamelessly that outsiders can never accuse them of anything illegal or morally reprehensible. If one endures legal prosecution, it should be only "as a Christian" (4:14–16).

Although many scholars formerly regarded 1 Peter as a baptismal sermon, to which editors later attached an opening (1:1–2) and conclusion (4:12–5:14) to give it the formal appearance of a letter, this interpretation has been generally abandoned. The writer does allude to his recipients as "new born infants" (2:2) whom God has granted a "new birth" (1:3; cf 1:23), as if they had been only recently baptized, but the significance of baptism is not his main theme. Some commentators regard the trials and sufferings inherent in leading a Christian life in a generally hostile society as the author's principal concern (see below). Still others emphasize the importance of hope (cf. 1:13). Taken as a whole, the epistle seems to posit an intimate parallel between the life and sufferings of Christ and the present experience of his followers, who endure similar hardship and persecution but who can also look forward to sharing in Christ's post resurrection "splendor" (1:6–12). As recipients of what Israel's prophets only dimly foresaw, the faithful, through the Holy Spirit, now enjoy an understanding of God's purpose that even angels may envy (1:12).

As a basic summary of Christian ideals and ethics, 1 Peter can be divided into three sections:

1. The privileges and values of the Christian calling (1:3–2:10)
2. The obligations and responsibilities of Christian life (2:11–4:11)
3. The ethical meaning of suffering as a Christian (4:12–5:11)

The Privileges and Values of the Christian Calling

Addressing believers who had not known the historical Jesus, Peter stresses the rarity and inestimable value of the faith recently transmitted to them. They must regard their present trials and difficulties as opportunities to display the depth of their commitment and the quality of their love (1:3–7). By remaining faithful, they will attain the salvation of which the Hebrew prophets spoke (1:9–12). Proper appreciation for Christ's sacrifice, which makes him the "living stone" of the heavenly temple, will also make believers a living part of the eternal sanctuary (2:4–8). Christians, including Gentiles, are the new "chosen race"—"a royal priesthood, a dedicated nation, and a people claimed by God for his own" (2:9–10).

The Obligations and Responsibilities of Christian Life

Scholars have noted that 1 Peter contains many Pauline ideas, particularly on matters of Christian behavior and obedience to the Roman state. In the second section (2:11–4:11), the author focuses on the responsibilities and moral conduct of God's people, who should act in a way that even nonbelievers admire (2:12). Echoing Romans 13, 1 Peter advises peaceful submission to governmental authorities (3:13–15). In the writer's social and political hierarchy, slaves and servants are subject to their masters (2:18), and wives to their husbands (3:1–2). Those who suffer unjustly must bear it as Jesus bore his sufferings (1:19–25; 3:13–18; 4:1–5).

In alluding to Christ's crucifixion, the author includes two fascinating references to Jesus' descent into the Underworld (Hades), presumably during the interval between his death and his resurrection (3:18–20; 4:6). Suggesting the existence of a rich early Christian lore surrounding Jesus' posthumous experiences, Peter's brief allusions inspired a later tradition that after his death Jesus entered hell and rescued the souls of faithful Israelites who had been imprisoned there before the way to heaven was open (see Box 18.2).

The Ethical Meaning of Suffering as a Christian

References to suffering occur throughout 1 Peter, but the author does not directly address the meaning of suffering as a Christian until the third part of his epistle (4:12–5:11). In his introduction, he notes that his audience

BOX 18.2 Jesus' Descent into the Underworld

Only the author of Luke-Acts describes Jesus' post resurrection ascent to heaven (Acts 1:10–11), and only the Petrine epistles* explicitly refer to a tradition about Jesus' postmortem descent into the Underworld:

> In the body he was put to death; in the spirit he was brought to life. And in the spirit he went and made his proclamation to the imprisoned spirits. They had refused obedience long ago while God waited patiently in the days of Noah . . .
> (1 Pet. 3:19–20)

According to a common interpretation, the "imprisoned spirits" are the "sons of the gods" (presumably angels) who "fell" from heaven when they trespassed divinely set boundaries by mating with the fair "daughters of men," thus producing "the heroes of old, men of renown" (Gen. 6:1–4). Although Genesis says nothing about the divine "sons'" subsequent fate, extrabiblical tradition states that God had confined these rebels in a dark and fiery prison, where they awaited the final judgment (1 Enoch 6–10). The author of 2 Peter apparently adopts that tradition, declaring that "God did not spare the angels who sinned, but consigned them to the dark pit of hell" (2:4). (The word here translated as "hell" is *Tartarus,* in Greek myth the subterranean dungeon housing fallen gods; see Box 4.1, "The Three-Story Universe.") In some views, 1 Peter's cryptic allusion to preaching "the Gospel" to "the dead" (4:6) refers to Jesus' "harrowing of Hell," when he descended into the Underworld to offer a message of redemption to persons who had perished before his death and resurrection had made salvation possible. (For a discussion of pre-Christian gods and heroes, such as Dionysus and Orpheus, who died, descended into Hades' realm, and then ascended to immortal life in heaven, see Chapter 4.)

*Ephesians may indirectly allude to the descent tradition (Eph. 4:10).

presently endures "trials of many kinds," tests of character that he compares to the process by which a refiner's fire separates pure gold from dross (1:6–7). In chapter 4, he reminds believers that because they are Christ's disciples they must expect to suffer as he did—and to acquire a mental attitude like his, voluntarily submitting to the divine will. Because "the end of all things" is near, Christians must lead "an ordered and sober life," ready for "the fiery ordeal" that lies before them (4:7, 12). Whatever form such persecution takes, they must accept it with "joy," for sharing Christ's pain also means sharing in his imminent "glory" (4:13–14). "If anyone suffers as a Christian," it should be welcomed as an opportunity to "confess [Jesus'] name" and thus honor God (4:16).

The author interprets Christians' present afflictions as evidence that "the [final] judgment" has already begun, starting with the church, "God's own household." If the righteous are but narrowly saved, what will happen to the wicked (4:17–19)? In this crisis, elders must shepherd the flock with loving care; younger people must submit humbly to their rule (5:1–7). Everyone must remain alert because the devil, "like a roaring lion, prowls round looking for someone to devour." The faithful who resist him will partake of Christ's reward (5:8–11).

Jude

Placed last among the general epistles, Jude is less a letter than a tract denouncing an unidentified group of heretics. Its primary intent is to persuade the (also unidentified) recipients to join the writer in defending orthodox Christian traditions (v. 3). Rather than specify his opponents' doctrinal errors or refute their arguments, the writer instead threatens the heretics with apocalyptic punishment drawn from both biblical and nonbiblical sources.

Authorship and Date

The author refers to himself as Jude (Judas), a servant of Jesus Christ and brother of James (v. 1)—and presumably also a kinsman of Jesus (Matt. 13:55; Mark 6:3). According to Eusebius, Jude, whom he describes as "the brother, humanly speaking, of the Savior," left descendants who played an important role in the Jerusalem church even after the Romans destroyed the city in 70 CE. Eusebius quotes an older historian, Hegesippus, who reported that during Domitian's reign the emperor ordered Jude's two grandsons to appear before him. Worried that their Davidic ancestry might make them potential leaders of another Jewish uprising, Domitian released the two when they demonstrated that they were only hardworking peasants with no pretensions to royalty (*History* 3.20) (see Box 12.3).

Scholars believe that Jude is not the work of Jesus' "brother" but rather is a pseudonymous work that entered the canon because of its presumed association with the Lord's family. Like James, the author shows no personal familiarity with Jesus and cites none of his characteristic teachings. He refers to Christianity as a fixed body of beliefs that the faithful already possess (v. 3) and to the apostles as prophets of a former age (vv. 17–18). This indicates that the book was composed significantly after the historical Jude's time. Most scholars suggest a date between about 100 and 125 CE.

Style and Content

The letter of Jude represents a kind of rhetoric known as **invective**—an argument characterized by verbal abuse and insults. Without describing their teachings, Jude calls the heretics "brute beasts" (v. 10), "enemies of religion" who have wormed their way into the church to pervert it with their "licentiousness" (v. 4). A "blot on [Christian] love feasts" (v. 12), they are doomed to suffer divine wrath as did Cain, Balaam, Korah, and other villains of the Hebrew Bible. Because the author does not try to explain his reasons for disagreeing with his opponents, but merely calls them names, accuses them of immorality, and predicts their future destruction, Jude has been called the least theologically creative book in the New Testament.

Apocalyptic Judgment

Jude views the heretics' misbehavior as fulfilling the apostles' predictions about End time (v. 18). Because their **apostasy** proves the nearness of the Last Judgment (an idea also expressed in 1 John 2:18), Jude reminds his audience of earlier punishments of the wicked, citing the plagues in Egypt (v. 5), the fallen angels of Genesis (v. 6), and the fiery destruction of Sodom and Gomorrah (vv. 6–7).

Use of Noncanonical Writings Jude is the only New Testament writer to go beyond the Hebrew Bible and quote directly from the **Pseudepigrapha,** Jewish religious works not included in the biblical canon. Citing the Book of 1 Enoch (1:9) verbatim, Jude reproduces a passage describing the Lord's negative judgment on "the ungodly" (v. 15). From copies of Enoch preserved among the Dead Sea Scrolls, we know that the Essenes studied the work. Jude's quotation, as well as several other allusions to the work (1 Enoch 1:1–9; 5:4; 18:12, 14–16; 27:2; 60:8; 93:2), suggests that some early Christian groups also regarded Enoch as authoritative.

In addition, Jude's allusion to a postbiblical legend about the archangel Michael contending with the devil for Moses' body (v. 9) may be taken from the incompletely preserved Assumption of Moses, another late noncanonical work. (When a later writer incorporated much of Jude into chapter 2 of 2 Peter, he deleted all references to the noncanonical writings.)

Exhortation to the Faithful Jude's advice to his orthodox recipients is as general as his denunciation of the false teachers. Counseling them to pray and live anticipating Jesus' return (vv. 20–21), he concedes that some involved with the heretics deserve pity and can be helped. Others are pitiable but corrupted by sensuality. The author's opinion that the clothing (or bodies) of such persons must be despised (v. 23) suggests that Jude advocates a strict asceticism—a self-discipline that denies physical appetites or comforts.

To balance its largely vindictive tone, the work closes with a particularly lyric doxology praising "the only God our Savior" (vv. 24–25).

2 Peter

Like Jude, 2 Peter was written for the double purpose of condemning false teachers and warning of the imminent world judgment. Theologically, its importance lies in the author's attempt to explain why God allows evil to continue and to reassert the early Christian belief that Jesus' Second Coming is near (3:1–15). Offering a theory that human history is divided into three distinct chronological epochs, or "worlds," 2 Peter is the only New Testament book to argue that the present world will be entirely consumed by fire.

Authorship and Date

Whereas many scholars defend Petrine authorship of 1 Peter, virtually none believe that 2 Peter was written by Jesus' chief disciple. The pseudonymous author, however, takes pains to claim Peter's identity (1:1), asserting that he was present at Christ's transfiguration (1:17–18) and that he wrote an earlier letter, presumably 1 Peter (3:1). Under the great fisherman's name, he writes to reaffirm his concept of the true apostolic teaching in the face of heretical misinterpretation of it. Portraying the church leader as about to face death, the writer offers

this epistle as Peter's last will and testament, a final exposition of the apostolic faith (1:14–15).

The pseudonymous author's claims are not persuasive, however, because 2 Peter contains too many indications that it was written long after Peter's martyrdom in about 64 or 65 CE. The letter's main intent—to reestablish the apostolic view of the Parousia—shows that the writer is addressing a group that lived long enough after the original apostles' day to have given up believing that Christ would return soon. The author's opponents deny the Parousia doctrine because the promised Second Coming has not materialized even though the "fathers" (first-generation disciples) have long since passed away. In addition, the writer makes use of Jude, itself an early-second-century document, incorporating most of it into his work.

The work also refers to Paul's letters as Scripture (3:16), a status they did not achieve until well into the second century. A late date is also indicated by the author's insistence on divinely inspired Scripture as the principal teaching authority (1:20–21). This tendency to substitute a fixed written text for the Spirit's operation or the "living voice" of the gospel also appears in the Pastor's letters (2 Tim. 3:15–16), which are similarly products of the second century.

Finally, many leaders of the early church doubted 2 Peter's apostolic origins, resulting in the epistle's absence from numerous lists of "approved" books. Not only was 2 Peter one of the last works to gain entrance into the New Testament, but scholars believe that it was also the last canonical book written. Composed at some point after 100 CE, it may not have appeared until as late as about 140 CE.

Organization and Purpose

A brief work, 2 Peter can be divided into three main sections:

1. The writer's apostolic authority and eschatological purpose (1:1–32)
2. Condemnations of false teachers (based on Jude) (2:1–22)

3. Defense of the Parousia doctrine, including a theodicy, and exhortation to behavior appropriate to End time (3:1–18)

The Delayed Parousia

Chapter 2 is devoted to invective. It is a brutal attack on false teachers whom the author describes as "slaves of corruption" and compares to dogs that eat their own vomit (2:1–22). Like the authors of Jude and 1 John, the writer seems unaware of any incongruity between the teaching of Christian love on the one hand and the savage abuse of fellow believers who disagree with him on the other. To him, dissenters have no more claim to respect than wild animals that are born only to be trapped and slaughtered (2:12).

It is not clear whether the opponents castigated in chapter 2 are the same skeptics who deny the Parousia in 3:3–4. In any case, the author's primary goal is to reinstate the early Christian apocalyptic hope. To convince his hearers, he reminds them that one world has already perished under a divine judgment—the world destroyed in Noah's flood (3:5–6). The present "heavens and earth" are reserved for burning, a divine act that will destroy unbelieving persons, presumably including the writer's opponents.

In his prediction of this world's coming incineration, the author apparently borrows the Stoic philosophers' theory that the cosmos undergoes cycles of destruction and renewal. Employing Stoic images and vocabulary, 2 Peter foretells a cosmic conflagration in which heaven will be swept away in a roaring fire and the earth will disintegrate, exposing all its secrets (3:10).

Because the entire universe is destined to fall apart in a cosmic catastrophe, the author advises his recipients to prepare for an imminent judgment. They should work hard to hurry it along, the implication being that correct human behavior will influence God to accelerate his schedule for the End (3:11–12).

Citing either Revelation's vision (21:1–3) or the Isaiah passages on which it is based (Isa. 65:17; 66:22), the author states that a third world will replace the previous two destroyed, respectively, by water and fire. "New heavens and a new earth" will host true justice (3:13), the eschatological kingdom of God.

Peter's Theodicy   The author is aware that some Christians who doubt the Parousia may do so because God, despite the arrival, death, and ascension to heaven of the Messiah, has not acted to conquer evil. God's seeming delay, however, has a saving purpose. Holding back judgment, the Deity allows time for more people to repent and be spared the coming holocaust (3:9, 15). Although exercising his kindly patience in the realm of human time, God himself dwells in eternity, where "a thousand years is like one day." From his vantage point, the Parousia is not delayed; his apparent slowness to act is really a manifestation of his will to save all people (3:8–9).

Paul's Letters   The author returns to criticizing his opponents in a famous reference to Paul's letters. Admitting that the Pauline correspondence contains unclear passages, he accuses immature Christians of twisting their meaning. Although he refers to Paul as a friend and brother, he clearly does not approve of the way in which some groups interpret Paul's teachings (3:15–16). Some critics suggest that if 2 Peter originated in Rome the writer may be referring to Marcion or other teachers who based their doctrines on a collection of Paul's letters. As in the case of Jude, the author does not give us enough information to identify his opponents with any certainty.

As the last-written New Testament book, 2 Peter affirms the primitive Christian hope that Jesus would soon return to establish his kingdom and eliminate evil from the universe. Although predicting that our world will disappear in a fiery cataclysm, 2 Peter foresees a renewed creation in which righteousness prevails. While they await the Lord's return to bring about the promised New Age, Christians must cling to the apostles' original teachings, avoiding heretical misinterpretations and by their good works shortening the time before the final day arrives (3:10–15). Although 2 Peter adopts the Stoic view that the present universe must perish in flames (an extreme belief that even Revelation does not advocate), it also shares Revelation's ultimately optimistic vision of the final and complete triumph of absolute good.

Letters from the Johannine Community

Three documents from a leader of the Johannine community reveal problems that beset his group perhaps a decade or two after the Gospel of John was first published. The Gospel author is concerned about believers' expulsion from the synagogue (cf. John 9:22; 12:42) and about the threat of external violence—people who seek to kill believers imagine they are "performing a religious duty" (John 16:1–3)—but the author of the letters of 1, 2, and 3 John is concerned only about conditions *within* the group. Instead of persecutions from the outside world, the letter writer, whose community has perhaps moved to a new geographical location, deals with internal dissensions and what he regards as the false teachings of some fellow Christians.

Authorship

Like the Fourth Gospel, the Johannine epistles are traditionally ascribed to the apostle John. Whereas 1 John, which is actually a treatise outlining standards of belief and behavior, is anonymous, 2 and 3 John, which are genuine letters, are attributed merely to "the elder [Greek, *presbyteros*]." Most scholars believe that neither the apostle John nor the Evangelist responsible for the Gospel wrote the epistles. Because of similarities in style, vocabulary, and theology, however, most agree that the same unidentified "elder" wrote all three documents. In these writings we see unfolded one the great ironies of religious history: the community of the Beloved Disciple, which was to be distinguished by the mutual love of its members (John 13:34–35), splintered and divided amid bitter controversy.

1 John

The longest epistle, 1 John contains the elder's defense of his community's most characteristic teachings: the historical Jesus' physical humanity, his **Incarnation** "in the flesh," and the necessity of showing love for fellow believers. Echoing the Gospel's opening hymn to the Word (*Logos*), the writer emphasizes his community's sensory experience of "the word of life . . . made visible." Using the plural "we," the author insists that Johannine believers have "seen it with our own eyes" and "felt it with our own hands," presumably referring to the corporal presence of the incarnate Christ among them (1 John 1:1–4). By identifying his intended audience as persons who "give their allegiance to the Son of God" (5:13), the **elder** probably addresses a core group whom he wishes to join him in opposing the alleged false teachers who were then breaking up the "brotherhood" (John 21:23). While summarizing his group's essential teachings—about Jesus' dual nature and the love connecting believers—the writer illustrates how John's Gospel traditions should be understood, interpreting them in a way that made the Fourth Gospel acceptable to the emerging doctrines of Christian orthodoxy (see the discussion of Gnosticism below).

The author's task was difficult because, like Paul's early charismatic churches, the Johannine communities took seriously the operation of the Holy Spirit among them. Paul asks Christians to "test the spirits," the unseen forces inspiring individual revelations, but offers no specific instructions for doing so (1 Thess. 5:19–21). Writing perhaps sixty or more years later, the elder similarly advises his group not to "trust any and every spirit" but to "test the spirits, to see whether they are from God" (4:1). In urging believers to "distinguish the spirit of truth from the spirit of error" (4:6), however, the elder goes further than Paul by giving his audience a set of standards, both doctrinal and ethical, by which to separate religious truth from falsehood. He is the first Christian known to provide such criteria.

The elder explains that his message is essentially the familiar foundation upon which the Johannine church is built: He gives believers "no new command," but only "the old command which you always had before you . . . the message which you heard in the beginning" (2:7). Evoking the same moral **dualism** that pervades the Gospel, the elder first affirms his community's basic teaching: "Here is the message we heard from him and pass on to you: that God is light" (1:5). Whereas his people now walk in light, the dissenters—who have demonstrated their unworthiness by leaving the elder's congregation—walk in darkness, a declaration reflecting the Gospel's pervasive light-dark dichotomy (compare 1 John 1:5–7; 2:9–11 with John 1:5; 3:19; 8:12; 12:46). Persons who left the community betray their mental darkness by rejecting the unique Johannine doctrine of incarnation. The secessionists fail to pass the doctrinal test when they do not "acknowledge that Jesus Christ has come in the flesh" (4:1–2). For thus denying Jesus' material humanity, the elder labels the secessionists "Antichrist," literally "opponents of Christ," adding that there are now many such "antichrists" abroad (2:18–19; 4:3).

The proliferation of these "false prophets," whom the elder also calls "[children] of the devil" (3:8), "proves to us that this is indeed the last hour," an indication that in his group the Gospel's concept of realized eschatology may have coexisted with more traditional ideas about the End (cf. 2:28). Besides failing the doctrinal test, the secessionists also flunk behavioral ethics. They do not "live as Christ himself lived," showing love for others (2:6). The writer's exposition of his community's cardinal rule, to "love one another as he [Jesus] commanded" (3:23), is one of the New Testament's most celebrated insights. Perceiving that "love is from God" and that "everyone who loves is a child of God," the elder offers the Bible's singular definition of God: "God is love" (4:9, 17). Although the writer implores his audience seven times to love their fellow Christians and asserts that believers "are bound to lay down [their] lives for our brothers" (3:16; cf. John 15:12–14), he cites only one concrete example of how love is expressed, by rescuing people from dire poverty (3:17).

A Response to Gnosticism?

Many commentators suggest that the secessionists whom John denounced were proto-Gnostics, forerunners of the **Gnosticism** that competed with other forms of Christianity from the second through the fifth centuries CE. Although some scholars object that full-blown Gnosticism had not yet developed at the time the Johannine letters were composed, others point out that the seeds of Gnostic ideas probably existed well before Gnosticism evolved into a distinct movement (see Box 18.3). Extremely varied in its myths about creation and the spirit realm, Gnosticism nonetheless consistently took a dualistic view of the cosmos, typically insisting that only the spirit was pure and good and that the physical world, the creation of an inferior god, was inherently corrupt. Imprisoned in physical bodies, humans could escape the world of decaying matter only through precious knowledge (Greek, *gnosis*) of the higher realm. As a revealer of divine truth who descended from

BOX 18.3 Gnosticism

Although often lumped together as an undifferentiated movement, Gnosticism was extremely complex and took many different forms. Most Gnostic groups, however, held in common a belief that *gnosis* (knowledge) of spiritual truths opened the way to personal salvation. Knowledge or conscious awareness that one's true nature did not consist of the physical body but of an immortal spirit was a first step in ultimately returning to one's original home, the invisible dimension of pure spirit.

Many Gnostics reinterpreted Genesis to explain the origin of the inferior material world, the production of a limited creator god. This deity's ignorance of the higher spirit realm results in the cosmic defects of sin, suffering, death, and decay. Some Gnostic teachers developed elaborate mythologies to illustrate the evolutionary process by which entities from the spirit world—such as Sophia or Wisdom—inadvertently helped to generate the deeply flawed material world, in which divine souls are trapped in dying bodies. To Christian Gnostics, Jesus had descended from the highest heaven to reveal the true nature of being and to help others escape from fleshly bondage. Because Jesus was an immortal spirit uncontaminated by physical qualities, some Gnostics theorized that he only seemed to be a mortal human. Instead of dying on the cross, he simply re-ascended to heaven, his place of origin. Many scholars think it likely that former members of the Johannine community who withdrew from the elder's group were proto-Gnostics who denied Jesus' physical humanity. Certainly the Johannine assertion that Jesus had preexisted as the eternal Word of God before descending to earth made this work extremely popular in Gnostic circles, which produced the first known commentary on John's Gospel.

---

heaven, Jesus was pure spirit; he merely *appeared* to be human.

In this line of thought, members of the Johannine church who denied that Jesus came "in the flesh" espoused a brand of Gnosticism known as **Docetism.** Derived from a Greek term meaning "to seem," Docetism held that Jesus did not suffer physically and die, but simply returned to heaven, his spiritual home. When the elder insists that "Jesus Christ came *in the flesh* (4:2, emphasis added), he asserts that the preexistent Word was also fully human, that the man who died on the cross and the exalted heavenly Christ are one. By placing this theological limit on interpreting Jesus spiritually, the author of 1 John demonstrated that the Gospel of John—with its unique emphasis on Jesus' divinity—was consistent with teachings of the mainstream church.

The Issue of Sin Considering the secessionists and other promulgators of false doctrine as sinners, the elder devotes considerable space to the problem of sin, which he defines as "lawlessness," the willful breaking of divine commands (3:4). In his initial discussion of sin, he categorically states that anyone who claims to be "sinless" is "self-deceived" because all people sin. He then reassures believers that Jesus, who functions as "the remedy for the defilement" of all sin, can be trusted to forgive the sinner (1:4–2:2). Later in his essay, however, the writer apparently contradicts himself when he declares that "a child of God does not commit sin"; the Christian "cannot be a sinner because he is God's child" (3:9–10). Conversely, "the man who sins is a child of the devil" (3:8). In his essay's conclusion, the elder further complicates his argument when he remarks that "a brother" may "commit sin" but not be guilty of "deadly [mortal] sin," and then somewhat illogically repeats that "no child of God is a sinner" (5:16–18). The writer may be trying to distinguish between different degrees of error, but most readers find his statements confusing.

2 John

Although containing only thirteen verses, 2 John is a true letter; some scholars regard it as a cover letter intended to accompany 1 John, though this is uncertain. It is addressed to "the Lady chosen by God" (v. 1), probably a house church belonging to the Johannine network of congregations. As in 1 John, the writer's purpose is to warn readers of "**the Antichrist,** the arch-deceiver," who falsely teaches that Jesus Christ did not live as a material human being (vv. 7–8). Urging his recipients to separate themselves entirely from any "deceiver" (false teacher), the elder orders congregation leaders not to "welcome him into your house" or even to greet him, for, in the elder's opinion, "anyone who gives him a greeting is an accomplice in his wicked deeds" (vv. 10–11). The elder concludes with a wish to visit the house church, adding that believers from his "sister" congregation send their greetings.

3 John

In a private note to his friend Gaius, the shortest document in the New Testament, the elder asks him to extend hospitality to some Johannine missionaries led by Demetrius (otherwise unknown). The writer encourages Gaius to welcome these travelers, who had also visited his home congregation, honoring their community's tradition of supporting those who labor to spread their version of "the truth" (v. 8).

Adding an ironic twist on his policy of denying hospitality to Christians whose opinions he deplores, the elder complains indignantly about Diotrephes, a "would-be [congregation]

leader," who "refuses to receive our friends" and "tries to expel them" from the group (vv. 9–10). Accusing Diotrephes of behaving "spitefully," the writer seems unaware that his fellow leader is merely carrying out the same exclusionary procedures outlined in 2 John 10–11.

The Epistles' Legacy

Readers of the Johannine letters, with their exhortations to express love interspersed with scorching denunciations of former fellow Christians (people who had left the elder's community), may come away with mixed feelings. Is it possible to manifest divine love and simultaneously call dissenters "deceivers," spawn of the devil, and "antichrists"? Moreover, why does the Johannine tradition exhort us to love only believers who fully agree with our doctrines, whereas the Synoptic tradition presented a Jesus who commanded followers to "love [their] enemies" as well (Matt. 5:44–45; Luke 6:35)? What fear of doctrinal contamination inspires the elder to insist that true believers must utterly reject Christians who hold different opinions? Why does he demand that the orthodox refuse them a place in the congregation or even the courtesy of a greeting, essentially denying their common humanity? The charge that anyone who extends hospitality to a dissenter becomes "an accomplice in his wicked deeds" would probably surprise Jesus, who was notoriously "a friend of tax gatherers and sinners" (Luke 7:33–35, 39–40).

The elder's harsh methods to control the spread of what he considers false teaching may have seemed necessary to him, but the general adoption of his exclusionary tactics in the later church, when bishops—overseers of a whole region—tended to exercise iron discipline over their flocks, is ethically problematic. The elder's approach to church authority thus presents a troubling paradox in religious history: A community founded on the principle of mutual love later became rife with dissension that triggered a most unloving response.

Summary

A diverse anthology of early Christian literature roughly comparable to the miscellaneous "writings" of the Hebrew Bible, this section of the New Testament reflects the variety of ideas and practices prevailing in different parts of the international Christian community during the late first and early second centuries CE. The three documents traditionally ascribed to John, son of Zebedee, provide a window on the evolving Johannine community, which was apparently split between the writer's group and proto-Gnostic opponents. Writing in the names of the three apostolic "pillars"—Peter, James, and John—to whom Paul alluded in Galatians, pseudonymous writers dispatched letters and tracts to defend their positions on church order and beliefs. Probably the last-written book in the Judeo-Christian Bible, 2 Peter warns against "misinterpretations" of Paul's letters and defends traditional Christian eschatology—expectation of the Parousia.

Questions for Review

1. Define the term *catholic epistles*, and describe the general nature of these seven documents. According to tradition, to what specific group of authors are these works attributed? Why do many scholars believe that all seven are pseudonymous?

2. Identify and explain the major themes in Hebrews. How does the author's belief in a dualistic universe—an unseen spirit world that parallels the visible cosmos—affect his teaching about Jesus as an eternal High Priest officiating in heaven?

3. Almost every book in this unit of the New Testament—Hebrews and the catholic epistles—contains a theme or concept not found in any other canonical document. For example, only Hebrews presents Jesus as a celestial High Priest foreshadowed by Melchizedek; it is also unique in being the only New Testament work to define faith (11:1). Indicate which of the catholic epistles contains the following definitions or statements:

a. A definition of religion
b. A belief that Jesus descended into Hades (the Underworld) and preached to spirits imprisoned there
c. A definition of God's essential nature
d. A set of standards by which to determine the truth of a religious teaching
e. An argument that actions are more important than faith
f. A concept that human history is divided into three separate stages, or "worlds"
g. A defense of the early apocalyptic hope involving Jesus' Second Coming (the Parousia)
h. Citations from the noncanonical books of the Pseudepigrapha, including the Book of Enoch
i. The New Testament's most severe denunciation of the rich

Questions for Discussion and Reflection

1. Hebrews presents certain biblical characters like Melchizedek and Israel's High Priest as foreshadowing the later role of Jesus. Explain the author's methods of biblical interpretation, including his uses of typology, allegory, and symbolism. According to his view, what is the relation of Israel's sacrificial ritual to the death and ascension of Jesus?

2. From your readings in the catholic epistles, what seem to be the principal concerns of Christian writers during the last decades of the first century CE and the first part of the second century CE? In what ways is the Christian community striving to define itself and preserve its message in a sometimes hostile world?

Terms and Concepts to Remember

Aaron	the Incarnation
the anti-Christ	invective
apostasy	Melchizedek
catholic epistles	Parousia (delay in)
Docetism	Pseudepigrapha
dualism	Tabernacle
epistle	tithes
expiation	typology
Gnosticism	wisdom literature

Recommended Reading

Hebrews

Attridge, Harold W. "Hebrews." In M. D. Coogan, ed. *The Oxford Encyclopedia of the Books of the Bible,* Vol. 1, pp. 361–367. New York, Oxford University Press, 2011. Analyzes the book's date, origin, and theology.

Bourke, Myles M. "The Epistle to the Hebrews." In R. E. Brown et al., eds., *The New Jerome Biblical Commentary,* 2nd ed., pp. 920–941. Englewood Cliffs, N.J.: Prentice-Hall, 1990. A helpful introduction.

Buchanan, G. W., ed. and trans. *Hebrews.* Vol. 36 of the Anchor Bible. Garden City, N.Y.: Doubleday, 1972. Provides the editor's translation and commentary.

DeSilva, David A. "Hebrews, Letters to the." In K. D. Sakenfeld, ed. *The New Interpreter's Dictionary of the Bible,* Vol. 2, p. 779–786. Nashville: Abingdon Press, 2007. Combines a general overview with a close analysis of the text.

Donelson, Lewis. *From Hebrews to Revelation: A Theological Introduction.* Louisville, Ky.: Westminster John Knox, 2000.

Johnson, Luke Timothy. *Hebrews: A Commentary.* New Testament Library. Louisville, Ky.: Westminster John Knox Press, 2006. A theological emphasis.

Kasemann, E. *The Wandering People of God: An Investigation of the Letter to the Hebrews.* Minneapolis: Augsburg, 1984. A classic study.

James

Johnson, Luke Timothy. *Brother of Jesus, Friend of God: Studies in the Letter of James.* Grand Rapids, Mich.: Eerdmans, 2004. A series of essays on James's origin and relevance to our understanding of early Palestianian Christianity.

———. *The Letter of James: A New Translation with Introduction and Commentary.* Vol. 37a of the Anchor Bible. New York: Doubleday, 1995. Argues that the author was Jesus' brother.

Lockett, Darian R. "James." In M. D. Coogan, ed., *The Oxford Encyclopedia of the Books of the Bible,* Vol. 1, pp. 411–414. New York: Oxford UP, 2011, Argues that Jesus' brother is the author.

Moo, Douglas J. *The Letter of James.* Pillar New Testament Commentary. Grand Rapids, Mich.: Eerdmans, 2000. Emphasizes the applicability of James to contemporary life.

Painter, John. "James, Letter of." In K. D. Sakenfeld, ed., *The New Interpreter's Bible,* Vol. 3, pp. 189–194. Nashville: Abingdon Press, 2008. Concludes that the book represents Jewish-Christian concerns of the Diaspora sometime after 70 CE, or even after the second destruction of Jerusalem (c. 135 CE).

1 and 2 Peter and Jude

Achtemeir, Paul. "Peter, First Letter of." In K. D. Sakenfeld, ed., *The New Interpreter's Dictionary of the Bible,* Vol. 4, pp. 462–468. Nashville: Abingdon Press, 2009. Carefully examines the letter's pseudonymous authorship and major themes.

Boring, M. Eugene. "1 Peter." In M. D. Coogan, ed., *The Oxford Encyclopedia of the Books of the Bible,* Vol. 2, pp. 155–157. New York: Oxford University Press, 2011. Argues that the work is pseudonymous and was composed in the late first century CE.

Brown, R. E.; Donfried, K.; and Reumann, J., eds. *Peter in the New Testament; A Collaborative Assessment by Protestant and Roman Catholic Scholars.* Minneapolis: Augsburg, 1973. A recommended study of Peter's role in the New Testament tradition and literature.

Dalton, William J. "The First Epistle of Peter." In R. E. Brown et al., eds., *The New Jerome Biblical Commentary,* 2nd ed., pp. 903–908. Englewood Cliffs, N.J.: Prentice-Hall, 1990.

Neyrey, Jerome H. "The Epistle of Jude." In R. E. Brown et al., eds., *The New Jerome Biblical Commentary,* 2nd ed., pp. 917–919. Englewood Cliffs, N.J.: Prentice-Hall, 1990.

———. "The Second Epistle of Peter." In R. E. Brown et al., eds., *The New Jerome Biblical Commentary,* 2nd ed., pp. 1017–1022. Englewood Cliffs, N.J.: Prentice-Hall, 1990.

Perkins, Pheme. *First and Second Peter, James, and Jude.* Interpretation, a Bible Commentary for Teaching and Preaching. Louisville, Ky.: Westminster John Knox Press, 1995 (reprint 2012). A good introduction to the catholic epistles.

Perry, Peter S. "2 Peter." In M. D. Coogan, ed., *The Oxford Encyclopedia of the Books of the Bible,* Vol. 2, pp. 137–160. New York: Oxford University Press, 2011. Concludes that the letter was written pseudonymously in the early second century.

Richard, Earl. "Peter, Second Letter of." In K. D. Sakenfeld, ed., *The New Interpreter's Dictionary of the Bible,* Vol. 4, pp. 469–475. Nashville: Abingdon Press, 2009. Concisely surveys the letter's main topics.

1, 2 and 3 John

Brown, R. E. *The Epistles of John,* Vol. 30 of the Anchor Bible. Garden City, N.Y.: Doubleday, 1982. A scholarly translation and commentary on the letters of John.

Mitchell, Margaret. "John, Letters of," In K. D. Sakenfeld, ed., *The New Interpreter's Dictionary of the Bible,* Vol. 3, pp. 370–374. Nashville: Abingdon

Press, 2008. Surveys the authorship, themes, theology, and historical context of the three documents, emphasizing the tension between the Johannine command to love and the sectarian in-fighting they reveal.

Stott, John R. W. *The Letters of John.* Tyndale New Testament Commentaries. Downers Grove, Ill.: Inter-Varsity Press, 2007. An Evangelical interpretation.

Van der Watt, Jan G. "1, 2, and 3 John." In M. D. Coogan, ed., *The Oxford Encyclopedia of the Books of the Bible,* Vol. 1, pp. 472–477. Explores the probable setting and date of the letters and their connection to John's Gospel.

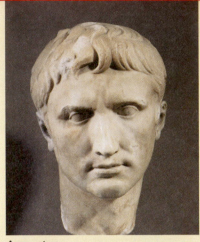

Augustus

The Faces of Roman Power

By the time John of Patmos recorded his apocalyptic visions (about 95 CE), Rome's emperors had wielded absolute power over a vast empire for more than a century, sparking a conflict with a tiny minority of Christians who regarded Jesus, now enthroned in heaven, as their real king. Born during Augustus's reign, Jesus was crucified by Pontius Pilate, the agent of Tiberius. Nero, the first emperor to persecute Jesus' followers, according to church tradition, executed the apostles Peter and Paul in the mid-60s CE. When Jews revolted against Roman domination (66–73 CE), Nero dispatched his general (later emperor) Vespasian to crush the

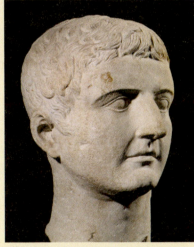

Tiberius

Vespasian

Nero (*far left*), Titus (*left*)

rebellion; Vespasian's son Titus completed the military operation, destroying Jerusalem and its Temple in 70 CE. Vespasian's younger son, Domitian, during whose reign John wrote Revelation, reputedly demanded worship as "lord and god." In John's view, the spiritual battle between good and evil will culminate in the fall of imperial Rome, shown below in a scale model (Rev. 17:1–19:2).

Domitian

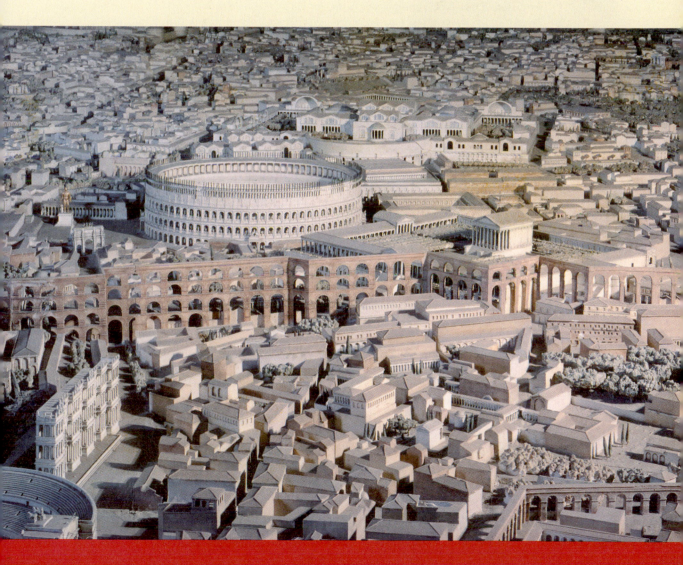

CHAPTER 19

Continuing the Apocalyptic Hope
The Book of Revelation and Other Jewish/Christian Apocalyptic Works

Then I saw a new heaven and a new earth, for the first heaven and the first earth had vanished. . . . Now at last God has his dwelling among men! Revelation 21:1, 3

Key Topics/Themes Revelation affirms Christianity's original hope for an immediate transformation of the world and assures the faithful that God's prearranged plan, including the destruction of evil and the advent of Christ's universal reign, is soon to be accomplished. The book presents an *apokalypsis* (unveiling) of unseen realities, both in heaven as it is now and on earth as it will be in the future. Placing governmental tyranny and Christian suffering in cosmic perspective, Revelation conveys its message of hope for believers in the cryptic language of metaphor and symbol.

A study of Hellenistic-Jewish apocalyptic writings, such as 1 Enoch and 2 Esdras (the latter written at almost the same time as Revelation), helps to place the New Testament's only apocalyptic work in its literary context. A second-century-CE Christian work, the Apocalypse of Peter, reveals a historical shift from cosmic to personal eschatology, focusing on the condition of souls in the afterlife.

Although Revelation was not the last New Testament book written, its position at the end of the canon is thematically appropriate. The first Christians believed that their generation would witness the end of the present wicked age and the beginning of God's direct rule over the earth. Revelation expresses that apocalyptic hope more powerfully than any other Christian writing. Looking forward to a "new heaven and a new earth" (21:1), it envisions the glorious completion of God's creative work begun in the first book of the Bible. In this sense, it provides the **omega** (the last letter of the Greek alphabet) to the **alpha** (the first letter) of Genesis.

Revelation's climactic placement is also fitting because it reintroduces Jesus as a major character. Its depiction of an all-powerful heavenly Jesus provides a counterweight to the Gospels' portrayal of the human Jesus' earthly career. In Revelation, Jesus is no longer Mark's suffering servant or John's embodiment of divine Wisdom. Revelation's Jesus is the Messiah of popular expectations, a conquering warrior-king who slays his enemies and proves beyond all doubt his right to universal rule. In striking contrast to the Gospel portraits, the Jesus of Revelation comes not to forgive sinners and instruct them in a higher righteousness but to

430

inflict a wrathful punishment upon his opponents (19:11–21).

Revelation's depiction of Jesus' character and function, qualitatively different from that presented in the Gospels, derives partly from the author's apocalyptic view of human history. Like the authors of Jude and 2 Peter, the writer perceives a sharp contrast between the present world, which he regards as hopelessly corrupt, and God's planned future world, a realm of ideal purity. In the author's opinion, the righteous new order can be realized only through God's direct intervention in human affairs, an event that requires Jesus to act as God's Judge and Destroyer of the world as we know it. To understand Revelation's emphasis on violence and destruction, with its correspondingly harsher picture of Jesus' cosmic rule, we must remember that the author belongs to a particular branch of the Jewish and Christian apocalyptic movement.

Revelation and the Apocalyptic Tradition

The Apocalypse

"Revelation" translates the Greek term *apokalypsis*, which means "an uncovering, an unveiling, a stripping naked of what was formerly covered." An **apocalypse** is thus a literary work that discloses things previously hidden, particularly unseen realities of the spirit world (Heb. 11:1) and future events. Apocalyptic writers typically describe visions or dreams in which they encounter supernatural beings ranging from hideous monsters to angels who communicate God's future intentions (2 Esd. 3–9; Dan. 7–12). Sometimes, apocalyptists are carried out of their bodies to behold the Deity's heavenly throne or other celestial regions normally invisible to human eyes. Although some late contributors to the Hebrew Bible and many New Testament writers share an apocalyptic worldview, only two—the authors of Daniel and

Revelation

Author: John of Patmos.
Date: About 95 CE.
Place of composition: Western Asia Minor.
Audience: Seven churches of Asia Minor.

Revelation—frame their visions in the literary form of an apocalypse (see below).

The apocalyptic tradition to which Revelation belongs is commonly regarded as an outgrowth of the prophetic movement in ancient Israel. Israel's great prophets had delivered Yahweh's messages to the people during the period of the Davidic monarchy (c. 1000–587 BCE). Following the monarchy's end and the Babylonian captivity (587–538 BCE), however, prophecy declined rapidly. Eventually, many Jews came to believe that authentic prophecy had ceased after the time of Ezra (c. 400 BCE). Priests took the place of prophets as Israel's spiritual leaders.

During the last two centuries before the Christian epoch, and for at least a century after, numerous Jewish writers attempted to fill the vacuum left by the prophets' disappearance. They composed innumerable books in the names of Israel's leaders who had lived before the death of Ezra. These pseudonymous works were attributed to figures like Enoch, Moses, Isaiah, David, Solomon, and Ezra. Many of them are apocalypses, containing visions of End time, such as Daniel (the only such work to become part of the Hebrew Bible), 1 and 2 Enoch, 2 Esdras, 2 Baruch, and the Essene War Scroll from Qumran. (Some noncanonical apocalypses are discussed later in the chapter.)

During the early centuries CE, many Christian writers contributed to the apocalyptic genre. We have already discussed the apocalyptic elements in the Gospels, especially Mark 13 and its parallels in Matthew 24 and Luke 21, as well as Paul's eschatological concerns in his letters to the Thessalonians and the Corinthians. Besides these canonical works, other Christian authors composed apocalyptic books, typically attributing them to prominent apostles, including Peter, John, James, Thomas, and Paul. The canonical

Revelation is unique in being ascribed, not to a figure of the distant past, but to a contemporary member of the first-century church named John. The work is also unique in being the only surviving document by a Christian prophet (1:3), which was a common function or office in the early church (Acts 2:15–17; 1 Thess. 5:19–20; 1 Cor. 12:10; 14:22, 24–25, 31–33).

Characteristics of Apocalyptic Writing

Besides the mystical, otherworldly quality of its content, **apocalyptic literature** is distinguished by several characteristics. The writers who chose the literary category of the apocalypse in which to express their views adopted most of the following assumptions of the apocalyptic worldview.

Universality In contrast to prophetic oracles, which focus almost exclusively on Israel and its immediate neighbors, apocalyptic visions are universal in scope. Although the writers' religious communities (Israel or the church) stand at the center of their concern, their work encompasses the whole of human history and surveys events both in heaven and on earth. Apocalyptists view all spirit beings, as well as all nations and peoples, as swept together in a conflict of cosmic proportions.

Cosmic Dualism The apocalyptic worldview borrows much of its cosmology from Greek philosophical ideas about parallel worlds of matter and spirit (see Figure 19.1). Postulating a dualistic two-dimensional universe composed of visible earth and invisible heaven, apocalyptists see human society profoundly influenced by unseen forces—angels and demons—operating in a celestial realm. Events on earth, such as persecution of the righteous, reflect the machinations of these heavenly beings.

Chronologic Dualism Besides dividing the universe into two opposing domains of physical matter and ethereal spirit, apocalyptists regard all history as separated into two mutually exclusive

periods of time, a current wicked era and a future age of perfection. Seeing the present world situation as too thoroughly evil to reform, apocalyptists expect a sudden and violent change in which God or his Messiah imposes divine rule by force. In the apocalyptic vision, there is no normal historical progression from one age to the next and no real continuity between them. Thus, the Book of Daniel depicts God's kingdom as abruptly interrupting the ordinary flow of time, shattering all worldly governments with the impact of a colossal meteorite (Dan. 2:31–45).

Ethical Dualism In the apocalyptic view, there are only two kinds of human beings, just as there are only two epochs of world history and two levels of existence, material and spiritual. Apocalyptists see humanity as being divided into two opposing camps of intrinsically different ethical quality. The vast majority of people walk in spiritual darkness and are doomed victims of God's wrath. Only a tiny minority—the religious group to which the writers belong and direct their message—remain faithful and receive salvation. Deeply conscious of human imperfection and despairing of humanity's ability to meet God's standards, apocalyptists consistently see most people as destined to eternal condemnation.

Predestination Whereas most biblical writers emphasize that historical events are the consequence of our moral choices (e.g., Deut. 28–29; Josh. 24; Ezek. 18), apocalyptists view history as running in a straight line toward a predetermined end. Just as the rise and fall of worldly empires occur according to God's plan (Dan. 2, 7–8), so will the End take place at a time God has already set. Human efforts, no matter how well intended, cannot avert the coming disaster or influence God to change his mind. The vast complexity of human experience means nothing when confronted with the divinely prearranged schedule.

Exclusivism Many apocalypses, including Daniel and Revelation, were composed to encourage the faithful to maintain integrity and resist temptations to compromise with "worldly" values or

FIGURE 19.1 *Christ over New York City.* In this painting on a steel door, an unknown Ukrainian-American artist projects the image of a cosmic Christ above the skyscrapers of Manhattan. Depicting two dimensions of reality, the painter contrasts New York's towers of cold steel and concrete—monuments to modern commerce and banking—with his vision of Jesus' unseen presence. Encompassing the largely unaware inhabitants of America's secular society in his spiritual embrace, Christ extends his arms in a gesture that is both protective and beseeching. In his apocalyptic visions, John of Patmos exhibited a similar, if somewhat less compassionate, view of Christ's relation to the Roman Empire.

customs. Apocalyptists typically equate religious fidelity with a total rejection of the ordinary goals, ambitions, social attachments, and other pursuits of unbelieving society. Regarding most people as condemned, apocalyptists commonly urge their audience to adopt a rigidly sectarian attitude, avoiding all association with unbelievers.

Limited Theology Consistent with this strict division of history and people into divinely approved or disapproved units, apocalyptists usually show little sympathy for differing viewpoints or compassion for nonbelievers. All modes of life are either black or white, with no psychological or spiritual shades of gray in between. As a result of the authors' mind-sets, the apocalyptic picture of God is ethically limited. The Deity is almost invariably portrayed as an enthroned monarch, an omnipotent authority who brings history to a violent conclusion in order to demonstrate his sovereignty, confound his enemies, and preserve his few worshipers. The notion that God might regard all humans as his children or that he might establish his kingdom by less catastrophic means does not appeal to the apocalyptic temperament or satisfy the apocalyptic yearning.

Portrait of a Violent God Assuming that the Deity achieves control over heaven and earth through a cataclysmic battle with a formidable opponent (the Dragon of Chaos or, in the New Testament, Satan), apocalyptists imagine this transference of power by picturing God as a destroyer who exterminates much of his sentient creation. Using the Exodus story of the ten plagues Yahweh inflicted on Egypt as their model, apocalyptists typically show God angrily punishing disobedient humanity with a devastating series of natural disasters, famines, and loathsome diseases. That the use of evil to defeat evil is ethically questionable does not seem to trouble the apocalyptic mentality.

Eschatological Preoccupations In addition to uncovering the mysteries of the invisible world, apocalyptists reveal the posthumous fate of people facing God's terrifying judgment. Because they were commonly written at a time when fidelity brought no earthly rewards but only potential imprisonment, torture, and death, apocalyptic works pioneered the way in popularizing new beliefs about compensatory blessings in the New Age. Apocalyptists were the first biblical writers to speculate about the nature of the afterlife, which they commonly portrayed as resurrection of the body rather than survival of an immortal soul (Dan. 12:1–3). The apocalyptists' rejection of the old Hebrew belief that human souls were consigned to eternal oblivion in Sheol (the Underworld) and their insistence that God makes moral distinctions between virtuous and wicked lives marked a theological innovation that was adopted by several later Jewish groups, including the Pharisees, Essenes, and early Christians.

The Use of Symbols and Code Words Perhaps because they are the work of sages immersed in arcane learning, almost all apocalypses contain deliberately obscure language that veils as well as expresses the authors' meaning. In addition, most were written during periods of crisis or persecution, which encouraged apocalyptists to use terms and images that their original audiences could understand but that will bewilder outsiders. In Enoch, Daniel, Revelation, and other apocalypses, the authors employ symbols from a wide variety of sources, both pagan and biblical.

In its broadest sense, a **symbol** is a sign that represents something other than itself, typically an abstract quality or religious concept. Symbols take the form of persons, places, objects, or actions that suggest an association or connection with another dimension of meaning. Both Daniel and Revelation depict Gentile nations as animals because, to the authors, they resemble wild beasts in their savage, irrational behavior. Kings who demand worship are symbolized as idols, and paying homage to them is seen as idolatry. Using code words for a pagan opponent, such as "Babylon" or "the beast," helps shield the apocalyptist's seditious message.

Authorship and Date

Who was the writer who created the bedazzling kaleidoscope of images in Revelation? According to some late-second-century traditions, he is the apostle John, the same person who wrote the Gospel and letters of John. However, other early Christian sources recognized the immense differences in thought, language, and theology between Revelation and the Fourth Gospel and concluded that they could not have originated with the same author. Eusebius suggests that another John, known only as the "Elder," an official of the late-first-century Ephesian church, may have written the Apocalypse (*History* 3.39.1–11).

Virtually all modern scholars agree that the Gospel and Revelation stem from different authors. A few accept Eusebius's theory about John the Elder of Ephesus, but the scholarly majority notes that we have no evidence to link the book with that obscure figure. Most scholars prefer to accept no more than the writer's own self-identification: He simply calls himself

FIGURE 19.2 Church on Patmos. According to Christian tradition, this domed church marks the site where John, banished to the island of Patmos, experienced the eschatological visions described in Revelation.

John, a "servant" of Jesus Christ (1:2). Because he does not profess apostolic authority and never claims to have known the earthly Jesus, most analysts conclude that he is not one of the Twelve, whom he categorizes as different from himself. In the author's day, the apostles had already become "cornerstones" of the heavenly Temple (21:14). Exiled to the island of **Patmos** (see Figure 19.2) in the eastern Aegean Sea, where he received his visions (1:9), the author perhaps is best described as John of Patmos, a mystic who regarded himself as a Christian prophet and his book as a highly symbolic preview of future events (1:1–3; 22:7–10).

By studying the contents of his work, scholars can infer something of John's background. He is intimately familiar with internal conditions in the seven churches addressed (Rev. 2:1–3:23), even though he seems to belong to none of them (see Figure 19.3). To some commentators, this indicates that John was an itinerant Christian prophet who traveled among widely scattered churches. Although he held no congregational office, his recognized stature as a mystic and visionary gave him considerable influence in the communities to which he directed his apocalypse.

Because he writes Greek as if it were a second language, phrasing idiosyncratically in a Semitic style, most scholars believe that John was a native of Palestine, or at least had spent much time there. A few critics suggest that he had some connection with the Johannine community, for, like the author of John's Gospel, he refers to Christ as Logos (Word), Lamb, Witness, Shepherd, Judge, and Temple. Both Revelation and the Gospel express a duality of spirit and matter, good and evil, God and the devil. Both regard Christ as present in the church's liturgy, and both view his death as a saving victory. Important differences range from the quality of the Greek—excellent in the Gospel and awkward in the Apocalypse—to the writers' respective theologies. Whereas the Gospel presents God's love as his primary motive in dealing with humanity (John 3:15–16), Revelation mentions divine love only once. The Johannine Jesus' preeminent command to love is conspicuously absent from Revelation.

Writing about 180 CE, the churchman Irenaeus stated that Revelation was composed late in the reign of Domitian, who was emperor from 81 to 96 CE. Internal references to government hostilities toward Christians (1:9; 2:10, 13;

FIGURE 19.3 The seven churches in Asia Minor (western Turkey) addressed in Revelation 1–3. These sites (printed in red) include Ephesus, one of the major seaports of the Roman Empire, and Sardis, once capital of the older Lydian Empire (sixth century BCE). John pictures the heavenly Christ dictating letters to seven angels who act as invisible guardians of the individual churches. With this image, John reminds his audience that the tiny groups of Christians scattered throughout the Roman Empire do not stand alone. Although seemingly weak and insignificant, they are part of God's mighty empire of the spirit and are destined to triumph over their earthly oppressors.

6:9–11; 14:12; 16:6; 21:4), policies then associated with Domitian's administration, support Irenaeus's assessment. Most scholars date the work to about 95 or 96 CE.

The Emperor Cult

Domitian was the son of Vespasian and the younger brother of Titus, the general who crushed the Jewish Revolt against Rome and demolished the Jerusalem Temple (see Figure 19.4). After Titus's brief reign (79–81 CE), Domitian inherited the imperial throne, accepting divine honors offered him and allowing himself to be worshiped as a god in various parts of the empire. We have no real evidence that Domitian personally enforced a universal observance of the emperor cult, but in certain areas—especially

Asia Minor—some governors and other local officials demanded public participation in the cult as evidence of citizens' loyalty and patriotism. During this period, persecution of Christians for refusing to honor the national leader seems to have been local and sporadic. Despite the lack of a concentrated official assault on the faith, however, John clearly feels a growing tension between church and state, a sense of impending conflict that makes him regard Rome as a new Babylon, destroyer of God's people (see the discussion of the ruler cult in Chapter 5).

Because Rome had recognized their religion's monotheism, Jews were generally exempted from the emperor cult. Jewish and Gentile Christians, however, were not. To most Romans, their "stubborn" refusal to honor any of the many Greco-Roman gods or deified emperors

FIGURE 19.4 Bust of Domitian, emperor of Rome from 81 to 96 CE. Many historians believe that an overzealous cult of emperor worship in Asia Minor stimulated the attacks on Christians described in Revelation. To what extent Domitian personally encouraged his subjects to honor him as a god is uncertain. Most Greco-Roman historians thoroughly disliked Domitian's policies and presented him as a tyrant. This ancient prejudice makes it difficult for modern scholars to evaluate his reign objectively.

was not only unpatriotic but also likely to bring the gods' wrath upon the whole community. Early Christians denied the existence of the Hellenistic deities and rejected offers to participate in Roman religious festivals and other communal events. They became known as unsocial "atheists" and "haters of humankind." Rumors spread that they met secretly to drink blood and perform cannibalistic rites (a distortion of the sacramental ingesting of Jesus' blood and body). Labeled as a seditious secret society dangerous to the general welfare, early Christian groups endured social ostracism and hostility. When they also refused to pledge their allegiance to the emperor as a symbol of the Roman state, many local governors and other magistrates had them arrested, imprisoned, tortured, and even executed.

Only a few decades after John composed Revelation, Pliny the Younger, a Roman governor of Bithynia (located in the same general region as Revelation's seven churches), wrote to the emperor Trajan inquiring about the government's official policy toward Christians. Pliny's description of the situation as it was about 112 CE may also apply to John's slightly earlier time.

Although a humane and sophisticated thinker, Pliny reports that he did not hesitate to torture two slave women, "deacons" of a local church, and execute other believers. If Christians held Roman citizenship, he sent them to Rome for trial. Trajan replied that, although his governors were not to seek out Christians or to accept anonymous accusations, self-confessed believers were to be punished. Both the emperor and Pliny clearly regarded Christians as a threat to the empire's security (Pliny, *Letters* 10.96–97).

Purpose and Organization

The Christians for whom John writes were experiencing a real crisis. They were faced with Jewish hostility, public suspicion, and sporadic governmental persecution, imprisonment, and even execution. Many believers must have been tempted to renounce Christ, as Pliny asked his prisoners to do, and conform to the norms of Roman society. Recognizing that the costs of remaining Christian were overwhelmingly high, John recorded his visions of cosmic conflict to strengthen those whose faith wavered, assuring them that death is not defeat but victory. In the light of eternity, Rome's power was insignificant, but its victims, slaughtered for their fidelity, gained everlasting life and the power to judge the fates of their former persecutors.

Despite its many complexities, we can outline Revelation as follows:

1. Prologue: the author's self-identification and the basis for his authority—divine revelation (1:1–20)
2. Jesus' letters to the seven churches of Asia Minor (2:1–3:22)
3. Visions from heaven: a scroll with seven seals; seven trumpets (4:1–11:19)

4. Signs in heaven: visions of the woman, the Dragon, the beast, the Lamb, and the seven plagues (12:1–16:21)

5. Visions of the "great whore" and the fall of Babylon (Rome) (17:1–18:24)

6. Visions of heavenly rejoicing, the warrior Messiah, the imprisonment of the beast and Satan, judgment of the dead, and the final defeat of evil (19:1–20:15)

7. Visions of the "new heaven and new earth" and the establishment of a new Jerusalem on earth (21:1–22:5)

8. Epilogue: authenticity of the author's prophetic visions and the nearness of their fulfillment (22:6–21)

From this outline, we observe that John begins his work in the real world of exile and suffering (1:1–10) and then takes his readers on a visionary tour of the spirit world—including a vivid dramatization of the imminent fall of satanic governments and the triumph of Christ. He returns at the end to earth and gives final instructions to his contemporary audience (22:6–21). The book's structure thus resembles a vast circle starting and ending in physical reality but encompassing a panorama of the unseen regions of heaven and the future.

Alone among New Testament writers, John claims divine inspiration for his work. He reports that on "the Lord's day"—Sunday—he "was caught up by the Spirit" to hear and see heaven's unimaginable splendors (1:9). His message derives from God's direct revelation to Jesus Christ, who in turn transmits it through an angel to him (1:1–2). John's visions generate an intense urgency, for they reveal the immediate future (1:1). Visionary previews of Jesus' impending return convince the author that what he sees is about to happen (1:3). This warning is repeated at the book's conclusion when Jesus proclaims that his arrival is imminent (22:7, 10, 12).

Revelation's Use of Symbols

John's Prophetic Style Revelation's opening chapter gives a representative example of John's writing style. It shows how profoundly he was influenced by the Hebrew Bible and how he utilizes its vivid images to construct his fantastic symbols. Without ever citing specific biblical books, John fills his sentences with metaphors and phrases borrowed from all parts of the Hebrew Bible. Scholars have counted approximately 500 such verbal allusions. (The Jerusalem Bible helps readers recognize John's biblical paraphrases by printing them in italics.)

In his first symbolic depiction of a heavenly being (1:12–16), John describes a male figure with snow-white hair, flaming eyes, incandescent brass feet, and a sharp sword protruding from his mouth. These images derive largely from Daniel (chs. 7 and 10). To universalize this figure, John adds astronomical features to his biblical symbols. Like a Greek mythological hero transformed into a stellar constellation, the figure is described as holding seven stars in his hand and shining with the brilliance of the sun.

The next verses (1:17–19) reveal the figure's identity. As the "first and the last" who has died but now lives forever, he is the crucified and risen Christ. The author's purpose in combining biblical and nonbiblical imagery is now clear: In strength and splendor, the glorified Christ surpasses rival Greco-Roman deities like Mithras, Apollo, Helios, Amon-Ra, and other solar gods worshiped throughout the Roman Empire.

John further explains his symbols in 1:20. There, Christ identifies the stars as angels and the lampstands standing nearby as the seven churches of John's home territory. This identification reassures the author that his familiar earthly congregations do not exist solely on a material plane but are part of a larger visible/invisible duality in which angelic spirits protectively oversee assembled Christians. The symbols also serve John's characteristic purpose in uncovering the spiritual reality behind physical appearance. To John, the seven churches are as precious as the golden candelabrum that once stood in the Jerusalem sanctuary. Like the eternal stars above, they shed Christ's light on a benighted world.

The Lamb and the Dragon In asking us to view the universe as God sees it, John challenges his

FIGURE 19.5 Mesopotamian god battling a seven-headed dragon. Revelation's image of the archangel Michael's defeating a "great red dragon with seven heads" has a long pedigree, extending at least as far back as the Sumerian Early Dynastic period (c. 2800–2600 BCE), when this plaque showing a divine warrior battling the primal monster of chaos was designed. Biblical writers preserved aspects of this ancient conflict myth in references to Yahweh's struggles with Leviathan, another name for the primeval serpent (Ps. 74:12–14; Job 14:1–34; Isa. 27:1). Apocalyptic writers commonly reapplied traditions about the precreation struggles between forces of order and chaos to events of End time, as does John of Patmos, who also identifies the "original serpent" with Satan and the devil (Rev. 12:9).

readers to respond emotionally and intuitively, as well as intellectually, to his symbols. Thus, he depicts invisible forces of good and evil in images that evoke an instinctively positive or negative reaction. Using a tradition also found in the Fourth Gospel, the author portrays Christ as the Lamb of God, whose death "takes away the sin of the world" (John 1:29, 36; Rev. 4:7–14; 5:6; 7:10, 14). Harmless and vulnerable, the Lamb is appealing; his polar opposite, the **Dragon,** elicits feelings of fear and revulsion. A reptilian monster with seven heads and ten horns, he is equated with "that serpent of old . . . whose name is Satan, or the Devil" (12:3, 9). (In the Eden story, the **serpent** that tempted Eve to disobey God is not described as evil. The Genesis serpent's identification with Satan is a much later development in Jewish thought [Wisd. of Sol. 2:23–24].)

In his vision of the Dragon waging war and being thrown down from heaven (12:1–12), John evokes one of the world's oldest conflict myths. Dating back to ancient Sumer and Babylon, the dragon image represents the forces of chaos—darkness, disorder, and the original void—that preceded the world's creation (see Figure 19.5). In the Babylonian creation story the *Enuma Elish,* the young god Marduk must defeat and kill Tiamat, the Dragon of Chaos, before the orderly cosmos can be brought into being. Echoes of these primordial creation myths appear in the Hebrew Bible, including the symbol of the dark, watery abyss (Gen. 1:2) and passages in which Yahweh defeats the chaotic monsters Rahab, Behemoth, and Leviathan (Pss. 74:13–17; 89:9–10; Job 26:5–14; Isa. 51:9). Consistent with the ancient chaos myth, the defeat of the Dragon in Revelation returns him to the original **abyss**—the dark void that represents forces opposing God's light and creative purpose (20:1–3, 7).

To unspiritual eyes, the Lamb—tiny and vulnerable—might appear a ridiculously inadequate opponent of the Dragon, particularly because John views Satan as possessing immense power on earth as he wages war against the Lamb's people, the church (12:13–17). Although nations that the Dragon controls, figuratively called Sodom and Egypt (11:8), have already slain the Lamb (when Rome crucified Jesus), God uses this apparent weakness to eliminate evil both in heaven and on earth. John wishes his readers to draw comfort from this paradox: Christ's sacrificial death guarantees his ultimate victory over the Dragon and all he represents.

The Lamb's death and rebirth to immortal power also delivers his persecuted followers. The church will overcome the seemingly invincible strength of its oppressors; the blood of its faithful martyrs confirms that God will preserve it (6:9–11; 7:13–17). Although politically and socially as weak as a lamb, the Christian community embodies a potential strength that is unrecognized by its enemies. John expresses this belief in the image of an angel carrying a golden censer, an incense burner used in Jewish and Christian worship services. He interprets the censer's symbolism very simply: Smoke rising upward from the burning incense represents Christians' prayers ascending to heaven, where they have an astonishing effect. In the next image, the angel throws the censer to earth, causing thunder and an earthquake. The meaning is that the prayers of the faithful can figuratively shake the world (8:3–5). The author gives many of his most obscure or grotesque symbols a comparably down-to-earth meaning.

Limited space permits us to discuss here only a few of John's most significant visions. We focus on those in which he pictures the cosmic tension between good and evil, light and dark, Christ and Satan. In commenting on the notorious beast whose "human" number is 666 (13:1–18)—a favorite topic for many of today's apocalyptists—we also briefly review the author's use of numerology, the occult art of assigning arcane meanings to specific numbers.

Jesus' Letters to the Seven Churches

Having validated his prophetic authority through the divine source of his prophecy, John now surveys the disparate churches of Asia Minor, the seven lamps that contrast with the world's darkness. Like the contemporary author of 2 Esdras (14:22–48), John presents himself as a secretary recording the dictation of a divine voice, conveying the instructions of a higher power.

Christ's messages to the seven communities all follow the same pattern. After he commands John to write, Jesus identifies himself as the speaker and then employs the formula "I know," followed by a description of the church's spiritual condition. A second formula, "but I have it against you," then introduces a summary of the church's particular weaknesses. Each letter also includes a prophetic call for repentance, a promise that the Parousia will occur soon, an exhortation to maintain integrity, a directive to "hear," and a final pledge to reward the victorious.

After reading Jesus' messages to **Ephesus** (2:1–7), **Smyrna** (2:8–11), **Pergamum** (2:12–17), **Thyatira** (2:18–29), **Sardis** (3:1–6), **Philadelphia** (3:7–13), and **Laodicea** (3:14–22), the student will have a good idea of John's method. Church conditions in each of these cities are rendered in images that represent the spiritual reality underlying those conditions. Thus, Pergamum is labeled the site of Satan's throne (2:13), probably because it was the first center of the emperor cult. (John sees any worldly ruler who claims divine honors as an agent of Satan, and hence an anti-Christ, the enemy of Jesus.) The Balaam referred to here was a Canaanite prophet hired to curse Israel (Num. 22–24), and hence a false teacher, like those who advocate eating meat previously sacrificed to Greco-Roman gods (2:14). John's strict refusal to tolerate the consumption of animals slaughtered in non-Christian rituals (which included virtually all meats sold in most Roman cities) is typical of his exclusivism and contrasts with Paul's more flexible attitude on the same issue (1 Cor. 8:1–13).

Visions in Heaven

John's initial vision made visible and audible the invisible presence of Christ; his second (4:1–11:19) opens the way to heaven. After the Spirit carries him to God's throne, John is shown images of events about to occur (4:1–2). It is important to remember, however, that John's purpose is not merely to predict future happenings but to remove the material veil that shrouds heavenly truths and allow his readers to see that God retains full control of the universe. The visions that follow are intended to reassure Christians that their sufferings are temporary and their deliverance is certain.

Breaking the Seven Seals

John conveys this assurance in two series of seven visions involving seven seals and seven trumpets. Seen from the perspective of God's heavenly throne (depicted in terms of Isa. 6 and Ezek. 1 and 10), the opening of the seven seals reveals that the future course of events has already been recorded on a heavenly scroll. In John's day, almost all writing was done on long, narrow strips of paper that were then rolled up around a stick, forming a scroll. Important communications from kings or other officials were commonly sealed with hot wax, which was imprinted while still soft with the sender's identifying seal. Because the scroll could not be opened without breaking the seal, the wax imprint effectively prevented anyone from knowing the scroll's contents until the intended recipient opened it.

In John's vision, the Lamb opens each of the seven seals in sequence, disclosing either a predestined future event or God's viewpoint on some important matter. (Breaking the seventh seal is an exception, producing only an ominous silence in heaven—the calm preceding the Lord's Final Judgment [8:1].) Breaking the first four seals unleashes four horses and riders—the famous Four Horsemen of the Apocalypse—representing, respectively, conquest, war, food shortages (including monetary inflation), and death, the "sickly pale" rider, followed closely by Hades (the grave or Underworld) (6:1–8).

Breaking the fifth seal makes visible the souls of persons executed for their Christian faith. While crying for divine vengeance, they are given white clothing and told to rest until the full number of predestined martyrs has been killed (6:9–11). In such scenes, John indicates that believers' willingness to die for their religion earns them the white garment of spiritual purity—and that God soon will act to avenge their deaths.

Showing how terrifying the great day of God's vengeance will be, John portrays it in terms of astronomical catastrophes. Apparently borrowing from the same apocalyptic tradition that the Synoptic Gospel writers used to predict Jesus' Second Coming (Mark 13; Matt. 24–25; Luke 21), the author predicts that the sun will turn black, the moon will turn a bloody red, and the stars will fall to earth as the sky vanishes into nothingness (6:12–14). As he clothes Jesus in astronomical images, so John also paints the End in livid colors of cosmic dissolution.

As the earth's population hides in fear, angels appear with God's distinctive seal to mark believers on the forehead, an apocalyptic device borrowed from Ezekiel 9. The symbolic number of those marked for salvation is 144,000 (a multiple of 12), the number representing the traditional twelve tribes of Israel. This indicates that John sees his fellow Jews redeemed at End time (compare Paul's view in Rom. 9:25–27). In chapter 14, the 144,000 are designated the first ingathering of God's harvest (14:1–5). Accompanying this group is a huge crowd from every nation on earth, probably signifying the countless multitudes of Gentile Christians. Both groups wear white robes and stand before God's throne. (In contrast, see John's description of those marked by the demonic "beast" [13:16–17].)

Sounding the Seven Trumpets

As if answering the churches' prayers (symbolized by the censer in 8:4–5), seven angels blow seven trumpets of doom. The first six announce catastrophes reminiscent of the ten plagues on Egypt. The initial trumpet blast triggers a hail of fire and blood, causing a third of the earth to burn (8:6–7). The second causes a fire-spewing mountain to be hurled into the sea, perhaps a reference to the volcanic island of Thera, which was visible from Patmos (8:8–9). Devastating volcanic eruptions like that of Vesuvius in 79 CE were commonly regarded as expressions of divine judgment.

The third and fourth trumpets introduce more astronomical disasters, including a blazing comet or meteorite called Wormwood (perhaps representing Satan's fall from heaven) and causing the sun, moon, and stars to lose a third of their light (8:10–12). After the fifth trumpet blast, the fallen star opens the abyss, releasing columns of smoke that produce a plague of locusts, similar to those described in Exodus (10:12–15) and Joel (1:4; 2:10). Persons not angelically marked are tormented with unbearable agonies but are unable to die to end their pain (9:1–6). These disasters, in which the locusts may represent barbarian soldiers invading the Roman Empire (9:7–11), are equivalent to the first disaster predicted (8:13; 9:12).

Despite the unleashing of further hordes as the sixth trumpet sounds (9:14–19), John does not believe that such afflictions will stop humanity's bad behavior. People who survive the plagues will continue committing crimes and practicing false religion (9:20–21). In fact, John presents the world's suffering as gratuitous and essentially without moral purpose. Revelation's various plagues compound human misery, but they fail to enlighten their victims about the divine nature or produce a single act of regret or repentance.

Eating the Scroll

Just as he borrowed his device of marking the saved from Ezekiel 9, John now draws upon the same prophet to describe the symbolic eating of a little scroll that tastes like honey but turns bitter in the stomach (Ezek. 2:8–3:3). The scroll represents the dual nature of John's message: sweet to the faithful but sour to the disobedient (10:8–11).

In the next section, John is told to measure the Jerusalem Temple, which will continue under Gentile (pagan) domination for forty-two months. In the meantime, two witnesses are appointed to prophesy for 1,260 days—the traditional period of persecution or tribulation established in Daniel (7:25; 9:27; 12:7). The witnesses are killed and, after three and a half days, resurrected and taken to heaven. (The executed prophets may refer to Moses and Elijah, to Peter and Paul, or, collectively, to all Christian martyrs whose testimony caused their deaths.) After the martyrs' ascension, an earthquake kills 7,000 inhabitants of the great city whose ethical reality is represented by Sodom and Egypt. Sodom, guilty of violence and inhospitality, was consumed by fire from heaven; Egypt, which enslaved God's people, was devastated by ten plagues. So Rome, the tyrannical state that executed Jesus and persecutes his disciples (11:1–13), suffers deserved punishment.

The seventh trumpet does not introduce a specific calamity but proclaims God's sovereignty and the eternal reign of his Christ. With the Messiah invisibly reigning in the midst of his enemies (Ps. 2:1–12), God's heavenly sanctuary opens to view amid awesome phenomena recalling Yahweh's presence in Solomon's Temple (1 Kings 8:1–6).

Signs in Heaven: The Woman, the Dragon, the Beast, and the Seven Plagues

Chapter 12 introduces a series of unnumbered visions dramatizing the cosmic battle between the Lamb and the Dragon. In this section (12:1–16:21), John links unseen events in heaven with their consequences on earth. The opening war in the spirit realm (12:1–12) finds its earthly counterpart in the climactic battle of **Armageddon** (16:12–16). Between these two analogous conflicts, John mixes inspirational visions of the Lamb's domain with warnings about "the beast" and God's negative judgment upon disobedient humanity.

The Celestial Woman, the Dragon, and the Beast from the Sea

This section's first astronomical sign reveals a woman dressed in the sun, moon, and stars—resembling Hellenistic portraits of the Egyptian goddess Isis. Despite its nonbiblical astrological features, however, John probably means the figure to symbolize Israel, historically the parent of Christ. Arrayed in "twelve stars" suggesting the traditional twelve tribes, the woman labors painfully giving birth to the Messiah. John's fellow first-century apocalyptist, the author of 2 Esdras, similarly depicted Israel's holy city, Jerusalem, the mother of all believers, as a persecuted woman (2 Esd. 9:38–10:54). Like most of John's symbols, this figure can be interpreted in many ways, including the view that it represents the Virgin.

The Dragon, whom the archangel **Michael** hurls from heaven, wages war against the woman's children, identified as the faithful who witness to Jesus' sovereignty (12:13–17). Lest they despair, however, John has already informed his hearers that this satanic attack on the church is really a sign of the Dragon's last days. His expulsion from heaven and his wrathful conduct on earth signify that Christ has already begun to rule (see Figure 19.6). Satan can no longer accuse the faithful of unworthiness to God as he did in Job's time (Job 1–2). In John's mystic vision, the Lamb's sacrificial death and believers' testimony about it have conquered the Dragon and overthrown evil (12:10–12).

His activities now limited to human society, the Dragon appears in the form of a "beast," a monster with ten horns and seven heads. The reversed number of heads and horns shows the beast's kinship to the Dragon, who gives him his power (13:1–4). As scholars such as Richard Bauckham have pointed out, John's symbols

FIGURE 19.6   *The Fall of Satan from Heaven.* In this painting by Luca Giordano (1632–1705), inspired by Revelation's eschatological scenario, the archangel Michael, Israel's guardian "prince," expels Satan from the divine presence, along with a full third of his fellow members of the heavenly council. According to John of Patmos, Satan's expulsion signals the triumph of God's "sovereignty and power, when his Christ comes to his rightful rule" (Rev. 12:10). A revolutionary event in biblical eschatology, God's banishment of Satan from the celestial assembly represents his permanent rejection of "the accuser of our [human] brothers," the figure whose function was to plant doubts of humanity's value in the divine mind (Job 1–2).

of the "beast" and the "harlot" who rides on the beast (17:3) are a two-pronged attack on the power of Rome, a deliberate refutation of Roman political propaganda that presented the Roman Empire as sustained by heaven's highest gods and as a benefactor of humankind (see Figure 19.7). Particularly repellent, in John's view, were the public cults that honored the emperors as if they were divine, a practice that

FIGURE 19.7 *The Whore of Babylon.* In his vision of spiritual reality, John depicted the great city of Rome as "a woman mounted on a scarlet beast," a symbol of imperial corruption who brandishes "a gold cup, full of obscenities" (Rev. 17:1–14). Because Roman armies had destroyed Jerusalem (70 CE), Rome has become the "new Babylon," archetype of governmental opposition to God. From the Apocalypse series of woodcuts by Albrecht Dürer, c. 1498.

economy, a burdensome system that benefits the wealthy ruling class and condemns the majority to unending poverty. Although the "kings of the earth" revel in the "wine" of her economic prosperity, she is doomed to public exposure and disgrace because she greedily amassed enormous riches with no thought for the poor (17:9–18:20). Like the man wallowing in luxury who ignored the beggar Lazarus (Luke 16:19–31), the harlot's excessive possessions—unshared with the destitute—reveal her as no friend to God (cf. James 5:1–6).

In interpreting the beast's "mortal wound [that] was healed" (13:3–4), Bauckham suggests that the widespread political disorder following Nero's suicide in 68 CE represented a potential "death blow" to the imperial system, as the government threatened to disintegrate into chaos. When Vespasian finally became emperor a year later and founded a new dynasty, the Flavian, however, the imperial rulership was reborn, resuscitating Rome's "monstrous" tyranny—as well as the practice of deifying emperors.

A second beast then emerges, not from the sea like the first, but from the earth, to work miracles and promote public worship of the first beast. This duplicate monster, also called the false prophet (16:13; 19:20), proceeds to enforce the imperial cult by erecting an "image" of the beast. According to Bauckham, this perverse ascribing of godlike qualities to an idol probably signifies the policies of the state priests who encouraged emperor worship in the cities of Asia Minor, including those to which John wrote (see Bauckham in "Recommended Reading"). In a parody of the angelic sealing, the earth-monster allows no one to conduct business unless he bears the beast's mark. John then adds a key to this bestial riddle: The beast's number is that of a "man's name," and the "numerical value of its letters is six hundred and sixty-six" (13:14–18).

John's Numerical Symbols

The reader is aware by this point that John's use of particular numbers is an important part

many Asian cities apparently promoted. John asks his readers to view Rome as God does—a vicious "beast" that built its sovereignty on brutal conquest and maintains its military supremacy through violence against and intimidation of its subject peoples. The beast is "blasphemous" because it promotes itself as humanity's political savior, a hideous distortion of God's kingdom.

Whereas the beast appears to represent tyrannical government, the "harlot" of chapters 17–18, who is closely associated with the beast, symbolizes Rome's exploitation of the world of his symbolism. In this respect, John is typical of the Hellenistic age in which he lived. For centuries before his time, Greco-Roman thinkers regarded certain numbers as possessing a special kind of meaning. The Greek philosopher Pythagoras speculated that the universe was structured on a harmony of numerical relationships and that certain combinations of numbers held a mystical signification.

In the Jewish tradition, seven represented the days of creation, culminating in God's Sabbath ("seventh-day") rest (Gen. 1). Hence, seven stood for earthly completion or perfection. In contrast, six may represent that which is incomplete or imperfect. When John depicts divine activities affecting earth, as in the seven seals or seven trumpets, he signifies that God's actions are perfectly completed. When he wishes to represent a personification of human inadequacy or corruption, he applies the number six, tripling it for emphasis.

The Mystical Number of the Beast To calculate the beast's numerical symbol, we must remember that in the author's day all numbers, whether in Hebrew, Aramaic, or Greek, were represented by letters of the alphabet. Thus, each letter in a person's name was also a number. By adding up the sum of all letters in a given name, we arrive at its "numerical value." (The awkward system of having letters double for numbers continued until the Arabs introduced their Arabic numerals to Europeans during the Middle Ages.)

John's hint that the beast's cryptic number could be identified with a specific person has inspired more irresponsible speculation than almost any other statement in his book. In virtually every generation from John's day until ours, apocalyptists have found men or institutions that they claimed fit the beast's description and thus filled the role of anti-Christ, whose appearance confirmed that the world was near its End.

In contrast, most New Testament scholars believe that John (or the source he employs) refers to a historical personage—or a human

FIGURE 19.8 Coin portrait bust of Nero, emperor of Rome from 54 to 68 CE. According to the Roman historian Tacitus, Nero was the first emperor to persecute Christians. Nero's violence toward believers made him seem to some the image of bestiality in his savage attacks on God's people. In depicting the "beast" who demands his subjects' worship, John of Patmos may have had Nero—and other worldly rulers who imitated the emperor's methods—in mind.

political institution—of his own time. Who that person or institution might have been, however, is still hotly debated. Some historians believe that the man who best fits John's description of the beast was **Nero**, the first Roman head of state to torture and execute Christians (see Figure 19.8). Following Nero's suicide in 68 CE, popular rumors swept the empire that he was not dead but in hiding and planned to reappear at the head of a barbarian army to reassert his sovereignty. Or, as Bauckham has proposed, it was the revival of imperial rulership after Vespasian's ascent to power in 69 CE. (Both views explain the beast's recovery from its "death-blow" and his execution of those Christians who refused to acknowledge his divinity.) Proponents of this hypothesis point to the fact that in Aramaic the "numerical value" of the name Nero Caesar is 666.

Although it is widely accepted, the theory identifying John's beast with Nero leaves much unexplained. We have no evidence that the author intended us to use Aramaic letters in computing the name's mystical significance. Other historians suggest that John intended to imply that Nero was figuratively reborn in Domitian, his vicious spirit ascending "out of the abyss" (17:8) to torment Christians in a new human form. Still others observe that we do not have "the key" (13:18) necessary to understand John's meaning.

Historians' speculations about the beast's identity have been disappointingly inconclusive. Whatever contemporary figure the author had in mind, his achievement was to create a symbol of timeless significance. Every age has its beast, a distortion of the divine image in which God created humanity (Gen. 1:27), who somehow gains the power to perpetrate evil on a large scale. In the universality of his symbols, John achieves a continuing relevance.

Methods of Interpretation

First Method Our brief scrutiny of John's mysterious beast illustrates the more general challenge of trying to find a reliable method of interpreting Revelation's complex system of symbols. In the tentative identifications mentioned previously, we have already touched on two possible methods. The first approach, favored by scholars, assumes that Revelation was composed for a first-century-CE audience familiar with apocalyptic imagery and that its chief purpose was to give an eschatological interpretation of then-current events. Reasoning that the book could not have been written or understood well enough to have been preserved had it not had considerable immediate significance to its original audience, the scholar looks to contemporary Roman history to supply the primary meanings of John's symbols. According to this scholarly method, Babylon (18:2, 10) is Rome, the beast personifies the empire's blasphemous might (represented in human form by the emperors), and the various plagues described are metaphorically intensified versions of wars, invasions, famines, earthquakes, and other disasters experienced (or feared) during this era.

Second Method According to a second view, favored by apocalyptists, Revelation is largely predictive. The visions may have had a contemporary application in Roman times, but John's main purpose was to prophesy about future events. Invariably, apocalyptist interpreters regard their own time as that which John predicted. During the past several centuries, such interpreters, comparing Daniel's use of "times," "years," and "days" with similar terms in Revelation (12:6, 14; 13:5, etc.), have tried to calculate the exact year of the End. In the United States alone, the years 1843, 1844, 1874, 1914, 1975, 1984, and 2000 were announced by different apocalyptic groups as the year in which Christ would return to judge the earth, slaughter the wicked, or establish a new world. Thus far, all such groups have been wrong, probably because apocalypses like John's were not intended to be blueprints of the future. To try to construct a paradigm of End time from Daniel's or Revelation's chronological or numerical symbols is to miss their purpose, as well as to ignore Paul's advice about computing "dates and times" (1 Thess. 5:1). Given human nature, however, it is unlikely that their predecessors' repeated failures will deter future apocalyptists from publicizing their ingeniously revised schedules of the End.

Third Method Although historians' attempts to correlate Revelation's images and symbols with conditions in the first-century Roman Empire are helpful, they do not exhaust the book's potential meaning. A third method recognizes that John's visions have a vitality that transcends any particular time or place. John's lasting achievement lies in the universality of his symbols and parabolic dramas. His visions continue to appeal, not because they apply explicitly to his or some future era, but because they reflect some of the deepest hopes and terrors of the human imagination. As long as dread of evil and longing for justice and peace motivate human beings, Revelation's promise of the ultimate triumph of divine rule over chaos will remain pertinent. John's visions speak directly to the human condition as thousands of generations experience it.

In surveying Revelation's last chapters (17–22), we focus on those aspects of the book that dramatize the ever-repeated struggle and make John's visions relevant not merely to his End time but to ours as well. Readers may have noted that John's method in presenting his visions is to retell the same event in different terms, using different symbols to illustrate the same concept. Thus, to dramatize Christ's victory over evil, he does not proceed in a straight line from the opening battle to the devil's final defeat but turns back to narrate the conflict again and again.

After the seventh trumpet blast, we are told that Jesus is victorious and now reigns as king over the world (11:15). However, another battle ensues in chapter 12, after which John declares that Christ has now achieved total sovereignty (12:10). Yet, still another conflict follows—the infamous Battle of Armageddon (16:13–16)—after which the angel repeats, "'It is over!'" (16:18). But it is not finished, for Satan's earthly kingdom—Babylon—has yet to fall (chs. 17–18). When she does and a fourth victory is proclaimed (19:1–3), the empowered Christ must repeat his conquest again (19:11–21). In John's cyclic visions, evil does not stay defeated but must be fought time after time. Similarly, life is a continual battleground in which the contestants must struggle to defend previous victories and combat the same opponents in new guises.

Visions of the Final Triumph

In contrast to the cyclic repetitions of earlier sections, after chapter 20, John apparently (we cannot be sure) pursues a linear narration, presenting a chronological sequence of events. In this final eschatological vision (20:1–22:5), events come thick and fast. An angel hurls the Dragon into the abyss, the primordial void that existed before God's creative light ordered the visible world (20:1–3). With the Dragon temporarily imprisoned, Christ's reign at last begins. Known as the

Millennium because it lasts 1,000 years, even this triumph is impermanent because at its conclusion Satan is again released to wage war on the faithful (see Box 19.1). The only New Testament writer to present a 1,000-year prelude to Christ's kingdom, John states that during the millennium the martyrs who resisted the beast's influence are resurrected to rule with Christ (20:4–6).

The Dragon's release and subsequent attack on the faithful (based on Ezekiel's prophetic drama involving the mythical **Gog** and **Magog,** symbols of Israel's enemies [Ezek. 38–39]) ends with fire from heaven destroying the attackers. A resurrection of all the dead ensues. Released from the control of death and Hades (the Underworld), they are judged according to their deeds (20:7–13).

The Lake of Fire John's eschatology includes a place of punishment represented by a lake of fire, an image drawn from popular Jewish belief (see Josephus's *Discourse on Hades* in Whiston's edition). Defined as "the second death" (20:15), it receives a number of symbolic figures, including death, Hades, the beast, the false prophet, and persons or human qualities not listed in God's book of life (19:20; 20:14–15). Earlier, John implied that persons bearing the beast's fatal mark would be tormented permanently amid burning sulphur (14:9–11), a destiny similar to that described for the rich man in Luke (17:19–31).

John's fiery lake also parallels that depicted in 2 Esdras (written c. 100 CE):

> Then the place of torment shall appear, and over against it the place of rest; the furnace of hell shall be displayed, and on the opposite side the paradise of delight . . . here are rest and delight, there fire and torments.
>
> (2 Esd. 7:36–38)

Although John uses his image of torture to encourage loyalty to Christ, his metaphor of hell incites many commentators to question the author's understanding of divine love. (For a discussion of other eschatological visions of the afterlife, see the next section.)

BOX 19.1 The Millennium

Although most religious groups recognize that John of Patmos consistently uses symbols and other forms of figurative language to portray his visions of heaven and the future, some interpreters take John's description of Christ's 1,000-year reign—the Millennium—literally. According to this view, after hurling Satan into the "abyss" (the primal "deep" that preceded creation in both Mesopotamian and biblical creation myths [Gen. 1:2]), the triumphant Christ will preside over a peaceful earth, to which the faithful dead will be resurrected (Rev. 20:1–6). When Christ's millennial rule is over, "the rest of the dead" are also resurrected, only to be tested severely when Satan emerges from the abyss to "seduce the nations," which seem to have survived the catastrophic plagues and other disasters John so vividly narrated earlier (Rev. 20:7–21:8).

Presenting Revelation's eschatological images as actual future events, the popular *Left Behind* novels by Jerry Jenkins and Tim LaHaye envision an imminent conflict between Christ and Satan in which the vast majority of humans are doomed. In this version of the apocalypse, Jesus rescues his true followers from a pre-Armageddon seven-year "tribulation" afflicting the rest of humanity by bodily taking them up to heaven in "the rapture," a term that occurs nowhere in the New Testament. Based on a nineteenth-century interpretation of Paul's description of Jesus' Parousia, the rapture concept is extremely popular among many Protestant fundamentalists. Most biblical scholars, however, reject this notion as a misreading of 1 Thessalonians 4–5 (see Chapter 14 for a discussion of the Roman analogy that Paul apparently uses in depicting Jesus' reappearance). As for a literalist view of the Millennium, most contemporary scholars agree with the early church historian Eusebius, who dismissed it as a failure to understand John's "mystic and symbolic language" (Eusebius, *Ecclesiastical History,* 3.39).

The Wedding of the Lamb and the Holy City

John's primary purpose is to demonstrate the truth of a divine power great enough to vanquish evil for all time and create the new universe described in chapters 21–22. The author combines images from Isaiah and other Hebrew prophets to portray an oasis of peace contrasting with the violent and bloody battlefields of his previous visions. Borrowing again from ancient myth, in which epics of conflict commonly end with a union of supernatural entities, John describes a sacred marriage of the Lamb with the holy city that descends from heaven to earth.

The wedding of a city to the Lamb may strike readers as a strange metaphor, but John attains great heights of poetic inspiration describing the union. The brilliance of the heavenly Jerusalem is rendered in terms of gold and precious stones, the jewel-like city illuminated by the radiance of God himself. John draws again on Ezekiel's vision of a restored Jerusalem Temple to describe a crystal stream flowing from God's throne to water the tree of life. Growing in a new Eden, the tree's fruits restore humanity to full health. The renewed and purified faithful can now look directly upon God (21:1–22:5). With his dazzling view of the heavenly city, portrayed in the earthy terms of the Hebrew prophets (Isa. 11, 65, 66), John completes his picture of a renewed and completed creation. God's will is finally done on earth as it is in heaven.

Warning that his visions represent the immediate future and that the scrolls on which they are written are not to be sealed (because their contents will soon be fulfilled), John adds a curse upon anyone who tampers with his manuscript (22:6, 10, 18–19). In his final address to the reader, John again invokes Jesus' speedy return, a reminder of the intense fervor with which many early Christians—generations after Jesus' death—awaited their Master's Second Coming.

Other Hellenistic-Jewish and Christian Apocalypses

With its images of a warring Dragon, celestial woman, lake of fire, and bejeweled city descending from heaven, Revelation has such a strong impact on readers' imaginations that many people think of the book as unique. As noted at the beginning of this chapter, however, Revelation is only one of many similar apocalyptic works that Hellenistic-Jewish or early Christian writers produced between about 300 BCE and 200 CE. To place Revelation in historical perspective, it is helpful to review some other books representing the apocalyptic genre to which Revelation belongs: 1 Enoch, a composite work written in several stages by different authors from about 300 BCE to the first century CE; 2 Esdras (4 Ezra), a Jewish apocalypse composed about the same time as Revelation (c. 100 CE); and the Apocalypse of Peter, a Christian work dating from the second century CE.

These three apocalyptic books are noteworthy not only because they employ the same kinds of imagery used in Revelation but also because their portrayals of the spirit world and the fate of souls after death have been extraordinarily influential on Christian thought. Almost two millennia after they were written, the eschatology they present continues to shape popular beliefs about divine judgment, heaven, and hell. The persistence of these eschatological speculations about postmortem existence— particularly the Apocalypse of Peter's detailed descriptions of fiery torments afflicting the damned—results, at least in part, from their views of the afterlife being later incorporated into masterpieces of Western literature, such as Dante's *Divine Comedy* and Milton's *Paradise Lost*. In contemporary Western culture, any student who has figuratively descended into Dante's Inferno or visited "the darkness visible" of Milton's hell has encountered ideas that were vividly articulated by the authors of 1 Enoch and the Apocalypse of Peter. (Traditions embodied in the Apocalypse of Peter were known to Dante through a late-fourth-century work, the Apocalypse of Paul, which incorporated concepts expressed in the earlier apocalyptic work.)

In tracing the chronological evolution of eschatological ideas expressed in both canonical and noncanonical apocalypses, readers will find a major shift in emphasis over time. The earliest apocalyptic visions, such as the previews of world history contained in 1 Enoch and the Book of Daniel (the only apocalypse admitted to the Hebrew Bible canon), tend to be cosmic in scope, presenting the rise and fall of political empires and the ultimate triumph of God's kingdom (cf. 1 Enoch 91:12–17; 93:1–10; Dan. 2; 7–11). Focusing on God-ordained changes in the macrocosm (the great world), Daniel says little about the microcosm (the smaller world of individual humans). Almost as an afterthought, Daniel's visions conclude with the Hebrew Bible's first explicit prophecy of an afterlife for both righteous and wicked persons: "Of those who lie sleeping in the dust of the earth many will awake, some to everlasting life, some to shame and everlasting disgrace" (Dan. 12:3, Jerusalem Bible). Other than this terse allusion to physical resurrection of the dead, Daniel (c. 165 BCE) says nothing about the nature of their future lives. By the close of the first century CE, however, when Revelation and 2 Esdras were written, ideas about personal eschatology (the posthumous fate of individuals) receive greater attention. Destinies of good and evil persons are now sharply distinguished, with the former enjoying eternal bliss and the latter condemned to everlasting pain. By the time the Apocalypse of Peter was composed, in the second century CE, typical apocalyptic concerns about the future of the cosmos had been subordinated to microcosmic preoccupations with the unspeakable agonies awaiting those who have offended God (see Figure 19.9).

The historical transition from apocalypses devoted to global eschatology to those emphasizing personal eschatology may reflect a concurrent change in the church's evolving beliefs about Jesus' Second Coming. As the Christian

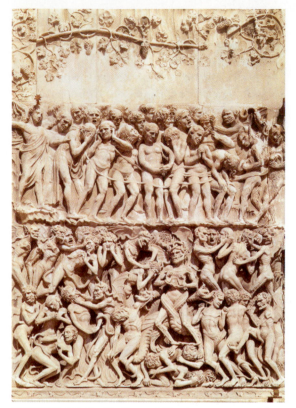

FIGURE 19.9   *The Damned.* The terror and anguish of souls condemned to hell are graphically rendered in this Christian bas-relief depicting the Last Judgment.

found in an Ethiopic translation in the eighteenth century, 1 Enoch was once widely read. Aramaic fragments of the book have been found among the Dead Sea Scrolls and at Masada, the Herodian fortress where the last survivors of the Jewish Revolt against Rome perished about 73 CE. Apparently accepted in some Christian circles, 1 Enoch is quoted as Scripture in Jude (see Chapter 18). Many scholars believe that traditions embodied in 1 Enoch also influenced the eschatological thought of Paul and the Synoptic authors.

First Enoch is the oldest of three extant books ascribed to the biblical Enoch, listed in Genesis as one of the patriarchs who lived before Noah's flood. A person of exemplary righteousness, Enoch did not experience ordinary human death because "God took him," presumably transporting him alive to heaven (Gen. 5:24). The tradition of Enoch's mysterious ascension into the divine presence inspired a host of legends about his unparalleled knowledge of celestial secrets, which are supposedly revealed in the books bearing his name. (A volume called 2 Enoch, describing Enoch's mystical journey through the ten levels of heaven, was composed in the first century CE; 3 Enoch dates from a much later period.)

church gradually accepted the idea that Christ's Parousia would be indefinitely delayed, its attention inevitably moved from expectations of the world's End and universal judgment to contemplation of the posthumous judgment of individual souls (see the discussion of the Apocalypse of Peter).

1 Enoch (Ethiopic Book of Enoch)

A composite work including both cosmic and personal eschatology, 1 Enoch incorporates diverse material composed as early as the third century BCE and as late as the first century CE. Although the book, originally written in Hebrew and/or Aramaic, had fallen out of use centuries before the only complete copy was

The Pseudepigrapha Long before Christian writers ascribed letters and other documents to Paul, Peter, John, James, and other leaders associated with the early Jerusalem church, Hellenistic Jews had developed a widespread practice of pseudonymity (see Chapter 17). A collection of pseudonymous Jewish writings that were included in neither the Hebrew Bible (Tanakh) nor the Apocrypha, the **Pseudepigrapha** are Hellenistic works attributed to eminent figures of the biblical past, such as Enoch, Noah, Moses, Abraham, Isaiah, and Ezra. (Contemporary English translations of all extant pseudepigraphal writings, including the three books ascribed to Enoch, are contained in Charlesworth's *The Old Testament Pseudepigrapha;* see "Recommended Reading.")

Incorporating some of the oldest examples of Jewish apocalyptic literature, the earliest parts of 1 Enoch anticipate visions of the spirit world and predictions of End time that later appear in Daniel and Revelation. Like the author of Daniel, the writer of 1 Enoch refers to angels as "the Watchers" and describes sessions of God's heavenly court. Written about 170 BCE, the section known as the Ten Weeks Apocalypse (91:12–17; 93:1–10) divides human history into epochs symbolically represented by successive "weeks," or years, culminating in eschatological separation of the righteous from the wicked. The book's latest segment, which many scholars think was added during the first century CE or slightly earlier, is the Book of Similitudes (Parables), which describes a heavenly figure called the "Son of Man," the designation that Mark applies to Jesus in his Gospel. In 1 Enoch, however, the "Son of Man" is identified as Enoch himself, the one whom God transported to heaven and who is allowed to reveal its sacred mysteries.

An ancient compiler, or editor, arranged 1 Enoch into five parts, perhaps to emulate the fivefold division of the Pentateuch and Book of Psalms. The first section, the Watchers (chs. 1–36), expands on the Genesis account of "sons of God" who mated with mortal women, producing a hybrid race of giants and heroes (cf. Gen. 6:1–4). Describing the fall of these rebellious divine "sons," Enoch is represented as making a tour of heaven and Sheol (the biblical Underworld), where he views a flaming abyss in which the fallen angels are punished (chs. 17–18, 21; cf. 108:3–7, 15). Enoch's portrayal of the angels' incandescent dungeon resembles the older Greek myth concerning the imprisonment of the Titans, divine giants whom Zeus overthrew and confined in Tartarus, the pit below Hades' realm (see Box 4.1).

Enoch's second section (chs. 37–71) contains a series of "similitudes," parables on a variety of topics, including the Messiah, the rewards of the virtuous, the coming judgment by the Son of Man, and other eschatological concerns. The third part, the Astronomical Writings (chs. 72–82), is a miscellaneous compilation of Hellenistic scientific ideas, including accounts of planetary and lunar movements that presuppose earth as the center of the solar system. In the fourth section, the Dream Visions (chs. 83–90), the author indulges in a typically apocalyptic device, surveying past events as if they were prophecies of the future, predicting the (then-imminent) global deluge. Having confirmed his prophetic authority, Enoch then offers an allegorical narrative of world history that portrays the covenant people as tame (and gentle) animals and the Gentile nations as wild beasts, symbolism also used in Daniel and Revelation. His account begins with Adam, signified by a white bull, and ends with the appearance of the Messiah as a "lamb" who becomes a "great animal" with black horns.

The final section, the Epistle of Enoch (chs. 91–107), incorporates some of the book's oldest material, including fragments from a Book of Noah or Book of Lamech that describe miracles attending the patriarch's birth. It also includes an eschatological vision of a new world order anticipating that in Revelation and 2 Peter:

> And the first heavens shall depart and pass away,
> And a new heaven shall appear. . . .
> And all shall be in goodness and righteousness,
> And sin shall no more be mentioned forever.
>
> (1 Enoch 91:16, 17; cf. Rev. 21:1–3; 2 Pet. 3:13)

The book concludes with Enoch's last words of encouragement for the pious who await their God's day of reckoning, a passage that foreshadows Revelation's invocation of Jesus' return.

2 Esdras

Unlike 1 Enoch, the Book of 2 Esdras is included in some modern editions of the Bible, such as the New Revised Standard Version and the Revised English Bible, where it is placed among the Apocrypha. Written about 100 CE, too late to be included in the Septuagint, it appeared in Catholic versions of the Old Testament until the Council of Trent in the sixteenth century, when it was dropped from the canon. Because it was composed within a few years of Revelation and deals with similar apocalyptic themes and symbols, 2 Esdras provides valuable insight into the worldview that John of Patmos also expressed, particularly the tensions among Jews, Christians, and their Roman oppressors.

The present Book of 2 Esdras is a composite work; the central core (chs. 3–14) was written by a Jewish apocalyptist in either Hebrew or Aramaic about thirty years after the Romans had destroyed Jerusalem in 70 CE. After the book was translated into Greek, an anonymous Christian editor added the first two chapters (c. 150 CE). Approximately a century later, another Christian redactor appended chapters 15 and 16, providing a Christian framework to this first-century Jewish apocalypse.

Ezra's Theodicy   Attributed to Ezra (Greek, Esdras), the priestly scribe credited with assembling the Mosaic Torah while exiled in Babylon (c. 557 BCE), the central section was actually composed by an unknown Jewish author who lived more than six centuries after Ezra's time. Like his ancestors during the Babylonian exile, the author of 2 Esdras 3–14 had witnessed the humiliating overthrow of Judaism's holy city and Temple, a catastrophic triumph of Gentile power over the covenant people that called God's justice into question. The pseudonymous writer, who finds himself in a position analogous to that of the historical Ezra, draws on the resources of apocalyptic discourse to find some meaning or purpose in the national disaster. Chapters 3–14 present a series of seven eschatological visions, of which the first three are cast in the form of philosophical dialogues between Ezra and various angels who defend God's handling of historical events. These angelic messengers counter Ezra's repeated questioning of divine ethics with attempts to justify the Deity's ways to humans. Most readers find Ezra's questions more penetrating than the conventional answers he receives.

If Babylon (Rome) is God's chosen instrument to punish people, Ezra asks, why are

Babylonians (Romans) so much worse behaved than the Jews whom they oppress? Why has God allowed an enemy nation that mocks him to annihilate those who at least try to worship him (3:25–32)? Is it not better to remain unborn than to live and suffer without knowing why (4:12)? The angels' replies express the apocalyptic stereotype: God will dispense justice in good time. The flourishing of wickedness is only temporary; it will be terminated according to a foreordained timetable (4:27–32), and the divine schedule is not humanity's concern. As Ezra observes, however, he does not presume to inquire into celestial mysteries, only to learn that which human intelligence is able to comprehend:

> To what end has the capacity for understanding been given me? For I did not mean to ask about ways above [exclusively God's domain], but about things which pass by us every day, why Israel . . . whom you love [is] given to godless tribes.
> (2 Esd. 4:22–23)

The wrenching disparity between the divine promises to Israel and the miserable historical reality constitutes a paradox that God does not explain.

The Afterlife   Ezra is concerned about not only the earthly plight of his people but also the condition of their souls after death. Reluctantly agreeing that many act wrongly while only a few are righteous, he nonetheless disputes the justice of condemning sinners to unending torment without any further chance of repentance. Chapter 7, vividly detailing the blessings of salvation and the agonies of the damned, offers the most complete description of eschatological judgment and the afterlife in the Old Testament Apocrypha.

In addition, 2 Esdras gives us perhaps the oldest biblical statement about original sin—the doctrine that all humanity inherits Adam's sinful nature and is therefore born deserving death, concepts that have been used to interpret Paul's views on the consequences of

Adam's disobedience (5:21–26; 7:46–48, 70–72; cf. Rom. 5:12–17; see Chapter 15). This belief in humankind's innate propensity toward vice has since become dogma in many Christian denominations (see Box 15.3).

Eschatological Future In chapter 9, the book changes from a Job-like theodicy to a more purely apocalyptic preview of the "last days." Ezra's fourth vision depicts a woman who, mourning her dead son, is suddenly transformed into a thriving city. Uriel, one of the book's angelic mediators, explains that the woman is Jerusalem, her lost son the destroyed Temple, and the splendid city a future glorified Zion (chs. 9–10; cf. Rev. 21–22). Chapters 11 and 12, with their portrait of a mighty eagle, evoke John's avian imagery in Revelation. This proud eagle (Rome) that now dominates the earth is destined to disappear when a lion (the Messiah) appears to judge it for its persecution of the righteous (11:38–12:34), an eventuality that John also prophesies (Rev. 17–19). The sixth vision emphasizes the certainty of the Messiah's expected appearance and his just overthrow of unbelievers who oppress Jerusalem (ch. 13).

The two final chapters, a Christian appendix from the third century CE, dramatize the Deity's coming vengeance on the wicked. Predicting a swarm of terrors and calamities (again reminiscent of Revelation's anti-Roman stance), the book assures readers that the ungodly nation (Rome), as well as all other empires that persecute the faithful, will fall and that the guilty will be consumed by fire (chs. 15–16).

The Apocalypse of Peter and the Shift from Cosmic to Personal Eschatology

Although it was ultimately excluded from the New Testament, the pseudonymous Apocalypse of Peter once stood on the margins of accepted Christian Scripture. The Muratorian Canon (late second to early fourth century CE), a list of books that the author regarded as canonical,

does not mention such works as Hebrews, James, 1 and 2 Peter, or 3 John. But it does include the apocalypse ascribed to Peter, an originally Greek work that survives complete only in an Ethiopic translation discovered in the late nineteenth century. Despite the popularity this work formerly enjoyed—and its usefulness in converting people who hoped to escape the terrors of eternal punishment it describes—the church, probably because of its pseudonymity, rejected it, along with numerous other writings, such as the Gospel of Peter, also incorrectly assigned to Jesus' leading disciple. (The present New Testament, however, does contain two Petrine documents that most scholars believe are also pseudonymous; see Chapter 18.)

The Apocalypse of Peter opens with a familiar Gospel scene: On the Mount of Olives, Jesus' disciples ask about the "signs" of his Parousia and "the end of the world" (cf. Mark 13; Matt. 24). After first reiterating Jesus' warnings about false messiahs and future persecutions, the author soon switches to his main interest: the eschatological consequences of Jesus' return and the judgment of individual souls. The writer's point of departure is a phrase from Matthew's parable in which the Son of Man returns to divide all humanity into two classes, "sheep" and "goats." Judged adversely, the goats are dispatched to "the eternal fire that is ready for the devil and his angels" (Matt. 25:41). In the Synoptic Gospels, Jesus makes several references to Gehenna and "eternal punishment" (see Box 8.5), but the Evangelists do not explore the implications of these allusions to posthumous suffering—an oversight that the author of the Apocalypse enthusiastically addresses.

Quickly moving from the Parousia to visions of the next world, the writer devotes the main part of his work to surveying the tortures endured by various kinds of sinners, in general following a principle of retributive justice in which the punishment supposedly fits the crime. It is difficult to be certain whether Jesus actually takes Peter on a tour of hell, as the spirit of the poet Virgil later guides Dante through the Inferno, or whether Christ simply describes the different sinners' torments so graphically that Peter can virtually "see" them. In any case, the fate of those who have displeased God is to feel maximum pain with no hope of release, to suffer the highest pitch of agony imaginable for all eternity.

As many commentators have recognized, the Apocalypse of Peter focuses largely on sexual sins, punishing erotic behaviors with "cataracts of fire." Women who beautified themselves with cosmetics to seduce men hang by their hair (regarded as the chief feminine attraction) in a dark fiery pit. Expectant mothers who aborted their babies are submerged in pools of flaming excrement, while the spirits of their dead children stand nearby, piercing their mothers' eyes with lightning bolts. Men who enjoyed sex outside of marriage are strung up by their genitals over glowing coals. Souls who "doubted" God's "righteousness" are tortured with "red hot irons" that bore into their eyes, while other sinners, their bodies aflame, are devoured by immortal worms. Slaves who dared to disobey their masters gnaw on their own tongues (the organ of impudence) while immersed in fire. When souls try to repent of their misdeeds and cry to God for mercy, the angel Tatirokos suddenly appears to increase their suffering, angrily declaring that the "time for repentance" has passed—the Deity has made no provision to redeem souls in hell.

Endeavoring to account for the vindictive, sadistic tone of the Apocalypse of Peter, some interpreters have suggested that it reflects some Christians' negative response to Roman persecutions of their faith during the second century CE. Widespread persecution of Christians in Gaul (France) during the late second century CE involved brutal interrogations, mutilations, and other tortures. To some Christians, the Roman practice of burning martyrs alive invited divine retaliation, in which the persecutors would suffer the same kinds of torture, with the difference that their pain would not end at death. Tertullian, a Christian theologian of the late second and early third centuries CE,

looked forward to an eschatological reversal in which familiar figures from Roman society would soon be writhing in hellish agony, providing an entertaining spectacle for the souls of their former victims. Anticipating the day of judgment, Tertullian states that he will not know whether to "laugh" or "applaud" at the sight of Roman administrators who had ordered Christians burnt at the stake now "melting in flames fiercer than those they had kindled for brave Christians." He delights at the prospect of "philosophers and their students" (promoters of rival beliefs) burning together, while tragic actors who had enraptured audiences in Roman theaters will bellow their lines in genuine anguish (see Fox and Turner in "Recommended Reading"). Offering better entertainment than any of Rome's circuses or athletic events, Tertullian's fantasy makes beholding the suffering of the damned one of the major rewards of the faithful. (It should also be remembered that in the only Gospel parable about the afterlife Lazarus's paradise is in full view of the rich man's fiery torments [Luke 16:19–31]; 2 Esdras portrays a similar juxtaposition of joy and suffering [2 Esd. 7:36–38].)

Summary

In Revelation, John asks his readers to see the course of human history from God's perspective. John's series of visions unveil the spiritual realities of the universe that are ordinarily hidden from human eyes. The visions disclose that events on earth are only part of a universal drama in which invisible forces of good and evil contend for control of human society. John shows that the battle between good and evil is an ongoing process by portraying the struggle as a cycle of repeated conflicts. God's forces win, only to find their evil opponents reappearing in a new guise. In combating spiritual and social evil, the faithful must be prepared to fight again and again.

Despite the cyclic nature of the struggle against chaotic powers, John assures his audience, through Christ's death God has already determined the outcome. The last part of Revelation shows the Dragon finally defeated and creation renewed. The Lamb's marriage to heavenly Jerusalem, descended to earth, reveals that the end purpose of history is the joyous union of humanity with the presence and image of God. In John's ultimate vision, the original goal and essential goodness of creation are realized. In contrast to Revelation's emphasis on cosmic events and the ultimate completion of God's purpose, some later Christian apocalypses focus largely on personal eschatology. This shift from macrocosmic to microcosmic concerns is particularly evident in the Apocalypse of Peter, a second-century-CE work that graphically depicts the consequences of Jesus' Second Coming for individual sinners. Expanding imaginatively on Revelation's image of a "lake of fire," this pseudonymous apocalypse graphically describes the sufferings of the damned, a portrayal of eternal torment that influenced many later Western writers, including Dante and Milton.

Questions for Review

1. Define the term *apocalypse* as a literary genre, and explain how the Book of Revelation unveils realities of the unseen spirit world and previews future events.
2. Identify and discuss the characteristics of apocalyptic literature. When and where did this type of visionary writing originate, and what is its main purpose?
3. Connect John's visions with conditions prevailing in his own time. What events taking place during the late first century CE would cause Christians to despair of the present evil world and hope for divine intervention in the near future?
4. Identify and explain some of the myths of cosmic conflict that John incorporates into his vision of the universal struggle between good and evil. In the ancient view of the world, why is disorder commonly identified with evil and an orderly creation synonymous with good?
5. Why did Hellenistic-Jewish apocalyptists select Enoch as the bearer of eschatological revelations? What topics does the Book of 1 Enoch address?
6. In what way is 2 Esdras a theodicy, confronting issues about divine justice as it is manifested in Israel's historical sufferings? What portrayals of the afterlife do 2 Esdras and the Apocalypse of Peter provide?

Questions for Discussion and Reflection

1. Discuss John's use of symbols and cryptic language. Do you think that the author deliberately made his mystical visions difficult to understand in order to confuse "outsiders" who might be hostile to his group?
2. Martin Luther thought that Revelation did not truly reveal the nature of God and Christ. Discuss the ethical strengths and religious limitations of John's view of the Deity and the divine purpose.
3. Revelation repeatedly shows God's kingdom triumphing only to be engaged again in further battles with evil, until the symbol and source of evil—the Dragon of Chaos—is finally exterminated by fire. Do you think that Revelation's frequently repeated battles between good and evil indicate a continuing cycle in which divine rule (the kingdom) alternates with wicked influences on humanity—a cycle in which each nation and individual participates until the final judgment? Cite specific passages to support your answer.
4. Apocalyptic works such as 1 Enoch, Revelation, 2 Esdras, and the Apocalypse of Peter contain horrific visions of the afterlife in which condemned souls suffer unending torment in hell. How do you reconcile Christianity's belief in an infinitely loving God with a doctrine of eternal punishment for sinners? If suffering on earth can be a learning process that brings insight and wisdom, what ethical purpose does the pain of the damned serve? Would a sane human father condemn a disobedient child to unendurable torment—without hope of release? Why do many religions ascribe this practice to God? In what ways do officially endorsed fears about the afterlife tend to support religious authorities and institutions?
5. Although their suggestions were later condemned by the church, some early Christian leaders, such as Origin, believed that God's unlimited love would eventually result in the redemption of all human souls. If God desires the salvation of all souls, how do you think he would accomplish this objective? How would Origin's doctrine of universal salvation work to enhance human appreciation of divine glory?

Terms and Concepts to Remember

the abyss	Magog
alpha	Michael
apocalypse (literary form)	Millennium
	Nero
apocalyptic literature	Patmos
Armageddon	Pergamum
Domitian	Philadelphia
Dragon	Pseudepigrapha
Enoch	Sardis
Ephesus	Serpent
Ezra	Smyrna
Gog	symbol
Laodicea	Thyatira

Recommended Reading

Revelation

Barr, David L., ed. *Reading the Book of Revelation: A Resource for Students.* Atlanta: Society of Biblical Literature, 2003. A collection of essays analyzing Revelation in its historical and social context.

Batto, Bernard F. *Slaying the Dragon: Mythmaking in the Biblical Tradition.* Louisville, Ky.: Westminster John Knox Press, 1992. Devoted mainly to the Hebrew Bible; also shows how New Testament writers used archetypal myths to express their understanding of Christ and the cosmic battle between God and the primordial Dragon of Chaos.

Bauckham, Richard. *The Theology of the Book of Revelation.* Cambridge: Cambridge University Press, 1993.

Collins, A. Y. "The Apocalypse (Revelation)." In R. E. Brown et al., eds., *The New Jerome Biblical Commentary,* 2nd ed., pp. 996–1016. Englewood Cliffs, N.J.: Prentice-Hall, 1990. A close reading of the text that places John's visions in their original Greco-Roman social and historical context.

———. *Crisis and Catharsis: The Power of the Apocalypse.* Philadelphia: Westminster Press, 1984. A carefully researched, clearly written, and rational analysis of the sociopolitical and theological forces affecting the composition of John's visions.

Collins, J. J. *The Encyclopedia of Apocalypticism,* Vol. 1: *The Origins of Apocalypticism in Judaism and Christianity.* New York: Continuum, 2002. A collection of essays, many insightful, on the apocalyptic worldview.

Duff, Paul B. "Revelation." In M.D. Coogan, ed., *The Oxford Encyclopedia of the Books of the Bible,* Vol. 2, pp. 256–271. New York: Oxford University Press, 2011. Examines the book's historical context and reviews traditional and scholarly interpretations.

Fiorenza, Elizabeth Schussler. *The Book of Revelation: Justice and Judgment.* Philadelphia: Fortress Press, 1985.

Josephus, Flavius. "Josephus' Discourse to the Greeks Concerning Hades." In *Josephus: Complete Works.* Translated by W. Whiston. Grand Rapids, Mich.: Kregel, 1960. Presents first-century Jewish views of the afterlife similar to those postulated in the Synoptic Gospels and Revelation.

Metzger, Bruce M. *Breaking the code: Understanding the Book of Revelation.* Nashville: Abingdon Press, 1993 (reprint, 2006). A concise and accessible introduction to the book's complexities, emphasizing the author's use of symbolism.

Osborne, Grant O. *Revelation.* Grand Rapids, Mich.: Baker, 2002. Argues that the apostle John wrote Revelation and that the book is a prophecy of future events, views different from those presented in our text.

Perkins, Pheme. *The Book of Revelation.* Collegeville, Minn.: Liturgical Press, 1983. A brief and readable introduction for Roman Catholic and other students.

1 Enoch

Charlesworth, James H., ed. *The Old Testament Pseudepigrapha,* Vol. 1: *Apocalyptic Literature and Testaments,* pp. 5–89. Garden City, N.Y.: Doubleday, 1983. Includes a translation and extensive explication of 1 Enoch (the later books of 2 and 3 Enoch are also included).

Nickelsburg, George W. E., and Vanderkam, James C. *I Enoch.* Minneapolis: Augsburg Fortress, 2004. A new English translation based on all available texts, including the Dead Sea Scrolls.

2 Esdras

Humphrey, Edith M. "Esdras, Second Book of." In K. D. Sakenfeld, ed., *The New Interpreter's Dictionary of the Bible,* Vol. 2, p. 309–313. Nashville: Abingdon Press, 2007. A perceptive reading of the Jewish apocalypse, with attention to the later Christian additions.

Meyers, Jacob M. *1 and 2 Esdras.* Anchor Bible. Garden City, N.Y.: Doubleday, 1974. Translations with helpful commentary.

The Apocalypse of Peter

Bernstein, Alan E. *The Formation of Hell: Death and Retribution in the Ancient and Early Christian Worlds.*

Ithaca, N.Y.: Cornell University Press, 1993. A comprehensive study of evolving ideas about the afterlife and the influence of Greco-Roman beliefs on Christian eschatology.

Ehrman, Bart D., ed. *The New Testament and Other Early Christian Writings: A Reader.* New York: Oxford University Press, 1998. Includes the complete text of the Apocalypse of Peter.

Fox, Robin Lane. *Pagans and Christians.* New York: Knopf, 1987. Includes discussion of Christian eschatology, the legal basis of Roman persecutions, and the cult of martyrdom.

Turner, Alice. *The History of Hell.* New York: Harcourt Brace, 1993. Discusses the social and legal environment of Rome in the second century CE that provides a context for Christian ideas about hell.

CHAPTER 20

Outside the Canon: Other Early Christian Literature

Key Topics/Themes Particularly during the late first and throughout the second century CE, Christian writers produced a large body of literature that reflected a wide variety of theological viewpoints. Most of these writings are modeled on the same literary genres found in the canonical New Testament: Gospels, "acts" of various apostles, and letters. The majority of noncanonical documents are attributed to leading figures of the early Christian era, such as the Gospels ascribed to Thomas, Peter, James, and Judas. Except for Thomas, which contains 114 sayings of the risen Jesus, most Gospels survive only in manuscript fragments. Although several works that once stood on the margins of the biblical canon—including 1 Clement, the Didache, and the Epistle of Barnabas—present ideas that eventually became part of orthodox teaching, many other compositions, such as the Acts of Paul and Thecla—which celebrates the accomplishments of a woman leader—did not win church approval.

In Chapter 2, we noted that many early Christian writings competed for acceptance in the New Testament canon and that the slow progress of canonization took several centuries to complete. Whereas Paul's letters, the four Gospels, and Acts were almost universally accepted, many other works, including Revelation, James, and 2 Peter, were contested. Until late in the fourth century CE, different church lists of "recognized" books varied considerably, with some lists including documents such as 1 Clement and the Apocalypse of Peter that were ultimately excluded from the Christian Scriptures. As the proliferation of pseudonymous Gospels and legendary accounts of various apostles reveals, early Christianity was not a monolithic movement but a phenomenon that embraced a multitude of spiritualities. Because of the abundance of early Christian writings, we will examine only a few representative works, beginning with the excluded Gospels and then surveying several documents that once hovered on the fringes of the canon.

Noncanonical Gospels

The Gospel of Thomas

In 1945, an Egyptian farmer named Mohammed Ali made what is perhaps the most important New Testament archaeological find of the modern era.

While Ali and his brother were digging for fertilizer near the village of Nag Hammadi, they unearthed an ancient pottery jar. Breaking it open, they found inside thirteen leather-bound codices—papyrus books—containing more than fifty individual documents. As scholars who later studied and translated the manuscripts learned,

458

their contents are extraordinarily varied, ranging from excerpts from Plato's *Republic* to dozens of noncanonical texts, mostly of Gnostic origin, such as the Gospel of Truth, the Gospel of the Egyptians, the Apocryphon of John, the Acts of Peter and the Twelve Apostles, and the Apocalypse of Peter. Of greatest significance, however, was the complete manuscript of the **Gospel of Thomas,** a work previously known only from a few Greek fragments.

Like the other documents from Nag Hammadi, the Gospel of Thomas had been translated from its original Greek into **Coptic,** a form of the Egyptian language (written in Greek letters) used by early Christians in Egypt. Although the Coptic manuscript of Thomas was copied about 350 CE, older fragments of the Gospel in Greek, found in Egypt almost fifty years before, have been dated to about 200 CE. Scholarly estimates for the Gospel's date of composition range from about 50 CE to the mid-second century CE; a growing number of scholars now believe that an early version of Thomas may have been compiled before 100 CE, perhaps about the same time as the Synoptic Gospels.

Unlike the canonical Gospels, the Gospel of Thomas contains no narrative of Jesus' miracles or other deeds; it consists solely of 114 sayings. According to the opening statement, "These are the secret sayings that the living Jesus spoke and Didymos Judas Thomas recorded." Although this Gospel does not even mention Jesus' death or resurrection, the "living" speaker in Thomas is the risen Jesus, who transmits spiritual enlightenment to his disciples. The sayings are "secret" because their true meaning is evident only to those who can understand them correctly, a life-giving "interpretation" that saves spiritually aware persons from "tasting death" (G. Thom. 1; cf. sayings 18, 19, 85, and 111). (John's Gospel, which shares several themes with the Gospel of Thomas, makes similar connections between knowing Jesus' message and achieving immortality: "In very truth I tell you, if anyone obeys my teachings he shall never know what it is to die" [John 8:51–52]; similarly, Jesus tells Lazarus's sister Martha that "no one who is alive and has faith will ever die" [John 11:25–26; cf. 17:3].)

The Ostensible Author

The "Didymos Judas Thomas" credited with compiling Jesus' words is commonly identified with the Thomas who appears prominently in John's Gospel. Because both "Didymos" (a Greek term) and "Thomas" (an Aramaic word) mean "twin," it seems significant that John's Thomas is repeatedly identified as "the Twin" (John 11:16; 20:24; 21:4). Best known as "doubting Thomas" (John 20: 24–29), this figure is also named in each list of the twelve chief disciples (Mark 3:18; Luke 6:15; Acts 1:13). Some commentators have suggested, however, that the reputed author of the Gospel of Thomas may have had an even closer relationship to Jesus than that of disciple. According to the noncanonical Acts of Thomas, "Judas Thomas" is the same Judas (Jude) whom Mark names as one of Jesus' "brothers" (Mark 6:3), and thus the twin of Jesus himself! Because this claim of Thomas's unique connection to Jesus appears nowhere in the New Testament or in any other credible source, scholars do not take it seriously.

The Gospel of Thomas reserves its highest praise, not for Thomas, Jesus' alleged twin, but for another of Jesus' "brothers," James. When the disciples ask Jesus who their leader will be after Jesus' departure, he replies that wherever the disciples are they must consult "James the Just, for whose sake heaven and earth came into being" (G. Thom. 12). Called "the just [righteous]" in early Christian Jewish circles for his strict observance of the Mosaic Law, James was also known as a "pillar" of the Jerusalem church, a leader to whom Peter deferred and from whom even the independent Paul reportedly took advice (Gal. 2:1–20; Acts 15:1–29; 21:17–26). Many scholars believe that Thomas's emphasis on James, representative of a Jewish Christianity that rapidly lost influence after Jerusalem's destruction in 70 CE, is another indication of the Gospel's early date of composition (mid-to-late first century).

Thomas's Diverse Contents

In browsing through Thomas, readers will find approximately 79 statements (out of the 114 into which scholars have divided the text) that resemble passages in the Synoptics, as well as some imagery and themes that otherwise appear only in John. Some of Jesus' sayings, particularly those that parallel statements in the Synoptics, are remarkably clear and terse:

> No prophet is welcome on his home turf.
>
> (G. Thom. 31; cf. Mark 6:4; Matt. 13:57; Luke 4:24; John 4:44 [all Thomas quotations are taken from the Scholars Version (SV), published in *The Five Gospels;* see "Recommended Reading"])

> One who seeks will find, and for [one who knocks] it will be opened.
>
> (G. Thom. 94; cf. Matt. 7:7–8; Luke 11:9–10)

> If you have money, don't lend it at interest. Rather, give [it] to someone from whom you won't get it back.
>
> (G. Thom. 95; cf. Matt. 5:42; Luke 6:34–35)

Other sayings, however, particularly those for which there is no real parallel in the canonical accounts, are more enigmatic. When the disciples ask Jesus how their "end" will come, Jesus replies:

> Have you found the beginning, then, that you are looking for the end? You see, the end will be where the beginning is. Congratulations to the one who stands at the beginning; that one will know the end and will not taste death.
>
> (G. Thom. 18)

The disciples also pose a variation of Matthew's question about the Second Coming (cf. Matt. 24:3), inquiring when Jesus will "appear" so that they can "see" him. But Jesus' reply, unlike that in Matthew, is thoroughly nonapocalyptic, turning attention from himself to the disciples' own future development:

> Jesus said, "When you strip without being ashamed, and you take your clothes and put

> them under your feet like little children and trample them, then [you] will see the son of the living one and you will not be afraid."
>
> (G. Thom. 37)

Assuming that Thomas 37 is a brief allegory expressing Gnostic ideas, most commentators regard "clothes" as symbolizing the physical body, which is stripped away at death to liberate the soul, returning the disciples to a spiritual purity ("like little children") and allowing them to be spiritually reunited with Jesus.

Although it is also commonly given a Gnostic interpretation, some critics have recently suggested that Jesus' statement in Thomas 18 about the "beginning" and "end" is actually directing the disciples' attention toward the world's origin and purpose, as described in Genesis 1–2. According to Stevan Davies, Jesus' many allusions to the "light" and the "beginning" suggest that God's first creation, the "light" of Genesis 1:3, still permeates both the created world and the souls of human beings. Fashioned in God's "image" and "likeness" (Gen. 1:27; 5:1–3) and containing elements of the divine light within, people who discover this inner divinity are then able to perceive the universe as it was when God first created it. Guided by and into the divine light that illuminates the immediacy of God's presence and rule, people awakened to this realization of the divine–human bond transcend both sexual gender and worldly delusions:

> Jesus said, "Images are visible to people, but the light within them is hidden in the image of the Father's light. He will be disclosed, but his image is hidden by his light."
>
> (G. Thom. 83; cf. G. Thom. 22)

After reaching a new state of spiritual growth in which the divine image, "the light within," is revealed, the initiated then can see what others, still "drunk" on the material, sensory world, cannot. Like Jesus, they now observe the kingdom of God "spread out upon the earth":

> It [the Father's kingdom] will not come by watching for it [in apocalyptic expectation]. It

will not be said, "Look here!" or "Look there!" Rather the Father's imperial rule is spread out upon the earth, and people don't see it.

(G. Thom. 113)

As Thomas's next-to-last saying, this declaration of the kingdom's presence balances a similar statement placed near the Gospel's beginning:

Jesus said, "If your leaders say to you, 'Look, the (Father's) imperial rule is in the sky,' then the birds of the sky will precede you. If they say to you, 'It is in the sea,' then the fish will precede you. Rather, the (Father's) imperial rule is within you and it is outside you."

(G. Thom. 3; cf. Luke 17:20–21)

Both a divine spark "within" and a power "outside," emanating from creation's eternal light, God's rule is universal, encompassing both internal and external states of being. Jesus continues:

When you know yourselves [the inner divine image], then you will be known, and you will understand that you are children of the living Father. But if you do not know yourselves, then you live in poverty, and you are the poverty [lacking awareness of both inner spirit and divine omnipresence].

(G. Thom. 3)

One of the principal differences between Thomas and the canonical Gospels is the relative absence in Thomas of a developed Christology. In Thomas, Jesus is not a savior, a human sacrifice given in atonement for sin, or even the Jewish Messiah. Only a few passages allude to Jesus' role as revelator of heavenly wisdom; in one rare statement, however, Jesus appears to associate himself with the source of divine light:

I am the light that is over all things. I am all: from me all came forth, and to me all attained. Split a piece of wood; I am there. Lift up the stone, and you will find me there.

(G. Thom. 77; cf. John 8:12; 10:7)

The first statement parallels a declaration of the Johannine Jesus: "I am the light of the world" (John 8:12); the second resembles another distinctively Johannine concept, adapted from the Jewish wisdom tradition, that Jesus is God's agent of creation and channel of divine light (John 1:1–5). The third, which has no parallel in the canonical tradition, implies that the truths that Jesus represents can be discovered through common actions and objects, mundane avenues to higher realities.

In one of Thomas's few extended dialogues between Jesus and his disciples, the compiler presents his version of a tradition that appears prominently in the canonical Gospels—the disciples' speculation about Jesus' true identity. In the Synoptics, when Jesus asks, "Who do people say I am?" his followers offer a variety of suggestions, culminating in Peter's recognition that he is the Messiah (Christ) (Mark 8:27–30; Matt. 16:13–20; Luke 9:18–21). As one would expect, Thomas's Jesus phrases the question differently, asking them, in effect, to make a parable of him: "Compare me to something and tell me what I am like" (G. Thom. 13). The disciples' responses also vary, with Peter comparing Jesus to a "just angel" and Matthew comparing him to a "wise philosopher." But when Thomas confesses that he is "utterly unable to say what [Jesus] is like," Jesus is apparently pleased, observing that he is no longer Thomas's "teacher," because Thomas has already drunk from "the bubbling spring that [Jesus] has tended," successfully internalizing the Master's teaching. Jesus then speaks privately with Thomas, confiding "three sayings" that Thomas later tells his fellow disciples are so offensive that they would stone him if he repeated them (G. Thom. 13). (Some commentators think that the three sayings are actually reproduced in Thomas 14, where Jesus advises against fasting, praying, and charitable giving. Because these three actions represent fundamental elements of Jewish religious practice, Jesus' criticism of them could be regarded as heretical.)

Independence of the Canonical Gospels

For many scholars, one of the most valuable aspects of Thomas's Gospel is that some of its parables *may* represent earlier forms of Jesus' teachings than many of those in the Synoptics. Of Thomas's fourteen parables, eleven have clear parallels in Mark, Matthew, or Luke, but they tend to be shorter, simpler, and less extensively edited by their compilers than the canonical versions. The author of Thomas does not fit the parables into a narrative context, apply them to Jesus' biography, or generally give them allegorical interpretations as the Synoptic writers do. Whereas Thomas simply recounts the parable of the sower, without commentary (G. Thom. 9), Mark interprets it allegorically, comparing the sowing of seed to the church's later preaching (Mark 4).

One of the most problematical sayings in Thomas is the last. Although it has no parallel in the canonical Gospels and is almost certainly not from the historical Jesus, it probably reflects a controversial issue affecting many different branches of the Christian community. In this final anecdote, Peter is represented as trying to banish Mary from the circle of disciples, "for females don't deserve life." Jesus permits Mary to remain in the group, but only because he will transform her female nature to make her the equal of the male disciples:

> Jesus said, "Look, I will guide her to make her male, so that she too may become a living spirit resembling you males. For every female who makes herself male will enter the domain of Heaven."
>
> (G. Thom. 114)

This Thomas saying echoes the distrust of women that permeated much of Greco-Roman society, an attitude that identified the female with humanity's "lower" nature (irrationality and physical passion) and the male with a "higher" nature (rational thought and spiritual power). In the New Testament, the authors of 1 Peter and the pastoral epistles (1 and 2 Tim., and Titus) voice similar opinions, urging the subordination of women to male leaders (see Chapters 17 and 18).

In an earlier Thomas saying about the necessity of transcending gender, the principle of transformation is applied to both sexes, who are to become like "nursing babies" in order to enter the kingdom:

> Jesus said to them, "When you make the two into one, and when you make the inner like the outer and the outer like the inner, and the upper like the lower, and when you make the male and female into a single one, so that the male will not be male nor the female be female, when you make . . . an image in place of an image, then you will enter [the (Father's) domain]."
>
> (G. Thom. 22)

In urging them to achieve a full integration of existence, combining "inner" and "outer" and "upper" and "lower" dimensions of being, Thomas asks the disciples to replicate the status of the first human, before Adam lost his primal unity by being divided into two sexes (Gen. 2). They can then enter the domain of God as it was at the beginning, before sin appeared.

Although scholars largely agree that the Gospel of Thomas may preserve some forms of Jesus' teachings that are as old as, if not older than, those in the canonical Gospels, it is not known how much, if any, material unique to this Gospel stems from the historical Jesus. In addition to its value in the comparative study of the canonical Gospels, Thomas demonstrates that some groups of early Christians regarded Jesus' teachings, as opposed to his actions, as the most important part of his legacy. Emphasizing Jesus' wisdom, Thomas shows that it was possible to create a Gospel without including a narrative and without even alluding to Jesus' exorcisms, miraculous cures, confrontations with Roman authorities, trial, crucifixion, death, or ascent from the grave. A sayings collection very similar in form to what scholars imagine the hypothetical Q to have been, Thomas also shows that some followers could revere Jesus exclusively for his liberating insights and his perceptions of elusive spiritual realities, without also presenting him as a human sacrifice or an incarnate divinity. In Thomas, Jesus' redemptive work is accomplished through his teaching rather than his death, a factor that probably helps to explain why the mainstream church, with its emerging orthodoxy, did not preserve this Gospel.

The Gospel of Judas

To the surprise of the scholarly world, yet another ancient Gospel recovered from Egypt's desert sands came to light in the early twenty-first century. Lost for almost 1,700 years, a papyrus manuscript of the **Gospel of Judas** was probably discovered in a cave near El Minya, Egypt, about 1978, after which it passed anonymously through the hands of various antiquities dealers. Because it was written in Coptic, its identity and value were not generally recognized, and for sixteen years, the fragile manuscript lay crumbling in a safe-deposit box on Long Island, New York. Because of its rapid deterioration, in 2001 the owner brought it to the Foundation for Ancient Art in Basel, Switzerland, where the disintegrating papyrus text could be preserved and made available to scholars. The National Geographic Society, which consulted with specialists who were able to radiocarbon date the papyrus and verify the manuscript's authenticity, published the first English translation in 2006 (see Kasser, Meyer, and Wurst in "Recommended Reading").

Although scholars had long known that a Gospel of Judas once existed—the church leader Irenaeus of Lyon had denounced it as heretical in 180 CE—no one knew its contents. (Most scholars seem confident that the newly recovered Gospel is the one that Irenaeus condemned.) Composed originally in Greek about 140–160 CE and translated into Coptic about 290–300 CE, the Gospel portrays Judas Iscariot as radically different from the greedy, treacherous figure depicted in the canonical Gospels. Rather than a false disciple who betrays Jesus to his enemies for personal gain, in the Coptic text, many scholars believe, Judas is portrayed as Jesus' truest friend, a man of spiritual stature exceeding that of the other apostles. He is the only follower who correctly perceives that Jesus derives from the celestial realm of pure spirit. In this account, Jesus implicitly asks Judas to facilitate his death: "for you will sacrifice the man that clothes me." Only by sacrificing his physical body can Jesus liberate his divine spirit to return to heaven (a similar view appears in John's Gospel; cf. John 14:28; 16:5–8, 28). By making possible Jesus' crucifixion, Judas—as Jesus forewarns him—will suffer persecution from the uncomprehending disciples, who will despise him as the foulest of traitors. This universal denigration Judas voluntarily accepts for his Master's sake.

As scholars immediately realized, the unknown author of the Gospel of Judas expounds a variant of early Christianity known as Sethian Gnosticism, which postulates a dualistic universe containing many ranks of spirit beings. According to the Sethian view, the true God—which Jesus teaches Judas to seek—has nothing to do with the physical world, which is the deeply flawed creation of the imperfect biblical deity, Yahweh, and is the source of ignorance, death, and corruption. Unlike Judas, to whom Jesus has imparted knowledge (*gnosis*) and spiritual enlightenment, the other disciples can recognize only "their god [the biblical Yahweh]," misleading them to found a church modeled on their misunderstanding of true divinity. In the Judas Gospel, salvation comes not because Jesus gives his life to pay for human sins, but because Jesus reveals the sacredness of the divine spark that dwells in many human souls and shows persons so endowed the way to discover the supreme God.

Some scholars, however, challenge the notion that this Gnostic Gospel actually places Judas in a positive light. Arguing that the National Geographic edition mistranslates the word *daimon* as "spirit" rather than "demon" (the text calls Judas the "thirteenth daimon") and that the translators omitted a crucial negative (Judas will "*not* ascend to the holy generation"), April DeConick proposes that the Coptic writer portrays Judas as an evil figure (see DeConick in "Recommended Reading"). According to this interpretation, Judas is actually serving a malign god when he turns Jesus over to be crucified. The Gospel writer is not trying to rehabilitate Judas, but perhaps seeking to show a Gnostic Jesus mocking his errant disciple's self-deceptions. Because the Judas manuscript is so poorly preserved, with many gaps and missing passages that make it extremely difficult to ascertain the author's original meaning, scholarly controversies over the Gospel's interpretation are likely to continue.

The Case of Secret Mark

Few noncanonical texts attract such fierce controversy as that now raging over the brief document known as the Gospel of **Secret Mark.** Discovered in 1958 by New Testament scholar Morton Smith while cataloguing manuscripts at the Mar Saba monastery near Jerusalem, Secret Mark describes Jesus' resuscitation of a rich young man, to whom he later privately teaches "the mystery of God's domain." Whereas many scholars judge the work a forgery, others defend its authenticity (see the works by Smith, Brown, and Carlson in "Recommended Reading"). If genuine, Secret Mark may preserve an early version of John's famous account of the raising of Lazarus, indicating that this miracle story was also once part of the Synoptic tradition.

The narrative passages constituting Secret Mark are quotations in a letter purportedly written about 200 CE by Clement, a prominent church leader in Alexandria, Egypt. According to Morton Smith, Clement's letter—the existence of which was previously unknown—was transcribed around 1750 on the blank pages of a book in the monastery library. In the letter, directed to a Christian named Theodore, Clement states that, after composing his Gospel for the general public, Mark wrote a revised version for more spiritually mature believers, including Jesus' esoteric teachings about God's kingdom. The longer of the two excerpts, Clement notes, appeared between canonical Mark 10:34 and 10:35. In the context of Secret

Mark, the youth whom Jesus revives may have been the same wealthy young man to whom Jesus' "heart [had] warmed" a few verses earlier in the same chapter. Upon rising from the tomb, "the young man looked at Jesus, loved him, and began to beg to be with him" (v. 8). Six days later, Jesus summons the youth, "dressed only in a linen cloth," to "[spend] the night with him," during which time Jesus "taught him the mystery of God's domain"—the same phrase translated as "the secret of the kingdom of God" in canonical Mark 4:11. A similar nocturnal ritual, perhaps involving a special intimacy with Jesus, as well as baptism, may explain the presence in canonical Mark of a "young man with nothing on but a linen cloth." When Jesus is arrested at Gethsemane, this youth escapes from the soldiers by "[slipping] out of the linen cloth and [running] away naked," an incident that appears only in Mark's Gospel (14:51–52). Some commentators suggest that this unnamed disciple at Gethsemane is the same as the "youth sitting on the right-hand side [of Jesus' empty tomb], wearing a white robe," who announces Jesus' resurrection on the first Easter Sunday (Mark 16:5–7).

At present, many in the scholarly community are still weighing the evidence for and against the authenticity of Secret Mark. If a majority eventually agrees that Clement's letter is genuine—and that he does indeed quote from a subsequently lost edition of Mark—we may have not only a precedent for the resuscitation of Lazarus but perhaps also a clue to the identity of "the disciple [Jesus] loved" (cf. John 11:35–36; 13:13–23).

The Gospel of Peter

Like Secret Mark, the **Gospel of Peter** is a narrative work that offers a brief glimpse into mysteries that the canonical authors merely allude to—in this case, the moment of Jesus' actual rising from his tomb. Although longer than Secret Mark, the Gospel (incorrectly) ascribed to Peter, Jesus' chief disciple, is only partially preserved, beginning and ending in midsentence. Found in 1886, the extant portion is a Passion account, dramatically narrating Jesus' trial, crucifixion, burial, and resurrection. Because of the manuscript's fragmentary state, we do not know if the original Gospel also included a report on Jesus' public ministry and miracles; the narrative ends abruptly with Peter fishing at the Sea of Galilee, apparently about to witness an appearance of the risen Lord.

The Gospel of Peter resembles Matthew's Gospel in many respects, including the story of Pilate's posting Roman soldiers to guard Jesus' grave, but it contains even more spectacularly supernatural, even bizarre, phenomena. Late Saturday night, while Pilate's guards watch in awe, the predawn heavens part, and two celestial beings descend to earth in a blaze of light and cause the massive stone that sealed the tomb entrance to roll away. The transformed Jesus is then shown emerging from the sepulchre, supported on each side by the two towering celestial beings, whose heads reach the sky. Standing even taller than his angelic companions, Jesus' head "reached beyond the skies." When a heavenly voice, reminiscent of that at the Transfiguration, asks if Christ has brought his message to the subterranean realm of the dead, a cross, the fourth figure in Jesus' triumphal procession, testifies that he has. The tradition of a speaking cross, an inanimate object suddenly given life to vocalize the Christian *kerygma,* is unique to this account.

Although scholars agree that the historical Peter had nothing to do with the Gospel attributed to him, they are sharply divided about the document's importance to the Jesus tradition. Whereas a majority see it as a secondary document, derived primarily from Matthew and other canonical sources, others, such as John D. Crossan, argue that in its earliest edition the Gospel of Peter may represent the first Passion story on which the canonical accounts, at least in part, are based. In the extant version, the Gospel exhibits several Gnostic touches. Jesus' silence during the Crucifixion intimates that (as pure spirit) he does not feel physical pain. Also, instead of lamenting that God has forsaken him (as in Mark and Matthew), he complains that his "Power" has deserted him (perhaps indicating the departure of the supernatural Being that had previously dwelt within him). Jesus's death, moreover, is expressed euphemistically, for he is described as "taken up," implying a divine rescue or escape to the spirit world (Gosp. Pet. 2:1; 5:5).

The cross's testimony that Jesus devoted the interval between his (assumed) death and visible resurrection to preaching in the netherworld also suggests that this Gospel's author saw Jesus' spiritual existence, in this life and the next, as a continuum. (The two canonical letters ascribed to Peter also refer to Jesus' postmortem activities in the Underworld [1 Pet. 3:19; 4:6; cf. 2 Pet. 2:4].)

Gospels About Jesus' Infancy and Childhood

Early Christians not only composed Gospels that recounted some mystical revelations of the risen Jesus (Gospel of Thomas), private communications with his betrayer (Gospel of Judas), and the dazzling splendor of his resurrection (Gospel of Peter); they also explored the mystery of Jesus' early life. If Jesus was the Son of God, possessing supernatural knowledge and power, what was he like as a child? Although Matthew and Luke provide infancy narratives, and Luke briefly mentions an incident when the twelve-year-old Jesus visited the Jerusalem Temple, no canonical author preserves any information about the period between Jesus' birth and his baptism by John, when he was "about thirty years old" (Luke 3:23).

The Infancy Gospel of Thomas

During the second century, curiosity about Jesus' boyhood prompted several narratives that attempted to fill in the "missing years" of

Jesus' youth. The **Infancy Gospel of Thomas,** dating from about 150 CE, is ascribed to the apostle Thomas. Unrelated to the Gospel of Thomas, the first edition of which may have been written much earlier, this account of incidents from Jesus' childhood uncritically incorporates popular legends and speculations about the Messiah's youthful character and behavior. Opening with anecdotes about the five-year-old Jesus performing mischievous tricks in his home village, the Gospel closes with a retelling of Luke's story about Jesus, at age twelve, visiting the Temple in Jerusalem. It says nothing, however, about Jesus' young manhood, leaving blank the eighteen years that pass before the adult Jesus comes to John for baptism.

Modern readers are likely to be perplexed by this Infancy Gospel's portrait of Jesus, who as a mere child possesses God-like powers that he at first seems too inexperienced or undisciplined to use wisely. Acutely aware that he merits respect and deference from everyone, the young Jesus is easily angered by even casual slights and repeatedly employs his superhuman abilities to punish the offenders. When a playmate disrupts pools of water that Jesus had formed in a stream, he furiously curses the child, withering him into a state of premature aging. When another boy, running through the village, accidentally bumps into Jesus, Jesus strikes him dead. After the dead boy's parents demand that Joseph teach his son to bless people rather than to curse them, and Joseph privately warns Jesus about the negative effects of his conduct, Jesus causes those who criticized him to go blind (chs. 3–5).

The Nazareth teachers who attempt to give Jesus a formal education fare little better. When his first teacher, Zaccheus, tries to instruct Jesus in the alphabet, the pupil calls his master a "hypocrite" for not knowing all the "allegorical" traditions surrounding each letter (chs. 6–7). After totally demoralizing Zaccheus, an old man "conquered by a child," Jesus is sent to another teacher, who makes the mistake of hitting Jesus on the head for speaking impertinently. The boy's curse sends the man crashing

to the ground in an apparent paralytic stroke (14:1–3). Jesus' third teacher, "a good friend of Joseph," who evidently has learned from the experiences of his predecessors, does not presume to instruct his charge but instead wins Jesus' approval by praising the boy, recognizing that he is "full of much grace and wisdom." Because his new instructor has perceived and honored Jesus' divine nature, the boy lifts the curse from his previous teachers.

In the meantime, Jesus' neighbors in Nazareth are appalled at the child's antics, for he is, literally, a holy terror. They indignantly ask Joseph, "What kind of child do you have who does such things?" (3:3). "Grief-stricken," Joseph privately tells Mary not to let Jesus out of the house "because anyone who angers him dies" (14:3).

As Jesus grows somewhat older, however, the beneficial aspects of his powers begin to outweigh the destructive. After his public shaming of Zaccheus, "all those who had fallen under his curse" are healed, and Jesus begins a series of miraculous cures and resuscitations. When a playmate dies after falling off a roof and Jesus is held responsible, he revives the boy to testify to his innocence (9:1–3). He also heals a young woodcutter whose misplaced axe blow had nearly severed his foot (10:1–2) and saves his brother James from death by a poisonous snake bite (16:1–2). In the last two reported miracles, Jesus resuscitates a dead child (17:1–2) and a deceased workman (18:1–2). Witnessing these deeds, the villagers now recognize Jesus' special status: "This is a heavenly child, for he saved many souls from death, and can save them all his life" (18:2).

In the Infancy Gospel's first episode, Jesus had "profaned" the Sabbath by shaping twelve sparrows from clay, technically violating the commandment to refrain from all work on the day of rest. When Joseph confronts him, Jesus claps his hands and, instantly, the twelve clay birds fly away, removing the evidence of his misdemeanor. In the Gospel's final incident, set in the Temple, Jesus' precocity has deepened into a wisdom that foreshadows the man he will become. Seated in the sanctuary, amid the "elders and teachers of the people," Jesus (as in Luke) amazes them with his ability to solve "the chief problems of the Law and the parables of the prophets" (19:1–5). As the narrator concludes, Jesus *grew* in wisdom . . . and grace" (emphasis added), perhaps suggesting that even God's son—future Judge of all humanity—underwent a learning process characteristic of the human condition.

The Infancy Gospel of James

Also called the Book of James or Protoevangelium of James, this Gospel supplies background information on Jesus' parents and family, covering events that occurred up to and including his birth. Based partly on the infancy accounts in Matthew and Luke and partly on oral tradition, this prologue to Jesus' life story may include a few historical facts among its purely legendary components. The work states that its author is James, who in this Gospel is identified as Jesus' older stepbrother, the son of Joseph by a former marriage. The story focuses on the personal history of Mary, Jesus' future mother, who is born to a previously childless couple—Joachim, a wealthy herdsman, and his wife, Anna (Anne). At age three, Mary is taken to the Jerusalem Temple, where she is raised by priests until her sexual maturation makes her ritually impure and disqualifies her from dwelling in the sanctuary. The priests then consign the twelve-year-old Mary to the care of Joseph, a widower with children, who functions as her guardian and strictly respects her virginity.

The genealogies in Matthew and Luke both trace Jesus' Davidic ancestry through his presumed father, Joseph. In contrast, the **Infancy Gospel of James** states that Mary, too, descended from David. Thus, her virgin-born son inherits his messianic heritage directly from her. Written during the mid-second century CE when veneration of Mary and curiosity about her origins were growing trends in many Christian circles, this Gospel provides not only the names of Mary's parents and the manner of

her extraordinary birth and upbringing but also a doctrine of her perpetual virginity.

Divided into three approximately equal parts, the Infancy Gospel of James is largely a prose hymn of praise to Mary the Virgin, regarded as the most divinely favored of all women. The first section recounts the divine intervention that resulted in Mary's miraculous birth to Joachim and Anna and the immaculate purity of her Temple childhood; the second part explores the perplexities that Mary and Joseph faced in their unusual life together. Although the narrator emphasizes that Joseph is only Mary's devoted protector, not her husband, their relationship becomes particularly complicated after an angel visits Mary, announcing that she will bear a child conceived by the Holy Spirit. When Joseph returns home after a long absence at work to find that Mary is six months pregnant, he agonizes over his apparent failure to protect her virginity. Composing a lively conversation between the almost equally bewildered—and celibate—pair, the author creates a scene that combines sensitivity to the plight of a human couple caught up in forces beyond their control and the inescapable humor inherent in their strange predicament.

Interspersing elements from the canonical infancy stories with his own special material, the narrator devotes the final third of his Gospel to an account of Jesus' birth at Bethlehem, closing with Herod's murderous attempts to eliminate a future rival. As if to guarantee the historicity of his account, the writer then reveals that he is none other than James (whom Paul calls "the Lord's brother"), the son of Joseph by his deceased wife. This final section contains a scene in which two midwives examine Mary after she has given birth to Jesus, discovering, to their astonishment, that she is still physically a virgin.

Traditional lore about Mary incorporated into the Infancy Gospel of James probably contributed significantly to the unique position that Jesus' mother eventually held in both the Greek Orthodox and Roman Catholic churches. Its immense popularity in the church is reflected in the Gospel's survival in over 130 Greek manuscripts. Although never officially admitted to the New Testament canon, in some Christian groups the book has exerted as much influence in shaping orthodox belief as have the canonical Gospels.

1 Clement

Although the author does not reveal his identity in the main text, 1 Clement is traditionally attributed to an early bishop of Rome. The letter resembles the Pastoral Epistles in its concern for a strongly organized church that could withstand the assaults of false teachers or other troublemakers. (2 Clement, a later document, has a different author.) Written "from the Church of God at Rome" to the "Church of God at Corinth," 1 Clement may have been composed in the mid-90s CE, although a few scholars date it about two decades later. Aware that Paul had founded the Corinthian congregation and that he had directed some of his most memorable correspondence to it, the author cites Paul as "the greatest of all examples of endurance," and provides the oldest extant allusion to the martyrdoms of both Paul and Peter. Contrary to later legend, however, he does not specifically claim that *both* apostles died in Rome (ch. 5). The author (whom we call Clement) implicitly appropriates Paul's apostolic authority in denouncing the Corinthians' recent change in leadership. It appears that the Corinthians had overthrown their presbyters (elders) and replaced them with new leaders of their own choosing, an act that Clement finds totally "unacceptable."

The major historical importance of Clement's letter is twofold: As a church leader in Rome, he shows no hesitation in intervening in the affairs of a church in faraway Greece and he resolutely sets down the rules by which legitimate church leaders are appointed. For Clement, the issue of legitimacy is paramount and defending its implementation is the purpose of his letter.

From the writer's perspective, the Corinthians' unauthorized demoting of their previous leaders violates an important principle—the orderly transmission of church authority—that would eventually emerge in the late second century as an official policy of apostolic succession.

According to Clement, there must be a direct line of succession from Jesus and his original apostles to current church supervisors if those leaders are to be seen as truly legitimate. This principle is most cogently expressed in chapters 42–44, where Clement lays out his concept of a church leadership that ultimately stems from God himself. After "Christ received his commission from God," the apostles received theirs from Christ; in turn, the apostles then conferred authority upon selected converts who were worthy to lead congregations. Originating with God and Christ, this human chain of leadership appointments continues from generation to generation, extending indefinitely into the future. Because this succession is divinely authorized, those who resist it—as the Corinthians did by ousting their former overseers—are actually opposing God. Submission to properly authorized leaders is thus required of all Christians (chs. 45–46).

Urging the Corinthians to remember Paul's famous discourse on love (1 Cor. 13), Clement orders them to restore their former leaders, avoiding preference for any others. Although he gives no information about why the Corinthians had rejected the former presbyters and set up new supervisors, Clement asks any potential opponents to remove themselves from the fray, if necessary going into voluntary exile to end dissension and restore peace to the congregation. By showing nobility and "compassion," those who withdraw will "earn a great name for [themselves] in Christ" (chs. 54–59). Praising the virtues of humility, patience, and submission to duly constituted authority, Clement ends his letter by appealing to the Corinthians for cooperation, which will bring the church "peace and joy."

Perhaps because of its usefulness in church administration, 1 Clement was highly respected in antiquity. Irenaeus, bishop of Lyon in Gaul, refers to it as "scripture" and it was included in the Codex Alexandrinus, a Greek edition of the Bible from the fifth century CE.

The Teaching (Didache) of the Twelve Apostles

Didache, which means "teaching," is part of a longer title, The Teaching of the Lord Through the Twelve Apostles to the Gentiles. Probably compiled about 100 CE—at an earlier date than the composition of several catholic epistles—this document is an invaluable resource for understanding the rituals of worship practiced in the early Christian community. Providing guidelines for rites of baptism, fasting, and holy communion, the Didache is a composite work, incorporating oral traditions that may be even older than the written Gospels. As scholars have recently emphasized, it seems to reflect a Jewish Christianity similar to that which produced the Gospel of Matthew.

Although known to early Christian leaders, such as Clement of Alexandria and the church historian Eusebius, the Didache was thought to have been lost until a copy was discovered in Constantinople in 1873. A two-part volume, the Didache's first section outlines the "Two Ways of Life and Death." The second part includes a primitive manual of church ritual and discipline, featuring instructions for performing baptism, saying prayers, and celebrating the Eucharist (partaking of the bread and wine commemorating Jesus' final meal with his disciples). Although some scholars believe that the Didache may have originated in Egypt, scholarly opinion now favors Syria—perhaps the city of Antioch—as the place of composition. In his introduction, the author cites typically Matthean versions of Jesus' teachings; since Matthew's Gospel was probably written in Antioch, it seems likely that the Didache also derives from the same general locale.

Opening with a survey of the opposing behaviors that lead either to "Life" or to "Death,"

the Didache borrows from a previously existing treatise on the "Two Ways" that was apparently well known in the early church (a slightly different version also appears in the noncanonical Epistle of Barnabas). Devoting only one of the six brief chapters in this section to misdeeds that are spiritually fatal, the author takes four chapters to emphasize the life-giving benefits of following Jesus' injunctions to love not only God and neighbor but enemies as well. As some scholars have observed, this rephrasing of passages from Matthew's Sermon on the Mount may reflect the oral traditions behind the written Gospel rather than a direct knowledge of the document itself, another indication of the Didache's early date.

In interpreting Jesus' teachings about behaving generously, the writer translates them into simple, direct commands. Loving others means refraining from wrong actions, such as lying, stealing, or killing; it also demands positive action, such as giving freely to the poor and sharing possessions with fellow believers. After dealing briefly with the "Ways of Death"—which include turning away from God, oppressing the needy, supporting only the rich, and committing infanticide—the writer concludes with a strikingly pragmatic bit of advice: Those who can obey Jesus' words entirely will be "perfect," but if full compliance is beyond them, they should simply "do as much as [they] can."

For historians of Christianity, particularly of its **liturgy** (the customary rites observed in public worship), the second part of the Didache is of particular interest. In this section (chs. 7–16), the author prescribes the correct procedures for church rituals and practices, ranging from the proper way to perform baptism or hold communion to practical ways of dealing with traveling "apostles and prophets," differentiating genuine servants of Christ from others who exploit the faithful. According to this very early form of the Christian liturgy, baptisms should occur in cold "running water" (a river or stream) or in "warm" water (indoor pools?). If such are not available, however, the person performing the rite should sprinkle

FIGURE 20.1 Early Christian baptistery. This baptistery (pool for performing baptisms) belongs to St. John's Basilica in Ephesus, traditionally the city where John, son of Zebedee, spent his last years and where he allegedly wrote the Gospel and letters bearing his name (a view disputed by most scholars). According to the author of the Didache (late first century CE), cold river water was the preferred medium for baptisms, but "warm" indoor pools, or even sprinkling, could also be used in the ritual by which new members were initiated into the church.

water three times on the convert's head, reciting the Matthean formula "in the name of the Father, and the Son, and the Holy Spirit" (Matt. 28:19–20) (see Figure 20.1). As in Matthew's community, Christians are to fast, but they are to go without food on Wednesdays and Fridays to distinguish them from Jews (here called "hypocrites," as in Matt. 23), who observe the biblical rule on Mondays and Thursdays.

Christians are also to recite the Lord's Prayer (reproduced here in a version almost identical to that in Matthew) three times daily.

The Didache's regulations for the Eucharist differ slightly from those reported in the Gospel tradition. Whereas in Mark Jesus first breaks bread and then passes the cup of wine, in the Didache the wine is offered before the bread. Interestingly, by the time the Didache was written, an elaborate series of prayers and set responses from the congregation had already been established for the Eucharist ceremony. Both praise of God and petitions for the welfare of the church are included.

Chapters 11–15 contain instructions on how churches are to deal with itinerant teachers, prophets, and "apostles," who, if they are true servants of the faithful, are to be welcomed as if they were Jesus himself. True prophets will accept a congregation's hospitality for no more than two days before moving on; if they decide to stay permanently to strengthen the church with sound teaching and spiritual guidance, they are to be treated like the priest of ancient Israel, receiving a portion of the group's income. False prophets can be distinguished by their indolence or greed; no one who asks for money or refuses to work will be tolerated.

The Didache concludes with an eschatological warning in which the author urges Christians to be prepared at all times for Jesus' return, which will occur unexpectedly. Echoing the apocalyptic scenario given in 2 Thessalonians (or the Jewish oracles on which it was based), the writer outlines the sequence of events that will take place at history's End: Deceivers will mislead the church, introducing "lawlessness" and attempts to change Christian love to "hate," after which an anti-Christ will seize control of the world. Believers will be subjected to a "fiery" test of faith (perhaps government persecution), which "multitudes" will fail. Then, in rapid order, the eschatological climax will be achieved: The heavens will open, the final trumpet will sound, the righteous dead will rise from their graves, and the "whole world" will behold Christ appearing in clouds of glory.

The Epistle of Barnabas

Although second-century Christians attributed this work to Paul's mentor and traveling companion—calling it the Epistle of Barnabas—the text itself makes no such claim. It also resembles a tract or sermon rather than an epistle, opening with a brief greeting to an unidentified audience but showing few other traits of the letter form. Anonymous rather than pseudonymous, this document presents a sustained attack on the Jewish religion (chs. 1–17), arguing that Jews fail to understand their own Scriptures, which should be interpreted prophetically as foreshadowing Christ. The much shorter second part (chs. 18–20) incorporates a preexisting text, the "Two Ways" (here called the opposite paths of "Light" and "Darkness") that also appears in the Didache (see above).

Heaping scorn on Jewish religious practices, the anonymous author radically reinterprets the Hebrew Bible, insisting that Torah requirements about sacrifice, diet, and ritual purity should be viewed as allegories that figuratively anticipate the coming of Christ. Similarly, biblical history must be seen exclusively as prophecies of Jesus' theological significance. Divine promises made to Israel for land, a covenant relationship, and kingship are really symbolic pledges fulfilled in Jesus' incarnation, crucifixion, and heavenly reign. Every text that Jews read literally, including Mosaic precepts from fasting to animal sacrifice, was intended to be read symbolically. Denying Judaism any intrinsic religious value, the author views the Jewish Scriptures as entirely a Christian book.

Readers familiar with Paul's letter to the Galatians will think it strange that second-century Christians ascribed this anti-Judaism tirade to Barnabas. According to Paul, the historical Barnabas was a Torah-abiding Jew who felt conscience-bound to observe Jewish dietary regulations. When delegates "from James," Jesus' rigorously law-observant brother, inspected the mixed Jewish-Gentile church at Antioch in Syria, both Peter and Barnabas, who previously had been sharing food with Gentiles, suddenly withdrew from non-Jewish association and henceforth ate their meals only with fellow Jews. As Paul laments, "even Barnabas was carried away and played false like the rest," siding with Peter and James against Paul's "gospel" of freedom from Mosaic regulations (Gal. 2:11–14; cf. 1:19). Despite the incongruity of assigning this treatise to Paul's observant mentor, this association with the premier missionary to the Gentiles gave the work considerable authority. Extremely influential, the Epistle of Barnabas was included in the Codex Sinaiticus, a fourth-century CE Greek edition of both the Old and the New Testament.

Interestingly, the Epistle includes a variation on the "Two Ways" text that the Didache, which probably originated in a Jewish-Christian group, had previously incorporated. Most scholars now believe that this description of the "Ways" leading to life or death is an adaptation of an older Jewish text, perhaps integrating ideas about the opposing forces of God's "Light" and Satan's "Darkness" that characterized many Essene writings (see Chapter 3). Perhaps without realizing it, the author appropriated Jewish religious insights into his sectarian attack on the Jewish faith.

The Acts of Paul and Thecla

An important narrative that apparently appealed to many women within the early Christian fold, the Acts of Paul and Thecla was probably composed in the mid–second century CE, although the anecdotes it relates about the apostle and a female disciple named Thecla may have circulated in oral form considerably earlier. In form and content, which dramatizes family conflict, exile, travel to strange places, and near-death experiences, this apocryphal tale resembles other popular Greco-Roman novels, such as the *Satyricon* and (later) *The Golden Ass*. It may be the same document that Tertullian, an influential church leader, condemned about 200 CE, citing its author as a "presbyter" who so admired Paul that he invented entirely new missionary adventures for him. If so, it may be that Tertullian objected to the work's celebration of a young woman who embraces a life of sexual abstinence, not only refusing to marry—and thereby asserting her independence from male domination—but also boldly following in the apostle's

footsteps by becoming a Christian missionary and teacher. (The historical Paul had reminded the Corinthians that it is better to remain unmarried, because single persons can better "serve the Lord," particularly in the light of an imminent Parousia [1 Cor. 7]. He did not, however, make celibacy a precondition of Christian redemption.)

Paul's conversion of Thecla, an aristocratic young virgin whose family has already engaged her to a local nobleman, is inadvertent: When Thecla, listening at an upper window of her house, secretly overhears Paul publicly preaching a doctrine of absolute celibacy, she enthusiastically dons the psychological armor of impregnable chastity. Rejected by his beloved, Thecla's outraged fiancé Thamyris then denounces Paul to the authorities as an enemy to marriage and an affront to the social order, persuading the city officials to throw Paul in jail. After the municipal governor expels Paul from the city, and Thecla, defying parental commands, persists in rejecting Thamyris, her own mother asks the governor to have Thecla burned at the stake as an example of incorrigible filial disobedience. At this point in the story, supernatural forces come to Thecla's rescue: A sudden rainstorm puts out the fire before it can touch her. (The Greek historian Herodotus tells a similar tale about Apollo sending rain to save King Croesus of Lydia when Cyrus the Great of Persia was about to burn him alive; see *Histories,* Bk. 1.86–89.)

After Thecla joins Paul (who was then hiding out in a tomb), the apostle takes her with him to Antioch in Syria, where Thecla's beauty draws the unwelcome attentions of a new suitor, Alexander. After she publicly humiliates Alexander, her second rejected lover appeals to Antioch's governor, who orders Thecla to be thrown into the local arena, where wild beasts will tear her to pieces. When Antioch's women protest the unfairness of Thecla's death sentence, a wealthy widow, Tryphaena (encouraged by her deceased daughter's ghost), takes the young virgin under her protection. Even so, Thecla must again stand naked to face savage beasts—lions, bears, flesh-eating seals, and, finally, fierce bulls—none of which attack the devout girl. So clearly do invisible powers protect Thecla from harm that even the governor at last recognizes her special virtue and pardons her, causing the arena crowds to praise her God. (The beasts' refusal to devour Thecla echoes the account of Daniel's miraculous deliverance from the lion's den [Dan. 6:5–24].)

After instructing Tryphaena in Christian doctrine and converting her household, Thecla again seeks out Paul, who commissions her to "teach the word of God," an apostolic empowerment of women that may have been the source of the Acts' popularity among its female audience. Returning to her home city, Thecla makes peace with her mother, after which she permanently leaves her family and native region to teach strangers abroad, an autonomous vocation she pursues until "she rested in a glorious sleep." As an imaginative account of a courageous and committed woman whom God repeatedly spares from death so that she can pursue her calling (apparently free of male control), the Acts of Paul and Thecla may represent the kind of works that the pseudonymous author of 1 Timothy contemptuously dismisses as "godless myths, fit only for old women" (1 Tim. 4:7; cf. 1 Tim. 2:11–15). This legend's popularity in the early church—and its survival to the present—however, indicates its lasting appeal.

Christians also composed apocalypses attributed to apostles and other leaders of the early church. For a discussion of the pseudonymous Apocalypse of Peter, which once appeared on several canonical lists, see Chapter 19.

Summary

The innumerable Gospels composed during the early Christian centuries reveal the multiplicity of worldviews that the Jesus movement produced—as well as the fact that believers did not quickly or unanimously settle on a single view of Jesus. As we have seen, even the canonical portraits of Jesus varied widely, from Mark's anguished servant and eschatological prophet to John's serene incarnation of divine wisdom. Noncanonical accounts range even more widely, from Thomas's revealer of mystical spirituality, to Secret Mark's confider of divine secrets, to the Gospel of Judas's apparent reversal of Jesus' relationship to his disciple/betrayer. This diversity suggests that many different branches of Christianity struggled creatively to understand Jesus' significance and that many of these groups claimed the authority to interpret him.

Other Christian writers focused on communal ways of living appropriate to believers. Insisting on an orderly appointment of leaders in Christian communities, the author of 1 Clement first articulated a doctrine of apostolic succession that characterized the international church from the late second century on. Prescribing rules and guidelines for the practice of rites such as baptism and the Eucharist, the Didache or Teaching of the Twelve Apostles drew on preexisting Jewish rituals for adaption into the Jewish-Christian church. By contrast, the anonymous writer of the Epistle of Barnabas argued for a total break with Jewish customs, advocating so radical a reinterpretation of the Hebrew Bible that it became a repository of Christian themes. Unlike the other general works mentioned in this paragraph, the Acts of Paul and Thecla, despite its widespread popularity, did not appear on canonical lists of "recognized" books. Nonetheless, this tale of a brave and determined woman who renounced family, marriage, and male dominance to become a leading missionary won a wide readership and elicited numerous favorable comments—even from some church fathers.

Questions for Review

1. Describe some early Christian Gospels, such as the Gospel of Thomas, the Gospel of Judas, and the Gospel of Peter, that were not included in the New Testament canon. Why do you think that these and other Gospels were not officially approved? In what ways do they differ from the canonical accounts of Jesus' life?
2. What distinctive elements appear in the Gospel of Judas and the Gospel of Peter?
3. Describe the character and actions of the young Jesus in the Infancy Gospel of Thomas. How does Jesus appear to mature in the handling of his divine powers as he grows older?

4. What is the author's main purpose in 1 Clement? Explain his concept of the legitimate transfer of authority in church leadership and its relation to the later doctrine of apostolic succession. Why did a church overseer in Rome feel authorized to intervene in a church so geographically remote from his?

5. What does the Didache (Teaching of the Twelve Apostles) contribute to our knowledge of early Christian liturgy and church practices? Describe the Didache's recommendations for performing baptisms and celebrating the Eucharist.

6. In the Acts of Paul and Thecla, how does Thecla's example illuminate the roles of women in the early church? How is her insistence on preserving her virginity related to her social independence?

Questions for Discussion and Reflection

1. What do you think we can learn from the use of traditions about Jesus in the early church? How diverse in their teaching about Jesus were some of these Christian communities?

2. Do you think that the New Testament canon is irrevocably closed? What are the possibilities that existing noncanonical writings—or even books not yet written—will eventually be added to the church's approved list? Describe the effect on Christian doctrine if such works as the Gospel of Thomas, Secret Mark, or the Didache were officially approved to be read in church as examples of legitimate Christian thought and experience.

Terms and Concepts to Remember

Barnabas	Judas Iscariot
Coptic	liturgy
Eucharist	Thomas
James	

Recommended Reading

Noncanonical Gospels

Brown, Scott G. *Mark's Other Gospel: Rethinking Morton Smith's Discovery*. Waterloo, Ontario: Wilfrid Laurier University Press, 2005. Analyzes evidence for Secret Mark's authenticity.

Carlson, Stephen C. *The Gospel Hoax: Morton Smith's Invention of Secret Mark*. Baylor, Tex.: Baylor University Press, 2005. Argues that Smith deliberately forged the Clement letter to deceive the scholarly community.

Crossan, John D. *The Cross That Spoke: The Origins of the Passion Narrative*. San Francisco: Harper & Row, 1988. Analyzes the Gospel of Peter as source for the canonical Gospels.

Davies, Stevan. *The Gospel of Thomas: Annotated and Explained*. Woodstock, Vt.: SkyLight Paths, 2002. Offers a close, insightful reading of the text.

———. "Thomas, Gospel of." In M. D. Coogan, ed., *The Oxford Encyclopedia of the Books of the Bible*, Vol. 2, pp. 414–422. New York: Oxford University Press, 2011. An insightful analysis of the work's historical importance.

DeConick, April D. *The Thirteenth Apostle: What the Gospel of Judas Really Says*. London: Continuum International, 2007. Includes a fresh translation that presents Judas as a demonic figure.

Ehrman, Bart D. *The Lost Gospel of Judas Iscariot: A New Look at Betrayer and Betrayed*. New York: Oxford University Press, 2006. A readable interpretation.

———. *Lost Scriptures: Books That Did Not Make It into the New Testament*. New York: Oxford University Press, 2003.

———. *The New Testament and Other Early Christian Writings: A Reader*. New York: Oxford University Press, 1998. Anthologizes both canonical and noncanonical writings composed by the mid-second century CE.

Eusebius. *The History of the Church from Christ to Constantine*. Translated with an introduction by G. A. Williamson. Baltimore: Penguin Books, 1965. Read with caution, provides excellent atmospheric background for the early church and fascinating traditions about the apostles and second-century church leaders.

Funk, Robert W.; Hoover, Roy W.; and the Jesus Seminar, *The Five Gospels: The Search for the Authentic Words of Jesus*. Macmillan, 1993. Features colloquial translations and extensive scholarly arguments for likely authenticity of each saying ascribed to Jesus.

Kasser, Rudolphe; Meyer, Marvin; and Wurst, Gregor, eds. *The Gospel of Judas*. Washington, D.C.: National Geographic, 2006. An English translation of the recently discovered text, with critical commentary.

Miller, Robert J., ed. *The Complete Gospels*, 4th ed. Salem, Ore.: Polebridge Press, 2010. All known Gospels, including complete texts of the Gospel of Thomas, Infancy Gospel of Thomas, Infancy Gospel of James, Gospel of Peter, and Secret Gospel of Mark, and numerous fragmentary works.

Pagels, Elaine. *The Gnostic Gospels.* New York: Random House, 1979. Argues that the church suppressed Gnostic Christianity on political grounds.

Robinson, James M., ed. *The Nag Hammadi Library,* 3rd ed. San Francisco: Harper & Row, 1988. Contains English translations of Christian documents found at Nag Hammadi.

Smith, Morton. *The Secret Gospel: The Discovery of the Secret Gospel According to Mark,* 3rd ed. Middletown, Calif.: Dawn Horse Press, 2005. A reprint of Smith's original publication, with a foreword by Elaine Pagels.

I Clement and The Didache

Del Verme, Marcello. "Didache." In M. D. Coogan, ed., *The Oxford Encyclopedia of the Books of the Bible,* Vol. 1, pp. 209–213. New York: Oxford University Press, 2011. Views this composite series of Christian guidelines as adapting older Jewish customs of worship.

———. *Didache and Judaism: Jewish Roots of an Ancient Christian-Jewish Work.* New York: T & T Clark International, 2004. Marshals evidence for Jewish origins of worship in early Jewish-Christian communities.

Jefford, Clayton N. "Clement, Letters of." In M. D. Coogan, ed., *The Oxford Encyclopedia of the Books of the Bible,* Vol. 1, pp. 132–136. New York: Oxford University Press, 2011. Examines the Jewish-Christian context of I Clement and the work's reliance on the Jewish Scriptures.

Epistle of Barnabas and the Acts of Paul and Thecla

Brock, Ann Graham. "Paul and Thecla, Acts of." In M. D. Coogan, ed., *The Oxford Encyclopedia of the Books of the Bible,* Vol. 2, pp. 138–144. New York: Oxford University Press, 2011. Reviews authorship, date, and contents and notes the work's widespread popularity and influence.

Rhodes, James N. "Barnabas, Epistle of." In K. D. Sakenfeld, ed., *The New Interpreter's Dictionary of the Bible,* Vol. 1, pp. 399–400. Nashville, Tenn.: Abingdon Press, 2006. Emphasizes the work's polemical anti-Jewish character.

Glossary of New Testament Terms and Concepts

Aaron In the Hebrew Bible, the brother of Moses and first High Priest of Israel (Exod. 4:14; 6:20, 26; Lev. 8; Num. 3:1–3). In the Book of Hebrews, the High Priest's function is said to foreshadow that of Christ (Heb. 5:1–4; 8:1–10:18).

Abba The Aramaic word for "father," used by Jesus and other early Christians to address God (Mark 14:36; Rom. 8:15; Gal. 4:6).

Abraham The founder of the Hebrew nation. In Genesis 12–24, Abraham (at first called Abram, meaning "exalted father") is the supreme example of obedience to Yahweh. All Jews were believed to be Abraham's descendants through his son Isaac.

Abraham's bosom In Luke's parable about Lazarus and the rich man, a term used to denote a position of divine favor (Luke 16:19–31).

abyss In the Hebrew Bible, a term designating the primal chaos "[watery] deep" that preceded creation (Gen. 1:2); in the New Testament, it denotes the place of the dead (Rom. 10:7) and/or the prison where the devil is confined for 1,000 years (Rev. 20:1–3).

Academy of Jamnia See **Jamnia, Academy of.**

Adam In Genesis 2–3, the first human being. In Paul's letters, Adam is a prototype of all humanity (1 Cor. 15:21–49; Rom. 5:12–21).

Alexander the Great The son of King Philip of Macedonia and conqueror of most of the known world. Alexander (356–323 BCE) united Greece and the vast territories of the Persian Empire as far east as India. The period of cultural assimilation and synthesis inaugurated by his conquests is called Hellenistic.

Alexandria A major port city and cultural center founded by Alexander on the Egyptian coast. The home of a large Jewish colony during the Hellenistic period, Alexandria nourished a fusion of Jewish and Greek ideas, one result of which was the Greek Septuagint edition of the Hebrew Bible (begun about 250 BCE).

allegory A literary narrative in which persons, places, and events are given a symbolic meaning.

Some Hellenistic-Jewish scholars, like Philo of Alexandria, interpreted the Hebrew Bible allegorically, as Paul does the story of Abraham, Sarah, and Hagar (Gal. 4:21–31).

alpha The first letter of the Greek alphabet, presented as a symbol of creation (Genesis). See also **omega.**

Ananias

1. The High Priest who presided over the full council (Sanhedrin) before which Paul was brought by Claudius Lycias for creating a "riot" in the Jerusalem Temple (Acts 22:22–23:22).

2. An early Christian who with his wife, Sapphira, attempted to defraud the Jerusalem church (Acts 5:1–10).

Andrew A disciple of Jesus and brother of Simon Peter, he was a Galilean fisherman (Mark 1:16–18) who may first have been a follower of John the Baptist (John 1:35–42).

angel From a Greek word meaning "messenger," a spirit being commonly regarded in biblical times as a member of God's heavenly council who served God by communicating his will to humanity (Luke 1–2; Matt. 1).

Annas A former High Priest before whom Jesus was brought for trial (John 18:13). Annas was father-in-law to Caiaphas, then the reigning High Priest (see also Luke 3:2 and Acts 4:6).

Annunciation The angel Gabriel's declaration to Mary of Nazareth that she was to bear a son, Jesus, who would inherit David's throne (Luke 1:28–32).

anthropomorphism The practice of attributing human qualities to something not human; in particular, ascribing human shape and form to a deity.

anti-Christ The ultimate enemy of Jesus Christ, who, according to Christian apocalyptic traditions, will manifest himself at the End of time to corrupt many of the faithful, only to be vanquished at Christ's Second Coming. The term appears only in 2 and 3 John but is clearly referred to in 2 Thessalonians (2:1–2) and Revelation 13.

antinomianism The belief and practice of certain early Christian groups who argued that faith in Christ absolves the believer from obeying moral laws; literally, "opponents of law." Paul attacks this libertarian attitude in Galatians (5:13–6:10; see also 1 and 2 John).

Antioch

1. In Syria, the capital of the Macedonian Seleucid kings and, under Roman rule, a province of the same name. According to Acts, the first predominantly Gentile church was founded in Antioch (Acts 11:20, 21), where followers of "the way" were first called Christians (Acts 11:26). Paul began all three of his missionary tours from here.

2. Pisidian Antioch, a major city in Galatia (in Asia Minor); also the site of an important early church that Paul and Barnabas founded (Acts 13:14–50).

Antiochus The name of several Syrian monarchs who inherited power from Seleucus I, a general and successor of Alexander the Great. The most famous were Antiochus III, who gained control of Palestine in 198–197 BCE, and Antiochus IV (Epiphanes, or "God Manifest") (175–163 BCE), whose persecution of the Jews led to the Maccabean Revolt.

Antipater A nobleman (c. 100–43 BCE) of Idumea and father of Herod the Great who intervened in Judean politics and fostered alliances with Rome.

antitheses The section of Matthew's Sermon on the Mount (Matt. 5:21–48) in which Jesus contrasts selected provisions of the Mosaic Torah with his own ethical directives. The term refers to a rhetorical structure in which contrasting ideas are presented in parallel arrangements of words, phrases, or sentences.

Antonius Felix See **Felix, Antonius.**

aphorism A terse, memorable statement that expresses a (commonly ignored) truth about human experience. Jesus frequently spoke in aphorisms, proverblike sayings that were typically concise, vivid, and paradoxical.

apocalypse A literary form that discloses spiritual realities or truths that are normally hidden—in the future or in the invisible world of spirit beings; from the Greek *apokalypsis*, meaning "to uncover," "to reveal."

apocalyptic An adjective derived from *apocalypse*, it typically refers to visions of the unseen world, such as God's heavenly throne, the habitation of angels, or the Underworld, as well as to the Deity's future plans for human history. See also **eschatology.**

apocalyptic literature

1. A body of Hellenistic-Jewish writings produced between about 300 BCE and 200 CE, including canonical works such as Daniel and noncanonical books such as 1 and 2 Enoch and 2 and 3 Baruch. These visionary books purport to reveal spiritual realities hidden from ordinary eyes, typically predicting future catastrophes heralding the defeat of God's enemies and the ultimate triumph of Israel.

2. Apocalyptic themes dominate much of early Christian literature, including Paul's letters, the Synoptic Gospels, 2 Peter, and Revelation, all of which emphasize Christ's role as God's eschatological agent.

apocalypticism A belief that God, through visions to chosen seers or prophets, reveals his hitherto hidden purpose for humanity, particularly his plan to bring human history to a cataclysmic End in a final climactic battle between both material and spiritual forces of good and evil.

Apocrypha A body of Jewish religious writings dating from about 200 BCE to 100 CE that were included in Greek editions of the Hebrew Bible but not in the official Hebrew Bible canon. The term *apocrypha,* meaning "hidden," was applied to these deuterocanonical works by Jerome, who excluded them from his Latin (Vulgate) translation of the Hebrew and Christian Scriptures. Later editions included them.

Apollos A Hellenistic Jew of Alexandria, Egypt, noted for his eloquence. Originally a follower of John the Baptist, he later became a Christian associate of Paul (Acts 18:24–28; 1 Cor. 1:12; 3:4–6, 22–23; 4:6).

apology A form of literature in which the author defends and explains his particular worldview and behavior.

apostasy The act of abandoning or rejecting a previously held religious belief; from a Greek term meaning "to revolt." An apostate is one who has defected from or ceased to practice his or her religion.

apostle A person sent forth or commissioned as an envoy or messenger, such as (but not restricted to) the Twelve whom Jesus selected to follow him. According to Acts 1, in the early Jerusalem church an apostle was defined as one who had accompanied Jesus during his earthly ministry and had seen the resurrected Lord. Lists of the original Twelve differ from account to account (Matt. 10:2–5; Mark 3:16–19; Luke 6:13–16; Acts 1:13–14).

apothegm In biblical criticism, a brief saying or instructive proverb found in the Gospels. See also **pericope.**

Aquila A prominent early Christian (apparently) expelled from Rome with his wife, Priscilla, by Claudius's edict (c. 49 CE). Aquila is often associated with Paul (Acts 18; Rom. 16:3–5; 1 Cor. 16:19).

Aramaic The language of the Arameans (ancient Syrians), a West Semitic tongue used in parts of Mesopotamia from about 1000 BCE. After the Babylonian captivity (538 BCE), it became the common language of Palestinian Jews and was probably the language spoken by Jesus.

archetype The primal form or original pattern from which all other things of a like nature are descended. The term refers to characters, ideas, or actions that represent the supreme and/or essential examples of a universal type, as Moses is the archetypal model of prophet and lawgiver and Paul is the archetypal missionary.

Areopagus The civic court in Athens and the location of an important legal council of the Athenian democracy where, according to Acts 17, Paul introduced Christianity to some Athenian intellectuals.

ark of the covenant According to Israelite tradition, the portable wooden chest built in Mosaic times to contain artifacts of the Mosaic faith, such as Aaron's staff and the stone tablets of the Decalogue (Exod. 25:10–22). Sometimes carried into battle (Josh. 6: 4–11; 1 Sam. 4), the ark was eventually housed in Solomon's Temple. Its fate after the Temple's destruction (587 BCE) is unknown.

Armageddon A Greek transliteration of the Hebrew place-name *Har-Megiddon,* or "Mountain of Megiddo," a famous battlefield in the Plain of Jezreel in ancient Israel (Judg. 5:19; 2 Kings 9:27; 23:29). In Revelation (16:16), it is the symbolic site of the ultimate war between good and evil.

Artemis The Greek goddess of wildlife, the hunt, and childbirth, whose magnificent temple at Ephesus was one of the Seven Wonders of the Ancient World (see Acts 19). The Romans called her Diana and associated her with the moon.

Ascension, the The resurrected Jesus' ascent to heaven (Acts 1:6–11).

Asclepius The son of a mortal woman, Coronis, and Apollo, the Greek god of prophecy, health, disease, and purification, he was the first physician, the founder and patron of medicine. Posthumously deified, he allegedly effected miraculous cures at shrines throughout the Greco-Roman world.

Athanasius A leading Christian theologian (c. 295–373 CE) who participated in the Council of Nicaea (325 CE) and who was later bishop of Alexandria, Egypt. His Easter Letter (367 CE) is the earliest document to list all the canonical books of the New Testament.

Athens Greece's dominant city-state and cultural capital in the fifth century BCE. Athens remained a leading intellectual center during Hellenistic and Roman times. Acts 17 depicts Paul debating Stoic and Epicurean philosophers there.

Atonement, Day of (Yom Kippur) A solemn, annual Jewish observance in which Israel's High Priest offered blood sacrifices ("sin offerings") to effect a reconciliation between the Deity and his people (Lev. 16). The banishment of a "scapegoat" to which the priest had symbolically transferred the people's collective guilt climaxed the atonement rites. This day marked the priest's once-yearly entrance into the Temple's Holy of Holies, a ceremony that the author of Hebrews says is a foreshadowing of Jesus' sacrificial death and ascension to the heavenly Temple (Heb. 9).

Augustus (Augustus Caesar) The first emperor of Rome (27 BCE–14 CE), who brought peace to the Roman Empire after centuries of civil war. According to Luke 2, his decree ordering a census of "the whole world" was the device that brought about Jesus' birth in Bethlehem.

Babylon An ancient city on the middle Euphrates that was the capital of both the Old Babylonian and the Neo-Babylonian empires. In 587 BCE, Babylonian armies destroyed Jerusalem and its Temple. As the archetypal enemy of God's people, Babylon became the symbol of any earthly government that opposes the faithful (Rev. 14:8; 18:12).

baptism A religious ceremony first associated with John the Baptist (Mark 1:4; 11:30; Luke 7:29) and performed on converts in the infant Christian community (Acts 2:38–41; 19:3–5). Baptism may have derived from ritual cleansings with water practiced by the Essenes or from the use of it by some Pharisees as a conversion alternative to circumcision. In Christianity, it is the rite of initiation into the church (1 Pet.), in which initiates either are totally immersed in water or have water poured on their heads.

bar An Aramaic word used in names, meaning "son of."

bar Kochba The name (meaning "son of the star") that his supporters applied to the leader of the second Jewish Revolt against Rome (132–135 CE).

Barabbas A condemned murderer and possibly a revolutionary whom the Roman prefect Pontius

Pilate released instead of Jesus (Mark 15:6–15; Matt. 27:15–18; Luke 23:16–25; John 18:39–49).

Barnabas A prominent leader of the early churches in Jerusalem and Antioch, Paul's mentor and later his traveling companion (Acts 9:26–30; 11:22–30; 13:1–3, 44–52; 14:1–15:4; 15:22–40; Col. 4:10; 1 Cor. 9:6; Gal. 2:1–13).

Bartholomew One of Jesus' twelve chief disciples (Mark 3:16–19; Matt. 10:2–4; Luke 6:14–16; Acts 1:13), about whom virtually nothing is known. Because Bartholomew's name follows that of Philip in all three Synoptic apostolic lists and because Philip brings an otherwise unknown "Nathanael" to Jesus in the Fourth Gospel (which does not mention Bartholomew), some commentators speculate that Nathanael and Bartholomew are the same person.

Beatitudes The list of blessings or sources of happiness with which Jesus begins the Sermon on the Mount (Matt. 5:3–12). Luke gives a simpler version of these sayings (6:20–23).

ben A Hebrew word used in names, meaning "son of."

Bethlehem A village about five miles south of Jerusalem; birthplace of David (1 Sam. 17:12) and the traditional site of the Messiah's birth (Mic. 5:2; Matt. 2:5–6; Luke 2; John 7:42).

Bible A collection of Jewish and Christian sacred writings commonly divided into two main sections— the Hebrew Bible (Old Testament) and the later Christian Greek Scriptures (New Testament); from the Greek *biblia*, meaning "little books."

bishop The supervisor or presiding officer of a church; from the Greek *episcopos*, meaning "overseer."

Bithynia In New Testament times, a Roman province in northern Asia Minor (modern Turkey) along the Black Sea coast and the location of several Christian churches (Acts 16:7; 1 Pet. 1:1).

Boanerges "Sons of thunder," an epithet Jesus bestows upon the brothers James and John (Mark 3:17; Luke 9:52–56).

Caesar A hereditary name by which the Roman emperors commemorated Gaius Julius Caesar, great-uncle of Augustus, Rome's first emperor (Luke 2:1; 3:1; Mark 12:14; Acts 11:28; 25:11).

Caesarea An important Roman city, built by Herod the Great on the Palestinian coast about sixty-four miles northwest of Jerusalem and named in honor of Caesar Augustus. Caesarea was Pilate's administrative capital and later a Christian center (Acts 8:40; 10:1;

18:22; 21:18; 24). Paul was imprisoned there for two years (Acts 23–26).

Caesarea Philippi An inland city north of the Sea of Galilee built by Philip, son of Herod the Great, and named for the emperor Tiberius Caesar; the site of Peter's recognition that Jesus was the Messiah (Mark 8:27; Matt. 16:13).

Caiaphas Joseph Caiaphas, High Priest of Jerusalem during the reign of the emperor Tiberius (Matt. 26:3, 57–66; John 9:49; 18:13–28; Acts 4:6). Son-in-law to his immediate predecessor, Annas, he was appointed to the office by the prefect Valerius Gratus and presided over Jesus' hearing before the Sanhedrin.

Calvary The site outside Jerusalem's walls, exact location unknown, where Jesus was crucified (Luke 23:33). Calvary derives from the Latin word *calveria*, a translation of the Greek *kranion*, meaning "skull." Calvary was also called Golgotha, a name that comes from the Aramaic for "skull" (Matt. 27:33; John 19:17).

Canaan The Tanakh name for the territory of Palestine west of the Jordan River, from Egypt in the south to Syria in the north (Gen. 10:19); according to biblical tradition, the land God promised to Abraham's descendants (Gen. 15:7-21; 17:1-8).

canon

1. A list of books that a religious community finds sacred and authoritative; from the Greek *kanon*.

2. A standard by which religious beliefs or documents are judged acceptable.

Capernaum A small port on the northwest shore of the Sea of Galilee that Jesus used as headquarters for his Galilean ministry (Matt. 9:1, 9–11; Mark 1:21–29; 2:3–11; Luke 7; John 4:46–54).

catholic epistles Seven short New Testament documents that were addressed to the church as a whole and thus are described as general, or "catholic" (universal).

centurion A low-ranking officer in the Roman army in charge of a "century," or division of 80 or 100 men.

Cephas A name meaning "stone," bestowed by Jesus upon Simon Peter (John 1:42).

chaos In ancient Greco-Roman belief, the original chasm (the formless darkness) that existed before the ordered world (cosmos) came into being.

Christ The Messiah; from the Greek *Christos*, a translation of the Hebrew *mashiah* (messiah), meaning "anointed one." The term derives from Israel's practice of anointing (pouring oil on the heads of) kings at their coronation.

Christology The theological interpretation of the nature and function of Jesus, including doctrines about his divinity, his prehuman existence, and his role in creating the universe and in human salvation.

church In New Testament usage, the community of believers in Jesus Christ (Matt. 16:18; 18:17; Eph. 5:27; 1 Tim. 3:15; 1 Cor. 12:12–27; Col. 1:18). The term translates the Greek *ekklesia,* meaning "assembly of ones called out" (to be the people of God).

circumcision An ancient Semitic operation in which the foreskin of an eight-day-old male is removed as a ceremony of initiation into the covenant and community of Israel. Genesis represents the practice as beginning with Abraham (Gen. 17:10–14); Exodus implies that circumcision began with Moses (Exod. 4:24–46). The question of whether to circumcise Gentile converts to the early Christian church was an important source of dissension (Acts 15; Gal. 2).

Claudius The fourth Roman emperor (41–54 CE), who expelled the Jews from Rome (Acts 11:28; 18:2).

codex A manuscript book of an ancient biblical text, a form pioneered by Christians to replace the unwieldy scrolls on which the Scriptures were originally recorded.

Codex Sinaiticus An ancient Greek edition of the Bible (fourth century CE) that originally contained both Old and New Testaments, although about half of the former is now missing. This version of the New Testament also included the Epistle of Barnabas and Shepherd of Hermas. Written in uncial script on fine vellum, this manuscript is one of the oldest and most valuable texts of the Christian Scriptures.

Colossae An ancient Phrygian city situated on the south bank of the Lycus River in central Asia Minor, important for its position on the trade route between Ephesus and Mesopotamia (Col. 1:1–2; 4:13). Paul or a Pauline disciple composed a canonical letter to Christians there.

Constantine The Roman emperor (306–337 CE) who converted to Christianity and whose reign began the period of state support for the early church. Constantine issued the Edict of Milan in 313 CE, mandating general tolerance of Christianity, and he presided over the Council of Nicaea in 325 CE, establishing a precedent for imperial leadership of the church.

Coptic A term relating to the church or liturgical language of the Copts, a people reputedly descended from the ancient Egyptians who preserved an early form of Christianity. The Nag Hammadi library was written in Coptic, a form of the Egyptian language written in Greek letters.

Corinth A large and prosperous Greek city that the Romans first destroyed (146 BCE) and later rebuilt, making it the capital of the Roman province called Achaia (Greece). About 50 CE, Paul and his associates founded an important church there (Acts 18:24; 19:1; 1 and 2 Cor.).

Cornelius A Roman centurion associated with the synagogue in Caesarea who became the first Gentile convert to Christianity (Acts 10–11).

cosmos The Greek term for the ordered universe, a world system characterized by structure, stability, and harmony.

covenant A vow, agreement, or contract between two parties, a model of the relationship between God and his people. In Exodus, Yahweh makes a covenant with Israel in which the people agree to obey all his laws and instruction (the Torah) and to worship him exclusively (Exod. 20–24; 34; see also Deut. 28; Josh. 24). In Christian tradition, Jesus introduced a "New Covenant" with his disciples, making them the true Israel (Mark 14:22–25; Matt. 26:26–29; 1 Cor. 11:25).

cult The formalized practices of a religious group, particularly its system of worship and public (or secret) rites.

Damascus The capital of Syria and the terminus of ancient caravan routes in the Fertile Crescent. Damascus was the site of Paul's earliest experiences as a Christian (Acts 9; Gal. 1:17).

David A popular king of Israel and the second king of the united twelve-tribe monarchy (c. 1000–961 BCE). Son of Jesse (Ruth 4:18–22) and successor to Saul, David created an Israelite kingdom (1 Sam. 16; 2 Kings 2). After his short-lived kingdom disintegrated, later ages remembered his reign as a model of God's rule on earth and regarded David as a prototype of the divinely appointed monarch, whom the prophets foresaw as an heir to the Davidic throne (Isa. 9:5–7; 11:1–16; Jer. 23:5; 30:9; Ezek. 34:23–31; Matt. 1–2; Rom. 1:3, etc.).

Davidic Covenant The promise that Yahweh made to King David to maintain David's heirs on Israel's throne forever (2 Sam. 7:8–16; Ps. 89:10–37), the basis of Israel's messianic hopes.

Day of Atonement See **Atonement, Day of (Yom Kippur).**

Day of Judgment See **Judgment, Day of.**

deacon A church officer in early Christianity; the term refers to one who serves or ministers.

Dead Sea Scrolls A collection of ancient documents (dating from the second century BCE to the first century CE) found preserved in caves near Qumran on the northwest shore of the Dead Sea. The scrolls included copies (many in fragmental form) of all canonical books of the Hebrew Bible except Esther, works from the Apocrypha and the Pseudepigrapha, and commentaries and other writings of the Essene community.

Decalogue The Ten Commandments (Exod. 20; Deut. 5).

Dedication, Feast of An eight-day Jewish celebration (now known as Hanukkah) instituted in 165 BCE by Judas Maccabeus and held annually on the twenty-fifth day of Kislev (November–December). The holiday commemorates the cleansing and rededication of the Jerusalem Temple, which Antiochus IV had polluted. Referred to in John (10:22–38), it is also known as the Festival of Lights.

deuterocanon The fourteen Old Testament books (Apocrypha) eventually included in the Vulgate but not in the Hebrew Bible. The Catholic and Eastern Orthodox churches regard these works as deuterocanonical—that is, belonging to a second and later canon.

devil The English word commonly used to translate two Greek words with different meanings:

1. *diabolos,* "the accuser" (John 8:44).

2. *daimonion,* one of the many malign spirits inhabiting the world, who were thought to cause disease, madness, and other afflictions (see Matt. 10:25; Mark 3:22; Luke 8; 11:14–16). In Revelation 12:9, the devil is identified with the Hebrew Satan and the serpent of Genesis 3.

Diana of the Ephesians The Near Eastern form of the Greek goddess Artemis (identified by the Romans with Diana). She was worshiped in Ephesus, which in Paul's time was the capital of the Roman province of Asia (Acts 19).

Diaspora The distribution of Jews outside their Palestinian homeland, such as the many Jewish communities established throughout the Greco-Roman world; literally, a "scattering."

Dionysus The son of Zeus and the mortal Semele, princess of Thebes, he was the Greek god of wine, ecstasy, and emotional liberation. The only Olympian god to suffer death, a descent into the Underworld (Hades), resurrection, and ascension to heaven, he presided over mystery cults that apparently promised their adherents a future immortality.

disciple In the New Testament, a follower of a particular religious figure, such as Moses (John 9:28), John the Baptist (Luke 11:1; John 1:35), the Pharisees (Mark 2:18), or Jesus (Matt. 14:26; 20:17); from the Greek word meaning "learner."

Docetism The belief, commonly associated with Gnostic Christianity, that Jesus was pure spirit and only appeared to be physically human; from the Greek verb meaning "to seem."

Domitian A Roman emperor (81–96 CE), the younger son of Vespasian, who ascended the throne following the death of his brother Titus. The Book of Revelation was written late in his reign.

doxology In a religious writing or service, the formal concluding expression of praise ascribing glory to God.

Dragon The image applied in Revelation 12 to Satan, the embodiment of evil forces opposing God. Derived from ancient Near Eastern mythology, the symbol of the giant reptile represents the powers of darkness and disorder (the original chaos) that God first conquered in creating the ordered universe (cosmos).

dualism A philosophic or religious system that posits the existence of two parallel worlds, one of physical matter and the other of invisible spirit. Moral dualism views the universe as divided between powers of good and evil, light and dark, which contend for human allegiance.

Elijah The leader of Israel's prophetic movement during the ninth century BCE. Elijah fiercely championed the exclusive worship of Yahweh and opposed the Israelite cult of the Canaanite god Baal (1 Kings 17–19; 21; 2 Kings 1–2). Reportedly carried to heaven in a fiery chariot (2 Kings 2:1–13), he was expected to reappear shortly before the Day of Yahweh arrived (Mal. 4:5–6). Although some Christian writers identified John the Baptist with Elijah (Luke 1:17; Mark 9:12–13), some contemporaries viewed Jesus as Elijah returned (Mark 9:28; Matt. 16:14). Along with Moses, Elijah appears at Jesus' Transfiguration (Mark 9:4; Matt. 17:3; Luke 9:30).

Elizabeth The wife of the Levite priest Zechariah and mother of John the Baptist (Luke 1).

Emmaus A village (site disputed) near Jerusalem, along the road to which the resurrected Jesus appeared to two disciples (Luke 24:13–32).

emperor cult A widespread practice in the Roman Empire, particularly in its eastern half, of assigning divine honors, typically involving sacrifice and related rituals, to an emperor or member of the imperial family. In Asia Minor, some cities advocated publicly worshiping the ruler as if he were a god, a rite that Revelation condemns as idolatrous (Rev. 13, 17).

Enoch A son of Cain (Gen. 4:17) or Jared (Gen. 5:18) and father of Methuselah (Gen. 5:21), taken by God (apparently to heaven). Legends surrounding Enoch's mysterious fate gave rise to a whole body of noncanonical literature in which Enoch returns to earth to describe his experiences in the spirit world and foretell events leading to the End.

Epaphras An early Christian of Colossae who reported on the Colossian church to the imprisoned Paul (Col. 1:7; 4:12; Philem. 23).

Epaphroditus A Macedonian Christian from Philippi who assisted Paul in prison (Phil. 2:25–27).

Ephesus A wealthy Hellenistic city, in New Testament times the capital of the Roman province of Asia, site of the famous temple of Artemis (Diana) (Acts 19–20). Mentioned frequently in Paul's correspondence (1 Cor. 16:19; 2 Cor. 12:14; 13:1; 1 Tim. 3:1, etc.), the Ephesian church receives the author's favorable judgment in Revelation 2:1–7.

epiphany An appearance or manifestation, particularly of a divine being.

epistle A formal communication intended to be read publicly.

eschatology Beliefs about the supernaturally directed destiny of humanity and the universe; from the Greek word meaning "study of last things." Associated with an apocalyptic worldview, eschatology has both personal and general applications:

1. Beliefs about the individual soul following death, including divine judgment, heaven, hell, and resurrection.

2. Larger concerns about the fate of the cosmos, including convictions about a divinely guided renewal of the world and human society in the near future or in the present (realized eschatology).

eschaton From the Greek *eschatos,* meaning "last," a term designating the end of history or human life.

Essenes According to Josephus, one of the three major sects of Judaism in the first century CE. Characterized by apocalyptic beliefs in the world's imminent End, some of the group, as most scholars believe, founded monastic communities in the Judean desert, such as the Qumran settlement that produced the library known as the Dead Sea Scrolls.

Eucharist The Christian ceremony of consecrated bread and wine that Jesus initiated at the Last Supper (Mark 14:22–25; Matt. 26:26–29, etc.); from the Greek word meaning "gratitude" or "thanksgiving."

Eusebius A Christian scholar (c. 260–339 CE) famous for his *History of the Church* (through about 323 CE) and forty other works, including a biography of Constantine, the first Christian emperor, whom Eusebius served as chief theological adviser. Born in Palestine, where he spent most of his life, Eusebius was also bishop of Caesarea and a major participant at the Council of Nicaea.

Evangelist From the Greek *evangelion,* meaning "good news"; the writer of a Gospel.

Eve The first woman, wife of Adam, who derived her name from the Hebrew verb "to live," because she was "the mother of all those who live" (Gen. 3:30). Paul's interpretation of her role in humanity's alienation from God appears in 2 Corinthians 11:3; the Pastor's negative evaluation of her sex appears in 1 Timothy 2:11–15.

exegesis The close analysis and interpretation of a text to discover the original author's intent and exact meaning. Once the writer's primary intent has been established, other interpretations can be considered.

exorcism The act or practice of expelling a demon or evil spirit from a person or place (Tob. 8:1–3; Mark 1:23–27, 32–34; 5:1–20; Matt. 8:25–34; Acts 19:13–19, etc.).

expiation The act of making atonement for sin, usually by offering a sacrifice to appease divine wrath (Lev. 16; Heb. 9).

faith In biblical terms, the quality of trust, reliance on, and fidelity to God. Both the New Testament and Greek editions of the Hebrew Bible use two terms (*pistis, pisteurein*) to express the concept, which reaches its fullest development in Paul's doctrine of salvation through full confidence and trust in the saving power of Christ (Rom. 10:17; Gal. 3:5–29; 5:6, etc.).

Fall, the A postbiblical concept denoting humanity's loss of innocence and divine favor through the first human beings' sin of disobedience (Gen. 3). According to some interpretations of Pauline thought (Rom. 5:12–21; 1 Cor. 15:45–49), the Fall resulted in the transmission of death and a proclivity toward wrongdoing to the entire human race. As a medieval rhyme expressed it, "In Adam's fall, we sinned all."

Feast of Dedication See **Dedication, Feast of.**

Felix, Antonius The Roman procurator of Judea (52–59 CE) before whom Paul was tried at Caesarea (Acts 23:23–24:27).

Festus, Porcius The procurator of Judea (c. 59–62 CE) whom Nero appointed to succeed Felix and through whom Paul appealed to be tried by Caesar's court in Rome (Acts 24:27–26:32).

Flavius Josephus See **Josephus, Flavius.**

form criticism A method of biblical analysis that attempts to isolate, classify, and analyze individual units or characteristic forms contained in a literary text and to identify the probable preliterary form of these units before their incorporation into the written text; the term is an English rendition of the German *Formgeschichte.* Form criticism also attempts to discover the setting in life (*Sitz-im-Leben*) of each unit—that is, the historical, social, religious, and cultural environment from which it developed—and to trace or reconstruct the process by which various traditions evolved from their original oral state to their final literary form.

Fourth Gospel The Gospel of John, last-written of the four canonical Gospels; it differs markedly in form, order, and content from the three Synoptics.

fundamentalism A largely North American Protestant movement, beginning about 1900, that affirmed the literal factuality of all biblical statements and rejected post-Enlightenment questioning of biblical infallibility.

Gabriel In the Hebrew angelic hierarchy, one of the seven archangels whose duty it was to convey the Deity's messages. Gabriel explained Daniel's visions to him (Dan. 8:15–26; 9:20–27) and, in the New Testament, announced the births of John the Baptist and Jesus (Luke 1:15–17, 26–38). The name may mean "person of God" or "God has shown himself mighty."

Galatia A region in the interior of Asia Minor (Turkey) settled by Gauls; in New Testament times, a Roman province visited by Paul and his associates (Acts 16:6; 18:23; 1 Cor. 16:1; Gal. 1:2; 1 Pet. 1:1).

Galilee The region of northern Palestine lying west of the Jordan River, where Jesus grew up and carried out much of his public ministry (Mark 1–9; Matt. 2:23; Luke 4); from the Hebrew *Ghil-ha-goyim*, meaning "circle of Gentiles." In Jesus' day, Herod Antipas administered this region for the Romans (Luke 23:5–7).

Galilee, Sea of The major body of fresh water in northern Palestine, source of livelihood to many Galilean fishermen, such as Peter, Andrew, James, and John (Matt. 4:18–22).

Gallio A proconsul of Achaia (the Roman province of Greece) who dismissed charges brought against Paul by Corinthian Jews (Acts 18:12–17). Gallio was a brother of Seneca, the Stoic philosopher.

Gamaliel A leading Pharisee and scholar, a member of the Sanhedrin, the reputed teacher of Paul (Acts 5:34–40; 22:3), and an exponent of the liberal wing of the Pharisaic party developed by his grandfather, Hillel.

Gehenna The New Testament name for the "Valley of the Son [or Children] of Hinnom," a topographical depression that bordered Jerusalem on the south and west and that had been the site of human sacrifices to Molech and other Canaanite gods (Jer. 7:32; Lev. 18:21; 1 Kings 11:7; 2 Chron. 28:3; 33:6). Later used as a dump in which garbage was burned, the valley became a symbol of punishment in the afterlife and is cited as such by Jesus (Matt. 5:22; 10:28–29; 18:8; 25:30, 46; etc.). *Gehenna* is commonly translated as "hell" in the Gospels.

Gemara The second part of the Talmud, an extensive commentary, in Aramaic, on the Hebrew Mishnah.

Gentile A non-Jewish person, a member of "the nations" that are not in a covenant relationship with Yahweh. Jewish writers commonly refer to Gentiles as "the uncircumcised," persons not bearing the ritual mark of the covenant people.

Gethsemane The site of a garden or orchard on the Mount of Olives where Jesus took his disciples after the Last Supper; the place where he was arrested (Matt. 26:36–56; Mark 14:32–52; Luke 22:39–53; John 18:1–14).

glossolalia A religious phenomenon in which a person is inspired to speak in a language not his own. In Acts 2, this emotional "speaking in [foreign] tongues" symbolizes the multinational nature of the early Christian movement. In 1 Corinthians 14, Paul prefers rational communication to *glossolalia.*

gnosis The Greek word for "knowledge."

Gnosticism A widespread and extremely diverse movement in early Christianity. Followers of Gnosticism believed that salvation is gained through a special knowledge (*gnosis*) revealed through a spiritual savior (presumably Jesus) and is the property of an elite few who have been initiated into its mysteries. In its various forms, Gnosticism became a major movement in the early church, in spite of leaders' condemnation.

Gog In Ezekiel, a future leader of Israel's enemies (Ezek. 38) whose attack on the Jerusalem sanctuary will precipitate Yahweh's intervention and the ultimate destruction of the wicked (Rev. 20:8).

Gospel

1. The Christian message, literally meaning "good news."

2. The literary form of Christian narratives about Jesus or compilations of his teachings.

Gospel, Fourth The Gospel attributed to John.

Gospels, apocryphal Christian Gospels, such as those attributed to Peter, Thomas, James, or others, that were not admitted to the New Testament canon.

Gospels, canonical The Gospels of Matthew, Mark, Luke, and John.

Gospels, Synoptic The three canonical Gospels—Matthew, Mark, and Luke—that present Jesus' public life from a strikingly similar viewpoint, structuring their respective narratives so that the contents can be arranged in parallel columns.

Griesbach theory A solution to the Synoptic problem that views Mark as a conflation and abridgement of Matthew and Luke, a theory a small minority of scholars supports.

Hades In Greek religion, the name of the god of the Underworld, a mythic region that also came to be known by that name. In translating the Hebrew Bible into Greek, the Septuagint translators rendered *Sheol* (the Hebrew term for the subterranean abode of all the dead) as *Hades* (Gen. 42:38; 1 Sam. 2:6; Job 7:9; Prov. 27:20; Eccles. 9:10). New Testament writers also refer to the place of the dead as Hades (Rev. 1:18; 20:14). See also **Gehenna.**

Haggadah The imaginative interpretation of the nonlegal (historical and religious) passages of the Hebrew Bible. A collection of Haggadah, dating from the first centuries CE, appears in the Palestinian Talmud. See also **Halakah.**

Hagiographa The third major division of the Hebrew Bible, a miscellaneous collection of poetry, wisdom literature, history, and an apocalypse (Daniel); from the Greek term meaning "sacred writings."

Halakah The interpretation of the legal sections of the Mosaic Torah. The term derives from a Hebrew word meaning "to follow"; Halakah deals with rules that guide a person's life. Collections of halakic interpretations dating from the first centuries CE are incorporated into the Talmud. See also **Haggadah.**

Hanukkah The Feast of Dedication celebrating the Maccabees' restoration of the Jerusalem Temple about 165 BCE.

Hasidim Devout Jews who refused to forsake their religion during the persecution inflicted by Antiochus IV (second century BCE). The Jewish religious parties of the New Testament period are descended from the Hasidim.

Hasmoneans The Jewish royal dynasty founded by the Maccabees and named for Hasmon, an ancestor of Mattathias.

Hebrew Bible A collection of Jewish sacred writings originally written in the Hebrew language (although some later books are in Aramaic); known to Christians as the Old Testament. The Hebrew Bible is traditionally divided into three main parts: the Torah or Law (Genesis through Deuteronomy), the Prophets (Joshua through the twelve minor prophets), and the Writings (Psalms through Chronicles).

Hellenism The influence and adoption of Greek thought, language, values, and customs that began with the conquest of the eastern Mediterranean world by Alexander the Great and intensified under his Hellenistic successors and various Roman emperors.

Hellenistic Greek-like; pertaining to the historical period following Alexander's death in 323 BCE during which Greek language, ideas, and customs permeated the eastern Mediterranean and Near Eastern worlds.

Hellenists Jews living outside Palestine who adopted the Greek language and, to varying degrees, Greek customs and ideas (Acts 6:1; 9:29).

Hellenization The diffusion of Greek language and culture (Hellenism) throughout the Mediterranean region, beginning with the conquests of Alexander of Macedonia in the fourth century BCE. Enforced Hellenization of the Jews by Antiochus IV sparked the Maccabean Revolt.

heresy An opinion contrary to that officially endorsed by religious authorities or persons in power. Applied to early Christianity by its detractors (Acts 24:14), the term was not generally used in its modern sense during New Testament times except in the pastoral epistles (1 Tim. 1:3; Titus 3:10).

Herod The name of seven Palestinian rulers:

1. Herod I (the Great), the Idumean Roman-appointed ruler when Jesus was born (Matt. 2:1). An able administrator who lavishly reconstructed the Jerusalem Temple, he was notorious for reputed cruelty and was almost universally hated by the Jews.

2. Herod Antipas, son of Herod I, tetrarch of Galilee (Luke 3:1) and Perea (4 BCE–39 CE), frequently mentioned in the New Testament. Jesus, who called him "that fox" (Luke 13:31–32) and regarded him as a malign influence (Mark 8:15), was tried before him (Luke 9:7, 9; 23:7–15). Antipas was also responsible for executing John the Baptist (Matt. 14:1–12).

3. Herod Archelaus, ethnarch of Judea, Samaria, who so misruled his territory that he was recalled to Rome, an event to which Jesus apparently refers in Luke 19:12–27. Archelaus's evil reputation caused Joseph and Mary to avoid Judea and settle in Nazareth (Matt. 2:22–23).

4. Herod, a son of Herod the Great and half brother to Herod Antipas (Matt. 14:3; Mark 6:17).

5. Herod Philip II, son of Herod the Great and half brother of Herod Antipas, who ruled portions of northeastern Palestine and rebuilt the city of Caesarea Philippi near Mount Hermon (Luke 3:1).

6. Herod Agrippa I, son of Aristobulus and grandson of Herod the Great, who ingratiated himself at the imperial court in Rome and, under Claudius, was made king over most of Palestine (41–44 CE). A persecutor of Christians, he reportedly died a horrible death immediately after accepting divine honors (Acts 12:1–23).

7. Herod Agrippa II, son of Herod Agrippa I and great-grandson of Herod the Great, first king of Chalcis (50 CE) and then of the territory formerly ruled by Philip the Tetrarch, as well as of the adjoining area east of Galilee and the Upper Jordan. This was the Herod, together with his sister Bernice, before whom Paul appeared at Caesarea (Acts 25:13–26:32).

Herodians The name applied to members of an influential political movement in first-century-CE Judaism who supported Herod's dynasty, particularly that of Herod Antipas. Opposing messianic hopes (Mark 3:6), they conspired with some Pharisees to implicate Jesus in disloyalty to Rome (Mark 12:13; Matt. 22:16).

Herodias A granddaughter of Herod the Great, daughter of Aristobulus, and half sister of Herod Agrippa I. Herodias was criticized by John the Baptist for having deserted her first husband for her second, Herod Antipas, who divorced his wife to marry her. In revenge, she demanded the head of John the Baptist (Mark 6:17–29; Matt. 14:1–12; Luke 3:19–20).

Hinnom, Valley of A surface depression lying south and west of Jerusalem; also called the "Valley of the Son (or Children) of Hinnom" (Jer. 7:32; 2 Kings 23:10). Called Gehenna in the New Testament, it is a symbol of the place of posthumous torment. See also **Gehenna.**

historical criticism A critical method involving the analysis of a document to determine its relative historical accuracy and plausibility, including such matters as the author's purpose (or bias) and the sociohistorical context in which it emerged.

Holy of Holies The innermost and most sacred room of the Jerusalem Temple, where Yahweh was believed to be invisibly enthroned.

Holy Spirit The presence of God active in human life, a concept most explicitly set forth in John 14:16–26 and in the Pentecost miracle depicted in Acts 2. In post–New Testament times, the Holy Spirit was defined as the Third Person in the Trinity (see Matt. 28:19–20).

Idumea The name (meaning "pertaining to Edom") that the Greeks and Romans applied to the country of Edom, Judah's southern neighbor; the homeland of Herod the Great (Mark 3:8).

Immanuel The name (meaning "God is with us") that Isaiah gave to a child whose birth he predicted as a sign to King Ahaz during the late eighth century BCE. Although not originally presented as a messianic prophecy, it was later interpreted as such (Mic. 5:3; Matt. 1:22–23).

Incarnation The Christian doctrine that the prehuman Son of God became flesh, the man Jesus of Nazareth—a concept based largely on the Logos hymn that opens John's Gospel (John 1:1–18, especially 1:14).

Isaac The son of Abraham and Sarah (Gen. 21:1–7), child of the covenant promise by which Abraham's descendants would bring a blessing to all the earth's families (Gen. 17:15–22; 18:1–15) but whom Yahweh commanded to be sacrificed to him (Gen. 22:1–19). Reprieved by an angel, Isaac marries Rebekah (Gen. 24:1–67), who bears him twin sons, Esau and Jacob (Gen. 25:19–26), the latter of whom has his name changed to Israel. Paul interprets the near-sacrifice of Isaac as an allegory of Christ (Gal. 4:21–31).

Isis The Egyptian mother goddess who was worshiped in mystery cults throughout the Roman Empire. Images in which she nurses her infant son Horus anticipate later Christian renditions of the Madonna.

Israel

1. The name an angel (or Yahweh) gives to Jacob (cf. Gen. 32:28; 35:10).

2. The Israelite nation descended from Jacob's twelve sons, Yahweh's covenant people united under kings Saul, David, and Solomon.

3. The northern kingdom of Israel, as opposed to the southern state of Judah, during the divided monarchy (922–721 BCE); even after the Assyrians destroyed the northern kingdom in 721 BCE, the covenant people were known collectively as "Israel."

Jairus The head of a synagogue in Galilee who asked Jesus to heal his dying child, for which act of faith he was rewarded with the girl's miraculous cure (Luke 8:41–42, 49–56; Mark 5:35–43; Matt. 9:18–20, 23–26).

James

1. The son of Zebedee and brother of John, and one of the Twelve Apostles (Mark 1:19–20; 3:17; Matt. 4:21–22; 10:2; Luke 5:10; 6:14). A Galilean fisherman, he left his trade to follow Jesus and, with John and Peter, became a member of his inner circle. He was among the three disciples present at the Transfiguration (Mark 9:2–10; Matt. 17:1–9; Luke 9:28–36) and was at Jesus' side during the last hours before his arrest (Mark 14:32–42; Matt. 26:36–45). James and John used their intimacy to request a favored place in the messianic kingdom, thus arousing the other apostles' indignation (Mark 10:35–45). James was beheaded when Herod Agrippa I persecuted the Jerusalem church (41–44 CE) (Acts 12:2).

2. James, the eldest of Jesus' three "brothers" (or close male relatives) named in the Gospels (Mark 6:3; Matt. 13:55). He first opposed Jesus' work (Matt. 12:46–50; Mark 3:31–35; Luke 8:19–21; John 7:3–5) but was apparently converted by one of Jesus' post resurrection appearances (1 Cor. 15:7) and became a leader in the Jerusalem church (Acts 15:13–34; 21:18–26). According to legend, a Nazirite and upholder of the Mosaic Law, he apparently clashed with Paul over the latter's policy of absolving Gentile converts from circumcision and other Torah requirements (Gal. 1:18–2:12). The reputed author of the New Testament epistle of James, he was martyred at Jerusalem in the early 60s CE.

3. James, son of Alphaeus and Mary (Acts 1:13; Mark 16:1), one of the Twelve (Matt. 10:3–4), called "the less" or "the younger" (Mark 15:40).

Jamnia, Academy of According to tradition an assembly of eminent Palestinian rabbis and Pharisees held about 90 CE in the coastal village of Jamnia (Yavneh) to define and guide Judaism following the Roman destruction of Jerusalem and its Temple. In this tradition, a leading Pharisee named Yohanan ben Zakkai had escaped from the besieged city by simulating death and being carried out in a coffin by his disciples. Yohanan, who had argued that saving human lives was more important than success in the national rebellion against Rome, was given Roman support to set up an academy to study the Mosaic Law. Under his direction, the Pharisees not only preserved the Torah traditions but apparently provided authoritative leadership for postwar Judaism.

Jerusalem When David captured this ancient Canaanite city about 1000 BCE, he made it Israel's capital, where his son Solomon built a Temple to Yahweh. After the ten northern tribes' secession from the Davidic monarchy, it remained the capital of Judah. Jerusalem suffered three major destructions: by Babylon (587 BCE) and by Rome (70 CE and 135 CE).

Jerusalem church According to Luke-Acts, the original center of Christianity from which the "new way" spread outward to "the ends of the earth" (Acts 1–15). Inspired by the Spirit at Pentecost, the Jerusalem believers formed a commune led by three "pillars"—Peter (Cephas), John, and James, Jesus' kinsman (Gal. 1:18–2:10).

Jesus The English form of a Latin name derived from the Greek *Iesous,* which translated the Aramaic *Yeshua,* a later version of the Hebrew *Yehoshua* or *Joshua,* meaning "Yahweh is salvation." The name was borne by several biblical figures, including Joshua, leader of the conquest of Canaan; an ancestor of Jesus (Luke 3:29); and a Jewish Christian also called Justus (Col. 4:11). It was also the name of the author of Ecclesiasticus, Jesus ben Sirach.

Jesus Christ The name and title given the firstborn of Mary and Joseph (the child's legal father), the one whom Christians regard as the Spirit-begotten Son of God and Savior of the world (Matt. 1:21; Luke 1:31). The term *Christ* is not a proper name but the English version of the Greek *Christos,* a translation of the Aramaic *meshiha* and the Hebrew *mashiah* (messiah, meaning "anointed one").

Jew Originally, a member of the tribe or kingdom of Judah (2 Kings 16:6; 25:25). The term later included any Hebrew who returned from the Babylonian captivity (587–538 BCE), and it finally encompassed all the Covenant people scattered throughout the world (Matt. 2:2) during the Second Temple period (c. 515 BCE–70 CE).

Jewish Bible See **Hebrew Bible.**

Joanna The wife of Chuza, an administrator in Herod Antipas's Jerusalem household, who became a disciple of Jesus (Luke 8:3) and was among the women who discovered his empty tomb (Luke 23:55–24:11).

John

1. The Apostle, a Galilean fisherman, son of Zebedee and brother of the apostle James, called by Jesus to be among his twelve most intimate followers (Mark 1:19–20; Matt. 4:21–22). Jesus called James and John "Boanerges" (sons of thunder), possibly because of their impetuous temperaments (Mark 3:17; 9:38; Luke 9:52–56). Always among the first four in the Gospel lists of the Twelve (Mark 3:14–17; Matt. 10:2; Luke 6:3–14), John was present at the Transfiguration (Matt. 17:1; Mark 9:2; Luke 9:28) and at Gethsemane (Matt. 26:37; Mark 14:33). Tradition identifies him with the Beloved Disciple (John 13:23; 21:20) and as the author of the Gospel of John, a premise that most scholars believe is unlikely. Along with Peter and James, he was one of the triple "pillars" of the Jerusalem church (Acts 1:13; 3:1–4:22; 8:14–17; Gal. 2:9). He may have been martyred under Herod Agrippa, although a late-second-century tradition states that he lived to old age in Ephesus.

2. The Baptist, the son of Zechariah, a priest, and Elizabeth (Luke 1:5–24, 56–80), John was an ascetic who preached the imminence of judgment and baptized converts in the Jordan River as a symbol of their repentance from sin (Matt. 3:1–12; Mark 1:2–8; Luke 3:1–18). The Gospel writers viewed him as an Elijah figure and forerunner of the Messiah (Luke 1:17; Matt. 11:12–14; John 1:15, 9–34; 3:22–36) who baptized Jesus but also recognized his superiority (Matt. 3:13–17; Mark 1:9–11; Luke 3:21–22). When imprisoned by Herod Antipas, he inquired whether Jesus was the expected "one who is to come." Jesus' answer was equivocal, but he praised John's work as fulfilling prophecy (Matt. 11:2–19; Luke 7:24–35). At his stepdaughter Salome's request, Herod had John beheaded (Matt. 14:6–12; Mark 6:17–29). Some of John's disciples later became Christians (John 1:37; Acts 18:25).

3. The author of Revelation. Known as John of Patmos (the Aegean island to which he was exiled), he was a prophet and visionary who described heaven and future history (Rev. 1:1–4, 9; 22:8–9).

Joseph

1. The husband of Mary and legal father of Jesus, a descendant of the Bethlehemite David (Matt. 1:20) but resident of Nazareth (Luke 2:4), where he was a carpenter (Matt. 13:55). Little is known of him except for his piety (Luke 2:21–24, 41–42) and his wish to protect his betrothed wife from scandal (Luke 2:1–5). Because he does not appear among Jesus' family members during his (supposed) son's public ministry, it is assumed that he died before Jesus began his preaching career (Matt. 1:18–2:23; 13:55–56).

2. Joseph of Arimathea, a wealthy member of the Sanhedrin and, according to John 19:38, a secret follower of Jesus who claimed Jesus' crucified body from Pilate for burial in his private garden tomb (Matt. 27:57–60; Mark 15:42–46; Luke 23:50–53; John 19:38–42).

Josephus, Flavius An important Jewish historian (c. 37–100 CE) whose two major works—*Antiquities of the Jews* and *The Jewish War* (covering the revolt against Rome, 66–73 CE)—provide valuable background material for first-century Judaism and the early Christian period.

Judaeus, Philo See **Philo Judaeus.**

Judah

1. The fourth son of the patriarch Jacob and his wife Leah (Gen. 29:35), progenitor of the tribe of Judah.

2. The kingdom of Judah during the divided monarchy (922–721 BCE), ruled by the Davidic dynasty until the Babylonian conquest (587 BCE) brought it to an end.

Judaism The name applied to the religion of the people of Judah ("the Jews") after the Babylonian exile (587–538 BCE). By Jesus' day, it was extremely diverse.

Judas A late form of the name Judah, popular after the time of Judas ("the Jew") Maccabeus and borne by several New Testament figures:

1. The brother (or son) of James, one of the Twelve Apostles (Luke 6:16), who is sometimes identified with the Thaddeus of Matthew 10:3 or the Judas of John 14:22.

2. The "brother" or kinsman of Jesus (Mark 6:3; Matt. 13:55).

3. Judas Iscariot ("Judas the man of Kerioth"), son of Simon Iscariot (John 6:71; 13:26), the apostle who betrayed Jesus to the priests and Romans for thirty pieces of silver (Mark 3:19; 14:10; Luke 6:16; Matt. 26:14–16, 47; John 18:3) but later returned the blood money shortly before his death (Matt. 27:3–5; Acts 1:18–20). The Gospel writers little understood Judas's motives, attributing them to simple greed or to the influence of Satan (Luke 22:3; John 6:71; 12:1–8; 13:11, 27–29). The recently discovered non-canonical Gospel of Judas allegedly portrays him as Jesus' friend who betrays his master only to facilitate Jesus' return to heavenly glory.

Judas Maccabeus The third of five sons of the Judean priest Mattathias, leader of the successful Jewish uprising (c. 167–160 BCE) against the Syrian king Antiochus IV. The epithet Maccabeus is believed to mean "[God's] hammer," referring to Judas's effectiveness in striking blows for Jewish freedom. His story is told in 1 Maccabees.

Judas the Galilean A Jewish patriot from Galilee who led an unsuccessful insurrection against Rome in 6 CE (Acts 5:37).

Jude An Anglicized form of the name Judah or Judas; one of Jesus' "brothers" (or a close male relative) (Mark 6:3; Matt. 13:55), perhaps a son born to Joseph before his marriage to Mary. Jude is less prominent in the early Christian community than his brother James (Jude 1:1) and is the traditional author of the Epistle of Jude, though most scholars doubt this claim.

Judea The Greco-Roman designation for territory comprising the old kingdom of Judah. The name first occurs in Ezra 5:8, a reference to the "province of Judea." In the time of Jesus, Judea was the southernmost of the three divisions of the Roman province of western Palestine, the other two of which were Samaria and Galilee (Neh. 2:7; Luke 1:39; John 3:22; 11:7; Acts 1:1; Gal. 1:22).

Judgment, Day of A theological concept deriving from the ancient Hebrew belief that the Day of Yahweh would see Israel's triumph and the destruction of its enemies, a confidence the prophet Amos shattered by proclaiming that it would mean calamity for Israel, as for all who broke Yahweh's laws (Amos 5:18–20). This view prevails in Zephaniah 1:1–2; 3 and Malachi 3:1–6; 4:1–6. Isaiah also refers to "that day" of coming retribution (Isa. 11:10–16; 13:9, 13), and it is given an apocalyptic setting in Daniel 7:9–14, an idea developed in several apocryphal

and pseudepigraphal books as well as in the New Testament (Matt. 25; Rev. 20).

Jupiter Latin name of the chief Roman deity, counterpart of the Greek Zeus, king of the Olympian gods for whom some ignorant men of Lycaonia mistook Paul's companion Barnabas (Acts 14:12–18).

kavod Yahweh's presence in the Jerusalem Temple; a Hebrew term commonly translated as "glory" or "splendor."

kerygma The act of publicly preaching the Christian message; a Greek term meaning "proclamation."

kingdom of God The rule or dominion of God in human affairs; the translation of the Greek *basileia tou theou.*

koinē The common Greek in which the New Testament is written. *Koinē* Greek, following the conquests of Alexander, was the everyday language of the Hellenistic world.

L An abbreviation for special Lukan material, the scholarly term designating passages that appear only in the Gospel of Luke.

Laodicea A commercial city on the Lycus River in Asia Minor and one of the seven churches of Asia (Col. 4:15–16; Rev. 3:14–22).

Last Supper, the Jesus' final meal with his disciples. Depicted as a Passover observance in the Synoptic Gospels, it was the occasion at which Jesus instituted a "New Covenant" with his followers and inaugurated the ceremony of bread and wine (Holy Communion, or the Eucharist) (Mark 14:12–26; Matt. 26:20–29; Luke 22:14–23; 1 Cor. 11:23–26).

latter prophets The books of Isaiah, Jeremiah, Ezekiel, and the twelve minor prophets; also known as the "writing prophets."

Law The Torah ("teaching," "instruction"), contained in the first five books of the Bible and including the legal material traditionally ascribed to Moses.

Lazarus

1. The brother of Mary and Martha, a resident of Bethany whom Jesus resuscitated (John 11:1–12:10).

2. The beggar in Jesus' parable of rewards and punishments in the afterlife (Luke 16:20–25).

legend An unverifiable story or narrative cycle about a celebrated person or place of the past. Legends grow as the popular oral literature of a people. Their purpose is to provide, not historical accuracy, but entertainment; they illustrate cherished beliefs, expectations, and moral principles. Scholars consider much of the material associated with the stories of the patriarchs, Moses, and prophets as legendary.

Levites The Israelite tribe descended from Levi, son of Jacob (Num. 3; 1 Chron. 5:27–6:81) that was given priestly duties in lieu of landholdings when Israel conquered Canaan (Deut. 18:1–8). According to a priestly writer, only descendants of Aaron were to be priests (Exod. 28:1; Num. 18:7); the Levites were regarded as their assistants and servants (Num. 18:2–7; 20–32). They served as priests of secondary rank and as temple functionaries during the postexilic period, which was dominated by a priestly hierarchy (1 Chron. 24–26). Other stories involving Levites appear in Judges 19–21 and Luke 10:32.

lex talionis The law of strict retaliation, the principle of retributive justice expressed in the Torah command to exact "eye for eye, life for life" (Exod. 21:23–25; Lev. 24:19–20; Deut. 19:21), a practice that Jesus rejects (Matt. 5:38–39).

literary criticism A form of literary analysis that attempts to categorize or define literary types, the stages of composition from oral to written form, a text's characteristic rhetorical features, major themes, and the stages and degree of redaction (editing) of a text.

liturgy A body of rites, including both actions and spoken formulas, used in public worship, such as the ceremony of the Eucharist (Holy Communion). The Didache (c. 100 CE) describes some of the church's earliest liturgical practices, including baptism and Communion.

Logos A Greek term meaning both "word" and "reason," used by Greek philosophers to denote the rational principle that creates and informs the universe. Amplified by Philo Judaeus of Alexandria, Egypt, to represent the mediator between God and his material creation, as Wisdom had been in Proverbs 8:22–31, the term found its most famous expression in the prologue to the Fourth Gospel to denote the prehuman Jesus—"the Word became flesh and dwelt among us" (John 1:14).

Lord's Supper, the The final meal that Jesus held with his closest disciples the night before his death. Here he introduced the New Covenant and shared the bread and wine that symbolized his body and blood about to be sacrificed on behalf of humanity (Mark 14:22–25; Matt. 26:26–29; Luke 22:14–20). Paul first calls the Christian "love feast" (*agape*), or communion, by this name in 1 Corinthians 11:20, in which he describes the ceremony of the Eucharist (1 Cor. 11:23–26). John's version of the event (John 13:1–35) differs strikingly from that in the Synoptics. See **Last Supper, the.**

love In biblical usage, an inner quality expressed through generously seeking the welfare of others, a major principle of Torah obedience, which requires active love of God (Deut. 6:4) and love of one's fellow humans (Lev. 19:18), concepts that Jesus cites as the two greatest commandments (Mark 12:29–31). In the New Testament, love (Greek, *agape*) is the primary religious virtue (1 Cor. 13) and the quality that most fully distinguishes Jesus' followers (John 13:34–35; 15:12).

Lucifer An epithet applied to the king of Babylon and later mistakenly taken as a name for Satan before his expulsion from heaven. The term means "light bearer" and refers to the planet Venus when it is the morning star; the English name Lucifer translates the Hebrew word for "shining one" (Isa. 14:12).

Luke A physician and traveling companion of Paul (Col. 4:14; Philem. 24; 2 Tim. 4:11) to whom a late-second-century tradition ascribes the Gospel of Luke and the Book of Acts.

LXX A common abbreviation for the Septuagint, the Greek translation of the Hebrew Bible made in Alexandria, Egypt, during the last three centuries BCE.

Lycaonia A district in Asia Minor added to the Roman Empire around 25 BCE, where Paul endured persecution (Acts 13:50; 14:6–19).

Lycia A small province in southwestern Asia Minor, bordering the Mediterranean, which Paul visited on his missionary travels (Acts 21:1; 27:5–7).

Lystra A city in the Roman province of Galatia where Paul and Barnabas performed such successful healings that they were identified as Hermes and Zeus (Mercury and Jupiter) (Acts 14:6–19; 16:1; 18:23).

M An abbreviation for special Matthean material, the scholarly term designating passages found only in Matthew's Gospel.

Maccabees A name bestowed upon the family that won religious and political independence for the Jews from their Greek-Syrian oppressors. Judas, called Maccabeus ("[God's] hammer"), son of the aged priest Mattathias, led his brothers and other faithful Jews against the armies of Antiochus IV (Epiphanes) (175–163 BCE). The dynasty his brothers established was called Hasmonean (after an ancestor named Hasmon) and ruled Judea until 63 BCE, when the Romans occupied Palestine.

Macedonia The large mountainous district in northern Greece ruled by Philip of Macedon (359–336 BCE). Philip's son Alexander the Great (356–323 BCE) extended the Macedonian Empire over the entire ancient Near East as far as western India, incorporating all of the earlier Persian Empire. Conquered by Rome (168 BCE) and annexed as a province (146 BCE), Macedonia was the first part of Europe to be Christianized (Acts 16:10–17:9; 18:5; 19:29; 20:1–3).

Magdala A town on the northwest shore of the Sea of Galilee, home of Mary Magdalene (of Magdala) (Matt. 15:39).

Magnificat Mary's beautiful hymn of praise, recorded in Luke 1:46–55.

Magog In Ezekiel, a future leader, along with Gog, of Israel's enemies (Ezek. 39). In Revelation 20:8–10, God utterly destroys them.

Marcion An early dualistic Christian who attempted to establish a Christian Scripture distinct from the Hebrew Bible, which he rejected. Marcion's canon included only Luke's Gospel and the Pauline letters, the only documents he believed to reflect true belief. The church at Rome expelled him as a heretic about 140 CE.

Mark (John Mark) The son of Mary. A Jerusalem Jew who accompanied Barnabas (his cousin) and Paul on an early missionary journey (Acts 12:12–25; 13:5, 13; 15:37). For reasons unstated, he left them at Perga (Acts 13:13), which so angered Paul that he refused to allow Mark to join a later preaching campaign (Acts 15:38), though he and the apostle were later reconciled (Col. 4:10; Philem. 24). Some commentators identify Mark with the youth who ran away naked at the time of Jesus' arrest (Mark 14:51–52). An early tradition ascribes authorship of the Gospel of Mark to him, as Papias and Eusebius (*History* 3.39.15) testify.

Martha The sister of Mary and Lazarus of Bethany (Luke 10:38–42; John 11:1–12:2), whose home Jesus frequently visited.

martyr A "witness" for Christ who prefers to die rather than relinquish his or her faith. Stephen, at whose stoning Saul of Tarsus assisted, is known as the first Christian martyr (Acts 22:20; Rev. 2:13; 17:6).

Mary From the Latin and Greek *Maria* and the Hebrew *Miryam* (Miriam), a name borne by six women in the New Testament:

1. Mary the Virgin, wife of Joseph and mother of Jesus, who, the angel Gabriel informed her, was conceived by the Holy Spirit (Matt. 1:18–25; Luke 1:26–56; 2:21). From her home in Nazareth, Mary traveled to Bethlehem, where her first son was born (Luke 2:1–18), and thence into Egypt to escape Herod's persecution (Matt 2:1–18), returning to Nazareth in Galilee after Herod's death (4 BCE) (Matt. 2:19–23). She had one sister (John 18:25), probably Salome, wife of Zebedee, mother of James and John (Matt. 27:56), and was also related to Elizabeth, mother of John the Baptist (Luke 1:36). Gabriel's annunciation of the Messiah's birth occurs in Luke 1:26–36; the Magnificat, in Luke 1:46–55. Mary visited Jerusalem annually for the Passover (Luke 2:41) and reprimanded the twelve-year-old Jesus for lingering behind at the Temple (Luke 2:46–50). She may have been among family members convinced that Jesus' early preaching showed mental instability (Mark 3:21) and apparently humored his requests during the wedding celebration at Cana (John 2:1–12). Although Jesus showed his mother little deference during his ministry (Mark 3:31–35; Luke 11:27–28; John 2:4), on the cross he entrusted her care to his Beloved Disciple (John 19:25–27). Mary last appears in the upper room praying with the disciples just before Pentecost (Acts 1:13–14).

2. Mary Magdalene, a woman from Magdala, from whom Jesus cast out seven demons (Luke 8:1–2) and who became his follower. A common tradition asserts that she had been a prostitute whom Jesus had rescued from her former life (Mark 16:9; Luke 7:37–50), but this is incorrect. She was present at the Crucifixion (Mark 15:40; Matt. 15:47), visited Jesus' tomb early Sunday morning (Matt. 28:1; Mark 16:1; Luke 24:10; John 20:1), and was one of the first to see the risen Jesus (Matt. 28:9; Mark 16:9; John 20:11–18), although the male disciples refused to believe her (Luke 24:9–11).

3. Mary, sister of Lazarus and Martha, whose home at Bethany Jesus frequented (Luke 10:38–42; John 11:1–12:8).

4. Mary, wife of Clopas, mother of James the Less and Joseph (Joses), was a witness to Jesus' crucifixion, burial, and resurrection (Matt. 27:56–61; 28:1; Mark 15:40, 47; 16:1; Luke 24:10; John 19:25).

5. Mary, sister of Barnabas and mother of John Mark, provided her Jerusalem home as a meeting place for the disciples (Acts 12:12; Col. 4:10).

6. An otherwise anonymous Mary mentioned in Romans 16:6.

Masada A stronghold built by Herod the Great on a fortified plateau 800 feet above the Dead Sea.

Masada was captured by Zealots during the revolt against Rome (66 CE). According to a now-disputed account by Josephus, when the attacking Romans finally entered Masada (73 CE), they found only 7 women and children alive, 953 others having died in a suicide pact.

Masoretes Medieval Jewish scholars who copied, annotated, and added vowels to the text of the Hebrew Bible; from a Hebrew term meaning "tradition."

Masoretic Text (MT) The standard text of the Hebrew Bible as given final form by the Masoretes in the seventh through eleventh centuries CE.

Mattathias A Jewish priest who, with his sons John, Simon, Judas, Eleazar, and Jonathan, led a revolt against the oppressions of Antiochus IV (c. 168–167 BCE) (1 Macc. 2:1–70).

Matthew A Jewish tax collector working for Rome whom Jesus called to be one of the Twelve Apostles (Matt. 9:9; 10:3; Mark 2:13–17; 3:18; Luke 5:27–32; 6:15; Acts 1:13). Matthew (also called Levi) is the traditional author of the Gospel of Matthew, an attribution that most scholars reject.

Matthias The early Christian elected to replace Judas among the Twelve (Acts 1:23–26) about whom nothing else is known. The name means "gift of Yahweh."

Megiddo An old Palestinian city overlooking the Valley of Jezreel (Plain of Esdraelon), the site of numerous decisive battles in biblical history (Josh. 12:21; 2 Kings 9:27; 23:29–30; 2 Chron. 35:20–24; Zech. 12:11) and symbolic location of the climactic War of Armageddon (Rev. 16:16).

Melchizedek The king-priest of Canaanite Salem (probably the site of Jerusalem) to whom Abraham paid a tenth of his spoils of war (Gen. 14:17–20); cited by the author of Hebrews as foreshadowing Jesus Christ (Ps. 110:4; Heb. 5:6–10; 7:1–25).

Mercury The Roman name for Hermes, the highly mobile Greek god of persuasion, business, and trade and messenger of Zeus, for whom Paul was mistaken in Lystra (Acts 14:12).

Mesopotamia The territory between the Euphrates and Tigris rivers at the head of the Persian Gulf (modern Iraq); cradle of the Sumerian, Akkadian, Assyrian, and Neo-Babylonian civilizations (Gen. 24:10; Judg. 3:8–10; 1 Chron. 19:6; Acts 2:9; 7:2).

Messiah A Hebrew term (*mashiah*) meaning "anointed one," designating a king or priest of ancient Israel who

had been consecrated by having holy oil poured on his head, marking him as set apart for a special role. King David is the model of Yahweh's anointed ruler; all his descendants who ruled over Judah were Yahweh's messiahs (2 Sam. 7:1–29; Ps. 89:3–45). After the end of the Davidic monarchy (587 BCE), various Hebrew prophets applied the promises made to the Davidic dynasty to a future heir who would eventually restore the kingdom of David (Pss. 2; 110; Dan. 9:25–26). Christians believe that Jesus of Nazareth was the promised Messiah (Christ) as expressed in Peter's "confession" (Matt. 16:13–20; Mark 8:27–30; Luke 9:18–22; etc.).

messianic secret The phrase that the German scholar William Wrede used to describe a major theme in Mark's Gospel—Jesus' "hidden messiahship," particularly his oft-repeated injunction to persons he heals to keep quiet about his miraculous actions.

Michael The angel whom the Book of Daniel represents as being the spirit prince, guardian, and protector of Israel (Dan. 10:13, 21; 12:1). Jude 9 depicts him as an archangel fighting with Satan for Moses' body. In Revelation 12:7, he leads the war against the Dragon (Satan) and casts him from heaven. His name means "who is like God."

midrash A commentary on or interpretation of Hebrew Scripture. Collections of such haggadic or halakic expositions of the significance of the biblical text are called midrashim; from a Hebrew word meaning "to search out."

Millennium A 1,000-year epoch, particularly the period of Christ's universal reign (Rev. 20:1–8), during which Satan will be chained and the dead resurrected.

Mishnah A collection of Pharisaic oral interpretations (Halakah) of the Torah compiled and edited by Rabbi Judah ha-Nasi about 200 CE; from the Hebrew verb "to repeat."

Mithras The Persian savior god who killed a celestial bull and was worshiped in mystery cults throughout the Roman Empire. A serious rival to early Christianity, Mithraism was limited by the fact that only men were initiated into the religion.

money An imprinted piece of metal generally accepted as a medium of exchange. In early biblical times, before coins were first minted, value in business transactions was determined by weighing quantities of precious metals. In the early period, the term *shekel* refers not to a coin, but to a certain weight of silver. The use of coinage was first introduced in Palestine during the Persian era, when the daric or dram, named for Darius I (521–486 BCE), appeared. After Alexander's conquest of Persia, Greek coinage became the standard. The silver drachma (Luke 15:8), a coin of small value, was equivalent to the Roman denarius. The lepton was a small copper coin (Luke 12:59; 21:2), the least valuable in circulation, and one of the denominations coined by the Jews for use in the Temple. This was the "widow's mite" (Mark 12:42). The talent (Matt. 18:24) was not a coin, but money of account; it was divided into smaller units—60 minas or 6,000 drachmas—and was worth several thousand dollars. The denarius (Matt. 18:28), the basic unit in the New Testament, was a silver coin, the day's wage of a rural laborer (Matt. 20:20).

monotheism The belief in the existence of one God, a major theme of Second Isaiah (Isa. 40–46) and the central tenet of Judaism, Christianity, and Islam.

Mosaic Covenant In the Hebrew Bible, the pact between Yahweh and Israel mediated by Moses (Exod. 19–24). According to the terms of the pact, Yahweh's support of Israel was dependent on the people's obedience to his will, expressed in the laws and principles of the Torah (Deut. 28–29).

Moses The great Hebrew lawgiver, religious reformer, founder of the Israelite nation, and central figure of the Pentateuch. Adopted by pharaoh's daughter and raised at the Egyptian royal court (Exod. 2:5–10; Acts 7:22), he fled Egypt after killing an Egyptian bully and settled in Midian among the Kenites, where he encountered Yahweh at a burning bush (Exod. 3:1–4:17). He returned to Egypt (Exod. 4:18–31), interceded with pharaoh during the ten plagues (Exod. 5–11), and led the Israelites across a chaotic sea (Exod. 14–15) to Sinai. There, he mediated the Law covenant between Yahweh and Israel (Exod. 19–31). Moses figures prominently in Paul's theology (Rom. 5:14; 10:5; 1 Cor. 10:2; 2 Cor. 3:7; 3:15) and that of the author of Hebrews (Heb. 3:2; 7:14; 9:19; 11:23). Jude preserves an old tradition, probably derived from the pseudepigraphal Assumption of Moses, that Satan disputed the angel Michael for Moses' body (Jude 9; Rev. 15:3).

Mount of Olives See **Olives, Mount of.**

Muratorian canon A fragmentary document listing books of the New Testament that its author regarded as canonical. Although written in Latin during the eighth century CE, the fragment is a translation of a much older Greek work. Until recently, the Greek original was commonly dated to the late second century BCE, but some scholars now argue that it was compiled in the fourth century.

mystery Derived from a Greek word meaning "to initiate" or "to shut the eyes or mouth," probably referring to the secrets of Hellenistic "mystery religions," and used variously in the New Testament. Jesus speaks at least once of the "mystery" of the kingdom (Matt. 13:11; Mark 4:11; Luke 8:10), but Paul employs the term frequently as if the profounder aspects of Christianity were a religious secret into which the Spirit-directed believer becomes initiated (Rom. 11:5; 16:25; 1 Cor. 2:7; 4:1; 13:2; 14:2; 15:51; Col. 1:26; 2:2; 4:3; 2 Thess. 2:7; 1 Tim. 3:9; 3:16; see also Rev. 1:20; 10:7; 17:5–7).

myth A narrative expressing a profound psychological or religious truth that cannot be verified by historical inquiry or other scientific means; from the Greek *mythos,* meaning a "story." Scholars speak of the "myth of Eden," for example, to emphasize the Eden story's archetypal expression of humanity's sense of alienation from their divine source. Myths typically feature stories about gods and goddesses who represent natural or psychological forces that deeply influence humans but that they cannot control. The psychologist Carl Jung interpreted myth as humanity's inherited concept of a primeval event that persists in the unconscious mind and finds expression through repeated reenactments in ritual worship and other cultic practices. Israel's covenant renewal ceremonies and retellings of Yahweh's saving acts during the Exodus are examples of such cultic myths.

mythology A system or cycle of myths, such as those featuring the deities of ancient Greece or Rome. Once the embodiment of living religious beliefs, Greco-Roman and other mythologies are now seen as archetypal symbols that give philosophic meaning to universal human experiences. Mythologies are thus "falsehoods" only in the narrowest literal sense. They are probably akin to dreams in revealing persistent images and attitudes present in the human unconscious.

Nag Hammadi The Egyptian village where a collection of early Christian and Gnostic books, including the Gospel of Thomas, was discovered in 1945.

narrative criticism A critical methodology applied to analyzing a literary narrative, including its structure, the point of view from which it is told, the author's implied attitude toward his characters, and the work's assumed audience.

Nazarenes A name applied to early Christians (Acts 24:5).

Nazareth A town in Lower Galilee above the Plain of Esdraelon (Megiddo) where Jesus spent his youth and began his ministry (Matt. 2:23; Luke 1:26; 4:16; John 1:46).

Nero (Nero Claudius Caesar Augustus Germanicus) An emperor of Rome (54–68 CE), the Caesar by whom Paul wished to be tried in Acts 25:11 and under whose persecution Paul was probably beheaded (64–65 CE). A first-century superstition held that Nero, slain during a palace revolt, would return at the head of an army. Nero was regarded by some Christians as the anti-Christ, and his reappearance is perhaps suggested in Revelation 13:4–18.

Nicodemus A leading Pharisee and member of the Sanhedrin (John 3:1; 7:50; 19:39) who discussed spiritual rebirth with Jesus (John 3:1–21), visited him by night and defended him against other Pharisees (John 7:45–52), and, with Joseph of Arimathea, helped entomb his body (John 19:38–42).

Olives, Mount of (Olivet) A mile-long limestone ridge with several distinct summits paralleling the eastern section of Jerusalem, from which it is separated by the narrow Kidron Valley. Here David fled during Absalom's rebellion (2 Sam. 15:30–32), and according to Zechariah 14:3–5, here Yahweh will stand at the final eschatological battle, when the mountain will be torn asunder from east to west. From its summit, with its panoramic view of Jerusalem, Jesus delivered his eschatological judgment on the city that had rejected him (Matt. 24–25). He often retreated to its shady groves in the evening (John 7:53; 8:1), including the night before his death (Matt. 26:30–56; Mark 14:26; Luke 22:39; see also Matt. 21:1; Mark 11:1; Luke 19:29; Acts 1:12).

omega The last letter in the Greek alphabet, used with alpha (the first letter) as a symbol of the eternity of God (Rev. 1:8; 21:6) and Jesus (Rev. 1:17; 22:13), probably echoing Isaiah's description of Yahweh as "the first and the last" (Isa. 44:6; 48:12).

Onesimus The runaway slave of Philemon of Colossae whom Paul converted to Christianity and reconciled to his master (Philem. 8–21; Col. 4:7–9).

oracle

1. A divine message or utterance (Rom. 3:2; Heb. 5:12; 1 Pet. 4:11) or the person through whom it is conveyed (Acts 7:38).

2. An authoritative communication, such as that from a wise person (Prov. 31:1; 2 Sam. 16:23).

3. The inner sanctum of the Jerusalem Temple (1 Kings 6:5–6; 7:49; 8:6–8; Ps. 28:2).

4. The supposedly inspired words of a priest or priestess at such shrines as Delphi in ancient Greece and Cumae in Italy.

oral tradition Material passed from generation to generation by word of mouth before finding written form. Scholars believe that traditions about Jesus' teaching and miracles were transmitted orally for about forty years before being incorporated into Mark's Gospel.

original sin The concept that the entire human race has inherited from the first man (Adam) a tendency to sin. Some theologians, such as Augustine and Calvin, argued that humanity is born totally corrupt. The doctrine is based partly on an extremist interpretation of Romans 5:12.

orthodoxy Literally, "correct opinion," holding beliefs or doctrines established by a religious or political authority.

Palestine A strip of land bordering the eastern Mediterranean Sea, lying south of Syria, north of the Sinai Peninsula, and west of the Arabian Desert. During the patriarchal period, it was known as Canaan (Gen. 12:6–7; 15:18–21). Named for the Philistines, it was first called Palestine by the Greek historian Herodotus about 450 BCE.

pantheon The accepted list or roster of a people's chief gods, such as the Olympian family of Zeus worshiped in classical Greece. It is also the name of a famous temple in Rome, the house of "all the gods."

parable A short fictional narrative that compares something familiar to an unexpected spiritual value; from the Greek *parabole*, meaning "a placing beside," or "a comparison." In the Synoptic Gospels, Jesus typically uses a commonplace object or action to illustrate a religious principle (Matt. 13:3–53; 22:1; 24:32; Mark 4:2–3; 13:28; Luke 8:4–18; 13:18–21; 21:29). A recurrent tradition held that Jesus used parables to prevent most of his hearers from understanding his message (Matt. 13:10–15; Mark 4:10–12; Luke 8:9–10).

Paraclete A Greek term meaning "an advocate," used to denote the Holy Spirit in the Gospel of John as well as to denote the abiding spiritual presence of the risen Jesus. *Paraclete* is variously translated as "Comforter," "Helper," "Advocate," or "Spirit of Truth" (John 7:39; 14:12, 16–18; 15:26; 16:7; see also 1 John 2:1).

paradise Literally, a "park" or walled garden, the name applied to Eden (Gen. 2:8–17) and in post–Hebrew Bible times to the abode of the righteous dead, of which the lower part housed souls awaiting resurrection and the higher was the permanent home of the just. It is possible that Jesus referred to the lower paradise in his words to the thief on the cross (Luke 23:43); Paul's reference to being "caught up" into paradise may refer to the third of the seven heavens postulated in later Jewish eschatology (as in the books of Enoch) (2 Cor. 12:2–5). John's vision of the tree of life in "the garden of God" (Rev. 2:7; 22:1–3) depicts paradise earth.

Parousia A Greek term, meaning "presence" or "coming," that New Testament writers use to denote Jesus' reappearance on earth, when, as Israel's divinely empowered Messiah, he will judge all humanity and establish God's universal rule. Although both Paul (1 Thess.) and the Synoptic writers (Mark 13; Matt. 24–25; Luke 21) emphasize this apocalyptic vision, the author of John's Gospel (14:25–29) expresses a quietly realized eschatology, focusing on Jesus' abiding spiritual presence among believers rather than on a Second Coming of cosmic violence (John 5:24–26; 11:24–27; 14:25–29).

Passion The term commonly used to denote Jesus' suffering and death (Acts 1:3).

Passover An annual Jewish observance commemorating Israel's last night of bondage in Egypt, when the Angel of Death "passed over" Israelite homes marked with the blood of a sacrificial lamb to destroy the firstborn of every Egyptian household (Exod. 12:1–51). Beginning the seven-day Feast of Unleavened Bread, it is a ritual meal eaten on Nisan 14 (March–April) and includes roast lamb, unleavened bread, and bitter herbs (Exod. 12:15–20; 13:3–10; Lev. 23:5; Num. 9:5; 28:16; Deut. 16:1). According to the Synoptics, Jesus' Last Supper with the Twelve was a Passover celebration (Matt. 26; Mark 14; Luke 22) and the model for Christian communion (the Eucharist) (1 Cor. 11:17–27).

pastoral epistles The New Testament books of 1 and 2 Timothy and Titus, ascribed to the apostle Paul but probably composed by an anonymous disciple of Pauline thought living in the late first to mid-second century CE.

Patmos A small Aegean island off the coast of western Asia Minor (Turkey) where John, author of Revelation, was exiled by the emperor Domitian about 95 CE (Rev. 1:9).

patriarch The male head (father) of an ancient family line, a venerable tribal founder or leader, especially the immediate progenitors of Israel: Abraham,

Isaac, and Jacob. Acts 7:8–9 includes Jacob's twelve sons among the patriarchs.

patriarchy A social-political system in which male leadership and masculine values dominate. Biblical writers typically adopt the patriarchal assumptions of ancient Near Eastern and Greco-Roman societies, an outlook that tends to minimize the cultural values and contributions of women.

Paul The most influential apostle and missionary of the mid-first-century church and author of seven or nine New Testament letters. According to Acts, Saul of Tarsus was born in the capital of the Asia Minor province of Cilicia (Acts 9:11; 21:39; 22:3) into a family of Pharisees (Acts 23:6) of the tribe of Benjamin (Phil. 3:5) and had both Roman and Taurean citizenship (Acts 22:28). Suddenly converted to Christianity after persecuting early Christians (Acts 7:55–8:3; 9:1–30; 22:1–21; 26:1–23; 1 Cor. 9:1; 15:8; Gal. 1:11–24; Eph. 3:3; Phil. 3:12), he undertook at least three international missionary tours, presenting defenses of the new faith before Jewish and Gentile authorities (Acts 13:1–28:31). His emphasis on the insufficiency of the Mosaic Law for salvation (Gal. 3–5; Rom. 4–11) and the superiority of faith to Law (Rom. 4–11) and his insistence that Gentiles be admitted to the church without observing Jewish legal restrictions (Gal. 2; 5; Rom. 7–8) were decisive in determining the future development of the new religion. He was probably martyred in Rome about 64–65 CE.

Pella A Gentile city in Palestine east of the Jordan River, to which tradition says that Jesus' family and other Jewish Christians fled during the Jewish Revolt against Rome (66–73 CE). No writings from the Palestinian Christians survive, so the fate of the Pella community is not known.

Pentateuch The first five books of the Hebrew Bible, the Torah; from a Greek work meaning "five scrolls."

Pentecost

1. Also known as the Feast of Weeks (Exod. 34:22; Deut. 16:10), the Feast of Harvest (Exod. 23:16), and the Day of the First Fruits (Num. 28:26), a one-day celebration held fifty days after Passover at the juncture of May and June.

2. The occasion of the outpouring of the Holy Spirit on early Christians assembled in Jerusalem (Acts 2:1–41), regarded as the spiritual baptism of the church.

Pergamum A major Hellenistic city in western Asia Minor (modern Bergama in west Anatolian Turkey), site of a magnificent altar to Zeus, which some commentators believe is referred to as "Satan's Throne" in Revelation 2:13. Pergamum is one of the seven churches addressed to which Christ sends his message (Rev. 1:11; 2:12–17).

pericope In form criticism, a literary unit (a saying, anecdote, parable, or brief narrative) that forms a complete entity in itself and is attached to its context by later editorial commentary. Many of Jesus' pronouncements probably circulated independently as pericopes before they were incorporated into the written Gospel narratives.

pesher In Hebrew, an analysis or interpretation of Scripture. The term is applied to the commentaries (*persherim*) found among the Dead Sea Scrolls.

Peter The most prominent of Jesus' twelve chief disciples, also known as Simon (probably his surname), Simeon (Symeon), and Cephas (the Aramaic equivalent of *petros,* meaning "rock" or "stone") (John 1:40–42). The son of Jonas or John (Matt. 16:17; John 1:42; 21:15–17), brother of the apostle Andrew, and a native of Bethsaida, a fishing village on the Sea of Galilee (John 1:44), he was called by Jesus to be "a fisher of men" (Matt. 4:18–20; Mark 1:16–18; Luke 5:1–11). The first to recognize Jesus as the Messiah (Matt. 16:13–20; Mark 8:27–30; Luke 9:18–22), Peter later denied him three times (Matt. 26:69–75; Mark 14:66–72; Luke 22:54–62; John 18:15–18). Commanded to "feed [the resurrected Jesus'] sheep" (John 21:15–19), Peter became a leader of the Jerusalem church (Acts 1:15–26; 2:14–42; 15:6–12) and miracle worker (Acts 3:1–10). He was instrumental in bringing the first Gentiles into the church (Acts 10–11), although Paul regarded him as a conservative obstacle to this movement (Gal. 2:11–14). He appeared before the Sanhedrin (Acts 4:1–12) and was miraculously rescued from at least one imprisonment (Acts 5:17–42; 12:1–19). A married man (Matt. 8:14; Mark 1:30; Luke 4:8; 1 Cor. 9:5), Peter was to be the "rock" on which Jesus' church was built (Matt. 16:16–20). Although a minority of scholars regard him as the source of 1 Peter, virtually all experts deny Petrine authorship to the second epistle bearing his name. He was probably martyred under Nero about 64–65 CE.

Pharisees A leading religious movement or sect in Judaism during the last two centuries BCE and the first two centuries CE. The Pharisees were probably descendants of the Hasidim who opposed Antiochus IV's attempts to destroy the Mosaic faith. Their name may derive from the Hebrew *perisha* (separated) because their rigorous observance of the Law bred a separatist view toward common life. Although the New Testament typically presents them as Jesus' opponents, their views on resurrection and the afterlife anticipated Christian teachings. The "seven woes" against the Pharisees appear in Matthew 23:13–32. Paul was a Pharisee (Acts 23:6; 26:5; Phil. 3:5).

Philadelphia A city in Lydia (modern Turkey) about twenty-eight miles from Sardis, one of the seven churches addressed in Revelation 3:7–13.

Philemon A citizen of Colossae whose runaway slave, Onesimus, Paul converted to Christianity (Philem. 5; 10; 16; 19).

Philip

1. A king of Macedonia (359–336 BCE), and the father of Alexander the Great (1 Macc. 1:1; 6:2).

2. One of the Twelve, a man of Bethsaida in Galilee (Matt. 10:3; Mark 3:18; Luke 6:14; John 1:43–49; 12:21–22; 14:8–9; Acts 1:12–14).

3. An evangelist of the Jerusalem church who was an administrator (Acts 6:1–6), a preacher (Acts 8:4–8), and the converter of Simon the sorcerer (Acts 8:9–13) and of an Ethiopian eunuch (Acts 8:26–39). Paul visited him at Caesarea (Acts 21:8–15).

4. A son of Herod the Great and Palestinian tetrarch (4 BCE–34 CE) (Luke 3:1).

Philippi A city of eastern Macedonia, the first European center to receive the Christian message (Acts 16:10–40). Philippi became the apostle Paul's favorite church (Acts 20:6; Phil. 4:16; 2 Cor. 11:9); it is the one to which his letter to the Philippians is addressed.

Philo Judaeus The most influential philosopher of Hellenistic Judaism. Philo was a Greek-educated Jew living in Alexandria, Egypt (c. 20 BCE–50 CE), who promoted a method of interpreting the Hebrew Bible allegorically (which may have influenced Paul in such passages as 1 Corinthians 10:4 and Galatians 4:24, as well as the authors of the Fourth Gospel and Hebrews). His doctrine of the Logos (the divine creative Word) anticipated the prologue to the Gospel of John.

Phoebe A servant or deacon of the church at Cenchrae, a port of Corinth, whose good works Paul commends in Romans 16:1–2.

phylacteries One of two small leather pouches containing copies of four scriptural passages (Exod. 13:1–10, 11–16; Deut. 6:4–9; 11:13–21), worn on the left arm and forehead by Jewish men during weekday prayers (Exod. 13:9, 16; Deut. 6:8; 11:18; Matt. 23:5).

Pilate, Pontius The Roman prefect (governor) of Judea (26–36 CE) who presided at Jesus' trial for sedition against Rome and sentenced him to be crucified (Matt. 27:1–26; Mark 15:1–15; Luke 3:1; 13:1; 23:1–25; John 18:28–19:22; Acts 3:13; 13:28; 1 Tim. 6:13).

Plato The Athenian philosopher (427–347 BCE) who taught that the material world is only a flawed reflection of a perfect spiritual realm, from which the human soul descends to be born in a mortal body and to which it returns for judgment after death.

polytheism The belief in more than one god, the most common form of religion in the ancient world.

Pontius Pilate See **Pilate, Pontius.**

Porcius Festus See **Festus, Porcius.**

predestination The act of foreordaining or predetermining by divine decree the ultimate destiny of an individual or a people, a theological doctrine asserting the absolute, irresistible power and control of God. In the biblical tradition, particularly in apocalyptic literature, both divine predetermination of events and the individual's freedom of choice seem to operate simultaneously.

Prisca (Priscilla) The wife of Aquila and a leading member of the early church (Acts 18:18; Rom. 16:3; 2 Tim. 4:19).

proconsul A Roman governor or administrator of a province or territory, such as Gallio, proconsul of Achaia, before whom Paul appeared (Acts 18:12).

procurator The Roman title of the governor of a region before it became an administrative province. During the reigns of Augustus and Tiberius, Judea was governed by a prefect, the most famous of whom was Pontius Pilate. The office was upgraded to the level of procurator under Claudius.

Promised Land The popular term for the territory of Canaan that Yahweh vowed to give Abraham's heirs in perpetuity (Gen. 15:5–21; 17:1–8), traditionally the land area embraced in David's kingdom.

prophet One who preaches or proclaims the word or will of his or her deity (Amos 3:7–8; Deut. 18:9–22). A true prophet in Israel was regarded as divinely inspired.

Prophets The second major division of the Hebrew Bible, from Joshua through the twelve minor prophets and including the books of Samuel and Kings, Isaiah, Jeremiah, and Ezekiel.

proverb A concise saying that memorably expresses a familiar or useful bit of folk wisdom, usually of a practical or prudential nature.

providence The quasi-religious concept of God as a force sustaining and guiding human destiny. It assumes that events occur as part of a divine plan or purpose working for the ultimate triumph of good.

psalm A sacred song or poem used in praise or worship of the Deity, particularly those in the Book of Psalms.

Pseudepigrapha

1. Literally, books falsely ascribed to eminent biblical figures of the past, such as Enoch, Noah, Moses, or Isaiah.

2. A collection of religious books outside the Hebrew Bible canon or Apocrypha that were composed in Hebrew, Aramaic, or Greek from about 250 BCE to 200 CE.

pseudonymity A literary practice, common among Hellenistic-Jewish and early Christian writers, of writing or publishing a book in the name of a famous religious figure of the past. Thus, an anonymous author of about 168 BCE ascribed his work to Daniel, who supposedly lived during the 500s BCE. The pastoral epistles, 2 Peter, James, and Jude are thought to be pseudonymous books written in the mid-second century CE but attributed to eminent disciples connected with the first-century Jerusalem church.

psyche The Greek word for "soul," it refers to the mental, emotional, and psychological makeup of human beings. Although biblical concepts of the soul do not presume its inherent immortality, the Greek philosophical position that the psyche survives bodily death to experience rewards or penalties in the afterlife deeply influenced later Christian teachings on the subject.

Ptolemaic dynasty The royal dynasty that was established by Alexander's general Ptolemy I and that ruled Egypt from about 323 to 30 BCE. Ptolemaic Egypt controlled Palestine until shortly after 200 BCE.

Ptolemy

1. Ptolemy I (323–285 BCE), a Macedonian general who assumed rulership of Egypt after the death of Alexander the Great. The Ptolemaic dynasty controlled Egypt and its dominions until 30 BCE, when the Romans came to power.

2. Ptolemy II (285–246 BCE), a Hellenistic-Egyptian ruler who supposedly authorized the translation of the Hebrew Bible into Greek (the Septuagint).

publican In the New Testament, petty-tax collectors for Rome, despised by the Jews, from whom they typically extorted money (Matt. 9:10–13; 18:17; 21:31). Jesus dined with these "sinners" (Matt. 9:9–13) and called one, Levi (Matthew), to apostleship (Matt. 9:9–13; Luke 5:27–31). He also portrayed a publican as more religiously acceptable than a Pharisee (Luke 18:9–14).

purity laws Regulations defining the nature, cause, or state of physical, ritual, or moral contamination; according to the Book of Leviticus and other parts of the Torah, ritual impurity results from a variety of activities, including the eating of forbidden foods such as shellfish and physical contact with impure persons or objects, such as a corpse, a leper, or a menstruating woman, all of which render violators "unclean" and hence religiously unacceptable. The Torah also prescribes elaborate purification rites to restore ritually impure persons to participation in the community, a practice that the Essenes emphasized in their communities.

Q An abbreviation for *Quelle,* the German term for "source," a hypothetical document that many scholars believe contained a collection of Jesus' sayings (*logia*). The theory of its existence was formed to explain material common to both Matthew and Luke but absent from Mark's Gospel. It is assumed that Matthew and Luke drew on a single source (Q), assembled about 50–70 CE, for this shared material.

Qumran Ruins of a community (probably of Essenes) near the northwest corner of the Dead Sea, where (as most scholars believe) the Dead Sea Scrolls were produced.

rabbi A Jewish title (meaning "master" or "teacher") given to scholars learned in the Torah. Jesus was frequently addressed by this title (Matt. 23:8; 26:25, 49; Mark 8:5; 10:51; 11:21; 14:45; John 1:38, 49; 3:2; 4:31; 6:25; 9:2; 11:8; 20:16), as was John the Baptist (John 3:26), although Jesus supposedly forbade his followers to be so called (Matt. 23:7–8).

realized eschatology A belief that events usually associated with the *eschaton* (world End), such as divine judgment and resurrection to eternal life, are even now realized in or fulfilled by Jesus' spiritual presence among his followers (see John 5:24–25; 11:26; 14:12–21; 16:7–14).

redaction criticism A method of analyzing written texts to define the purpose and literary procedures of editors (redactors) who compile and edit older documents, transforming shorter works into longer ones, as did the redactors who collected and ordered independent traditions about Jesus to compose the present Gospels.

resurrection The returning of the dead to life, a late Hebrew Bible concept (Isa. 26:19; Dan. 12:2–3, 13) that first became prevalent in Judaism during the time of the Maccabees (after 168 BCE) and eventually a part of the Pharisees' doctrine. Like the prophets Elijah and Elisha (1 Kings 17:17–24; 2 Kings 4:18–37), Jesus performed several temporal resuscitations: of the widow of Nain's son (Luke 7:11–17), the daughter of Jairus (Mark 5:21–43), and Lazarus (John 11:1–44). Unlike these personages, however, Jesus ascended to heaven after his own resurrection (Acts 1:7–8). Paul gives the fullest discussions of bodily resurrection in the New Testament (1 Thess. 4; 1 Cor. 15), emphasizing the quasi-material nature of the transformed "spiritual body" (see also Rev. 20:11–15).

Roman Empire The international, multicultural government centered in Rome that conquered and administered the entire Mediterranean region from Gaul (France and southern Germany) in the northwest to Egypt in the southeast. The empire ruled the Jewish state in Palestine from 63 BCE until Hadrian's destruction of Jerusalem during the second Jewish War (132–135 CE).

Sabbath The seventh day of the Jewish week, sacred to Yahweh and dedicated to rest and worship. Enjoined upon Israel as a sign of Yahweh's covenant (Exod. 20:8–11; 23:12; 31:12–17; Lev. 23:3; 24:1–9; Deut. 5:12–15), the Sabbath was also a memorial of Yahweh's repose after six days of creation. Jesus was frequently criticized for his liberal attitude toward the Sabbath, which he contended was made for humanity's benefit (Matt. 12:1–12; Mark 2:23–28; Luke 6:1–9; John 5:18).

sacrifice In ancient religion, something precious—usually an unblemished animal, fruit, or grain—offered to a god and thereby made sacred. The Mosaic Law required the regular ritual slaughter of sacrificial animals and birds (Lev. 1:1–7:38; 16:1–17:14; Deut. 15:19–23), a major priestly function at the Jerusalem Temple.

Sadducees An ultraconservative Jewish sect of the first century BCE and first century CE composed largely of wealthy and politically influential landowners. Unlike the Pharisees, the Sadducees recognized only the Torah as binding and rejected the Prophets and the Writings, denying both resurrection and a judgment in the afterlife. An aristocracy controlling the priesthood and Temple, they cooperated with Roman rule of Palestine, a collusion that made them unpopular with the common people (Matt. 3:7; 16:1; 22:23; Mark 12:18; Luke 20:27; Acts 4:1; 5:17; 23:6).

saints Holy ones, persons of exceptional virtue and sanctity, believers outstandingly faithful despite persecution (Dan. 7:18–21; 8:13; Matt. 27:52; Acts 9:13; 26:10; Rom. 8:27; 1 Cor. 6:2; 1 Thess. 3:13; 2 Thess. 1:10; Heb. 13:24; Rev. 5:8; 13:7–10; 17:6; 20:9).

Salome

1. The daughter of Herodias and Herod (son of Herod the Great) and niece of Herod Antipas, before whom she danced to secure the head of John the Baptist (Matt. 14:3–11; Mark 6:17–28). She is anonymous in the New Testament; her name is given by Josephus (*Antiquities* 18.5.4).

2. A woman present at Jesus' crucifixion (Matt. 27:56; Mark 15:40) and at the empty tomb (Mark 16:1).

Samaria The capital of the northern kingdom (Israel), Samaria was founded by Omri (c. 876–869 BCE) (1 Kings 16:24–25) and destroyed by the Assyrians in 721 BCE (2 Kings 17).

Samaritans Inhabitants of the city or territory of Samaria, the central region of Palestine lying west of the Jordan River. According to a probably biased southern account in 2 Kings 17, the Samaritans were regarded by orthodox Jews as descendants of foreigners who had intermarried with survivors of the northern kingdom's fall to Assyria (721 BCE). Separated from the rest of Judaism after about 400 BCE, they had a Bible consisting of their own edition of the Pentateuch (Torah) and a temple on Mount Gerizim, which was later destroyed by John Hyrcanus (128 BCE) (Matt. 10:5; Luke 9:52; John 4:20–21). Jesus discussed correct worship with a woman at Jacob's well in Samaria (John 4:5–42) and made a "good Samaritan" the hero of a famous parable (Luke 10:29–37).

sanctuary A holy place dedicated to the worship of a god and often believed to confer personal security to those who take refuge in it. Yahweh's Temple on Mount Zion in Jerusalem was such a sacred edifice.

Sanhedrin The supreme judicial council of the Jews from about the third century BCE until the Romans destroyed Jerusalem in 70 CE. Its deliberations were led by the High Priest (2 Chron. 19:5–11). Jesus was tried before the Sanhedrin and condemned on charges of blasphemy (Matt. 26:59; Mark 14:55; 15:1; Luke 22:66; John 11:47). Stephen was stoned as a result of its verdict (Acts 6:12–15). Peter, John, and other disciples appeared before its court (Acts 4:5–21; 5:17–41), and Paul was charged there with violating the Mosaic Torah (Acts 22).

Sarah The wife and half sister of Abraham (Gen. 11:29; 16:1; 20:12). Sarah traveled with Abraham from Ur to Haran and ultimately to Canaan and, after a long period of barrenness, bore him a single son, Isaac (Gen. 18:9–15; 21:1–21). In Galatians 4:22–31, Paul refers to Sarah as the "free-born woman" who symbolizes the heavenly Jerusalem.

Sardis The capital of the kingdom of Lydia (modern Turkey), captured by Cyrus the Great (546 BCE); later part of the Roman province of Asia and the site of a cult of Cybele, a pagan fertility goddess (Rev. 3:1–6).

Satan In the Hebrew Bible, "the satan" appears as a prosecutor in the heavenly court among "the sons of God" (Job 1–2; Zech. 3:1–3) and only later as a tempter (1 Chron. 21:1; cf. 2 Sam. 24:1). Although the Hebrew Bible says virtually nothing about Satan's origin, the pseudepigraphal writings contain much legendary material about his fall from heaven and the establishment of a hierarchy of demons and devils. By the time the New Testament was written, he was believed to head a kingdom of evil and to seek the corruption of all people, including the Messiah (Matt. 4:1–11; Luke 4:1–13). Satan ("the opposer" or the "adversary") is also "the evil one" (Matt. 6:13; 13:19; Eph. 6:16; 1 John 2:13; 5:18–19), "the devil" (Matt. 4:1; 13:39; 25:41; John 8:44; Eph. 4:27), and the primordial serpent who tempted Eve (Rev. 12:9).

Savior One who saves from danger or destruction, a term applied to Yahweh in the Hebrew Bible (Ps. 106:21; Isa. 43:1–13; 63:79; Hos. 13:4) and to Jesus in the New Testament (Luke 2:11; John 4:42; Acts 5:31; 13:23; Phil. 3:20; 1 Tim. 4:10; 2 Tim. 1:10; 1 John 4:14).

scapegoat According to Leviticus 16, a sacrificial goat upon whose head Israel's High Priest placed the people's collective sins on the Day of Atonement, after which the goat was sent out into the desert to Azazel (possibly a demon). The term has come to signify anyone who bears the blame for others (see Isa. 53).

scribes Professional copyists who recorded commercial, royal, and religious texts and served as clerks, secretaries, and archivists at Israel's royal court and

Temple (2 Kings 12:10; 19:2; Ezra 4:8; 2 Chron. 34:8; Jer. 36:18). After the Jews' return from exile, professional teachers or "wise men" preserved and interpreted the Mosaic Torah (Ezra 7:6; Neh. 7:73–8:18). In the New Testament, scribes are often linked with Pharisees as Jesus' opponents (Matt. 7:29; 23:2, 13; Luke 11:44) who conspired to kill him (Mark 14:43; 15:1; Luke 22:2; 23:10), although some became his followers (Matt. 8:19; see also Acts 6:12; 23:9; 1 Cor. 1:20).

scripture A writing or collection of documents that a religion holds to be sacred and binding upon its adherents. The Hebrew Bible (Old Testament) is Scripture to both Jews and Christians; only Christians accord the status of Scripture to the New Testament.

scroll A roll of papyrus, leather, or parchment such as those on which the Hebrew Bible and New Testament were written. The rolls were made of sheets about 9 to 11 inches high and 5 or 6 inches wide, sewed together to make a strip up to 25 or 30 feet long, which was wound around a stick and unrolled when read (Isa. 34:4; Rev. 6:14; Jer. 36).

Sea of Galilee See **Galilee, Sea of.**

Second Coming The term (not found in the New Testament) denoting the risen Jesus' return to earth to establish the kingdom of God. See **Parousia.**

Seleucids The Macedonian Greek dynasty founded by Alexander's general Seleucus (ruled 312–280 BCE), centered in Syria with Antioch as its capital. After defeating the Ptolemies of Egypt, it controlled Palestine from 198 to 165 BCE, after which the Maccabeans defeated the forces of Antiochus IV and eventually drove the Syrians from Judea (142 BCE) (1 and 2 Macc.).

Seleucus The Macedonian general (ruled 312–280 BCE) of Alexander the Great who founded a ruling dynasty in Syria, with Antioch as its capital. After defeating the Ptolemies of Egypt, the Seleucid dynasty controlled Palestine from 198 to 165 BCE, after which the Maccabean Revolt eventually drove the Seleucid forces from Judea (142 BCE).

Semites According to Genesis 10:21–31, peoples descended from Noah's son Shem, whose progeny included Elam, Asshur, Arpacshad (Hebrews and Arabs), Lud (Lydians), and Aram (Syrians) (Gen. 10:22). In modern usage, the term applies to linguistic rather than to racial groups, such as those who employ one of a common family of inflectional languages, including Akkadian, Aramaic, Hebrew, and Arabic.

Septuagint (LXX) A Greek edition of the Hebrew Bible traditionally attributed to seventy or seventy-two Palestinian scholars during the reign of Ptolemy II (285–246 BCE), but actually the work of several generations of Alexandrine translators, begun about 250 BCE and not completed until the first century CE. The later additions to the Septuagint were deleted from the standard Hebrew Bible (Masoretic Text) but included in the Old Testament as the Apocrypha.

serpent A common symbol in Near Eastern fertility cults, the original tempter of humanity (Gen. 3–4). Revelation 12:9 identifies the serpent with the devil and Satan (the primordial Dragon).

seven messianic woes See **woes, seven messianic.**

Shema Judaism's supreme declaration of monotheistic faith, expressed in the words of Deuteronomy 6:4–9 beginning "Listen [Hebrew, *shema*, "hear"], Israel, Yahweh our God is the one Yahweh." The complete Shema also includes Deuteronomy 11:13–21 and Numbers 14:37–41 (cf. Mark 12: 29–34).

Sheol According to the Hebrew Bible, the subterranean region to which the "shades" of all the dead descended, a place of intense gloom, hopelessness, and virtual unconsciousness for its inhabitants. The term was translated *Hades* in the Greek Septuagint. In later Hellenistic times, it was regarded as an abode of the dead awaiting resurrection (Gen. 42:38; 1 Sam. 2:6; Job 7:9; 14:13–14; 26:6; Pss. 6:5; 16:10; 55:15; 139:8; Prov. 27:20; Eccles. 9:10; Isa. 14:15; 28:15; 38:10, 18; Hos. 13:14; Jon. 2:2; cf. references to Hades in Matt. 16:18; Luke 10:15; Acts 2:31; Rev. 1:18; 20:15). It is *not* the same theological concept as hell or Gehenna (Matt. 10:28; 23:33; Mark 9:43; Luke 12:5).

Signs Gospel A hypothetical early Christian document describing seven of Jesus' miraculous acts; according to one theory, it forms the principal narrative source for John's Gospel.

Silas The Semitic, perhaps Aramean, name of an early Christian prophet (Acts 15:32), otherwise called Silvanus, who accompanied Barnabas and Paul to Antioch with decrees from the Jerusalem council (Acts 15:1–35) and who joined Paul on his second missionary journey (Acts 16–18; 1 Thess. 1:1; 2 Thess. 1:1). He may have been the author of 1 Peter (1 Pet. 5:12).

Simeon

1. Another name for Simon Peter (Acts 15:14; 2 Pet. 1:1).

2. The devout old man who recognized the infant Jesus as the promised Messiah (Luke 2:22–34).

simile A comparison using "like" or "as," usually to illustrate an unexpected resemblance between a familiar object and novel idea. Jesus' parables about the kingdom of God are typically cast as similes (Matt. 13:31–35, 44–50; Mark 4:26–32; Luke 13:18–19).

Simon The name of several New Testament figures:

1. Simon Peter (Matt. 4:18; 10:2).

2. One of the Twelve Apostles, Simon the Zealot, perhaps so called for his religious zeal (Matt. 10:4; Mark 3:18; Luke 6:15; Acts 1:13).

3. One of Jesus' "brothers" (Matt. 13:55; Mark 6:3).

4. A leper whom Jesus cured (Mark 14:3–9).

5. The man from Cyrene in North Africa who was forced to carry Jesus' cross (Mark 15:21).

6. A Pharisee who entertained Jesus in his home (Luke 7:36–50).

7. Simon Iscariot, father of Judas the traitor (John 6:71; 13:26).

8. A leather tanner of Joppa with whom Peter stayed (Acts 9:43; 10).

Simon Magus A Samaritan sorcerer ("magus") who tried to buy the power of the Holy Spirit from Peter (Acts 8:9–24); thought by some to be the forerunner of the Faust figure. The sale of church offices is known as *simony,* after Simon Magus.

Sitz-im-Leben In form criticism, the social and cultural environment out of which a particular biblical unit grew and developed; German, "setting in life."

Smyrna An Aegean port city of western Asia Minor (Turkey), site of an early Christian church that the author of Revelation praises for its poverty and faithfulness (Rev. 1:11; 2:8–10).

Socrates The Athenian philosopher (c. 469–399 BCE) and friend and teacher of Plato, who was condemned to death for questioning assumptions deemed essential to maintain proper religious beliefs, civic order, and security. In Plato's dialogues, he is always the chief speaker.

Sodom Along with Gomorrah, Admah, Zebolim, and Zoar (Gen. 13:10–12; 14:2; Deut. 29:23), one of the "five cities of the plain" (near the south shore of the Dead Sea) destroyed by a great cataclysm attributed to Yahweh (Gen. 19:1–29). Later Bible writers cite it as a symbol of divine judgment upon wickedness (Isa. 3:9; Lam. 4:6; Matt. 10:15; 2 Pet. 2:6; Jude 7; Rev. 11:8).

Solomon The son of David and Bathsheba and Israel's third king (c. 961–922 BCE) (2 Sam. 12:24–25), he was famous for his wisdom (1 Kings 3:5–28).

Solomon's Porch A magnificent covered colonnade built along the east side of Herod's Temple in Jerusalem in which Jesus walked (John 10:23); the site of several apostolic miracles (Acts 3:11; 5:12).

Son of Man

1. A Hebrew Bible phrase used to denote a human being (Pss. 8:4; 80:17; 144:3; 146:3; Isa. 56:2; Jer. 51:43), including a plural usage (Pss. 31:19; 33:13; Prov. 8:4; Eccles. 3:18–19; 8:11; 9:12). The phrase is characteristic of the Book of Ezekiel, where it is commonly used to indicate the prophet himself (Ezek. 2:1).

2. In Daniel 7:12–14, a reference—"one like a [son of] man"—to Israel itself or to a divinely appointed future ruler of Israel, although this figure is not given specific messianic significance.

3. In certain pseudepigraphal writings, particularly the Similitudes of the Book of Enoch, he who serves as Yahweh's agent on the coming Day of Judgment, variously called "the Elect One," "the Anointed One," and "the Son of Man."

4. In the Gospels, a phrase always spoken by Jesus and in most cases applied to himself (Matt. 8:20; 9:6; 11:19; 12:8; 16:27–28; 19:28; 24:30; 28:31; Mark 2:28; 8:38; 9:31; 10:45; 13:26; Luke 12:8–10; 18:8; 21:27; 22:22; John 3:14). Outside the Gospels, it is used only once (Acts 7:56), although the author of Revelation echoes Daniel 7:13 (Rev. 14:14).

sons of thunder See **thunder, sons of.**

soul In Hebrew, *nephesh* (breath), meaning "the quality of being a living creature," applied to both humans and animals (Gen. 1:20; 2:7; 2:19; 9:4; Exod. 1:5; 1 Chron. 5:21). Nephesh was translated *psyche* in the Greek Septuagint, the same term used (commonly for "life" rather than the immortal personality) in the New Testament (Matt. 10:28; 16:26; Acts 2:27; 3:23; Phil. 1:27; Rev. 20:4).

source criticism The analysis of a document to discover its written sources. See also **form criticism.**

Stephen A Hellenistic Jew of Jerusalem who was stoned for his Christian preaching (Acts 6:8–60), thus becoming the first martyr of the early church. The name means "royal" or "crown."

Stoicism A Greek philosophy that became popular among the upper classes in Roman times. Stoicism emphasized duty, endurance, self-control, and service to the gods, the family, and the state. Its adherents believed in the soul's immortality, rewards and punishments after death, and a divine force (providence) that directs human destiny. Paul encountered Stoics when preaching in Athens (Acts 17:18–34), and Stoic ideas appear in both his letters and other parts of the New Testament (cf. John 4:23 and 5:30, James 1:10, and 1 Peter 2:17).

symbol In its broadest usage, anything that stands for something else; from the Greek *symbolon,* a "token" or "sign," and *symballein,* to "throw together" or "compare." For example, the star of David is a symbol of Judaism, and the cross is a symbol of Christianity. The use of symbols characterizes prophetic and apocalyptic writing. In Daniel, wild beasts symbolize pagan nations; in Ezekiel, Yahweh's presence is symbolized by his radiant "glory."

synagogue In Judaism, a gathering of no fewer than ten adult males assembled for worship, scriptural instruction, and administration of local Jewish affairs. Synagogues probably began forming during the Babylonian exile when the Jerusalem Temple no longer existed. Organization of such religious centers throughout the Diaspora played an important role in the faith's transmission and survival. The synagogue liturgy included lessons from the Torah, the Prophets, the Shema, Psalms, and eighteen prayers.

syncretism The blending of different religions, a term biblical scholars typically apply to the mingling of Canaanite rites and customs with the Israelites' Mosaic faith.

Synoptic Problem A term referring to scholars' attempts to discover the literary relationship among the three strikingly similar Synoptic Gospels: Mark, Matthew, and Luke.

Synoptics The first three Gospels, so named because they share a large quantity of material in common, allowing their texts to be viewed together "with one eye."

Syro-Phoenician A woman living near the Phoenician cities of Tyre and Sidon whose daughter Jesus healed (Matt. 15:21–28; Mark 7:24–30).

Tabernacle The portable tent-shrine, elaborately decorated, that housed the ark of the covenant (Exod. 25–31; 35–40; Num. 7–9) from the Exodus to the building of Solomon's Temple (1 Kings 6–8); used in both the Hebrew and Christian Bibles as a symbol of God's presence with humanity (Num. 9:5; Deut. 31:15; Pss. 15:1; 43:3; 61:4; 132:7; Isa. 4:6; 33:20; Hos. 12:9; Acts 7:46; Heb. 8:2; 9:11; 2 Pet. 1:14; Rev. 21:3).

Talmud A huge collection of Jewish religious traditions consisting of two parts: (1) the Mishnah (written editions of ancient oral interpretations of the Torah), published in Palestine by Judah ha-Nasi (died c. 220 CE) and his disciples, and (2) the Gemara, extensive commentaries on the Mishnah. The Palestinian version of the Talmud, which is incomplete, was produced about 450 CE; the Babylonian Talmud, nearly four times as long, was finished about 500 CE. Both Talmuds contain Mishnah and Gemara.

Tanakh A term designating the three divisions of the Hebrew Bible: *T* for Torah (Law, or Instruction), *N* for Nevi'im (Prophets), and *K* for Kethuvim (Writings).

Targum Interpretative translations of the Hebrew Bible into Aramaic, such as that made by Ezra after the Jews' return from the Babylonian exile (Neh. 8:1–18). The practice may have begun in the postexilic synagogues, where Hebrew passages were read aloud and then translated into Aramaic with interpretative comments added.

Tarsus Capital of the Roman province of Cilicia (southeastern Turkey) and birthplace of Paul (Saul) (Acts 9:11; 11:25; 21:39; 22:3); a thriving commercial center in New Testament times.

Temple

1. The imposing structure built by King Solomon (using Phoenician architects and craftsmen) on Mount Zion in Jerusalem to house the ark of the covenant in its innermost room (the Holy of Holies) (1 Kings 5:15–9:25). Later recognized as the only authorized center for sacrifice and worship of Yahweh, it was destroyed by Nebuchadnezzar's troops in 587 BCE (2 Kings 25:8–17; 2 Chron. 36:18–19).

2. The Second Temple, rebuilt by Jews returned from the Babylonian exile under Governor Zerubbabel, dedicated about 515 BCE (Ezra 1:1–11; 3:1–13; 4:24–6:22; Hag. 1–2; Zech. 1:1–8:13).

3. Herod's splendid Temple replaced the inferior edifice of Zerubbabel's time and took nearly a half-century to complete (John 2:20). Jesus, who visited the Temple as a child (Luke 2:22–38, 41–50) and often taught there (Matt. 21:23–24:1; Luke 20:1; John 7:14–52; 10:22–39), assaulted its money-changers (Matt. 21:12–17; Mark 11:15–19; Luke 19:45–46; John 2:13–22) and prophesied its destruction (Matt. 24:1–2; Mark 13:1–4; Luke 21:5–7), which was fulfilled when the Romans sacked Jerusalem in 70 CE. Until that event, the apostles continued to preach and worship there (Acts 3:1–26; 5:42; 21:26–22:29).

testament Either of the two main divisions of the Bible—the Old Testament (canonical Hebrew Scriptures) and the New Testament (Christian Greek Scriptures); from the Latin for "covenant."

tetragrammaton The four consonants (YHWH) making up the sacred name Yahweh, the God of Israel. Although the name appears almost 7,000 times in the canonical Hebrew Bible, some modern Bible translations continue the Jewish practice of inaccurately rendering it as "THE LORD."

textual criticism The comparison and analysis of ancient manuscripts to discover copyists' errors and, if possible, to reconstruct the true or original form of the document; also known as "lower criticism."

Thaddeus One of the most obscure of Jesus' apostles, listed among the Twelve in Matthew 10:3 and Mark 3:18 but not in Luke 7:16 or Acts 1:13.

theodicy A literary work that attempts to explain how an all-good, all-powerful god can permit the existence of evil and undeserved suffering; from a Greek term combining "god" and "justice." Job, 2 Peter, and 2 Esdras contain notable theodicies.

theology The study and interpretation of concepts about God's nature, will, and intentions toward humanity; from the Greek *theos,* meaning "god," and *logos,* "reason."

theophany An appearance of a god to a person, as when El wrestled with Jacob (Gen. 32:26–32), Yahweh appeared to Moses (Exod. 3:1–4:17; 6:2–13) and the elders of Israel (Exod. 24:9–11), or the resurrected Jesus revealed himself to Thomas (John 20:24–29) and Paul (Acts 9:3–9).

Theophilus The otherwise unknown man to whom the Gospel of Luke and the Book of Acts are addressed. He may have been a Roman official who became a Christian.

Thessalonica A major Macedonian city (modern Thessaloniki) where Paul and Silas converted "some" Jews, "many" Greeks and "Godfearers," and numerous "rich women" to Christianity (Acts 17:1–9). Paul later revisited it (1 Cor. 16:5) and wrote his earliest surviving letter to its congregation (1 Thess.).

Thomas One of the Twelve Apostles (Matt. 10:3; Mark 3:18; Luke 6:15; Acts 1:13), seldom mentioned in the Synoptics but relatively prominent in the Fourth Gospel, where he is called Didymus (twin) (John 11:16; 20:24; 21:2). Thomas doubted the other disciples' report of Jesus' resurrection, but when suddenly confronted with the risen Jesus, he pronounces the strongest confession of faith in the Gospel (John 20:24–29). He is the reputed author of the apocryphal Gospel of Thomas.

thunder, sons of An epithet (Boanerges) applied to the apostles James and John (Mark 3:17), possibly because of their impulsive temperaments (Luke 9:52–56).

Thyatira A city of ancient Lydia in Asia Minor (modern Turkey), original home of Lydia, Paul's first European convert (Acts 16:14) and one of the seven churches of Asia in Revelation 2:18–19.

Tiberias A city on the western shore of the Sea of Galilee founded by Herod Antipas and named after the emperor Tiberius; a well-known spa in Jesus' day.

Tiberius (Tiberius Claudius Nero) The stepson of Augustus and second emperor of Rome (14–37 CE). According to Luke 3:1, Jesus came to John for baptism in the fifteenth year of Tiberius's reign. Except for in Luke 2:1, he is the Caesar referred to in the Gospels (Matt. 22:17; Mark 12:14; Luke 20:22; John 19:12).

Timothy The younger friend and fellow missionary of Paul, who called him "beloved son" (1 Cor. 4:17; 1 Tim. 1:2–28; 2 Tim. 1:2), Timothy was the son of a Greek father and a devout Jewish mother (Acts 16:1; 2 Tim. 1:5). To please the Jews, Paul circumcised Timothy before taking him on his second missionary tour (Acts 16:1–4; 20:1–4). Paul later sent him to Macedonia (1 Thess. 3:6) and thence to Corinth to quiet the dissension there (Acts 19:22; 1 Cor. 4:17; 16:11), which he failed to do (2 Cor. 7:6, 13–14; 8:6, 16, 23; 12:18). The picture of Timothy in the pastoral epistles seems irreconcilable with what is known of him from Acts and Paul's genuine letters.

tithe A tenth of one's income paid in money, crops, or animals to support a government (1 Sam. 8:15–17) or religion (Lev. 27:30–33; Num. 18:24–28; Deut.

12:17–19; 14:22–29; Neh. 10:36–38); also, to pay such a part. Jesus apparently regarded tithing as an obligation of his people (Luke 11:42; 18:12).

Titus A Greek whom Paul converted and who became a companion on his missionary journeys (2 Cor. 8:23; Gal. 2:1–3; Tit. 1:4). Titus effected a reconciliation between Paul and the Corinthians (2 Cor. 7:5–7; 8:16–24; 12:18). A post-Pauline writer makes him the type of the Christian pastor (Tit. 1–3).

Titus, Flavius Sabinius Vespasianus The son and successor of Vespasian and emperor of Rome (79–81 CE); he directed the siege of Jerusalem, which culminated in the destruction of the city and Herodian Temple in 70 CE. His carrying of the Temple treasures to Rome is commemorated in the triumphal Arch of Titus that still stands in the Roman Forum.

Torah The Pentateuch (the first five books of the Hebrew Bible) and in a general sense all the Hebrew canonical writings, which are traditionally regarded as a direct oracle, or revelation, from Yahweh. *Torah* is a Hebrew term usually translated as "law," "instruction," or "teaching."

tradition

1. Collections of stories and interpretations transmitted orally from generation to generation typically embodying the religious history and beliefs of a people or community.

2. Oral explanations, interpretations, and applications of the written Torah (1 Chron. 4:22; Mark 7:5, 9; Matt. 15:2; Gal. 1:15), many of which were eventually compiled in the Mishnah.

3. In the New Testament, orally transmitted stories about Jesus circulated before being incorporated in the Gospels.

tradition criticism The analysis of the origin and development of specific biblical themes—such as the Exodus motif in the Tanakh and the eschatology of the kingdom of God in the New Testament—as presented by different biblical writers. In some cases, tradition criticism emphasizes the early and oral stages of development.

Trajan (Marcus Ulpius Nerva Trajanus) The emperor of Rome (98–117 CE) who was born in Spain about 53 CE, became a successful military leader, and brought the Roman Empire to its greatest geographical extent, annexing Dacia, Armenia, Mesopotamia, Assyria, and Arabia. Probably following the policies of Vespasian (69–79 CE), he conducted a persecution of Christians, although he wrote to Pliny the Younger, governor of Bithynia, that Christians were not to be sought out or denounced anonymously.

transcendence The quality of God expressing the Deity's inherent limitlessness and transcending of all physical and cosmic boundaries.

Transfiguration According to the Synoptic Gospels, a supernatural transformation of Jesus into a being of light, witnessed by Jesus' three closest disciples—Peter, James, and John—on an isolated mountaintop. In this awesome revelation of Jesus' divinity, the biblical figures Elijah and Moses also appear (Matt. 17:1–13; Mark 9:2–13; Luke 9:28–36).

Trinity The post–New Testament doctrine that God exists as three divine Persons in One—Father, Son, and Holy Spirit. After heated ecclesiastical debate on the subject had seriously divided the church, Constantine, the first Christian emperor of Rome but then unbaptized, called a council of church leaders in Nicaea to define the doctrine (325 CE). The council decreed the orthodoxy of the trinitarian formula, so that the mystery of Trinity in unity (although still opposed by Arian Christians for centuries thereafter) eventually became central to the Christian faith (Matt. 28:19–20; 2 Cor. 13:14; Gal. 1:1–5).

Twelve, the The Twelve Apostles whom Jesus specifically chose to follow him. Different names appear on different New Testament lists of the Twelve (Matt. 10:1–5; Mark 3:16–19; Luke 6:12–16; Acts 1:13–14).

Tychicus A loyal helper and companion of Paul who accompanied him through the Roman province of Asia on his third missionary journey (Acts 20:4). Tychicus delivered letters to the Colossians (Col. 4:7–9) and Ephesians (Eph. 6:21).

typology A form of biblical interpretation in which the narratives and teachings of the Hebrew Bible (Old Testament) are viewed as prophetic types or patterns for what Jesus was later to say and do.

Tyre An ancient Phoenician seaport famous for its commerce and wealth, originally built on a small offshore island about twenty-five miles south of Sidon. Alexander the Great sacked the city in 332 BCE, although it had been rebuilt by Jesus' day (Mark 7:24–31; Luke 3:8).

Valley of Hinnom See **Hinnom, Valley of.**

veil, the The elaborately decorated curtain separating the Holy Place from the Most Holy Place in the Tabernacle and the Jerusalem Temple (Exod. 26:31–37), which was reputedly rent in two at Jesus' crucifixion (Matt. 27:51; Heb. 6:19; 9–10).

Vespasian The emperor of Rome (69–79 CE) who led Roman legions into Judea during the Jewish Revolt (66–73 CE), the siege of Jerusalem passing to his son Titus when Vespasian became emperor.

Vulgate Jerome's Latin translation of the Bible (late fourth century CE), to which the Apocrypha was later added and which became the official edition of Roman Catholicism.

Wisdom In Proverbs 8, the personification of Yahweh's attribute of creative intelligence as a gracious woman who mediates between God and humanity. The Hebrew concept of divine Wisdom later merges with the Greek philosophical doctrine of the heavenly Logos in John's Gospel (John 1:1–18).

wisdom literature Biblical works dealing primarily with practical and ethical behavior and ultimate religious questions, such as God's relationship to humanity and the problem of evil. The books include Proverbs, Job, Ecclesiastes, Ecclesiasticus, and the Wisdom of Solomon. Habakkuk, 2 Esdras, and the New Testament Book of James also have characteristics of Wisdom writing.

woes, seven messianic The series of seven condemnations of scribes and Pharisees attributed to Jesus when he was rejected by official Judaism (Matt. 23:13–32).

Word

1. The "word" or "oracle" of Yahweh, a phrase characteristic of the Hebrew prophets, typically referring to a divine pronouncement, judgment, or statement of purpose that the prophet delivers in his God's name.

2. The preincarnate Jesus (John 1:1–3). See also **Logos.**

Yahweh A translation of the sacred name of Israel's God, represented almost 7,000 times in the canonical Hebrew Bible by the four consonants of the tetragrammaton (YHWH). According to Exodus 6:2–4, it was revealed for the first time to Moses at the burning bush; according to another account, it was used from the time of Enosh before the Flood (Gen. 4:26). Scholars have offered various interpretations of the origin and meaning of the divine name. According to a widely accepted theory, it is derived from the Hebrew verb "to be" and means "He is" or "He causes to be," implying that Yahweh is the maker of events and shaper of history.

Yom Kippur See **Atonement, Day of.**

Zealots A fiercely nationalistic Jewish party dedicated to freeing Judea from foreign domination that coalesced about 67–68 CE during the great rebellion against Rome (66–73 CE). According to Josephus's possibly biased account, their intransigence led to the destruction of Jerusalem and the Temple.

Zebedee A Galilean fisherman, husband of Salome, and father of the apostles James and John (Matt. 27:56; Mark 1:19–20; 3:17; 14:33; 15:40).

Zechariah

1. A Judean priest married to Elizabeth, a descendant of Aaron, whose long, childless marriage was blessed in old age by the birth of the future John the Baptist (Luke 1:5–25, 57–80; 3:2). A vision foretelling the birth rendered Zechariah temporarily paralyzed, but he recovered his speech in time to name the child and to utter a prayer of thanksgiving—the Benedictus (Luke 1:67–79).

2. A Jewish martyr mentioned in Jesus' phrase "from Abel to Zecharias" (Matt. 23:35; Luke 11:51), usually identified with Zechariah, son of Jehoiada in 2 Chronicles 24:20–24.

Zeus In Greek mythology, the son of Cronus and Rhea, king of the Olympian gods, and patron of civic order. A personification of storm and other heavenly powers, he ruled by wielding a thunderbolt. The Romans identified him with Jupiter (Jove). Some people of Lystra compared Barnabas to Zeus and Paul to Hermes (Acts 14:12). The erection of an altar to Zeus in the Jerusalem Temple courts helped spark the Maccabean Revolt (c. 168 BCE).

Zion The name, probably meaning "citadel," for a rocky hill in old Jerusalem, originally a Jebusite acropolis that David captured and upon which he built his palace and housed the ark of the covenant (Judg. 19:11–12; 2 Sam. 5:6–12; 6:12–17; 1 Chron. 11:5–8).

Zoroastrianism A dualistic religion established by the east Iranian prophet Zoroaster about the late sixth century BCE. Zoroaster saw the universe as a duality of spirit and matter, light and darkness, good and evil. The present age witnesses the conflict between Ahura-Mazda, a deity of light, and his evil spirit opponents. This conflict eventually will culminate in a cosmic battle in which good finally triumphs. Zoroastrian ideas about angels, demons, and the end of the present world appear to have influenced both Jewish and Christian writers, particularly in the realm of apocalyptic thought.

Photo Credits

Part 1 Opener: © Leemage/Getty; Figure 1.3: © Leemage/Getty; Figure 1.4: © Jewish Museum, London; Figure 2.1: © Archive Timothy McCarthy/ Art Resource, NY; Figure 2.2: Reproduced by courtesy of the University Librarian and and Director, The John Rylands Library, The University of Manchester; Figure 2.3: © The British Library Board; Figure 2.4: © Erich Lessing/ Art Resource, NY; Part 2 Opener: © Zev Radovan/ www.BibleLandPictures.com; p. 42 top right: © Zev Radovan/www.BibleLandPictures.com; p. 42 top left: © David Rubinger/CORBIS; p. 42 bottom: Neil Beer/Getty Images; p. 43 top: © Richard T. Nowitz/CORBIS; p. 43 bottom left: © Scala/ Art Resource, NY; p. 43 bottom right: © Roger Wood/CORBIS; Figure 3.2: © Zev Radovan/www .BibleLandPictures.com; Figure 3.3: © The Israel Museum, Jerusalem; Figure 3.4: © Richard T. Nowitz/CORBIS; Figure 3.5: © Richard Nowitz; Figure 3.6: © Erich Lessing/PhotoEdit; Figure 4.2: © The Trustees of the British Museum/Art Resource, NY; Figure 4.3: © Nimatallah/Art Resource, NY; Figure 4.4: © Gianni Dagli Orti/ Corbis; Figure 4.5: © Erich Lessing/Art Resource, NY; Figure 4.6: © Bridgeman Art Library International; Figure 4.7: © Erich Lessing/Art Resource, NY; Figure 4.8: © bpk, Berlin/ Aegyptisches Museum/Staatliche Museen/Art Resource, NY; Figure 5.1: © The Trustees of the British Museum/Art Resource, NY; Figure 5.3: © Erich Lessing/Art Resource, NY; Figure 5.6: Image copyright © The Metropolitan Museum of Art. Image source: Art Resource, NY; Figure 5.8: © Scala/Art Resource, NY; Figure 5.9: © Erich Lessing/Art Resource, NY; Figure 5.10: © Scala/ Art Resource, NY; Figure 5.12: © SEF/Art Resource, NY; Figure 5.13: Per Karlsson—BKWine .com/Alamy; Part 3 Opener: © Erich Lessing/Art Resource, NY; p. 112 top: Time & Life Pictures/ Getty Images; p. 112 bottom: © AP Photo/Kevin Frayer; p. 113 top: © Erich Lessing/Art Resource, NY; p. 113 bottom left: © Photri Images; p. 113 bottom right: Getty Images; p. 114 top: © Zev Radovan/www.BibleLandPictures.com; p. 114 bottom: © Zev Radovan/www.BibleLandPictures .com; Figure 6.1: © Scala/Art Resource, NY; Figure 7.3: Image copyright © The Metropolitan Museum of Art. Image source: Art Resource, NY; Figure 7.4: © Erich Lessing/PhotoEdit; Figure 7.5: © Zev Radovan/www.BibleLandPictures.com; Figure 7.6: © Bridgeman Art Library International; Figure 7.7: © Erich Lessing/Art Resource, NY; Figure 7.8: National Gallery of Art; Figure 8.1: "The Holy Family" © 1992 Fr. John Giuliani, Reproductions at www.BridgeBuilding.com; Figure 8.2: © Scala/ Art Resource, NY; Figure 8.3: © Scala/Art Resource, NY; Figure 9.1: © Bridgeman Art Library International; Figure 9.2: © Bridgeman Art Library International; Figure 9.3: © Fernando Botero, courtesy Marlborough Gallery, New York; Figure 9.4: © Erich Lessing/Art Resource, NY; Figure 9.5: © The Trustees of the British Museum/Art Resource, NY; p. 228 top: © Scala/Art Resource, NY; p. 228 bottom: © Pierre Perrin/Zoko/Sygma/ Corbis; p. 229 top: © The Trustees of the British Museum/Art Resource, NY; p. 229 center: © Scala/Art Resource, NY; p. 229 bottom: © Erich Lessing/Art Resource, NY; p. 230 top: © Erich Lessing/Art Resource, NY; p. 230 center: © Scala/ Art Resource, NY; p. 230 bottom left: © Scala/Art Resource, NY; p. 230 bottom right: © Scala/Art Resource, NY; Figure 10.2: © Scala/Art Resource, NY; Figure 10.3: © Erich Lessing/Art Resource, NY; Figure 10.4: © Bridgeman Art Library International; Figure 11.1: © Erich Lessing/Art Resource, NY; Figure 11.2: © Bridgeman Art Library International; Part 4 Opener: © akg-images; p. 282 top: © Scala/Art Resource, NY; p. 282 bottom left: © Erich Lessing/Art Resource, NY; p. 282 bottom right: © Erich Lessing/Art Resource, NY; p. 283 top: © Erich Lessing/Art Resource, NY; p. 283 bottom: Adam Crowley/ Getty Images; p. 284 top: © Anthony Pidgeon; p. 284 center: © Richard T. Nowitz/CORBIS;

Index

Bold page numbers indicate definitions and/or main discussion.